Why Do You Need This New Edition?

If you're wondering why you should buy this new edition of *The Blair Reader*, here are a few great reasons!

❶ Forty-six new reading selections will stimulate student interest and introduce them to challenging issues they will confront as citizens. These new selections include articles, book excerpts, speeches, fiction, and poetry.

❷ Twenty-two new images for analysis are reproduced in the chapter openers and Focus Units.

❸ A new Chapter Eight, "Saving the Planet," provides background on a crucial contemporary issue.

❹ A new Focus Unit, "How Can We Create a More Sustainable Environment?" appears in the new Chapter Eight.

❺ A new Focus Unit, "Is Texting Destroying the English Language?" appears in Chapter Three.

❻ A new Focus Unit, "Does Social Networking Connect Us or Keep Us Apart?" appears in Chapter Four.

❼ A new series of questions, "Reacting to Visual Texts," in the Introduction helps students approach and better understand visuals. These questions are accompanied by a sample visual with student annotations.

THE BLAIR READER

EXPLORING ISSUES AND IDEAS

SEVENTH EDITION

EDITED BY

LAURIE G. KIRSZNER

University of the Sciences in Philadelphia

STEPHEN R. MANDELL

Drexel University

Prentice Hall

Boston   Columbus   Indianapolis   New York   San Francisco   Upper Saddle River
Amsterdam   Cape Town   Dubai   London   Madrid   Milan   Munich   Paris   Montreal   Toronto
Delhi   Mexico City   Sao Paulo   Sydney   Hong Kong   Seoul   Singapore   Taipei   Tokyo

Senior Acquisitions Editor: Brad Potthoff
Senior Marketing Manager: Sandra McGuire
Project Coordination, Text Design, and Electronic Page Makeup: Laserwords
Art Director: Anne Nieglos/Pat Smythe
Cover Illustration/Photo: Getty Images (journalists)/PhotoLibrary (twitter)/
    iStock photo (windmills)
Image Permission Coordinator: Nancy Seise
Photo Researcher: Pearson Image Resource Center/Sheila Norman
Operations Specialist: Mary Ann Gloriande
Printer and Binder: Courier Companies
Cover Printer: Lehigh-Phoenix Color Hagerstown

For permission to use copyrighted material, grateful acknowledgment is made to the copyright holders on pages 673–680, which are hereby made part of this copyright page.

Library of Congress Cataloging-in-Publication Data

The Blair reader : exploring issues and ideas / edited by Laurie G. Kirszner, Stephen R. Mandell. — 7th ed.

   p. cm.
  Includes index.
  ISBN 0-205-72844-8
  1. College readers. 2. English language—Rhetoric—Problems, exercises, etc. 3. Report writing—Problems, exercises, etc. I. Kirszner, Laurie G. II. Mandell, Stephen R.
  PE1417.B54 2010
  808'.0427—dc22

                             2009038636

1 2 3 4 5 6 7 8 9 10—CRS—12 11 10 09

Prentice Hall
is an imprint of

ISBN-13: 978-0-205-72844-2
ISBN-10:   0-205-72844-8

CONTENTS

Topical Clusters

Generation Gap

Government and Misgovernment

Social and Economic Class

Stereotyping

Speeches

Note: Speeches are listed in alphabetical order.

Rhetorical Table of Contents

Note: Essays are listed alphabetically within categories.

Argument & Persuasion

PREFACE

After many years of teaching composition, we have come to see reading and writing as interrelated activities: if students are going to write effectively, they must first be able to read actively and critically. In addition, we see writing as both a private and a public act. As a private act, it enables students to explore their feelings and reactions and to discover their ideas about subjects that are important to them. As a public act, writing enables students to see how their own ideas fit into larger discourse communities, where ideas gain meaning and value. We believe that students are enriched and engaged when they view the reading and writing they do as a way of participating in ongoing public discussions about ideas that matter to them. From the beginning, our goal in *The Blair Reader* has always been to encourage students to contribute to these discussions in the wider world by responding to the ideas of others.

The core of *The Blair Reader* is, of course, its reading selections. As we selected the readings for this book, our goal was to introduce students to the enduring issues they confront as citizens in the twenty-first century. Many of these readings are very contemporary; many are also quite provocative. Whenever possible, however, we include classic readings that give students the historical context they need. For example, Chapter 2, "Issues in Education," includes "School Is Bad for Children" by John Holt; Chapter 3, "The Politics of Language," includes "Learning to Read and Write" by Frederick Douglass; and Chapter 6, "The American Dream," includes the Declaration of Independence. It was also important to us that the selections *The Blair Reader* represent a wide variety of rhetorical patterns and types of discourse as well as a variety of themes, issues, and positions. In addition to essays and articles from print and electronic sources, *The Blair Reader* includes speeches, short stories, and poems. It is our hope that exposure to this wide variety of formats, topics, and viewpoints can help students discover their own voices and express their own ideas.

As teachers, we—like you—expect a thematic reader to include compelling reading selections that involve instructors and students in spirited exchanges. We also expect readings that reflect the diversity of ideas that characterizes our society and questions that challenge students to respond critically to what they have read. In short, we expect a book that stimulates discussion and that encourages students to discover new ideas and see familiar ideas in new ways. These expectations guided us as we initially created *The Blair Reader*, and they continued to guide us as we worked on this new seventh edition.

What's New in the Seventh Edition?

In response to the thoughtful comments of the many instructors who generously shared with us their reactions (and their students' reactions) to the *The Blair Reader*, we have made many changes in this new edition, adding a new thematic unit, new readings, new study questions and writing prompts, and new visuals.

- **A new thematic unit,** "Saving the Planet," provides background on an important contemporary issue, including essays by writers such as Leslie Marmon Silko, Rachel Carson, and John Muir and a Focus section on the question, "How Can We Create a More Sustainable Environment?"

- **New Focus sections** showcase related essays that examine contemporary concerns, zeroing in on questions such as "Is Texting Destroying the English Language?" and "Does Social Networking Connect Us or Keep Us Apart?"

- **Updated treatment of visual literacy** draws attention to this important skill. In the Introduction to the text, "Reacting to Visual Texts" offers a series of questions to help students approach and understand visuals and includes a sample visual with student annotations. In addition, we include a full-color photo essay in Chapter 2, "Issues in Education," as well as new visuals in chapter openers and Focus sections.

- **New readings** have been added to stimulate student interest and to introduce them to some of the challenging issues that they confront as students and as citizens. Among the many essays that are new to this edition are Sandra Cisneros's "The Storyteller," Charles Murray's "Should the Obama Generation Drop Out?," Sherman Alexie's "What Sacagawea Means to Me," and Lasantha Wickrematunge's "And Then They Came for Me." New fiction, such as John Updike's "A & P" and Steven Millhauser's "The Invasion from Outer Space"; new poetry, such as Linda Hogan's "Heritage" and Louise Erdrich's "Dear John Wayne"; and new speeches, such as James Howard Kunstler's "Where Evil Dwells," a commencement address by David Foster Wallace, and John F. Kennedy's classic Houston speech, have also been added.

Resources for Students

We designed the apparatus in *The Blair Reader* to involve students and to encourage them to respond critically to what they read. These responses can lay the groundwork for the more focused thinking that they will do when they write. In order to help students improve their critical reading and writing skills, we have included the following features:

- **Introduction: Becoming a Critical Reader** explains and illustrates the process of reading and reacting critically to texts (including visual texts) and formulating original responses.

- **Paired visuals** introduce each thematic chapter. These visuals engage students by encouraging them to identify parallels and contrasts. In addition, they introduce students to the themes that they will be considering as they read the essays in the chapter.

- A brief **chapter introduction** places each chapter's broad theme in its social, historical, or political context, helping students to understand the complexities of the issues being discussed. This chapter introduction is followed by **Preparing to Read and Write**, a list of questions designed to help students to focus their responses to individual readings and to relate these responses to the chapter's larger issues.

- **Headnotes** that introduce each selection provide biographical and other background information as well as insight into the writer's purpose.

- **Responding to Reading** questions that follow each selection address thematic and rhetorical considerations. By encouraging students to think critically, these questions help them to see reading as an interactive and intellectually stimulating process.

- A **Responding in Writing** prompt after each reading selection gives students the opportunity to write an informal response.

- A **Focus** section in Chapters 2 through 9 is introduced by a provocative question related to the chapter's theme, followed by a visual that is accompanied by **Responding to the Image** questions and a writing prompt. The heart of the Focus section is a group of readings that take a variety of positions on the issue, encouraging students to add their voices to the debate and demonstrating that complex issues elicit different points of view. Each reading is followed by "Responding to Reading" questions and a "Responding in Writing" prompt.

- At the end of each Focus section, a **Widening the Focus** feature includes a writing prompt ("For Critical Thinking and Writing") that asks students to tie the readings together; a list of essays in other chapters of the book that also address the issues raised by the Focus question; and a research assignment.

- **Writing** suggestions at the end of each chapter ask students to respond to one or more of the chapter's readings.

- A **Rhetorical Table of Contents,** located at the front of the book on pages xx–xxvii, groups the text's readings according to the way they arrange material: narration, description, process, comparison and contrast, and so on.

- **Topical Clusters,** narrowly focused thematic units (pp. x–xix), offer students and teachers additional options for grouping readings.

Additional Resources for Instructors and Students

Instructor's Manual (0-205-72846-4)

Because we wanted *The Blair Reader* to be a rich and comprehensive resource for instructors, a thoroughly revised and updated Instructor's Resource Manual has been developed to accompany the text. Designed to be a useful and all-inclusive tool, the manual contains teaching strategies, collaborative activities, and suggested answers for "Responding to Reading" questions. The manual includes Web and/or multimedia teaching resources for almost every reading. It also contains new questions for stimulating classroom discussions of the new chapter-opening images. Contact your local Pearson representative for details.

MyCompLab™

MyCompLab empowers student writers and facilitates writing instruction by uniquely integrating a composing space and assessment tools with market-leading instruction, multimedia tutorials, and exercises for writing, grammar, and research.

Students can use MyCompLab on their own, benefiting from self-paced diagnostics and a personal study plan that recommends the instruction and practice each student needs to improve her writing skills. The composing space and its integrated resources, tools, and services (such as online tutoring) are also available to each student as he writes.

MyCompLab is an eminently flexible application that instructors can use in ways that best complement their course and teaching style. They can recommend it to students for self-study, set up courses to track student progress, or leverage the power of administrative features to be more effective and save time. The assignment builder and commenting tools, developed specifically for writing instruction, bring instructors closer to their student writers, make managing assignments and evaluating papers more efficient, and put powerful assessment tools within reach. Students receive feedback within the context of their own writing, which encourages critical thinking and revision and helps them to develop skills based on their individual needs.

Learn more at www.mycomplab.com.

Acknowledgments

The Blair Reader is the result of a fruitful collaboration between the two of us, between us and our students, between us and Pearson, and between us and you—our colleagues who told us what you wanted in a reader.

At Pearson we want to thank Brad Potthoff, Senior Acquisitions Editor, and Joe Opiela, Editorial Director. We also appreciate the efforts of Nancy C. Lee, Editorial Assistant, as well as our copyeditor, Kathy Whittier.

Karen R. Mauk, our wonderful developmental editor, spent a great deal of time and effort making this book as good as it is. As always, her patience, professionalism, and hard work are greatly appreciated. At Laserwords Maine, we want to thank Karen Berry, Production Editor, for seeing this book through to completion.

In preparing *The Blair Reader*, Seventh Edition, we benefited at every stage from the assistance and suggestions from colleagues from across the country: Lisa Beckelhimer, University of Cincinnati; Anne Fernald, Fordham University; Web Freeman, Ozarks Technical Community College; Janet P. Gerstner, San Juan College; Lisa Gordon, Columbus State Community College; Judy A. Hayden, University of Tampa; Jessica Hyatt, Ozarks Technical Community College; Robert S. Imbur, University of Toledo; JoAnne James, Pitt Community College; Amanda Jerome, Saddleback College; Dani McLean, Saddleback College; Jeannette E. Riley, UMass Dartmouth; Margaret Simonton, East Arizona College; Katie Singer, Fairleigh Dickinson University; and Mary Ellen Williams, UC Davis.

We would also like to thank the following reviewers of previous editions for their valuable insight: Jacob Agatucci, Central Oregon

Community College; Jesse T. Airaudi, Baylor University; Linda A. Archer, Green River Community College; Anthony Armstrong, Richland College; Stephen R. Armstrong, Eastern Carolina University; Patricia Baldwin, Pitt Community College; Chere Berman, College of the Canyons; Charlene Bunnell, University of Delaware; Jason Chaffin, Cape Fear Community College; Peggy Cole, Arapahoe Community College; Carla L. Dando, Idaho State University; Rosemary Day, Albuquerque Community College; Emily Dial-Driver, Rogers State University; Janet Eldred, University of Kentucky; Anne Fernald, Fordham University; Robert G. Ford, Houston Community College; Ruth Gerik, University of Texas at Arlington; Janet Gerstner, San Juan College; David Holper, College of the Redwoods; Pamela Howell, Midland College; Tara Hubschmitt, Lakeland College; Lu Ellen Huntley, University of North Carolina at Wilmington; James Jenkins, Mt. San Antonio College; Terry Jolliffe, Midland College; Alan Kaufman, Bergen Community College; Dimitri Keriotis, Modesto Junior College; Robert Leston, University of Texas at Arlington; John Lucarelli, Community College of Allegheny County; Camilla Mortensen, University of Oregon; Kathryn Neal, York Technical College; Paul Northam, Johnson County Community College; Marguerite Parker, Eastern Carolina University; Andrea Penner, San Juan College; Angie Pratt, Montgomery College; CC Ryder, West L.A. College; Debra Shein, Idaho State University; Darlene Smith-Worthington, Pitt Community College; Derek Soles, Drexel University; Lori Ann Stephens, Richland College; Sharon Strand, Black Hills State University; Diane Sweet, Wentworth Institute of Technology; Cara Unger, Portland Community College; Jennifer Vanags, Johnson County Community College; Stephen H. Wells, Community College of Allegheny County; Mary Williams, Midland College; and K. Siobhan Wright, Carroll Community College.

On the home front, we once again "round up the usual suspects" to thank—Mark, Adam, and Rebecca Kirszner and Demi, David, and Sarah Mandell. And, of course, we thank each other: it really has been a "beautiful friendship."

Laurie G. Kirszner
Stephen R. Mandell

THE BLAIR READER

INTRODUCTION: BECOMING A CRITICAL READER

In his autobiographical essay "The Library Card" (p. 330), Richard Wright describes his early exposure to the world of books. He says, "The plots and stories in the novels did not interest me so much as the point of view revealed. I gave myself over to each novel without reserve, without trying to criticize it; it was enough for me to see and feel something different. Reading was like a drug."

It is a rare person today for whom reading can hold this magic or inspire this awe. Most of us take the access to books for granted. As a student, you've probably learned to be pragmatic about your reading. In fact, "reading a book" may have come to mean just reading assigned pages in a textbook. Whether the book's subject is modern American history, principles of corporate management, or quantum mechanics, you probably tend to read largely for information, expecting a book's ideas to be accessible and free of ambiguity and the book to be clearly written and logically organized.

In addition to reading textbooks, however, you also read essays and journal articles, fiction and poetry, Web sites and blogs. These texts present special challenges because you read them not just for information but also to discover your own ideas about what the writer is saying—what the piece of writing means to you, how you react to it, why you react as you do, and how your reactions differ from the responses of other readers. And, because the writers express opinions and communicate impressions as well as facts, your role as a reader must be more active than it is when you read a textbook. Here, reading becomes not only a search for information, but also a search for meaning.

Reading and Meaning

Like many readers, you may assume that the meaning of a text is hidden somewhere between the lines and that you only have to ask the right questions or unearth the appropriate clues to discover exactly what the writer is getting at. But reading is not a game of hide-and-seek in which you search for ideas that have been hidden by the writer. As current reading theory demonstrates, meaning is created by the interaction of a reader with a text.

One way to explain this interactive process is to draw an analogy between a text—a work being read—and a word. A word is not the natural equivalent of the thing it signifies. The word *dog,* for example, does not evoke the image of a furry, four-legged animal in all parts of the world. To speakers of Spanish, the word *perro* elicits the same mental picture *dog* does in English-speaking countries. Not only does the word *dog* have meaning only in a specific cultural context, but even within that context it evokes different images in different people. Some people may picture a collie, others a poodle, and still others a particular pet.

Like a word, a text can have different meanings in different cultures—or even in different historical time periods. Each reader brings to the text associations that come from the cultural community in which he or she lives. These associations are determined by readers' experience and education as well as by their ethnic group, class, religion, gender, and many other factors that contribute to how they view the world. Each reader also brings to the text beliefs, expectations, desires, and biases that influence how he or she reacts to and interprets it. Thus, it is entirely possible for two readers to have very different, but equally valid, interpretations of the same text. (This does not mean, of course, that a text can mean whatever any individual reader wishes it to mean. To be valid, an interpretation must be supported by the text itself.)

To get an idea of the range of possible interpretations that can be suggested by a single text, consider some of the responses different readers might have to E. B. White's classic essay "Once More to the Lake" (p. 24).

In "Once More to the Lake," White tells a story about his visit with his son to a lake in Maine in the 1940s, comparing this visit with those he made as a boy with his own father in 1904. Throughout the essay, White describes the changes that have occurred since his first visit. Memories from the past flood his consciousness, causing him to remember things that he did when he was a boy. At one point, after he and his son have been feeding worms to fish, he remembers doing the same thing with his father and has trouble separating the past from the present. Eventually, White realizes that he will soon be just a memory in his son's mind—just as his father is only a memory in his.

White had specific goals in mind when he wrote this essay. His title, "Once More to the Lake," indicates that he intended to compare his childhood and adult visits to the lake. The organization of ideas in the essay, the use of flashbacks, and the choice of particular transitional phrases reinforce this purpose. In addition, descriptive details—such as the image of the tarred road that replaced the dirt road—remind readers, as well as White himself, that the years have made the lake site different from what it once was. The essay ends with White suddenly feeling the "chill of death."

Despite White's specific intentions, each person reading "Once More to the Lake" will respond to it somewhat differently. Young male readers might identify with the boy. If they have ever spent a vacation at a lake, they might have experienced the "peace and goodness and jollity" of the whole summer scene. Female readers might also want to share these experiences, but they might feel excluded because only males are described in the essay. Readers who have never been on a fishing trip might not feel the same nostalgia for the woods that White feels. To them, living in the woods away from the comforts of home might seem an unthinkably uncomfortable ordeal. Older readers might identify with White, sympathizing with his efforts as an adult to recapture the past and seeing his son as naively innocent of the challenges of life.

Thus, although each person who reads White's essay will read the same words, each will be likely to interpret it differently and to see different things as important. This is because much is left open to interpretation. All essays leave blanks or gaps—missing ideas or images—that readers have to fill in. In "Once More to the Lake," for example, readers must imagine what happened in the years that separated White's last visit to the lake with his father and the trip he took with his son.

These gaps in the text create ambiguities—words, phrases, descriptions, or ideas that need to be interpreted by the reader. For instance, when you read the words "One summer, along about 1904, my father rented a camp on a lake," how do you picture the camp? White's description of the setting contains a great deal of detail, but no matter how much information he supplies, he cannot paint a complete verbal picture of the lakeside camp. He must rely on the reader's ability to visualize the setting and to supply details from his or her own experience.

Readers also bring their emotional associations to a text. For example, how readers react to White's statement above depends, in part, on their feelings about their own fathers. If White's words bring to mind a parent who is loving, strong, and protective, they will most likely respond favorably; if the essay calls up memories of a parent who is distant, bad-tempered, or even abusive, they may respond negatively.

Because each reader views the text from a slightly different angle, each may also see a different focus as central to "Once More to the Lake." Some might see nature as the primary element in the essay and believe that White's purpose is to condemn the encroachment of human beings on the environment. Others might see the passage of time as the central focus. Still others might see the initiation theme as being the most important element of the essay: each boy is brought to the lake by his father, and each eventually passes from childhood innocence to adulthood and to the awareness of his own mortality.

Finally, each reader may evaluate the essay differently. Some readers might think "Once More to the Lake" is boring because it has little action and deals with a subject in which they have no interest. Others might believe the essay is a brilliant meditation that makes an impact through its vivid description and imaginative figurative language. Still others might see the essay as falling between these two extremes—for example, granting that White is an excellent stylist but also seeing him as self-centered and self-indulgent. After all, they might argue, the experiences he describes are available only to relatively privileged members of society and are irrelevant to others.

Reading Critically

Reading critically means interacting with a text, questioning the text's assumptions, and formulating and reformulating judgments about its ideas. Think of reading as a dialogue between you and the text: sometimes the author will assert himself or herself; at other times, you will dominate the conversation. Remember, though, that a critical voice is a thoughtful and responsible one, not one that shouts down the opposition. Linguist Deborah Tannen makes this distinction clear in an essay called "The Triumph of the Yell":

> In many university classrooms, "critical thinking" means reading someone's life work, then ripping it to shreds. Though critique is surely one form of critical thinking, so are integrating ideas from disparate fields and examining the context out of which they grew. Opposition does not lead to truth when we ask only "What's wrong with this argument?" and never "What can we use from this in building a new theory, a new understanding?"

In other words, being a critical reader does not necessarily mean arguing and contradicting; more often, it means asking questions and exploring your reactions—while remaining open to new ideas.

Asking the following questions as you read will help you to become aware of the relationships between the writer's perspective and your own:

- **Who is the writer addressing?** Who is the writer's intended audience? For example, the title of John Holt's essay on early childhood education, "School Is Bad for Children" (p. 64), suggests that Holt expects his readers to have preconceived notions about the value of a traditional education—notions his essay will challenge.

- **What is the writer's purpose?** Exactly what is the writer trying to accomplish in the essay? For example, is the writer attempting to explain, persuade, justify, evaluate, describe, debunk, entertain, preach, browbeat, threaten, or frighten? Or, does the writer have some other purpose (or combination of purposes)? For example, is the writer trying to explain causes and effects, as Marie Winn is in "Television: The Plug-In Drug" (p. 207)? To reflect on his or her life, as Sandra Cisneros is in "The Storyteller" (p. 50)? Or to move readers to action, as Arlie Hochschild is in "The Second Shift" (p. 415)? What strategies does the writer use to achieve his or her purpose? For example, does the writer rely primarily on logic or on emotion? Does the writer appeal to the prejudices or fears of his or her readers or in any other way attempt to influence readers unfairly?

- **What voice does the writer use?** Does the writer seem to talk directly to readers? If so, does the writer's subjectivity get in the way, or does it help to involve readers? Does the writer's voice seem distant or formal? Different voices have different effects on readers. For example, an emotional tone, like the one Martin Luther King, Jr., uses in "I Have a Dream" (p. 383), can inspire; an intimate tone, like the one Lynda Barry uses in "The Sanctuary of School" (p. 61), can create reader identification and empathy; a straightforward, forthright voice, like that of John F. Kennedy in his 1960 speech to the Greater Houston Ministerial Association, can make ideas seem reasonable and credible. An ironic tone can either amuse readers or alienate them; a distant, reserved tone can evoke either respect or discomfort.

- **What emotional response is the writer trying to create?** In "Letter from Birmingham Jail" (p. 608), Martin Luther King, Jr., maintains a calm, unemotional tone even though he is writing about injustices that have wounded him deeply. By maintaining a dignified tone and avoiding bitterness and resentment, he succeeds in inspiring sympathy and respect. Other writers may attempt to elicit other emotional responses: amusement, nostalgia, curiosity, wonder over the grandeur or mystery of the world that surrounds us, or even anger or fear.

- **What position does the writer take on the issue?** The choice of the word *war* in Christina Hoff Sommers's title "The War against Boys" (p. 309) clearly reveals her position on society's attitude toward boys; in the same way, the title of John Humphrys's essay "I h8 txt msgs" (p. 185) conveys his attitude toward texting. In the Declaration of Independence (p. 375), Thomas Jefferson presents his position in equally unambiguous terms when he asserts that the colonists have a right to defy the king. Keep in mind, though, that a writer's position may not always be as obvious as it is in these three examples. As you read, look carefully for statements that suggest the writer's position on a particular subject or issue—and be sure you understand how you feel about that position, particularly if it is an unusual or controversial one. Do you agree or disagree? Can you explain your reasoning? Of course, a writer's advocacy of a position that is at odds with your own does not automatically render the work suspect or its ideas invalid. Remember, ideas that you might consider shocking or absurd may be readily accepted by many other readers. Unexpected, puzzling, or even repellent positions should encourage you to read carefully and thoughtfully, trying to understand the larger historical and cultural context of a writer's ideas.

- **How does the writer support his or her position?** What kind of support is provided? Is it convincing? Does the writer use a series of individual examples, as Alleen Pace Nilsen does in "Sexism in English: Embodiment and Language" (p. 150), or an extended example, as Claire McCarthy does in "Dog Lab" (p. 632)? Does the writer use statistics, as Christina Hoff Sommers does in "The War against Boys" (p. 309), or does he or she rely primarily on personal experiences, as Brent Staples does in "Just Walk On By" (p. 354)? Does the writer quote experts, as Deborah Tannen does in "Marked Women" (p. 294), or present anecdotal information, as Jonathan Kozol does in "The Human Cost of an Illiterate Society" (p. 164)? Why does the writer choose a particular kind of support? Does he or she supply enough information to support the essay's points? Are the examples given relevant to the issues being discussed? Is the writer's reasoning valid, or do the arguments seem forced or unrealistic? Are any references in the work unfamiliar to you? If so, do they arouse your curiosity, or do they discourage you from reading further?

- **What beliefs, assumptions, or preconceived ideas do you have that color your responses to a work?** Does the writer challenge any ideas that you accept as "natural" or "obvious"? For example, do the experiments described in Stanley Milgram's "The Perils of Obedience" (p. 639) shock you or violate your sense of fairness? Does the fact that you are opposed to home schooling prevent you from appreciating arguments presented in Daniel H. Pink's "School's Out" (p. 87)?

- **Does your background or experience give you any special insights that enable you to understand or interpret the writer's ideas?** Are the writer's experiences similar to your own? Is the writer like you in terms of age, ethnic background, gender, and social class? How do the similarities between you and the writer affect your reaction to the work? For example, you may be able to understand Amy Tan's "Mother Tongue" (p. 140) better than other students because you, like Tan, speak one language at home and another in public. You may have a unique perspective on the problems Lynda Barry describes in "The Sanctuary of School" (p. 61) because you also had a difficult childhood. Or, your volunteer work at a shelter may have helped you understand the plight of the homeless as described by Lars Eighner in "On Dumpster Diving" (p. 358). Any experiences you may have had can help you to understand a writer's ideas and shape your response to them.

Recording Your Reactions

It is a good idea to read a work at least twice: first to get a general sense of the writer's ideas and then to react critically to these ideas. As you read critically, you interact with the text and respond in ways that will help you to interpret it. This process of coming to understand the text will prepare you to discuss the work with others and, perhaps, to write about it.

As you read and reread, record your responses; if you don't, you may forget some of your best ideas. Two activities can help you keep a record of the ideas that come to you as you read: **highlighting** (using a system of symbols and underlining to identify key ideas) and **annotating** (writing down your responses and interpretations in the margins of the text).

When you react to what you read, don't be afraid to question the writer's ideas. As you read and make annotations, you may disagree with or even challenge some of these ideas; when you have time, you can think more about what you have written. These informal responses may be the beginning of a thought process that will lead you to original insights.

Highlighting and annotating helped a student to understand the passage on page 8, which is excerpted from Brent Staples's essay "Just Walk On By" (p. 354). As she prepared to write about the essay, the student identified and summarized the writer's key points and made a connection with another essay, Judith Ortiz Cofer's "The Myth of the Latin Woman" (p. 346). As she read, she underlined some of the passage's important words and ideas, using arrows to indicate relationships between them. She also circled a few words to remind her to look up their meanings later on, and she wrote down questions and comments as they occurred to her.

Still applies today?

⑦

<u>The fearsomeness mistakenly attributed to me in public places often has a perilous flavor.</u> The most frightening of these confusions occurred in the <u>late 1970s and early 1980s</u> when I worked as a journalist in Chicago. One day, rushing into the office of a magazine I was writing for with a deadline story in hand, I was mistaken for a burglar. The office manager called security and, with an (ad hoc) posse, pursued me through the (labyrinthine) halls, nearly to my editor's door. I had no way of proving who I was. I could only move briskly toward the company of someone who knew me.

(Fear creates danger)

First experience

⑦

(Another time) I was on assignment for a local paper and killing time before an interview. I entered a jewelry store on the city's affluent Near North Side. The proprietor excused herself and returned with an enormous red Doberman pinscher straining at the end of a leash. She stood, the dog extended toward me, silent to my questions, her eyes bulging nearly out of her head. I took a cursory look around, nodded, and (bade) her good night. Relatively speaking, however, I never fared as badly as another black male journalist. He went to nearby Waukegan, Illinois, a couple of summers ago to work on a story about a murderer who was born there. Mistaking the reporter for the killer, police hauled him from his car at gunpoint and but for his press credentials would probably have tried to book him. <u>Such episodes are not uncommon. Black men trade tales like this all the time.</u>

Second experience

⑦

Compare with Cofer's experience w/ stereotypes

*

Reacting to Visual Texts

Many of the written texts you read—from newspapers and magazines to Web sites to textbooks like this one—include visuals. Some of these visuals (charts, tables, maps, graphs, scientific diagrams, and the like) are designed primarily to present information; others (fine art, photographs, cartoons, and advertisements, for example) may be designed to have an emotional effect on readers or even to persuade them.

Visuals may be analyzed, interpreted, and evaluated just as written texts are. You begin this process by looking critically at the visual, identifying its most important elements, and considering the relationships of various elements to one another and to the image as a whole. Then, you try to identify the purpose for which the image was created, and you consider your own personal response to the image.

As you examine a visual text, finding answers to the following questions will help you to understand it better:

- **What audience is the visual aimed at?** Does the visual seem to address a wide general audience or some kind of specialized audience, such as new parents, runners, or medical professionals? Is it aimed at adults or at children? Does it seem likely to appeal mainly to people from a particular region or ethnic group, or is it likely to resonate with a broad range of people? Often, knowing where a visual appeared—in a popular magazine, a political blog, a professional journal, or a trade publication, for example—will help you identify the audience the visual is trying to reach.

- **What is the purpose of the visual?** Is the visual designed to evoke an emotional response—fear or guilt, for example? Is it designed to be humorous? Or is its purpose simply to present information? To understand a visual's purpose, you need to consider not only its source but also what images it contains and how it arranges them. (Sometimes you will have to consider written text as well.)

- **What elements does the visual use to achieve its purpose?** What is the most important image? Where is it placed? What other images are present? Does the visual depict people? How much space is left blank? How does the visual use color and shadow? Does it include written text? How are words and images juxtaposed? For example, a visual designed to be primarily informative may use written text and straightforward graphics (such as graphs or scientific diagrams), while one that aims to persuade may use a single eye-catching image surrounded by blank space.

- **Does the visual make a point?** If so, how does it use images to get its message across? What other elements help to convey that message? Is the visual designed to convince its audience of something—for example, to change unhealthy behavior, donate to a charity, vote for a candidate, or buy a product? Exactly how does it communicate this message? For example, a photograph of starving children on a charity's Web site might convey the idea that a donation will bring them food, but statistics about infant mortality might make the image even more persuasive. Moreover, a close-up of one hungry child might be more convincing than a distant photo of a crowd. Similarly, an ad might appeal to consumers either by showing satisfied customers using a product or by presenting a memorable slogan against a contrasting background.

- **Do you have any beliefs or assumptions that affect your response to the visual?** Is there anything in your background or experience that influences your reaction? Just as with written texts, different people react differently to different visual texts. For example, if you have expertise in economics, you may approach a chart depicting economic trends with greater interest—or greater skepticism—than a general audience. If you know very little about fine art, your reaction to a painting is more likely to be emotional than analytical. And, as a loyal Democrat or Republican, you may react negatively to a political cartoon that is critical of your party. Finally, if you or a family member has struggled with illness or addiction, you might not respond favorably to a visual that took a superficial, light-hearted, or satirical approach to such a problem.

The following visual is a parody of an ad for Marlboro cigarettes. The visual, which appeared on the Web site www.adbusters.org, was annotated by a student who was assigned to analyze it. As he examined the ad, he identified its key elements and recorded his reactions in hand-written notes.

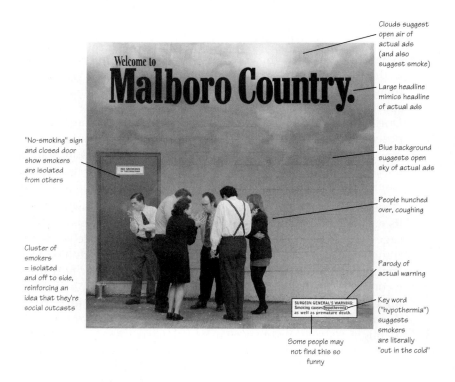

Reading to Write

Much of the reading you will do as a student will be done to prepare you for writing. Writing helps you focus your ideas about various issues; in addition, the process of writing can lead you in unexpected directions, thereby enabling you to discover new ideas. With this in mind, we have included in *The Blair Reader* a number of features that will help you as you read and prepare to write about its selections.

The readings in *The Blair Reader* (classic and contemporary essays as well as speeches, fiction, and poetry) are arranged in ten thematic chapters, each offering a variety of different vantage points from which to view the chapter's central theme. Each chapter opens with a brief introduction, which provides a context for the chapter's theme and includes a list of **Preparing to Read and Write** questions to guide your thinking as you read. These questions will help you to sharpen your critical skills and begin to apply those skills effectively. Each chapter introduction also includes a pair of contrasting visual images—photographs, advertisements, Web pages, and so on—designed to introduce you to the chapter's theme and to help you begin thinking about the issues it suggests.

Following each reading are three questions that encourage you to think about and respond to what you have read. These **Responding to Reading** questions ask you to think critically about the writer's ideas, perhaps focusing on a particular strategy the writer has used to achieve his or her purpose. In some cases, these questions may ask you to examine your own ideas or beliefs. Following the **Responding to Reading** questions is a **Responding in Writing** prompt that asks you to write a brief informal response. These prompts may ask you to link the writer's experiences or ideas to your own; to do some kind of writing exercise, such as making a list, writing a summary, or drafting an email; or to respond more critically to the writer's ideas.

Following the essays on each chapter's general theme is a **Focus** section that zeroes in on a specific issue related to that theme. (Chapters 1 and 10 do not include Focus sections.) The **Focus** section's central question—for example, "Who Has It Harder, Girls or Boys?" (Chapter 5) or "Is Outsourcing Bad for America?" (Chapter 7)—introduces a cluster of thought-provoking essays that take different positions on a single complex issue; a related visual image is also included in this Focus section. Each **Focus** essay is accompanied by three **Responding to Reading** questions and one **Responding in Writing** prompt; **Responding to the Image** questions follow each visual. The **Focus** section ends with **Widening the Focus,** which includes a writing prompt, a list of related readings in other chapters of the book, and a guided research assignment.

At the end of each chapter are suggestions for writing assignments that are longer and more formally structured than those suggested by the **Responding in Writing** prompts. These writing assignments ask you to examine some aspect of the chapter's theme by analyzing, interpreting, or evaluating ideas explored in various essays, sometimes considering parallels and contrasts with other essays in the book—or with your own life experiences.

As you read and write about the selections in this book, remember that you are learning how to think about yourself and about the world. By considering and reconsidering the ideas of others, by rejecting easy answers, by considering a problem from many different angles, and by appreciating the many factors that can influence your responses, you will develop critical thinking skills that you will use throughout your life. In addition, by writing about the themes discussed in this book, you will participate in an ongoing conversation within the community of scholars and writers who care deeply about the issues that shape our world.

1

FAMILY AND MEMORY

The ties that bind us to family, and to our family history, are like no other human connections. In this chapter, writers search their memories, trying to understand, recapture, or re-create the past, to see across the barriers imposed by time. In some cases, memories appear in sharp focus; in others, they are blurred, confused, or even partially invented. Many writers focus on themselves; others focus on their parents or other family members, struggling to close generational gaps, to replay events, to see through the eyes of others—and in this way to understand their families and themselves more fully.

Amy Ma's grandparents, Ma Ching-rei (left) and Lu Xiao-fang (right).

Alice Walker with her mother, Minnie Lou Walker, 1979.

────────── **PREPARING TO READ AND WRITE** ──────────

As you read and prepare to write about the selections in this chapter, you may consider the following questions:

- How does the writer define *family?*

- Does the writer focus on a single person, on a relationship between two people, or on larger family dynamics?

- How important is the setting in which the events the writer describes take place?

- Do you think the writer's perspective is *subjective* (shaped by his or her emotional responses or personal opinions) or *objective* (based mainly on observation and fact rather than on personal impressions)?

- What insights does the writer have that he or she did not have when the events occurred? What has the writer learned—and how?

- Are the memories generally happy or unhappy ones?

- Are family members presented in a favorable, unfavorable, neutral, or ambivalent way?

Gary Shteyngart with his father at Disney World, 1986.

Sandra Cisneros with her father, Alfred Cisneros Del Moral, 1995.

- Does the writer feel close to or distant from family members? Does the writer identify with a particular family member?

- Does one family member seem to have had a great influence over the writer? If so, is this influence positive or negative?

- What social, political, economic, or cultural forces influenced the family dynamics?

- What is the writer's primary purpose? For example, is the writer's purpose to observe? explore? discover? explain? persuade?

- Do you identify with the writer or with another person the writer describes? What makes you identify with that person?

- Which selections seem most similar in their views of family? How are they similar?

- Which selections seem most different in their views of family? How are they different?

- Which family seems most like your own? Why?

HERITAGE
Linda Hogan
1947–

A Chickasaw Native American, Linda Hogan writes poetry, novels, plays, and essays. She has published numerous works, including the 2008 poetry collection Rounding the Human Corners *and the novel* People of the Whale. *In the following poem, Hogan explores the complexity of her heritage.*

From my mother, the antique mirror
where I watch my face take on her lines.
She left me the smell of baking bread
to warm fine hairs in my nostrils,
she left the large white breasts that weigh down   5
my body.

From my father I take his brown eyes,
the plague of locusts that leveled our crops,
they flew in formation like buzzards.

From my uncle the whittled wood   10
that rattles like bones
and is white
and smells like all our old houses
that are no longer there. He was the man
who sang old chants to me, the words   15
my father was told not to remember.

From my grandfather who never spoke
I learned to fear silence.
I learned to kill a snake
when you're begging for rain.   20

And grandmother, blue-eyed woman
whose skin was brown,
she used snuff.
When her coffee can full of black saliva
spilled on me   25
it was like the brown cloud of grasshoppers
that leveled her fields.
It was the brown stain
that covered my white shirt,
my whiteness a shame.   30
That sweet black liquid like the food
she chewed up and spit into my father's mouth

when he was an infant.
It was the brown earth of Oklahoma
35   stained with oil.
She said tobacco would purge your body of poisons.
It has more medicine than stones and knives
against your enemies.

That tobacco is the dark night that covers me.
40   She said it is wise to eat the flesh of deer
so you will be swift and travel over many miles.
She told me how our tribe has always followed a stick
that pointed west
that pointed east.

45   From my family I have learned the secrets
of never having a home.

Responding to Reading

1. What has the speaker inherited from her parents? from her grandparents? from her tribe? Which inheritance does she seem to value most? Why?
2. What do you think the speaker means in the poem's last lines when she says, "From my family I have learned the secrets / of never having a home"?
3. What feelings does the speaker have about her family's past? Do you see these as mixed feelings?

Responding in Writing

In lines 21–38, the speaker describes her grandmother in terms of the colors she associates with her. Write a paragraph in which you describe a family member in this way.

THOSE WINTER SUNDAYS
Robert Hayden
1913–1980

Robert Hayden's work includes poems about slave rebellions and the histori-
cal roots of racism as well as about more personal subjects. Hayden's first book
of poetry, Heart-Shaped in the Dust, *was published in 1940. Other works*
include Angle of Ascent; New and Selected Poems *(1975), in which "Those*
Winter Sundays" appeared, and Complete Poems *(1985). In the following*
poem, the speaker expresses his ambivalence about his father's sacrifices.

Sundays too my father got up early
and put his clothes on in the blueblack cold,
then with cracked hands that ached
from labor in the weekday weather made
banked fires blaze. No one ever thanked him.   5

I'd wake and hear the cold splintering, breaking,
When the rooms were warm, he'd call,
and slowly I would rise and dress,
fearing the chronic angers of that house,

Speaking indifferently to him,   10
who had driven out the cold
and polished my good shoes as well.
What did I know, what did I know
of love's austere and lonely offices?

Responding to Reading

1. Other than having "driven out the cold," what has the father done for his
    son? To what might "chronic angers" (line 9) refer?
2. What important lessons has the speaker learned? When do you think he
    learned them? Do you see these lessons as primarily theoretical or practical?
3. In what respects does this poem sound like conversational speech? In what
    respects is it "poetic"?

Responding in Writing

What do you now know about your parents' responsibilities and sacrifices that
you did not know when you were a child? How has this knowledge changed
your feelings about your parents?

MY GRANDMOTHER'S DUMPLING

Amy Ma

Based in Hong Kong, Amy Ma writes about her Chinese heritage. In "My Grandmother's Dumpling," Ma describes how a yearly family tradition has shaped generations.

There was no denying a dumpling error. If the meat tumbled out of a poorly made one as it cooked, Grandmother could always tell who made it because she had personally assigned each of us a specific folding style at the onset of our dumpling-making education. In our house, a woman's folding style identified her as surely as her fingerprints.

"From now on, you and only you will fold it in this way," she instructed me in our Taipei kitchen in 1994, the year I turned 13. That is when I had reached a skill level worthy of joining the rest of the women—10 in all, from my 80-year-old grandmother, Lu Xiao-fang, to my two middle-aged aunts, my mother and the six children of my generation—in the folding of *jiao zi*, or dumplings, for Chinese New Year. Before then, I had been relegated to prep work: mixing the meat filling or cutting the dough and flattening it.

Cousin Mao Mao, the eldest daughter of my grandmother's first son, had been away for four years at college in the U.S. But with casual ease, she fashioned her dumplings in the style of the rat, tucking in the creases and leaving a small tail that pinched together at one end. Two distinct pleats in a fan-shaped dumpling marked the work of Aunt Yee, Mao Mao's mother, who had just become a grandmother herself with the birth of a grandson. A smaller purse-like dumpling with eight folds toward the center was my mother's. Grandmother's dumplings were the simplest of the bunch—flat, crescent-shaped with no creases and a smooth edge. And as I was the youngest in my generation, she'd thought it appropriate to make my signature design a quirky variation of her own, with an added crimping to create a rippling *hua bian,* or flower edge.

"A pretty little edge, for a pretty little girl," she said.

5   While dumplings graced our tables year-round, they were a requisite dish during the Lunar New Year holidays. The Spring Festival, as it is known in China—*chun jie*—is arguably the most important celebration of the year: It is a time to be with family, to visit friends and start life anew—and eat dumplings.

The length of observance varies. Today in Taiwan, the national holiday stretches to nine days—including two weekends—with all businesses and government offices closed. In mainland China, officials rearrange the working calendar to give the public seven consecutive days off, while in Hong Kong there are three public holidays and in Singapore, two. Unofficially, many Chinese people consider the traditional period of the first 15 days appropriate to welcome the new year.

My family celebrated the first three days of the Spring Festival in a traditional way: Everyone came "home," which meant to my grandfather's house. We were already home—my father, mother, brother and I lived in Taipei with my father's parents, who had moved from China in the late 1940s. Most of my father's family lived nearby. On *chu yi*, the first day of the new year, friends came to our house to extend greetings. For *chu er*, the second day, married women returned to their parents' house. The third day, *chu san*, was always celebrated united, as a family. And on each of those days, dumplings were the main food served during lunch and dinner. There might be other side dishes—leftovers from New Year's Eve—but no other food was prepared from scratch during the holiday. It was considered bad luck to do any work during this time; to ensure a peaceful year ahead, you had to rest and that meant no cooking.

Though it isn't known exactly when dumplings came into being, author and Chinese food expert Fuchsia Dunlop says jiao zi date as far back as 1,100 years ago. "In the city of Turpan, a tomb was uncovered that had boiled dumplings from the Tang dynasty (618–907) preserved in much the same shape with similar fillings as they are today," says Ms. Dunlop.

Many people believe the practice of eating these dumplings on Chinese New Year became popular in the Yuan and Ming dynasties, which stretched from 1271 to 1644, when *yuan bao*—gold and silver ingots—began to take hold as currency in China; the dumplings take the shape of those coins. During new year celebrations, filling your stomach with edible replicas of ingots was thought to ensure a year of prosperity ahead. The packaged bites also celebrated a letting go of the past, since the word "*jiao*" also means "the end of something."

Traditions have relaxed: Not every family eats only dumplings for three days. They also vary regionally: In the south of China, *nian gao*, or rice cakes, are often served instead of these dough-swaddled morsels at Chinese New Year. Still, hefty portions of dumplings undoubtedly remain a big attraction this time of year in many Chinese households.

Even now, that initial bite of any dumpling transports me back to our Taipei kitchen: the women packed like sardines working on their craft with a Zen-like rhythm, the flour-dusted countertops, the air redolent with the scent of dough, and the faded brown ceramic tiles on the floor polished smooth by countless footsteps over the years.

The great dumpling cook-off commenced each year following Lunar New Year's Eve dinner, a family meal of Grandmother's best dishes—sweet soy-braised pork, *ru yi cai* (10 vegetables tossed together with a soy-sauce vinaigrette), and always steamed fish since its term in Mandarin, "*yu*," is a homonym for "plenty." By 9 P.M., the plates were cleared and washed, and the women were clustered in the kitchen.

The men, forbidden to enter the cooking area, dispersed to their separate corners to talk politics and play dice or mahjong while awaiting the countdown to midnight. Every room of the house swelled with

festivity as the whole family of more than 30 members—four generations—gathered for this night in my grandparents' house.

Amid the bustle, the kitchen alone had an air of serenity and purpose
as the women worked through the night. Before dawn of the next morning, there would be enough dumplings to cover two large dining room
tables and every kitchen countertop.

15   To start, Grandmother unloaded from the refrigerator the large ball
of dough made from flour, cold water and a dash of egg white (her secret
ingredient) that she had prepared the day before. Setting it onto the
butcher block with her plump and sturdy hands, she ripped off two large
balls and rolled each into a log, starting her gentle kneading from the center and stretching out to both sides. The remaining dough she kept covered under a damp towel.

Meanwhile, the rest of the women—my mother and two aunts and
my cousins and me—picked over bunches of coriander and peeled off
the wilted layers of scallions and cabbages. A liberal douse of salt sprinkled over the cabbage drew out the excess water, and the chopped
confetti-like bits were hand-squeezed to prevent a watery dumpling filling. The butcher knife rocked repeatedly back and forth on the ginger
and garlic until it was almost a paste. Likewise, the vegetables had to be
diced as finely as possible so they would be evenly spread through every
bite of the final product.

Ignoring the slew of innovative options for fillings popular in contemporary restaurants—shrimp and chives, shark's fin and vermicelli—
we filled our no-frills dumplings with minced pork. Into the pink ground
meat went the chopped speckles of vegetables and herbs along with sesame
oil, Shaoxin wine, salt, soy sauce, a pinch of sugar, white pepper, five-spice
powder and an egg. Nothing was measured, yet it always tasted the same.

"That's enough mixing," Grandmother cautioned. My mother was using
a pair of wooden chopsticks to combine the ingredients in large circular
motions. Grandmother insisted on only combing through the filling in one
direction—clockwise—so as to not over-mix, which would make it tough.

Then like a carefully orchestrated master plan, a natural assembly
line formed. First, Grandmother cut off equal-size segments of her log
of dough and then passed them to my mother, who used a wooden
roller to flatten them into circles, a process called *gan mien*. Two aunts
continued to fashion new dough into logs on one end of the kitchen
counter, and three cousins lined up on the other end to begin filling and
folding dumplings. The positions would alternate periodically, and
makers would move up the line over the years as their skills improved.
At 5 years old, my job had been the menial task of pressing the just-cut
dough segments into flat disks so they would be easier to roll out, but
I had since graduated to a dumpling folder. All together, we women
stood, each ready to play her part in this culinary theater.

20   "Every step requires its own *kung fu*," Grandmother instructed in
Mandarin. She was short, but her chubby silhouette held the solid stance

of a symphony conductor. The process was tedious, but a mere mention of serving a frozen dumpling from a supermarket would be confronted with a gaze that screamed: uncultured, unbelievable, un-*Chinese*. The matriarch in her kitchen was doing more than just cooking; she was training the next generation of wives, daughters and mothers as her mother-in-law had taught her.

"Use your palm to control the roller, not your fingertips," she barked. "Keep a steady rhythm, consistent like your pulse." The dumpling skins weren't flattened in one fell swoop like a pie crust. Each one had to be rolled just around the rim and rotated so that the resulting circle was thinner on the edges than in the center. When folded in half the two sides met, the dumpling skin was uniform in thickness. It was a painstaking task when repeated over the span of many hours, and my mother once showed me her swollen palms after a night of gan mien.

The amount of meat filling had to be just right. Not too much—"too greedy!"—and not too little: "too stingy!"

And dumplings had to be folded with both hands. "It's a superstition," Grandmother told us. "Women who fold dumplings with one hand won't have children. Your right and left hand have to work together to be a good mother." Grandmother demonstrated how she used the fleshy part of the index finger and thumb to press together the dough. Fresh dough, unlike frozen dough, didn't need water to seal the seams. Only a firm pinch.

"Beautifully folded," Grandmother commented on the dumpling of the newest granddaughter-in-law, Mei Fang. "But it took you too long to make. What good is a wife who makes lovely dumplings if there's not enough to feed everyone?" Grandmother asked.

The women smirked at the acrid words—she had been equally harsh 25 to all of them when they first joined the family. Grandmother had taken her lumps, too: After she married grandfather, her mother-in-law had harrassed her on the ways of making a proper dumpling. Now, Grandmother reigned over her kitchen; it was a classroom and crucible we all endured.

"It's better that I am more strict on you girls now," she sighed. "Lest you get criticized by someone else even worse than me." My mother looked over her shoulder to check on me, her only daughter, and smiled when I gave her an assuring nod.

When no one was looking, Grandmother washed a small coin and hid it in one of the dumplings to be discovered by a lucky winner, who was said to be blessed with extra good fortune for the new year. Despite my best efforts, I never chanced upon it.

Working until the early hours of the next morning in the kitchen brought out the juicier stories, ones laced with family secrets, scandals, gossips and tall-tales, all soaked up by my youthful ears.

"Did you hear? Second uncle's daughter got a tattoo."

"So-and-so's sister is really her daughter." 30

By the time the echoes of popping firecrackers filled the streets signaling the stroke of midnight, hundreds of dumplings, ready for boiling, were lined up on the kitchen sheet pans like tiny soldiers pending a final command.

With only the boiling of the dumplings left to do, the women then took turns cleaning up and bathing, all the while trailing after their children and lulling them to bed. But the majority of the family didn't sleep. The custom of *shou sui,* or staying up all night to symbolize having unlimited energy for the upcoming year, was usually followed.

Around 5 A.M., the tables were set in preparation for the midmorning dumpling brunch. But there was no counting of bowls or chopsticks. "You're not allowed to count anything during the first day of the year," reminded Grandmother. "If you don't count anything today, then the amount of possessions you have will be countless for next year." So we grabbed chopsticks by the handfuls—some wooden, some metal, all mixed in a pile—and laid them on the table alongside stacks of blue and white porcelain bowls and plates.

Before long, the first doorbell rang, and along with it came the boisterous greetings from guests, friends and neighbors. The words *gong xi fa cai* ("congratulations and be prosperous") were audible even from inside the kitchen, and they drew out the younger girls, who were eager for their *hong bao,* or red packets. These waxy packets stuffed with money were given by elders to children as a gift, and the youngest in the house could often rack up what seemed to them a small fortune. Their flour-covered fingerprints dotted the envelopes as they calculated the year's gains.

35   At 9 A.M. or when the guest count reached 10—enough to fill a table—we slid the dumplings into the stainless steel pot, careful not to let the boiling water splatter onto our bare toes, peeking out from house slippers. Grandmother insisted on never stirring the pot, and to ensure the dumplings wouldn't stick together, she slid a spatula through the bubbling broth just once in a pushing motion. Thrice the water came to a boil and each time we added more water. By the fourth time, the dumplings bobbed merrily on the surface. They were done.

Grandmother fished out the broken dumplings before turning to Cousin Jia Yin, often the culprit, in half jest. "Ah . . . thanks to you, the dumpling soup will be especially tasty this year since you've flavored it with all the filling that busted out." The casualties were fished out and quickly disposed of; broken dumplings are considered bad luck if served. To save Jia Yin's face, her father, grandmother's second son, often said at the table, "Dumplings are great, but my favorite is still the dumpling soup," ladling up another bowl.

Guests and grandparents ate first and the two large tables in the dining room were seated by gender. My grandfather took the head seat at one table with his friends, and my grandmother with hers at the other. After they ate, the tables were reset and the second generation took its turn, with my father and uncles at one table, my mother and aunts at the other. The third and fourth generations had less strict table assignments and took whatever empty chairs opened up—it could be two or three hours before it was our turn to eat.

Steaming plates were heaped high with dumplings still glistening from their hot-water bath. Diners readied themselves with their own taste-tinkering rituals in concocting the perfect dipping sauce—a combination of soy sauce, vinegar, minced garlic and sometimes sesame oil or chili paste. Grandmother's special *la ba* vinegar, marinated with whole garlic cloves, was the most coveted condiment.

Before the first bite, everyone gathered around Grandfather, who made a toast—usually with tea though sometimes he would sneak in some Chinese wine—to ring in the new year. Then, he took the first pick of the dumplings—something of an honor among the women, who held their breath in hopes that his choice of the perfect dumpling would be their own. It would have to have the ideal skin-to-filling ratio, every bite an equal portion of meat and dough, and expert craftsmanship—a balanced and symmetrical shape with firmly sealed seams.

"This one looks good to me," my grandfather decided, gently lift- 40 ing the plump parcel with the tips of his chopsticks. It was Grandmother's dumpling, and she stood poker-faced next to him, not revealing her triumph.

She remembered a time when her dumplings were the only ones on the platter. As her family grew, so too did the styles of dumplings until the plate resembled an eclectic family tree, and each doughy pouch carried within it the cross-generational memoirs of its maker. The dumpling ritual slowly faded after Grandmother's passing in 1999; Grandfather died soon after and the family scattered. But every Chinese New Year, I still make dumplings in Grandmother's way, repeating her lessons in my head.

"Eat more! Eat more! There's magic in these dumplings," Grandmother would say. And she meant it truly.

Responding to Reading

1. Given the amount and kind of information Ma provides about the Chinese New Year, and about Chinese culture in general, what kind of audience do you think she is writing for? What do you think she wants this audience to learn from her essay?
2. What do you see as the true subject of this essay? Family? Chinese New Year? Rituals? Tradition? Female roles? Something else? How do you know?
3. How would you characterize Ma's grandmother? What lessons (apart from how to make dumplings) do you think she taught her children and grandchildren?

Responding in Writing

Reread paragraph 11. Then, try to picture a scene in your own family's kitchen that might be inspired by a taste of a particular food. Write a paragraph or two describing the atmosphere of this scene.

ONCE MORE TO THE LAKE

E. B. White

1899–1985

Well known for his children's stories, Elwyn Brooks White was also a talented essayist and a witty observer of contemporary society. His expansion of Will Strunk's The Elements of Style *remains one of the most popular and concise grammar and style texts in use today. White wrote for the* New Yorker *and* Harper's Magazine, *and his essays are collected in* Essays of E. B. White *(1977). In 1939, he moved to a farm in North Brooklin, Maine, where he wrote the children's classics* Stuart Little *(1945) and* Charlotte's Web *(1952). As a youth, White vacationed with his family on a lake in Maine. It is to this lake that he returned with his son, and he describes his experience in the following essay.*

One summer, along about 1904, my father rented a camp on a lake in Maine and took us all there for the month of August. We all got ringworm from some kittens and had to rub Pond's Extract on our arms and legs night and morning, and my father rolled over in a canoe with all his clothes on; but outside of that the vacation was a success and from then on none of us ever thought there was any place in the world like that lake in Maine. We returned summer after summer—always on August 1st for one month. I have since become a salt-water man, but sometimes in summer there are days when the restlessness of the tides and the fearful cold of the sea water and the incessant wind which blows across the afternoon and into the evening make me wish for the placidity of a lake in the woods. A few weeks ago this feeling got so strong I bought myself a couple of bass hooks and a spinner and returned to the lake where we used to go, for a week's fishing and to revisit old haunts.

I took along my son, who had never had any fresh water up his nose and who had seen lily pads only from train windows. On the journey over to the lake I began to wonder what it would be like. I wondered how time would have marred this unique, this holy spot—the coves and streams, the hills that the sun set behind, the camps and the paths behind the camps. I was sure the tarred road would have found it out and I wondered in what other ways it would be desolated. It is strange how much you can remember about places like that once you allow your mind to return into the grooves which lead back. You remember one thing, and that suddenly reminds you of another thing. I guess I remembered clearest of all the early mornings, when the lake was cool and motionless, remembered how the bedroom smelled of the lumber it was made of and of the wet woods whose scent entered through the screen. The partitions in the camp were thin and did not extend clear to the top of the rooms, and as I was always the first up I would dress softly so as not to wake the others, and sneak out into the sweet outdoors and start out in the canoe, keeping close along the shore in the long shadows of the pines. I remembered being very careful never to rub my paddle against the gunwale for fear of disturbing the stillness of the cathedral.

The lake had never been what you would call a wild lake. There were cottages sprinkled around the shores, and it was in farming country although the shores of the lake were quite heavily wooded. Some of the cottages were owned by nearby farmers, and you would live at the shore and eat your meals at the farmhouse. That's what our family did. But although it wasn't wild, it was a fairly large and undisturbed lake and there were places in it which, to a child at least, seemed infinitely remote and primeval.

I was right about the tar: it led to within half a mile of the shore. But when I got back there, with my boy, and we settled into a camp near a farmhouse and into the kind of summertime I had known, I could tell that it was going to be pretty much the same as it had been before—I knew it, lying in bed the first morning, smelling the bedroom, and hearing the boy sneak quietly out and go off along the shore in a boat. I began to sustain the illusion that he was I, and therefore, by simple transposition, that I was my father. This sensation persisted, kept cropping up all the time we were there. It was not an entirely new feeling, but in this setting it grew much stronger. I seemed to be living a dual existence. I would be in the middle of some simple act, I would be picking up a bait box or laying down a table fork, or I would be saying something, and suddenly it would be not I but my father who was saying the words or making the gesture. It gave me a creepy sensation.

We went fishing the first morning. I felt the same damp moss covering the worms in the bait can, and saw the dragonfly alight on the tip of my rod as it hovered a few inches from the surface of the water. It was the arrival of this fly that convinced me beyond any doubt that everything was as it always had been, that the years were a mirage and there had been no years. The small waves were the same, chucking the rowboat under the chin as we fished at anchor, and the boat was the same boat, the same color green and the ribs broken in the same places, and under the floor-boards the same freshwater leavings and débris— the dead helgramite,[1] the wisps of moss, the rusty discarded fishhook, the dried blood from yesterday's catch. We stared silently at the tips of our rods, at the dragonflies that came and went. I lowered the tip of mine into the water, tentatively, pensively dislodging the fly, which darted two feet away, poised, darted two feet back, and came to rest again a little farther up the rod. There had been no years between the ducking of this dragonfly and the other one—the one that was part of memory. I looked at the boy, who was silently watching his fly, and it was my hands that held his rod, my eyes watching. I felt dizzy and didn't know which rod I was at the end of.

[1]The nymph of the May-fly, used as bait. [Eds.]

We caught two bass, hauling them in briskly as though they were mackerel, pulling them over the side of the boat in a businesslike manner without any landing net, and stunning them with a blow on the back of the head. When we got back for a swim before lunch, the lake was exactly where we had left it, the same number of inches from the dock, and there was only the merest suggestion of a breeze. This seemed an utterly enchanted sea, this lake you could leave to its own devices for a few hours and come back to, and find that it had not stirred, this constant and trustworthy body of water. In the shallows, the dark, water-soaked sticks and twigs, smooth and old, were undulating in clusters on the bottom against the clean ribbed sand, and the track of the mussel was plain. A school of minnows swam by, each minnow with its small individual shadow, doubling the attendance, so clear and sharp in the sunlight. Some of the other campers were in swimming, along the shore, one of them with a cake of soap, and the water felt thin and clear and unsubstantial. Over the years there had been this person with the cake of soap, this cultist, and here he was. There had been no years.

Up to the farmhouse to dinner through the teeming, dusty field, the road under our sneakers was only a two-track road. The middle track was missing, the one with the marks of the hooves and the splotches of dried, flaky manure. There had always been three tracks to choose from in choosing which track to walk in; now the choice was narrowed down to two. For a moment I missed terribly the middle alternative. But the way led past the tennis court, and something about the way it lay there in the sun reassured me; the tape had loosened along the backline, the alleys were green with plantains and other weeds, and the net (installed in June and removed in September) sagged in the dry noon, and the whole place steamed with midday heat and hunger and emptiness. There was a choice of pie for dessert, and one was blueberry and one was apple, and the waitresses were the same country girls, there having been no passage of time, only the illusion of it as in a dropped curtain—the waitresses were still fifteen; their hair had been washed, that was the only difference—they had been to the movies and seen the pretty girls with the clean hair.

Summertime, oh summertime, pattern of life indelible, the fade-proof lake, the woods unshatterable, the pasture with the sweetfern and the juniper forever and ever, summer without end; this was the background, and the life along the shore was the design, the cottagers with their innocent and tranquil design, their tiny docks with the flagpole and the American flag floating against the white clouds in the blue sky, the little paths over the roots of the trees leading from camp to camp and the paths leading back to the outhouses and the can of lime for sprinkling, and at the souvenir counters at the store the miniature birch-bark canoes and the post cards that showed things looking a little better than they looked. This was the American family at play, escaping the city heat, wondering whether the newcomers in the camp at the head of the cove were "common" or "nice," wondering whether it was true that the people who drove up for Sunday dinner at the farmhouse were turned away because there wasn't enough chicken.

It seemed to me, as I kept remembering all this, that those times and those summers had been infinitely precious and worth saving. There had been jollity and peace and goodness. The arriving (at the beginning of August) had been so big a business in itself, at the railway station the farm wagon drawn up, the first smell of the pine-laden air, the first glimpse of the smiling farmer, and the great importance of the trunks and your father's enormous authority in such matters, and the feel of the wagon under you for the long ten-mile haul, and at the top of the last long hill catching the first view of the lake after eleven months of not seeing this cherished body of water. The shouts and cries of the other campers when they saw you, and the trunks to be unpacked, to give up their rich burden. (Arriving was less exciting nowadays, when you sneaked up in your car and parked it under a tree near the camp and took out the bags and in five minutes it was all over, no fuss, no loud wonderful fuss about trunks.)

Peace and goodness and jollity. The only thing that was wrong now, 10 really, was the sound of the place, an unfamiliar nervous sound of the outboard motors. This was the note that jarred, the one thing that would sometimes break the illusion and set the years moving. In those other summertimes all motors were inboard; and when they were at a little distance, the noise they made was a sedative, an ingredient of summer sleep. They were one-cylinder and two-cylinder engines, and some were make-and-break and some were jump-spark,[2] but they all made a sleepy sound across the lake. The one-lungers throbbed and fluttered, and the twin-cylinder ones purred and purred, and that was a quiet sound too. But now the campers all had outboards. In the daytime, in the hot mornings, these motors made a petulant, irritable sound; at night, in the still evening when the afterglow lit the water, they whined about one's ears like mosquitoes. My boy loved our rented outboard, and his great desire was to achieve singlehanded mastery over it, and authority, and he soon learned the trick of choking it a little (but not too much), and the adjustment of the needle valve. Watching him I would remember the things you could do with the old one-cylinder engine with the heavy flywheel, how you could have it eating out of your hand if you got really close to it spiritually. Motor boats in those days didn't have clutches, and you would make a landing by shutting off the motor at the proper time and coasting in with a dead rudder. But there was a way of reversing them, if you learned the trick, by cutting the switch and putting it on again exactly on the final dying revolution of the flywheel, so that it would

---

[2]Methods of ignition timing. [Eds.]

kick back against compression and begin reversing. Approaching a dock in a strong following breeze, it was difficult to slow up sufficiently by the ordinary coasting method, and if a boy felt he had complete mastery over his motor, he was tempted to keep it running beyond its time and then reverse it a few feet from the dock. It took a cool nerve, because if you threw the switch a twentieth of a second too soon you would catch the flywheel when it still had speed enough to go up past center, and the boat would leap ahead, charging bull-fashion at the dock.

We had a good week at the camp. The bass were biting well and the sun shone endlessly, day after day. We would be tired at night and lie down in the accumulated heat of the little bedrooms after the long hot day and the breeze would stir almost imperceptibly outside and the smell of the swamp drift in through the rusty screens. Sleep would come easily and in the morning the red squirrel would be on the roof, tapping out his gay routine. I kept remembering everything, lying in bed in the mornings—the small steamboat that had a long rounded stern like the lip of a Ubangi, and how quietly she ran on the moonlight sails, when the older boys played their mandolins and the girls sang and we ate dough-nuts dipped in sugar, and how sweet the music was on the water in the shining night, and what it had felt like to think about girls then. After breakfast we would go up to the store and the things were in the same place—the minnows in a bottle, the plugs and spinners disarranged and pawed over by the youngsters from the boys' camp, the fig newtons and the Beeman's gum. Outside, the road was tarred and cars stood in front of the store. Inside, all was just as it had always been, except there was more Coca-Cola and not so much Moxie and root beer and birch beer and sarsaparilla. We would walk out with a bottle of pop apiece and sometimes the pop would backfire up our noses and hurt. We explored the streams, quietly, where the turtles slid off the sunny logs and dug their way into the soft bottom; and we lay on the town wharf and fed worms to the tame bass. Everywhere we went I had trouble making out which was I, the one walking at my side, the one walking in my pants.

One afternoon while we were there at that lake a thunderstorm came up. It was like the revival of an old melodrama that I had seen long ago with childish awe. The second-act climax of the drama of the electrical disturbance over a lake in America had not changed in any important respect. This was the big scene, still the big scene. The whole thing was so familiar, the first feeling of oppression and heat and a general air around camp of not wanting to go very far away. In midafternoon (it was all the same) a curious darkening of the sky, and a lull in everything that had made life tick; and then the way the boats suddenly swung the other way at their moorings with the coming of a breeze out of the new quarter, and the premonitory rumble. Then the kettle drum, then the snare, then the bass drum and cymbals, then crackling light against the dark, and the gods grinning and licking their chops in the hills. Afterward the calm, the rain steadily rustling in the calm lake, the return of light and hope and spirits, and the campers running out in joy and relief to go swimming in the rain, their bright cries perpetuating the deathless joke about how they were getting simply drenched, and the children scream- ing with delight at the new sensation of bathing in the rain, and the joke about getting drenched linking the generations in a strong indestructible chain. And the comedian who waded in carrying an umbrella.

When the others went swimming my son said he was going in too. He pulled his dripping trunks from the line where they had hung all through the shower, and wrung them out. Languidly, and with no thought of going in, I watched him, his hard little body, skinny and bare, saw him wince slightly as he pulled up around his vitals the small, soggy, icy garment. As he buckled the swollen belt suddenly my groin felt the chill of death.

Responding to Reading

1. How is White's "holy spot" different when he visits it with his son from how it was when he visited it with his father?
2. Is this essay primarily about a time, a place, or a relationship? Explain.
3. Why does White feel "the chill of death" as he watches his son? Do you identify more with White the father or White the son?

Responding in Writing

Write two short paragraphs about a place that was important to you as a child: one from the point of view of your adult self, and one from the point of view of your childhood self. How are the two paragraphs different?

NO NAME WOMAN

Maxine Hong Kingston

1940–

Maxine Hong Kingston was born in Stockton, California, the daughter of Chi- nese immigrants who ran a gambling house and, later, a laundry where she and her five siblings worked. Since her first book, The Woman Warrior: Mem- oirs of a Girlhood among Ghosts *(1976), was published, Kingston has been acclaimed as a writer of fiction and nonfiction. Her most recent novel is* The Fifth Book of Peace *(2003). In the following autobiographical essay from* The Woman Warrior, *Kingston speculates about the life and death of a fam- ily member she has never met.*

"You must not tell anyone," my mother said, "what I am about to tell you. In China your father had a sister who killed herself. She jumped into the family well. We say that your father has all brothers because it is as if she had never been born.

"In 1924 just a few days after our village celebrated seventeen hurry-up weddings—to make sure that every young man who went 'out on the road' would responsibly come home—your father and his brothers and your grandfather and his brothers and your aunt's new husband sailed for America, the Gold Mountain. It was your grandfather's last trip. Those lucky enough to get contracts waved good-bye from the decks. They fed and guarded the stowaways and helped them off in Cuba, New York, Bali, Hawaii. 'We'll meet in California next year,' they said. All of them sent money home.

"I remember looking at your aunt one day when she and I were dressing; I had not noticed before that she had such a protruding melon of a stomach. But I did not think, 'She's pregnant,' until she began to look like other pregnant women, her shirt pulling and the white tops of her black pants showing. She could not have been pregnant, you see, because her husband had been gone for years. No one said anything. We did not discuss it. In early summer she was ready to have the child, long after the time when it could have been possible.

"The village had also been counting. On the night the baby was to be born the villagers raided our house. Some were crying. Like a great saw, teeth strung with lights, files of people walked zigzag across our land, tearing the rice. Their lanterns doubled in the disturbed black water, which drained away through the broken bunds. As the villagers closed in, we could see that some of them, probably men and women we knew well, wore white masks. The people with long hair hung it over their faces. Women with short hair made it stand up on end. Some had tied white bands around their foreheads, arms, and legs.

5   "At first they threw mud and rocks at the house. Then they threw eggs and began slaughtering our stock. We could hear the animals scream their deaths—the roosters, the pigs, a last great roar from the ox. Familiar wild heads flared in our night windows; the villagers encircled us. Some of the faces stopped to peer at us, their eyes rushing like searchlights. The hands flattened against the panes, framed heads, and left red prints.

"The villagers broke in the front and the back doors at the same time, even though we had not locked the doors against them. Their knives dripped with the blood of our animals. They smeared blood on the doors and walls. One woman swung a chicken, whose throat she had slit, splattering blood in red arcs about her. We stood together in the middle of our house, in the family hall with the pictures and tables of the ancestors around us, and looked straight ahead.

"At the time the house had only two wings. When the men came back, we would build two more to enclose our courtyard and a third one to begin a second courtyard. The villagers pushed through both wings, even your grandparents' rooms, to find your aunt's, which was also mine until the men returned. From this room a new wing for one of the younger families would grow. They ripped up her clothes and shoes and broke her combs, grinding them underfoot. They tore her work from the loom. They scattered the cooking fire and rolled the new weaving in it. We could hear them in the kitchen breaking our bowls and banging the pots. They overturned the great waist-high earthenware jugs; duck eggs, pickled fruits, vegetables burst out and mixed in acrid torrents. The old woman from the next field swept a broom through the air and loosed the spirits-of-the-broom over our heads. 'Pig.' 'Ghost.' 'Pig,' they sobbed and scolded while they ruined our house.

"When they left, they took sugar and oranges to bless themselves. They cut pieces from the dead animals. Some of them took bowls that were not broken and clothes that were not torn. Afterward we swept up the rice and sewed it back up into sacks. But the smells from the spilled preserves lasted. Your aunt gave birth in the pigsty that night. The next morning when I went for the water, I found her and the baby plugging up the family well.

"Don't let your father know that I told you. He denies her. Now that you have started to menstruate, what happened to her could happen to you. Don't humiliate us. You wouldn't like to be forgotten as if you had never been born. The villagers are watchful."

Whenever she had to warn us about life, my mother told stories that 10 ran like this one, a story to grow up on. She tested our strength to establish realities. Those in the emigrant generations who could not reassert brute survival died young and far from home. Those of us in the first American generations have had to figure out how the invisible world the emigrants built around our childhoods fit in solid America.

The emigrants confused the gods by diverting their curses, misleading them with crooked streets and false names. They must try to confuse their offspring as well, who, I suppose, threaten them in similar ways—always trying to get things straight, always trying to name the unspeakable. The Chinese I know hide their names; sojourners take new names when their lives change and guard their real names with silence.

Chinese-Americans, when you try to understand what things in you are Chinese, how do you separate what is peculiar to childhood, to poverty, insanities, one family, your mother who marked your growing with stories, from what is Chinese? What is Chinese tradition and what is the movies?

If I want to learn what clothes my aunt wore, whether flashy or ordinary, I would have to begin, "Remember Father's drowned-in-the-well sister?" I cannot ask that. My mother has told me once and for all the useful parts. She will add nothing unless powered by Necessity, a riverbank that guides her life. She plants vegetable gardens rather than lawns; she carries the odd-shaped tomatoes home from the fields and eats food left for the gods.

Whenever we did frivolous things, we used up energy; we flew high kites. We children came up off the ground over the melting cones our parents brought home from work and the American movie on New Year's Day—*Oh, You Beautiful Doll* with Betty Grable one year, and *She Wore a Yellow Ribbon* with John Wayne another year. After the one carnival ride each, we paid in guilt; our tired father counted his change on the dark walk home.

15   Adultery is extravagance. Could people who hatch their own chicks and eat the embryos and the heads for delicacies and boil the feet in vinegar for party food, leaving only the gravel, eating even the gizzard lining—could such people engender a prodigal aunt? To be a woman, to have a daughter in starvation time was a waste enough. My aunt could not have been the lone romantic who gave up everything for sex. Women in the old China did not choose. Some man had commanded her to lie with him and be his secret evil. I wonder whether he masked himself when he joined the raid on her family.

Perhaps she encountered him in the fields or on the mountain where the daughters-in-law collected fuel. Or perhaps he first noticed her in the marketplace. He was not a stranger because the village housed no strangers. She had to have dealings with him other than sex. Perhaps he worked an adjoining field, or he sold her the cloth for the dress she sewed and wore. His demand must have surprised, then terrified her. She obeyed him; she always did as she was told.

When the family found a young man in the next village to be her husband, she stood tractably beside the best rooster, his proxy, and promised before they met that she would be his forever. She was lucky that he was her age and she would be the first wife, an advantage secure now. The night she first saw him, he had sex with her. Then he left for America. She had almost forgotten what he looked like. When she tried to envision him, she only saw the black and white face in the group photograph the men had had taken before leaving.

The other man was not, after all, much different from her husband. They both gave orders: she followed. "If you tell your family, I'll beat you. I'll kill you. Be here again next week." No one talked sex, ever. And she might have separated the rapes from the rest of living if only she did not have to buy her oil from him or gather wood in the same forest. I want her fear to have lasted just as long as rape lasted so that the fear could have been contained. No drawn-out fear. But women at sex hazarded birth and hence lifetimes. The fear did not stop but permeated everywhere. She told the man, "I think I'm pregnant." He organized the raid against her.

On nights when my mother and father talked about their life back home, sometimes they mentioned an "outcast table" whose business they still seemed to be settling, their voices tight. In a commensal[1] tradition,

---

[1]Eating at the same table; sharing meals as table companions. [Eds.]

where food is precious, the powerful older people made wrongdoers eat alone. Instead of letting them start separate new lives like the Japanese, who could become samurais and geishas, the Chinese family, faces averted but eyes glowering sideways, hung on to the offenders and fed them leftovers. My aunt must have lived in the same house as my parents and eaten at an outcast table. My mother spoke about the raid as if she had seen it, when she and my aunt, a daughter-in-law to a different household, should not have been living together at all. Daughters-in-law lived with their husbands' parents, not their own; a synonym for marriage in Chinese is "taking a daughter-in-law." Her husband's parents could have sold her, mortgaged her, stoned her. But they had sent her back to her own mother and father, a mysterious act hinting at disgraces not told me. Perhaps they had thrown her out to deflect the avengers.

She was the only daughter; her four brothers went with her father, husband, and uncles "out on the road" and for some years became western men. When the goods were divided among the family, three of the brothers took land, and the youngest, my father, chose an education. After my grandparents gave their daughter away to her husband's family, they had dispensed all the adventure and all the property. They expected her alone to keep the traditional ways, which her brothers, now among the barbarians, could fumble without detection. The heavy, deep-rooted women were to maintain the past against the flood, safe for returning. But the rare urge west had fixed upon our family, and so my aunt crossed boundaries not delineated in space.

The work of preservation demands that the feelings playing about in one's guts not be turned into action. Just watch their passing like cherry blossoms. But perhaps my aunt, my forerunner, caught in a slow life, let dreams grow and fade and after some months or years went toward what persisted. Fear at the enormities of the forbidden kept her desires delicate, wire and bone. She looked at a man because she liked the way the hair was tucked behind his ears, or she liked the question-mark line of a long torso curving at the shoulder and straight at the hip. For warm eyes or a soft voice or a slow walk—that's all—a few hairs, a line, a brightness, a sound, a pace, she gave up family. She offered us up for a charm that vanished with tiredness, a pigtail that didn't toss when the wind died. Why, the wrong lighting could erase the dearest thing about him.

It could very well have been, however, that my aunt did not take subtle enjoyment of her friend, but, a wild woman, kept rollicking company. Imagining her free with sex doesn't fit, though. I don't know any women like that, or men either. Unless I see her life branching into mine, she gives me no ancestral help.

To sustain her being in love, she often worked at herself in the mirror, guessing at the colors and shapes that would interest him, changing them frequently in order to hit on the right combination. She wanted him to look back.

On a farm near the sea, a woman who tended her appearance reaped a reputation for eccentricity. All the married women blunt-cut their hair in flaps about their ears or pulled it back in tight buns. No nonsense. Neither style blew easily into heart-catching tangles. And at their weddings they displayed themselves in their long hair for the last time. "It brushed the backs of my knees," my mother tells me. "It was braided, and even so, it brushed the backs of my knees."

25   At the mirror my aunt combed individuality into her bob. A bun could have been contrived to escape into black streamers blowing in the wind or in quiet wisps about her face, but only the older women in our picture album wear buns. She brushed her hair back from her forehead, tucking the flaps behind her ears. She looped a piece of thread, knotted into a circle between her index fingers and thumbs, and ran the double strand across her forehead. When she closed her fingers as if she were making a pair of shadow geese bite, the string twisted together catching the little hairs. Then she pulled the thread away from her skin, ripping the hairs out neatly, her eyes watering from the needles of pain. Opening her fingers, she cleaned the thread, then rolled it along her hairline and the tops of her eyebrows. My mother did the same to me and my sisters and herself. I used to believe that the expression "caught by the short hairs" meant a captive held with a depilatory string. It especially hurt at the temples, but my mother said we were lucky we didn't have to have our feet bound when we were seven. Sisters used to sit on their beds and cry together, she said, as their mothers or their slave removed the bandages for a few minutes each night and let the blood gush back into their veins. I hope that the man my aunt loved appreciated a smooth brow, that he wasn't just a tits-and-ass man.

Once my aunt found a freckle on her chin, at a spot that the almanac said predestined her for unhappiness. She dug it out with a hot needle and washed the wound with peroxide.

More attention to her looks than these pullings of hairs and pickings at spots would have caused gossip among the villagers. They owned work clothes and good clothes, and they wore good clothes for feasting the new seasons. But since a woman combing her hair hexes beginnings, my aunt rarely found an occasion to look her best. Women looked like great sea snails—the corded wood, babies, and laundry they carried were the whorls on their backs. The Chinese did not admire a bent back; goddesses and warriors stood straight. Still there must have been a marvelous freeing of beauty when a worker laid down her burden and stretched and arched.

Such commonplace loveliness, however, was not enough for my aunt. She dreamed of a lover for the fifteen days of New Year's, the time for families to exchange visits, money, and food. She plied her secret comb. And sure enough she cursed the year, the family, the village, and herself.

Even as her hair lured her imminent lover, many other men looked at her. Uncles, cousins, nephews, brothers would have looked, too, had they been home between journeys. Perhaps they had already been restraining their curiosity, and they left, fearful that their glances, like a field of nesting birds, might be startled and caught. Poverty hurt, and that was their first reason for leaving. But another, final reason for leaving the crowded house was the never-said.

She may have been unusually beloved, the precious only daughter, 30 spoiled and mirror gazing because of the affection the family lavished on her. When her husband left, they welcomed the chance to take her back from the in-laws; she could live like the little daughter for just a while longer. There are stories that my grandfather was different from other people, "crazy ever since the little Jap bayoneted him in the head." He used to put his naked penis on the dinner table, laughing. And one day he brought home a baby girl, wrapped up inside his brown western-style greatcoat. He had traded one of his sons, probably my father, the youngest, for her. My grandmother made him trade back. When he finally got a daughter of his own, he doted on her. They must have all loved her, except perhaps my father, the only brother who never went back to China, having once been traded for a girl.

Brothers and sisters, newly men and women, had to efface their sexual color and present plain miens.[2] Disturbing hair and eyes, a smile like no other, threatened the ideal of five generations living under one roof. To focus blurs, people shouted face to face and yelled from room to room. The immigrants I know have loud voices, unmodulated to American tones even after years away from the village where they called their friendships out across the fields. I have not been able to stop my mother's screams in public libraries or over telephones. Walking erect (knees straight, toes pointed forward, not pigeon-toed, which is Chinese-feminine) and speaking in an inaudible voice, I have tried to turn myself American-feminine. Chinese communication was loud, public. Only sick people had to whisper. But at the dinner table, where the family members came nearest one another, no one could talk, not the outcasts nor any eaters. Every word that falls from the mouth is a coin lost. Silently they gave and accepted food with both hands. A preoccupied child who took his bowl with one hand got a sideways glare. A complete moment of total attention is due everyone alike. Children and lovers have no singularity here, but my aunt used a secret voice, a separate attentiveness.

She kept the man's name to herself throughout her labor and dying; she did not accuse him that he be punished with her. To save her inseminator's name she gave silent birth.

He may have been somebody in her own household, but intercourse with a man outside the family would have been no less abhorrent. All

---

[2]Appearances. [Eds.]

the village were kinsmen, and the titles shouted in loud country voices never let kinship be forgotten. Any man within visiting distance would have been neutralized as a lover—"brother," "younger brother," "older brother"—one hundred and fifteen relationship titles. Parents researched birth charts probably not so much to assure good fortune as to circumvent incest in a population that has but one hundred surnames. Everybody has eight million relatives. How useless then sexual mannerisms, how dangerous.

As if it came from an atavism[3] deeper than fear, I used to add "brother" silently to boys' names. It hexed the boys, who would or would not ask me to dance, and made them less scary and as familiar and deserving of benevolence as girls.

35   But, of course, I hexed myself also—no dates. I should have stood up, both arms waving, and shouted out across libraries, "Hey, you! Love me back." I had no idea, though, how to make attraction selective, how to control its direction and magnitude. If I made myself American-pretty so that the five or six Chinese boys in the class fell in love with me, everyone else—the Caucasian, Negro, and Japanese boys—would too. Sisterliness, dignified and honorable, made much more sense.

Attraction eludes control so stubbornly that whole societies designed to organize relationships among people cannot keep order, not even when they bind people to one another from childhood and raise them together. Among the very poor and the wealthy, brothers married their adopted sisters, like doves. Our family allowed some romance, paying adult brides' prices and providing dowries so that their sons and daughters could marry strangers. Marriage promises to turn strangers into friendly relatives—a nation of siblings.

In the village structure, spirits shimmered among the live creatures, balanced and held in equilibrium by time and land. But one human being flaring up into violence could open up a black hole, a maelstrom that pulled in the sky. The frightened villagers, who depended on one another to maintain the real, went to my aunt to show her a personal, physical representation of the break she had made in the "roundness." Misallying couples snapped off the future, which was to be embodied in true offspring. The villagers punished her for acting as if she could have a private life, secret and apart from them.

If my aunt had betrayed the family at a time of large grain yields and peace, when many boys were born, and wings were being built on many houses, perhaps she might have escaped such severe punishment. But the men—hungry, greedy, tired of planting in dry soil, cuckolded— had had to leave the village in order to send food-money home. There were ghost plagues, bandit plagues, wars with the Japanese, floods. My Chinese brother and sister had died of an unknown sickness. Adultery,

---

[3]The reappearance of a characteristic after a long absence. [Eds.]

perhaps only a mistake during good times, became a crime when the village needed food.

The round moon cakes and round doorways, the round tables of graduated size that fit one roundness inside another, round windows and rice bowls—these talismans had lost their power to warn this family of the law: a family must be whole, faithfully keeping the descent line by having sons to feed the old and the dead, who in turn look after the family. The villagers came to show my aunt and her lover-in-hiding a broken house. The villagers were speeding up the circling of events because she was too shortsighted to see that her infidelity had already harmed the village, that waves of consequences would return unpredictably, sometimes in disguise, as now, to hurt her. This roundness had to be made coin-sized so that she would see its circumference: punish her at the birth of her baby. Awaken her to the inexorable. People who refused fatalism because they could invent small resources insisted on culpability. Deny accidents and wrest fault from the stars.

After the villagers left, their lanterns now scattering in various directions toward home, the family broke their silence and cursed her. "Aiaa, we're going to die. Death is coming. Death is coming. Look what you've done. You've killed us. Ghost! Dead ghost! Ghost! You've never been born." She ran out into the fields, far enough from the house so that she could no longer hear their voices, and pressed herself against the earth, her own land no more. When she felt the birth coming, she thought that she had been hurt. Her body seized together. "They've hurt me too much," she thought. "This is gall, and it will kill me." With forehead and knees against the earth, her body convulsed and then relaxed. She turned on her back, lay on the ground. The black well of sky and stars went out and out and out forever; her body and her complexity seemed to disappear. She was one of the stars, a bright dot in blackness, without home, without a companion, in eternal cold and silence. And agoraphobia[4] rose in her, speeding higher and higher, bigger and bigger; she would not be able to contain it; there would be no end to fear.

Flayed, unprotected against space, she felt pain return, focusing her body. This pain chilled her—a cold, steady kind of surface pain. Inside, spasmodically, the other pain, the pain of the child, heated her. For hours she lay on the ground, alternately body and space. Sometimes a vision of normal comfort obliterated reality: she saw the family in the evening gambling at the dinner table, the young people massaging their elders' backs. She saw them congratulating one another, high joy on the mornings the rice shoots came up. When these pictures burst, the stars drew yet further apart. Black space opened.

She got to her feet to fight better and remembered that old-fashioned women gave birth in their pigsties to fool the jealous, pain-dealing gods,

40

---

[4]Pathological fear of being helpless or embarrassed in a public situation, characterized by avoidance of public places. [Eds.]

who do not snatch piglets. Before the next spasms could stop her, she ran to the pigsty, each step a rushing out into emptiness. She climbed over the fence and knelt in the dirt. It was good to have a fence enclosing her, a tribal person alone.

Laboring, this woman who had carried her child as a foreign growth that sickened her every day, expelled it at last. She reached down to touch the hot, wet, moving mass, surely smaller than anything human, and could feel that it was human after all—fingers, toes, nails, nose. She pulled it up on to her belly, and it lay curled there, butt in the air, feet precisely tucked one under the other. She opened her loose shirt and buttoned the child inside. After resting, it squirmed and thrashed and she pushed it up to her breast. It turned its head this way and that until it found her nipple. There, it made little snuffling noises. She clenched her teeth at its preciousness, lovely as a young calf, a piglet, a little dog.

She may have gone to the pigsty as a last act of responsibility: she would protect this child as she had protected its father. It would look after her soul, leaving supplies on her grave. But how would this tiny child without family find her grave when there would be no marker for her anywhere, neither in the earth nor the family hall? No one would give her a family hall name. She had taken the child with her into the wastes. At its birth the two of them had felt the same raw pain of separation, a wound that only the family pressing tight could close. A child with no descent line would not soften her life but only trail after her, ghost-like, begging her to give it purpose. At dawn the villagers on their way to the fields would stand around the fence and look.

45   Full of milk, the little ghost slept. When it awoke, she hardened her breasts against the milk that crying loosens. Toward morning she picked up the baby and walked to the well.

Carrying the baby to the well shows loving. Otherwise abandon it. Turn its face into the mud. Mothers who love their children take them along. It was probably a girl; there is some hope of forgiveness for boys.

"Don't tell anyone you had an aunt. Your father does not want to hear her name. She has never been born." I have believed that sex was unspeakable and words so strong and fathers so frail that "aunt" would do my father mysterious harm. I have thought that my family, having settled among immigrants who had also been their neighbors in the ancestral land, needed to clean their name, and a wrong word would incite the kinspeople even here. But there is more to this silence: they want me to participate in her punishment. And I have.

In the twenty years since I heard this story I have not asked for details nor said my aunt's name; I do not know it. People who can comfort the dead can also chase after them to hurt them further—a reverse ancestor worship. The real punishment was not the raid swiftly inflicted by the villagers, but the family's deliberately forgetting her. Her betrayal so maddened them, they saw to it that she would suffer forever, even after death. Always hungry, always needing, she would have to beg food from other ghosts, snatch and steal it from those whose living descendants give them gifts. She would have to fight the ghosts massed at crossroads for the buns a few thoughtful citizens leave to decoy her away from village and home so that the ancestral spirits could feast unharassed. At peace, they could act like gods, not ghosts, their descent lines providing them with paper suits and dresses, spirit money, paper houses, paper automobiles, chicken, meat, and rice into eternity—essences delivered up in smoke and flames, steam and incense rising from each rice bowl. In an attempt to make the Chinese care for people outside the family, Chairman Mao[5] encourages us now to give our paper replicas to the spirits of outstanding soldiers and workers, no matter whose ancestors they may be. My aunt remains forever hungry. Goods are not distributed evenly among the dead.

My aunt haunts me—her ghost drawn to me because now, after fifty years of neglect, I alone devote pages of paper to her, though not origamied into houses and clothes. I do not think she always means me well. I am telling on her, and she was a spite suicide, drowning herself in the drinking water. The Chinese are always very frightened of the drowned one, whose weeping ghost, wet hair hanging and skin bloated, waits silently by the water to pull down a substitute.

Responding to Reading

1. How accurate do you imagine Kingston's "facts" are? Do you think strict accuracy is important in this essay? Why or why not?
2. Kingston never met her aunt; in fact, she doesn't even know her name. Even so, in what sense is this essay about her relationship with her aunt (and with other family members, both known and unknown)?
3. In paragraph 49, Kingston says, "My aunt haunts me—." Why do you think Kingston is "haunted" by her aunt's story?

Responding in Writing

Write a one-paragraph biographical sketch of a family member whose memory "haunts" you. Or, write a short obituary of a deceased relative.

---

[5]Mao Zedong (1893–1976), founder and leader of the communist People's Republic of China from 1949 until his death. [Eds.]

BEAUTY: WHEN THE OTHER DANCER IS THE SELF

Alice Walker

1944–

Alice Walker, best known for her award-winning novel The Color Purple
*(1982), is recognized as an important voice among African-American women
writers. Born in Georgia, the daughter of sharecroppers, Walker received scholarships to Spelman College in Atlanta and Sarah Lawrence College in
Bronxville, New York. Her work, which often focuses on racism and sexism,
includes poetry, novels, short stories, essays, criticism, a biography of Langston
Hughes, and an edition of Zora Neale Hurston's collection* I Love Myself
When I Am Laughing *(1979). Walker's most recent work is the children's
book* Why War Is Never a Good Idea *(2007). Like much of her writing, the
following essay moves from pain and despair to self-celebration.*

It is a bright summer day in 1947. My father, a fat, funny man with beautiful eyes and a subversive wit, is trying to decide which of his eight
children he will take with him to the county fair. My mother, of course,
will not go. She is knocked out from getting most of us ready: I hold my
neck stiff against the pressure of her knuckles as she hastily completes
the braiding and then beribboning of my hair.

My father is the driver for the rich old white lady up the road. Her
name is Miss Mey. She owns all the land for miles around, as well as the
house in which we live. All I remember about her is that she once offered
to pay my mother thirty-five cents for cleaning her house, raking up
piles of her magnolia leaves, and washing her family's clothes, and that
my mother—she of no money, eight children, and a chronic earache—
refused it. But I do not think of this in 1947. I am two and a half years old.
I want to go everywhere my daddy goes. I am excited at the prospect of
riding in a car. Someone has told me fairs are fun. That there is room in
the car for only three of us doesn't faze me at all. Whirling happily in my
starchy frock, showing off my biscuit-polished patent-leather shoes and
lavender socks, tossing my head in a way that makes my ribbons bounce,
I stand, hands on hips, before my father. "Take me, Daddy," I say with
assurance; "I'm the prettiest!"

Later, it does not surprise me to find myself in Miss Mey's shiny
black car, sharing the back seat with the other lucky ones. Does not surprise me that I thoroughly enjoy the fair. At home that night I tell the
unlucky ones all I can remember about the merry-go-round, the man
who eats live chickens, and the teddy bears, until they say: "That's
enough, baby Alice. Shut up now, and go to sleep."

It is Easter Sunday, 1950. I am dressed in a green, flocked, scalloped-hem dress (handmade by my adoring sister, Ruth) that has its own smooth satin petticoat and tiny hot-pink roses tucked into each scallop. My shoes, new T-strap patent leather, again highly biscuit-polished. I am six years old and have learned one of the longest Easter speeches to be heard that day, totally unlike the speech I said when I was two: "Easter lilies/pure and white/blossom in/the morning light." When I rise to give my speech I do so on a great wave of love and pride and expectation. People in the church stop rustling their new crinolines. They seem to hold their breath. I can tell they admire my dress, but it is my spirit, bordering on sassiness (womanishness), they secretly applaud.

"That girl's a little *mess*," they whisper to each other, pleased.   5

Naturally I say my speech without stammer or pause, unlike those who stutter, stammer, or, worst of all, forget. This is before the word "beautiful" exists in people's vocabulary, but "Oh, isn't she the *cutest* thing!" frequently floats my way. "And got so much sense!" they gratefully add . . . for which thoughtful addition I thank them to this day.

It was great fun being cute. But then, one day, it ended.

I am eight years old and a tomboy. I have a cowboy hat, cowboy boots, checkered shirt and pants, all red. My playmates are my brothers, two and four years older than I. Their colors are black and green, the only difference in the way we are dressed. On Saturday nights we all go to the picture show, even my mother; Westerns are her favorite kind of movie. Back home, "on the ranch," we pretend we are Tom Mix, Hopalong Cassidy, Lash LaRue (we've even named one of our dogs Lash LaRue); we chase each other for hours rustling cattle, being outlaws, delivering damsels from distress. Then my parents decide to buy my brothers guns. These are not "real" guns. They shoot "BBs," copper pellets my brothers say will kill birds. Because I am a girl, I do not get a gun. Instantly I am relegated to the position of Indian. Now there appears a great distance between us. They shoot and shoot at everything with their new guns. I try to keep up with my bow and arrows.

One day while I am standing on top of our makeshift "garage"—pieces of tin nailed across some poles—holding my bow and arrow and looking out toward the fields, I feel an incredible blow in my right eye. I look down just in time to see my brother lower his gun.

Both brothers rush to my side. My eye stings, and I cover it with my   10 hand. "If you tell," they say, "we will get a whipping. You don't want that to happen, do you?" I do not. "Here is a piece of wire," says the older brother, picking it up from the roof; "say you stepped on one end of it and the other flew up and hit you." The pain is beginning to start. "Yes," I say, "Yes, I will say that is what happened." If I do not say this is what happened, I know my brothers will find ways to make me wish I had. But now I will say anything that gets me to my mother.

Confronted by our parents we stick to the lie agreed upon. They place me on a bench on the porch and I close my left eye while they examine the right. There is a tree growing from underneath the porch that climbs past the railing to the roof. It is the last thing my right eye sees. I watch as its trunk, its branches, and then its leaves are blotted out by the rising blood.

I am in shock. First there is intense fever, which my father tries to break using lily leaves bound around my head. Then there are chills: my mother tries to get me to eat soup. Eventually, I do not know how, my parents learn what has happened. A week after the "accident" they take me to see a doctor. "Why did you wait so long to come?" he asks, looking into my eye and shaking his head. "Eyes are sympathetic," he says. "If one is blind, the other will likely become blind too."

This comment of the doctor's terrifies me. But it is really how I look that bothers me most. Where the BB pellet struck there is a glob of whitish scar tissue, a hideous cataract, on my eye. Now when I stare at people—a favorite pastime, up to now—they will stare back. Not at the "cute" little girl, but at her scar. For six years I do not stare at anyone, because I do not raise my head.

Years later, in the throes of a mid-life crisis, I ask my mother and sister whether I changed after the "accident." "No," they say, puzzled. "What do you mean?"

15 *What do I mean?*

I am eight, and, for the first time, doing poorly in school, where I have been something of a whiz since I was four. We have just moved to the place where the "accident" occurred. We do not know any of the people around us because this is a different county. The only time I see the friends I knew is when we go back to our old church. The new school is the former state penitentiary. It is a large stone building, cold and drafty, crammed to overflowing with boisterous, ill-disciplined children. On the third floor there is a huge circular imprint of some partition that has been torn out.

"What used to be here?" I ask a sullen girl next to me on our way past it to lunch.

"The electric chair," says she.

At night I have nightmares about the electric chair, and about all the people reputedly "fried" in it. I am afraid of the school, where all the students seem to be budding criminals.

20 "What's the matter with your eye?" they ask, critically.

When I don't answer (I cannot decide whether it was an "accident" or not), they shove me, insist on a fight.

My brother, the one who created the story about the wire, comes to my rescue. But then brags so much about "protecting" me, I become sick.

After months of torture at the school, my parents decide to send me back to our old community, to my old school. I live with my grandparents and the teacher they board. But there is no room for Phoebe, my cat. By the time my grandparents decide there *is* room, and I ask for my cat, she cannot be found. Miss Yarborough, the boarding teacher, takes me under her wing, and begins to teach me to play the piano. But soon she marries an African—a "prince," she says—and is whisked away to his continent.

At my old school there is at least one teacher who loves me. She is the teacher who "knew me before I was born" and bought my first baby clothes. It is she who makes life bearable. It is her presence that finally helps me turn on the one child at the school who continually calls me "one-eyed bitch." One day I simply grab him by his coat and beat him until I am satisfied. It is my teacher who tells me my mother is ill.

My mother is lying in bed in the middle of the day, something I have 25 never seen. She is in too much pain to speak. She has an abscess in her ear. I stand looking down on her, knowing that if she dies, I cannot live. She is being treated with warm oils and hot bricks held against her cheek. Finally a doctor comes. But I must go back to my grandparents' house. The weeks pass but I am hardly aware of it. All I know is that my mother might die, my father is not so jolly, my brothers still have their guns, and I am the one sent away from home.

"You did not change," they say.

Did I imagine the anguish of never looking up?

I am twelve. When relatives come to visit I hide in my room. My cousin Brenda, just my age, whose father works in the post office and whose mother is a nurse, comes to find me. "Hello," she says. And then she asks, looking at my recent school picture, which I did not want taken, and on which the "glob," as I think of it, is clearly visible, "You still can't see out of that eye?"

"No," I say, and flop back on the bed over my book.

That night, as I do almost every night, I abuse my eye. I rant and 30 rave at it, in front of the mirror. I plead with it to clear up before morning. I tell it I hate and despise it. I do not pray for sight. I pray for beauty.

"You did not change," they say.

I am fourteen and baby-sitting for my brother Bill, who lives in Boston. He is my favorite brother and there is a strong bond between us. Understanding my feelings of shame and ugliness he and his wife take me to a local hospital, where the "glob" is removed by a doctor named O. Henry. There is still a small bluish crater where the scar tissue was, but the ugly white stuff is gone. Almost immediately I become a different person from the girl who does not raise her head. Or so I think. Now that I've raised my head I win the boyfriend of my dreams. Now that I've raised my head I have plenty of friends. Now that I've raised my head classwork comes from my lips as faultlessly as Easter speeches did, and I leave high school as valedictorian, most popular student, and *queen,* hardly believing my luck. Ironically, the girl who was voted most beautiful in our class (and was) was later shot twice through the chest by a male companion, using a "real" gun, while she was pregnant. But that's another story in itself. Or is it?

"You did not change," they say.

It is now thirty years since the "accident." A beautiful journalist comes to visit and to interview me. She is going to write a cover story for her magazine that focuses on my latest book. "Decide how you want to look on the cover," she says. "Glamorous, or whatever."

35   Never mind "glamorous," it is the "whatever" that I hear. Suddenly all I can think of is whether I will get enough sleep the night before the photography session: if I don't, my eye will be tired and wander, as blind eyes will.

At night in bed with my lover I think up reasons why I should not appear on the cover of a magazine. "My meanest critics will say I've sold out," I say. "My family will now realize I write scandalous books."

"But what's the real reason you don't want to do this?" he asks.

"Because in all probability," I say in a rush, "my eye won't be straight."

"It will be straight enough," he says. Then, "Besides, I thought you'd made your peace with that."

40   And I suddenly remember that I have.

I remember:

I am talking to my brother Jimmy, asking if he remembers anything unusual about the day I was shot. He does not know I consider that day the last time my father, with his sweet home remedy of cool lily leaves, chose me, and that I suffered and raged inside because of this. "Well," he says, "all I remember is standing by the side of the highway with Daddy, trying to flag down a car. A white man stopped, but when Daddy said he needed somebody to take his little girl to the doctor, he drove off."

I remember:

I am in the desert for the first time. I fall totally in love with it. I am so overwhelmed by its beauty, I confront for the first time, consciously, the meaning of the doctor's words years ago: "Eyes are sympathetic. If one is blind, the other will likely become blind too." I realize I have dashed about the world madly, looking at this, looking at that, storing up images against the fading of the light. *But I might have missed seeing the desert!* The shock of that possibility—and gratitude for over twenty-five years of sight—sends me literally to my knees. Poem after poem comes—which is perhaps how poets pray.

On Sight

I am so thankful I have seen
The Desert
And the creatures in the desert
And the desert Itself.

The desert has its own moon
Which I have seen
With my own eye.
There is no flag on it.

Trees of the desert have arms
All of which are always up
That is because the moon is up
The sun is up
Also the sky
The stars
Clouds
None with flags.

If there were flags, I doubt
the trees would point.
Would you?

But mostly, I remember this: 45

I am twenty-seven, and my baby daughter is almost three. Since her birth I have worried about her discovery that her mother's eyes are different from other people's. Will she be embarrassed? I think. What will she say? Every day she watches a television program called "Big Blue Marble." It begins with a picture of the earth as it appears from the moon. It is bluish, a little battered-looking, but full of light, with whitish clouds swirling around it. Every time I see it I weep with love, as if it is a picture of Grandma's house. One day when I am putting Rebecca down for her nap, she suddenly focuses on my eye. Something inside me cringes, gets ready to try to protect myself. All children are cruel about physical differences, I know from experience, and that they don't always mean to be is another matter. I assume Rebecca will be the same.

But no-o-o-o. She studies my face intently as we stand, her inside and me outside her crib. She even holds my face maternally between her dimpled little hands. Then, looking every bit as serious and lawyerlike as her father, she says, as if it may just possibly have slipped my attention: "Mommy, there's a *world* in your eye." (As in, "Don't be alarmed, or do anything crazy.") And then, gently, but with great interest: "Mommy, where did you get that world in your eye?"

For the most part, the pain left then. (So what, if my brothers grew up to buy even more powerful pellet guns for their sons and to carry real guns themselves. So what, if a young "Morehouse man"[1] once nearly fell off the steps of Trevor Arnett Library because he thought my eyes were blue.) Crying and laughing I ran to the bathroom, while Rebecca mumbled and sang herself off to sleep. Yes indeed, I realized, looking into the mirror. There was a world in my eye. And I saw that it was possible to love it: that in fact, for all it had taught me of shame and anger and inner vision, I *did* love it. Even to see it drifting out of orbit in boredom, or rolling up out of fatigue, not to mention floating back at attention in excitement (bearing witness, a friend has called it), deeply suitable to my personality, and even characteristic of me.

That night I dream I am dancing to Stevie Wonder's song "Always" (the name of the song is really "As," but I hear it as "Always"). As I dance, whirling and joyous, happier than I've ever been in my life, another bright-faced dancer joins me. We dance and kiss each other and hold each other through the night. The other dancer has obviously come through all right, as I have done. She is beautiful, whole and free. And she is also me.

Responding to Reading

1. Although she is remembering past events, Walker uses present tense ("It is a bright summer day in 1947") to tell her story. Why do you think she does this? Is the present tense more effective than the past tense ("It *was* a bright summer day in 1947") would be? Explain.
2. At several points in the essay, Walker repeats the words her relatives used to reassure her: "You did not change." Why does she repeat this phrase? Were her relatives correct?
3. What circumstances or individuals does Walker blame for the childhood problems she describes? Who do you think is responsible for her misery? Would you be as forgiving as Walker seems to be?

Responding in Writing

Using present tense, write a paragraph or two about a painful incident from your childhood. Begin with a sentence that tells how old you are ("I am _____.").

---

[1]A student at Morehouse College, a historically black college in Atlanta, Georgia. [Eds.]

SIXTY-NINE CENTS
Gary Shteyngart
1972–

Born in Leningrad (now called Saint Petersburg), Russia, Gary Shteyngart immigrated to the United States when he was seven years old. The author of two highly acclaimed novels, Shteyngart has published numerous essays and short stories in publications such as the New York Times Magazine, *the* New Yorker, Esquire, *and* GQ. *In the following essay, Shteyngart recalls his mixed feelings about his family on a childhood trip to Disney World.*

When I was fourteen years old, I lost my Russian accent. I could, in theory, walk up to a girl and the words "Oh, hi there" would not sound like Okht Hyzer, possibly the name of a Turkish politician. There were three things I wanted to do in my new incarnation: go to Florida, where I understood that our nation's best and brightest had built themselves a sandy, vice-filled paradise; have a girl, preferably native-born, tell me that she liked me in some way; and eat all my meals at McDonald's. I did not have the pleasure of eating at McDonald's often. My parents believed that going to restaurants and buying clothes not sold by weight on Orchard Street[1] were things done only by the very wealthy or the very profligate, maybe those extravagant "welfare queens" we kept hearing about on television. Even my parents, however, as uncritically in love with America as only immigrants can be, could not resist the iconic pull of Florida, the call of the beach and the Mouse.

And so, in the midst of my Hebrew-school winter vacation, two Russian families crammed into a large used sedan and took I-95 down to the Sunshine State. The other family—three members in all—mirrored our own, except that their single offspring was a girl and they were, on the whole, more ample; by contrast, my entire family weighed three hundred pounds. There's a picture of us beneath the monorail at EPCOT Center, each of us trying out a different smile to express the déjà-vu feeling of standing squarely in our new country's greatest attraction, my own megawatt grin that of a turn-of-the-century Jewish peddler scampering after a potential sidewalk sale. The Disney tickets were a freebie, for which we had had to sit through a sales pitch for an Orlando time-share. "You're from Moscow?" the time-share salesman asked, appraising the polyester cut of my father's jib.

"Leningrad."

"Let me guess: mechanical engineer?"

"Yes, mechanical engineer. . . . Eh, please Disney tickets now."   5

---

[1] A shopping street on New York City's Lower East Side, a destination for generations of immigrants. [Eds.]

The ride over the MacArthur Causeway to Miami Beach was my real naturalization ceremony. I wanted all of it—the palm trees, the yachts bobbing beside the hard-currency mansions, the concrete-and-glass condominiums preening at their own reflections in the azure pool water below, the implicit availability of relations with amoral women. I could see myself on a balcony eating a Big Mac, casually throwing fries over my shoulder into the sea-salted air. But I would have to wait. The hotel reserved by my parents' friends featured army cots instead of beds and a half-foot-long cockroach evolved enough to wave what looked like a fist at us. Scared out of Miami Beach, we decamped for Fort Lauderdale, where a Yugoslav woman sheltered us in a faded motel, beach-adjacent and featuring free UHF reception. We always seemed to be at the margins of places: the driveway of the Fontainebleau Hilton, or the glassed-in elevator leading to a rooftop restaurant where we could momentarily peek over the "Please Wait to Be Seated" sign at the endless ocean below, the Old World we had left behind so far and yet deceptively near.

To my parents and their friends, the Yugoslav motel was an unquestioned paradise, a lucky coda to a set of difficult lives. My father lay magnificently beneath the sun in his red-and-black striped imitation Speedo while I stalked down the beach, past baking Midwestern girls. "Oh, hi there." The words, perfectly American, not a birthright but an acquisition, perched between my lips, but to walk up to one of those girls and say something so casual required a deep rootedness to the hot sand beneath me, a historical presence thicker than the green card embossed with my thumbprint and freckled face. Back at the motel, the *Star Trek* reruns looped endlessly on Channel 73 or 31 or some other prime number, the washed-out Technicolor planets more familiar to me than our own.

On the drive back to New York, I plugged myself firmly into my Walkman, hoping to forget our vacation. Sometime after the palm trees ran out, somewhere in southern Georgia, we stopped at a McDonald's. I could already taste it: The sixty-nine-cent hamburger. The ketchup, red and decadent, embedded with little flecks of grated onion. The uplift of the pickle slices; the obliterating rush of fresh Coca-Cola; the soda tingle at the back of the throat signifying that the act was complete. I ran into the meat-fumigated coldness of the magical place, the larger Russians following behind me, lugging something big and red. It was a cooler, packed, before we left the motel, by the other mother, the kindly, round-faced equivalent of my own mother. She had prepared a full Russian lunch for us. Soft-boiled eggs wrapped in tinfoil; *vinigret*, the Russian beet salad, overflowing a reused container of sour cream; cold chicken served between crisp white furrows of a *bulka*.[2] "But it's not allowed," I pleaded. "We have to buy the food here."

---

[2]Russian bread roll. [Eds.]

I felt coldness, not the air-conditioned chill of southern Georgia but the coldness of a body understanding the ramifications of its own demise, the pointlessness of it all. I sat down at a table as far away from my parents and their friends as possible. I watched the spectacle of the newly tanned resident aliens eating their ethnic meal—jowls working, jowls working—the soft-boiled eggs that quivered lightly as they were brought to the mouth; the girl, my coeval, sullen like me but with a hint of pliant equanimity; her parents, dishing out the chunks of beet with plastic spoons; my parents, getting up to use free McDonald's napkins and straws while American motorists with their noisy towheaded children bought themselves the happiest of meals.

My parents laughed at my haughtiness. Sitting there hungry and all 10 alone—what a strange man I was becoming! So unlike them. My pockets were filled with several quarters and dimes, enough for a hamburger and a small Coke. I considered the possibility of redeeming my own dignity, of leaving behind our beet-salad heritage. My parents didn't spend money, because they lived with the idea that disaster was close at hand, that a liver-function test would come back marked with a doctor's urgent scrawl, that they would be fired from their jobs because their English did not suffice. We were all representatives of a shadow society, cowering under a cloud of bad tidings that would never come. The silver coins stayed in my pocket, the anger burrowed and expanded into some future ulcer. I was my parents' son.

Responding to Reading

1. In paragraph 8, Shteyngart describes in detail the "full Russian lunch" his mother served the family. Why does he include this information?
2. This is an essay that contrasts the familiar world of Shteyngart's home and family with the unfamiliar world of Miami. List some of the contrasts he identifies. What other differences would you imagine exist between these two worlds?
3. How do you suppose Shteyngart's memories of this trip differ from his parents' memories?

Responding in Writing

Shteyngart's longing for a McDonald's hamburger and a Coke parallels his longing to be "American." What other products and brand names do you see as typically American? Why?

THE STORYTELLER

Sandra Cisneros

1954–

A highly acclaimed novelist, poet, and essayist, Sandra Cisneros frequently writes about her Mexican-American roots. Her works include The House on Mango Street *(1983),* My Wicked Wicked Ways *(1987),* Woman Hollering Creek and Other Stories *(1991),* Loose Woman: Poems *(1994), and* Caramelo, or, Puro Cuento: A Novel *(2002). In the following essay, which was adapted from the introduction to the twenty-fifth anniversary edition of* The House on Mango Street, *Cisneros explores the role of family and memory in shaping a writer.*

The young woman in [a photograph I remember is] me when I was writing *The House on Mango Street*. She's in her office, a room that had probably been a child's bedroom when families lived in this apartment. It has no door and is only slightly wider than the walk-in pantry. But it has great light and sits above the hallway door downstairs, so she can hear her neighbors come and go. She's posed as if she's just looked up from her work for a moment, but in real life she never writes in this office. She writes in the kitchen, the only room with a heater.

It's Chicago, 1980, in the down-at-the-heels Bucktown neighborhood before it's discovered by folks with money. The young woman lives at 1814 N. Paulina, second floor front. Nelson Algren[1] once wandered these streets. Saul Bellow's[2] turf was over on Division Street, walking distance away. It's a neighborhood that reeks of beer and urine, of sausage and beans.

The young woman fills her "office" with things she drags home from the flea market at Maxwell Street. Antique typewriters, alphabet blocks, asparagus ferns, bookshelves, ceramic figurines from Occupied Japan, wicker baskets, birdcages, hand-painted photos. Things she likes to look at. It's important to have this space to look and think. When she lived at home, the things she looked at scolded her and made her feel sad and depressed. They said, "Wash me." They said, "Lazy." They said, "You ought." But the things in her office are magical and invite her to play. They fill her with light. It's the room where she can be quiet and still and listen to the voices inside herself. She likes being alone in the daytime.

As a girl, she dreamed about having a silent home, just to herself, the way other women dreamed of their weddings. Instead of collecting

---

[1]American writer (1909–1981). [Eds.]
[2]American writer (1915–2005). [Eds.]

lace and linen for her trousseau,[3] the young woman buys old things from the thrift stores on grimy Milwaukee Avenue for her future house-of-her-own—faded quilts, cracked vases, chipped saucers, lamps in need of love.

The young woman returned to Chicago after graduate school and moved   5 back into her father's house, 1754 N. Keeler, back into her girl's room with its twin bed and floral wallpaper. She was 23 and a half. Now she summoned her courage and told her father she wanted to live alone again, like she did when she was away at school. He looked at her with that eye of the rooster before it attacks, but she wasn't alarmed. She'd seen that look before and knew he was harmless. She was his favorite, and it was only a matter of waiting.

The daughter claimed she'd been taught that a writer needs quiet, privacy, and long stretches of solitude to think. The father decided too much college and too many gringo friends had ruined her. In a way he was right. In a way she was right. When she thinks to herself in her father's language, she knows sons and daughters don't leave their parents' house until they marry. When she thinks in English, she knows she should've been on her own since 18.

For a time father and daughter reached a truce. She agreed to move into the basement of a building where the oldest of her six brothers and his wife lived, 4832 W. Homer. But after a few months, when the big brother upstairs turned out to be Big Brother, she got on her bicycle and rode through the neighborhood of her high school days until she spotted an apartment with fresh-painted walls and masking tape on the windows. Then she knocked on the storefront downstairs. That's how she convinced the landlord she was his new tenant.

Her father can't understand why she wants to live in a hundred-year-old building with big windows that let in the cold. She knows her apartment is clean, but the hallway is scuffed and scary, though she and the woman upstairs take turns mopping it regularly. The hall needs paint, and there's nothing they can do about that. When the father visits, he climbs up the stairs muttering with disgust. Inside, he looks at her books arranged in milk crates, at the futon on the floor in a bedroom with no door, and whispers, "Hippie," in the same way he looks at boys hanging out in his neighborhood and says, "Drogas."[4] When he sees the space heater in the kitchen, the father shakes his head and sighs, "Why did I work so hard to buy a house with a furnace so she could go backward and live like this?"

---

[3]Collection of a bride's belongings. [Eds.]
[4]Spanish for *drugs*. [Eds.]

When she's alone, she savors her apartment of high ceilings and windows that let in the sky, the new carpeting and walls white as typing paper, the walk-in pantry with empty shelves, her bedroom without a door, her office with its typewriter, and the big front-room windows with their view of a street, rooftops, trees, and the dizzy traffic of the Kennedy Expressway.

10   Her father calls every week to say, "*Mija*,[5] when are you coming home?" What does her mother say about all this? She puts her hands on her hips and boasts, "She gets it from me." When the father is in the room, the mother just shrugs and says, "What can I do?" The mother doesn't object. She knows what it is to live a life filled with regrets, and she doesn't want her daughter to live that life, too. She always supported the daughter's projects, so long as she went to school. The mother who painted the walls of their Chicago homes the color of flowers; who planted tomatoes and roses in her garden; sang arias; practiced solos on her son's drum set; boogied along with the *Soul Train* dancers; glued travel posters on her kitchen wall with Karo syrup; herded her kids weekly to the library, to public concerts, to museums; wore a button on her lapel that said FEED THE PEOPLE NOT THE PENTAGON; who never went beyond the ninth grade. *That* mother. She nudges her daughter and says, "Good lucky you studied."

The father wants his daughter to be a weather girl on television, or to marry and have babies. She doesn't want to be a TV weather girl. Nor does she want to marry and have babies. Not yet. Maybe later, but there are so many other things she must do in her lifetime first. Travel. Learn how to dance the tango. Publish a book. Live in other cities. Win a National Endowment for the Arts Award. See the northern lights. Jump out of a cake.

She stares at the ceilings and walls of her apartment the way she once stared at the ceilings and walls of the apartments she grew up in, inventing pictures in the cracks in the plaster, inventing stories to go with these pictures. At night, under the circle of light from a cheap metal lamp clamped to the kitchen table, she sits with paper and a pen and pretends she's not afraid. She's trying to live like a writer.

The woman I am in the photo was working on a series of vignettes, little by little, along with her poetry. I already had a title—*The House on Mango Street*. Fifty pages had been written, but I still didn't think of it as a novel. It was just a jar of buttons, like the mismatched embroidered pillowcases and monogrammed napkins I tugged from the bins at the Goodwill. I wrote these things and thought of them as "little stories," though I sensed they were connected to each other. I hadn't heard of story cycles yet. I hadn't read Ermilo Abreu Gómez's *Canek*,

---

[5]Spanish term of endearment for *daughter.* [Eds.]

Elena Poniatowska's *Lilus Kikus,* Gwendolyn Brooks's *Maud Martha,*
Nellie Campobello's *My Mother's Hands.* That would come later, when
I had more time and solitude to read.

The young woman is modeling her book-in-progress after *Dreamtigers,* by
Jorge Luis Borges—a writer she'd read since high school, story fragments
that ring like Hans Christian Andersen, or Ovid, or entries from the encyclopedia. She wants to write stories that ignore borders between genres,
between written and spoken, between highbrow literature and children's
nursery rhymes, between New York and the imaginary village of
Macondo, between the United States and Mexico. It's true, she wants the
writers she admires to respect her work, but she also wants people who
don't usually read books to enjoy these stories, too. She doesn't want to
write a book that a reader won't understand and would feel ashamed for
not understanding.

She thinks stories are about beauty. Beauty that is there to be admired [15]
by anyone, like a herd of clouds grazing overhead. She thinks people
who are busy working for a living deserve beautiful little stories, because
they don't have much time and are often tired. She has in mind a book
that can be opened at any page and will still make sense to the reader
who doesn't know what came before or comes after.

She experiments, creating a text that is as succinct and flexible as
poetry, snapping sentences into fragments so that the reader pauses,
making each sentence serve her and not the other way round, abandoning quotation marks to streamline the typography and make the
page as simple and readable as possible. So that the sentences are pliant
as branches and can be read in more ways than one.

Sometimes the woman I once was goes out on weekends to meet
with other writers. Sometimes I invite these friends to come to my apart-
ment to workshop each other's writing. We come from black, white,
Latino communities. What we have in common is our sense that art
should serve our communities. Together we publish an anthology—
Emergency Tacos, because we finish our collaborations in the early hours
before dawn and gather at the same 24-hour taqueria on Belmont
Avenue, like a multicultural version of Hopper's *Nighthawks* painting.
The *Emergency Tacos* writers organize monthly arts events at my brother
Keek's apartment—Galeria Quique. We do this with no capital except
our valuable time. We do this because the world we live in is a house on
fire and the people we love are burning.

The young woman in the photograph gets up in the morning to
go to the job that pays the rent on her Paulina Street apartment. She
teaches at a school in Pilsen, her mother's old neighborhood on
Chicago's South Side, a Mexican neighborhood where the rent is cheap
and too many families live crowded together. Landlords and the city
take no responsibility for the rats, trash that isn't collected often

enough, porches that collapse, apartments without fire escapes, until a tragedy happens and several people die. Then they hold investigations for a little while, but the problems go on until the next death, the next investigation, the next bout of forgetting.

The young woman works with students who have dropped out of high school but have decided to try again for their diplomas. She learns from her students that they have more difficult lives than her storyteller's imagination can invent. Her life has been comfortable and privileged compared with theirs. She never had to worry about feeding her babies before she went to class. She never had a father or boyfriend who beat her at night and left her bruised in the morning. She didn't have to plan an alternative route to avoid gangs in the school hallway. Her parents didn't plead with her to drop out of school so she could help them earn money.

20   The young woman's teaching job leads to the next, and now she finds herself a counselor/recruiter at her alma mater, Loyola University, on the north side, in Rogers Park. I have health benefits. I don't bring work home anymore. My workday ends at 5 P.M. Now I have evenings free to do my own work. I feel like a real writer.

On the weekends, if I can sidestep guilt and avoid my father's demands to come home for Sunday dinner, I'm free to stay home and write. I feel like a bad daughter ignoring my father, but I feel worse when I don't write. Either way, I never feel completely happy.

Often all I have is a title with no story—"The Family of Little Feet"—and I have to make the title kick me in the behind to get me going. Or sometimes all I've got is a first sentence—"You can never have too much sky." One of my Pilsen students said I had said this, and she never forgot it. Good thing she remembered and quoted it back to me. "They came with the wind that blows in August. . . ." This line came to me in a dream. Sometimes the best ideas come in dreams. Sometimes the worst ideas come from there, too!

Whether the idea came from a sentence I heard buzzing around somewhere and saved in a jar, or from a title I picked up and pocketed, the stories always insist on telling me where they want to end. They often surprise me by stopping when I had every intention of galloping along a little further. They're stubborn. They know best when there's no more to be said. The last sentence must ring like the final notes at the end of a mariachi song—*tan-tán*—to tell you when the song is done.

I meet Norma Alarcón. She is to become one of my earliest publishers and my lifetime friend. The first time she walks through the rooms of the apartment on N. Paulina, she notices the quiet rooms, the collection of typewriters, the books and Japanese figurines, the windows with the view of freeway and sky. She walks as if on tiptoe, peering into every room, even the pantry and closet as if looking for something. "You live here . . ." she asks, "alone?"

"Yes."   25

"So . . ." She pauses. "How did you do it?"

Eventually I took a job in San Antonio. Left. Came back. And left again. I kept coming back lured by cheap rent. Affordable housing is essential to an artist. I could, in time, even buy my own first house, a hundred-year-old home once periwinkle, but now painted a Mexican pink.

Two years ago my office went up in my backyard, a building created from my Mexican memories. I am writing this today from this very office, Mexican marigold on the outside, morning-glory violet on the inside. Wind chimes ring from the terrace. Trains moan in the distance all the time, ours is a neighborhood of trains. The same San Antonio River tourists know from the Riverwalk wends its way behind my house to the Missions and beyond until it empties into the Gulf of Mexico. From my terrace you can see the river where it bends into an S.

White cranes float across the sky like a scene painted on a lacquered screen. The river shares the land with ducks, raccoons, possums, skunks, buzzards, butterflies, hawks, turtles, snakes, owls, even though we're walking distance to downtown. And within the confines of my own garden there are plenty of other creatures too—yappy dogs, kamikaze cats, one lovesick parrot with a crush on me.

This is my house.   30

Bliss.

Responding to Reading

1. Although she is writing largely about past events in her own life, Cisneros often uses third person and present tense: "The young woman fills her 'office' . . ." (3); "It's Chicago, 1980 . . ." (2). Why? Where does she use first person? Where does she use past tense? Can you explain these shifts?

2. What is the source of Cisneros's conflict with her father? What does he want for her? What does she want for herself? Is this conflict ever resolved?

3. Do you think the primary focus of this essay is on Cisneros's life as a writer, her life as a daughter, or her life as a woman? Explain.

Responding in Writing

Cisneros focuses on a variety of places that were important to her—for example, her first "office" (3), her "apartment of high ceilings and windows that let in the sky" (9), and her house in San Antonio. Write a few paragraphs about places that have been important to you. Introduce each place with a "snapshot" sentence that identifies and describes it.

—————————— WRITING ——————————

Family and Memory

1. What exactly is a family? Is it a group of people bound together by love? by marriage? by blood? by history? by shared memories? by economic dependency? by habit? What unites family members, and what divides them? Does *family* denote only a traditional nuclear family or also a family broken by divorce and blended by remarriage? Define *family* as it is portrayed in several of the readings in this chapter.

2. Leo Tolstoy's classic Russian novel *Anna Karenina* opens with this sentence: "Happy families are all alike; every unhappy family is unhappy in its own way." Write an essay in which you agree with or challenge this statement, supporting your position with references to several of the readings in this chapter.

3. In a sense, memories are like snapshots: a series of disconnected candid pictures, sometimes unflattering, often out of focus, gradually fading. Writers of autobiographical memoirs often explore this similarity. For example, Alice Walker (p. 40) sees her painful childhood as a series of snapshots, and Sandra Cisneros (p. 50) also refers to photographs as she remembers her past. Using information from your own family life as well as from your reading, discuss the relationship between memories and photographs. If you like, you may describe and discuss some of your own family photographs. (You might begin by examining the photographs that open this chapter.)

4. In "No Name Woman" (p. 29), Maxine Hong Kingston presents a detailed biographical sketch of a family member she never knew. Using her essay as a guide, write a detailed biographical essay about a member of your own family (living or deceased). Prepare for this assignment by interviewing several family members.

5. When you think about your childhood and your young adulthood, what music do you imagine playing in the background? Write a musical autobiography that gives readers a sense of who you were at different times of your life. Try to help readers understand the times you grew up in and the person you were (and became). Or, remember the smells and tastes of the food you grew up with, as Amy Ma (p. 18) does, and write a culinary autobiography instead.

6. How do your parents' notions of success and failure affect you? Do you think your parents tend to expect too much of you? too little? Explore these ideas in an essay, referring to readings in this chapter and in Chapter 6, "The American Dream."

7. What traits, habits, and values (positive or negative) have you inherited from your parents? What qualities do you think you will pass on to your children? Read the poem "Heritage" (p. 15), and then write a letter to your parents in which you answer these two questions. Be sure to illustrate the characteristics you discuss with examples of specific incidents.

8. "Those Winter Sundays" (p. 17), told from the point of view of an adult looking back on his childhood, views the parent–child relationship with a mixture of regret and resignation. Write an essay exploring the similarly ambivalent feelings this work—and others in this chapter—convey about the relationship between child and parent.

2

ISSUES IN EDUCATION

In the nineteenth century, people had little difficulty defining the purpose of education: they assumed it was the school's job to prepare students for the roles they would play as adults. To accomplish this end, public school administrators made sure that the elementary school curriculum gave students a good dose of the basics: arithmetic, grammar, spelling, reading, composition, and penmanship. High school students studied literature, history, geography, and civics. At the elite private schools, students studied subjects that would prepare them for the leadership positions that they would eventually occupy as adults. They learned physics, rhetoric, and elocution—as well as Latin and Greek so that they could read the classics in the original.

Today, educators seem to have a great deal of difficulty agreeing on what purpose schools are supposed to serve. No longer can a group of

Fifth-grade students working together in a traditional classroom

school administrators simply proscribe a curriculum. Parents, students, politicians, academics, special interest groups, and religious leaders all attempt to influence what is taught. The result, according to some educators, is an environment in which it is almost impossible for any real education to take place. In fact, in many of today's schools, more emphasis seems to be placed on increasing self-esteem, avoiding controversy, and passing standardized tests than on challenging students to discover new ways of thinking about themselves and about the world. In this milieu, classic books are censored or rewritten to eliminate passages that might offend, ideas are presented as if they all have equal value, and the curriculum is revised so that teachers can "teach to the test." The result is an educational environment that has all the intellectual appeal of elevator music. Many people—educators included—seem to have forgotten that ideas must be unsettling if they are to make us think. After all, what is education but a process that encourages us to think critically about our world and to develop a healthy skepticism—to question, evaluate, and reach conclusions about ideas and events?

The Focus section of this chapter (p. 111) addresses the question, "How Much Do a College's Facilities Really Matter?" The essays and accompanying images in this section contrast two colleges in Iowa—one with a very large endowment and the other with a relatively small one. In addition to pointing out some obvious differences between these two colleges, the essays and the images raise some important questions about

Children being home schooled

higher education in the United States. For example, what educational advantages does a wealthy college provide? Do state-of-the-art facilities, such as those at Grinnell, actually enhance learning, or do they exist primarily to attract students? Can students get a good education from a college with more modest facilities, such as Clarke? Finally, do affluent colleges actually perpetuate the educational divide that separates the rich from the poor in the United States?

PREPARING TO READ AND WRITE

As you read and prepare to write about the selections in this chapter, you may consider the following questions:

- How does the writer define *education*? Is this definition consistent with yours?

- What does the writer think the main goals of education should be? Do you agree?

- Which does the writer believe is more important, formal or informal education?

- On what aspect or aspects of education does the writer focus?

- Who does the writer believe bears primary responsibility for a student's education? The student? The family? The school? The community? The government?

- Does the writer use personal experience to support his or her points? Does he or she use facts and statistics or expert opinion as support? Do you find the writer's ideas convincing?

- What changes in the educational system does the writer recommend? Do you agree with these recommendations?

- Are the writer's educational experiences similar to or different from yours? How do these similarities or differences affect your response to the essay?

- In what way is the essay similar to or different from other essays in this chapter?

The Sanctuary of School
Lynda Barry
1956–

Lynda Barry grew up as part of an extended Filipino family (her mother was Filipino, her father an alcoholic Norwegian-Irishman). The first member of her family to pursue higher education, she majored in art and began her career as a cartoonist shortly after graduation. Barry is known as a chronicler of adolescent angst both in her syndicated comic strip Ernie Pook's Comeek *and in the semi-autobiographical* One Hundred Demons *(2002). Her latest collections are* What Is It *(2008) and* Nearsighted Monkey *(2009). Barry has also written a novel,* The Good Times Are Killing Me *(1988), which was turned into a successful musical. In the following essay, Barry remembers her Seattle grade school in a racially mixed neighborhood as a nurturing safe haven from her difficult family life.*

I was 7 years old the first time I snuck out of the house in the dark. It was winter and my parents had been fighting all night. They were short on money and long on relatives who kept "temporarily" moving into our house because they had nowhere else to go.

My brother and I were used to giving up our bedroom. We slept on the couch, something we actually liked because it put us that much closer to the light of our lives, our television.

At night when everyone was asleep, we lay on our pillows watching it with the sound off. We watched Steve Allen's mouth moving. We watched Johnny Carson's mouth moving. We watched movies filled with gangsters shooting machine guns into packed rooms, dying soldiers hurling a last grenade and beautiful women crying at windows. Then the sign-off finally came and we tried to sleep.

The morning I snuck out, I woke up filled with a panic about needing to get to school. The sun wasn't quite up yet but my anxiety was so fierce that I just got dressed, walked quietly across the kitchen and let myself out the back door.

It was quiet outside. Stars were still out. Nothing moved and no one was 5 in the street. It was as if someone had turned the sound off on the world.

I walked the alley, breaking thin ice over the puddles with my shoes. I didn't know why I was walking to school in the dark. I didn't think about it. All I knew was a feeling of panic, like the panic that strikes kids when they realize they are lost.

That feeling eased the moment I turned the corner and saw the dark outline of my school at the top of the hill. My school was made up of about 15 nondescript portable classrooms set down on a fenced concrete lot in a rundown Seattle neighborhood, but it had the most beautiful view of the Cascade Mountains. You could see them from anywhere on the playfield and you could see them from the windows of my classroom—Room 2.

I walked over to the monkey bars and hooked my arms around the cold metal. I stood for a long time just looking across Rainier Valley. The sky was beginning to whiten and I could hear a few birds.

In a perfect world my absence at home would not have gone unnoticed. I would have had two parents in a panic to locate me, instead of two parents in a panic to locate an answer to the hard question of survival during a deep financial and emotional crisis.

10   But in an overcrowded and unhappy home, it's incredibly easy for any child to slip away. The high levels of frustration, depression and anger in my house made my brother and me invisible. We were children with the sound turned off. And for us, as for the steadily increasing number of neglected children in this country, the only place where we could count on being noticed was at school.

"Hey there, young lady. Did you forget to go home last night?" It was Mr. Gunderson, our janitor, whom we all loved. He was nice and he was funny and he was old with white hair, thick glasses and an unbelievable number of keys. I could hear them jingling as he walked across the playfield. I felt incredibly happy to see him.

He let me push his wheeled garbage can between the different portables as he unlocked each room. He let me turn on the lights and raise the window shades and I saw my school slowly come to life. I saw Mrs. Holman, our school secretary, walk into the office without her orange lipstick on yet. She waved.

I saw the fifth-grade teacher Mr. Cunningham, walking under the breezeway eating a hard roll. He waved.

And I saw my teacher, Mrs. Claire LeSane, walking toward us in a red coat and calling my name in a very happy and surprised way, and suddenly my throat got tight and my eyes stung and I ran toward her crying. It was something that surprised us both.

15   It's only thinking about it now, 28 years later, that I realize I was crying from relief. I was with my teacher, and in a while I was going to sit at my desk, with my crayons and pencils and books and classmates all around me, and for the next six hours I was going to enjoy a thoroughly secure, warm and stable world. It was a world I absolutely relied on. Without it, I don't know where I would have gone that morning.

Mrs. LeSane asked me what was wrong and when I said "Nothing," she seemingly left it at that. But she asked me if I would carry her purse for her, an honor above all honors, and she asked if I wanted to come into Room 2 early and paint.

She believed in the natural healing power of painting and drawing for troubled children. In the back of her room there was always a drawing table and an easel with plenty of supplies, and sometimes during the day she would come up to you for what seemed like no good reason and quietly ask if you wanted to go to the back table and "make some pictures for Mrs. LeSane." We all had a chance at it—to sit apart from the class for a while to paint, draw and silently work out impossible problems on 11×17 sheets of newsprint.

Drawing came to mean everything to me. At the back table in Room 2, I learned to build myself a life preserver that I could carry into my home.

We all know that a good education system saves lives, but the people of this country are still told that cutting the budget for public schools is necessary, that poor salaries for teachers are all we can manage and that art, music and all creative activities must be the first to go when times are lean.

Before- and after-school programs are cut and we are told that pub- 20 lic schools are not made for baby-sitting children. If parents are neglectful temporarily or permanently, for whatever reason, it's certainly sad, but their unlucky children must fend for themselves. Or slip through the cracks. Or wander in a dark night alone.

We are told in a thousand ways that not only are public schools not important, but that the children who attend them, the children who need them most, are not important either. We leave them to learn from the blind eye of a television, or to the mercy of "a thousand points of light"[1] that can be as far away as stars.

I was lucky. I had Mrs. LeSane. I had Mr. Gunderson. I had an abundance of art supplies. And I had a particular brand of neglect in my home that allowed me to slip away and get to them. But what about the rest of the kids who weren't as lucky? What happened to them?

By the time the bell rang that morning I had finished my drawing and Mrs. LeSane pinned it up on the special bulletin board she reserved for drawings from the back table. It was the same picture I always drew—a sun in the corner of a blue sky over a nice house with flowers all around it.

Mrs. LeSane asked us to please stand, face the flag, place our right hands over our hearts and say the Pledge of Allegiance. Children across the country do it faithfully. I wonder now when the country will face its children and say a pledge right back.

Responding to Reading

1. What information about her school does Barry provide? What information does she not provide? How can you explain these omissions?
2. In paragraph 22, Barry asks two questions. Why doesn't she answer them? What do you think the answers to these questions might be?
3. Barry's essay ends on a cynical note. How effective is this conclusion? What does Barry gain or lose with this concluding strategy?

Responding in Writing

Has school been a sanctuary for you as it was for Barry? Write a paragraph or two in which you answer this question.

---

[1]Catchphrase for President George H. W. Bush's plan to substitute volunteerism for government programs. [Eds.]

School Is Bad for Children

John Holt

1923–1985

John Holt, a teacher and education theorist, believed that traditional schooling suppresses children's natural curiosity about life. In his writings about education, Holt suggested that students be allowed to pursue whatever interests them. Holt worked for an international peace group, traveled in Europe, and then worked at the private Colorado Rocky Mountain School in Carbondale, Colorado, where he taught high school English, French, and mathematics and coached soccer and baseball. His many books include How Children Fail *(1964),* How Children Learn *(1967),* Education *(1976), and* Learning All the Time *(1989). In the following essay, first published in 1969, Holt makes a plea to free children from the classroom, a "dull and ugly place, where nobody ever says anything very truthful," and to "give them a chance to learn about the world at first hand." Holt was also a major supporter of the Home Schooling movement.*

Almost every child, on the first day he sets foot in a school building, is smarter, more curious, less afraid of what he doesn't know, better at finding and figuring things out, more confident, resourceful, persistent and independent than he will ever be again in his schooling—or, unless he is very unusual and very lucky, for the rest of his life. Already, by paying close attention to and interacting with the world and people around him, and without any school-type formal instruction, he has done a task far more difficult, complicated and abstract than anything he will be asked to do in school, or than any of his teachers has done for years. He has solved the mystery of language. He has discovered it—babies don't even know that language exists—and he has found out how it works and learned to use it. He has done it by exploring, by experimenting, by developing his own model of the grammar of language, by trying it out and seeing whether it works, by gradually changing it and refining it until it does work. And while he has been doing this, he has been learning other things as well, including many of the "concepts" that the schools think only they can teach him, and many that are more complicated than the ones they do try to teach him.

In he comes, this curious, patient, determined, energetic, skillful learner. We sit him down at a desk, and what do we teach him? Many things. First, that learning is separate from living. "You come to school to learn," we tell him, as if the child hadn't been learning before, as if living were out there and learning were in here, and there were no connection between the two. Secondly, that he cannot be trusted to learn and is no good at it. Everything we teach about reading, a task far simpler than many that the child has already mastered, says to him, "If we don't make you read, you won't, and if you don't do it exactly the way we tell you, you can't." In short, he comes to feel that learning is a passive process, something that someone else does *to* you, instead of something you do for yourself.

In a great many other ways he learns that he is worthless, untrustworthy, fit only to take other people's orders, a blank sheet for other people to write on. Oh, we make a lot of nice noises in school about respect for the child and individual differences, and the like. But our acts, as opposed to our talk, say to the child, "Your experience, your concerns, your curiosities, your needs, what you know, what you want, what you wonder about, what you hope for, what you fear, what you like and dislike, what you are good at or not so good at—all this is of not the slightest importance, it counts for nothing. What counts here, and the only thing that counts, is what we know, what we think is important, what we want you to do, think and be." The child soon learns not to ask questions—the teacher isn't there to satisfy his curiosity. Having learned to hide his curiosity, he later learns to be ashamed of it. Given no chance to find out who he is—and to develop that person, whoever it is—he soon comes to accept the adults' evaluation of him.

He learns many other things. He learns that to be wrong, uncertain, confused, is a crime. Right Answers are what the school wants, and he learns countless strategies for prying these answers out of the teacher, for conning her into thinking he knows what he doesn't know. He learns to dodge, bluff, fake, cheat. He learns to be lazy. Before he came to school, he would work for hours on end, on his own, with no thought of reward, at the business of making sense of the world and gaining competence in it. In school he learns, like every buck private, how to goldbrick, how not to work when the sergeant isn't looking, how to know when he is looking, how to make him think you are working even when he is looking. He learns that in real life you don't do anything unless you are bribed, bullied or conned into doing it, that nothing is worth doing for its own sake, or that if it is, you can't do it in school. He learns to be bored, to work with a small part of his mind, to escape from the reality around him into daydreams and fantasies— but not like the fantasies of his preschool years, in which he played a very active part.

The child comes to school curious about other people, particularly 5 other children, and the school teaches him to be indifferent. The most interesting thing in the classroom—often the only interesting thing in it— is the other children, but he has to act as if these other children, all about him, only a few feet away, are not really there. He cannot interact with them, talk with them, smile at them. In many schools he can't talk to other children in the halls between classes; in more than a few, and some of these in stylish suburbs, he can't even talk to them at lunch. Splendid training for a world in which, when you're not studying the other person to figure out how to do him in, you pay no attention to him.

In fact, he learns how to live without paying attention to anything going on around him. You might say that school is a long lesson in how to turn yourself off, which may be one reason why so many young people, seeking the awareness of the world and responsiveness to it they had when they were little, think they can only find it in drugs. Aside from being boring, the school is almost always ugly, cold, inhuman— even the most stylish, glass-windowed, $20-a-square-foot schools.

And so, in this dull and ugly place, where nobody ever says anything very truthful, where everybody is playing a kind of role, as in a charade, where the teachers are no more free to respond honestly to the students than the students are free to respond to the teachers or each other, where the air practically vibrates with suspicion and anxiety, the child learns to live in a daze, saving his energies for those small parts of his life that are too trivial for the adults to bother with, and thus remain his. It is a rare child who can come through his schooling with much left of his curiosity, his independence or his sense of his own dignity, competence and worth.

So much for criticism. What do we need to do? Many things. Some are easy—we can do them right away. Some are hard, and may take some time. Take a hard one first. We should abolish compulsory school attendance. At the very least we should modify it, perhaps by giving children every year a large number of authorized absences. Our compulsory school-attendance laws once served a humane and useful purpose. They protected children's right to some schooling, against those adults who would otherwise have denied it to them in order to exploit their labor, in farm, store, mine or factory. Today the laws help nobody, not the schools, not the teachers, not the children. To keep kids in school who would rather not be there costs the schools an enormous amount of time and trouble—to say nothing of what it costs to repair the damage that these angry and resentful prisoners do every time they get a chance. Every teacher knows that any kid in class who, for whatever reason, would rather not be there not only doesn't learn anything himself but makes it a great deal tougher for anyone else. As for protecting the children from exploitation, the chief and indeed only exploiters of children these days *are* the schools. Kids caught in the college rush more often than not work 70 hours or more a week, most of it on paper busywork. For kids who aren't going to college, school is just a useless time waster, preventing them from earning some money or doing some useful work, or even doing some true learning.

Objections. "If kids didn't have to go to school, they'd all be out in the streets." No, they wouldn't. In the first place, even if schools stayed just the way they are, children would spend at least some time there because that's where they'd be likely to find friends; it's a natural meeting place for children. In the second place, schools wouldn't stay the way they are, they'd get better, because we would have to start making them what they ought to be right now—places where children would *want* to be. In the third place, those children who did not want to go to school could find, particularly if we stirred up our brains and gave them a little help, other things to do—the things many children now do during their summers and holidays.

There's something easier we could do. We need to get kids out of the school buildings, give them a chance to learn about the world at first hand. It is a very recent idea, and a crazy one, that the way to teach our young people about the world they live in is to take them out of it and shut them up in brick boxes. Fortunately, educators are beginning to realize this. In Philadelphia and Portland, Oreg., to pick only two places I happen to have heard about, plans are being drawn up for public schools that won't have any school buildings at all, that will take the students out into the city and help them to use it and its people as a learning resource. In other words, students, perhaps in groups, perhaps independently, will go to libraries, museums, exhibits, court rooms, legislatures, radio and TV stations, meetings, businesses and laboratories to learn about their world and society at first hand. A small private school in Washington is already doing this. It makes sense. We need more of it.

As we help children get out into the world, to do their learning there, we get more of the world into the schools. Aside from their parents, most children never have any close contact with any adults except people whose sole business is children. No wonder they have no idea what adult life or work is like. We need to bring a lot more people who are *not* full-time teachers into the schools and into contact with the children. In New York City, under the Teachers and Writers Collaborative, real writers, working writers—novelists, poets, playwrights—come into the schools, read their work, and talk to the children about the problems of their craft. The children eat it up. In another school I know of, a practicing attorney from a nearby city comes in every month or so and talks to several classes about the law. Not the law as it is in books but as he sees it and encounters it in his cases, his problems, his work. And the children love it. It is real, grown-up, true, not *My Weekly Reader*, not "social studies," not lies and baloney.

Something easier yet. Let children work together, help each other, learn from each other and each other's mistakes. We now know, from the experience of many schools, both rich-suburban and poor-city, that children are often the best teachers of other children. What is more important, we know that when a fifth- or sixth-grader who has been having trouble with reading starts helping a first-grader, his own reading sharply improves. A number of schools are beginning to use what some call Paired Learning. This means that you let children form partnerships with other children, do their work, even including their tests, together, and share whatever marks or results this work gets—just like grownups in the real world. It seems to work.

Let the children learn to judge their own work. A child learning to talk does not learn by being corrected all the time—if corrected too much, he will stop talking. *He* compares, a thousand times a day, the difference between language as he uses it and as those around him use it. Bit by bit, he makes the necessary changes to make his language like other people's. In the same way, kids learning to do all the other things they learn without adult teachers—to walk, run, climb, whistle, ride a bike, skate, play games, jump rope—compare their own performance with what more skilled people do, and slowly make the needed changes. But in school we never give a child a chance to detect his mistakes, let alone correct them. We do it all for him. We act as if we thought he would never notice a mistake unless it was pointed out to him, or correct it unless he was made to. Soon he becomes dependent on the expert. We should let him do it himself. Let him figure out, with the help of other children if he wants it, what this word says, what is the answer to that problem, whether this is a good way of saying or doing this or that. If right answers are involved, as in some math or science, give him the answer book, let him correct his own papers. Why should we teachers waste time on such donkey work? Our job should be to help the kid when he tells us that he can't find a way to get the right answer. Let's get rid of all this nonsense of grades, exams, marks. We don't know now, and we never will know, how to measure what another person knows or understands. We certainly can't find out by asking him questions. All we find out is what he doesn't know—which is what most tests are for, anyway. Throw it all out, and let the child learn what every educated person must someday learn, how to measure his own understanding, how to know what he knows or does not know.

We could also abolish the fixed, required curriculum. People remember only what is interesting and useful to them, what helps them make sense of the world, or helps them get along in it. All else they quickly forget, if they ever learn it at all. The idea of a "body of knowledge," to be picked up in school and used for the rest of one's life, is nonsense in a world as complicated and rapidly changing as ours. Anyway, the most important questions and problems of our time are not *in* the curriculum, not even in the hotshot universities, let alone the schools.

15   Children want, more than they want anything else, and even after years of miseducation, to make sense of the world, themselves, and other human beings. Let them get at this job, with our help if they ask for it, in the way that makes most sense to them.

Responding to Reading

1. In what ways does Holt believe schools fail children?
2. According to Holt, what should schools do to correct their shortcomings? Do you think his suggestions are realistic? Why or why not?

3. In paragraph 13, Holt says, "Let's get rid of all this nonsense of grades, exams, marks." Do you agree? What would be the advantages and disadvantages of this course of action?

Responding in Writing

What would your ideal elementary school be like? How would it be like the schools you attended? How would it be different?

GRADUATION

Maya Angelou

1928–

Maya Angelou was raised in Arkansas by her grandmother, who ran a general store. She began a theatrical career when she toured with Porgy *and* Bess *in 1954–1955. Angelou is now a poet, writer, lecturer, and teacher. She read her poem "On the Pulse of Morning" at the 1993 presidential inauguration of Bill Clinton. Angelou's most recent book is* Letter to My Daughter *(2008). In "Graduation," excerpted from her autobiography* I Know Why the Caged Bird Sings *(1969), Angelou remembers the anger and pride of graduation day at her segregated school in Stamps, Arkansas.*

The children in Stamps trembled visibly with anticipation. Some adults were excited too, but to be certain the whole young population had come down with graduation epidemic. Large classes were graduating from both the grammar school and the high school. Even those who were years removed from their own day of glorious release were anxious to help with preparations as a kind of dry run. The junior students who were moving into the vacating classes' chairs were tradition-bound to show their talents for leadership and management. They strutted through the school and around the campus exerting pressure on the lower grades. Their authority was so new that occasionally if they pressed a little too hard it had to be overlooked. After all, next term was coming, and it never hurt a sixth grader to have a play sister in the eighth grade, or a tenth-year student to be able to call a twelfth grader Bubba. So all was endured in a spirit of shared understanding. But the graduating classes themselves were the nobility. Like travelers with exotic destinations on their minds, the graduates were remarkably forgetful. They came to school without their books, or tablets or even pencils. Volunteers fell over themselves to secure replacements for the missing equipment. When accepted, the willing workers might or might not be thanked, and it was of no importance to the pregraduation rites. Even teachers were respectful of the now quiet and aging seniors, and tended to speak to them, if not as equals, as beings only slightly lower than themselves. After tests were returned and grades given, the student body, which acted like an extended family, knew who did well, who excelled, and what piteous ones had failed.

Unlike the white high school, Lafayette County Training School distinguished itself by having neither lawn, nor hedges, nor tennis court, nor climbing ivy. Its two buildings (main classrooms, the grade school and home economics) were set on a dirt hill with no fence to limit either its boundaries or those of bordering farms. There was a large expanse to the left of the school which was used alternately as a baseball diamond or basketball court. Rusty hoops on swaying poles represented the permanent recreational equipment, although bats and balls could be borrowed from the P.E. teacher if the borrower was qualified and if the diamond wasn't occupied.

Over this rocky area relieved by a few shady tall persimmon trees the graduating class walked. The girls often held hands and no longer bothered to speak to the lower students. There was a sadness about them, as if this old world was not their home and they were bound for higher ground. The boys, on the other hand, had become more friendly, more outgoing. A decided change from the closed attitude they projected while studying for finals. Now they seemed not ready to give up the old school, the familiar paths and classrooms. Only a small percentage would be continuing on to college—one of the South's A & M (agricultural and mechanical) schools, which trained Negro youths to be carpenters, farmers, handymen, masons, maids, cooks and baby nurses. Their future rode heavily on their shoulders, and blinded them to the collective joy that had pervaded the lives of the boys and girls in the grammar school graduating class.

Parents who could afford it had ordered new shoes and ready-made clothes for themselves from Sears and Roebuck or Montgomery Ward. They also engaged the best seamstresses to make the floating graduating dresses and to cut down secondhand pants which would be pressed to a military slickness for the important event.

5   Oh, it was important, all right. Whitefolks would attend the ceremony, and two or three would speak of God and home, and the Southern way of life, and Mrs. Parsons, the principal's wife, would play the graduation march while the lower-grade graduates paraded down the aisles and took their seats below the platform. The high school seniors would wait in empty classrooms to make their dramatic entrance.

In the Store I was the person of the moment. The birthday girl. The center. Bailey[1] had graduated the year before, although to do so he had had to forfeit all pleasures to make up for his time lost in Baton Rouge.

---

[1]Angelou's brother. The store was run by Angelou's grandmother, whom she called Momma, and Momma's son, Uncle Willie. [Eds.]

My class was wearing butter-yellow piqué dresses, and Momma launched out on mine. She smocked the yoke into tiny crisscrossing puckers, then shirred the rest of the bodice. Her dark fingers ducked in and out of the lemony cloth as she embroidered raised daisies around the hem. Before she considered herself finished she had added a crocheted cuff on the puff sleeves, and a pointy crocheted collar.

I was going to be lovely. A walking model of all the various styles of fine hand sewing and it didn't worry me that I was only twelve years old and merely graduating from the eighth grade. Besides, many teachers in Arkansas Negro schools had only that diploma and were licensed to impart wisdom.

The days had become longer and more noticeable. The faded beige of former times had been replaced with strong and sure colors. I began to see my classmates' clothes, their skin tones, and the dust that waved off pussy willows. Clouds that lazed across the sky were objects of great concern to me. Their shiftier shapes might have held a message that in my new happiness and with a little bit of time I'd soon decipher. During that period I looked at the arch of heaven so religiously my neck kept a steady ache. I had taken to smiling more often, and my jaws hurt from the unaccustomed activity. Between the two physical sore spots, I suppose I could have been uncomfortable, but that was not the case. As a member of the winning team (the graduating class of 1940) I had outdistanced unpleasant sensations by miles. I was headed for the freedom of open fields.

Youth and social approval allied themselves with me and we tram- 10 meled memories of slights and insults. The wind of our swift passage remodeled my features. Lost tears were pounded to mud and then to dust. Years of withdrawal were brushed aside and left behind, as hanging ropes of parasitic moss.

My work alone had awarded me a top place and I was going to be one of the first called in the graduating ceremonies. On the classroom blackboard, as well as on the bulletin board in the auditorium, there were blue stars and white stars and red stars. No absences, no tardinesses, and my academic work was among the best of the year. I could say the preamble to the Constitution even faster than Bailey. We timed ourselves often: "WethepeopleoftheUnitedStatesinordertoformamoreperfectunion . . ." I had memorized the Presidents of the United States from Washington to Roosevelt in chronological as well as alphabetical order.

My hair pleased me too. Gradually the black mass had lengthened and thickened, so that it kept at last to its braided pattern, and I didn't have to yank my scalp off when I tried to comb it.

Louise and I had rehearsed the exercises until we tired out ourselves. Henry Reed was class valedictorian. He was a small, very black boy with hooded eyes, a long, broad nose and an oddly shaped head.

I had admired him for years because each term he and I vied for the best grades in our class. Most often he bested me, but instead of being disappointed I was pleased that we shared top places between us. Like many Southern Black children, he lived with his grandmother, who was as strict as Momma and as kind as she knew how to be. He was courteous, respectful and soft-spoken to elders, but on the playground he chose to play the roughest games. I admired him. Anyone, I reckoned, sufficiently afraid or sufficiently dull could be polite. But to be able to operate at a top level with both adults and children was admirable.

His valedictory speech was entitled "To Be or Not to Be." The rigid tenth-grade teacher had helped him write it. He'd been working on the dramatic stresses for months.

15   The weeks until graduation were filled with heady activities. A group of small children were to be presented in a play about buttercups and daisies and bunny rabbits. They could be heard throughout the building practicing their hops and their little songs that sounded like silver bells. The older girls (nongraduates, of course) were assigned the task of making refreshments for the night's festivities. A tangy scent of ginger, cinnamon, nutmeg and chocolate wafted around the home economics building as the budding cooks made samples for themselves and their teachers.

In every corner of the workshop, axes and saws split fresh timber as the woodshop boys made sets and stage scenery. Only the graduates were left out of the general bustle. We were free to sit in the library at the back of the building or look in quite detachedly, naturally, on the measures being taken for our event.

Even the minister preached on graduation the Sunday before. His subject was, "Let your light so shine that men will see your good works and praise your Father, Who is in Heaven." Although the sermon was purported to be addressed to us, he used the occasion to speak to backsliders, gamblers and general ne'er-do-wells. But since he had called our names at the beginning of the service we were mollified.

Among Negroes the tradition was to give presents to children going only from one grade to another. How much more important this was when the person was graduating at the top of the class. Uncle Willie and Momma had sent away for a Mickey Mouse watch like Bailey's. Louise gave me four embroidered handkerchiefs. (I gave her crocheted doilies.) Mrs. Sneed, the minister's wife, made me an undershirt to wear for graduation, and nearly every customer gave me a nickel or maybe even a dime with the instruction "Keep on moving to higher ground," or some such encouragement.

Amazingly the great day finally dawned and I was out of bed before I knew it. I threw open the back door to see it more clearly, but Momma said, "Sister, come away from that door and put your robe on."

I hoped the memory of that morning would never leave me. Sun- 20
light was itself young, and the day had none of the insistence maturity
would bring it in a few hours. In my robe and barefoot in the backyard,
under cover of going to see about my new beans, I gave myself up to
the gentle warmth and thanked God that no matter what evil I had done
in my life He had allowed me to live to see this day. Somewhere in my
fatalism I had expected to die, accidentally, and never have the chance
to walk up the stairs in the auditorium and gracefully receive my hard-
earned diploma. Out of God's merciful bosom I had won reprieve.

Bailey came out in his robe and gave me a box wrapped in Christmas paper. He said he had saved his money for months to pay for it. It
felt like a box of chocolates, but I knew Bailey wouldn't save money to
buy candy when we had all we could want under our noses.

He was as proud of the gift as I. It was a soft-leather-bound copy
of a collection of poems by Edgar Allan Poe, or, as Bailey and I called
him, "Eap." I turned to "Annabel Lee" and we walked up and down
the garden rows, the cool dirt between our toes, reciting the beautifully sad lines.

Momma made a Sunday breakfast although it was only Friday.
After we finished the blessing, I opened my eyes to find the watch on
my plate. It was a dream of a day. Everything went smoothly and to
my credit I didn't have to be reminded or scolded for anything. Near
evening I was too jittery to attend to chores, so Bailey volunteered to do
all before his bath.

Days before, we had made a sign for the Store, and as we turned out
the lights Momma hung the cardboard over the doorknob. It read
clearly: CLOSED. GRADUATION.

My dress fitted perfectly and everyone said that I looked like a sun- 25
beam in it. On the hill, going toward the school, Bailey walked behind
with Uncle Willie, who muttered, "Go on, Ju." He wanted him to walk
ahead with us because it embarrassed him to have to walk so slowly.
Bailey said he'd let the ladies walk together, and the men would bring
up the rear. We all laughed, nicely.

Little children dashed by out of the dark like fireflies. Their crepe-
paper dresses and butterfly wings were not made for running and we
heard more than one rip, dryly, and the regretful "uh uh" that followed.

The school blazed without gaiety. The windows seemed cold and
unfriendly from the lower hill. A sense of ill-fated timing crept over me,
and if Momma hadn't reached for my hand I would have drifted back
to Bailey and Uncle Willie, and possibly beyond. She made a few slow
jokes about my feet getting cold, and tugged me along to the now-
strange building.

Around the front steps, assurance came back. There were my fellow
"greats," the graduating class. Hair brushed back, legs oiled, new

dresses and pressed pleats, fresh pocket handkerchiefs and little hand-bags, all homesewn. Oh, we were up to snuff, all right. I joined my com-rades and didn't even see my family go in to find seats in the crowded auditorium.

The school band struck up a march and all classes filed in as had been rehearsed. We stood in front of our seats, as assigned, and on a signal from the choir director, we sat. No sooner had this been accom-plished than the band started to play the national anthem. We rose again and sang the song, after which we recited the pledge of allegiance. We remained standing for a brief minute before the choir director and the principal signaled to us, rather desperately I thought, to take our seats. The command was so unusual that our carefully rehearsed and smooth-running machine was thrown off. For a full minute we fumbled for our chairs and bumped into each other awkwardly. Habits change or solid-ify under pressure, so in our state of nervous tension we had been ready to follow our usual assembly pattern: the American national anthem, then the pledge of allegiance, then the song every Black person I knew called the Negro National Anthem. All done in the same key, with the same passion and most often standing on the same foot.

30   Finding my seat at last, I was overcome with a presentiment of worse things to come. Something unrehearsed, unplanned, was going to hap-pen, and we were going to be made to look bad. I distinctly remember being explicit in the choice of pronoun. It was "we," the graduating class, the unit, that concerned me then.

The principal welcomed "parents and friends" and asked the Bap-tist minister to lead us in prayer. His invocation was brief and punchy, and for a second I thought we were getting on the high road to right action. When the principal came back to the dais, however, his voice had changed. Sounds always affected me profoundly and the principal's voice was one of my favorites. During assembly it melted and lowed weakly into the audience. It had not been in my plan to listen to him, but my curiosity was piqued and I straightened up to give him my attention.

He was talking about Booker T. Washington, our "late great leader," who said we can be as close as the fingers on the hand, etc. . . . Then he said a few vague things about friendship and the friendship of kindly people to those less fortunate than themselves. With that his voice nearly faded, thin, away. Like a river diminishing to a stream and then to a trickle. But he cleared his throat and said, "Our speaker tonight, who is also our friend, came from Texarkana to deliver the commencement address, but due to the irregularity of the train schedule, he's going to, as they say, 'speak and run.'" He said that we understood and wanted the man to know that we were most grateful for the time he was able to give us and then something about how we were willing always to adjust to another's program, and without more ado—"I give you Mr. Edward Donleavy."

Not one but two white men came through the door off-stage. The shorter one walked to the speaker's platform, and the tall one moved to the center seat and sat down. But that was our principal's seat, and already occupied. The dislodged gentleman bounced around for a long breath or two before the Baptist minister gave him his chair, then with more dignity than the situation deserved, the minister walked off the stage.

Donleavy looked at the audience once (on reflection, I'm sure that he wanted only to reassure himself that we were really there), adjusted his glasses and began to read from a sheaf of papers.

He was glad "to be here and to see the work going on just as it was in the other schools." 35

At the first "Amen" from the audience I willed the offender to immediate death by choking on the word. But Amens and Yes, sir's began to fall around the room like rain through a ragged umbrella.

He told us of the wonderful changes we children in Stamps had in store. The Central School (naturally, the white school was Central) had already been granted improvements that would be in use in the fall. A well-known artist was coming from Little Rock to teach art to them. They were going to have the newest microscopes and chemistry equipment for their laboratory. Mr. Donleavy didn't leave us long in the dark over who made these improvements available to Central High. Nor were we to be ignored in the general betterment scheme he had in mind.

He said that he had pointed out to people at a very high level that one of the first-line football tacklers at Arkansas Agricultural and Mechanical College had graduated from good old Lafayette County Training School. Here fewer Amen's were heard. Those few that did break through lay dully in the air with the heaviness of habit.

He went on to praise us. He went on to say how he had bragged that "one of the best basketball players at Fisk[2] sank his first ball right here at Lafayette County Training School."

The white kids were going to have a chance to become Galileos and Madame Curies and Edisons and Gauguins,[3] and our boys (the girls weren't even in on it) would try to be Jesse Owenses and Joe Louises.[4] 40

Owens and the Brown Bomber were great heroes in our world, but what school official in the white-goddom of Little Rock had the right to decide that those two men must be our only heroes? Who decided that for Henry Reed to become a scientist he had to work like George Washington Carver, as a bootblack, to buy a lousy microscope? Bailey was obviously always going to be too small to be an athlete, so which concrete

---

[2]Highly regarded, historically black university in Nashville. [Eds.]
[3]Inventors, scientists, and artists. [Eds.]
[4]The black track star and Olympic gold medalist, and the longtime world heavyweight boxing champion known as the "Brown Bomber." [Eds.]

angel glued to what country seat had decided that if my brother wanted to become a lawyer he had to first pay penance for his skin by picking cotton and hoeing corn and studying correspondence books at night for twenty years?

The man's dead words fell like bricks around the auditorium and too many settled in my belly. Constrained by hard-learned manners I couldn't look behind me, but to my left and right the proud graduating class of 1940 had dropped their heads. Every girl in my row had found something new to do with her handkerchief. Some folded the tiny squares into love knots, some into triangles, but most were wadding them, then pressing them flat on their yellow laps.

On the dais, the ancient tragedy was being replayed. Professor Parsons sat, a sculptor's reject, rigid. His large, heavy body seemed devoid of will or willingness, and his eyes said he was no longer with us. The other teachers examined the flag (which was draped stage right) or their notes, or the windows which opened on our now-famous playing diamond.

Graduation, the hush-hush magic time of frills and gifts and congratulations and diplomas, was finished for me before my name was called. The accomplishment was nothing. The meticulous maps, drawn in three colors of ink, learning and spelling decasyllabic words, memorizing the whole of *The Rape of Lucrece*[5]—it was for nothing. Donleavy had exposed us.

45   We were maids and farmers, handymen and washerwomen, and anything higher that we aspired to was farcical and presumptuous.

Then I wished that Gabriel Prosser and Nat Turner[6] had killed all whitefolks in their beds and that Abraham Lincoln had been assassinated before the signing of the Emancipation Proclamation, and that Harriet Tubman[7] had been killed by that blow on her head and Christopher Columbus had drowned in the *Santa Maria*.

It was awful to be a Negro and have no control over my life. It was brutal to be young and already trained to sit quietly and listen to charges brought against my color with no chance of defense. We should all be dead. I thought I should like to see us all dead, one on top of the other. A pyramid of flesh with the whitefolks on the bottom, as the broad base, then the Indians with their silly tomahawks and teepees and wigwams and treaties, the Negroes with their mops and recipes and cotton sacks and spirituals sticking out of their mouths. The Dutch children should all stumble in their wooden shoes and break their necks. The French should choke to death on the Louisiana Purchase (1803) while silkworms ate all the Chinese with their stupid pigtails. As a species, we were an abomination. All of us.

---

[5]*The Rape of Lucrece* is a long narrative poem by Shakespeare. [Eds.]

[6]Prosser and Turner both led slave rebellions. [Eds.]

[7]Harriet Tubman (1820–1913) was an African-American abolitionist who became one of the most successful guides on the Underground Railroad. [Eds.]

Donleavy was running for election, and assured our parents that if he won we could count on having the only colored paved playing field in that part of Arkansas. Also—he never looked up to acknowledge the grunts of acceptance—also, we were bound to get some new equipment for the home economics building and the workshop.

He finished, and since there was no need to give any more than the most perfunctory thank-you's, he nodded to the men on the stage, and the tall white man who was never introduced joined him at the door. They left with the attitude that now they were off to something really important. (The graduation ceremonies at Lafayette County Training School had been a mere preliminary.)

The ugliness they left was palpable. An uninvited guest who 50 wouldn't leave. The choir was summoned and sang a modern arrangement of "Onward, Christian Soldiers," with new words pertaining to graduates seeking their place in the world. But it didn't work. Elouise, the daughter of the Baptist minister, recited "Invictus,"[8] and I could have cried at the impertinence of "I am the master of my fate, I am the captain of my soul."

My name had lost its ring of familiarity and I had to be nudged to go and receive my diploma. All my preparations had fled. I neither marched up to the stage like a conquering Amazon, nor did I look in the audience for Bailey's nod of approval. Marguerite Johnson,[9] I heard the name again, my honors were read, there were noises in the audience of appreciation, and I took my place on the stage as rehearsed.

I thought about colors I hated: ecru, puce, lavender, beige and black.

There was shuffling and rustling around me, then Henry Reed was giving his valedictory address, "To Be or Not to Be." Hadn't he heard the whitefolks? We couldn't *be*, so the question was a waste of time. Henry's voice came out clear and strong. I feared to look at him. Hadn't he got the message? There was no "nobler in the mind" for Negroes because the world didn't think we had minds, and they let us know it. "Outrageous fortune"? Now, that was a joke. When the ceremony was over I had to tell Henry Reed some things. That is, if I still cared. Not "rub," Henry, "erase." "Ah, there's the erase." Us.

Henry had been a good student in elocution. His voice rose on tides of promise and fell on waves of warnings. The English teacher had helped him to create a sermon winging through Hamlet's soliloquy. To be a man, a doer, a builder, a leader, or to be a tool, an unfunny joke, a crusher of funky toadstools. I marveled that Henry could go through with the speech as if we had a choice.

---

[8]An inspirational poem written in 1875 by William Ernest Henley (1849–1903). Its defiant and stoic sentiments made it extremely popular with nineteenth-century readers. [Eds.]
[9]Angelou's given name. [Eds.]

55   I had been listening and silently rebutting each sentence with my eyes closed; then there was a hush, which in an audience warns that something unplanned is happening. I looked up and saw Henry Reed, the conservative, the proper, the A student, turn his back to the audience and turn to us (the proud graduating class of 1940) and sing, nearly speaking,

> "Lift ev'ry voice and sing
> Till earth and heaven ring
> Ring with the harmonies of Liberty . . ."

It was the poem written by James Weldon Johnson. It was the music composed by J. Rosamond Johnson. It was the Negro national anthem. Out of habit we were singing it.

Our mothers and fathers stood in the dark hall and joined the hymn of encouragement. A kindergarten teacher led the small children onto the stage and the buttercups and daisies and bunny rabbits marked time and tried to follow:

> "Stony the road we trod
> Bitter the chastening rod
> Felt in the days when hope, unborn, had died.
> Yet with a steady beat
> 5   Have not our weary feet
> Come to the place for which our fathers sighed?"

Each child I knew had learned that song with his ABC's and along with "Jesus Loves Me This I Know." But I personally had never heard it before. Never heard the words, despite the thousands of times I had sung them. Never thought they had anything to do with me.

On the other hand, the words of Patrick Henry had made such an impression on me that I had been able to stretch myself tall and trembling and say, "I know not what course others may take, but as for me, give me liberty or give me death."

60   And now I heard, really for the first time:

> "We have come over a way that with tears
> has been watered,
> We have come, treading our path through
> the blood of the slaughtered."

While echoes of the song shivered in the air, Henry Reed bowed his head, said "Thank you," and returned to his place in the line. The tears that slipped down many faces were not wiped away in shame.

We were on top again. As always, again. We survived. The depths had been icy and dark, but now a bright sun spoke to our souls. I was no longer simply a member of the proud graduating class of 1940; I was a proud member of the wonderful, beautiful Negro race.

Oh, Black known and unknown poets, how often have your auctioned pains sustained us? Who will compute the lonely nights made less lonely by your songs, or the empty pots made less tragic by your tales?

If we were a people much given to revealing secrets, we might raise monuments and sacrifice to the memories of our poets, but slavery cured us of that weakness. It may be enough, however, to have it said that we survive in exact relationship to the dedication of our poets (include preachers, musicians and blues singers).

Responding to Reading

1. Angelou's graduation took place in 1940. What expectations did educators have for Angelou and her classmates? How were these expectations different from the expectations Angelou and her fellow students had?
2. In what sense did Mr. Donleavy's speech "educate" the graduates? How did Angelou's thinking change as she listened to him?
3. In paragraph 62, Angelou says, "We were on top again." In what sense were she and the graduates "on top"? Do you think Angelou is being overly optimistic in light of what she had just experienced?

Responding in Writing

In the 1954 *Brown v. Board of Education* decision, the Supreme Court of the United States ruled that the "separate but equal" education that Angelou experienced was unconstitutional. How do you suppose her education would have been different had she attended high school in 1960 instead of in 1940?

THE GOOD IMMIGRANT STUDENT

Bich Minh Nguyen

1974–

Bich Minh Nguyen is an associate professor of English at Purdue University and winner of the PEN American Center's 2005 PEN/Jerard Award in nonfiction for her memoir, Stealing Buddha's Dinner *(2007). She has also coedited three anthologies and written for* Gourmet *magazine, the* Chicago Tribune, *and other publications. Her latest work is a novel,* Short Girls *(2009). In the following essay, Nguyen explores the implications of bilingual education for immigrants in America.*

My stepmother, Rosa, who began dating my father when I was three years old, says that my sister and I used to watch *Police Woman* and rapturously repeat everything Angie Dickinson said. But when the show was over Anh and I would resume our Vietnamese, whispering together, giggling in accents. Rosa worried about this. She had the idea that she could teach us English and we could teach her Vietnamese. She would make us lunch or give us baths, speaking slowly and asking us how to say *water*, or *rice*, or *house*.

After she and my father married, Rosa swept us out of our falling-down house and into middle-class suburban Grand Rapids, Michigan. Our neighborhood surrounded Ken-O-Sha Elementary School and Plaster Creek, and was only a short drive away from the original Meijer's Thrifty Acres. In the early 1980s, this neighborhood of mismatching street names—Poinsettia, Van Auken, Senora, Ravanna—was home to families of Dutch heritage, and everyone was Christian Reformed, and conservative Republican. Except us. Even if my father hadn't left his rusted-through silver Mustang, the first car he ever owned, to languish in the driveway for months we would have stuck out simply because we weren't white. There was my Latina stepmother and her daughter, Cristina, my father, sister, grandmother, and I, refugees from Saigon; and my half-brother born a year after we moved to the house on Ravanna Street.

Although my family lived two blocks from Ken-O-Sha, my stepmother enrolled me and Anh at Sherwood Elementary, a bus ride away, because Sherwood had a bilingual education program. Rosa, who had a master's in education and taught ESL and community ed in the public school system, was a big supporter of bilingual education. School mornings, Anh and I would be at the bus stop at the corner of our street quite early, hustled out of the house by our grandmother who constantly feared we would miss our chance. I went off to first grade, Anh to second. At ten o'clock, we crept out of our classes, drawing glances and whispers from the other students, and convened with a group of Vietnamese kids from other grades to learn English. The teachers were Mr. Ho, who wore a lot of short-sleeved button-down shirts in neutral hues, and Miss Huong, who favored a maroon blouse with puffy shoulders and slight ruffles at the high neck and wrists, paired with a tweed skirt that hung heavily to her ankles. They passed out photocopied booklets of Vietnamese phrases and their English translations, with themes such as "In the Grocery Store." They asked us to repeat slowly after them and took turns coming around to each of us, bending close to hear our pronunciations.

Anh and I exchanged a lot of worried glances, for we had a secret that we were quite embarrassed about: we already knew English. It was the Vietnamese part that gave us trouble. When Mr. Ho and Miss Huong gave instructions, or passed out homework assignments, they did so in Vietnamese. Anh and I received praise for our English, but were reprimanded for failing to complete our assignments and failing to pay attention. After a couple of weeks of this Anh announced to Rosa that we didn't need bilingual education. Nonsense, she said. Our father just shrugged his shoulders. After that, Anh began skipping bilingual classes, urging me to do the same, and then we never went back. What was amazing was that no one, not Mrs. Eunice, my first grade teacher, or Mrs. Hankins, Anh's teacher, or even Mr. Ho or Miss Huong said anything directly to us about it. Or if they did, I have forgotten it entirely. Then one day my parents got a call from Miss Huong. When Rosa came to talk to me and Anh about it we were watching television the way kids do, sitting alarmingly close to the screen. Rosa confronted us with "Do you girls know English?" Then she suddenly said, "Do you know Vietnamese?" I can't remember what we replied to either question.

For many years, a towering old billboard over the expressway   5 downtown proudly declared Grand Rapids "An All-American City." For me, that all-American designation meant all-white. I couldn't believe (and still don't) that they meant to include the growing Mexican-American population, or the sudden influx of Vietnamese refugees in 1975. I often thought it a rather mean-spirited prank of some administrator at the INS, deciding with a flourish of a signature to send a thousand refugees to Grand Rapids, a city that boasted having more churches per square mile than other city in the United States. Did that administrator know what Grand Rapids was like? That in school, everywhere I turned, and often when I closed my eyes, I saw blond blond blond? The point of bilingual education was assimilation. To my stepmother, the point was preservation: she didn't want English to take over wholly, pushing the Vietnamese out of our heads. She was too ambitious. Anh and I were Americanized as soon as we turned on the television. Today, bilingual education is supposed to have become both a method of assimilation and a method of preservation, an effort to prove that kids can have it both ways. They can supposedly keep English for school and their friends and keep another language for home and family.

In Grand Rapids, Michigan, in the 1980s, I found that an impossible task.

I transferred to Ken-O-Sha Elementary in time for third grade, after Rosa finally admitted that taking the bus all the way to Sherwood was pointless. I was glad to transfer, eager to be part of a class that wasn't, in my mind, tainted with the knowledge of my bilingual stigma. Third grade was led by Mrs. Alexander, an imperious, middle-aged woman of many plaid skirts held safe by giant gold safety pins. She had a habit of turning her wedding ring around and around her finger while she stood at the chalkboard. Mrs. Alexander had an intricate system of rewards for good grades and good behavior, denoted by colored star stickers on a piece of poster board that loomed over us all. One glance and you could see who was behind, who was striding ahead.

I was an insufferably good student, with perfect Palmer cursive and the highest possible scores in every subject. I had learned this trick at Sherwood. That the quieter you are, the shyer and sweeter and better-at-school you are, the more the teacher will let you alone. Mrs. Alexander should have let me alone. For, in addition to my excellent marks, I was nearly silent, deadly shy, and wholly obedient. My greatest fear was being called on, or in any way standing out more than I already did in the class that was, except for me and one black student, dough-white. I got good grades because I feared the authority of the teacher; I felt that getting in good with Mrs. Alexander would protect me, that she would protect me from the frightful rest of the world. But Mrs. Alexander was not agreeable to this notion. If it was my turn to read aloud during reading circle, she'd interrupt me to snap, "You're reading too fast" or demand, "What does that word mean?" Things she did not do to the other students. Anh, when I told her about this, suggested that perhaps Mrs. Alexander liked me and wanted to help me get smarter. But neither of us believed it. You know when a teacher likes you and when she doesn't.

Secretly, I admired and envied the rebellious kids, like Robbie Andrews who came to school looking bleary-eyed and pinched, like a hungover adult; Robbie and his ilk snapped back at teachers, were routinely sent to the principal's office, were even spanked a few times with the principal's infamous red paddle (apparently no one in Grand Rapids objected to corporal punishment). Those kids made noise, possessed something I thought was confidence, self-knowledge, allowing them to marvelously question everything ordered of them. They had the ability to challenge the given world.

10   Toward the middle of third grade Mrs. Alexander introduced a stuffed lion to the pool of rewards: the best student of the week would earn the privilege of having the lion sit on his or her desk for the entire week. My quantity of gold stars was neck and neck with that of my two competitors, Brenda and Jennifer, both sweet-eyed blond girls with pastel-colored monogrammed sweaters and neatly tied Dock-Sides. My family did not have a lot of money and my stepmother had terrible taste. Thus I attended school in such ensembles as dark red parachute pants and a nubby pink sweater stitched with a picture of a unicorn rearing up. This only propelled me to try harder to be good, to make up for everything I felt was against me: my odd family, my race, my very face. And I craved that stuffed lion. Week after week, the lion perched on Brenda's desk or Jennifer's desk. Meanwhile, the class spelling bee approached. I didn't know I was such a good speller until I won it, earning a scalloped-edged certificate and a candy bar. That afternoon I started toward home, then remembered I'd forgotten my rain boots in my locker. I doubled back to school and overheard Mrs. Alexander in the classroom talking to another teacher. "Can you believe it?" Mrs. Alexander was saying. "A foreigner winning our spelling bee!"

I waited for the stuffed lion the rest of that year, with a kind of patience I have no patience for today. To no avail. In June, on the last day of school, Mrs. Alexander gave the stuffed lion to Brenda to keep forever.

The first time I had to read aloud something I had written—perhaps it was in fourth grade—I felt such terror, such a need not to have any attention upon me, that I convinced myself that I had become invisible, that the teacher could never call on me because she couldn't see me.

More than once, I was given the assignment of writing a report about my family history. I loathed this task, for I was dreadfully aware that my history could not be faked; it already showed on my face. When my turn came to read out loud the teacher had to ask me several times to speak louder. Some kids, a few of them older, in different classes, took to pressing back the corners of their eyes with the heels of their palms while they chanted, "Ching-chong, ching-chong!" during recess. (This continued until Anh, who was far tougher than me, threatened to beat them up.)

I have no way of telling what tortured me more: the actual snickers and remarks and watchfulness of my classmates, or my own imagination, conjuring disdain. My own sense of shame. At times I felt sickened by my obedience, my accumulation of gold stickers, my every effort to be invisible.

Yet Robbie Andrews must have felt the same kind of claustrophobia, 15 trapped in his own reputation, in his ability to be otherwise. I learned in school that changing oneself is not easy, that the world makes up its mind quickly.

I've heard that Robbie dropped out of high school, got a girl pregnant, found himself in and out of first juvenile detention, then jail.

What comes out of difference? What constitutes difference? Such questions, academic and unanswered, popped up in every other course description in college. But the idea of difference is easy to come by, especially in school; it is shame, the permutations and inversions of difference and self-loathing, that we should be worrying about.

Imagined torment, imagined scorn. When what is imagined and what is desired turn on each other.

Some kids want to rebel; other kids want to disappear. I wanted to disappear. I was not brave enough to shrug my shoulders and flaunt my difference; because I could not disappear into the crowd, I wished to disappear entirely. Anyone might have mistaken this for passivity.

Once, at the end of my career at Sherwood Elementary, I disappeared 20 on the bus home. Mine was usually the third stop, but that day the bus driver thought I wasn't there, and she sailed right by the corner of

Ravanna and Senora. I said nothing. The bus wove its way downtown, and for the first time I got to see where other children lived, some of them in clean orderly neighborhoods, some near houses with sagging porches and boarded-up windows. All the while, the kid sitting across the aisle from me played the same cheerful song over and over on his portable boom box. *Pass the doochee from the left hand side, pass the doochee from the left hand side.* He and his brother turned out to be the last kids off the bus. Then the bus driver saw me through the rearview mirror. She walked back to where I was sitting and said, "How come you didn't get off at your stop?" I shook my head, don't know. She sighed and drove me home.

I was often doing that, shaking my head silently or staring up wordlessly. I realize that while I remember so much of what other people said when I was a child, I remember little of what I said. Probably because I didn't say much at all.

I recently came across in the stacks of the University of Michigan library *A Manual for Indochinese Refugee Education 1976–1977.* Some of it is silly, but much of it is a painstaking, fairly thoughtful effort to let school administrators and teachers know how to go about sensitively handling the influx of Vietnamese children in the public schools. Here is one of the most wonderful items of advice: "The Vietnamese child, even the older child, is also reported to be afraid of the dark, and more often than not, believes in ghosts. A teacher may have to be a little more solicitous of the child on gloomy, wintery days." Perhaps if Mrs. Alexander had read this, she would not have upbraided me so often for tracking mud into the classroom on rainy days. In third grade I was horrified and ashamed of my muddy shoes. I hung back, trying to duck behind this or that dark-haired boy. In spite of this, in spite of bilingual education, and shyness, and all that wordless shaking of my head, I was sent off every Monday to the Spectrum School for the Gifted and Talented. I still have no idea who selected me, who singled me out. Spectrum was (and still is) a public school program that invited students from every public elementary school to meet once a week and take specialized classes on topics such as the Middle Ages, Ellis Island, and fairy tales. Each student chose two classes, a major and minor, and for the rest of the semester worked toward final projects in both. I loved going to Spectrum. Not only did the range of students from other schools prove to be diverse, I found myself feeling more comfortable, mainly because Spectrum encouraged individual work. And the teachers seemed happy to be there. The best teacher at Spectrum was Mrs. King, whom every student adored. I still remember the soft gray sweaters she wore, her big wavy hair, her art-class handwriting, the way she'd often tell us to close our eyes when she read us a particular story or passage.

I believe that I figured out how to stop disappearing, how to talk and answer, even speak up, after several years in Spectrum. I was still deeply self-conscious, but I became able, sometimes, to maneuver around it.

Spectrum may have spoiled me a little, because it made me think about college and freedom, and thus made all the years in between disappointing and annoying.

In seventh grade I joined Anh and Cristina at the City School, a seventh through twelfth grade public school in the Grand Rapids system that served as an early charter school; admission was by interview, and each grade had about fifty students. The City School had the advantage of being downtown, perched over old cobblestone roads, and close to the main public library. Art and music history were required. There were no sports teams. And volunteering was mandatory. But kids didn't tend to stay at City School; as they got older they transferred to one of the big high schools nearby, perhaps wishing to play sports, perhaps wishing to get away from City's rather brutal academic system. Each half semester, after grades were doled out, giant dot-matrix printouts of everyone's GPAs were posted in the hallways.

I didn't stay at City, either. When my family moved to a different suburb, my stepmother promptly transferred me to Forest Hills Northern High School. Most of the students there came from upper-middle-class or very well-to-do families; the ones who didn't stood out sharply. The rich kids were the same as they were anywhere in America: they wore a lot of Esprit and Guess, drove nice cars, and ran student council, prom, and sports. These kids strutted down the hallways; the boys sat in a row on the long windowsill near a group of lockers, whistling or calling out to girls who walked by. Girls gathered in bathrooms with their Clinique lipsticks.

High school was the least interesting part of my education, but I did accomplish something: I learned to forget myself a little. I learned the sweetness of apathy. And through apathy, how to forget my skin and body for a minute or two, almost not caring what would happen if I walked into a room late and all heads swiveled toward me. I learned the pleasure that reveals itself in the loss, no matter how slight, of self-consciousness. These things occurred because I remained the good immigrant student, without raising my hand often or showing off what I knew. Doing work was rote, and I went along to get along. I've never gotten over the terror of being called on in class, or the dread in knowing that I'm expected to contribute to class discussion. But there is a slippage between being good and being unnoticed, and in that sliver of freedom I learned what it could feel like to walk in the world in plain, unself-conscious view.

I would like to make a broad, accurate statement about immigrant children in schools. I would like to speak for them (us). I hesitate; I cannot. My own sister, for instance, was never as shy as I was. Anh disliked

25

school from the start, choosing rebellion rather than silence. It was a good arrangement: I wrote papers for her and she paid me in money or candy; she gave me rides to school if I promised not to tell anyone about her cigarettes. Still, I think of an Indian friend of mine who told of an elementary school experience in which a blond schoolchild told the teacher, "I can't sit by her. My mom said I can't sit by anyone who's brown." And another friend, whose family immigrated around the same time mine did, whose second grade teacher used her as a vocabulary example: "Children, this is what a *foreigner* is." And sometimes I fall into thinking that kids today have the advantage of so much more wisdom, that they are so much more socially and politically aware than anyone was when I was in school. But I am wrong, of course. I know not every kid is fortunate enough to have a teacher like Mrs. King, or a program like Spectrum, or even the benefit of a manual written by a group of concerned educators; I know that some kids want to disappear and disappear until they actually do. Sometimes I think I see them, in the blurry background of a magazine photo, or in a gaggle of kids following a teacher's aide across the street. The kids with heads bent down, holding themselves in such a way that they seem to be self-conscious even of how they breathe. Small, shy, quiet kids, such good, good kids, *immigrant, foreigner,* their eyes watchful and waiting for whatever judgment will occur. I reassure myself that they will grow up fine, they will be okay. Maybe I cross the same street, then another, glancing back once in a while to see where they are going.

Responding to Reading

1. What does Nguyen mean when she says that today bilingual education is supposed to be "both a method of assimilation and a method of preservation" (5)? Does she believe this assessment is accurate?
2. In paragraph 17, Nguyen asks, "What comes out of difference? What constitutes difference?" How does she answer these questions? In what way does her own sense of difference affect her education?
3. What is "the good immigrant student"? How did Nguyen's education reinforce this stereotype? How did it help her move beyond it?

Responding in Writing

In paragraph 28, Nguyen says, "I would like to make a broad, accurate statement about immigrant children in schools. I would like to speak for them (us). I hesitate; I cannot." What do you think she means? Why can't she make "a broad, accurate statement"?

SCHOOL'S OUT
Daniel H. Pink
1964–

Daniel H. Pink worked from 1995 to 1997 as chief speechwriter to Vice Pres-
ident Al Gore. Pink writes mainly about business, work, and economic trans-
formation. His articles and essays have appeared in Wired, *the* New York
Times, *the* New Republic, Slate, *and other publications. Currently, he is a*
contributing editor to Wired *magazine. His latest books are* A Whole New
Mind: Moving from The Informational Age to the Conceptual Age
(2005) and The Adventures of Johnny Bunko: The Last Career Guide
You Will Ever Need *(2008), illustrated by Rob Ten Pas. The following essay,*
taken from Pink's book Free Agent Nation: How America's New Independent Workers Are Transforming the Way We Live *(2001), shows how*
traditional public schools are unable to prepare students for the challenges of
the twenty-first century.

Here's a riddle of the New Economy: Whenever students around the
world take those tests that measure which country's children know the
most, American kids invariably score near the bottom. No matter the subject, when the international rankings come out, European and Asian
nations finish first while the U.S. pulls up the rear. This, we all know,
isn't good. Yet by almost every measure, the American economy outperforms those very same nations of Asia and Europe. We create greater
wealth, deliver more and better goods and services, and positively kick
butt on innovation. This, we all know, *is* good.

Now the riddle: If we're so dumb, how come we're so rich? How
can we fare so poorly on international measures of education yet perform so well in an economy that depends on brainpower? The answer
is complex, but within it are clues about the future of education—and
how "free agency" may rock the school house as profoundly as it has
upended the business organization.

We are living in the founding of what I call "free agent nation."
Over the past decade, in nearly every industry and region, work has
been undergoing perhaps its most significant transformation since
Americans left the farm for the factory a century ago. Legions of Americans, and increasingly citizens of other countries as well, are abandoning one of the Industrial Revolution's most enduring legacies—the
"job"—and forging new ways to work. They're becoming self-employed
knowledge workers, proprietors of home-based businesses, temps and
permatemps, freelancers and e-lancers, independent contractors and
independent professionals, micropreneurs and infopreneurs, part-time
consultants, interim executives, on-call troubleshooters, and full-time
soloists.

In the U.S. today, more than 30 million workers—nearly one-fourth of the American workforce—are free agents. And many others who hold what are still nominally "jobs" are doing so under terms closer in spirit to free agency than to traditional employment. They're telecommuting. They're hopping from company to company. They're forming ventures that are legally their employers', but whose prospects depend largely on their own individual efforts.

5   In boom times, many free agents—fed up with bad bosses and dysfunctional workplaces and yearning for freedom—leapt into this new world. In leaner times, other people—clobbered by layoffs, mergers, and downturns—have been pushed. But these new independent workers are transforming the nation's social and economic future. Soon they will transform the nation's education system as well.

The Homogenizing Hopper

Whenever I walk into a public school, I'm nearly toppled by a wave of nostalgia. Most schools I've visited in the 21st century look and feel exactly like the public schools I attended in the 1970s. The classrooms are the same size. The desks stand in those same rows. Bulletin boards preview the next national holiday. The hallways even *smell* the same. Sure, some classrooms might have a computer or two. But in most respects, the schools American children attend today seem indistinguishable from the ones their parents and grandparents attended.

At first, such déjà vu warmed my soul. But then I thought about it. How many other places look and feel exactly as they did 20, 30, or 40 years ago? Banks don't. Hospitals don't. Grocery stores don't. Maybe the sweet nostalgia I sniffed on those classroom visits was really the odor of stagnation. Since most other institutions in American society have changed dramatically in the past half-century, the stasis of schools is strange. And it's doubly peculiar because school itself is a modern invention, not something we inherited from antiquity.

Through most of history, people learned from tutors or their close relatives. In 19th-century America, says education historian David Tyack, "the school was a voluntary and incidental institution." Not until the early 20th century did public schools as we know them—places where students segregated by age learn from government-certified professionals—become widespread. And not until the 1920s did attending one become compulsory. Think about that last fact a moment. Compared with much of the world, America is a remarkably hands-off land. We don't force people to vote, or to work, or to serve in the military. But we do compel parents to relinquish their kids to this institution for a dozen years, and threaten to jail those who resist.

Compulsory mass schooling is an aberration in both history and modern society. Yet it was the ideal preparation for the Organization

Man economy, a highly structured world dominated by large, bureaucratic corporations that routinized the workplace. Compulsory mass schooling equipped generations of future factory workers and middle managers with the basic skills and knowledge they needed on the job. The broader lessons it conveyed were equally crucial. Kids learned how to obey rules, follow orders, and respect authority—and the penalties that came with refusal.

This was just the sort of training the old economy demanded. 10 Schools had bells; factories had whistles. Schools had report card grades; offices had pay grades. Pleasing your teacher prepared you for pleasing your boss. And in either place, if you achieved a minimal level of performance, you were promoted. Taylorism—the management philosophy, named for efficiency expert Frederick Winslow Taylor, that there was One Best Way of doing things that could and should be applied in all circumstances—didn't spend all its time on the job. It also went to class. In the school, as in the workplace, the reigning theory was One Best Way. Kids learned the same things at the same time in the same manner in the same place. Marshall McLuhan once described schools as "the homogenizing hopper into which we toss our integral tots for processing." And schools made factory-style processing practically a religion—through standardized testing, standardized curricula, and standardized clusters of children. (Question: When was the last time *you* spent all day in a room filled exclusively with people almost exactly your own age?)

So when we step into the typical school today, we're stepping into the past—a place whose architect is Frederick Winslow Taylor and whose tenant is the Organization Man. The one American institution that has least accommodated itself to the free agent economy is the one Americans claim they value most. But it's hard to imagine that this arrangement can last much longer—a One Size Fits All education system cranking out workers for a My Size Fits Me economy. Maybe the answer to the riddle I posed at the beginning is that we're succeeding *in spite of* our education system. But how long can that continue? And imagine how we'd prosper if we began educating our children more like we earn our livings. Nearly 20 years ago, a landmark government report, *A Nation at Risk*, declared that American education was "being eroded by a rising tide of mediocrity." That may no longer be true. Instead, American schools are awash in a rising tide of irrelevance.

Don't get me wrong. In innumerable ways, mass public schooling has been a stirring success. Like Taylorism, it has accomplished some remarkable things—teaching immigrants both English and the American way, expanding literacy, equipping many Americans to succeed beyond their parents' imaginings. In a very large sense, America's schools have been a breathtaking democratic achievement.

But that doesn't mean they ought to be the same as they were when we were kids. Parents and politicians have sensed the need for reform, and have pushed education to the top of the national agenda. Unfortunately, few of the conventional remedies—standardized testing, character training, recertifying teachers—will do much to cure what ails American schools, and may even make things worse. Free agency, though, will force the necessary changes. Look for free agency to accelerate and deepen three incipient movements in education—home schooling, alternatives to traditional high school, and new approaches to adult learning. These changes will prove as pathbreaking as mass public schooling was a century ago.

The Home-Schooling Revolution

"School is like starting life with a 12-year jail sentence in which bad habits are the only curriculum truly learned." Those are the words of John Taylor Gatto, who was named New York state's Teacher of the Year in 1991. Today he is one of the most forceful voices for one of the most powerful movements in American education—home schooling. In home schooling, kids opt out of traditional school to take control of their own education and to learn with the help of parents, tutors, and peers. Home schooling is free agency for the under-18 set. And it's about to break through the surface of our national life.

15   As recently as 1980, home schooling was illegal in most states. In the early 1980s, no more than 15,000 students learned this way. But Christian conservatives, unhappy with schools they considered God-free zones and eager to teach their kids themselves, pressed for changes. Laws fell, and home schooling surged. By 1990, there were as many as 300,000 American home-schoolers. By 1993, home schooling was legal in all 50 states. Since then, home schooling has swum into the mainstream—paddled there by secular parents dissatisfied with low-quality, and even dangerous, schools. In the first half of the 1990s, the home-schooling population more than doubled. Today some 1.7 million children are home-schoolers, their ranks growing as much as 15 percent each year. Factor in turnover, and one in 10 American kids under 18 has gotten part of his or her schooling at home.

Home schooling has become perhaps the largest and most successful education reform movement of the last two decades:

- While barely 3 percent of American schoolchildren are now home-schoolers, that represents a surprisingly large dent in the public school monopoly—especially compared with private schools. For every four kids in private school, there's one youngster learning at home. The home-schooling population is roughly equal to all the school-age children in Pennsylvania.

- According to *The Wall Street Journal,* "Evidence is mounting that home-schooling, once confined to the political and religious fringe, has achieved results not only on par with public education, but in some ways surpassing it." Home-schooled children consistently score higher than traditional students on standardized achievement tests, placing on average in the 80th percentile in all subjects.

- Home-schooled children also perform extremely well on nearly all measures of socialization. One of the great misconceptions about home schooling is that it turns kids into isolated loners. In fact, these children spend more time with adults, more time in their community, and more time with children of varying ages than their traditional-school counterparts. Says one researcher, "The conventionally schooled tended to be considerably more aggressive, loud, and competitive than the home educated."

"Home schooling," though, is a bit of a misnomer. Parents don't re-create the classroom in the living room any more than free agents re-create the cubicle in their basement offices. Instead, home schooling makes it easier for children to pursue their own interests in their own way—a My Size Fits Me approach to learning. In part for this reason, some adherents—particularly those who have opted out of traditional schools for reasons other than religion—prefer the term "unschooling."

The similarities to free agency—having an "unjob"—are many. Free agents are independent workers; home-schoolers are independent learners. Free agents maintain robust networks and tight connections through informal groups and professional associations; home-schoolers have assembled powerful groups—like the 3,000-family Family Unschoolers Network—to share teaching strategies and materials and to offer advice and support. Free agents often challenge the idea of separating work and family; home-schoolers take the same approach to the boundary between school and family.

Perhaps most important, home schooling is almost perfectly consonant with the four animating values of free agency: having freedom, being authentic, putting yourself on the line, and defining your own success. Take freedom. In the typical school, children often aren't permitted to move unless a bell rings or an adult grants them permission. And except for a limited menu of offerings in high school, they generally can't choose what to study or when to study it. Home-schoolers have far greater freedom. They learn more like, well, children. We don't teach little kids how to talk or walk or understand the world. We simply put them in nurturing situations and let them learn on their own. Sure, we impose certain restrictions. ("Don't walk in the middle of the street.") But we don't go crazy. ("Please practice talking for 45 minutes until a bell rings.") It's the same for home-schoolers. Kids can become agents of their own education rather than merely recipients of someone else's noble intentions.

20   Imagine a 5-year-old child whose current passion is building with Legos. Every day she spends up to an hour, maybe more, absorbed in complex construction projects, creating farms, zoos, airplanes, spaceships. Often her friends come over and they work together. No one assigns her this project. No one tells her when and how to do it. And no one will give her creation a grade. Is she learning? Of course. This is how many home-schoolers explore their subjects.

Now suppose some well-intentioned adults step in to teach the child a thing or two about Lego building. Let's say they assign her a daily 45-minute Lego period, give her a grade at the end of each session, maybe even offer a reward for an A+ building. And why not bring in some more 5-year-olds to teach them the same things about Legos? Why not have them all build their own 45-minute Lego buildings at the same time, then give them each a letter grade, with a prize for the best one? My guess: Pretty soon our 5-year-old Lego lover would lose her passion. Her buildings would likely become less creative, her learning curve flatter. This is how many conventional schools work—or, I guess, *don't work*.

The well-meaning adults have squelched the child's freedom to play and learn and discover on her own. She's no longer in control. She's no longer having fun. Countless studies, particularly those by University of Rochester psychologist Edward L. Deci, have shown that kids and adults alike—in school, at work, at home—lose the intrinsic motivation and the pure joy derived from learning and working when somebody takes away their sense of autonomy and instead imposes some external system of reward and punishment. Freedom isn't a detour from learning. It's the best pathway toward it.

Stay with our Lego lass a moment and think about authenticity— the basic desire people have to be who they are rather than conform to someone else's standard. Our young builder has lost the sense that she is acting according to her own true self. Instead, she has gotten the message. You build Legos for the same reason your traditionally employed father does his work assignments: because an authority figure tells you to.

Or take accountability. The child is no longer fully accountable for her own Lego creating. Whatever she has produced is by assignment. Her creations are no longer truly hers. And what about those Lego grades? That A+ may motivate our girl to keep building, but not on her own terms. Maybe she liked the B− building better than the A+ creation. Oh well. Now she'll probably bury that feeling and work to measure up—to someone else's standards. Should she take a chance—try building that space shuttle she's been dreaming about? Probably not. Why take that risk when, chances are, it won't make the grade? Self-defined success has no place in this regime. But for many home-schoolers, success is something they can define themselves. (This is true even though, as I mentioned, home-schoolers score off the charts on conventional measures of success—standardized tests in academic subjects.)

To be sure, some things most kids should learn are not intrinsi- 25 cally fun. There are times in life when we must eat our Brussels sprouts. For those subjects, the punishment-and-reward approach of traditional schooling may be in order. But too often, the sheer thrill of learning a new fact or mastering a tough equation is muted when schools take away a student's sense of control. In home schooling, kids have greater freedom to pursue their passions, less pressure to conform to the wishes of teachers and peers—and can put themselves on the line, take risks, and define success on their own terms. As more parents realize that the underlying ethic of home schooling closely resembles the animating values of free agency, home schooling will continue to soar in popularity.

Free Agent Teaching

Several other forces will combine to power home schooling into greater prominence. One is simply the movement's initial prominence. As more families choose this option, they will make it more socially acceptable—thereby encouraging other families to take this once-unconventional route. The home-schooling population has already begun to look like the rest of America. While some 90 percent of home-schoolers are white, the population is becoming more diverse, and may be growing fastest among African Americans. And the median income for a home-school family is roughly equal to the median income for the rest of the country; about 87 percent have annual household incomes under $75,000.

Recent policy changes—in state legislatures and principals' offices—will further clear the way. Not only is home schooling now legal in every state, but many public schools have begun letting home-schoolers take certain classes or play on school teams. About two-thirds of American colleges now accept transcripts prepared by parents, or portfolios assembled by students, in lieu of an accredited diploma.

Another force is free agency itself. Thanks to flexible schedules and personal control, it's easier for free agents than for traditional employees to home-school their children. Free agents will also become the professionals in this new world of learning. A carpenter might hire herself out to teach carpentry skills to home-schoolers. A writer might become a tutor or editor to several home-schoolers interested in producing their own literary journal. What's more, the huge cadre of teachers hired to teach the baby boom will soon hit retirement age. However, perhaps instead of fully retiring, many will hire themselves out as itinerant tutors to home-schoolers—and begin part-time careers as free agent educators. For many parents, of course, the responsibility and time commitment of home schooling will be daunting. But the wide availability of teachers and tutors might help some parents overcome the concern that they won't be able to handle this awesome undertaking by themselves.

The Internet makes home schooling easier, too. Indeed, home-schoolers figured out the Internet well before most Americans. For example, my first Internet connection was a DOS-based Compuserve account I acquired in 1993. Before the wide acceptance of the Internet and the advent of the World Wide Web, the most active discussion groups on Compuserve were those devoted to home schooling. Using the Web, home-schoolers can do research and find tutors anywhere in the world. There are now even online ventures—for instance, the Christa McAuliffe Academy (www.cmacademy.org) in Washington state and ChildU.com in Florida—that sell online courses and provide e-teachers for home-schoolers. Physical infrastructure might also accelerate this trend. Almost three-fourths of America's public school buildings were built before 1969. School administrations might be more likely to encourage some amount of home schooling if that means less strain on their crowded classrooms and creaky buildings.

30   I don't want to overstate the case. Home schooling, like free agency, won't be for everyone. Many parents won't have the time or the desire for this approach. And home schooling won't be for all time. Many students will spend a few years in a conventional school and a few years learning at home—just as some workers will migrate between being a free agent and holding a job. But home schooling is perhaps the most robust expression of the free agent way outside the workplace, making its continued rise inevitable.

The End of High School

One other consequence of the move toward home schooling will be something many of us wished for as teenagers: the demise of high school. It wasn't until the 1920s that high school replaced work as the thing most Americans did in their teens. "American high school is obsolete," says Bard College president Leon Botstein, one of the first to call for its end. He says today's adolescents would be better off pursuing a college degree, jumping directly into the job market, engaging in public service, or taking on a vocational apprenticeship. Even the National Association of Secondary School Principals, which has blasted home schooling, concedes that "high schools continue to go about their business in ways that sometimes bear startling resemblance to the flawed practices of the past."

In the future, expect teens and their families to force an end to high school as we know it. Look for some of these changes to replace and augment traditional high schools with free-agent-style learning—and to unschool the American teenager:

- **A renaissance of apprenticeships.** For centuries, young people learned a craft or profession under the guidance of an experienced master. This method will revive and expand to include skills like computer programming and graphic design. Imagine a 14-year-old taking two or three academic courses each week, and spending the rest of her time apprenticing as a commercial artist. Traditional high schools tend to separate learning and doing. Free agency makes them indistinguishable.

- **A flowering of teenage entrepreneurship.** Young people may become free agents even before they get their driver's licenses—and teen entrepreneurs will become more common. Indeed, most teens have the two crucial traits of a successful entrepreneur: a fresh way of looking at the world and a passionate intensity for what they do. In San Diego County, 8 percent of high school students already run their own online business. That will increasingly become the norm and perhaps even become a teenage rite of passage.

- **A greater diversity of academic courses.** Only 16 states offer basic economics in high school. That's hardly a sound foundation for the free agent workplace. Expect a surge of new kinds of "home economics" courses that teach numeracy, accounting, and basic business.

- **A boom in national service.** Some teenagers will seek greater direction than others and may want to spend a few years serving in the military or participating in a domestic service program. Today, many young people don't consider these choices because of the pressure to go directly to college. Getting people out of high school earlier might get them into service sooner.

- **A backlash against standards.** A high school diploma was once the gold standard of American education. No more. Yet politicians seem determined to make the diploma meaningful again by erecting all sorts of hurdles kids must leap to attain one—standardized subjects each student must study, standardized tests each student must pass. In some schools, students are already staging sit-ins to protest these tests. This could be American youth's new cause célèbre. ("Hey hey, ho ho. Standardized testing's got to go.")

Most politicians think the answer to the problems of high schools is to exert more control. But the real answer is *less* control. In the free agent future, our teens will learn by less schooling and more doing.

The Unschooling of Adults

For much of the 20th century, the U.S. depended on what I call the Thanksgiving turkey model of education. We placed kids in the oven of formal education for 12 years, and then served them up to employers. (A select minority got a final, four-year basting at a place called college.) But this model doesn't work in a world of accelerated cycle times, shrinking company half-lives, and the rapid obsolescence of knowledge and skills. In a free agent economy, our education system must allow people to learn throughout their lives.

35   Home schooling and alternatives to high school will create a nation of self-educators, free agent learners, if you will. Adults who were home-schooled youths will know how to learn and expect to continue the habit throughout their lives.

For example, how did anybody learn the Web? In 1993, it barely existed. By 1995, it was the foundation of dozens of new industries and an explosion of wealth. There weren't any college classes in Web programming, HTML coding, or Web page design in those early years. Yet somehow hundreds of thousands of people managed to learn. How? They taught themselves—working with colleagues, trying new things, and making mistakes. That was the secret to the Web's success. The Web flourished almost entirely through the ethic and practice of self-teaching. This is not a radical concept. Until the first part of this century, most Americans learned on their own—by reading. Literacy and access to books were an individual's ticket to knowledge. Even today, according to my own online survey of 1,143 independent workers, "reading" was the most prevalent way free agents said they stay up-to-date in their field.

In the 21st century, access to the Internet and to a network of smart colleagues will be the ticket to adult learning. Expect more of us to punch those tickets throughout our lives. Look for these early signs:

- **The devaluation of degrees.** As the shelf life of a degree shortens, more students will go to college to acquire particular skills than to bring home a sheepskin. People's need for knowledge doesn't respect semesters. They'll want higher education just in time—and if that means leaving the classroom before earning a degree, so be it. Remember: Larry Ellison, Steve Jobs, and Steven Spielberg never finished college.

THE FIRST DAY
Edward P. Jones
1950–

Edward P. Jones studied writing at the University of Virginia. His book Lost
in the City *(1992) is a collection of stories set in the hometown of his childhood, Washington, D.C., a city of working-class black men and women who
struggle heroically in their daily lives. The book was nominated for the National
Book Award and lauded by critics both for addressing racial issues and for
transcending them. His first novel,* The Known World, *published in 2003,
was chosen as one of the year's nine best books (and four best novels) by the
editors of the* New York Times Book Review. The Known World *also won
the fiction prize of the National Book Critics Circle and the 2004 Pulitzer Prize
for fiction. His latest book,* All Aunt Hagar's Children *(2006), is a collection of stories. The short story that follows, from* Lost in the City, *is the
poignant story of a mother who takes her daughter to her first day of school.*

In an otherwise unremarkable September morning, long before I learned
to be ashamed of my mother, she takes my hand and we set off down
New Jersey Avenue to begin my very first day of school. I am wearing a
checkeredlike blue-and-green cotton dress, and scattered about these colors are bits of yellow and white and brown. My mother has uncharacter-
istically spent nearly an hour on my hair that morning, plaiting and
replaiting so that now my scalp tingles. Whenever I turn my head quickly,
my nose fills with the faint smell of Dixie Peach hair grease. The smell is
somehow a soothing one now and I will reach for it time and time again
before the morning ends. All the plaits, each with a blue barrette near the
tip and each twisted into an uncommon sturdiness, will last until I go to
bed that night, something that has never happened before. My stomach
is full of milk and oatmeal sweetened with brown sugar. Like everything
else I have on, my pale green slip and underwear are new, the underwear
having come three to a plastic package with a little girl on the front who
appears to be dancing. Behind my ears, my mother, to stop my whining,
has dabbed the stingiest bit of her gardenia perfume, the last present my
father gave her before he disappeared into memory. Because I cannot smell
it, I have only her word that the perfume is there. I am also wearing yellow socks trimmed with thin lines of black and white around the tops.
My shoes are my greatest joy, black patent-leather miracles, and when one
is nicked at the toe later that morning in class, my heart will break.

I am carrying a pencil, a pencil sharpener, and a small ten-cent tablet
with a black-and-white speckled cover. My mother does not believe that a

girl in kindergarten needs such things, so I am taking them only because of my insistent whining and because they are presents from our neighbors, Mary Keith and Blondelle Harris. Miss Mary and Miss Blondelle are watching my two younger sisters until my mother returns. The women are as precious to me as my mother and sisters. Out playing one day, I have overheard an older child, speaking to another child, call Miss Mary and Miss Blondelle a word that is brand new to me. This is my mother: When I say the word in fun to one of my sisters, my mother slaps me across the mouth and the word is lost for years and years.

All the way down New Jersey Avenue, the sidewalks are teeming with children. In my neighborhood, I have many friends, but I see none of them as my mother and I walk. We cross New York Avenue, we cross Pierce Street, and we cross L and K, and still I see no one who knows my name. At I Street, between New Jersey Avenue and Third Street, we enter Seaton Elementary School, a timeworn, sad-faced building across the street from my mother's church, Mt. Carmel Baptist.

Just inside the front door, women out of the advertisements in *Ebony* are greeting other parents and children. The woman who greets us has pearls thick as jumbo marbles that come down almost to her navel, and she acts as if she had known me all my life, touching my shoulder, cupping her hand under my chin. She is enveloped in a perfume that I only know is not gardenia. When, in answer to her question, my mother tells her that we live at 1227 New Jersey Avenue, the woman first seems to be picturing in her head where we live. Then she shakes her head and says that we are at the wrong school, that we should be at Walker-Jones.

5   My mother shakes her head vigorously. "I want her to go here," my mother says. "If I'da wanted her someplace else, I'da took her there." The woman continues to act as if she has known me all my life, but she tells my mother that we live beyond the area that Seaton serves. My mother is not convinced and for several more minutes she questions the woman about why I cannot attend Seaton. For as many Sundays as I can remember, perhaps even Sundays when I was in her womb, my mother has pointed across I Street to Seaton as we come and go to Mt. Carmel. "You gonna go there and learn about the whole world." But one of the guardians of that place is saying no, and no again. I am learning this about my mother: The higher up on the scale of respectability a person is—and teachers are rather high up in her eyes—the less she is liable to let them push her around. But finally, I see in her eyes the closing gate, and she takes my hand and we leave the building. On the steps, she stops as people move past us on either side.

"Mama, I can't go to school?"

She says nothing at first, then takes my hand again and we are down the steps quickly and nearing New Jersey Avenue before I can blink. This is my mother: She says, "One monkey don't stop no show."

Walker-Jones is a larger, newer school and I immediately like it because of that. But it is not across the street from my mother's church, her rock, one of her connections to God, and I sense her doubts as she absently rubs her thumb over the back of her hand. We find our way to the crowded auditorium where gray metal chairs are set up in the middle of the room. Along the wall to the left are tables and other chairs. Every chair seems occupied by a child or adult. Somewhere in the room a child is crying, a cry that rises above the buzz-talk of so many people. Strewn about the floor are dozens and dozens of pieces of white paper, and people are walking over them without any thought of picking them up. And seeing this lack of concern, I am all of a sudden afraid.

"Is this where they register for school?" my mother asks a woman at one of the tables.

The woman looks up slowly as if she has heard this question once 10 too often. She nods. She is tiny, almost as small as the girl standing beside her. The woman's hair is set in a mass of curlers and all of those curlers are made of paper money, here a dollar bill, there a five-dollar bill. The girl's hair is arrayed in curls, but some of them are beginning to droop and this makes me happy. On the table beside the woman's pocketbook is a large notebook, worthy of someone in high school, and looking at me looking at the notebook, the girl places her hand possessively on it. In her other hand she holds several pencils with thick crowns of additional erasers.

"These the forms you gotta use?" my mother asks the woman, picking up a few pieces of the paper from the table. "Is this what you have to fill out?"

The woman tells her yes, but that she need fill out only one.

"I see," my mother says, looking about the room. Then: "Would you help me with this form? That is, if you don't mind."

The woman asks my mother what she means.

"This form. Would you mind helpin me fill it out?" 15

The woman still seems not to understand.

"I can't read it. I don't know how to read or write, and I'm askin you to help me." My mother looks at me, then looks away. I know almost all of her looks, but this one is brand new to me. "Would you help me, then?"

The woman says Why sure, and suddenly she appears happier, so much more satisfied with everything. She finishes the form for her daughter and my mother and I step aside to wait for her. We find two chairs nearby and sit. My mother is now diseased, according to the girl's eyes, and until the moment her mother takes her and the form to the front of the auditorium, the girl never stops looking at my mother. I stare back at her. "Don't stare," my mother says to me. "You know better than that."

Another woman out of the *Ebony* ads takes the woman's child away. Now, the woman says upon returning, let's see what we can do for you two.

My mother answers the questions the woman reads off the form. 20 They start with my last name, and then on to the first and middle names. This is school, I think. This is going to school. My mother slowly enunciates each word of my name. This is my mother: As the questions go on, she takes from her pocketbook document after document, as if they will support my right to attend school, as if she has been saving them up for just this moment. Indeed, she takes out more papers than I have ever seen her do in other places: my birth certificate, my baptismal record, a doctor's letter concerning my bout with chicken pox, rent receipts, records of immunization, a letter about our public assistance payments, even her marriage license—every single paper that has anything even remotely to do with my five-year-old life. Few of the papers are needed here, but it does not matter and my mother continues to pull out the documents with the purposefulness of a magician pulling out a long string of scarves. She has learned that money is the beginning and end of everything in this world, and when the woman finishes, my mother offers her fifty cents, and the woman accepts it without hesitation. My mother and I are just about the last parent and child in the room.

My mother presents the form to a woman sitting in front of the stage, and the woman looks at it and writes something on a white card, which she gives to my mother. Before long, the woman who has taken the girl with the drooping curls appears from behind us, speaks to the sitting woman, and introduces herself to my mother and me. She's to be my teacher, she tells my mother. My mother stares.

We go into the hall, where my mother kneels down to me. Her lips are quivering. "I'll be back to pick you up at twelve o'clock. I don't want you to go nowhere. You just wait right here. And listen to every word she say." I touch her lips and press them together. It is an old, old game between us. She puts my hand down at my side, which is not part of the game. She stands and looks a second at the teacher, then she turns and walks away. I see where she has darned one of her socks the night before. Her shoes make loud sounds in the hall. She passes through the doors and I can still hear the loud sounds of her shoes. And even when the teacher turns me toward the classrooms and I hear what must be the singing and talking of all the children in the world, I can still hear my mother's footsteps above it all.

Responding to Reading

1. Why does the narrator's mother want to enroll her in Seaton Elementary School? Why is she unable to? What does the mother's reaction to this situation tell you about her?
2. What are the mother's limitations? What are her strengths?
3. Do you think that this story is primarily about the mother or her daughter? How do you explain the mother's reaction as she leaves her daughter? Why does the daughter still remember this reaction years later as she is telling this story? Why do you think the story ends with the sound of the mother's footsteps?

Responding in Writing

Write a paragraph describing your earliest memory of school.

--------------------------- FOCUS ---------------------------

How Much Do a College's Facilities Really Matter?

IN IOWA, 2 COLLEGES SEPARATED BY 150 MILES AND $1.37 BILLION: GRINNELL COLLEGE

Goldie Blumenstyk

A senior writer for the Chronicle of Higher Education, *Goldie Blumenstyk reports on issues related to business and information technology in higher education. In the following essay, Blumenstyk examines the advantages and disadvantages of attending an affluent Iowa college.*

Grinnell, Iowa—In its 160-year history, Grinnell College has been rich and it has been strapped. As the many generously paid professors and well-subsidized students here today will readily tell you, being rich is better.

With an endowment that has grown from about $44-million in 1980 to about $1.4-billion today, Grinnell is the wealthiest liberal-arts college in the country and has the 35th-largest endowment over all.

For its 1,500 students, Grinnell's prosperity means paid summer research projects with professors on the campus, college-financed internships off the campus, and hands-on classroom experience in first-class facilities where equipment and supplies—whether expensive reagents for an introductory chemistry course or ink in the printmaking studio—are never in short supply.

"Especially if you are a science major," says Priya Malik, a senior from Delhi, India, "you definitely are under the impression that you are going to a rich college."

The signs and sounds of the college's affluence are unmistakable on   5 this immaculately tended 120-acre campus, with its mix of low-slung Tudor residence halls, turreted academic buildings, and Modernist architecture.

At the campus's northern edge is the rumble of heavy equipment at the side-by-side construction sites of a new Cesar Pelli–designed student center and an expansion of the science building. And at the south are the haunting tones of the Javanese iron gamelan[1] in the college's world-music collection, housed in the elegant arts complex. (This arts complex, replete with a gallery and a recording studio, was also designed by the Pelli firm and opened in 1999.)

The $43-million science addition and the $42-million student center, which will feature a soaring glass wall and several styles of brick,

---

[1]Indonesian orchestra. [Eds.]

stone, and handmade tile, are part of a $163-million building boom that began in 2000. It has also included a dormitory, a fitness center, and an angular glass, steel, and limestone building for the admissions and financial-aid offices.

Money from the endowment paid for most of it, except for about $50-million from gifts.

Grinnell is among the lucky few colleges in the country that rarely, if ever, worry about meeting enrollment targets and instead have the luxury of focusing on how best to deploy their ever-increasing endowments to attract the most desirable students. But even as such colleges have been growing richer, the students who get to enjoy their high-tech science centers, palatial fitness complexes, and intimate classes are still mostly from wealthy and middle-class families.

10   Grinnell and other such colleges do provide financial aid. But critics argue that it and others should do more to make their colleges more accessible to students from poor families.

When it comes to serving poor students, "Grinnell gets a solid failing grade from us," says Thomas G. Mortenson, senior scholar at the Pell Institute for the Study of Opportunity in Higher Education. "Other elite schools do, too."

Mr. Mortenson, who happens to live in Iowa, is an unapologetic advocate for expanding access to higher education to underrepresented students. "Some of the rich schools are out there to pad their endowment," says Mr. Mortensen, "rather than serve the public interest."

One college that recently answered the call is Amherst College, pledging to provide admission—and the requisite financial aid—for as many as 120 students a year who come from families needy enough to qualify for Pell Grants.

Grinnell says it is paying attention, too. The college is one of a diminishing number that still meets the full financial need of all American students, its officials note, although in some cases, some of that aid comes through low-interest loans from the college or a required campus job.

15   And Grinnell's president has begun hinting that it, too, may be preparing a big move to make the college more affordable to needy students, even as it moves aggressively over the next few years to increase tuition.

Not Thinking "Rich"

Grinnell's striking buildings by celebrity architects are only the most visible signs of the college's prosperity. Grinnell provides need-based financial aid to 65 percent of its students and merit scholarships to an additional 25 percent, at a total cost of nearly $21-million this year (nearly 30 percent of its overall budget). For faculty members, it offers not only nationally competitive salaries but also a semester of paid leave to new professors after their third year of teaching, to help them keep abreast of their fields before they come up for tenure review.

The college even sponsors its own Peace Corps–style program, Grinnell Corps, which sends as many as 15 graduating seniors overseas for a year to teach English in places like Nanjing, in China, and Lesotho.

"The reason we can do it is because of the endowment," says Russell K. Osgood, Grinnell's president. The college depends on its endowment for nearly half of its $69-million annual budget, an unusually high proportion even for a college with a big endowment.

But Mr. Osgood, who assumed the post in 1998, says wealth also brings challenges. "If you say, 'We're a rich college,' you'll be undisciplined" about finances. The college's spending is focused, he says, on trying to ensure that all students can take part in the college's offerings, no matter their income, and to overcome some of the limitations of Grinnell's location "in a little town in Iowa."

He adds, "We don't sit around and think, How can we rain money 20 down on our students?"

Despite the spending here on programs and facilities, Grinnell does have an unassuming air. Students seem serious about their studies (at least during midterm week), few drive flashy cars, and for most last month's spring break seemed to involve a trip home, a visit with friends, or a community-service project, rather than a fling in Cancun. But Grinnell's wealth comes into play here, too: Students participating in many of the "alternative spring break" projects receive a subsidy from the college.

Warren Buffett and Joseph Who?

The story of Grinnell's endowment growth begins with Joseph F. Rosenfield, Class of 1925. A college trustee from 1941 until his death in 2000, Mr. Rosenfield was a department-store executive turned investor who occasionally bailed out the college when it was unable to pay its bills and who, along with his friend Warren E. Buffett, helped to guide Grinnell's investment miracle. (Mr. Buffett, the storied investor, was active on the board from 1968 until 1987.)

Thanks to Mr. Rosenfield—once described by *Money* magazine as "the best investor you've never heard of"—Grinnell was an early investor in a semiconductor company founded by another alumnus, Robert N. Noyce, that would later become Intel. Grinnell also made a splash in 1976 when, at Mr. Buffett's suggestion, it acquired a commercial television station in Dayton, Ohio, for about $13-million—an unusual investment for a college, particularly at that time—and then sold it, five years later, for $49-million.

Since 1980 the college has had only one fiscal year, 2000, when investment returns declined, and only six other years in which its

CHAPTER 2   FOCUS

returns fell below 10 percent. In 15 different years, it had returns of more than 15 percent, and in 12 of those years, its returns exceeded 20 percent.

25   Grinnell reveals few details about its idiosyncratic approach to investing. David S. Clay, the college's treasurer, does say that its endowment is probably far less diversified than other colleges' and far less rigid about asset allocation. He says the institution has succeeded by taking a long-term view, looking for opportunities at low prices, and being willing to allocate big stakes when it found them. Two of its most successful investments have been Freddie Mac and the Sequoia Fund.

Mark Montgomery, a professor of economics, says the college's investment success is a curse as well as a blessing. "There's almost a cult of the endowment at Grinnell," he says, and for all of the college's success, "we have not taken advantage of our wealth to really lower the burden on our students."

Eli Zigas, a senior from Washington, D.C., says Grinnell could be a small part of the solution to the growing economic divide in the country. Today only 11.5 percent of Grinnell students come from families with incomes that would qualify them for Pell Grants.

With its endowment, Grinnell "could make an enormous statement," say Mr. Zigas, a student leader with a deeper-than-typical understanding of the college's finances. On a recent evening, over pizza in the snack bar of the college's 1960s-vintage student center, he shared his affection for what the college offers and his frustration for what it doesn't: "We should and can be different," he says, "because we have the cushion."

It is a view that Mr. Montgomery and many of his colleagues share. Still, as the economics professor readily acknowledges, the endowment has transformed Grinnell, "and our lives are all the better for that."

The Good Life

30   Grinnell professors receive not only generous leaves and salaries that match those at colleges where the cost of living is lot higher, but also, typically, stipends to attend at least one academic conference a year. Usually, there is enough left over to bring along a few students.

Faculty members teach in first-rate facilities like the stone-and-glass Bucksbaum Center for the Arts, which anchors the southern tip of this rectangular campus. There, in one wing, students study world music in a two-story room festooned with exotic instruments hanging like tools in a garage. In another, participants in a physics class called "Bridges, Towers, and Skyscrapers" come to examine the designs of famous Swiss architects now on display in the sleek, light-filled gallery. The gallery routinely draws a half-dozen visiting exhibits each year, in addition to shows by students and faculty members.

Neither does Grinnell skimp at the opposite end of the campus, in the Robert N. Noyce Science Center. Introductory-science courses require students to work in small teams in hands-on experiments, and they do so with some of the most modern laboratory benches, electronic microscopes, and measuring instruments available.

"I have everything I need, and I'm not in a cheap field," says Leslie Gregg-Jolly, an associate professor of biology, who on a recent March day was supervising freshmen in the lab as they fertilized sea urchins.

Ms. Gregg-Jolly also relishes working with the high-caliber students here, who can handle the rigors of the curriculum. "Students in my molecular lab are doing work that would lead to publication," she says.

And Grinnell's academic program is about to expand. As part of a 35 strategic plan adopted a year ago, the college will add 12 new full-time faculty positions over the next five years in several new interdisciplinary fields.

Learning Off the Grid

The emphasis on hands-on experiences, through research programs and internships, is another hallmark of the undergraduate experience made possible by the endowment. Students working on research projects are paid as much as $3,200 a semester; those in internships receive up to $2,400. Altogether, about 250 students take part in the programs each year, at an overall cost of $750,000.

The idea is "to do something they can't do within our curriculum and that they couldn't do without the money," says Steve Langerud, associate dean for experiential education, who oversees the internships. Students have worked in rare-book stores in England, studied HIV in Zambia, and apprenticed with a sports agent in Oklahoma, he says. "We really push them to things that are off the grid."

The endowment also makes possible a program that brings nationally and internationally known speakers to the campus for short symposia on major issues in human rights and public affairs. This semester the topic was the genocide in the Darfur region of Sudan, and speakers included Nicholas D. Kristof, a columnist for The New York Times. Later this spring, another symposium will focus on the avian flu.

Alexey Hartlieb-Shea, a senior from Burlington, Vt., who takes in his share of the visitors' talks, as well as exhibits in the art gallery, says those are the kinds of extras he loves most at Grinnell. "I can't imagine I could get a better education anywhere else," he says.

But Mr. Hartlieb-Shea, caught between sets during his evening work- 40 out at the airy two-story fitness center, says he is uneasy about the college's direction. While he enjoys lifting weights beneath a balcony holding rows of high-end elliptical machines, treadmills, rowing

CHAPTER 2   FOCUS

machines, and stationary bicycles, he wonders if facilities like the new student center are necessary. "At the end of the day, you go to college because of the education you're going to get, and the experiences," he says.

And he laments that Grinnell has become more expensive. During his four years here, the cost has gone up by $5,000.

That trend is going to continue. As part of the strategic plan, Grinnell is raising its tuition by 12 percent over the next two years to be more in line with its three Midwestern peers: Carleton, Macalester, and Oberlin Colleges.

Meanwhile, the rate of spending from the endowment is going down. Three years ago it was 4.5 percent. Next year it will be 4 percent. The moves are part of a conscious pricing plan to keep revenue sources in balance and to send a message to students and parents that Grinnell believes its education is worth the price. For those who can afford it, "we don't want to be a bargain," says Mr. Osgood, the president.

"Moving Boldly"

While it raises its price, Grinnell will continue to take steps to become more racially and economically diverse, say Mr. Osgood and James Sumner, dean of admission and financial aid. About 67 percent of the students are white. Three years ago the college began accepting students from inner-city high schools through a program run by the Posse Foundation, which helps colleges admit students in groups of about 10 and provides mentors for them. By next year, when Posse students will be enrolled in all four undergraduate classes, the program will cost Grinnell about $1.8-million, mostly for financial aid.

45   This month the college will also sponsor two "Grinnell on Our Dime" weekends, when it pays the travel costs for campus visits for admitted prospective freshmen who are the first generation of their families to go to college, are students of color, or are financially needy enough to qualify for Pell Grants. The college expects about 60 students.

Grinnell is also proud that its students with Pell Grants, many of whom came from high schools that don't offer top-tier preparation, graduate at essentially the same rate as the student body as a whole.

Mr. Osgood says the policies have helped to make Grinnell more diverse than its peers, even while he acknowledges that most of those colleges aren't all that diverse themselves. "If we had a lot of truly poor people, I guess I'd be a little more proud of it," the president concedes.

Nordahl L. Brue, chairman of the Board of Trustees, says Grinnell's spending and pricing policies have been well directed. To be a great liberal-arts college, "you have to have great facilities," he says. And those financially needy students who must borrow to pay for Grinnell still graduate carrying less debt, on average, than do graduates of Iowa's public colleges. (The average for Grinnell students is about $16,000; the University of Iowa about $17,000; and Iowa State University about $27,000.)

But Mr. Brue, who is probably better known as the founder of Bruegger's bagel chain, says he realizes Grinnell could soon have even more endowment earnings at its disposal because construction on the campus is winding down.

The college's leaders also recognize that other wealthy institutions, 50 including Amherst College and Princeton and Stanford Universities, have recently begun making high-profile commitments to serve larger numbers of needy students by replacing loans with grants.

Mr. Osgood says that in the not-so-distant future, Grinnell might use the endowment to make "dramatic increases" in the amounts it provides needy students, probably in the form of forgivable loans from the college. The program, which is far from a done deal, would most likely be adopted in conjunction with Grinnell's first-ever major fund-raising campaign.

Mr. Brue says Grinnell trustees are open to new ideas. As much as they seek to protect the endowment for the benefit of the college, he insists that they also recognize the college's broader obligations. "Our job is to look at the horizon, not at the foreground," he says. "But I don't think that will keep us from moving boldly."

Responding to Reading

1. How did Grinnell become such a wealthy school?
2. What advantages does its wealth give Grinnell? How do both students and professors benefit from this wealth? Are there any disadvantages?
3. What does Grinnell intend to do to become more racially and economically diverse? Do you think the school will succeed?

Responding in Writing

Do you think wealthy colleges like Grinnell have an obligation to attract a more economically diverse student body? If so, what steps should they take to enroll such students?

IN IOWA, 2 COLLEGES SEPARATED BY 150 MILES AND $1.37 BILLION: CLARKE COLLEGE

Sara Hebel

An editor at the Chronicle of Higher Education, *Sara Hebel reports on various social and political issues related to higher education, including issues surrounding the accessibility and affordability of a college education. In the following essay, Hebel discusses the challenges faced by one small private Iowa college.*

Dubuque, Iowa—Sitting atop a bluff along the Mississippi River here, Clarke College is a place where students call their professors by first names, where people rarely fail to greet each other in the hallways, and where, once a semester, faculty and staff members flip more than 20 pounds of pancakes to serve students a late-night snack.

The intimate interaction among faculty members, administrators, and students is central to the character of Clarke, a Roman Catholic liberal-arts institution with a full-time enrollment of 1,068. The college's mission statement says that it strives to be a "caring, learning community," following in the tradition of the Sisters of Charity of the Blessed Virgin Mary, who founded Clarke in 1843. And the personal attention is an advantage that many similar, small liberal-arts colleges across the nation tout as a quality that sets them apart from larger public and private institutions in the American higher-education landscape.

But paying close attention to each individual, and to recruiting and retaining them, isn't just a philosophical nicety for colleges like Clarke. It's a financial necessity.

At Clarke, more than three-fifths of the $18-million operating budget comes from tuition and fees, and another fifth comes from auxiliary services such as residence halls and food service. With an endowment of only $17-million, Clarke doesn't have much of a financial cushion to help pay the bills when it misses enrollment targets, even by handfuls of students.

5   Clarke "defines almost every private college that has less than 1,500 enrollment and less than a $50-million endowment," says Thomas C. Longin, an independent consultant for colleges on strategic planning. He estimates that about 800 institutions, roughly half of the nation's four-year private colleges, face budget scenarios similar to Clarke's.

He argues that those institutions are not necessarily on the brink of demise but that their futures are bleak. It is extraordinarily difficult, he and other college-planning experts say, for the Clarke Colleges of the nation to transcend a pattern of budget planning that focuses on scraping by from year to year.

"They've got a real cash-flow problem," says Mr. Longin. "And it is really hard to take strategic initiatives when they are not able to carve out any money."

Fighting to Grow

Over the years, Clarke has added academic programs and facilities to foster growth and to better serve its market, which is heavily focused on students who live in the rural region that surrounds this river city. To its undergraduate programs, Clarke has added master's programs in business administration, education, nursing, and physical therapy. This year it began its first doctoral program, also in physical therapy.

And the college is searching for ways to attract money from new sources, such as foundations, and to build up its endowment. Clarke officials acknowledge that they were slow to focus on developing an endowment because leaders relied for many years on the value of contributed services of the nuns who work at the college. As the number of nuns working at the college has shrunk, so has the value of their salaries to the bottom line. Now, that value accounts for only 2 percent of revenues.

Clarke has survived a fire, which destroyed about a third of its 10 buildings in 1984. The college used the opportunity to build a modern, signature campus structure that serves as a central gathering place. Its 56-foot-tall glass atrium—where the library, chapel, art gallery, and administrative offices meet—encloses a courtyard that has wireless Internet access and a softly bubbling fountain.

Over the past 12 years, the college has added other facilities to improve student life, including a dormitory with apartment-style living, which provides students with individual rooms in suites that include kitchens, as well as a new student-activities center and a sports complex with a bigger gym and indoor track, racquetball courts, and dirt-floored batting cages.

But for all the upgrades Clarke has made, tight budgets have still limited the college's ability to offer some of the amenities that help attract students to a campus. Most incoming students move into two dormitories that were built in the 1960s and that lack such modern features as air-conditioning. The college's fitness center is small and situated over half of an old basketball court, and some of its athletics teams, like baseball, must use public parks and other off-campus facilities as their home fields.

Annual Anxiety

Sister Catherine Dunn, Clarke's president, says college officials pride themselves on doing the best they can with facilities, keeping them clean and making improvements when possible. And she says she places her priority on protecting academic programs and has been largely able to avoid laying off faculty members (though she has left some positions open) during her 22-year tenure, no matter how tight the budgets.

This spring, once again, Sister Catherine is planning for another year of very tight budgets. Financial-aid offers have just gone out to prospective students, and she is anxiously waiting to learn how many deposits for next fall's class will come in.

15   "This is always a nervous time for me," says Sister Catherine, who is retiring at the end of June.

So far this year, the numbers are running ahead of last year, when Clarke officials missed their enrollment goal by about 20 students. The result: about $500,000 less revenue.

While wealthy colleges could make up such a shortfall by using reserves or taking more from their endowment, Clarke had little choice but to tighten the purse strings across the campus. Spending on travel, subscriptions, and other expenses has been pared, and departments' budgets for supplies and other items are receiving more scrutiny. Faculty-salary increases that would have otherwise been given out this spring are being delayed until final enrollments are known in the fall.

The financial pressures on Clarke, and institutions like it, to enroll as many students as possible often lead them to make admissions offers more attractive by providing generous amounts of institutional aid. That is one area in which Clarke's interim vice president for business affairs is encouraging the college to cut back.

"People get carried away with tuition discounting," says Edward Whalen, who took over the position in January. "If you're not careful, you end up giving away more money than it costs you to educate per student."

20   On average, Clarke provides its students institutional aid worth about 38 percent of the price of tuition. Incoming freshmen receive even more, an average of about 47 percent, and some students receive as much as 60 percent. On average, private four-year colleges of a size similar to Clarke discount their undergraduate students' tuition by 35.5 percent and their freshman students' tuition by 39.9 percent, according to a study by the National Association of College and University Business Officers.

Mr. Whalen has urged Clarke to be more selective about tuition discounting and to focus on using the practice to lure truly exceptional students.

Admissions officials are also scaling back their generosity in other ways. For example, Clarke had routinely tried to find institutional funds for Iowa applicants who had missed a deadline for need-based grants, worth up to $4,000, that the state provides its residents at in-state private institutions. Clarke is stopping that practice and doing more to encourage students to meet the state deadline.

Seeking a Niche

Clarke officials are also seeking new ways to draw students and raise money. Administrators and faculty members are hoping to do both through an undergraduate program in bioinformatics Clarke is establishing this year.

Clarke's admissions officers are reporting that at many college fairs, Clarke is the only institution that offers the major, a discipline that combines the study of computer science, biology, and chemistry to analyze large databases, such as those on genomes. And Melba Rodriguez, Clarke's vice president for institutional advancement, says the program is already attracting attention from at least one foundation that has not looked at Clarke before.

Last month she learned that the W.M. Keck Foundation, a Los 25 Angeles–based fund that provides grants for science, engineering, and medical research, wanted to visit Clarke, a sign that the group was seriously considering the college's application for a $766,600 grant. Clarke applied for the money to finance a project through its bioinformatics program that would allow students to help develop advanced Web-based tools to analyze data on HIV.

"To get a foundation's attention is very exciting," Ms. Rodriguez says. Winning a grant from a nationally known foundation, she adds, could help a college like Clarke gain a higher profile, and possibly make it easier to attract money from other private and governmental sources in the future.

But even as Clarke is adding programs, it is also seeking funds to make basic improvements in some of its core disciplines that limited budgets have not allowed. The college is undertaking a campaign to raise $5-million to update its 40-year-old science laboratories, which need better ventilation and plumbing so more students can work in them.

Clarke's chemistry professors and students say they also need better equipment to conduct more-accurate experiments. Their wish list includes a cold-room facility, to help them better control temperatures than they can with Styrofoam buckets of ice that they now use, and a mass spectrometer, an instrument that identifies separate components of materials.

Ellen Reisch, a senior from Dubuque who is majoring in chemistry, is trying to examine the active ingredients in herbal medications, a task that she says is very difficult without a spectrometer to help her isolate those ingredients from other matter. "There are so many other things in there that I don't know what they are," she says. And without better instruments, "I don't even know where to begin to identify them."

CHAPTER 2   FOCUS

Ideas for Reform

30   When a college is stretched as thin as Clarke is, it must continually evaluate what programs are essential to support. If an undergraduate major does not have at least 20 students, it is put on a watch list and given three years to grow. If it does not, the major is reshaped or phased out, as is now happening with Clarke's sociology program.

Clarke's incoming president, Sister Joanne Burrows, says she plans to seek reforms that will refine the college's academic mission, to focus it more sharply on market needs. Sister Joanne, who is chief academic officer at Saint Mary-of-the-Woods College, says she may consider adding more graduate programs and incorporating distance education into some offerings. She says she does not yet know Clarke well enough to offer a specific plan for broader changes at the institution.

"We may need to stop being all things to all people," she says, "and find real opportunities to serve the market."

Mr. Longin, the independent consultant, agrees that small private colleges need to reinvent themselves in bold ways if they want to have even a chance at escaping their cycles of minimal budgets.

He suggests that such colleges consider thematic changes to serve emerging markets and needs in academe. For example, an institution might try to improve how American students understand global issues by adapting the college's entire curriculum to include more international perspectives and analysis.

35   Without changes that can bring more distinction to the hundreds of small liberal-arts colleges that survive on the margins, Mr. Longin says, he worries that academic quality will suffer at many of these institutions and that they will not be serving society as effectively or efficiently as they could.

"I do see a value to these places," he says, "but I don't see a lot of will among many of them to really get significantly better."

But other higher-education experts emphasize that society will need to continue to rely on many of these liberal-arts colleges. Larry Goldstein, president of Campus Strategies, a company that consults on business affairs for colleges, praises liberal-arts institutions for their role in serving a wide spectrum of students, including those who do not learn well in large environments and those who may be shut out of increasingly competitive public institutions. The individualized attention at these colleges, he says, can be particularly helpful to low-income students and those whose parents never attended college.

"I won't call these colleges a safety net, but in fact, for many people they do end up being a safety net," Mr. Goldstein says.

Offering Support

At Clarke, almost one-third of the undergraduates are eligible for federal Pell Grants, and more than one-third are among the first in their families to attend college.

CHAPTER 2   FOCUS

Nick Marlette, a sophomore from Waverly, Iowa, who is majoring 40 in social work at Clarke, plans to be the first in his family to earn a four-year degree. His mother is a secretary, and his father works as a mechanic.

Clarke appealed to him, he says, because it offered the chance to play soccer and because the college environment provided him the academic and personal support he sought. "The people are great," he says, raving about many one-on-one interactions with his professors and the constant stream of friendly hellos he gets when he crosses campus. "Everyone is real close."

The intimacy of Clarke has helped many of its students find their place. Now Clarke must develop a niche for itself, if it, too, is to thrive.

Responding to Reading

1. What percentage of Clarke's budget comes from tuition? from other sources? How is Clarke's situation different from that of Grinnell?
2. How do Clarke's financial difficulties affect students and instructors?
3. What steps is Clarke taking to ensure that it will survive? How successful do you think these measures will be?

Responding in Writing

What resources does Clarke offer that Grinnell doesn't? How important are these resources to you? All things considered, which college would you prefer to attend?

CHAPTER 2 FOCUS

PHOTO ESSAY, FROM *THE CHRONICLE* OF *HIGHER EDUCATION*

The eight photographs that follow show the campuses of the two Iowa colleges discussed in the essays on pages 111–123: Grinnell College and Clarke College. Grinnell is an extremely wealthy college, with a $1.4 billion endowment; Clarke has a small endowment and therefore depends on tuition for most of its income.

Look closely at the photographs on the pages that follow, and read the captions that accompany them. Then, answer the questions below.

Responding to the Images

1. What do you consider to be a college's most important physical resources? Are any of these not pictured here?
2. On a tour of a college campus, what resources and facilities (other than the ones pictured here) would a tour guide show you? Are any of these items more important to you than the ones depicted on the pages that follow? Why?
3. On a sheet of paper, list the differences you see between the two labs, dining halls, fitness centers, and art galleries pictured here. Which differences are most striking in each case?
4. How important do you think a state-of-the-art fitness center is? Do you see it as important just for recruitment of new students, or do you think it adds in any way to the quality of a student's education?
5. Which of the items pictured here do you see as *most* important? Why? Which do you see as *least* important?
6. Do you think it necessarily follows that the school with the more impressive physical plant offers a superior education? Why or why not?

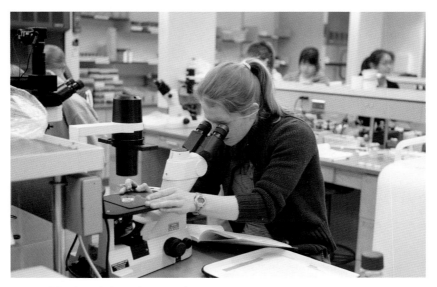

Grinnell biology lab with up-to-date equipment.

Clarke science lab, slated for updating when funds are available.

Traditional dining hall at Grinnell (to be replaced by dining venues in new student center).

Clarke dining hall.

Grinnell's state-of-the-art fitness center.

Clarke fitness center (in old gym).

Grinnell art museum, part of art center complex that includes three theaters.

Clarke art gallery.

WIDENING THE FOCUS

For Critical Thinking and Writing

Assume that you have been accepted at both Grinnell and Clarke. Your finances are limited, and neither school has offered you financial aid. You know that Grinnell has more resources and a bigger endowment, but Grinnell's tuition, fees, and room and board will cost you almost $10,000 a year more than Clarke's. Which school would you choose? Is it possible to get an equally strong education at either school? In making your decision, think carefully about whether it is worth the money to attend Grinnell instead of Clarke. What other factors—besides the physical appearance of the campus and the resources offered in the labs, dining halls, fitness centers, and art galleries depicted in this Focus section—would you consider in making your decision?

For Further Reading

The following readings can suggest additional perspectives for thinking and writing about the subject of inequality in education.

- Maya Angelou, "Graduation" (p. 69)

- Jim Sagel, "Baca Grande" (p. 131)

- Jonathan Kozol, "The Human Cost of an Illiterate Society" (p. 164)

- Robert Frost, "The Road Not Taken" (p. 599)

For Focused Research

To what extent does a college's Web site convey the college's quality of education? Visit Grinnell College's site at http://www.grinnell.edu/ and Clarke College's site at http://www.clarke.edu/ and read about some of the resources and facilities the two sites advertise. Then, write an essay in which you evaluate the schools' self-images as projected by the two sites. Which site makes its college more appealing? Be sure to support your position with examples and evidence from both sites.

—————————— WRITING ——————————

Issues in Education

1. Both Lynda Barry (p. 61) and Maya Angelou (p. 69) describe personal experiences related to their education. Write an essay in which you describe a positive or negative experience you have had with your own education. Be specific, and make sure you include plenty of vivid descriptive details.

2. Many of the essays in this chapter try to define exactly what constitutes a "good" education. Write an essay in which you define a good education. Explain your view with specific references to essays in this chapter by John Holt (p. 64) and Daniel H. Pink (p. 87), as well as with examples from your own experience.

3. According to Christina Hoff Sommers (p. 104), instructors with conservative political views are being systematically excluded from many American colleges and universities. Write a letter to Sommers in which you agree or disagree with her contentions. Make sure that you address Sommers's specific points and that you use examples from both the essay and your own experience to support your position.

4. In his short story "The First Day" (p. 107), Edward P. Jones tells the story of a child attending school for the first time. Write an essay in which you discuss your own first impressions of school. In what way have your impressions changed? How have they stayed the same? Do you agree with John Holt (p. 64) that traditional methods of education do more to hurt students than to help them?

5. In his essay "Should the Obama Generation Drop Out?" (p. 99), Charles Murray questions the idea that every student should be encouraged to go to college. In "Is College Worth the Money?" (p. 102), Daniel S. Cheever, Jr., asks if students are getting their money's worth in college. Write an essay in which you address one (or both) of these issues. Be specific, and use examples from your own experience as well as the essays to support your points.

6. In her essay "The Good Immigrant Student" (p. 79), Bich Minh Nguyen discusses the difficulties immigrant students face in American schools. At one point in her essay she says that she has never "gotten over the terror of being called on in class, or the dread in knowing that I'm expected to contribute to class discussion" (27). Assume that you are a tutor in your school's writing center and that you have been asked to write an essay to be included in an orientation booklet. In this essay, your goal is to address the concerns that Nguyen expresses. Be supportive, and give specific advice for overcoming these problems.

7. Define your educational philosophy. Then, choose one grade level and design a curriculum that reflects your philosophy. Finally, write a proposal in which you present your ideal curriculum, referring to the ideas of at least one of the writers in this chapter.

8. All the writers in this chapter believe in the power of education to change a person. For many people, this process begins with a teacher who has a profound influence on them. Write an essay in which you discuss such a teacher. What, in your opinion, made this teacher so effective? In what ways did contact with this teacher change you?

9. Write an essay in which you develop a definition of good teaching, considering the relationship of the teacher to the class, the standards teachers should use to evaluate students, and what students should gain from their educational experience. Make sure you refer to the ideas of John Holt (p. 64) and Daniel H. Pink (p. 87) in your essay.

3

THE POLITICS OF LANGUAGE

During the years he spent in prison, political activist Malcolm X became increasingly frustrated by his inability to express himself in writing, so he began the tedious and often frustrating task of copying words from the dictionary—page by page. The eventual result was that, for the first time, he could pick up a book and read it with understanding: "Anyone who has read a great deal," he says, "can imagine the new world that opened." In addition, by becoming a serious reader, Malcolm X was able to develop the ideas about race, politics, and economics that he presented so forcefully after he was released from prison.

In our society, language is constantly being manipulated for political ends. This fact should come as no surprise if we consider the potential

Man protesting against bill to crack down on illegal immigrants

power of words. Often, the power of a word comes not from its dictionary definition, or *denotation,* but from its *connotations,* the associations that surround it. These connotations can be subtle, giving language the power to confuse and even to harm. For example, whether a doctor who performs an abortion is "terminating a pregnancy" or "murdering a preborn child" is not just a matter of semantics. It is also a political issue, one that has provoked both debate and violence. This potential for misunderstanding, disagreement, deception, and possibly danger makes careful word choice very important.

The Focus section of this chapter (p. 184) addresses the question, "Is Texting Destroying the English Language?" As the essays in this section illustrate, the answer to this question is neither straightforward nor simple. In "I h8 txt msgs: How Texting Is Wrecking Our Language," John Humphrys makes the point that texting is ruining our language and must be stopped. In "2b or not 2b?" David Crystal disagrees with Humphrys; far from ruining the language, he says, texting is enriching it by encouraging people to experiment and to be linguistically creative. And finally, in "Thumbspeak: Is Texting Here to Stay?" Louis Menand claims that, contrary to Crystal's assertion, texting will have little effect on our language because it is an interim technology that will soon be obsolete.

People demonstrating against illegal immigrants

—————————— PREPARING TO READ AND WRITE ——————————

As you read and prepare to write about the essays in this chapter, you may consider the following questions:

- Does the selection deal primarily with written or spoken language?

- Does the writer place more emphasis on the denotations or the connotations of words?

- Does the writer make any distinctions between language applied to males and language applied to females? Do you consider such distinctions valid?

- Does the writer discuss language in the context of a particular culture? Does he or she see language as a unifying or a divisive factor?

- In what ways would the writer like to change or reshape language? What do you see as the possible advantages or disadvantages of such change?

- Does the writer believe that people are shaped by language or that language is shaped by people?

- Does the writer see language as having a particular social or political function? In what sense?

- Does the writer see language as empowering?

- Does the writer make assumptions about people's status on the basis of their use of language? Do these assumptions seem justified?

- Does the writer make a convincing case for the importance of language?

- Is the writer's focus primarily on language's ability to help or its power to harm?

- In what ways are your ideas about the power of words similar to or different from the writer's?

- How is the essay like and unlike other essays in this chapter?

BACA GRANDE[1]

Jim Sagel

1947–1998

Poet, playwright, fiction and nonfiction writer, and bilingual educator, Jim Sagel often focused on the language and culture of northern New Mexico in his numerous works. Of Prussian descent, Sagel knew no Spanish when he came to New Mexico. With the help of his wife and her family, he learned Spanish and began to write in both English and Spanish. Because his ethnicity made him difficult to categorize, Sagel became a controversial figure in the Chicano literary community even though he received praise for his writing. The recipient of several awards, Sagel won the 1997 El Premio Literario Cuidad de San Sebastián, Spain, for the best Spanish play. The following poem, "Baca Grande," explores the ways in which language shapes experience.

Una vaca se topó con un ratón y le dice:
"Tú—¿tan chiquito y con bigote?" Y le responde el ratón:
"Y tú tan grandota—¿y sin brassiere?"[2]

It was nearly a miracle
James Baca remembered anyone at all
from the old hometown gang
having been two years at Yale
  no less   5
and halfway through law school
at the University of California at Irvine
They hardly recognized him either
in his three-piece grey business suit
and surfer-swirl haircut   10
with just the menacing hint
of a tightly trimmed Zapata moustache
  for cultural balance
and relevance

He had come to deliver the keynote address   15
to the graduating class of 80

---

[1]*Baca Grande: Baca* is both a phonetic spelling of the Spanish word *vaca* (cow) and the last name of one of the poem's characters. *Grande* means "large." [Eds.]

[2]*Una . . . brassiere?:* A cow ran into a rat and said: "You—so small and with a moustache?" The rat responded: "And you—so big and without a bra?" [Eds.]

at his old alma mater
and show off his well-trained lips
which laboriously parted
20   each Kennedyish "R"
and drilled the first person pronoun
through the microphone
like an oil bit
with the slick, elegantly honed phrases
25 that slid so smoothly
off his meticulously bleached
        tongue
He talked Big Bucks
with astronautish fervor and if he
30   the former bootstrapless James A. Baca
could dazzle the ass
off the universe
then even you
        yes you

35 Joey Martinez toying with your yellow
        tassle
and staring dumbly into space
could emulate Mr. Baca someday
        possibly
40 well
there was of course
such a thing
as being an outrageously successful
gas station attendant too
45   let us never forget
it doesn't really matter what you do
so long as you excel
never believing a word
of it
50 for he had already risen
        as high as they go

Wasn't nobody else
from this deprived environment
who'd ever jumped
55   straight out of college
into the Governor's office
and maybe one day
he'd sit in that big chair
        himself

and when he did   60
he'd forget this damned town
and all the petty little people
in it
once and for all

That much he promised himself   65

Responding to Reading

1. Who is the poem's speaker? What can you infer about the speaker from his
   language? How is his language different from James Baca's?
2. Why is Baca visiting the speaker's school? What ideas is he supposed to convey to his audience? What ideas do you think he actually conveys?
3. List the words and phrases that identify this poem's diction as informal. Do
   you think this informality is a strength or a weakness?

Responding in Writing

What comment does the poem make about James Baca? What comment does it
make about the social divisions between the speaker and Baca? Do you think the
speaker's observations are valid?

ARIA[1]

Richard Rodriguez

1944–

*The son of Mexican-American immigrants, Richard Rodriguez earned a Ph.D.
in Renaissance literature from the University of California at Berkeley (1975).
His most recent books include* Days of Obligation: An Argument with My
Mexican Father *(1992) and* Brown: The Last Discovery of America
*(2002). Currently a journalist and author, Rodriguez is a frequent contribu-
tor to National Public Radio and an editor for the Pacific News Service (PNS)
as well as a contributing editor for* Harpers' *Magazine,* U.S. News and
World Report, *and the* Los Angeles Times. *In 1997, he won a George Foster
Peabody Award for his* NewsHour *essays on American life. The following
selection is from Rodriguez's first book,* The Hunger of Memory: The Education of Richard Rodriguez *(1982). In this memoir, he writes about the
experience of growing up in a Spanish-speaking home and adapting to the
English-speaking community around him.*

Supporters of bilingual education today imply that students like me
miss a great deal by not being taught in their family's language. What

---

[1]Solo vocal piece with instrumental accompaniment or melody. [Eds.]

they seem not to recognize is that, as a socially disadvantaged child. I considered Spanish to be a private language. What I needed to learn in school was that I had the right—and the obligation—to speak the public language of *los gringos*.[2] The odd truth is that my first-grade classmates could have become bilingual, in the conventional sense of that word, more easily than I. Had they been taught (as upper-middle-class children are often taught early) a second language like Spanish or French, they could have regarded it simply as that: another public language. In my case such bilingualism could not have been so quickly achieved. What I did not believe was that I could speak a single public language.

Without question, it would have pleased me to hear my teachers address me in Spanish when I entered the classroom. I would have felt much less afraid. I would have trusted them and responded with ease. But I would have delayed—for how long postponed?—having to learn the language of public society, I would have evaded—and for how long could I have afforded to delay?—learning the great lesson of school, that I had a public identity.

Fortunately, my teachers were unsentimental about their responsibility. What they understood was that I needed to speak a public language. So their voices would search me out, asking me questions. Each time I'd hear them, I'd look up in surprise to see a nun's face frowning at me. I'd mumble, not really meaning to answer. The nun would persist, "Richard, stand up. Don't look at the floor. Speak up. Speak to the entire class, not just to me!" But I couldn't believe that the English language was mine to use. (In part, I did not want to believe it.) I continued to mumble. I resisted the teacher's demands. (Did I somehow suspect that once I learned public language my pleasing family life would be changed?) Silent, waiting for the bell to sound, I remained dazed, diffident, afraid.

Because I wrongly imagined that English was intrinsically a public language and Spanish an intrinsically private one, I easily noted the difference between classroom language and the language of home. At school, words were directed to a general audience of listeners. ("Boys and girls.") Words were meaningfully ordered. And the point was not self-expression alone but to make oneself understood by many others. The teacher quizzed: "Boys and girls, why do we use that word in this sentence? Could we think of a better word to use there? Would the sentence change its meaning if the words were differently arranged? And wasn't there a better way of saying much the same thing?" (I couldn't say. I wouldn't try to say.)

5   Three months. Five. Half a year passed. Unsmiling, ever watchful, my teachers noted my silence. They began to connect my behavior with the difficult progress my older sister and brother were making. Until one Saturday morning three nuns arrived at the house to talk to our parents.

---

[2]Foreigners, especially Americans. [Eds.]

Stiffly, they sat on the blue living room sofa. From the doorway of another room, spying the visitors, I noted the incongruity—the clash of two worlds, the faces and voices of school intruding upon the familiar setting of home. I overheard one voice gently wondering, "Do your children speak only Spanish at home, Mrs. Rodriguez?" While another voice added, "That Richard especially seems so timid and shy."

That Rich-heard!

With great tact the visitors continued, "Is it possible for you and your husband to encourage your children to practice their English when they are home?" Of course, my parents complied. What would they not do for their children's well-being? And how could they have questioned the Church's authority which those women represented? In an instant, they agreed to give up the language (the sounds) that had revealed and accentuated our family's closeness. The moment after the visitors left, the change was observed, "*Ahora*, speak to us *en inglés*,"[3] my father and mother united to tell us.

At first, it seemed a kind of game. After dinner each night, the family gathered to practice "our" English. (It was still then *inglés*, a language foreign to us, so we felt drawn as strangers to it.) Laughing, we would try to define words we could not pronounce. We played with strange English sounds, often overanglicizing our pronunciations. And we filled the smiling gaps of our sentences with familiar Spanish sounds. But that was cheating, somebody shouted. Everyone laughed. In school, meanwhile, like my brother and sister, I was required to attend a daily tutoring session. I needed a full year of special attention. I also needed my teachers to keep my attention from straying in class by calling out, *Rich-heard*—their English voices slowly prying loose my ties to my other name, its three notes, *Ri-car-do*. Most of all I needed to hear my mother and father speak to me in a moment of seriousness in broken—suddenly heartbreaking—English. The scene was inevitable: One Saturday morning I entered the kitchen where my parents were talking in Spanish. I did not realize that they were talking in Spanish however until, at the moment they saw me, I heard their voices change to speak English. Those *gringo* sounds they uttered startled me. Pushed me away. In that moment of trivial misunderstanding and profound insight, I felt my throat twisted by unsounded grief. I turned away quickly and left the room. But I had no place to escape to with Spanish. (The spell was broken.) My brother and sisters were speaking English in another part of the house.

Again and again in the days following, increasingly angry, I was obliged to hear my mother and father: "Speak to us *en inglés*" (*Speak.*) Only then did I determine to learn classroom English. Weeks after, it happened: One day in school I raised my hand to volunteer an answer.

---

[3]"Now, speak to us in English." [Eds.]

I spoke out in a loud voice. And I did not think it remarkable when the entire class understood. That day, I moved very far from the disadvantaged child I had been only days earlier. The belief, that calming assurance that I belonged in public, had at last taken hold.

10   Shortly after, I stopped hearing the high and loud sounds of *los gringos*. A more and more confident speaker of English, I didn't trouble to listen to *how* strangers sounded, speaking to me. And there simply were too many English-speaking people in my day for me to hear American accents anymore. Conversations quickened. Listening to persons who sounded eccentrically pitched voices, I usually noted their sounds for an initial few seconds before I concentrated on *what* they were saying. Conversations became content-full. Transparent. Hearing someone's *tone* of voice—angry or questioning or sarcastic or happy or sad—I didn't distinguish it from the words it expressed. Sound and word were thus tightly wedded. At the end of a day, I was often bemused, always relieved, to realize how "silent," though crowded with words, my day in public had been. (This public silence measured and quickened the change in my life.)

At last, seven years old, I came to believe what had been technically true since my birth; I was an American citizen.

But the special feeling of closeness at home was diminished by then. Gone was the desperate, urgent, intense feeling of being at home, rare was the experience of feeling myself individualized by family intimates. We remained a loving family, but one greatly changed. No longer so close; no longer bound tight by the pleasing and troubling knowledge of our public separateness. Neither my older brother nor sister rushed home after school anymore. Nor did I. When I arrived home there would often be neighborhood kids in the house. Or the house would be empty of sounds.

Following the dramatic Americanization of their children, even my parents grew more publicly confident. Especially my mother. She learned the names of all the people on our block. And she decided we needed to have a telephone installed in the house. My father continued to use the word *gringo*. But it was no longer charged with the old bitterness of distrust. (Stripped of any emotional content, the word simply became a name for those Americans not of Hispanic descent.) Hearing him, sometimes, I wasn't sure if he was pronouncing the Spanish word *gringo* or saying gringo in English.

Matching the silence I started hearing in public was a new quiet at home. The family's quiet was partly due to the fact that, as we children learned more and more English, we shared fewer and fewer words with our parents. Sentences needed to be spoken slowly when a child addressed his mother or father. (Often the parent wouldn't understand.) The child would need to repeat himself. (Still the parent misunderstood.) The young voice, frustrated, would end up saying, "Never mind"—the subject was closed. Dinners would be noisy with the clinking of knives and forks against dishes. My mother would smile softly between her remarks; my father at the other end of the table would chew and chew at his food, while he stared over the heads of his children.

My *mother!* My *father!* After English became my primary language, 15 I no longer knew what words to use in addressing my parents. The old Spanish words (those tender accents of sound) I had used earlier—*mamá* and *papá*—I couldn't use anymore. They would have been too painful reminders of how much had changed in my life. On the other hand, the words I heard neighborhood kids call their parents seemed equally unsatisfactory. *Mother* and *Father; Ma, Papa, Pa, Dad, Pop* (how I hated the all-American sound of that last word especially)—all these terms I felt were unsuitable, not really terms of address for my parents. As a result, I never used them at home. Whenever I'd speak to my parents, I would try to get their attention with eye contact alone. In public conversations, I'd refer to "my parents" or "my mother and father."

My mother and father, for their part, responded differently, as their children spoke to them less. She grew restless, seemed troubled and anxious at the scarcity of words exchanged in the house. It was she who would question me about my day when I came home from school. She smiled at small talk. She pried at the edges of my sentences to get me to say something more. (What?) She'd join conversations she overheard, but her intrusions often stopped her children's talking. By contrast, my father seemed reconciled to the new quiet. Though his English improved somewhat, he retired into silence. At dinner he spoke very little. One night his children and even his wife helplessly giggled at his garbled English pronunciation of the Catholic Grace before Meals. Thereafter he made his wife recite the prayer at the start of each meal, even on formal occasions, when there were guests in the house. Hers became the public voice of the family. On official business, it was she, not my father, one would usually hear on the phone or in stores, talking to strangers. His children grew so accustomed to his silence that, years later, they would speak routinely of his shyness. (My mother would often try to explain: Both his parents died when he was eight. He was raised by an uncle who treated him like little more than a menial servant. He was never encouraged to speak. He grew up alone. A man of few words.) But my father was not shy, I realized, when I'd watch him speaking Spanish with relatives. Using Spanish, he was quickly effusive. Especially when talking with other men, his voice would spark, flicker, flare alive with sounds. In Spanish, he expressed ideas and feelings he rarely revealed in English. With firm Spanish sounds, he conveyed confidence and authority English would never allow him.

The silence at home, however, was finally more than a literal silence. Fewer words passed between parent and child, but more profound was the silence that resulted from my inattention to sounds. At about the time I no longer bothered to listen with care to the sounds of English in public, I grew careless about listening to the sounds family members made when they spoke. Most of the time I heard someone speaking at home and didn't distinguish his sounds from the words people uttered in public. I didn't even pay much attention to my parents' accented and ungrammatical speech. At least not at home. Only when I was with them in public would I grow alert to their accents. Though, even then, their sounds caused me less and less concern. For I was increasingly confident of my own public identity.

I would have been happier about my public success had I not sometimes recalled what it had been like earlier, when my family had conveyed its intimacy through a set of conveniently private sounds. Sometimes in public, hearing a stranger, I'd hark back to my past. A Mexican farmworker approached me downtown to ask directions to somewhere, "¿*Hijito* . . . ?"[4] he said. And his voice summoned deep longing. Another time, standing beside my mother in the visiting room of a Carmelite convent, before the dense screen which rendered the nuns shadowy figures, I heard several Spanish-speaking nuns—their busy, singsong overlapping voices—assure us that yes, yes, we were remembered, all our family was remembered in their prayers. (Their voices echoed faraway family sounds.) Another day, a dark-faced old woman—her hand light on my shoulder—steadied herself against me as she boarded a bus. She murmured something I couldn't quite comprehend. Her Spanish voice came near, like the face of a never-before-seen relative in the instant before I was kissed. Her voice, like so many of the Spanish voices I'd hear in public, recalled the golden age of my youth. Hearing Spanish then, I continued to be a careful, if sad, listener to sounds. Hearing a Spanish-speaking family walking behind me, I turned to look. I smiled for an instant, before my glance found the Hispanic-looking faces of strangers in the crowd going by.

Today I hear bilingual educators say that children lose a degree of "individuality" by becoming assimilated into public society. (Bilingual schooling was popularized in the seventies, that decade when middle-class ethnics began to resist the process of assimilation—the American melting pot.) But the bilingualists simplistically scorn the value and necessity of assimilation. They do not seem to realize that there are *two* ways a person is individualized. So they do not realize that while one suffers a diminished sense of *private* individuality by becoming assimilated into public society, such assimilation makes possible the achievement of *public* individuality.

20   The bilingualists insist that a student should be reminded of his difference from others in mass society, his heritage. But they equate

---

[4]"Little boy . . . ?" [Eds.]

mere separateness with individuality. The fact is that only in private—with intimates—is separateness from the crowd a prerequisite for individuality. (An intimate draws me apart, tells me that I am unique, unlike all others.) In public, by contrast, full individuality is achieved, paradoxically, by those who are able to consider themselves members of the crowd. Thus it happened for me: Only when I was able to think of myself as an American, no longer an alien in *gringo* society, could I seek the rights and opportunities necessary for full public individuality. The social and political advantages I enjoy as a man result from the day that I came to believe that my name, indeed, is *Rich-heard Road-ree-guess.* It is true that my public society today is often impersonal. (My public society is usually mass society.) Yet despite the anonymity of the crowd and despite the fact that the individuality I achieve in public is often tenuous—because it depends on my being one in a crowd—I celebrate the day I acquired my new name. Those middle-class ethnics who scorn assimilation seem to me filled with decadent self-pity, obsessed by the burden of public life. Dangerously, they romanticize public separateness and they trivialize the dilemma of the socially disadvantaged.

My awkward childhood does not prove the necessity of bilingual education. My story discloses instead an essential myth of childhood—inevitable pain. If I rehearse here the changes in my private life after my Americanization, it is finally to emphasize the public gain. The loss implies the gain: The house I returned to each afternoon was quiet. Intimate sounds no longer rushed to the door to greet me. There were other noises inside. The telephone rang. Neighborhood kids ran past the door of the bedroom where I was reading my school-books—covered with shopping-bag paper. Once I learned public language, it would never again be easy for me to hear intimate family voices. More and more of my day was spent hearing words. But that may only be a way of saying that the day I raised my hand in class and spoke loudly to an entire roomful of faces, my childhood started to end.

Responding to Reading

1. What distinction does Rodriguez make between public and private languages? What point does this distinction help him make?
2. What does Rodriguez say he gains by speaking English? What does he say he loses? Do you agree with his assessment?
3. What is Rodriguez's main argument against those who support bilingual education? What evidence does he use to support his argument? How convincing is he?

Responding in Writing

Do you agree with Rodriguez's opposition to bilingual education, or do you think that children who do not speak English should be taught in their native language?

Mother Tongue

Amy Tan

1952–

Amy Tan was born to parents who had emigrated from China only a few years earlier. (Her given name is actually An-mei, which means "blessing from America.") A workaholic, Tan began writing stories as a means of personal therapy, and these stories eventually became the highly successful The Joy Luck Club *(1987), a novel about Chinese-born mothers and their American-born daughters that was later made into a widely praised film. Tan's other books include four more novels—*The Kitchen God's Wife *(1991),* The Hundred Secret Senses *(1995),* The Bonesetter's Daughter *(2001), and* Saving Fish from Drowning *(2005)—and a work of nonfiction,* The Opposite of Fate: A Book of Musings *(2003) as well as two illustrated children's books. In the following essay, which was originally delivered as a speech, Tan considers her relationship with her own mother, concentrating on the different "Englishes" they use to communicate with each other and with the world.*

I am not a scholar of English or literature. I cannot give you much more than personal opinions on the English language and its variations in this country or others.

I am a writer. And by that definition, I am someone who has always loved language. I am fascinated by language in daily life. I spend a great deal of my time thinking about the power of language—the way it can evoke an emotion, a visual image, a complex idea, or a simple truth. Language is the tool of my trade. And I use them all—all the Englishes I grew up with.

Recently, I was made keenly aware of the different Englishes I do use. I was giving a talk to a large group of people, the same talk I had already given to half a dozen other groups. The nature of the talk was about my writing, my life, and my book, *The Joy Luck Club*. The talk was going along well enough, until I remembered one major difference that made the whole talk sound wrong. My mother was in the room. And it was perhaps the first time she had heard me give a lengthy speech, using the kind of English I have never used with her. I was saying things like, "The intersection of memory upon imagination" and "There is an aspect of my fiction that relates to thus-and-thus"—a speech filled with carefully wrought grammatical phrases, burdened, it suddenly seemed to me, with nominalized forms, past perfect tenses, conditional phrases, all the forms of standard English that I had learned in school and through books, the forms of English I did not use at home with my mother.

Just last week, I was walking down the street with my mother, and I again found myself conscious of the English I was using, and the English I do use with her. We were talking about the price of new and used

furniture and I heard myself saying this: "Not waste money that way."
My husband was with us as well, and he didn't notice any switch in
my English. And then I realized why. It's because over the twenty years
we've been together I've often used that same kind of English with him,
and sometimes he even uses it with me. It has become our language of
intimacy, a different sort of English that relates to family talk, the language I grew up with.

So you'll have some idea of what this family talk I heard sounds   5
like, I'll quote what my mother said during a recent conversation which
I videotaped and then transcribed. During this conversation, my mother
was talking about a political gangster in Shanghai who had the same last
name as her family's, Du, and how the gangster in his early years
wanted to be adopted by her family, which was rich by comparison.
Later, the gangster became more powerful, far richer than my mother's
family, and one day showed up at my mother's wedding to pay his
respects. Here's what she said in part:

"Du Yusong having business like fruit stand. Like off the street kind.
He is Du like Du Zong—but not Tsung-ming Island people. The local
people call putong, the river east side, he belong to that side local people. The man want to ask Du Zong father take him in like become own
family. Du Zong father wasn't look down on him, but didn't take seriously, until that man big like become a mafia. Now important person,
very hard to inviting him. Chinese way, came only to show respect,
don't stay for dinner. Respect for making big celebration, he shows up.
Mean gives lots of respect. Chinese custom. Chinese social life that way.
If too important won't have to stay too long. He come to my wedding.
I didn't see, I heard it. I gone to boy's side, they have YMCA dinner.
Chinese age I was nineteen."

You should know that my mother's expressive command of English
belies how much she actually understands. She reads the Forbes report,
listens to *Wall Street Week,* converses daily with her stockbroker, reads all
of Shirley MacLaine's[1] books with ease—all kinds of things I can't begin
to understand. Yet some of my friends tell me they understand 50 percent
of what my mother says. Some say they understand 80 to 90 percent.
Some say they understand none of it, as if she were speaking pure
Chinese. But to me, my mother's English is perfectly clear, perfectly natural. It's my mother tongue. Her language, as I hear it, is vivid, direct, full
of observation and imagery. That was the language that helped shape
the way I saw things, expressed things, made sense of the world.

Lately, I've been giving more thought to the kind of English my
mother speaks. Like others, I have described it to people as "broken" or
"fractured" English. But I wince when I say that. It has always bothered

---

[1]Actress known for her autobiographical books, in which she traces her many past lives. [Eds.]

me that I can think of no way to describe it other than "broken," as if it were damaged and needed to be fixed, as if it lacked a certain wholeness and soundness. I've heard other terms used, "limited English," for example. But they seem just as bad, as if everything is limited, including people's perceptions of the limited English speaker.

I know this for a fact, because when I was growing up, my mother's "limited" English limited *my* perception of her. I was ashamed of her English. I believed that her English reflected the quality of what she had to say. That is, because she expressed them imperfectly her thoughts were imperfect. And I had plenty of empirical evidence to support me: the fact that people in department stores, at banks, and at restaurants did not take her seriously, did not give her good service, pretended not to understand her, or even acted as if they did not hear her.

10   My mother has long realized the limitations of her English as well. When I was fifteen, she used to have me call people on the phone to pretend I was she. In this guise, I was forced to ask for information or even to complain and yell at people who had been rude to her. One time it was a call to her stockbroker in New York. She had cashed out her small portfolio and it just so happened we were going to go to New York the next week, our very first trip outside California. I had to get on the phone and say in an adolescent voice that was not very convincing, "This is Mrs. Tan."

And my mother was standing in the back whispering loudly, "Why he don't send me check, already two weeks late. So mad he lie to me, losing me money."

And then I said in perfect English, "Yes, I'm getting rather concerned. You had agreed to send the check two weeks ago, but it hasn't arrived."

Then she began to talk more loudly. "What he want, I come to New York tell him front of his boss, you cheating me?" And I was trying to calm her down, make her be quiet, while telling the stockbroker, "I can't tolerate any more excuses. If I don't receive the check immediately, I am going to have to speak to your manager when I'm in New York next week." And sure enough, the following week there we were in front of this astonished stockbroker, and I was sitting there red-faced and quiet, and my mother, the real Mrs. Tan, was shouting at his boss in her impeccable broken English.

We used a similar routine just five days ago, for a situation that was far less humorous. My mother had gone to the hospital for an appointment, to find out about a benign brain tumor a CAT scan had revealed a month ago. She said she had spoken very good English, her best English, no mistakes. Still, she said, the hospital did not apologize when they said they had lost the CAT scan and she had come for nothing. She said they did not seem to have any sympathy when she told them she was anxious to know the exact diagnosis, since her husband and son had both died of brain tumors. She said they would not give her any more information until the next time and she would have to make another appointment for that. So she said she would not leave until the doctor called her daughter. She wouldn't budge. And when the doctor finally called her daughter, me, who spoke in perfect English—lo and behold—we had assurances the CAT scan would be found, promises that a conference call on Monday would be held, and apologies for any suffering my mother had gone through for a most regrettable mistake.

I think my mother's English almost had an effect on limiting my 15 possibilities in life as well. Sociologists and linguists probably will tell you that a person's developing language skills are more influenced by peers. But I do think that the language spoken in the family, especially in immigrant families which are more insular, plays a large role in shaping the language of the child. And I believe that it affected my results on achievement tests, IQ tests, and the SAT. While my English skills were never judged as poor, compared to math, English could not be considered my strong suit. In grade school I did moderately well, getting perhaps B's, sometimes B-pluses, in English and scoring perhaps in the sixtieth or seventieth percentile on achievement tests. But those scores were not good enough to override the opinion that my true abilities lay in math and science, because in those areas I achieved A's and scored in the ninetieth percentile or higher.

This was understandable. Math is precise; there is only one correct answer. Whereas, for me at least, the answers on English tests were always a judgment call, a matter of opinion and personal experience. Those tests were constructed around items like fill-in-the-blank sentence completion, such as, "Even though Tom was _____, Mary thought he was _____." And the correct answer always seemed to be the most bland combinations of thoughts, for example, "Even though Tom was shy, Mary thought he was charming," with the grammatical structure "even though" limiting the correct answer to some sort of semantic opposites, so you wouldn't get answers like, "Even though Tom was foolish, Mary thought he was ridiculous." Well, according to my mother, there were very few limitations as to what Tom could have been and what Mary might have thought of him. So I never did well on tests like that.

The same was true with word analogies, pairs of words in which you were supposed to find some sort of logical, semantic relationship— for example, "*Sunset* is to *nightfall* as _____ is to _____." And here you would be presented with a list of four possible pairs, one of which showed the same kind of relationship: *red* is to *stoplight, bus* is to *arrival, chills* is to *fever, yawn* is to *boring.* Well, I could never think that way. I knew what the tests were asking, but I could not block out of my mind the images already created by the first pair, "*sunset* is to *nightfall*"—and I would see a burst of colors against a darkening sky, the moon rising, the lowering of a curtain of stars. And all the other pairs of words—red, bus, stoplight, boring—just threw up a mass of confusing images, making it impossible for me to sort out something as logical as saying: "A sunset precedes nightfall" is the same as "a chill precedes a fever." The only way I would have gotten that answer right would have been to imagine an associative situation, for example, my being disobedient and staying out past sunset, catching a chill at night, which turns into feverish pneumonia as punishment, which indeed did happen to me.

I have been thinking about all this lately, about my mother's English, about achievement tests. Because lately I've been asked, as a writer, why there are not more Asian Americans represented in American literature. Why are there few Asian Americans enrolled in creative writing programs? Why do so many Chinese students go into engineering? Well, these are broad sociological questions I can't begin to answer. But I have noticed in surveys—in fact, just last week—that Asian students, as a whole, always do significantly better on math achievement tests than in English. And this makes me think that there are other Asian-American students whose English spoken in the home might also be described as "broken" or "limited." And perhaps they also have teachers who are steering them away from writing and into math and science, which is what happened to me.

Fortunately, I happen to be rebellious in nature and enjoy the challenge of disproving assumptions made about me. I became an English major my first year in college, after being enrolled as pre-med. I started writing nonfiction as a freelancer the week after I was told by my former boss that writing was my worst skill and I should hone my talents toward account management.

20   But it wasn't until 1985 that I finally began to write fiction. And at first I wrote using what I thought to be wittily crafted sentences, sentences that would finally prove I had mastery over the English language. Here's an example from the first draft of a story that later made its way into *The Joy Luck Club*, but without this line: "That was my mental quandary in its nascent state." A terrible line, which I can barely pronounce.

Fortunately, for reasons I won't get into today, I later decided I should envision a reader for the stories I would write. And the reader I decided upon was my mother, because these were stories about mothers. So with this reader in mind—and in fact she did read my early drafts—I began to write stories using all the Englishes I grew up with: the English I spoke to my mother, which for lack of a better term might be described as "simple"; the English she used with me, which for lack of a better term might be described as "broken"; my translation of her Chinese, which could certainly be described as "watered down"; and what I imagined to be her translation of her Chinese if she could speak in perfect English, her internal language, and for that I sought to preserve the essence, but neither an English nor a Chinese structure. I wanted to capture what language ability tests can never reveal: her intent, her passion, her imagery, the rhythms of her speech and the nature of her thoughts.

Apart from what any critic had to say about my writing, I knew I had succeeded where it counted when my mother finished reading my book and gave me her verdict: "So easy to read."

Responding to Reading

1. Why does Tan begin her essay with the disclaimer, "I am not a scholar of English or literature. I cannot give you much more than personal opinions" (1)? Do these statements add to her credibility or detract from it? Explain.
2. Tan implies that some languages are more expressive than others. Do you agree? Are there some ideas you can express in one language that are difficult or impossible to express in another? Give examples if you can.
3. Do you agree with Tan's statement in paragraph 15 that the kind of English spoken at home can have an effect on a student's performance on IQ tests and the SAT?

Responding in Writing

Do you think the English you speak at home has had a positive or a negative effect on your performance in school?

LEARNING TO READ AND WRITE

Frederick Douglass

1817?–1895

Frederick Douglass was born a slave in rural Talbot County, Maryland, and later served a family in Baltimore. After escaping to the North in 1838, he settled in Bedford, Massachusetts, where he became active in the abolitionist movement. He recounts these experiences in his most famous work, Narrative of the Life of Frederick Douglass *(1845). After spending almost two years in England and Europe on a lecture tour, Douglass returned to the United States and purchased his freedom. In 1847, he launched the antislavery newspaper* The North Star *and became a vocal supporter of both Abraham Lincoln and the Civil War. Throughout his life, Douglass believed that the United States Constitution, if interpreted correctly, would enable African Americans to become full participants in the economic, social, and intellectual life of America. In the following excerpt from his* Narrative, *Douglass writes of outwitting his owners to become literate, thereby finding "the pathway from slavery to freedom."*

I lived in Master Hugh's family about seven years. During this time, I succeeded in learning to read and write. In accomplishing this, I was compelled to resort to various stratagems. I had no regular teacher. My mistress, who had kindly commenced to instruct me, had, in compliance with the advice and direction of her husband, not only ceased to instruct, but had set her face against my being instructed by any one else. It is due, however, to my mistress to say of her, that she did not adopt this course of treatment immediately. She at first lacked the depravity indispensable to shutting me up in mental darkness. It was at least necessary for her to have some training in the exercise of irresponsible power, to make her equal to the task of treating me as though I were a brute.

My mistress was, as I have said, a kind and tender-hearted woman; and in the simplicity of her soul she commenced, when I first went to live with her, to treat me as she supposed one human being ought to treat another. In entering upon the duties of a slaveholder, she did not seem to perceive that I sustained to her the relation of a mere chattel,[1] and that for her to treat me as a human being was not only wrong, but dangerously so. Slavery proved as injurious to her as it did to me. When I went there, she was a pious, warm, and tender-hearted woman. There was no sorrow or suffering for which she had not a tear. She had bread for the hungry, clothes for the naked, and comfort for every mourner that came within her reach. Slavery soon proved its ability to divest her of these heavenly qualities. Under its influence, the tender heart became stone, and the lamblike disposition gave way to one of tigerlike fierceness. The first step in her downward course was in her ceasing to instruct me. She now commenced to practice her husband's precepts. She finally became even more violent in her opposition than her husband himself. She was not satisfied with simply doing as well as he had commanded; she seemed anxious to do better. Nothing seemed to make her more angry than to see me with a newspaper. She seemed to think that here lay the danger. I have had her rush at me with a face made all up of fury, and snatch from me a newspaper, in a manner that fully revealed her apprehension. She was an apt woman; and a little experience soon demonstrated, to her satisfaction, that education and slavery were incompatible with each other.

From this time I was most narrowly watched. If I was in a separate room any considerable length of time, I was sure to be suspected of having a book, and was at once called to give an account of myself. All this, however, was too late. The first step had been taken. Mistress, in teaching me the alphabet, had given me the *inch,* and no precaution could prevent me from taking the *ell.*

The plan which I adopted, and the one by which I was most successful, was that of making friends of all the little white boys whom I met in the street. As many of these as I could, I converted into teachers. With their kindly aid, obtained at different times and in different

---

[1] Property. [Eds.]

places, I finally succeeded in learning to read. When I was sent on errands, I always took my book with me, and by going one part of my errand quickly, I found time to get a lesson before my return. I used also to carry bread with me, enough of which was always in the house, and to which I was always welcome; for I was much better off in this regard than many of the poor white children in our neighborhood. This bread I used to bestow upon the hungry little urchins, who, in return, would give me that more valuable bread of knowledge. I am strongly tempted to give the names of two or three of those little boys, as a testimonial of the gratitude and affection I bear them; but prudence forbids;—not that it would injure me, but it might embarrass them; for it is almost an unpardonable offense to teach slaves to read in this Christian country. It is enough to say of the dear little fellows, that they lived on Philpot Street, very near Durgin and Bailey's ship-yard. I used to talk this matter of slavery over with them. I would sometimes say to them, I wished I could be as free as they would be when they got to be men. "You will be free as soon as you are twenty-one, *but I am a slave for life!* Have not I as good a right to be free as you have?" These words used to trouble them; they would express for me the liveliest sympathy, and console me with the hope that something would occur by which I might be free.

I was now about twelve years old, and the thought of being *a slave*   5
for life began to bear heavily upon my heart. Just about this time, I got hold of a book entitled "The Columbian Orator."[2] Every opportunity I got, I used to read this book. Among much of other interesting matter, I found in it a dialogue between a master and his slave. The slave was represented as having run away from his master three times. The dialogue represented the conversation which took place between them, when the slave was retaken the third time. In this dialogue, the whole argument in behalf of slavery was brought forward by the master, all of which was disposed of by the slave. The slave was made to say some very smart as well as impressive things in reply to his master—things which had the desired though unexpected effect; for the conversation resulted in the voluntary emancipation of the slave on the part of the master.

In the same book, I met with one of Sheridan's might speeches on and in behalf of Catholic emancipation.[3] These were choice documents to me. I read them over and over again with unabated interest. They gave tongue to interesting thoughts of my own soul, which had frequently flashed through my mind, and died away for want of utterance. The moral which I gained from the dialogue was the power of

---

[2]A popular textbook that taught the principles of effective public speaking. [Eds.]
[3]Richard Brinsley Sheridan (1751–1816), British playwright and statesman who made speeches supporting the right of English Catholics to vote. Full emancipation was not granted to Catholics until 1829. [Eds.]

truth over the conscience of even a slaveholder. What I got from Sheridan was a bold denunciation of slavery, and a powerful vindication of human rights. The reading of these documents enabled me to utter my thoughts, and to meet the arguments brought forward to sustain slavery; but while they relieved me of one difficulty, they brought on another even more painful than the one of which I was relieved. The more I read, the more I was led to abhor and detest my enslavers. I could regard them in no other light than a band of successful robbers, who had left their homes, and gone to Africa, and stolen us from our homes, and in a strange land reduced us to slavery. I loathed them as being the meanest as well as the most wicked of men. As I read and contemplated the subject, behold! that very discontentment which Master Hugh had predicted would follow my learning to read had already come, to torment and sting my soul to unutterable anguish. As I writhed under it, I would at times feel that learning to read had been a curse rather than a blessing. It had given me a view of my wretched condition, without the remedy. It opened my eyes to the horrible pit, but to no ladder upon which to get out. In moments of agony, I envied my fellow-slaves for their stupidity. I have often wished myself a beast. I preferred the condition of the meanest reptile to my own. Any thing, no matter what, to get rid of thinking! It was the everlasting thinking of my condition that tormented me. There was no getting rid of it. It was pressed upon me by every object within sight or hearing, animate or inanimate. The silver trump of freedom had roused my soul to eternal wakefulness. Freedom now appeared, to disappear no more forever. It was heard in every sound, and seen in every thing. It was ever present to torment me with a sense of my wretched condition. I saw nothing without seeing it, I heard nothing without hearing it, and felt nothing without feeling it. It looked from every star, it smiled in every calm, breathed in every wind, and moved in every storm.

I often found myself regretting my own existence, and wishing myself dead; and but for the hope of being free, I have no doubt but that I should have killed myself, or done something for which I should have been killed. While in this state of mind, I was eager to hear any one speak of slavery. I was a ready listener. Every little while, I could hear something about the abolitionists. It was some time before I found what the word meant. It was always used in such connections as to make it an interesting word to me. If a slave ran away and succeeded in getting clear, or if a slave killed his master, set fire to a barn, or did any thing very wrong in the mind of a slaveholder, it was spoken of as the fruit of *abolition*. Hearing the word in this connection very often, I set about learning what it meant. The dictionary afforded me little or no help. I found it was "the act of abolishing"; but then I did not know what was to be abolished. Here I was perplexed. I did not dare to ask any one about its meaning, for I was satisfied that it was something they wanted me to know very little about. After a patient waiting, I got one of our city papers, containing an account of the number of petitions from the north, praying for the abolition of slavery in the District of Columbia, and of the slave trade between the States. From this time I understood the words *abolition* and *abolitionist,* and always drew near when that word was spoken, expecting to hear something of importance to myself and fellow-slaves. The light broke in upon me by degrees. I went one day down on the wharf of Mr. Waters; and seeing two Irishmen unloading a scow of stone, I went, unasked, and helped them. When we had finished, one of them came to me and asked me if I were a slave. I told him I was. He asked, "Are ye a slave for life?" I told him that I was. The good Irishman seemed to be deeply affected by the statement. He said to the other that it was a pity so fine a little fellow as myself should be a slave for life. He said it was a shame to hold me. They both advised me to run away to the north; that I should find friends there, and that I should be free. I pretended not to be interested in what they said, and treated them as if I did not understand them; for I feared they might be treacherous. White men have been known to encourage slaves to escape, and then, to get the reward, catch them and return them to their masters. I was afraid that these seemingly good men might use me so; but I nevertheless remembered their advice, and from that time I resolved to run away. I looked forward to a time at which it would be safe for me to escape. I was too young to think of doing so immediately; besides, I wished to learn how to write, as I might have occasion to write my own pass. I consoled myself with the hope that I should one day find a good chance. Meanwhile, I would learn to write.

The idea as to how I might learn to write was suggested to me by being in Durgin and Bailey's ship-yard, and frequently seeing the ship carpenters, after hewing, and getting a piece of timber ready for use, write on the timber the name of that part of the ship for which it was intended. When a piece of timber was intended for the larboard side, it would be marked thus—"L." When a piece was for the starboard side, it would be marked thus—"S." A piece for the larboard side forward, would be marked thus—"L. F." When a piece was for starboard side forward, it would be marked thus—"S. F." For larboard aft, it would be marked thus—"L. A." For starboard aft, it would be marked thus—"S. A." I soon learned the names of these letters, and for what they were intended when placed upon a piece of timber in the shipyard. I immediately commenced copying them, and in a short time was able to make the four letters named. After that, when I met with any boy who I knew could write, I would tell him I could write as well as he. The next word would be, "I don't believe you. Let me see you try it." I would then make the letters which I had been so fortunate as to learn, and ask him to beat that. In this way I got a good many lessons in writing, which it is quite possible I should never have gotten in any other way. During this time, my copy-book was the board fence, brick wall, and pavement; my pen and ink was a lump of chalk. With these, I learned mainly how to write. I then commenced and continued copying the Italics in Webster's Spelling Book, until I could make them all without looking on the book. By this time, my little Master Thomas had gone to school, and learned how to write, and had written over a number of copy-books. These had been brought home, and shown to some of our near neighbors, and then laid aside. My mistress used to go to class meeting at the Wilk Street meetinghouse every Monday afternoon, and leave me to take care of the house. When left thus, I used to spend the time in writing in the spaces left in Master Thomas's copy-book, copying what he had written. I continued to do this until I could write a hand very similar to that of Master Thomas. Thus, after a long, tedious effort for years, I finally succeeded in learning how to write.

Responding to Reading

1. What does Douglass mean in paragraph 2 when he says that slavery proved as harmful to his mistress as it did to him? In spite of his owners' actions, what strategies did Douglass use to learn to read?
2. Douglass escaped from slavery in 1838 and became a leading figure in the antislavery movement. How did reading and writing help him develop his ideas about slavery? In what way did language empower him?
3. What comment do you think Douglass's essay makes on the condition of African Americans in the mid-nineteenth century?

Responding in Writing

Does this essay, written over 150 years ago, have relevance today? Explain.

SEXISM IN ENGLISH: EMBODIMENT AND LANGUAGE

Alleen Pace Nilsen

1936–

Alleen Pace Nilsen is an educator and essayist. Her most recent book, coauthored with her husband, is Names and Naming in Young Adult Literature *(2007). When Nilsen lived in Afghanistan in the 1960s, she observed the subordinate position of women in that society. When she returned to the United States, she studied American English for its cultural biases toward men and women. Nilsen says of that project, "As I worked my way through the dictionary, I concentrated on the way particular usages, metaphors, slang terms, and definitions reveal society's attitude toward males and females." The following essay is an updated version of Nilsen's findings from her dictionary study.*

During the late 1960s, I lived with my husband and three young children in Kabul, Afghanistan. This was before the Russian invasion, the Afghan civil war, and the eventual taking over of the country by the Taleban Islamic movement and its resolve to return the country to a strict Islamic dynasty, in which females are not allowed to attend school or work outside their homes.

But even when we were there and the country was considered moderate rather than extremist, I was shocked to observe how different were the roles assigned to males and females. The Afghan version of the *chaderi*[1] prescribed by Moslem women was particularly confining. Women in religious families were required to wear it whenever they were outside their family home, with the result being that most of them didn't venture outside.

The household help we hired were made up of men, because women could not be employed by foreigners. Afghan folk stories and jokes were blatantly sexist, as in this proverb: "If you see an old man, sit down and take a lesson; if you see an old woman, throw a stone."

But it wasn't only the native culture that made me question women's roles, it was also the American community within Afghanistan.

Most of the American women were like myself—wives and mothers whose husbands were either career diplomats, employees of USAID, or college professors who had been recruited to work on various contract teams. We were suddenly bereft of our traditional roles: The local economy provided few jobs for women and certainly none for foreigners; we were isolated from former friends and the social goals we had grown up with. Some of us became alcoholics, others got very good at bridge, while still others searched desperately for ways to contribute either to our families or to the Afghans.

When we returned in the fall of 1969 to the University of Michigan in Ann Arbor, I was surprised to find that many other women were also questioning the expectations they had grown up with. Since I had been an English major when I was in college, I decided that for my part in the feminist movement I would study the English language and see what it could tell me about sexism. I started reading a desk dictionary and making note cards on every entry that seemed to tell something different about male and female. I soon had a dog-eared dictionary, along with a collection of note cards filling two shoe boxes.

The first thing I learned was that I couldn't study the language without getting involved in social issues. Language and society are as intertwined as a chicken and an egg. The language a culture uses is telltale evidence of the values and beliefs of that culture. And because there is a lag in how fast a language changes—new words can easily be introduced, but it takes a long time for old words and usages to disappear—a careful look at English will reveal the attitudes that our

---

[1]A *chaderi* is a heavily draped cloth covering the entire head and body. [Eds.]

ancestors held and that we as a culture are therefore predisposed to hold. My note cards revealed three main points. While friends have offered the opinion that I didn't need to read a dictionary to learn such obvious facts, the linguistic evidence lends credibility to the sociological observations.

Women Are Sexy; Men Are Successful

First, in American culture a woman is valued for the attractiveness and sexiness of her body, while a man is valued for his physical strength and accomplishments. A woman is sexy. A man is successful.

A persuasive piece of evidence supporting this view are the eponyms—words that have come from someone's name—found in English. I had a two-and-a-half-inch stack of cards taken from men's names but less than a half-inch stack from women's names, and most of those came from Greek mythology. In the words that came into American English since we separated from Britain, there are many eponyms based on the names of famous American men: Bartlett pear, boysenberry, Franklin stove, Ferris wheel, Gatling gun, mason jar, sideburns, sousaphone, Schick test, and Winchester rifle. The only common eponyms that I found taken from American women's names are Alice blue (after Alice Roosevelt Longworth), bloomers (after Amelia Jenks Bloomer), and Mae West jacket (after the buxom actress). Two out of the three feminine eponyms relate closely to a woman's physical anatomy, while the masculine eponyms (except for "sideburns" after General Burnsides) have nothing to do with the namesake's body, but, instead, honor the man for an accomplishment of some kind.

10   In Greek mythology women played a bigger role than they did in the biblical stories of the Judeo-Christian cultures, and so the names of goddesses are accepted parts of the language in such place names as Pomona, from the goddess of fruit, and Athens, from Athena, and in such common words as *cereal* from Ceres, *psychology* from Psyche, and *arachnoid* from Arachne. However, there is the same tendency to think of women in relation to sexuality as shown through the eponyms *aphrodisiac* from Aphrodite, the Greek name for the goddess of love and beauty, and *venereal disease* from Venus, the Roman name for Aphrodite.

Another interesting word from Greek mythology is *Amazon*. According to Greek folk etymology, the *a-* means "without," as in *atypical* or *amoral*, while *-mazon* comes from *mazos*, meaning "breast," as still seen in *mastectomy*. In the Greek legend, Amazon women cut off their right breasts so they could better shoot their bows. Apparently, the storytellers had a feeling that for women to play the active, "masculine" role the Amazons adopted for themselves, they had to trade in part of their femininity.

This preoccupation with women's breasts is not limited to the Greeks; it's what inspired the definition and the name for "mammals" (from Indo-European *mammae* for "breasts"). As a volunteer for the University of Wisconsin's *Dictionary of American Regional English (DARE)*, I read a western trapper's diary from the 1830s. I was to make notes of any unusual usages or language patterns. My most interesting finding was that the trapper referred to a range of mountains as "The Teats," a metaphor based on the similarity between the shapes of the mountains and women's breasts. Because today we use the French wording "The Grand Tetons," the metaphor isn't as obvious, but I wrote to mapmakers and found the following listings: Nipple Top and Little Nipple Top near Mount Marcy in the Adirondacks; Nipple Mountain in Archuleta County, Colorado; Nipple Peak in Coke County, Texas; Nipple Butte in Pennington, South Dakota; Squaw Peak in Placer County, California (and many other locations); Maiden's Peak and Squaw Tit (they're the same mountain) in the Cascade Range in Oregon; Mary's Nipple near Salt Lake City, Utah; and Jane Russell Peaks near Stark, New Hampshire.

Except for the movie star Jane Russell, the women being referred to are anonymous—it's only a sexual part of their body that is mentioned. When topographical features are named after men, it's probably not going to be to draw attention to a sexual part of their bodies but instead to honor individuals for an accomplishment.

Going back to what I learned from my dictionary cards, I was surprised to realize how many pairs of words we have in which the feminine word has acquired sexual connotations while the masculine word retains a serious businesslike aura. For example, a callboy is the person who calls actors when it is time for them to go on stage, but a callgirl is a prostitute. Compare sir and madam. *Sir* is a term of respect, while *madam* has acquired the specialized meaning of a brothel manager. Something similar has happened to master and mistress. Would you rather have a painting "by an old master" or "by an old mistress"?

It's because the word *woman* had sexual connotations, as in "She's   15 his woman," that people began avoiding its use, hence such terminology as ladies' room, lady of the house, and girl's school or school for young ladies. Those of us who in the 1970s began asking that speakers use the term *woman* rather than *girl* or *lady* were rejecting the idea that *woman* is primarily a sexual term.

I found two-hundred pairs of words with masculine and feminine forms; for example, *heir/heiress, hero/heroine, steward/stewardess, usher/usherette*. In nearly all such pairs, the masculine word is considered the base, with some kind of a feminine suffix being added. The masculine form is the one from which compounds are made; for example, from *king/queen* comes *kingdom* but not *queendom*, from *sportsman/sports-lady* comes *sportsmanship* but not *sportsladyship*. There is one—and only one—semantic area in which the masculine word is not the base or more powerful word. This is in the area dealing with sex, marriage, and motherhood. When someone refers to a virgin, a listener will probably think of a female unless the speaker specifies male or uses a masculine pronoun. The same is true for *prostitute.*

In relation to marriage, linguistic evidence shows that weddings are more important to women than to men. A woman cherishes the wedding and is considered a bride for a whole year, but a man is referred to as a groom only on the day of the wedding. The word *bride* appears in *bridal attendant, bridal gown, bridesmaid, bridal shower,* and even *bridegroom. Groom* comes from the Middle English *grom,* meaning "man," and in that sense is seldom used outside of the wedding. With most pairs of male/female words, people habitually put the masculine word first: *Mr. and Mrs., his and hers, boys and girls, men and women, kings and queens, brothers and sisters, guys and dolls, and host and hostess.* But it is the bride and groom who are talked about, not the groom and bride.

The importance of marriage to a woman is also shown by the fact that when a marriage ends in death, the woman gets the title of widow. A man gets the derived title of widower. This term is not used in other phrases or contexts, but widow is seen in widowhood, widow's peak, and widow's walk. A widow in a card game is an extra hand of cards, while in typesetting it is a leftover line of type.

Changing cultural ideas bring changes to language, and since I did my dictionary study three decades ago the word *singles* has largely replaced such gender-specific and value-laden terms as *bachelor, old maid, spinster, divorcee, widow,* and *widower.* In 1970 I wrote that when people hear a man called "a professional," they usually think of him as a doctor or a lawyer, but when people hear a woman referred to as "a professional," they are likely to think of her as a prostitute. That's not as true today because so many women have become doctors and lawyers, it's no longer incongruous to think of women in those professional roles.

20   Another change that has taken place is in wedding announcements. They used to be sent out from the bride's parents and did not even give the name of the groom's parents. Today, most couples choose to list either all or none of the parents' names. Also it is now much more likely that both the bride and groom's picture will be in the newspaper, while twenty years ago only the bride's picture was published on the "Women's" or the "Society" page. In the weddings I have recently attended, the official has pronounced the couple "husband and wife" instead of the traditional "man and wife," and the bride has been asked if she promises to "love, honor, and cherish," instead of to "love, honor, and obey."

Women Are Passive; Men Are Active

However, other wording in the wedding ceremony relates to a second point that my cards showed, which is that women are expected to play a passive or weak role while men play an active or strong role. In the traditional ceremony, the official asks, "Who gives the bride away?" and the father answers, "I do." Some fathers answer, "Her mother and I do," but that doesn't solve the problem inherent in the question. The idea that a bride is something to be handed over from one man to another bothers people because it goes back to the days when a man's servants, his children, and his wife were all considered to be his property. They were known by his name because they belonged to him, and he was responsible for their actions and their debts.

The grammar used in talking or writing about weddings as well as other sexual relationships shows the expectation of men playing the active role. Men *wed* women while women *become* brides of men. A man *possesses* a woman; he *deflowers* her; he *performs*; he *scores*; he *takes away* her virginity. Although a woman can *seduce* a man, she cannot offer him her virginity. When talking about virginity, the only way to make the woman the actor in the sentence is to say that "she lost her virginity," but people lose things by accident rather than by purposeful actions, and so she's only the grammatical, not the real-life, actor.

The reason that women brought the term Ms. into the language to replace Miss and Mrs. relates to this point. Many married women resent being identified in the "Mrs. Husband" form. The dictionary cards showed what appeared to be an attitude on the part of the editors that it was almost indecent to let a respectable woman's name march unaccompanied across the pages of a dictionary. Women were listed with male names whether or not the male contributed to the woman's reason for being in the dictionary or whether or not in his own right he was as famous as the woman. For example:

Charlotte Brontë = Mrs. Arthur B. Nicholls
Amelia Earhart = Mrs. George Palmer Putnam
Helen Hayes = Mrs. Charles MacArthur
Jenny Lind = Mme. Otto Goldschmit
Cornelia Otis Skinner = daughter of Otis
Harriet Beecher Stowe = sister of Henry Ward Beecher
Dame Edith Sitwell = sister of Osbert and Sacheverell[2]

Only a small number of rebels and crusaders got into the dictionary without the benefit of a masculine escort: temperance leaders Frances

[2]Charlotte Brontë (1816–1855), author of *Jane Eyre*; Amelia Earhart (1898–1937), first woman to fly over the Atlantic; Helen Hayes (1900–1993), actress; Jenny Lind (1820–1887), Swedish soprano; Cornelia Otis Skinner (1901–1979), actress and writer; Harriet Beecher Stowe (1811–1896), author of *Uncle Tom's Cabin*; Edith Sitwell (1877–1964), English poet and critic. [Eds.]

Elizabeth Caroline Willard and Carry Nation, women's rights leaders Carrie Chapman Catt and Elizabeth Cady Stanton, birth control educator Margaret Sanger, religious leader Mary Baker Eddy, and slaves Harriet Tubman and Phillis Wheatley.

Etiquette books used to teach that if a woman had Mrs. in front of her name, then the husband's name should follow because Mrs. is an abbreviated form of Mistress and a woman couldn't be a mistress of herself. As with many arguments about "correct" language usage, this isn't very logical because Miss is also an abbreviation of Mistress. Feminists hoped to simplify matters by introducing Ms. as an alternative to both Mrs. and Miss, but what happened is that Ms. largely replaced Miss to become a catch-all business title for women. Many married women still prefer the title Mrs., and some even resent being addressed with the term Ms. As one frustrated newspaper reporter complained, "Before I can write about a woman I have to know not only her marital status but also her political philosophy." The result of such complications may contribute to the demise of titles, which are already being ignored by many writers who find it more efficient to simply use names; for example, in a business letter: "Dear Joan Garcia," instead of "Dear Mrs. Joan Garcia," "Dear Ms. Garcia," or "Dear Mrs. Louis Garcia."

25   Titles given to royalty show how males can be disadvantaged by the assumption that they always play the more powerful role. In British royalty, when a male holds a title, his wife is automatically given the feminine equivalent. But the reverse is not true. For example, a count is a high political officer with a countess being his wife. The same pattern holds true for a duke and a duchess and a king and a queen. But when a female holds the royal title, the man she marries does not automatically acquire the matching title. For example, Queen Elizabeth's husband has the title of prince rather than king, but when Prince Charles married Diana, she became Princess Diana. If they had stayed married and he had ascended to the throne, then she would have become Queen Diana. The reasoning appears to be that since masculine words are stronger, they are reserved for true heirs and withheld from males coming into the royal family by marriage. If Prince Phillip were called "King Phillip," British subjects might forget who had inherited the right to rule.

The names that people give their children show the hopes and dreams they have for them, and when we look at the differences between male and female names in a culture, we can see the cumulative expectations of that culture. In our culture girls often have names taken from small, aesthetically pleasing items; for example, Ruby, Jewel, and Pearl. Esther and Stella mean "star," and Ada means "ornament." One of the few women's names that refers to strength is Mildred, and it means "mild strength." Boys often have names with meanings of power and strength; for example, Neil means "champion"; Martin is from Mars, the God of war; Raymond means "wise protection"; Harold means "chief of the army"; Ira means "vigilant"; Rex means "king"; and Richard means "strong king."

We see similar differences in food metaphors. Food is a passive substance just sitting there waiting to be eaten. Many people have recognized this and so no longer feel comfortable describing women as "delectable morsels." However, when I was a teenager, it was considered a compliment to refer to a girl (we didn't call anyone a "woman" until she was middle-aged) as a cute tomato, a peach, a dish, a cookie, honey, sugar, or sweetie-pie. When being affectionate, women will occasionally call a man honey or sweetie, but in general, food metaphors are used much less often with men than with women. If a man is called "a fruit," his masculinity is being questioned. But it's perfectly acceptable to use a food metaphor if the food is heavier and more substantive than that used for women. For example, pin-up pictures of women have long been known as "cheesecake," but when Burt Reynolds posed for a nude centerfold the picture was immediately dubbed "beefcake," that is, a hunk of meat. That such sexual references to men have come into the language is another reflection of how society is beginning to lessen the differences between their attitudes toward men and women.

Something similar to the fruit metaphor happens with references to plants. We insult a man by calling him a "pansy," but it wasn't considered particularly insulting to talk about a girl being a wallflower, a clinging vine, or a shrinking violet, or to give girls such names as Ivy, Rose, Lily, Iris, Daisy, Camelia, Heather, and Flora. A positive plant metaphor can be used with a man only if the plant is big and strong; for example, Andrew Jackson's nickname of Old Hickory. Also, the phrases *blooming idiots* and *budding geniuses* can be used with either sex, but notice how they are based on the most active thing a plant can do, which is to bloom or bud.

Animal metaphors also illustrate the different expectations for males and females. Men are referred to as studs, bucks, and wolves, while women are referred to with such metaphors as kitten, bunny, beaver, bird, chick, and lamb. In the 1950s, we said that boys went "tom catting," but today it's just "catting around," and both boys and girls do it. When the term foxy, meaning that someone was sexy, first became popular it was used only for females, but now someone of either sex can be described as a fox. Some animal metaphors that are used predominantly with men have negative connotations based on the size and/or strength of the animals; for example, beast, bull-headed, jackass, rat, loanshark, and vulture. Negative metaphors used with women are based on smaller animals; for example, social butterfly, mousey, catty, and vixen. The feminine terms connote action, but not the same kind of large scale action as with the masculine terms.

Women Are Connected with Negative Connotations;
Men with Positive Connotations

30 The final point that my note cards illustrated was how many positive connotations are associated with the concept of masculinity, while there are
either trivial or negative connotations connected with the corresponding
feminine concept. An example from the animal metaphors makes a good
illustration. The word *shrew* taken from the name of a small but especially
vicious animal was defined in my dictionary as "an ill-tempered scolding
woman," but the word *shrewd* taken from the same root was defined as
"marked by clever, discerning awareness" and was illustrated with the
phrase "a shrewd businessman."

Early in life, children are conditioned to the superiority of the masculine role. As child psychologists point out, little girls have much
more freedom to experiment with sex roles than do little boys. If a little girl acts like a tomboy, most parents have mixed feelings, being at
least partially proud. But if their little boy acts like a sissy (derived
from *sister*), they call a psychologist. It's perfectly acceptable for a little girl to sleep in the crib that was purchased for her brother, to wear
his hand-me-down jeans and shirts, and to ride the bicycle that he has
outgrown. But few parents would put a boy baby in a white-and-gold
crib decorated with frills and lace, and virtually no parents would have
their little boy wear his sister's hand-me-down dresses, nor would they
have their son ride a girl's pink bicycle with a flower-bedecked basket.
The proper names given to girls and boys show this same attitude.
Girls can have "boy" names—Cris, Craig, Jo, Kelly, Shawn, Teri, Toni,
and Sam—but it doesn't work the other way around. A couple of generations ago, Beverly, Frances, Hazel, Marion, and Shirley were common boys' names. As parents gave these names to more and more girls,
they fell into disuse for males, and some older men who have these
names prefer to go by their initials or by such abbreviated forms as
Haze or Shirl.

When a little girl is told to be a lady, she is being told to sit with
her knees together and to be quiet and dainty. But when a little boy is
told to be a man, he is being told to be noble, strong, and virtuous—
to have all the qualities that the speaker looks on as desirable. The
concept of manliness has such positive connotations that it used to be
a compliment to call someone a he-man, to say that he was doubly a
man. Today many people are more ambivalent about this term and
respond to it much as they do to the word *macho*. But calling someone
a manly man or a virile man is nearly always meant as a compliment.
Virile comes from the Indo-European *vir*, meaning "man," which is
also the basis of *virtuous*. Consider the positive connotations of both
virile and virtuous with the negative connotations of *hysterical*. The
Greeks took this latter word from their name for uterus (as still seen

in *hysterectomy*). They thought that women were the only ones who experienced uncontrolled emotional outbursts, and so the condition must have something to do with a part of the body that only women have. But how word meanings change is regularly shown at athletic events where thousands of *virtuous* women sit quietly beside their *hysterical* husbands.

Differences in the connotations between positive male and negative female connotations can be seen in several pairs of words that differ denotatively only in the matter of sex. Bachelor as compared to spinster or old maid has such positive connotations that women try to adopt it by using the term *bachelor-girl* or *bachelorette*. Old maid is so negative that it's the basis for metaphors: pretentious and fussy old men are called "old maids," as are the leftover kernels of unpopped popcorn and the last card in a popular children's card game.

Patron and *matron* (Middle English for "father" and "mother") have such different levels of prestige that women try to borrow the more positive masculine connotations with the word *patroness*, literally "female father." Such a peculiar term came about because of the high prestige attached to patron in such phrases as a *patron of the arts* or a *patron saint*. Matron is more apt to be used in talking about a woman in charge of a jail or a public restroom.

When men are doing jobs that women often do, we apparently try ₃₅ to pay the men extra by giving them fancy titles. For example, a male cook is more likely to be called a "chef" while a male seamstress will get the title of "tailor." The armed forces have a special problem in that they recruit under such slogans as "The Marine Corps builds men!" and "Join the Army! Become a Man." Once the recruits are enlisted, they find themselves doing much of the work that has been traditionally thought of as "women's work." The solution to getting the work done and not insulting anyone's masculinity was to change the titles as shown below:

waitress = orderly
nurse = medic or corpsman
secretary = clerk-typist
assistant = adjutant
dishwasher = KP (kitchen police) or kitchen helper

Compare *brave* and *squaw*. Early settlers in America truly admired Indian men and hence named them with a word that carried connotations of youth, vigor, and courage. But for Indian women they used an Algonquin slang term with negative sexual connotations that are almost opposite to those of brave. Wizard and witch contrast almost as much. The masculine *wizard* implies skill and wisdom combined with magic, while the feminine *witch* implies evil intentions combined with magic.

When witch is used for men, as in witch-doctor, many main-stream speakers feel some carry-over of the negative connotations.

Part of the unattractiveness of both witch and squaw is that they have been used so often to refer to old women, something with which our culture is particularly uncomfortable, just as the Afghans were. Imagine my surprise when I ran across the phrases *grandfatherly advice* and *old wives' tales* and realized that the underlying implication is the same as the Afghan proverb about old men being worth listening to while old women talk only foolishness.

Other terms that show how negatively we view old women as compared to young women are *old nag* as compared to *filly*, *old crow* or *old bat* as compared to *bird*, and being *catty* as compared to being *kittenish*. There is no matching set of metaphors for men. The chicken metaphor tells the whole story of a woman's life. In her youth she is a chick. Then she marries and begins feathering her nest. Soon she begins feeling cooped up, so she goes to hen parties where she cackles with her friends. Then she has her brood, begins to henpeck her husband, and finally turns into an old biddy.

I embarked on my study of the dictionary not with the intention of prescribing language change but simply to see what the language would tell me about sexism. Nevertheless, I have been both surprised and pleased as I've watched the changes that have occurred over the past three decades. I'm one of those linguists who believes that new language customs will cause a new generation of speakers to grow up with different expectations. This is why I'm happy about people's efforts to use inclusive languages, to say "he or she" or "they" when speaking about individuals whose names they do not know. I'm glad that leading publishers have developed guidelines to help writers use language that is fair to both sexes. I'm glad that most newspapers and magazines list women by their own names instead of only by their husbands' names. And I'm so glad that educated and thoughtful people no longer begin their business letters with "Dear Sir" or "Gentlemen," but instead use a memo form or begin with such salutations as "Dear Colleagues," "Dear Reader," or "Dear Committee Members." I'm also glad that such words as *poetess, authoress, conductress,* and *aviatrix* now sound quaint and old-fashioned and that *chairman* is giving way to *chair* or *head, mailman* to *mail carrier, clergyman* to *clergy,* and *stewardess* to *flight attendant.* I was also pleased when the National Oceanic and Atmospheric Administration bowed to feminist complaints and in the late 1970s began to alternate men's and women's names for hurricanes. However, I wasn't so pleased to discover that the change did not immediately erase sexist thoughts from everyone's mind, as shown by a headline about Hurricane David in a 1979 New York tabloid, "David Rapes Virgin Islands." More recently a similar metaphor appeared in a headline in the *Arizona*

Republic about Hurricane Charlie, "Charlie Quits Carolinas, Flirts with Virginia."

What these incidents show is that sexism is not something existing 40 independently in American English or in the particular dictionary that I happened to read. Rather, it exists in people's minds. Language is like an X-ray in providing visible evidence of invisible thoughts. The best thing about people being interested in and discussing sexist language is that as they make conscious decisions about what pronouns they will use, what jokes they will tell or laugh at, how they will write their names, or how they will begin their letters, they are forced to think about the underlying issue of sexism. This is good because as a problem that begins in people's assumptions and expectations, it's a problem that will be solved only when a great many people have given it a great deal of thought.

Responding to Reading

1. What point is Nilsen making about American culture? Does your experience support her conclusions?
2. Does Nilsen use enough examples to support her claims? What other examples can you think of? In what way do her examples—and your own—illustrate the power of language to define the way people think?
3. Many of the connotations of the words Nilsen discusses are hundreds of years old and are also found in languages other than English. Given these widespread and long-standing connotations, do you think attempts by Nilsen and others to change this linguistic situation can succeed?

Responding in Writing

List some words and phrases that you routinely use that reinforce the stereotypes Nilsen discusses. What alternatives could you employ? What would be gained and lost if you used these alternatives?

THE LOADED LANGUAGE OF SCIENCE

Joan M. Herbers

A professor of evolution, ecology, and organismal biology at the Ohio State University, Joan M. Herbers focuses her research on ant evolution and ecology, the study of how organisms interact with their environments. In the following essay, Herbers makes a plea to the scientific community to adopt a new language to discuss a particular scientific phenomenon.

I study ants.

In recent years I've focused my research on so-called "slavemaking ants"—species known for invading the colonies of other ant species, stealing their larvae and pupae, and killing those defending ants that try to protect their colony. The marauders then raise the stolen larvae and pupae as their own. Once fully grown into adult worker ants, those kidnapped "slaves" are put to work for their captors. This highly evolved behavior is fascinating to watch, and has become an important model of antagonistic co-evolution—the arms race between parasite and host that results in ever-accelerating adaptations to each other.

The problem is our scientific jargon. I have been repeatedly surprised by reactions to my use of the term "slavemaking" to define behavior and of "slave" to define the status of the captured ants in their captors' nests. On several occasions, individuals objected (usually after public talks, interviews with reporters, and scientific presentations, and usually anonymously) to the slave metaphor, and on many others I have been asked what my studies of ants tell us about the human condition (the answer to the latter is easy: nothing).

I did not invent this jargon, but I have certainly used it without thinking. Dulosis is the technical term, derived from the Greek *doulos,* or slave, and these terms have been in use to describe entomological phenomena for some 200 years (check out *The Oxford English Dictionary*). Given its long history of usage, and by no less august a figure than Charles Darwin himself, what is the problem?

I posed that question to a colleague who specializes in rhetorical studies of (human) slave narratives from the 18th and 19th centuries. She responded crisply: "We should be able to study ants without being reminded of race, for crying out loud," and then introduced me to Toni Morrison's essay collection *Playing in the Dark: Whiteness and the Literary Imagination.* Morrison suggests that an analysis of American literature is incomplete unless it confronts the essential truth that our writers have been immersed in a racialized society. Her discussion of how inattention to racial constructs has hampered literary criticism led me to consider the problem of how our use of loaded jargon might affect the scientific enterprise itself.

5   I, too, became uneasy with the slavery metaphor, and concluded that it might even be affecting my discipline's struggle to recruit scientists of color. That we have failed to attract young blacks, Hispanics, and Native Americans to science careers is indisputable, and has varying causes. Now I must confront the uncomfortable truth that our very jargon may be part of the problem: By appropriating the terminology of slavery, we scientists are in fact perpetuating racism. How can we (overwhelmingly white) scientists casually talk about slavemaking ants, with implicit messages of power, inequity, and subjugation, without recognizing that our very language is a powerful deterrent to recruiting descendants of slaves to appreciate our scientific work?

Discussing this issue with colleagues has provoked both bemusement and hostility. The most common reaction is that these words are part of our language and should not be considered offensive since we do not imply any parallel between what insects do and what humans continue to do around the globe; furthermore, the slave metaphor is a common one. I assert that a corollary to those arguments is that individuals who feel offended, even vaguely, are the ones with the problems.

But that attitude completely sidesteps Morrison's main point, when she calls for "a serious intellectual effort to see what racial ideology does to the mind, imagination, and behavior of masters." We must be open to the possibility that using racially loaded metaphors is inherently damaging to ourselves and to our work.

Fortunately, there is a precedent in behavioral ecology for just this kind of self-examination. For decades, biologists filed reports of sexual behavior in many animals that involved males forcing copulation on females. A quick review of the literature from the 1970s and early 1980s shows that biologists used the word "rape" to describe that behavior. However, a large, vocal group of feminist scientists protested the use of that metaphor, with the result that the term "rape" was rapidly dropped and replaced by "forced copulation." In other words, scientists who understood the emotional impact of words on themselves, on female colleagues, students, and the public changed their jargon.

So too do I now call for biologists to discard the use of slave metaphors to describe insect behavior. Not only are the terms damaging, but in fact they are not particularly accurate. Unlike human slaves, captive worker ants cannot breed, nor are they sold to other captors. Instead, the predatory species must repeatedly raid colonies to replenish its work force; indeed, voracious colonies can overexploit their captives and engender their own demise when there is no one left to do the work.

I propose, then, that we adopt a pirate metaphor to replace the slavery 10 jargon. Human pirates engage in behavior much like the ants I study: They attack ships to steal cargo, usually inflicting considerable mortality among the defending crew. We can therefore write about pirate ants, captive ants, raiding parties, and booty. Since we scientists love jargon, I further propose that we call this "leistic" behavior, from the Greek *leistos* for "pirate."

So pirate ants and leistic behavior it is, at least in my own publications, discussions with journalists, and presentations to the public. Piracy on the high seas or in clandestine software mills is illegal, and we can safely apply this metaphor to insects without perpetuating social injustice. In fact, biologists have discussed pirate perches, pirate spiders, and pirate crabs with impunity, and pirates the world over surely will not object to pirate ants.

Scientists like to think their work is unhampered by human conventions, an illusion fostered by their ignorance of the work of philosophers, historians, linguists, and rhetoricians who study the scientific enterprise.

I now understand that those delusions of objectivity can hamper our ability to further the progress to which we are passionately devoted. Scientists use language, and so must take responsibility for its rhetorical impact.

Responding to Reading

1. Herbers states her thesis at the end of paragraph 4. What does she try to accomplish in the first four paragraphs of her essay?
2. Why does Herbers want her fellow scientists to stop using the word *slave* to refer to insect behavior? What reasons does she give to support her objections to this term?
3. How do Herbers's colleagues react to her proposal? How does she respond to their criticisms?

Responding in Writing

Do you think that Herbers's criticisms have merit, or do you think she is overreacting? Do you agree that the "use of loaded jargon" (4) is damaging both to scientists and to their work?

THE HUMAN COST OF AN ILLITERATE SOCIETY

Jonathan Kozol

1936–

In 1964, Jonathan Kozol took a teaching job in the Boston Public Schools System. In 1967, he published his first book, Death at an Early Age: The Destruction of the Hearts and Minds of Negro Children in the Boston Public Schools. *Based on his experiences as a fourth-grade teacher in an inner-city school, a position from which he was fired for "curriculum deviation," this book won the National Book Award in 1968 and led to a number of specific reforms. Since then, Kozol has divided his time between teaching and social activism. His books include* Illiterate America *(1985),* Savage Inequalities *(1991),* The Shame of a Nation: The Restoration of Apartheid Schooling in America *(2005), and* Letters to a Young Teacher *(2008). In the following essay, a chapter from* Illiterate America, *Kozol exposes the problems facing the sixty million Americans who are unable to read and argues that their plight has important implications for the nation as a whole.*

PRECAUTIONS. READ BEFORE USING.
Poison: Contains sodium hydroxide (caustic soda-lye).
Corrosive: Causes severe eye and skin damage, may cause blindness.
Harmful or fatal if swallowed.
If swallowed, give large quantities of milk or water.
Do not induce vomiting.
Important: Keep water out of can at all times to prevent contents from violently erupting . . .

—warning on a can of Drano

Questions of literacy, in Socrates' belief, must at length be judged as matters of morality. Socrates could not have had in mind the moral compromise peculiar to a nation like our own. Some of our Founding Fathers did, however, have this question in their minds. One of the wisest of those Founding Fathers (one who may not have been most compassionate but surely was more prescient than some of his peers) recognized the special dangers that illiteracy would pose to basic equity in the political construction that he helped to shape.

"A people who mean to be their own governors," James Madison wrote, "must arm themselves with the power knowledge gives. A popular government without popular information or the means of acquiring it, is but a prologue to a farce or a tragedy, or perhaps both."

Tragedy looms larger than farce in the United States today. Illiterate citizens seldom vote. Those who do are forced to cast a vote of questionable worth. They cannot make informed decisions based on serious print information. Sometimes they can be alerted to their interests by aggressive voter education. More frequently, they vote for a face, a smile, or a style, not for a mind or character or body of beliefs.

The number of illiterate adults exceeds by 16 million the entire vote cast for the winner in the 1980 presidential contest. If even one third of all illiterates could vote, and read enough and do sufficient math to vote in their self-interest, Ronald Reagan would not likely have been chosen president. There is, of course, no way to know for sure. We do know this: Democracy is a mendacious[1] term when used by those who are prepared to countenance the forced exclusion of one third of our electorate. So long as 60 million people are denied significant participation, the government is neither of, nor for, nor by, the people. It is a government, at best, of those two thirds whose wealth, skin color, or parental privilege allows them opportunity to profit from the provocation and instruction of the written word.

The undermining of democracy in the United States is one "expense" 5 that sensitive Americans can easily deplore because it represents a contradiction that endangers citizens of all political positions. The human price is not so obvious at first.

Since I first immersed myself within this work I have often had the following dream: I find that I am in a railroad station or a large department store within a city that is utterly unknown to me and where I cannot understand the printed words. None of the signs or symbols is familiar. Everything looks strange: like mirror writing of some kind. Gradually I understand that I am in the Soviet Union. All the letters on the walls around me are Cyrillic. I look for my pocket dictionary but I find that it has been mislaid. Where have I left it? Then I recall that I forgot to bring it with me when I packed my bags in Boston. I struggle to

---

[1]Basely dishonest. [Eds.]

remember the name of my hotel. I try to ask somebody for directions. One person stops and looks at me in a peculiar way. I lose the nerve to ask. At last I reach into my wallet for an ID card. The card is missing. Have I lost it? Then I remember that my card was confiscated for some reason, many years before. Around this point, I wake up in a panic.

This panic is not so different from the misery that millions of adult illiterates experience each day within the course of their routine existence in the U.S.A.

Illiterates cannot read the menu in a restaurant.

They cannot read the cost of items on the menu in the *window* of the restaurant before they enter.

10   Illiterates cannot read the letters that their children bring home from their teachers. They cannot study school department circulars that tell them of the courses that their children must be taking if they hope to pass the SAT exams. They cannot help with homework. They cannot write a letter to the teacher. They are afraid to visit in the classroom. They do not want to humiliate their child or themselves.

Illiterates cannot read instructions on a bottle of prescription medicine. They cannot find out when a medicine is past the year of safe consumption; nor can they read of allergenic risks, warnings to diabetics, or the potential sedative effect of certain kinds of nonprescription pills. They cannot observe preventive health care admonitions. They cannot read about "the seven warning signs of cancer" or the indications of blood-sugar fluctuations or the risks of eating certain foods that aggravate the likelihood of cardiac arrest.

Illiterates live, in more than literal ways, an uninsured existence. They cannot understand the written details on a health insurance form. They cannot read the waivers that they sign preceding surgical procedures. Several women I have known in Boston have entered a slum hospital with the intention of obtaining a tubal ligation and have emerged a few days later after having been subjected to a hysterectomy.[2] Unaware of their rights, incognizant of jargon, intimidated by the unfamiliar air of fear and atmosphere of ether that so many of us find oppressive in the confines even of the most attractive and expensive medical facilities, they have signed their names to documents they could not read and which nobody, in the hectic situation that prevails so often in those overcrowded hospitals that serve the urban poor, had even bothered to explain.

Childbirth might seem to be the last inalienable right of any female citizen within a civilized society. Illiterate mothers, as we shall see, already have been cheated of the power to protect their progeny against the likelihood of demolition in deficient public schools and, as a result,

---

[2]A hysterectomy, the removal of the uterus, is a much more radical procedure than a tubal ligation, a method of sterilization that is a common form of birth control. [Eds.]

against the verbal servitude within which they themselves exist. Surgical denial of the right to bear that child in the first place represents an ultimate denial, an unspeakable metaphor, a final darkness that denies even the twilight gleamings of our own humanity. What greater violation of our biological, our biblical, our spiritual humanity could possibly exist than that which takes place nightly, perhaps hourly these days, within such over-burdened and benighted institutions as the Boston City Hospital? Illiteracy has many costs; few are so irreversible as this.

Even the roof above one's head, the gas or other fuel for heating that protects the residents of northern city slums against the threat of illness in the winter months become uncertain guarantees. Illiterates cannot read the lease that they must sign to live in an apartment which, too often, they cannot afford. They cannot manage check accounts and therefore seldom pay for anything by mail. Hours and entire days of difficult travel (and the cost of bus or other public transit) must be added to the real cost of whatever they consume. Loss of interest on the check accounts they do not have, and could not manage if they did, must be regarded as another of the excess costs paid by the citizen who is excluded from the common instruments of commerce in a numerate society.

"I couldn't understand the bills," a woman in Washington, D.C., 15 reports, "and then I couldn't write the checks to pay them. We signed things we didn't know what they were."

Illiterates cannot read the notices that they receive from welfare offices or from the IRS. They must depend on word-of-mouth instruction from the welfare worker—or from other persons whom they have good reason to mistrust. They do not know what rights they have, what deadlines and requirements they face, what options they might choose to exercise. They are half-citizens. Their rights exist in print but not in fact.

Illiterates cannot look up numbers in a telephone directory. Even if they can find the names of friends, few possess the sorting skills to make use of the yellow pages; categories are bewildering and trade names are beyond decoding capabilities for millions of nonreaders. Even the emergency numbers listed on the first page of the phone book— "Ambulance," "Police," and "Fire"—are too frequently beyond the recognition of nonreaders.

Many illiterates cannot read the admonition on a pack of cigarettes. Neither the Surgeon General's warning nor its reproduction on the package can alert them to the risks. Although most people learn by word of mouth that smoking is related to a number of grave physical disorders, they do not get the chance to read the detailed stories which can document this danger with the vividness that turns concern into determination to resist. They can see the handsome cowboy or the slim Virginia lady lighting up a filter cigarette; they cannot heed the words that tell them that this product is (not "may be") dangerous to their health. Sixty million men and women are condemned to be the unalerted, high-risk candidates for cancer.

Illiterates do not buy "no-name" products in the supermarkets. They must depend on photographs or the familiar logos that are printed on the packages of brand-name groceries. The poorest people, therefore, are denied the benefits of the least costly products.

20   Illiterates depend almost entirely upon label recognition. Many labels, however, are not easy to distinguish. Dozens of different kinds of Campbell's soup appear identical to the nonreader. The purchaser who cannot read and does not dare to ask for help, out of the fear of being stigmatized (a fear which is unfortunately realistic), frequently comes home with something which she never wanted and her family never tasted.

Illiterates cannot read instructions on a pack of frozen food. Packages sometimes provide an illustration to explain the cooking preparations; but illustrations are of little help to someone who must "boil water, drop the food—*within* its plastic wrapper—in the boiling water, wait for it to simmer, instantly remove."

Even when labels are seemingly clear, they may be easily mistaken. A woman in Detroit brought home a gallon of Crisco for her children's dinner. She thought that she had bought the chicken that was pictured on the label. She had enough Crisco now to last a year—but no more money to go back and buy the food for dinner.

Recipes provided on the packages of certain staples sometimes tempt a semiliterate person to prepare a meal her children have not tasted. The longing to vary the uniform and often starchy content of low-budget meals provided to the family that relies on food stamps commonly leads to ruinous results. Scarce funds have been wasted and the food must be thrown out. The same applies to distribution of food-surplus produce in emergency conditions. Government inducements to poor people to "explore the ways" in which to make a tasty meal from tasteless noodles, surplus cheese, and powdered milk are useless to nonreaders. Intended as benevolent advice, such recommendations mock reality and foster deeper feelings of resentment and of inability to cope. (Those, on the other hand, who cautiously refrain from "innovative" recipes in preparation of their children's meals must suffer the opprobrium of "laziness," "lack of imagination. . . .")

Illiterates cannot travel freely. When they attempt to do so, they encounter risks that few of us can dream of. They cannot read traffic signs and, while they often learn to recognize and to decipher symbols, they cannot manage street names which they haven't seen before. The same is true for bus and subway stops. While ingenuity can sometimes help a man or woman to discern directions from familiar landmarks, buildings, cemeteries, churches, and the like, most illiterates are virtually immobilized. They seldom wander past the streets and neighborhoods they know. Geographical paralysis becomes a bitter metaphor for their entire existence. They are immobilized in almost every sense we can imagine. They can't move up. They can't move out. They cannot see beyond. Illiterates may take an oral test for drivers' permits in most sections of America. It is a questionable concession. Where will they go? How will they get there? How will they get home? Could it be that some of us might like it better if they stayed where they belong?

Travel is only one of many instances of circumscribed existence. 25 Choice, in almost all its facets, is diminished in the life of an illiterate adult. Even the printed TV schedule, which provides most people with the luxury of preselection, does not belong within the arsenal of options in illiterate existence. One consequence is that the viewer watches only what appears at moments when he happens to have time to turn the switch. Another consequence, a lot more common, is that the TV set remains in operation night and day. Whatever the program offered at the hour when he walks into the room will be the nutriment that he accepts and swallows. Thus, to passivity, is added frequency—indeed, almost uninterrupted continuity. Freedom to select is no more possible here than in the choice of home or surgery or food.

"You don't choose," said one illiterate woman. "You take your wishes from somebody else." Whether in perusal of a menu, selection of highways, purchase of groceries, or determination of affordable enjoyment, illiterate Americans must trust somebody else: a friend, a relative, a stranger on the street, a grocery clerk, a TV copywriter.

"All of our mail we get, it's hard for her to read. Settin' down and writing a letter, she can't do it. Like if we get a bill . . . we take it over to my sister-in-law . . . My sister-in-law reads it."

Billing agencies harass poor people for the payment of the bills for purchases that might have taken place six months before. Utility companies offer an agreement for a staggered payment schedule on a bill past due. "You have to trust them," one man said. Precisely for this reason, you end up by trusting no one and suspecting everyone of possible deceit. A submerged sense of distrust becomes the corollary to a constant need to trust. "They are cheating me . . . I have been tricked . . . I do not know . . ."

Not knowing: This is a familiar theme. Not knowing the right word for the right thing at the right time is one form of subjugation. Not knowing the world that lies concealed behind those words is a more terrifying feeling. The longitude and latitude of one's existence are beyond all easy apprehension. Even the hard, cold stars within the firmament above one's head begin to mock the possibilities for self-location. Where am I? Where did I come from? Where will I go?

"I've lost a lot of jobs," one man explains. "Today, even if you're a 30 janitor, there's still reading and writing . . . They leave a note saying, 'Go to room so-and-so . . .' You can't do it. You can't read it. You don't know."

"The hardest thing about it is that I've been places where I didn't know where I was. You don't know where you are . . . You're lost."

"Like I said: I have two kids. What do I do if one of my kids starts choking? I go running to the phone . . . I can't look up the hospital phone number. That's if we're at home. Out on the street, I can't read the sign. I get to a pay phone. 'Okay, tell us where you are. We'll send an ambulance.' I look at the street sign. Right there, I can't tell you what it says. I'd have to spell it out, letter for letter. By that time, one of my kids would be dead . . . These are the kinds of fears you go with, every single day . . ."

"Reading directions, I suffer with. I work with chemicals . . . That's scary to begin with . . ."

"You sit down. They throw the menu in front of you. Where do you go from there? Nine times out of ten you say, 'Go ahead. Pick out something for the both of us.' I've eaten some weird things, let me tell you!"

35 Menus. Chemicals. A child choking while his mother searches for a word she does not know to find assistance that will come too late. Another mother speaks about the inability to help her kids to read: "I can't read to them. Of course that's leaving them out of something they should have. Oh, it matters. You *believe* it matters! I ordered all these books. The kids belong to a book club. Donny wanted me to read a book to him. I told Donny: 'I can't read,' He said: 'Mommy, you sit down. I'll read it to you.' I tried it one day, reading from the pictures. Donny looked at me. He said, 'Mommy, that's not right.' He's only five. He knew I couldn't read . . ."

A landlord tells a woman that her lease allows him to evict her if her baby cries and causes inconvenience to her neighbors. The consequence of challenging his words conveys a danger which appears, unlikely as it seems, even more alarming than the danger of eviction. Once she admits that she can't read, in the desire to maneuver for the time in which to call a friend, she will have defined herself in terms of an explicit impotence that she cannot endure. Capitulation in this case is preferable to self-humiliation. Resisting the definition of oneself in terms of what one cannot do, what others take for granted, represents a need so great that other imperatives (even one so urgent as the need to keep one's home in winter's cold) evaporate and fall away in face of fear. Even the loss of home and shelter, in this case, is not so terrifying as the loss of self.

"I come out of school. I was sixteen. They had their meetings. The directors meet. They said that I was wasting their school paper. I was wasting pencils . . ."

Another illiterate, looking back, believes she was not worthy of her teacher's time. She believes that it was wrong of her to take up space within her school. She believes that it was right to leave in order that somebody more deserving could receive her place.

Children choke. Their mother chokes another way: on more than chicken bones.

People eat what others order, know what others tell them, struggle 40 not to see themselves as they believe the world perceives them. A man in California speaks about his own loss of identity, of self-location, definition:

"I stood at the bottom of the ramp. My car had broke down on the freeway. There was a phone. I asked for the police. They was nice. They said to tell them where I was. I looked up at the signs. There was one that I had seen before. I read it to them: ONE WAY STREET. They thought it was a joke. I told them I couldn't read. There was other signs above the ramp. They told me to try. I looked around for somebody to help. All the cars was going by real fast. I couldn't make them understand that I was lost. The cop was nice. He told me: 'Try once more.' I did my best. I couldn't read. I only knew the sign above my head. The cop was trying to be nice. He knew that I was trapped. 'I can't send out a car to you if you can't tell me where you are.' I felt afraid. I nearly cried. I'm forty-eight years old. I only said: 'I'm on a one-way street . . .' "

The legal problems and the courtroom complications that confront illiterate adults have been discussed above. The anguish that may underlie such matters was brought home to me this year while I was working on this book. I have spoken, in the introduction, of a sudden phone call from one of my former students, now in prison for a criminal offense. Stephen is not a boy today. He is twenty-eight years old. He called to ask me to assist him in his trial, which comes up next fall. He will be on trial for murder. He has just knifed and killed a man who first enticed him to his home, then cheated him, and then insulted him—as "an illiterate subhuman."

Stephen now faces twenty years to life. Stephen's mother was illiterate. His grandparents were illiterate as well. What parental curse did not destroy was killed off finally by the schools. Silent violence is repaid with interest. It will cost us $25,000 yearly to maintain this broken soul in prison. But what is the price that has been paid by Stephen's victim? What is the price that will be paid by Stephen?

Perhaps we might slow down a moment here and look at the realities described above. This is the nation that we live in. This is a society that most of us did not create but which our President and other leaders have been willing to sustain by virtue of malign neglect. Do we possess the character and courage to address a problem which so many nations, poorer than our own, have found it natural to correct?

The answers to these questions represent a reasonable test of our 45 belief in the democracy to which we have been asked in public school to swear allegiance.

Responding to Reading

1. According to Kozol, how does illiteracy undermine democracy in the United States? Do you agree with him?
2. Do you think Kozol accurately describes the difficulties illiterates face in their daily lives, or does he seem to be exaggerating? If you think he is exaggerating, what motive might he have?
3. Kozol concludes his essay by asking whether we as a nation have "the character and courage to address" illiteracy (44). He does not, however, offer any concrete suggestions for doing so. Can you offer any suggestions?

Responding in Writing

Keep a log of your activities for a day. Then, write a few paragraphs discussing which of these activities you could and could not perform if you were illiterate.

POLITICS AND THE ENGLISH LANGUAGE
George Orwell
1903–1950

George Orwell was born Eric Arthur Blair in Bengal, India, the son of a British colonial civil servant. He joined the Indian Imperial Police in Burma, where he came to question the British methods of colonialism. (See "Shooting an Elephant" in Chapter 10.) An enemy of totalitarianism and a spokesperson for the oppressed, Orwell criticized totalitarian regimes in his bitterly satirical novels Animal Farm *(1945) and* 1984 *(1949). He wrote many literary essays and is much admired for his lucid prose style. The following essay was written at the end of World War II, when jingoistic praise for "our democratic institutions" and blindly passionate defenses of Marxist ideology were the two common extremes of public political discourse. Orwell's plea for clear thinking and writing at a time when "political language . . . [was] designed to make lies sound truthful and murder respectable, and to give an appearance of solidity to pure wind" is as relevant today as it was when it was written.*

Most people who bother with the matter at all would admit that the English language is in a bad way, but it is generally assumed that we cannot by conscious action do anything about it. Our civilization is decadent and our language—so the argument runs—must inevitably share in the general collapse. It follows that any struggle against the abuse of language is a sentimental archaism, like preferring candles to electric light or hansom cabs to airplanes. Underneath this lies the half-conscious belief that language is a natural growth and not an instrument which we shape for our own purposes.

Now, it is clear that the decline of a language must ultimately have political and economic causes: it is not due simply to the bad influence of this or that individual writer. But an effect can become a cause, reinforcing the original cause and producing the same effect in an intensified form, and so on indefinitely. A man may take to drink because he feels himself to be a failure, and then fail all the more completely because he drinks. It is rather the same thing that is happening to the English language. It becomes ugly and inaccurate because our thoughts are foolish, but the slovenliness of our language makes it easier for us to have foolish thoughts. The point is that the process is reversible. Modern English, especially written English, is full of bad habits which spread by imitation and which can be avoided if one is willing to take the necessary trouble. If one gets rid of these habits one can think more clearly, and to think clearly is a necessary first step towards political regeneration: so that the fight against bad English is not frivolous and is not the exclusive concern of professional writers. I will come back to this presently, and I hope that by that time the meaning of what I have said here will have become clearer. Meanwhile, here are five specimens of the English language as it is now habitually written.

These five passages have not been picked out because they are especially bad—I could have quoted far worse if I had chosen—but because they illustrate various of the mental vices from which we now suffer. They are a little below the average, but are fairly representative samples. I number them so that I can refer back to them when necessary:

> "(1) I am not, indeed, sure whether it is not true to say that the Milton who once seemed not unlike a seventeenth-century Shelley had not become, out of an experience ever more bitter in each year, more alien (*sic*) to the founder of that Jesuit sect which nothing could induce him to tolerate."
>
> Professor Harold Laski (Essay in *Freedom of Expression*).

> "(2) Above all, we cannot play ducks and drakes with a native battery of idioms which prescribes such egregious collocations of vocables as the Basic *put up with* for *tolerate* or *put at a loss* for *bewilder*."
>
> Professor Lancelot Hogben (*Interglossa*).

> "(3) On the one side we have the free personality: by definition it is not neurotic, for it has neither conflict nor dream. Its desires, such as they are, are transparent, for they are just what institutional approval keeps in the forefront of consciousness; another institutional pattern would alter their number and intensity; there is little in them that is natural, irreducible, or culturally dangerous. But *on the other side*, the social bond itself is nothing but the mutual reflection of these selfsecure integrities. Recall the definition of love. Is not this the very picture of a small academic? Where is there a place in this hall of mirrors for either personality or fraternity?"
>
> Essay on psychology in *Politics* (New York).

"(4) All the 'best people' from the gentlemen's clubs, and all the frantic fascist captains, united in common hatred of Socialism and bestial horror of the rising tide of the mass revolutionary movement, have turned to acts of provocation, to foul incendiarism, to medieval legends of poisoned wells, to legalize their own destruction of proletarian organizations, and rouse the agitated petty-bourgeoisie to chauvinistic fervor on behalf of the fight against the revolutionary way out of the crisis."

Communist pamphlet.

"(5) If a new spirit is to be infused into this old country, there is one thorny and contentious reform which must be tackled, and that is the humanization and galvanization of the B.B.C. Timidity here will bespeak cancer and atrophy of the soul. The heart of Britain may be sound and of strong beat, for instance, but the British lion's roar at present is like that of Bottom in Shakespeare's *Midsummer Night's Dream*—as gentle as any sucking dove. A virile new Britain cannot continue indefinitely to be traduced in the eyes, or rather ears, of the world by the effete languors of Langham Place, brazenly masquerading as 'standard English.' When the Voice of Britain is heard at nine o'clock, better far and infinitely less ludicrous to hear aitches honestly dropped than the present priggish, inflated, inhibited, school-ma'amish arch braying of blameless bashful mewing maidens!"

Letter in *Tribune*.

Each of these passages has faults of its own, but, quite apart from avoidable ugliness, two qualities are common to all of them. The first is staleness of imagery: the other is lack of precision. The writer either has a meaning and cannot express it, or he inadvertently says something else, or he is almost indifferent as to whether his words mean anything or not. This mixture of vagueness and sheer incompetence is the most marked characteristic of modern English prose, and especially of any kind of political writing. As soon as certain topics are raised, the concrete melts into the abstract and no one seems able to think of turns of speech that are not hackneyed: prose consists less and less of *words* chosen for the sake of their meaning, and more and more of *phrases* tacked together like the sections of a prefabricated hen-house. I list below, with notes and examples, various of the tricks by means of which the work of prose-construction is habitually dodged:

Dying Metaphors

5 A newly invented metaphor assists thought by evoking a visual image, while on the other hand a metaphor which is technically "dead" (e.g. *iron resolution*) has in effect reverted to being an ordinary word and can generally be used without loss of vividness. But in between these two

classes there is a huge dump of worn-out metaphors which have lost all evocative power and are merely used because they save people the trouble of inventing phrases for themselves. Examples are: *Ring the changes on, take up the cudgels for, toe the line, ride roughshod over, stand shoulder to shoulder with, play into the hands of, no axe to grind, grist to the mill, fishing in troubled waters, on the order of the day, Achilles' heel, swan song, hotbed.* Many of these are used without knowledge of their meaning (what is a "rift,"[1] for instance?), and incompatible metaphors are frequently mixed, a sure sign that the writer is not interested in what he is saying. Some metaphors now current have been twisted out of their original meaning without those who use them even being aware of the fact. For example, *toe the line* is sometimes written *tow the line.* Another example is the *hammer and the anvil,* now always used with the implication that the anvil gets the worst of it. In real life it is always the anvil that breaks the hammer, never the other way about: a writer who stopped to think what he was saying would be aware of this, and would avoid perverting the original phrase.

Operators or Verbal False Limbs

These save the trouble of picking out appropriate verbs and nouns, and at the same time pad each sentence with extra syllables which give it an appearance of symmetry. Characteristic phrases are: *render inoperative, militate against, make contact with, be subjected to, give rise to, give grounds for, have the effect of, play a leading part (role) in, make itself felt, take effect, exhibit a tendency to, serve the purpose of,* etc., etc. The keynote is the elimination of simple verbs. Instead of being a single word, such as *break, stop, spoil, mend, kill,* a verb becomes a *phrase,* made up of a noun or adjective tacked on to some general-purposes verb such as *prove, serve, form, play, render.* In addition, the passive voice is wherever possible used in preference to the active, and noun constructions are used instead of gerunds (*by examination of* instead of *by examining*). The range of verbs is further cut down by means of the *-ize* and *de-* formation, and the banal statements are given an appearance of profundity by means of the *not un-* formation. Simple conjunctions and prepositions are replaced by such phrases as *with respect to, having regard to, the fact that, by dint of, in view of, in the interests of, on the hypothesis that;* and the ends of sentences are saved from anticlimax by such resounding commonplaces as *greatly to be desired, cannot be left out of account, a development to be expected in the near future, deserving of serious consideration, brought to a satisfactory conclusion,* and so on and so forth.

---

[1]Originally *rift* referred to a geological fault or fissure. Now it is commonly used to indicate a breach or estrangement. [Eds.]

Pretentious Diction

Words like *phenomenon, element, individual* (as noun), *objective, categorical, effective, virtual, basic, primary, promote, constitute, exhibit, exploit, utilize, eliminate, liquidate,* are used to dress up simple statements and give an air of scientific impartiality to biased judgments. Adjectives like *epoch-making, epic, historic, unforgettable, triumphant, age-old, inevitable, inexorable, veritable,* are used to dignify the sordid processes of international politics, while writing that aims at glorifying war usually takes on an archaic color, its characteristic words being: *realm, throne, chariot, mailed fist, trident, sword, shield, buckler, banner, jackboot, clarion.* Foreign words and expressions such as *cul de sac, ancien régime, deus ex machina, mutatis mutandis, status quo, gleichschaltung, weltanschauung,* are used to give an air of culture and elegance. Except for the useful abbreviations *i.e., e.g.,* and *etc.,* there is no real need for any of the hundreds of foreign phrases now current in English. Bad writers, and especially scientific, political and sociological writers, are nearly always haunted by the notion that Latin or Greek words are grander than Saxon ones, and unnecessary words like *expedite, ameliorate, predict, extraneous, deracinated, clandestine, subaqueous* and hundreds of others constantly gain ground from their Anglo-Saxon opposite numbers.[2] The jargon peculiar to Marxist writing (*hyena, hangman, cannibal, petty bourgeois, these gentry, lacquey, flunkey, mad dog, White Guard,* etc.) consists largely of words and phrases translated from Russian, German or French; but the normal way of coining a new word is to use a Latin or Greek root with the appropriate affix and, where necessary, the *-ize* formation. It is often easier to make up words of this kind (*deregionalize, impermissible, extramarital, nonfragmentatory* and so forth) than to think up the English words that will cover one's meaning. The result, in general, is an increase in slovenliness and vagueness.

Meaningless Words

In certain kinds of writing, particularly in art criticism and literary criticism, it is normal to come across long passages which are almost completely lacking in meaning.[3] Words like *romantic, plastic, values, human,*

---

[2]An interesting illustration of this is the way in which the English flower names which were in use till very recently are being ousted by Greek ones, *snapdragon* becoming *antirrhinum, forget-me-not* becoming *myosotis,* etc. It is hard to see any practical reason for this change in fashion: it is probably due to an instinctive turning-away from the more homely word and a vague feeling that the Greek word is scientific.

[3]Example: "Comfort's catholicity of perception and image, strangely Whitmanesque in range, almost the exact opposite in aesthetic compulsion, continues to evoke that trembling atmospheric accumulative hinting at a cruel, an inexorably serene timelessness. . . . Wrey Gardiner scores by aiming at simple bull's-eyes with precision. Only they are not so simple, and through this contended sadness—runs more than the surface bittersweet of resignation" (*Poetry Quarterly*).

dead, sentimental, natural, vitality, as used in art criticism, are strictly meaningless in the sense that they not only do not point to any discoverable
object, but are hardly ever expected to do so by the reader. When one
critic writes, "The outstanding feature of Mr. X's work is its living quality," while another writes, "The immediately striking thing about Mr.
X's work is its peculiar deadness," the reader accepts this as a simple
difference of opinion. If words like *black* and *white* were involved, instead
of the jargon words *dead* and *living,* he would see at once that language
was being used in an improper way. Many political words are similarly
abused. The word *Fascism* has now no meaning except in so far as it signifies "something not desirable." The words *democracy, socialism, freedom, patriotic, realistic, justice,* have each of them several different
meanings which cannot be reconciled with one another. In the case of a
word like *democracy,* not only is there no agreed definition, but the
attempt to make one is resisted from all sides. It is almost universally felt
that when we call a country democratic we are praising it: consequently
the defenders of every kind of regime claim that it is a democracy, and
fear that they might have to stop using the word if it were tied down to
any one meaning. Words of this kind are often used in a consciously dishonest way. That is, the person who uses them has his own private definition, but allows his hearer to think he means something quite different.
Statements like *Marshal Pétain was a true patriot, The Soviet Press is the
freest in the world, The Catholic Church is opposed to persecution,* are almost
always made with intent to deceive. Other words used in variable meanings, in most cases more or less dishonestly, are: *class, totalitarian, science,
progressive, reactionary, bourgeois, equality.*

Now that I have made this catalogue of swindles and perversions,
let me give another example of the kind of writing that they lead to.
This time it must of its nature be an imaginary one. I am going to translate a passage of good English into modern English of the worst sort.
Here is a well-known verse from *Ecclesiastes:*

> "I returned and saw under the sun, that the race is not to the swift, nor
> the battle to the strong, neither yet bread to the wise, nor yet riches to
> men of understanding, nor yet favor to men of skill; but time and chance
> happeneth to them all."

Here it is in modern English: 10

> "Objective consideration of contemporary phenomena compels the con-
> clusion that success or failure in competitive activities exhibits no ten-
> dency to be commensurate with innate capacity, but that a considerable
> element of the unpredictable must invariably be taken into account."

This is a parody, but not a very gross one. Exhibit (3), above, for
instance, contains several patches of the same kind of English. It will be

seen that I have not made a full translation. The beginning and ending of the sentence follow the original meaning fairly closely, but in the middle the concrete illustrations—race, battle, bread—dissolve into the vague phrase "success or failure in competitive activities." This had to be so, because no modern writer of the kind I am discussing—no one capable of using phrases like "objective consideration of contemporary phenomena"—would ever tabulate his thoughts in that precise and detailed way. The whole tendency of modern prose is away from concreteness. Now analyze these two sentences a little more closely. The first contains forty-nine words but only sixty syllables, and all its words are those of everyday life. The second contains thirty-eight words of ninety syllables: eighteen of its words are from Latin roots, and one from Greek. The first sentence contains six vivid images, and only one phrase ("time and chance") that could be called vague. The second contains not a single fresh, arresting phrase, and in spite of its ninety syllables it gives only a shortened version of the meaning contained in the first. Yet without a doubt it is the second kind of sentence that is gaining ground in modern English. I do not want to exaggerate. This kind of writing is not yet universal, and outcrops of simplicity will occur here and there in the worst-written page. Still, if you or I were told to write a few lines on the uncertainty of human fortunes, we should probably come much nearer to my imaginary sentence than to the one from *Ecclesiastes*.

As I have tried to show, modern writing at its worst does not consist in picking out words for the sake of their meaning and inventing images in order to make the meaning clearer. It consists in gumming together long strips of words which have already been set in order by someone else, and making the results presentable by sheer humbug. The attraction of this way of writing is that it is easy. It is easier—even quicker, once you have the habit—to say *In my opinion it is a not unjustifiable assumption that* than to say *I think*. If you use ready-made phrases, you not only don't have to hunt about for words; you also don't have to bother with the rhythms of your sentences, since these phrases are generally so arranged as to be more or less euphonious. When you are composing in a hurry—when you are dictating to a stenographer, for instance, or making a public speech—it is natural to fall into a pretentious, Latinized style. Tags like *a consideration which we should do well to bear in mind* or *a conclusion to which all of us would readily assent* will save many a sentence from coming down with a bump. By using stale metaphors, similes and idioms, you save much mental effort, at the cost of leaving your meaning vague, not only for your reader but for yourself. This is the significance of mixed metaphors. The sole aim of a metaphor is to call up a visual image. When these images clash—as in *The Fascist octopus has sung its swan song, the jackboot is thrown into the melting pot*—it can be taken as certain that the writer is not seeing a mental image of the objects he is naming; in other words he is not really thinking. Look again at the examples I gave at the beginning of this essay. Professor Laski (1) uses five negatives in fifty-three words. One of these is superfluous, making nonsense of the whole passage, and in addition there is the slip *alien* for *akin,* making further nonsense, and several avoidable pieces of clumsiness which increase the general vagueness. Professor Hogben (2) plays ducks and drakes with a battery which is able to write prescriptions, and, while disapproving of the everyday phrase *put up with,* is unwilling to look *egregious* up in the dictionary and see what it means. (3), if one takes an uncharitable attitude towards it, is simply meaningless: probably one could work out its intended meaning by reading the whole of the article in which it occurs. In (4), the writer knows more or less what he wants to say, but an accumulation of stale phrases chokes him like tea leaves blocking a sink. In (5), words and meaning have almost parted company. People who write in this manner usually have a general emotional meaning—they dislike one thing and want to express solidarity with another—but they are not interested in the detail of what they are saying. A scrupulous writer, in every sentence that he writes, will ask himself at least four questions, thus: What am I trying to say? What words will express it? What image or idiom will make it clearer? Is this image fresh enough to have an effect? And he will probably ask himself two more: Could I put it more shortly? Have I said anything that is avoidably ugly? But you are not obliged to go to all this trouble. You can shirk it by simply throwing your mind open and letting the ready-made phrases come crowding in. They will construct your sentences for you—even think your thoughts for you, to a certain extent—and at need they will perform the important service of partially concealing your meaning even from yourself. It is at this point that the special connection between politics and the debasement of language becomes clear.

In our time it is broadly true that political writing is bad writing. Where it is not true, it will generally be found that the writer is some kind of rebel, expressing his private opinions and not a "party line." Orthodoxy, of whatever color, seems to demand a lifeless, imitative style. The political dialects to be found in pamphlets, leading articles, manifestos, White Papers and the speeches of under-secretaries do, of course, vary from party to party, but they are all alike in that one almost never finds in them a fresh, vivid, home-made turn of speech. When one watches some tired hack on the platform mechanically repeating the familiar phrases—*bestial atrocities, iron heel, bloodstained tyranny, free peoples of the world, stand shoulder to shoulder*—one often has a curious feeling that one is not watching a live human being but some kind of dummy: a feeling which suddenly becomes stronger at moments when the light catches the speaker's spectacles and turns them into blank discs which seem to have no eyes behind them. And this is not altogether fanciful. A speaker who uses that kind of phraseology has gone some distance towards turning himself into a machine. The appropriate noises are coming out of his larynx, but his brain is not involved as it would be if he were choosing his words for himself. If the speech he is making is one that he is accustomed to make over and over again, he may be almost unconscious of what he is saying, as one is when one utters the responses in church. And this reduced state of consciousness, if not indispensable, is at any rate favorable to political conformity.

In our time, political speech and writing are largely the defense of the indefensible. Things like the continuance of British rule in India, the Russian purges and deportations, the dropping of the atom bombs on Japan, can indeed be defended, but only by arguments which are too brutal for most people to face, and which do not square with the professed aims of political parties. Thus political language has to consist largely of euphemism, question-begging and sheer cloudy vagueness. Defenseless villages are bombarded from the air, the inhabitants driven out into the countryside, the cattle machine-gunned, the huts set on fire with incendiary bullets: this is called *pacification.* Millions of peasants are robbed of their farms and sent trudging along the roads with no more than they can carry: this is called *transfer of population* or *rectification of frontiers.* People are imprisoned for years without trial, or shot in the back of the neck or sent to die of scurvy in Arctic lumber camps: this is called *elimination of unreliable elements.* Such phraseology is needed if one wants to name things without calling up mental pictures of them. Consider for instance some comfortable English professor defending Russian totalitarianism. He cannot say outright, "I believe in killing off your opponents when you can get good results by doing so." Probably, therefore, he will say something like this:

15   "While freely conceding that the Soviet régime exhibits certain features which the humanitarian may be inclined to deplore, we must, I think, agree that a certain curtailment of the right to political opposition is an unavoidable concomitant of transitional periods, and that the rigors which the Russian people have been called upon to undergo have been amply justified in the sphere of concrete achievement."

The inflated style is itself a kind of euphemism. A mass of Latin words falls upon the facts like soft snow, blurring the outlines and covering up all the details. The great enemy of clear language is insincerity. When there is a gap between one's real and one's declared aims, one turns as it were instinctively to long words and exhausted idioms, like a cuttlefish squirting out ink. In our age there is no such thing as "keeping out of politics." All issues are political issues, and politics itself is a mass of lies, evasions, folly, hatred and schizophrenia. When the general atmosphere is bad, language must suffer. I should expect to find—this is a guess which I have not sufficient knowledge to verify—that the German, Russian and Italian languages have all dete-riorated in the last ten to fifteen years, as a result of dictatorship.

But if thought corrupts language, language can also corrupt thought. A bad usage can spread by tradition and imitation, even among people who should and do know better. The debased language that I have been discussing is in some ways very convenient. Phrases like *a not unjustifiable assumption, leaves much to be desired, would serve no good pur-pose, a consideration which we should do well to bear in mind,* are a contin-uous temptation, a packet of aspirins always at one's elbow. Look back through this essay, and for certain you will find that I have again and again committed the very faults I am protesting against. By this morn-ing's post I have received a pamphlet dealing with conditions in Germany. The author tells me that he "felt impelled" to write it. I open it at random, and here is almost the first sentence that I see: "(The Allies) have an opportunity not only of achieving a radical transformation of Germany's social and political structure in such a way as to avoid a nationalistic reaction in Germany itself, but at the same time of laying the foundations of a cooperative and unified Europe." You see, he "feels impelled" to write—feels, presumably, that he has something new to say—and yet his words, like cavalry horses answering the bugle, group themselves automatically into the familiar dreary pattern. This inva-sion of one's mind by ready-made phrases (*lay the foundations, achieve a radical transformation*) can only be prevented if one is constantly on guard against them, and every such phrase anesthetizes a portion of one's brain.

I said earlier that the decadence of our language is probably curable. Those who deny this would argue, if they produced an argument at all, that language merely reflects existing social conditions, and that we cannot influence its development by any direct tinkering with words and constructions. So far as the general tone or spirit of a language goes, this may be true, but it is not true in detail. Silly words and expressions have often disappeared, not through any evolutionary process but owing to the conscious action of a minority. Two recent examples were *explore every avenue* and *leave no stone unturned,* which were killed by the jeers of a few journalists. There is a long list of flyblown metaphors which could similarly be got rid of if enough people would interest themselves in the job; and it should also be possible to laugh the *not un-* formation out of existence,[4] to reduce the amount of Latin and Greek in the average sentence, to drive out foreign phrases and strayed sci-entific words, and, in general, to make pretentiousness unfashionable.

---

[4]One can cure oneself of the *not un-* formation by memorizing this sentence: *A not unblack dog was chasing a not unsmall rabbit across a not ungreen field.*

But all these are minor points. The defense of the English language implies more than this, and perhaps it is best to start by saying what it does *not* imply.

To begin with it has nothing to do with archaism, with the salvaging of obsolete words and turns of speech, or with the setting up of a "standard English" which must never be departed from. On the contrary, it is especially concerned with the scrapping of every word or idiom which has outworn its usefulness. It has nothing to do with correct grammar and syntax, which are of no importance so long as one makes one's meaning clear, or with the avoidance of Americanisms, or with having what is called a "good prose style." On the other hand it is not concerned with fake simplicity and the attempt to make written English colloquial. Nor does it even imply in every case preferring the Saxon word to the Latin one, though it does imply using the fewest and shortest words that will cover one's meaning. What is above all needed is to let the meaning choose the word and not the other way about. In prose, the worst thing one can do with words is to surrender to them. When you think of a concrete object, you think wordlessly, and then, if you want to describe the thing you have been visualizing you probably hunt about till you find the exact words that seem to fit. When you think of something abstract you are more inclined to use words from the start, and unless you make a conscious effort to prevent it, the existing dialect will come rushing in and do the job for you, at the expense of blurring or even changing your meaning. Probably it is better to put off using words as long as possible and get one's meaning as clear as one can through pictures or sensations. Afterwards one can choose—not simply accept—the phrases that will best cover the meaning, and then switch round and decide what impression one's words are likely to make on another person. This last effort of the mind cuts out all stale or mixed images, all prefabricated phrases, needless repetitions, and humbug and vagueness generally. But one can often be in doubt about the effect of a word or a phrase, and one needs rules that one can rely on when instinct fails. I think the following rules will cover most cases:

   (i)   Never use a metaphor, simile or other figure of speech which you are used to seeing in print.
  (ii)   Never use a long word where a short one will do.
 (iii)   If it is possible to cut a word out, always cut it out.
  (iv)   Never use the passive where you can use the active.
   (v)   Never use a foreign phrase, a scientific word, or a jargon word if you can think of an everyday English equivalent.
  (vi)   Break any of these rules sooner than say anything outright barbarous.

These rules sound elementary, and so they are, but they demand a 20 deep change of attitude in anyone who has grown used to writing in the style now fashionable. One could keep all of them and still write bad English, but one could not write the kind of stuff that I quoted in those five specimens at the beginning of this article.

I have not here been considering the literary use of language, but merely language as an instrument for expressing and not for concealing or preventing thought. Stuart Chase[5] and others have come near to claiming that all abstract words are meaningless, and have used this as a pretext for advocating a kind of political quietism. Since you don't know what Fascism is, how can you struggle against Fascism? One need not swallow such absurdities as this, but one ought to recognize that the present political chaos is connected with the decay of language, and that one can probably bring about some improvement by starting at the verbal end. If you simplify your English, you are freed from the worst follies of orthodoxy. You cannot speak any of the necessary dialects, and when you make a stupid remark its stupidity will be obvious, even to yourself. Political language—and with variations this is true of all political parties, from Conservatives to Anarchists—is designed to make lies sound truthful and murder respectable, and to give an appearance of solidity to pure wind. One cannot change this all in a moment, but one can at least change one's own habits, and from time to time one can even, if one jeers loudly enough, send some worn-out and useless phrase, some *jackboot, Achilles' heel, hotbed, melting pot, acid test, veritable inferno* or other lump of verbal refuse—into the dustbin where it belongs.

Responding to Reading

1. According to Orwell, what is the relationship between politics and the English language?
2. What does Orwell mean in paragraph 14 when he says, "In our time, political speech and writing are largely the defense of the indefensible"? Do you believe his statement applies to current political speech and writing as well?
3. Locate some examples of dying metaphors used in the popular press. Do you agree with Orwell that they undermine clear thought and expression? Why or why not?

Responding in Writing

As you listen to the local news on TV, write down several sentences that contain words and phrases that are vague, repetitious, or meaningless. Then, substitute your own clearer, more explicit words for the ones you identified.

---

[5]Writer known for his advocacy of clear writing and clear thinking. [Eds.]

FOCUS

Is Texting Destroying the English Language?

Responding to the Image

1. The image above shows someone writing a text message. What advantages does texting have over a phone call? What are the disadvantages of texting? Do you believe that the advantages of texting outweigh its disadvantages?
2. Do you think texting threatens your communication skills, or do you believe it enhances or expands them? How is texting different from the other types of writing you do?

I H8 TXT MSGS: HOW TEXTING IS WRECKING OUR LANGUAGE

John Humphrys

1943–

A radio presenter for the BBC and host of the BBC television game show Mastermind, *John Humphrys is an award-winning journalist and broadcaster. His books include* Devil's Advocate *(1999),* The Great Food Gamble *(2002),* Lost for Words: The Mangling and Manipulating of the English Language *(2004),* Beyond Words: How Language Reveals the Way We Live Now *(2006), and* In God We Doubt *(2007). In the following essay, Humphrys describes what he perceives as the drawbacks of texting.*

A good dictionary is a fine thing—I yield to no man in my love for one. If I stretch out my right arm as I type, I can pluck from my shelves the two volumes of the Shorter Oxford English Dictionary.

They are as close to my heart as they are to my desk because they are so much more than a useful tool.

Leafing through a good dictionary in search of a single word is a small voyage of discovery—infinitely more satisfying than looking something up on the internet.

It's partly the physical sensation—the feel and smell of good paper—and partly the minor triumph of finding the word you seek, but it's rare to open a dictionary without being diverted somewhere else.

The eye falls on a word you've never seen before or one whose 5 meaning you have always wanted to check, and you close the dictionary just a little bit richer for the experience.

But my lifetime love affair with the OED is at risk. The sixth edition has just been published and—I feel a small shudder as I write these words—it has fallen victim to fashion.

It has removed the hyphen from no fewer than 16,000 words.

So in future we are required to spell pigeon-hole, for instance, as pigeonhole and leap-frog as leapfrog. In other cases we have two words instead of one. Pot-belly shall henceforth be pot belly.

You may very well say: so what? Indeed, you may well have functioned perfectly well until now spelling leapfrog without a hyphen.

The spell-check (sorry: spellcheck) on my computer is happy with 10 both. But that's not why I feel betrayed by my precious OED.

It's because of the reason for this change. It has happened because we are changing the way we communicate with each other, which means, says the OED editor Angus Stevenson, that we no longer have time to reach for the hyphen key.

Have you ever heard anything quite so daft? No time to make one tiny key-stroke (sorry: key stroke).

Has it really come to this? Are our lives really so pressured, every minute occupied in so many vital tasks, every second accounted for, that we cannot afford the millisecond (no hyphen) it takes to tap that key?

Obviously not. No, there's another reason—and it's far more sinister and deeply troubling.

15   It is the relentless onward march of the texters, the SMS (Short Message Service) vandals who are doing to our language what Genghis Khan[1] did to his neighbours eight hundred years ago.

They are destroying it: pillaging our punctuation; savaging our sentences; raping our vocabulary. And they must be stopped.

This, I grant you, is a tall order. The texters have many more arrows in their quiver than we who defend the old way.

Ridicule is one of them. "What! You don't text? What century are you living in then, granddad? Need me to sharpen your quill pen for you?"

You know the sort of thing; those of us who have survived for years without a mobile phone have to put up with it all the time. My old friend Amanda Platell, who graces these pages on Saturdays, has an answerphone message that says the caller may leave a message but she'd *prefer* a text. One feels so inadequate.

20   (Or should that have been *ansafone*? Of course it should. There are fewer letters in that hideous word and think how much time I could have saved typing it.)

The texters also have economy on their side. It costs almost nothing to send a text message compared with a voice message. That's perfectly true. I must also concede that some voice messages can be profoundly irritating.

My own outgoing message asks callers to be very brief—ideally just name and number—but that doesn't stop some callers burbling on for ten minutes and always, always ending by saying: "Ooh—sorry I went on so long!"

But can that be any more irritating than those absurd little smiley faces with which texters litter their messages? It is 25 years since the emoticon (that's the posh word) was born.

It started with the smiley face and the gloomy face and now there are 16 pages of them in the texters' A–Z.

25   It has now reached the stage where my computer will not allow me to type the colon, dash and bracket without automatically turning it into a picture of a smiling face. Aargh!

---

[1]Mongolian emperor and conqueror (1162–1227). [Eds.]

Even worse are the grotesque abbreviations. It is interesting, in a masochistic sort of way, to look at how text language has changed over the years.

It began with some fairly obvious and relatively inoffensive abbreviations: 'tks' for 'thanks'; 'u' for 'you'; 4 for 'for'.

But as it has developed its users have sought out increasingly obscure ways of expressing themselves which, when you think about it, entirely defeats the purpose.

If the recipient of the message has to spend ten minutes trying to translate it, those precious minutes are being wasted. And isn't the whole point to 'save' time?

Then there's the problem of ambiguity. With my vast knowledge 30 of text language I had assumed LOL meant 'lots of love', but now I discover it means 'laugh out loud'. Or at least it did the last time I asked.

But how would you know? Instead of aiding communication it can be a barrier. I can work out BTW (by the way) but I was baffled by IMHO U R GR8. It means: "In my humble opinion you are great." But, once again, how would you know?

Let me anticipate the reaction to this modest little rant against the text revolution and the OED for being influenced by it. Its defenders will say language changes.

It is constantly evolving and anyone who tries to get in the way is a fuddy-duddy who deserves to be run down.

I agree. One of the joys of the English language and one of the reasons it has been so successful in spreading across the globe is that it is infinitely adaptable.

If we see an Americanism we like, we snaffle it—and so we should. 35 But texting and 'netspeak' are effectively different languages.

The danger—for young people especially—is that they will come to dominate. Our written language may end up as a series of ridiculous emoticons and everchanging abbreviations.

It is too late to save the hand-written letter. E-mailing has seen to that and I must confess that I would find it difficult to live without it. That does not mean I like it.

I resent the fact that I spend so much of my working day (and, even more regrettably, weekends) checking for e-mails—most of which are junk.

I am also cross with myself for the way I have adapted my own style. In the early days I treated e-mails as though they were letters. I tried to construct proper, grammatical sentences and used punctuation that would have brought a smile to the lips of that guardian of our language, Lynne Truss.

Now I find myself slipping into sloppy habits, abandoning capital 40 letters and using rows of dots.

But at least I have not succumbed to 'text-speak' and I wish the OED had not hoisted the white flag either. I recall a piece of doggerel which sums up my fears nicely: *Mary had a mobile.*

She texted day and night. But when it came to her exams She'd forgotten how to write.

To the editor of the OED I will simply say: For many years you've been GR8. Don't spoil it now. Tks.

Responding to Reading

1. Why is Humphrys so troubled by the fact that the *Oxford English Dictionary* has removed the hyphen from thousands of words? According to Humphrys, what is the reason for this change?
2. In what ways does Humphrys think texters have changed the English language? Are there any other changes that Humphrys has missed?
3. According to Humphrys, what is the danger of "text-speak"? Do you think he makes a valid point, or do you think he is overreacting?

Responding in Writing

In paragraph 16, Humphrys says that texters are "pillaging our punctuation; savaging our sentences; raping our vocabulary. And they must be stopped." Write an email to Humphrys in which you agree or disagree with this statement. Make sure you use specific examples to support your points.

2B OR NOT 2B?

David Crystal

1941–

An honorary professor of linguistics at the University of Wales at Bangor, David Crystal has written extensively on issues related to language and the Internet. His most recent books include As They Say in Zanzibar *(2008),* Think on My Words: Exploring Shakespeare's Language *(2008),* Txtng: The Gr8 Db8 *(2008),* The Future of Language *(2009), and* Just a Phrase I'm Going Through: My Life in Language *(2009). Crystal is the founder-editor of* Linguistics Abstracts, *the* Journal of Child Language, *and* Child Language Teaching and Therapy. *In the following essay, Crystal argues for the benefits of text messaging.*

Last year, in a newspaper article headed "I h8 txt msgs: How texting is wrecking our language", John Humphrys argued that texters are "vandals who are doing to our language what Genghis Khan did to his neighbours 800 years ago. They are destroying it: pillaging our punctuation; savaging our sentences; raping our vocabulary. And they must be stopped."

As a new variety of language, texting has been condemned as "textese", "slanguage", a "digital virus". According to John Sutherland of University College London, writing in this paper in 2002, it is "bleak, bald, sad shorthand. Drab shrinktalk . . . Linguistically it's all pig's ear . . . it masks dyslexia, poor spelling and mental laziness. Texting is penmanship for illiterates."

Ever since the arrival of printing—thought to be the invention of the devil because it would put false opinions into people's minds—people have been arguing that new technology would have disastrous consequences for language. Scares accompanied the introduction of the telegraph, telephone, and broadcasting. But has there ever been a linguistic phenomenon that has aroused such curiosity, suspicion, fear, confusion, antagonism, fascination, excitement and enthusiasm all at once as texting? And in such a short space of time. Less than a decade ago, hardly anyone had heard of it.

The idea of a point-to-point short message service (or SMS) began to be discussed as part of the development of the Global System for Mobile Communications network in the mid-1980s, but it wasn't until the early 90s that phone companies started to develop its commercial possibilities. Text communicated by pagers were replaced by text messages, at first only 20 characters in length. It took five years or more before numbers of users started to build up. The average number of texts per GSM customer in 1995 was 0.4 per month; by the end of 2000 it was still only 35.

The slow start, it seems, was because the companies had trouble   5 working out reliable ways of charging for the new service. But once procedures were in place, texting rocketed. In the UK, in 2001, 12.2bn text messages were sent. This had doubled by 2004, and was forecast to be 45bn in 2007. On Christmas Day alone in 2006, over 205m texts went out. World figures went from 17bn in 2000 to 250bn in 2001. They passed a trillion in 2005. Text messaging generated around $70bn in 2005. That's more than three times as much as all Hollywood box office returns that year.

People think that the written language seen on mobile phone screens is new and alien, but all the popular beliefs about texting are wrong. Its graphic distinctiveness is not a new phenomenon, nor is its use restricted to the young. There is increasing evidence that it helps rather than hinders literacy. And only a very tiny part of it uses a distinctive orthography.[1] A trillion text messages might seem a lot, but when we set these alongside the multi-trillion instances of standard orthography in everyday life, they appear as no more than a few ripples on the surface of the

---

[1]System of using letters to form words. [Eds.]

sea of language. Texting has added a new dimension to language use, but its long-term impact is negligible. It is not a disaster.

Although many texters enjoy breaking linguistic rules, they also know they need to be understood. There is no point in paying to send a message if it breaks so many rules that it ceases to be intelligible. When messages are longer, containing more information, the amount of standard orthography increases. Many texters alter just the grammatical words (such as "you" and "be"). As older and more conservative language users have begun to text, an even more standardised style has appeared. Some texters refuse to depart at all from traditional orthography. And conventional spelling and punctuation is the norm when institutions send out information messages, as in this university text to students: "Weather Alert! No classes today due to snow storm", or in the texts which radio listeners are invited to send in to programmes. These institutional messages now form the majority of texts in cyberspace—and several organisations forbid the use of abbreviations, knowing that many readers will not understand them. Bad textiquette.

Research has made it clear that the early media hysteria about the novelty (and thus the dangers) of text messaging was misplaced. In one American study, less than 20% of the text messages looked at showed abbreviated forms of any kind—about three per message. And in a Norwegian study, the proportion was even lower, with just 6% using abbreviations. In my own text collection, the figure is about 10%.

People seem to have swallowed whole the stories that youngsters use nothing else but abbreviations when they text, such as the reports in 2003 that a teenager had written an essay so full of textspeak that her teacher was unable to understand it. An extract was posted online, and quoted incessantly, but as no one was ever able to track down the entire essay, it was probably a hoax.

10   There are several distinctive features of the way texts are written that combine to give the impression of novelty, but none of them is, in fact, linguistically novel. Many of them were being used in chatroom interactions that predated the arrival of mobile phones. Some can be found in pre-computer informal writing, dating back a hundred years or more.

The most noticeable feature is the use of single letters, numerals, and symbols to represent words or parts of words, as with b "be" and 2 "to". They are called rebuses, and they go back centuries. Adults who condemn a "c u" in a young person's texting have forgotten that they once did the same thing themselves (though not on a mobile phone). In countless Christmas annuals, they solved puzzles like this one:

YY U R YY U B I C U R YY 4 ME
("Too wise you are . . .")

CHAPTER 3   FOCUS

Similarly, the use of initial letters for whole words (n for "no", gf for "girlfriend", cmb "call me back") is not at all new. People have been initialising common phrases for ages. IOU is known from 1618. There is no difference, apart from the medium of communication, between a modern kid's "lol" ("laughing out loud") and an earlier generation's "Swalk" ("sealed with a loving kiss").

In texts we find such forms as msg ("message") and xlnt ("excellent"). Almst any wrd cn be abbrvted in ths wy—though there is no consistency between texters. But this isn't new either. Eric Partridge published his Dictionary of Abbreviations in 1942. It contained dozens of SMS-looking examples, such as agn "again", mth "month", and gd "good"—50 years before texting was born.

English has had abbreviated words ever since it began to be written down. Words such as exam, vet, fridge, cox and bus are so familiar that they have effectively become new words. When some of these abbreviated forms first came into use, they also attracted criticism. In 1711, for example, Joseph Addison complained about the way words were being "miserably curtailed"—he mentioned pos (itive) and incog (nito). And Jonathan Swift thought that abbreviating words was a "barbarous custom".

What novelty there is in texting lies chiefly in the way it takes further some of the processes used in the past. Some of its juxtapositions create forms which have little precedent, apart from in puzzles. All conceivable types of feature can be juxtaposed—sequences of shortened and full words (hldmecls "hold me close"), logograms[2] and shortened words (2bctnd "to be continued"), logograms and nonstandard spellings (cu2nite) and so on. There are no less than four processes combined in iowan2bwu "I only want to be with you"—full word + an initialism + a shortened word + two logograms + an initialism + a logogram. And some messages contain unusual processes: in iohis4u "I only have eyes for you", we see the addition of a plural ending to a logogram. One characteristic runs through all these examples: the letters, symbols and words are run together, without spaces. This is certainly unusual in the history of special writing systems. But few texts string together long sequences of puzzling graphic units.

There are also individual differences in texting, as in any other linguistic domain. In 2002, Stuart Campbell was found guilty of the murder of his 15-year-old niece after his text message alibi was shown to be a forgery. He had claimed that certain texts sent by the girl showed he was innocent. But a detailed comparison of the vocabulary and other stylistic features of his own text messages and those of his niece showed that he had written the messages himself. The forensic possibilities have

[2]Letters or symbols that stand for words. [Eds.]

been further explored by a team at the University of Leicester. The fact that texting is a relatively unstandardised mode of communication, prone to idiosyncrasy, turns out to be an advantage in such a context, as authorship differences are likely to be more easily detectable than in writing using standard English.

Texters use deviant spellings—and they know they are deviant. But they are by no means the first to use such nonstandard forms as cos "because", wot "what", or gissa "give us a". Several of these are so much part of English literary tradition that they have been given entries in the Oxford English Dictionary. "Cos" is there from 1828 and "wot" from 1829. Many can be found in literary dialect representations, such as by Charles Dickens, Mark Twain, Walter Scott, DH Lawrence, or Alan Bleasdale ("Gissa job!").

Sending a message on a mobile phone is not the most natural of ways to communicate. The keypad isn't linguistically sensible. No one took letter-frequency considerations into account when designing it. For example, key 7 on my mobile contains four symbols, pqrs. It takes four key-presses to access the letter s, and yet s is one of the most frequently occurring letters in English. It is twice as easy to input q, which is one of the least frequently occurring letters. It should be the other way round. So any strategy that reduces the time and awkwardness of inputting graphic symbols is bound to be attractive.

Abbreviations were used as a natural, intuitive response to a technological problem. And they appeared in next to no time. Texters simply transferred (and then embellished) what they had encountered in other settings. We have all left notes in which we have replaced an and by an &, a three by a 3, and so on. Anglo-Saxon scribes used abbreviations of this kind.

20   But the need to save time and energy is by no means the whole story of texting. When we look at some texts, they are linguistically quite complex. There are an extraordinary number of ways in which people play with language—creating riddles, solving crosswords, playing Scrabble, inventing new words. Professional writers do the same—providing catchy copy for advertising slogans, thinking up puns in newspaper headlines, and writing poems, novels and plays. Children quickly learn that one of the most enjoyable things you can do with language is to play with its sounds, words, grammar—and spelling.

The drive to be playful is there when we text, and it is hugely powerful. Within two or three years of the arrival of texting, it developed a ludic dimension. In short, it's fun.

To celebrate World Poetry day in 2007, T-Mobile tried to find the UK's first "Txt laureate" in a competition for the best romantic poem in SMS. They had 200 entrants, and as with previous competitions the entries were a mixture of unabbreviated and abbreviated texts.

The winner, Ben Ziman-Bright, wrote conventionally:

The wet rustle of rain
can dampen today. Your text
buoys me above oil-rainbow puddles
like a paper boat, so that even
soaked to the skin
I am grinning.

The runner-up did not:

O hart tht sorz
My luv adorz
He mAks me liv
He mAks me giv
Myslf 2 him
As my luv porz

(The author of the latter was, incidentally, in her late 60s.)

The length constraint in text-poetry fosters economy of expression in much the same way as other tightly constrained forms of poetry do, such as the haiku or the Welsh englyn. To say a poem must be written within 160 characters at first seems just as pointless as to say that a poem must be written in three lines of five, seven, and five syllables. But put such a discipline into the hands of a master, and the result can be poetic magic. Of course, SMS poetry has some way to go before it can match the haiku tradition; but then, haikus have had a head-start of several hundred years.

There is something about the genre which has no parallel elsewhere. 25 This is nothing to do with the use of texting abbreviations. It is more to do with the way the short lines have an individual force. Reading a text poem, wrote Peter Sansom, who co-judged a Guardian competition in 2002, is "an urgent business . . . with a text poem you stay focused as it were in the now of each arriving line." The impact is evident even in one-liners, whose effect relies on the kind of succinctness we find in a maxim or proverb. UA Fanthorpe, Sansom's fellow judge, admired "Basildon: imagine a carpark." And they both liked "They phone you up, your mum and dad."

Several competitions have focussed on reworking famous lines, titles, or quotations:

txt me ishmael
zen & T @ f m2 cycl mn10nc

The brevity of the SMS genre disallows complex formal pattern-ing—of, say, the kind we might find in a sonnet. It isn't so easy to include more than a couple of images, such as similes, simply because there isn't

CHAPTER 3 FOCUS

the space. Writers have nonetheless tried to extend the potential of the medium. The SMS novel, for example, operates on a screen-by-screen basis. Each screen is a "chapter" describing an event in the story. Here is an interactive example from 2005, from an Indian website called "Cloakroom":

> Chptr 6: While Surching 4 Her Father, Rita Bumps In2 A Chaiwalla & Tea Spills On Her Blouse. She Goes Inside Da Washroom, & Da Train Halts @ A Station.

In Japan, an author known as Yoshi has had a huge success with his text-messaging novel *Deep Love*. Readers sent feedback as the story unfolded, and some of their ideas were incorporated into it. He went on to make a film of the novel.

A mobile literature channel began in China in 2004. The "m-novel", as it is called, started with a love story, "Distance", by writer and broadcaster Xuan Huang. A young couple get to know each other because of a wrongly sent SMS message. The whole story is 1008 Chinese characters, told in 15 chapters, with one chapter sent each day.

30   Plainly, there are severe limits to the expressive power of the medium, when it is restricted to a screen in this way. So it is not surprising that, very early on, writers dispensed with the 160-character constraint, and engaged in SMS creative writing of any length using hard copy. Immediately there was a problem. By taking the writing away from the mobile phone screen, how could the distinctiveness of the genre be maintained? So the stylistic character of SMS writing changed, and texting abbreviations, previously optional, became obligatory.

Several SMS poets, such as Norman Silver, go well beyond text-messaging conventions, introducing variations in line-shape, type-size, font, and colour that are reminiscent of the concrete poetry creations of the 1960s. They illustrate the way the genre is being shaped by the more powerful applications available on computers.

In 2007 Finnish writer Hannu Luntiala published The Last Messages, in which the whole 332-page narrative consists of SMS messages. It tells the story of an IT-executive who resigns his job and travels the world, using text messages to keep in touch with everyone. And the growing independence of the genre from its mobile-phone origins is well illustrated by the French novelist Phil Marso, who published a book in 2004 written entirely in French SMS shorthand, Pas Sage a Taba vo SMS—a piece of word-play intended to discourage young people from smoking. The next year he produced L, an SMS retelling of French poetic classics.

An extraordinary number of doom-laden prophecies have been made about the supposed linguistic evils unleashed by texting. Sadly, its creative potential has been virtually ignored. But five years of research has at last begun to dispel the myths. The most important finding is that texting does not erode children's ability to read and write. On the contrary, literacy improves. The latest studies (from a team at Coventry University) have found strong positive links between the use of text language and the skills underlying success in standard English in preteenage children. The more abbreviations in their messages, the higher they scored on tests of reading and vocabulary. The children who were better at spelling and writing used the most textisms. And the younger they received their first phone, the higher their scores.

Children could not be good at texting if they had not already developed considerable literacy awareness. Before you can write and play with abbreviated forms, you need to have a sense of how the sounds of your language relate to the letters. You need to know that there are such things as alternative spellings. If you are aware that your texting behaviour is different, you must have already intuited that there is such a thing as a standard. If you are using such abbreviations as lol and brb ("be right back"), you must have developed a sensitivity to the communicative needs of your textees.

Some people dislike texting. Some are bemused by it. But it is 35 merely the latest manifestation of the human ability to be linguistically creative and to adapt language to suit the demands of diverse settings. There is no disaster pending. We will not see a new generation of adults growing up unable to write proper English. The language as a whole will not decline. In texting what we are seeing, in a small way, is language in evolution.

Responding to Reading

1. Why does Crystal think that popular conceptions about the effect of texting on the English language are wrong? What examples does he use to support his position?
2. According to Crystal, what is truly novel about texting? How do his ideas contradict those of John Humphrys (p. 185)?
3. In his conclusion, Crystal says, "In texting what we are seeing, in a small way, is language in evolution" (35). What does he mean?

Responding in Writing

Crystal gives examples of text-poetry and a chapter of a text-novel. Write your own text-poem or text-story. Then, write a paragraph in which you describe the advantages and limitations of using the text-message format for this assignment.

THUMBSPEAK: IS TEXTING HERE TO STAY?

Louis Menand

1952–

A professor of English and American literature and language at Harvard University and a staff writer for the New Yorker, *Louis Menand researches American studies with a focus on nineteenth- and twentieth-century cultural history. His books include* The Marketplace of Ideas *(2001),* American Studies *(2002), and* The Story of the Soup Cans *(2006). His 2001 book* The Metaphysical Club *was the recipient of the 2002 Pulitzer Prize for history. In the following essay, a review of a book on texting by David Crystal (p. 188), Menand examines the rise and fall of texting.*

Is texting bringing us closer to the end of life as we currently tolerate it? Enough people have suggested that it is to have inspired David Crystal to produce "Txtng: The Gr8 Db8" (Oxford; $19.95). "I don't think I have ever come across a topic which has attracted more adult antagonism," he says. (On the other hand, Crystal has written more than a hundred books, so he does not require extraordinary encouragement to share his views.) Crystal is a professional linguist, and professional linguists, almost universally, do not believe that any naturally occurring changes in the language can be bad. So his conclusions are predictable: texting is not corrupting the language; people who send text messages that use emoticons, initialisms ("g2g," "lol"), and other shorthands generally know how to spell perfectly well; and the history of language is filled with analogous examples of nonstandard usage. It is good to know that the estimated three billion human beings who own cell phones, and who use them to send more than a trillion text messages every year, are having no effect on anything that we should care about. A trillion text messages, Crystal says, "appear as no more than a few ripples on the surface of the sea of language."

The texting function of the cell phone ought to have been the special province of the kind of people who figure out how to use the television remote to turn on the toaster: it's a huge amount of trouble relative to the results. In some respects, texting is a giant leap backward in the science of communication. It's more efficient than semaphore[1], maybe, but how much more efficient is it than Morse code[2]? With Morse code, to make an "s" you needed only three key presses. Sending a text message with a numeric keypad feels primitive

---

[1]System of communicating with the use of flags. [Eds.]
[2]System of communicating with dots and dashes developed by Samuel F. B. Morse (1791–1872). [Eds.]

and improvisational—like the way prisoners speak to each other by tapping on the walls of their cells in "Darkness at Noon," or the way the guy in "The Diving Bell and the Butterfly" writes a book. And, as Crystal points out, although cell phones keep getting smaller, thumbs do not. Usually, if you can text a person you can much more quickly and efficiently call that person. But people sometimes text when they are close enough to talk face to face. People *like* to text. Why is that?

Crystal's answer is that texting is, partly, a game. It's like writing a sonnet (well, sort of): the requirement is to adapt the message to immutable formal constraints. A sonnet can't have more than fourteen lines, and a mobile-phone message can't have more than a hundred and forty bytes, which is usually enough for a hundred and sixty characters. This is a challenge to ingenuity, not an invitation to anarchy.

Most of the shortcuts used in texting are either self-evident (@ for "at" and "b" for "be") or new initialisms on the model of the old "A.S.A.P.," "R.S.V.P.," and "B.Y.O.B.": "imho" for "in my humble opinion," and so on. More imaginatively, there are the elaborated emoticons, such as 7:-) for baseball cap, and pictograms, such as @(------ for a rose and ~(_8^(|) for Homer Simpson. These are for thumb-happy aficionados, though, not the ordinary texter notifying her partner that the flight is late. There is a dialect that is used mainly by kids: "prw" for "parents are watching"; "F?" for "Are we friends again?" But Crystal thinks that texting is not the equivalent of a new language. "People were playing with language in this way long before mobile phones were invented," he points out. "Texting may be using a new technology, but its linguistic processes are centuries old." Acronyms, contractions, abbreviations, and shortened words ("phone" for "telephone," and so forth) are just part of the language. Even back in the days when the dinosaurs roamed the earth and men wrote with typewriters, the language of the office memo was studded with abbreviations: "re:," "cc.," "F.Y.I." "Luv" for "love" dates from 1898; "thanx" was first used in 1936. "Wassup," Crystal notes, originally appeared in a Budweiser commercial. @(------ is something that E. E. Cummings might have come up with.

Still, despite what they say, size matters. A trillion of anything has to make some change in cultural weather patterns. Texting is international. It may have come late to the United States because personal computers became a routine part of life much earlier here than in other countries, and so people could e-mail and Instant Message (which shares a lot of texting lingo). Crystal provides lists of text abbreviations in eleven languages besides English. And it is clear from the lists that

5

different cultures have had to solve the problem of squeezing commonly delivered messages onto the cell-phone screen according to their own particular national needs. In the Czech Republic, for example, "hosipa" is used for *"Hovno si pamatuju"*: "I can't remember anything." One can imagine a wide range of contexts in which Czech texters might have recourse to that sentiment. French texters have devised "ght2v1," which means *"J'ai acheté du vin."* In Germany, "nok" is an efficient solution to the problem of how to explain *"Nicht ohne Kondom"*—"not without condom." If you receive a text reading "aun" from the fine Finnish lady you met in the airport lounge, she is telling you *"Älä unta nää"*—in English, "Dream on."

But the lists also suggest that texting has accelerated a tendency toward the Englishing of world languages. Under the constraints of the numeric-keypad technology, English has some advantages. The average English word has only five letters; the average Inuit word, for example, has fourteen. English has relatively few characters; Ethiopian has three hundred and forty-five symbols, which do not fit on most keypads. English rarely uses diacritical marks, and it is not heavily inflected. Languages with diacritical marks, such as Czech, almost always drop them in text messages. Portuguese texters often substitute "m" for the tilde. Some Chinese texters use Pinyin—that is, the practice of writing Chinese words using the Roman alphabet.

But English is also the language of much of the world's popular culture. Sometimes it is more convenient to use the English term, but often it is the aesthetically preferred term—the cooler expression. Texters in all eleven languages that Crystal lists use "lol," "u," "brb," and "gr8," all English-based shorthands. The Dutch use "2m" to mean "tomorrow"; the French have been known to use "now," which is a lot easier to type than *"maintenant."* And there is what is known as "code-mixing," in which two languages—one of them invariably English—are conflated in a single expression. Germans write "mbsseg" to mean "mail back *so schnell es geht"* ("as fast as you can"). So texting has probably done some damage to the planet's cultural ecology, to lingo-diversity. People are better able to communicate across national borders, but at some cost to variation.

The obvious appeal of texting is its speed. There is, as it happens, a Ten Commandments of texting, as laid down by one Norman Silver, the author of "Laugh Out Loud :-D"). The Fourth of these commandments reads, "u shall b prepard @ all times 2 tXt & 2 recv." This is the new decorum in communication: you can be sloppy and you can be blunt, but you have to be fast. To delay is to disrespect. In fact, delay is the only disrespect. Any other misunderstanding can be cleared up by a few more exchanges.

Back when most computing was done on a desktop, people used to complain about how much pressure they felt to respond quickly to e-mail. At least, in those days, it was understood that you might have walked away from your desk. There is no socially accepted excuse for being without your cell phone. "I didn't have my phone": that just does not sound believable. Either you are lying or you are depressed or you have something to hide. If you receive a text, therefore, you are obliged instantaneously to reply to it, if only to confirm that you are not one of those people who can be without a phone. The most common text message must be "k." It means "I have nothing to say, but God forbid that you should think that I am ignoring your message." The imperative to reply is almost addictive, which is probably one reason that texting can be not just rude (people continually sneaking a look at their cell phones, while you're talking with them, in case some message awaits) but deadly. It was reported that the engineer in the fatal Los Angeles commuter-train crash this fall was texting seconds before the accident occurred. The *Times* noted recently that four of ten teen-agers claim that they can text blindfolded. As long as they don't think that they can drive blindfolded.

A less obvious attraction of texting is that it uses a telephone to   10
avoid what many people dread about face-to-face exchanges, and even about telephones—having to have a real, unscripted conversation. People don't like to have to perform the amount of self-presentation that is required in a personal encounter. They don't want to deal with the facial expressions, the body language, the obligation to be witty or interesting. They just want to say "flt is lte." Texting is so formulaic that it is nearly anonymous. There is no penalty for using catchphrases, because that is the accepted glossary of texting. C. K. Ogden's "Basic English" had a vocabulary of eight hundred and fifty words. Most texters probably make do with far fewer than that. And there is no penalty for abruptness in a text message. Shortest said, best said. The faster the other person can reply, the less you need to say. Once, a phone call was quicker than a letter, and face-to-face was quicker than a phone call. Now e-mail is quicker than face-to-face, and texting, because the respondent is almost always armed with his or her device and ready to reply, is quicker than e-mail.

"For the moment, texting seems here to stay," Crystal concludes. Aun, as the Finns say. It's true that all technology is, ultimately, interim technology, but texting, in the form that Crystal studies, is a technology that is nearing its obsolescence. Once the numeric keypad is replaced by the QWERTY keyboard on most mobile messaging devices, and once the capacity of those devices increases, we are likely to see far fewer initialisms and pictograms. Discourse will migrate back up

CHAPTER 3   FOCUS

toward the level of e-mail. But it will still be important to reach out and touch someone. Nok, though. Danke.

Responding to Reading

1. According to Menand, why is texting "a giant leap backward in the science of communication" (2)? In what way does this statement contradict David Crystal (p. 188)?
2. Why, according to Crystal, do people like to text? In what way is texting like a game?
3. What does Menand see as the effect of texting? What does he mean when he says that texting "is a technology that is nearing its obsolescence" (11)?

Responding in Writing

Write a paragraph in which you analyze the texts you send each day. What different audiences do you text? How are the messages to each audience similar? How are they different? Why do you text rather than call or email?

WIDENING THE FOCUS

For Critical Thinking and Writing

Write an essay in which you answer the Focus question, "Is Texting Destroying the English Language?" In your essay, refer to the ideas in John Humphrys's "I h8 txt msgs: How Texting Is Wrecking Our Language," David Crystal's "2b or not 2b?" and Louis Menand's "Thumbspeak: Is Texting Here to Stay?"

For Further Reading

The following readings can suggest additional perspectives for thinking and writing about the effect of technology on language.

- Brent Staples, "What Adolescents Miss When We Let Them Grow Up in Cyberspace" (p. 241)

- Robert W. Lucky, "To Twitter or Not to Twitter?" (p. 244)

- Richard Wright, "The Library Card" (p. 330)

For Focused Research

Should the United States have an official language policy? According to *Ethnologue* http://www.ethnologue.com, 238 languages are spoken in the United States. How should the federal government respond to this situation? Do minority languages threaten our national interest and democratic traditions? Should the Congress introduce a constitutional amendment that makes English the official language of the United States? Or, do you see language diversity as a national asset? Should the government encourage speakers of other languages while providing them with ample opportunities to learn English? Write an essay in which you outline a national language policy, basing your argument on information from one of the following Web pages:

- "Bilingual Education: A Critique," an essay published by the Hoover Institution, http://www.hoover.org/publications/he/2896386.html

- James Crawford's Language Policy Web site: http://www.languagepolicy.net/

- The "Analysis and Information" pages of the Web site run by English for the Children, a group lobbying to end bilingual education nationwide, http://onenation.org/

CHAPTER 3   FOCUS

WRITING

The Politics of Language

1. Currently, there is a great deal of debate about the value of home schooling. What might Richard Rodriguez (p. 133) and Frederick Douglass (p. 145) think of this practice? What advantages do you think they would see? What problems do you think they would identify? Be specific, and use material from their essays as well as from Daniel Pink's "School's Out" (p. 87) to support your points.

2. According to some educators, texting is negatively affecting the quality of students' writing. Other educators disagree. They see texting as a good thing because it enables students to say what they want to say just the way they want to say it. Rather than dismissing this technology, they say, educators should explore ways of integrating it into the curriculum. Write an essay in which you suggest ways in which texting could be made part of your educational experience. Be specific, referring to the essays in the Focus section (p. 184) as well as to specific classes that you are taking.

3. In "Mother Tongue" (p. 140), Amy Tan distinguishes between the English she speaks to her mother and the English she speaks to the rest of the world. Write an essay in which you describe the various types of English you speak—at home, at school, at work, to your friends, and so on. In what ways are these Englishes alike, and in what ways are they different? What ideas are you able to express best with each type of English?

4. Over fifty years ago, George Orwell wrote an essay in which he discussed how governments use language to control their citizens. Write an essay in which you discuss how today's governments do this. Do you think such control is easier or more difficult to achieve than it was fifty years ago? In your essay, be sure you refer specifically to "Politics and the English Language" (p. 172).

5. Both Amy Tan in "Mother Tongue" (p. 140) and Richard Rodriguez in "Aria" (p. 133) talk about how education can change one's use of language. Write an essay discussing the effect education has had on your own spoken and written language. What do you think you have gained and lost as your language has changed?

6. Which of your daily activities would you be unable to carry out if, like the people Jonathan Kozol describes in "The Human Cost of an Illiterate Society" (p. 164), you could neither read nor write? Write an article for your local newspaper in which you report on a typical day, being sure to identify specific tasks you could not do. In addition,

explain some strategies you would use to hide the fact that you couldn't read or write.

7. In paragraph 21 of "Politics and the English Language" (p. 172), Orwell says, "Political language . . . is designed to make lies sound truthful and murder respectable, and to give an appearance of solidity to pure wind." Write an essay in which you agree or disagree with this statement. Support your position with examples of political language you find in newspapers and magazines, on TV, or on the Internet.

8. List some of the words you use to refer to women, minorities, and other groups. Then, write an email to Alleen Pace Nilsen (p. 150) in which you agree or disagree with her assertion that the words people use tell a lot about their values and beliefs. In addition to Nilsen's essay, consider Joan M. Herbers's essay "The Loaded Language of Science" (p. 161).

9. Recently, there has been a great deal of debate about the benefits and drawbacks of a multilingual society. Supporters say that a multilingual society allows people to preserve their own cultures and thus fosters pride. Detractors say that a multilingual society reinforces differences and ultimately tears a country apart. What do you see as the benefits and drawbacks of a multilingual society? As a country, what would we gain if we encouraged multilingualism? What would we lose? Refer to the essays in this chapter by Richard Rodriguez (p. 133) and Amy Tan (p. 140) to support your position.

4

MEDIA AND SOCIETY

Many forms of popular media—for example, books, newspapers, and magazines; radio, television, and film—have been around for a long time, and over the years, they have had a powerful impact on our lives. But the popular media have changed dramatically in our lifetimes.

Television is one medium that changed and yet managed to survive, and even thrive. Cable television brought us literally hundreds of stations, along with sitcom reruns that endlessly recycled our childhoods (and our parents' childhoods). Satellites brought immediacy, delivering news in real time around the clock. Other innovations also appeared on television: home shopping, reality TV, infomercials, music videos. And now, of course, television has become digital and interactive.

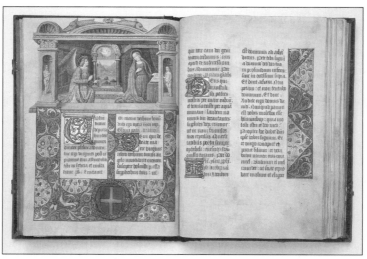

Fifteenth-century illuminated manuscript depicting the angel Gabriel speaking to Mary

Over the years, in response to emerging technology, other forms of media also reinvented themselves. Music evolved from vinyl records to cassettes to CDs to music downloaded onto MP3 players. Movies moved from silent to "talkies" and from black and white to color, enhanced by sophisticated computer animation and special digital effects. Professional journals and popular magazines became available online, and today, portable digital readers permit us to read paperless newspapers and even books. In an effort to hold on to readers, newspapers constructed Web sites and published online editions, but, despite these innovations, the Internet continues to threaten survival of the daily newspaper. (Even before the Internet existed, newspaper readership was on the decline; cities that once had several different daily newspapers, with a variety of editorial positions, now have only a few. In fact, over 98 percent of U.S. cities have just one major daily newspaper.)

Clearly, "new media" is a completely different entity from the media of even a decade ago, and this evolution has had negative as well as positive consequences. In recent years, the increasing power and scope of the Internet, and its ever-increasing ability to enable us to form networks, has changed everything. Today, our access to digital media has truly made the world into what Canadian cultural critic Marshall McLuhan once called a "global village": a world of nations—and, today, of individuals—that are more and more interconnected and interdependent. The Internet has made available a tremendous amount of information—and

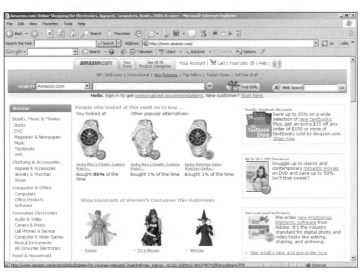

Amazon.com home page

the ability to communicate this information almost instantly to millions of people all over the planet. Now, we exchange ideas through blogs, chat rooms, bulletin boards, and email as well as through instant messaging, texting, YouTube, and Twitter. But the development of new media also has a dark side. The same tools that can unite, inform, instruct, entertain, and inspire can also isolate, misinform, frighten, deceive, stereotype, and even brainwash.

In this chapter's Focus section, "Does Social Networking Connect Us or Keep Us Apart?" writers debate whether digital social networking tools have created vibrant virtual communities or have actually replaced face-to-face communication—and led to a loss of true intimacy.

-------------------- **PREPARING TO READ AND WRITE** --------------------

As you read and prepare to write about the essays in this chapter, you may consider the following questions:

- Does the essay focus on one particular medium or on the media in general?

- Does the writer discuss traditional media, "new media," or both?

- Is the writer's purpose to present information or to persuade readers?

- Does the writer see the media as a positive, negative, or neutral force? Why?

- If the writer sees negative effects, where does he or she place blame? Do you agree?

- Does the writer make any recommendations for change? Do these recommendations seem reasonable?

- Is the writer focusing on the media's effects on individuals or on society?

- Does the writer discuss personal observations or experiences? If so, are they similar to or different from your own?

- When was the essay written? Has the situation the writer describes changed since then?

- Which writers' positions on the impact of the media (or on the media's shortcomings) are most alike? Most different? Most like your own?

TELEVISION: THE PLUG-IN DRUG
Marie Winn
1936–

Born in Prague, Marie Winn immigrated to the United States with her family in 1939. She has written on a variety of subjects, but she is probably best known for her three critiques of television's effects on children and families: The Plug-In Drug: Television, Children and Family *(1977, revised 2002), from which the following selection was taken;* Children Without Childhood *(1983); and* Unplugging the Plug-In Drug *(1987). Winn has also published* Red-Tails in Love: A Wildlife Drama in Central Park *(1998) and* Central Park in the Dark *(2004) as well as several children's books. In the following widely reprinted essay, Winn considers how television has affected the family.*

Not much more than fifty years after the introduction of television into American society, the medium has become so deeply ingrained in daily life that in many states the TV set has attained the rank of a legal necessity, safe from repossession in case of debt along with clothes and cooking utensils. Only in the early years after television's introduction did writers and commentators have sufficient perspective to separate the activity of watching television from the actual content it offers the viewer. In those days writers frequently discussed the effects of television on family life. However, a curious myopia afflicted those first observers: almost without exception they regarded television as a favorable, beneficial, indeed, wondrous influence upon the family.

"Television is going to be a real asset in every home where there are children," predicted a writer in 1949.

"Television will take over your way of living and change your children's habits, but this change can be a wonderful improvement," claimed another commentator.

"No survey's needed, of course, to establish that television has brought the family together in one room," wrote the *New York Times*'s television critic in 1949.

The early articles about television were almost invariably accom- 5 panied by a photograph or illustration showing a family cozily sitting together before the television set, Sis on Mom's lap, Buddy perched on the arm of Dad's chair, Dad with his arm around Mom's shoulder. Who could have guessed that twenty or so years later Mom would be watching a drama in the kitchen, the kids would be looking at cartoons in their room, while Dad would be taking in the ball game in the living room?

Of course television sets were enormously expensive when they first came on the market. The idea that by the year 2000 more than three quarters of all American families would own two or more sets would have seemed preposterous. The splintering of the multiple-set family was something the early writers did not foresee. Nor did anyone imagine the number of hours children would eventually devote to television, the changes television would effect upon child-rearing methods, the increasing domination of family schedules by children's viewing requirements—in short, the power of television to dominate family life.

As children's consumption of the new medium increased together with parental concern about the possible effects of so much television viewing, a steady refrain helped soothe and reassure anxious parents. "Television always enters a pattern of influences that already exist: the home, the peer group, the school, the church and culture generally," wrote the authors of an early and influential study of television's effects on children. In other words, if the child's home life is all right, parents need not worry about the effects of too much television watching.

But television did not merely influence the child; it deeply influenced that "pattern of influences" everyone hoped would ameliorate the new medium's effects. Home and family life have changed in important ways since the advent of television. The peer group has become television-oriented, and much of the time children spend together is occupied by television viewing. Culture generally has been transformed by television. Participation in church and community activities has diminished, with television a primary cause of this change. Therefore it is improper to assign to television the subsidiary role its many apologists insist it plays. Television is not merely one of a number of important influences upon today's child. Through the changes it has made in family life, television emerges as *the* important influence in children's lives today.

The Quality of Life

Television's contribution to family life has been an equivocal one. For while it has, indeed, kept the members of the family from dispersing, it has not served to bring them together. By its domination of the time families spend together, it destroys the special quality that distinguishes one family from another, a quality that depends to a great extent on what a family does, what special rituals, games, recurrent jokes, familiar songs, and shared activities it accumulates.

10   Yet parents have accepted a television-dominated family life so completely that they cannot see how the medium is involved in whatever problems they might be having. A first-grade teacher reports:

> I have one child in the group who's an only child. I wanted to find out more about her family life because this little girl was quite isolated from the group, didn't make friends, so I talked to her mother. Well, they don't have time to do anything in the evening, the mother said. The parents

come home after picking up the child at the baby-sitter's. Then the mother fixes dinner while the child watches TV. Then they have dinner and the child goes to bed. I said to this mother, "Well, couldn't she help you fix dinner? That would be a nice time for the two of you to talk," and the mother said, "Oh, but I'd hate to have her miss *Zoom*. It's such a good program!"

Several decades ago a writer and mother of two boys aged three and seven described her family's television schedule in a newspaper article. Though some of the programs her kids watched then have changed, the situation she describes remains the same for great numbers of families today:

> We were in the midst of a full-scale War. Every day was a new battle and every program was a major skirmish. We agreed it was a bad scene all around and were ready to enter diplomatic negotiations. . . . In principle we have agreed on $2\frac{1}{2}$ hours of TV a day, *Sesame Street, Electric Company* (with dinner gobbled up in between) and two half-hour shows between 7 and 8:30, which enables the grown-ups to eat in peace and prevents the two boys from destroying one another. Their pre-bedtime choice is dreadful, because, as Josh recently admitted, "There's nothing much on I really like." So . . . it's *What's My Line* or *To Tell the Truth*. . . . Clearly there is a need for first-rate children's shows at this time. . . .

Consider the "family life" described here: Presumably the father comes home from work during the *Sesame Street–Electric Company* stint. The children are either watching television, gobbling their dinner, or both. While the parents eat their dinner in peaceful privacy, the children watch another hour of television. Then there is only a half-hour left before bedtime, just enough time for baths, getting pajamas on, brushing teeth, and so on. The children's evening is regimented with an almost military precision. They watch their favorite programs, and when there is "nothing much on I really like," they watch whatever else is on—because *watching* is the important thing. Their mother does not see anything amiss with watching programs just for the sake of watching; she only wishes there were some first-rate children's shows on at those times.

Without conjuring up fantasies of bygone eras with family games and long, leisurely meals, the question arises: isn't there a better family life available than this dismal, mechanized arrangement of children watching television for however long is allowed them, evening after evening?

Of course, families today still do things together at times: go camping in the summer, go to the zoo on a nice Sunday, take various trips and expeditions. But their ordinary daily life together is diminished—those hours of sitting around at the dinner table, the spontaneous taking up of an activity, the little games invented by children on the spur of the moment when there is nothing else to do, the scribbling, the chatting, and even the quarreling, all the things that form the fabric of a family, that define a childhood. Instead, the children have their regular schedule of television programs and bedtime, and the parents have their peaceful dinner together.

15   The author of the quoted newspaper article notes that "keeping a family sane means mediating between the needs of both children and adults." But surely the needs of the adults in that family were being better met than the needs of the children. The kids were effectively shunted away and rendered untroublesome, while their parents enjoyed a life as undemanding as that of any childless couple. In reality, it is those very demands that young children make upon a family that lead to growth, and it is the way parents respond to those demands that builds the relationships upon which the future of the family depends. If the family does not accumulate its backlog of shared experiences, shared everyday experiences that occur and recur and change and develop, then it is not likely to survive as anything other than a caretaking institution.

Family Rituals

Ritual is defined by sociologists as "that part of family life that the family likes about itself, is proud of and wants formally to continue." Another text notes that "the development of a ritual by a family is an index of the common interest of its members in the family as a group."

What has happened to family rituals, those regular, dependable, recurrent happenings that gave members of a family a feeling of belonging to a home rather than living in it merely for the sake of convenience, those experiences that act as the adhesive of family unity far more than any material advantages?

Mealtime rituals, going-to-bed rituals, illness rituals, holiday rituals—how many of these have survived the inroads of the television set?

A young woman who grew up near Chicago reminisces about her childhood and gives an idea of the effects of television upon family rituals:

> As a child I had millions of relatives around—my parents both come from relatively large families. My father had nine brothers and sisters. And so every holiday there was this great swoop-down of aunts, uncles, and millions of cousins. I just remember how wonderful it used to be. These thousands of cousins would come and everyone would play and ultimately, after dinner, all the women would be in the front of the house, drinking coffee and talking, all the men would be in the back of the house, drinking and smoking, and all the kids would be all

over the place, playing hide and seek. Christmas time was particularly nice because everyone always brought all their toys and games. Our house had a couple of rooms with go-through closets, so there were always kids running in a great circle route. I remember it was just wonderful.

And then all of a sudden one year I remember becoming suddenly aware of how different everything had become. The kids were no longer playing Monopoly or Clue or the other games we used to play together. It was because we had a television set which had been turned on for a football game. All of that socializing that had gone on previously had ended. Now everyone was sitting in front of the television set, on a holiday, at a family party! I remember being stunned by how awful that was. Somehow the television had become more attractive.

As families have come to spend more and more of their time 20 together engaged in the single activity of television watching, those rituals and pastimes that once gave family life its special quality have become more and more uncommon. Not since prehistoric times, when cave families hunted, gathered, ate, and slept, with little time remaining to accumulate a culture of any significance, have families been reduced to such a sameness.

Real People

The relationships of family members to each other are affected by television's powerful competition in both obvious and subtle ways. For surely the hours that children spend in a one-way relationship with television people, an involvement that allows for no communication or interaction, must have some effect on their relationships with real-life people.

Studies show the importance of eye-to-eye contact, for instance, in real-life relationships, and indicate that the nature of one's eye-contact patterns, whether one looks another squarely in the eye or looks to the side or shifts one's gaze from side to side, may play a significant role in one's success or failure in human relationships. But no eye contact is possible in the child–television relationship, although in certain children's programs people purport to speak directly to the child and the camera fosters this illusion by focusing directly upon the person being filmed. How might such a distortion affect a child's development of trust, of openness, of an ability to relate well to *real* people?

Bruno Bettelheim suggested an answer:

Children who have been taught, or conditioned, to listen passively most of the day to the warm verbal communications coming from the TV screen, to the deep emotional appeal of the so-called TV personality, are often unable to respond to real persons because they arouse so much less feeling than the skilled actor. Worse, they lose the ability to learn from reality because life experiences are much more complicated than the ones they see on the screen. . . .

A teacher makes a similar observation about her personal viewing experiences:

I have trouble mobilizing myself and dealing with real people after watching a few hours of television. It's just hard to make that transition from watching television to a real relationship. I suppose it's because there was no effort necessary while I was watching, and dealing with real people always requires a bit of effort. Imagine, then, how much harder it might be to do the same thing for a small child, particularly one who watches a lot of television every day.

25   But more obviously damaging to family relationships is the elimination of opportunities to talk and converse, or to argue, to air grievances between parents and children and brothers and sisters. Families frequently use television to avoid confronting their problems, problems that will not go away if they are ignored but will only fester and become less easily resolvable as time goes on.

A mother reports:

I find myself, with three children, wanting to turn on the TV set when they're fighting. I really have to struggle not to do it because I feel that's telling them this is the solution to the quarrel—but it's so tempting that I often do it.

A family therapist discusses the use of television as an avoidance mechanism:

In a family I know the father comes home from work and turns on the television set. The children come and watch with him and the wife serves them their meal in front of the set. He then goes and takes a shower, or works on the car or something. She then goes and has her own dinner in front of the television set. It's a symptom of a deeper-rooted problem, sure. But it would help them all to get rid of the set. It would be far easier to work on what the symptom really means without the television. The television simply encourages a double avoidance of each other. They'd find out more quickly what was going on if they weren't able to hide behind the TV. Things wouldn't necessarily be better, of course, but they wouldn't be anesthetized.

A number of research studies done when television was a relatively new medium demonstrated that television interfered with family activities and the formation of family relationships. One survey showed that 78 percent of the respondents indicated no conversation taking place during viewing except at specified times such as commercials. The study noted: "The television atmosphere in most households is one of quiet absorption on the part of family members who are present. The nature of the family social life during a program could be described as 'parallel' rather than interactive, and the set does seem to dominate family life when it is on." Thirty-six percent of the respondents in another study indicated that television viewing was the only family activity participated in during the week.

The situation has only worsened during the intervening decades. When the studies were made, the great majority of American families had only one television set. Though the family may have spent more time watching TV in those early days, at least they were all together while they watched. Today the vast majority of all families have two or more sets, and nearly a third of all children live in homes with four or more TVs. The most telling statistic: almost 60 percent of all families watch television during meals, and not necessarily at the same TV set. When do they talk about what they did that day? When do they make plans, exchange views, share jokes, tell about their triumphs or little disasters? When do they get to be a real family?

Undermining the Family

Of course television has not been the only factor in the decline of family life in America. The steadily rising divorce rate, the increase in the number of working mothers, the trends towards people moving far away from home, the breakdown of neighborhoods and communities—all these have seriously affected the family.

Obviously the sources of family breakdown do not necessarily come from the family itself, but from the circumstances in which the family finds itself and the way of life imposed upon it by those circumstances. As Urie Bronfenbrenner[1] has suggested:

> When those circumstances and the way of life they generate undermine relationships of trust and emotional security between family members, when they make it difficult for parents to care for, educate, and enjoy their children, when there is no support or recognition from the outside world for one's role as a parent, and when time spent with one's family means frustration of career, personal fulfillment, and peace of mind, then the development of the child is adversely affected.

Certainly television is not the single destroyer of American family life. But the medium's dominant role in the family serves to anesthetize parents into accepting their family's diminished state and prevents them from struggling to regain some of the richness the family once possessed.

---

[1]Developmental psychologist who cofounded the U.S. Head Start program. [Eds.]

One research study alone seems to contradict the idea that television has a negative impact on family life. In their important book *Television and the Quality of Life,* sociologists Robert Kubey and Mihaly Csikszentmihalyi observe that the heaviest viewers of TV among their subjects were "no less likely to spend time with their families" than the lightest viewers. Moreover, those heavy viewers reported feeling happier, more relaxed, and satisfied when watching TV with their families than light viewers did. Based on these reports, the researchers reached the conclusion that "television viewing harmonizes with family life."

Using the same data, however, the researchers made another observation about the heavy and light viewers: ". . . families that spend substantial portions of their time together watching television are likely to experience greater percentages of their family time feeling relatively passive and unchallenged compared with families who spend small proportions of their time watching TV."

35   At first glance the two observations seem at odds: the heavier viewers feel happy and satisfied, yet their family time is more passive and unchallenging—less satisfying in reality. But when one considers the nature of the television experience, the contradiction vanishes. Surely it stands to reason that the television experience is instrumental in preventing viewers from recognizing its dulling effects, much as a mind-altering drug might do.

In spite of everything, the American family muddles on, dimly aware that something is amiss but distracted from an understanding of its plight by an endless stream of television images. As family ties grow weaker and vaguer, as children's lives become more separate from their parents', as parents' educational role in their children's lives is taken over by the media, the school, and the peer group, family life becomes increasingly more unsatisfying for both parents and children. All that seems to be left is love, an abstraction that family members know is necessary but find great difficulty giving to each other since the traditional opportunities for expressing it within the family have been reduced or eliminated.

Responding to Reading

1. Winn says, "Home and family life have changed in important ways since the advent of television" (8). How, according to Winn, has family life changed? What kind of support does she offer for this conclusion? Is it enough?
2. Do you agree with Winn that television is an evil, addictive drug that has destroyed cherished family rituals, undermined family relationships, and "[anesthetized] parents into accepting their family's diminished state and [prevented] them from struggling to regain some of the richness the family once possessed" (32)? Or, do you think she is exaggerating the dangers of TV?

3. Although it was updated in 2002, Winn's essay was written almost thirty years ago. In light of how much time has passed, do you think she needs to change any of her examples or add any new information?

Responding in Writing

Do you consider any other item—for example, your cell phone, iPod, or computer—to be a "plug-in drug" for you? Do you see any danger in your dependence on this object, or do you consider it just a routine part of your life?

REALITY TV: A DEARTH OF TALENT AND THE DEATH OF MORALITY

Salman Rushdie

1947–

Born in Bombay, India, Salman Rushdie is perhaps best known for his novel The Satanic Verses *(1988), which infuriated Muslims around the world. The book was banned in a dozen countries, caused riots in several, and led to a multimillion-dollar bounty being offered for Rushdie's assassination. In 1998, the* fatwa *(death sentence) was lifted by the Iranian government (although some fundamentalist Muslim groups increased the reward for killing him). Rushdie lives in seclusion and continues to publish articles, essays, and books, including* Fury *(2001),* Step Across This Line: Collected Nonfiction 1992–2002 *(2002),* Shalimar the Clown *(2005), and* The Enchantress of Florence: A Novel *(2008). In the following selection, which appeared in* The Guardian *in 2001, Rushdie offers his criticisms of reality TV and suggests some dangerous trends to come.*

I've managed to miss out on reality TV until now. In spite of all the talk in Britain about nasty Nick and flighty Mel, and in America about the fat, naked bastard Richard manipulating his way to desert-island victory, I have somehow preserved my purity. I wouldn't recognise Nick or Mel if I passed them in the street, or Richard if he was standing in front of me unclothed.

Ask me where the Big Brother house is, or how to reach Temptation Island, and I have no answer. I do remember the American *Survivor* contestant who managed to fry his own hand so that the skin peeled away until his fingers looked like burst sausages, but that's because he got on to the main evening news. Otherwise, search me. Who won? Who lost? Who cares?

The subject of reality TV shows, however, has been impossible to avoid. Their success is the media story of the (new) century, along with the ratings triumph of the big-money game shows such as *Who Wants to Be a Millionaire?* Success on this scale insists on being examined, because it tells us things about ourselves; or ought to.

And what tawdry narcissism is here revealed! The television set, once so idealistically thought of as our window on the world, has become a dime-store mirror instead. Who needs images of the world's rich otherness, when you can watch these half-familiar avatars of yourself—these half-attractive half-persons—enacting ordinary life under weird conditions? Who needs talent, when the unashamed self-display of the talentless is constantly on offer?

5   I've been watching *Big Brother 2,* which has achieved the improbable feat of taking over the tabloid front pages in the final stages of a general election campaign. This, according to the conventional wisdom, is because the show is more interesting than the election. The "reality" may be even stranger. It may be that *Big Brother* is so popular because it's even more boring than the election. Because it is the most boring, and therefore most "normal," way of becoming famous, and, if you're lucky or smart, of getting rich as well.

"Famous" and "rich" are now the two most important concepts in western society, and ethical questions are simply obliterated by the potency of their appeal. In order to be famous and rich, it's OK—it's actually "good"— to be devious. It's "good" to be exhibitionistic. It's "good" to be bad. And what dulls the moral edge is boredom. It's impossible to maintain a sense of outrage about people being so trivially self-serving for so long.

Oh, the dullness! Here are people becoming famous for being asleep, for keeping a fire alight, for letting a fire go out, for videotaping their cliched thoughts, for flashing their breasts, for lounging around, for quarrelling, for bitching, for being unpopular, and (this is too interesting to happen often) for kissing! Here, in short, are people becoming famous for doing nothing much at all, but doing it where everyone can see them.

Add the contestants' exhibitionism to the viewers' voyeurism and you get a picture of a society sickly in thrall to what Saul Bellow called "event glamour." Such is the glamour of these banal but brilliantly spotlit events that anything resembling a real value—modesty, decency, intelligence, humour, selflessness; you can write your own list—is rendered redundant. In this inverted ethical universe, worse is better. The show presents "reality" as a prize fight, and suggests that in life, as on TV, anything goes, and the more deliciously contemptible it is, the more we'll like it. Winning isn't everything, as Charlie Brown once said, but losing isn't anything.

The problem with this kind of engineered realism is that, like all fads, it's likely to have a short shelf-life, unless it finds ways of renewing itself. The probability is that our voyeurism will become more demanding. It won't be enough to watch somebody being catty, or weeping when evicted from the house of hell, or "revealing everything" on subsequent talk shows, as if they had anything left to reveal.

10   What is gradually being reinvented is the gladiatorial combat. The TV set is the Colosseum and the contestants are both gladiators and lions; their job is to eat one another until only one remains alive. But

how long, in our jaded culture, before "real" lions, actual dangers, are introduced to these various forms of fantasy island, to feed our hunger for more action, more pain, more vicarious thrills?

Here's a thought, prompted by the news that the redoubtable Gore Vidal[1] has agreed to witness the execution by lethal injection of the Oklahoma bomber Timothy McVeigh.[2] The witnesses at an execution watch the macabre proceedings through a glass window: a screen. This, too, is a kind of reality TV, and—to make a modest proposal—it may represent the future of such programmes. If we are willing to watch people stab one another in the back, might we not also be willing to actually watch them die?

In the world outside TV, our numbed senses already require increasing doses of titillation. One murder is barely enough; only the mass murderers make the front pages. You have to blow up a building full of people or machine-gun a whole royal family to get our attention. Soon, perhaps, you'll have to kill off a whole species of wildlife or unleash a virus that wipes out people by the thousand, or else you'll be small potatoes. You'll be on an inside page.

And as in reality, so on "reality TV." How long until the first TV death? How long until the second? By the end of Orwell's great novel 1984, Winston Smith has been brainwashed. "He loved Big Brother." As, now, do we. We are the Winstons now.

Responding to Reading

1. Salman Rushdie is a respected novelist with an international reputation, but he admits that he knows little about reality TV and has only recently begun to watch one reality show. Do you think he has the credibility to criticize reality TV?
2. Rushdie's fear is that "our voyeurism will become more demanding" (9), leading to shows that will "feed our hunger for more action, more pain, more vicarious thrills" (10). Has this fear been realized in any way since this essay was published in 2001? Do you think Rushdie is correct to be alarmed, or do you think viewers will continue to be satisfied with the present level of thrills and action?
3. How are the trends in reality TV shows that Rushdie describes similar to trends in television in general? Can you think of any dangerous trends that might develop on other kinds of TV shows?

Responding in Writing

Consulting TV listings in a newspaper or online, read the program descriptions of several different reality shows. List the features these programs seem to have in common. Then, write a paragraph in which you explain what it is about these shows that appeals to viewers.

---

[1]Novelist and essayist. [Eds.]

[2]Executed in 2001 for killing 168 people in the 1995 bombing of a government building (which housed a daycare center for employees) in Oklahoma City. [Eds.]

THE REVOLUTION WILL BE TELEVISED

Michael Hirschorn

A contributing editor and columnist for the Atlantic Monthly, *Michael Hirschorn writes about print and digital media. In 2008, he started Ish Entertainment, which produces reality television shows. Previously, he was the executive vice president of original programming and production for VH1, editor-in-chief of Inside.com, features editor at* Esquire *magazine, executive editor at* New York *magazine, and editor-in-chief of* Spin *magazine. In the following essay, Hirschorn explores the future of the television industry.*

One of the most exhausting things about new-media Moonies is their cultish conviction: either you "get it" or you don't. But they're right, up to a point. It's like when you're finding your way around a strange city: you have to see the whole thing in its full conceptual clarity before you can even begin to understand the particulars. The classic case study is how Steve Jobs shanghaied and basically destroyed the CD business. The major record labels, in giving Apple's iTunes the right to sell individual songs for 99 cents each, undermined their own business model— selling bundles of songs gathered together into something called an "album" for up to $20 a pop—because they didn't see that people were about to consume music in an entirely new way. The labels saw iTunes as free money; "ancillary," in the legal vernacular. Jobs took their cheap music and used it as a loss leader to sell his expensive iPods, and the traditional music business now lies in tatters.

Since I work in the traditional TV business, I'd been resolutely not seeing how the exact same thing is happening to video. Certainly, I'd been following the rise of Web-based video services like YouTube, Joost, and Hulu (the latter two being, to different degrees, Big Media–funded attempts to create satisfying experiences roughly analogous to watching TV, except on the Web). More recently, Miro, a nonprofit, launched a high-definition Web channel. And iTunes went video as well, offering a mix of professionally produced video and video podcasts from amateurs and quasi-amateurs. Like the record labels before them, TV networks and studios licensed some of their content to Apple, allowing iTunes to sell shows and movies with the same one-price strategy it had applied to music ($1.99 for TV shows; $9.99 for movies). The video iPod, competing with video-enabled cell phones and other viewing devices, allowed visual content to go mobile as well, auguring a period of video everywhere, immediately, all the time. All of this seemed like peripheral noise, digital noodling, because it was obvious: people love TV. They'll never stop watching TV. YouTube is popular, but doesn't count because it's not really TV: it's short-form crap. Produced TV is shinier, more pleasingly narrative. These are eternal values.

A recent visit to Houston, though, convinced me that I just hadn't been getting it. My friend Mike and his wife had done away with their TV entirely and instead had set up their 20-inch iMac widescreen as the focal point of a kind of jerry-rigged home theater; with no grievous loss in quality, they were feeding it with content from iTunes, various other Web-based media services, and DVDs. In doing so, they had dispensed with those hefty cable bills and had asserted an iconoclastic form of control over their media lives. It turns out, anecdotally at least, that lots of other people are doing the same. And that was my Homer Simpson "D'oh!" moment. Video without a TV console was not only possible, it was likely.

The traditional TV-viewing experience doesn't have to die (for reasons I'll get into later), but to save it, the media-industrial complex will have to act in non-traditional and uncomfortable ways—and will also have to rethink what "TV" is. Currently, it means watching a professionally produced video program—passively—on a television console that is fed with content delivered as part of a subscription to a cable or digital service. In the future, TV will mean a cacophony of professional and amateur short- and long-form content shipped via a variety of platforms to a variety of devices, only one of which is the Sony BRAVIA taking up too much space in your living room. Then, that content will be edited, poked at, commented on, parodied, and rebroadcast by you the former viewer—now "user"—to whomever you choose. Who gets paid by whom to deliver what to whom in this new dispensation is, as in every moment of grand tectonic digital shift, the $60 billion question.

And it's far from obvious that the people being paid now will be the people being paid a few years from now. The post–World War II model of expensive video driving a massively profitable content-production industry (that now-legendary $10 million pilot for *Lost,* those $200 million movies) is in some peril—much as, for the first time, it is conceivable that one or more of the major record labels could go out of business entirely. Among many other matters, the writers' strike (still ongoing at press time, possibly to be followed by an actors' strike this summer) is a final, great battle royal over content profits at what might be the last moment when such profits are worth fighting over—like steel workers' strikes in the '80s.

The story of digital video is not necessarily going to be the same as that of digital music, though the parallels between Napster and YouTube are fairly uncanny. It's not self-evident that watching long-running movies or TV shows on very small devices will become a mass behavior. According to a recent study, the majority of Internet users watch roughly 3 hours of video on the Web each month, compared to the average person's 4.5 hours of TV each *day.* For all the hype surrounding

Web video, it was not surprising that NBC, responsible for 40 percent of iTunes's video sales, had earned only $15 million last year on those sales, a point NBC Universal's chief, Jeff Zucker, made (uncontested) in announcing he would pull NBCU shows off iTunes at the end of last year. (This content is mostly going to Hulu.com, NBC's joint venture with Fox, where NBC hopes to sell advertising time much as it does on the air. How this will work better, given the still-unproven Web-video advertising market, remains undetermined.)

The video story is different from the music story in another crucial way. Being a music fan traditionally involved going to the record store (remember those?) or ordering from Amazon and committing a large sum of money to a product you knew about only via one or two songs, and then usually being disappointed by what you got. The iTunes music model, and the illegal-download model, represented a quantum leap in consumer satisfaction over the previous iteration: you could pay for only the songs you wanted (or not pay at all!), and there was a convenient sorting system that meant you could get rid of all those CDs and broken jewel cases. The traditional-TV model is altogether more user-friendly. It's free, or at least the costs are buried in cable bills (where, my Houston friends notwithstanding, years of learned behavior dictate that this is simply a cost to be borne), or they are buried in the more recent "triple play" offerings from Comcast and other companies that bundle cable with phone and high-speed Internet, obscuring the costs even more.

Watching video on the Web, contratrend, remains more of an analog experience than watching it on TV. On TV, you can click through hundreds of offerings instantly, or choose from dozens more you've recorded on your digital video recorder, and there's a handy electronic program guide to tell you what's on and when. On most Web video sites, however, clicking from show to show involves launching and relaunching players and then sitting through seemingly interminable "pre-roll" ads (and it's almost always the same ad). The quality remains subpar, with poor definition, small player windows, and unsynced audio and video. The selection is spotty, and there is no central guide to what is available where and when. It's easy to say these problems will be solved, but there's always the suspicion that the experience is intentionally being made unsatisfying so that people don't leave their TV sets too quickly. As Mark Cuban, the not-as-boorish-as-he-appears Internet entrepreneur-cum-Dallas Mavericks owner-cum-reality-TV star, has pointed out, the curve on Web innovation has stalled, even as band-width has begun to top out. In other words, only so much data can be thrust through the Internet's distributed nodes, and this structural limitation makes it unlikely that a satisfying, seamless Web-video experience will be on offer anytime soon. For these reasons, with great counterintuitive brio, Cuban last year pronounced the Web "dead and boring."

This is where the problem and opportunity lie for traditional TV. The flip side of the music business's obstinacy is a kind of we-need-to-be-down-with-the-kids type of herd mentality. It dictates that unless you throw everything online, you don't "get it." But "getting it" does not necessarily mean giving in to the braying of the digerati, especially when you will destroy your business in the process. In the past couple of years, the TV networks have thrown their shows onto the Web willy-nilly, some on their own sites, some via AOL, Yahoo, and so forth, and some on new ventures like the aforementioned Hulu. The logic is that if they don't, someone else will; indeed, a dedicated surfer can find most any show through sub-rosa peer-to-peer file-sharing systems that are used by an astonishing proportion of Web surfers, perhaps as much as 70 percent of the total. In the age of distributed media, you give the people what they want when they want it, where they want it. "If they want their show to succeed, they've got to get it out in front of as many people as possible," an analyst for the technology research firm Forrester said of the Big Four broadcast networks, articulating the moment's conventional wisdom and following it with a typical note of alarm: "The window is very short."

But as the music industry learned very quickly (and the newspaper 10 industry before it), this model swiftly turns you from a business to a charity, undermining the value of your product even as it brings your content to a larger audience. This is because advertisers and broadcasters have yet to settle on a protocol to sell advertising to accompany the near-infinitude of available content, and consumers are not yet ready to spend a lot of money paying for downloads. As NBCU's Zucker put it in announcing the end of the network's iTunes deal, "We don't want to replace the dollars we were making in the analog world with pennies on the digital side."

Conveniently, there's a solution, and it's right under the noses of the TV networks: make TV more like the Internet. In his various Web postings, Cuban has been promoting huge innovations coming in high-definition television, including the arrival of full Web functionality in next-generation TV sets and set-top cable boxes. "If the question is 'What's Next,' " he concluded in one, "the answer begins with 'Watch TV.' " Cuban co-owns a high-definition TV network, and may be accused of self-promotion, but I'm inclined to trust him on this one. This means, as Cuban suggested, embracing TV's Webby potential: near-infinite choice, the ability to manipulate and share content, deep and meaningful interactivity around professionally produced content, and a savvier, more "open source" strategy about how nonconventional content is allowed onto and promoted on the big screen. New set-top boxes recently announced separately by Comcast and Netflix suggest a strong push to connect TVs to the Web. Web-enabled TV would likely mean a profound loss of control for TV programmers, as the traditional prerogatives of scheduling became increasingly moot, and with them the meaning of "networks," since most shows would become equally accessible, no matter what network they were affiliated with.

As we move toward a fully on-demand culture (my 6-year-old son literally doesn't understand why I can't replay a song he just heard on the radio), TV does need to follow suit, no matter how fashionable that sounds. But it does not have to follow suit on the Internet (or at least not *only* on the Internet). There is no reason TV itself cannot compete as Cuban's next-generation version of the Web, offering endless choice (huge stockpiles of movies, entire seasons of TV shows), user editing and sharing capabilities (e.g., sending that *Gossip Girl* clip you just watched to your friend in Cleveland), playback, storage, and WiFi, whatever. And because the data all flow through the same pipes already, but without the destabilizing influence of the Internet, TV can offer brilliant resolution, even on a flat-screen 60-inch set.

A recent article in the trade publication *Multichannel News* warned that technical obstacles still prevent realizing this kind of vision, but serious technical problems bedevil Web video, too: as Cuban has been loudly blogging (the emperor has no clothes!), it's just not satisfying. This means TV has a buffer of a few years to figure out the bandwidth issues, the technical bugaboos, and the business model. But I would sit through ads, and maybe even pay more for cable, if I knew that I had some approximation of a Borgesian library[1] of video content available to me at home—content that I could talk back to, manipulate, and share.

And here's the final twist. As TV and the Internet converge into something generically known as broadband, the distinctions between the two will soon become nugatory from a consumer point of view. But will this resulting hybrid be more like TV, plus interactivity; or more like the Internet, plus TV? The distinction will be worth billions to whoever gets there first and organizes this mess in a fashion that's satisfying for consumers. The networks and cable companies, therefore, will need to move quickly to find a way to package the different streams— professional and user-made, broadcast and Internet—into a huge, interactive library, all easily and pleasingly accessible on demand and portable to whatever device people are overpaying for at that moment.

15   When they do, they can call it Web 3.0, and everyone will want to get it.

Responding to Reading

1. What similarities does Hirschorn see between the development of iTunes and the rise of YouTube and similar Web-based video services? In what sense does he see such media services as a threat to television?

---

[1]An endless library (reference to a fictional concept developed by Argentinean writer Jorge Luis Borges [1899–1986]). [Eds.]

2. In what respects does Hirschorn expect "the story of digital video" (6) to be different from the digital music story? Why does he see the "traditional-TV model" as "altogether more user-friendly" than the "iTunes music model" (7)?

3. What solution does Hirschorn recommend to help the television industry survive in the digital age? Is he optimistic that the television industry can be "saved"?

Responding in Writing

Do you think TV will endure in its present form, or do you expect that eventually it will be replaced by video content on the Web or on handheld electronic devices? Explain your position.

EMINEM IS RIGHT

Mary Eberstadt

Research fellow at the Hoover Institution and associate member of the Fellowship of Catholic Scholars, Mary Eberstadt is a consulting editor at Policy Review *and author of numerous magazine and newspaper articles on various American cultural issues. Originally published in her 2004 book* Home-Alone America: The Hidden Toll of Day Care, Behavioral Drugs, and Other Parent Substitutes, *the essay excerpted here examines the meanings and social implications of contemporary American popular music.*

If there is one subject on which the parents of America passionately agree, it is that contemporary adolescent popular music, especially the subgenres of heavy metal and hip-hop/rap, is uniquely degraded—and degrading—by the standards of previous generations. At first blush this seems slightly ironic. After all, most of today's baby-boom parents were themselves molded by rock and roll, bumping and grinding their way through adolescence and adulthood with legendary abandon. Even so, the parents are correct: Much of today's music *is* darker and coarser than yesterday's rock. Misogyny, violence, suicide, sexual exploitation, child abuse—these and other themes, formerly rare and illicit, are now as common as the surfboards, drive-ins, and sock hops of yesteryear.

In a nutshell, the ongoing adult preoccupation with current music goes something like this: *What is the overall influence of this deafening, foul, and often vicious-sounding stuff on children and teenagers?* This is a genuinely important question, and serious studies and articles, some concerned particularly with current music's possible link to violence, have lately been devoted to it. In 2000, the American Academy of Pediatrics, the American Medical Association, the American Psychological Association, and the American Academy of Child & Adolescent

Psychiatry all weighed in against contemporary lyrics and other forms of violent entertainment before Congress with a first-ever "Joint Statement on the Impact of Entertainment Violence on Children."

Nonetheless, this is not my focus here. Instead, I would like to turn that logic about influence upside down and ask this question: *What is it about today's music, violent and disgusting though it may be, that resonates with so many American kids?*

As the reader can see, this is a very different way of inquiring about the relationship between today's teenagers and their music. The first question asks what the music *does* to adolescents; the second asks what it *tells* us about them. To answer that second question is necessarily to enter the roiling emotional waters in which that music is created and consumed in other words, actually to listen to some of it and read the lyrics.

5   As it turns out, such an exercise yields a fascinating and little understood fact about today's adolescent scene. If yesterday's rock was the music of abandon, today's is that of abandon*ment*. The odd truth about contemporary teenage music—the characteristic that most separates it from what has gone before—is its compulsive insistence on the damage wrought by broken homes, family dysfunction, checked-out parents, and (especially) absent fathers. Papa Roach, Everclear, Blink-182, Good Charlotte, Eddie Vedder and Pearl Jam, Kurt Cobain and Nirvana, Tupac Shakur, Snoop Doggy Dogg, Eminem—these and other singers and bands, all of them award-winning top-40 performers who either are or were among the most popular icons in America, have their own generational answer to what ails the modern teenager. Surprising though it may be to some, that answer is: dysfunctional childhood. Moreover, and just as interesting, many bands and singers explicitly link the most deplored themes in music today—suicide, misogyny, and drugs—with that lack of a quasi-normal, intact-home personal past.

To put this perhaps unexpected point more broadly, during the same years in which progressive-minded and politically correct adults have been excoriating Ozzie and Harriet as an artifact of 1950s-style oppression, many millions of American teenagers have enshrined a new generation of music idols whose shared generational signature in song after song is to rage about what *not* having had a nuclear family has done to them. This is quite a fascinating puzzle of the times. The self-perceived emotional damage scrawled large across contemporary music may not be statistically quantifiable, but it is nonetheless among the most striking of all the unanticipated consequences of our home-alone world. . . .

[An] Example of the rage in contemporary music against irresponsible adults—perhaps the most interesting—is that of genre-crossing bad-boy rap superstar Marshall Mathers or Eminem (sometime stage persona "Slim Shady"). Of all the names guaranteed to send a shudder down the parental spine, his is probably the most effective. In fact, Eminem has single-handedly, if inadvertently, achieved the otherwise ideologically impossible: He is the object of a vehemently disapproving public consensus shared by the National Organization for Women, the Gay & Lesbian Alliance Against Defamation, William J. Bennett, Lynne Cheney, Bill O'Reilly, and a large number of other social conservatives as well as feminists and gay activists. In sum, this rapper—"as harmful to America as any al Qaeda fanatic," in O'Reilly's opinion—unites adult polar opposites as perhaps no other single popular entertainer has done.

There is small need to wonder why. Like other rappers, Eminem mines the shock value and gutter language of rage, casual sex, and violence. Unlike the rest, however, he appears to be a particularly attractive target of opprobrium for two distinct reasons. One, he is white and therefore politically easier to attack. (It is interesting to note that black rappers have not been targeted by name anything like Eminem has.) Perhaps even more important, Eminem is one of the largest commercially visible targets for parental wrath. Wildly popular among teenagers these last several years, he is also enormously successful in commercial terms. Winner of numerous Grammys and other music awards and a perpetual nominee for many more, he has also been critically (albeit reluctantly) acclaimed for his acting performance in the autobiographical 2003 movie *8 Mile.* For all these reasons, he is probably the preeminent rock/rap star of the last several years, one whose singles, albums, and videos routinely top every chart. His 2002 album, *The Eminem Show,* for example, was easily the most successful of the year, selling more than 7.6 million copies.

This remarkable market success, combined with the intense public criticism that his songs have generated, makes the phenomenon of Eminem particularly intriguing. Perhaps more than any other current musical icon, he returns repeatedly to the same themes that fuel other success stories in contemporary music: parental loss, abandonment, abuse, and subsequent child and adolescent anger, dysfunction, and violence (including self-violence). Both in his raunchy lyrics as well as in *8 Mile,* Mathers's own personal story has been parlayed many times over: the absent father, the troubled mother living in a trailer park, the series of unwanted maternal boyfriends, the protective if impotent feelings toward a younger sibling (in the movie, a baby sister; in real life, a younger brother), and the fine line that a poor, ambitious, and unguided young man might walk between catastrophe and success. Mathers plumbs these and related themes with a verbal savagery that leaves most adults aghast.

Yet Eminem also repeatedly centers his songs on the crypto-traditional 10 notion that children need parents and that *not* having them has made all hell break loose. In the song "8 Mile" from the movie soundtrack, for example, the narrator studies his little sister as she colors one picture after another of an imagined nuclear family, failing to understand that *"mommas got a new man."* *"Wish I could be the daddy that neither one of us had,"* he comments. Such wistful lyrics juxtapose oddly and regularly with Eminem's violent other lines. Even in one of his most infamous songs, "Cleaning Out My Closet (Mama, I'm Sorry)," what drives the vulgar narrative is the insistence on seeing abandonment from a child's point of view. *"My faggot father must have had his panties up in a bunch / 'Cause he split. I wonder if he even kissed me good-bye."*

As with other rappers, the vicious narrative treatment of women in some of Eminem's songs is part of this self-conception as a child victim. Contrary to what critics have intimated, the misogyny in current music does not spring from nowhere; it is often linked to the larger theme of having been abandoned several times—left behind by father, not nurtured by mother, and betrayed again by faithless womankind. One of the most violent and sexually aggressive songs in the last few years is "Kill You" by the popular metal band known as Korn. Its violence is not directed toward just any woman or even toward the narrator's girlfriend; it is instead a song about an abusive stepmother whom the singer imagines going back to rape and murder.

Similarly, Eminem's most shocking lyrics about women are not randomly dispersed; they are largely reserved for his mother and ex-wife, and the narrative pose is one of despising them for not being better women—in particular, better mothers. The worst rap directed at his own mother is indeed gut-wrenching: *"But how dare you try to take what you didn't help me to get? / You selfish bitch, I hope you f— burn in hell for this shit!"* It is no defense of the gutter to observe the obvious: This is not the expression of random misogyny but, rather, of primal rage over alleged maternal abdication and abuse.

Another refrain in these songs runs like this: Today's teenagers are a mess, and the parents who made them that way refuse to get it. In one of Eminem's early hits, for example, a song called "Who Knew," the rapper pointedly takes on his many middle- and upper-middle-class critics to observe the contradiction between their reviling him and the parental inattention that feeds his commercial success. *"What about the make-up you allow your 12 year-old daughter to wear?"* he taunts.

This same theme of AWOL parenting is rapped at greater length in another award-nominated 2003 song called "Sing for the Moment," whose lyrics and video would be recognized in an instant by most teenagers in America. That song spells out Eminem's own idea of what connects him to his millions of fans—a connection that parents, in his view, just don't (or is that won't?) understand. It details the case of one more "problem child" created by *"His f— dad walkin' out."* "Sing for the Moment," like many other songs of Eminem's, is also a popular video. The "visuals" show clearly what the lyrics depict—hordes of disaffected kids, with flashbacks to bad home lives, screaming for the singer who feels their pain. It concludes by rhetorically turning away from the music itself and toward the emotionally desperate teenagers who turn out for this music by the millions. If the demand of all those empty kids wasn't out there, the narrator says pointedly, then rappers wouldn't be supplying it the way they do.

If some parents still don't get it—even as their teenagers elbow up for   15 every new Eminem CD and memorize his lyrics with psalmist devotion— at least some critics observing the music scene have thought to comment on the ironies of all this. In discussing The *Marshall Mathers* LP in 2001 for Music Box, a daily online newsletter about music, reviewer John Metzger argued, "Instead of spewing the hate that he is so often criticized of doing, Eminem offers a cautionary tale that speaks to our civilization's growing depravity. Ironically, it's his teenage fans who understand this, and their all-knowing parents that miss the point." Metzger further specified "the utter lack of parenting due to the spend-thrift necessity of the two-income family."[1]

That insight raises the overlooked fact that in one important sense Eminem . . . would agree with many of today's adults about one thing: The kids *aren't* all right out there after all. Recall, for just one example, Eddie Vedder's rueful observation about what kind of generation would make him or Kurt Cobain its leader. Where parents and entertainers disagree is over who exactly bears responsibility for this moral chaos. Many adults want to blame the people who create and market today's music and videos. Entertainers, Eminem most prominently, blame the absent, absentee, and generally inattentive adults whose deprived and furious children (as they see it) have catapulted today's singers to fame. (As he puts the point in one more in-your-face response to parents: *"Don't blame me when lil' Eric jumps off of the terrace / You shoulda been watchin him—apparently you ain't parents."*)

The spectacle of a foul-mouthed bad-example rock icon instructing the hardworking parents of America in the art of child-rearing is indeed a peculiar one, not to say ridiculous. The single mother who is working frantically because she must and worrying all the while about what her 14-year-old is listening to in the headphones is entitled to a certain fury over lyrics like those. In fact, to read through most rap lyrics is to wonder which adults or political constituencies *wouldn't* take offense. Even so, the music idols who point the finger away from themselves and toward the emptied-out homes of America are telling a truth that some adults would rather not hear. In this limited sense at least, Eminem is right.

To say that today's popular music is uniquely concerned with broken homes, abandoned children, and distracted or incapable parents is not to say that this is what all of it is about. Other themes remain a constant,

---

[1]John Metzger, review of "Eminem: the Marshall Mathers I.P.," *Music Box* 8:6 (June 2001).

too, although somewhat more brutally than in the alleged golden era recalled by some baby boomers.

Much of today's metal and hip-hop, like certain music of yesterday, romanticizes illicit drug use and alcohol abuse, and much of current hip-hop sounds certain radical political themes, such as racial separationism and violence against the police. And, of course, the most elementally appealing feature of all, the sexually suggestive beat itself, continues to lure teenagers and young adults in its own right—including those from happy homes. Today as yesterday, plenty of teenagers who don't know or care what the stars are raving about find enough satisfaction in swaying to the sexy music. As professor and intellectual Allan Bloom observed about rock in his bestseller, *The Closing of the American Mind* (Simon & Schuster, 1987), the music "gives children, on a silver platter, with all the public authority of the entertaining industry, everything their parents always used to tell them they had to wait for until they grew up and would understand later."

20   Even so, and putting aside such obvious continuities with previous generations, there is no escaping the fact that today's songs are musically and lyrically unlike any before. What distinguishes them most clearly is the fixation on having been abandoned personally by the adults supposedly in charge, with consequences ranging from bitterness to rage to bad, sick, and violent behavior.

And therein lies a painful truth about an advantage that many teenagers of yesterday enjoyed but their own children often do not. Baby boomers and their music rebelled against parents *because* they were parents—nurturing, attentive, and overly present (as those teenagers often saw it) authority figures. Today's teenagers and their music rebel against parents because they are *not* parents—not nurturing, not attentive, and often not even there. This difference in generational experience may not lend itself to statistical measure, but it is as real as the platinum and gold records that continue to capture it. What those records show compared to yesteryear's rock is emotional downward mobility. Surely if some of the current generation of teenagers and young adults had been better taken care of, then the likes of Kurt Cobain, Eminem, Tupac Shakur, and certain other parental nightmares would have been mere footnotes to recent music history rather than rulers of it.

To step back from the emotional immediacy of those lyrics and to juxtapose the ascendance of such music alongside the long-standing sophisticated assaults on what is sardonically called "family values" is to meditate on a larger irony. As today's music stars and their raving fans likely do not know, many commentators and analysts have been rationalizing every aspect of the adult exodus from home—sometimes celebrating it full throttle, as in the example of working motherhood—longer than most of today's singers and bands have been alive.

Nor do they show much sign of second thoughts. Representative sociologist Stephanie Coontz greeted the year 2004 with one more op-ed piece aimed at burying poor metaphorical Ozzie and Harriet for good. She reminded America again that "changes in marriage and family life" are here to stay and aren't "necessarily a problem"; that what is euphemistically called "family diversity" is or ought to be cause for celebration. Many other scholars and observers—to say nothing of much of polite adult society—agree with Coontz. Throughout the contemporary nonfiction literature written of, by, and for educated adults, a thousand similar rationalizations about family "changes" bloom on.

Meanwhile, a small number of emotionally damaged former children, embraced and adored by millions of teenagers like them, rage on in every commercial medium available about the multiple damages of the disappearance of loving, protective, attentive adults—and they reap a fortune for it. If this spectacle alone doesn't tell us something about the ongoing emotional costs of parent–child separation on today's outsize scale, it's hard to see what could.

Responding to Reading

1. Eberstadt acknowledges in her first paragraph that "contemporary adolescent popular music, especially the subgenres of heavy metal and hip-hop/rap," commonly includes themes of "Misogyny, violence, suicide, sexual exploitation, [and] child abuse. . . ." How does she explain the presence of these themes? In what sense is Eminem "right"?

2. Eberstadt's focus here is not on the effects of music on adolescents but on what it reveals about them. In paragraph 3, she asks, *"What is it about today's music, violent and disgusting though it may be, that resonates with so many American kids?"* How does she answer this question? How would you answer it?

3. In what sense does Eberstadt see today's adolescent music as the music of "abandon*ment*" rather than as the "music of abandon" (5)? How does she believe what she calls "our home-alone world" (6) helps to explain Eminem's violent, misogynistic lyrics? Do you see this essay primarily as a defense of the music of performers like Eminem or as an attack on "irresponsible adults" (7)?

Responding in Writing

Elsewhere in her writing, Eberstadt discusses the lyrics of other musical artists who appeal to today's adolescents, and she argues that their lyrics, like Eminem's, also reveal a preoccupation with family dysfunction and abandonment by parents. Give examples of such lyrics in music you are familiar with, and explain how they support her position.

Editors of the *Rocky Mountain News*

Colorado's first daily newspaper, the Rocky Mountain News, *had been reporting the news for nearly 150 years before its closing in 2009. The following final
edition article, "Goodbye, Colorado," is written in the form of an obituary.*

It is with great sadness that we say
goodbye to you today. Our time
chronicling the life of Denver and Colorado, the nation and the world, is
over. Thousands of men and women
have worked at this newspaper since
William Byers produced its first edition on the banks of Cherry Creek on
April 23, 1859. We speak, we believe,
for all of them, when we say that it has
been an honor to serve you. To have
reached this day, the final edition of
the *Rocky Mountain News*, just 55 days
shy of its 150th birthday is painful. We
will scatter. And all that will be left are
the stories we have told, captured on
microfilm or in digital archives, devices unimaginable in those first days.
But what was present in the paper then and has remained to this day is a
belief in this community and the people who make it what it has become
and what it will be. We part in sorrow because we know so much lies ahead
that will be worth telling, and we will not be there to do so. We have celebrated life in Colorado, praising its ways, but we have warned, too, against
steps we thought were mistaken. We have always been a part of this special place, striving to reflect it accurately and with compassion. We hope
Coloradans will remember this newspaper fondly from generation to generation, a reminder of Denver's history—the ambitions, foibles and virtues
of its settlers and those who followed. We are confident that you will build
on their dreams and find new ways to tell your story. Farewell—and thank
you for so many memorable years together.

Responding to Reading

1. According to the editors, what general contributions has the *Rocky Mountain
    News* made both to Denver and to Colorado? Can you suggest some more
    specific ways in which the newspaper might have benefited the people of
    its city and state?
2. This article, written in the form of an obituary, does not blame anyone (or any-
    thing) for the newspaper's demise. Where do you place the blame? What, if
    anything, do you think could have been done to save the newspaper?
3. In the article's conclusion, the editors say, "We are confident that you will
    . . . find new ways to tell your story." What "new ways" are there to tell this story?

Do you think these "new ways" are as good as (or even better than) the old ways? Explain.

Responding in Writing

Using "Goodbye, Colorado" as a model, write an obituary for a newspaper in your city.

NEWS YOU CAN ENDOW
David Swensen
1954–
Michael Schmidt

David Swensen is the chief investment officer for Yale University, where he also teaches as an adjunct professor of finance. He is the author of Pioneering Portfolio Management: An Unconventional Approach to Institutional Investment *(2000) and* Unconventional Success: A Fundamental Approach to Personal Investment *(2005). Michael Schmidt is a financial analyst for Yale University. In the following essay, Swensen and Schmidt propose a plan to help keep print newspapers afloat in the digital age.*

"The basis of our governments being the opinion of the people, the very first object should be to keep that right," Thomas Jefferson wrote in January 1787. "And were it left to me to decide whether we should have a government without newspapers or newspapers without a government, I should not hesitate to prefer the latter."

Today, we are dangerously close to having a government without newspapers. American newspapers shoulder the burden of considerable indebtedness with little cash on hand, as their profit margins have diminished or disappeared. Readers turn increasingly to the Internet for information—even though the Internet has the potential to be, in the words of the chief executive of Google, Eric Schmidt, "a cesspool" of false information. If Jefferson was right that a well-informed citizenry is the foundation of our democracy, then newspapers must be saved.

Although the problems that the newspaper industry faces are well known, no one has offered a satisfactory solution. But there is an option that might not only save newspapers but also make them stronger: Turn them into nonprofit, endowed institutions—like colleges and universities. Endowments would enhance newspapers' autonomy while shielding them from the economic forces that are now tearing them down.

In the standard business model, newspapers rely on revenues from circulation and advertising to pay for news coverage and generate healthy profits. In the past decade, however, as Americans embraced the Internet, newspaper circulation has declined every year. Advertising revenues, which are tied to circulation levels, fell even faster. Classified ads, in particular, suffered as the Web offered cheaper, easier and more effective alternatives.

5   America's pre-eminent papers exemplify the distress. Average profit margins at *The Washington Post* over the past five years have been about 25 percent less than what they had been in the previous 15 years. At *The New York Times,* the decline was more than 50 percent. The debt-laden Tribune Company, which operates *The Chicago Tribune, The Los Angeles Times* and six other daily papers, has filed for bankruptcy protection.

Newspapers nationwide, struggling to survive the economic turmoil, seek to refinance debt, issue equity and dispose of nonessential assets. These actions are short-term solutions to a systemic problem, Band-Aids for a gaping wound.

News organizations have cut costs, with grave consequences. Over the past three years, *The New York Times, The Wall Street Journal, The Washington Post, The Chicago Tribune, The Los Angeles Times* and *The San Francisco Chronicle* have trimmed their staffs. The number of American correspondents reporting from abroad fell by 25 percent from 2002 to 2006, and only a handful of American newspapers now operate foreign bureaus.

In a move that would have been unthinkable just last year, *The New York Times* recently began selling display advertising on its front page. Some papers have even shrunk physically, eliminating sections and decreasing paper size.

As long as newspapers remain for-profit enterprises, they will find no refuge from their financial problems. The advertising revenues that newspaper Web sites generate are not enough to sustain robust news coverage. Though *The New York Times* Web site attracted 20 million unique users in October, Web-driven revenues support only an estimated 20 percent of the paper's current staff.

10   As newspapers go digital, their business model erodes. A 2008 research report from Sanford C. Bernstein & Company explained, "The notion that the enormous cost of real news-gathering might be supported by the ad load of display advertising down the side of the page, or by the revenue share from having a Google search box in the corner of the page, or even by a 15-second teaser from Geico prior to a news clip, is idiotic on its face."

By endowing our most valued sources of news we would free them from the strictures of an obsolete business model and offer them a permanent place in society, like that of America's colleges and universities. Endowments would transform newspapers into unshakable fixtures of American life, with greater stability and enhanced independence that would allow them to serve the public good more effectively.

As educational and literary organizations devoted to the "promotion of social welfare," endowed newspapers would benefit from Section 501(c)(3) of the I.R.S. code, which provides exemption from taxes on income and allows tax deductions for people who make contributions to eligible organizations.

One constraint on an endowed institution is the prohibition in the same law against trying to "influence legislation" or "participate in any campaign activity for or against political candidates." While endowed newspapers would need to refrain from endorsing candidates for public office, they would still be free to participate forcefully in the debate over issues of public importance. The loss of endorsements seems minor in the context of the opinion-heavy Web.

Aside from providing stability, an endowment would promote journalistic independence. The best-run news organizations insulate reporters from pressures to produce profits or to placate advertisers. But endowed news organizations would be in an ideal situation—with no pressure from stockholders or advertisers at all.

How large an endowment would a newspaper need? The news- 15 gathering operations at *The New York Times* cost a little more than $200 million a year. Assuming some additional outlay for overhead, it would require an endowment of approximately $5 billion (assuming a 5 percent annual payout rate). Newspapers with smaller newsrooms would require smaller endowments.

Note that just as endowed educational institutions charge tuition, endowed newspapers would generate incremental revenues from hardcopy sales and online subscriptions. If revenues were to exceed the costs of distribution, the endowment requirement would decline.

Many newspapers will not weather the digital storm on their own. Only a handful of foundations and wealthy individuals have the money required to endow, and thereby preserve, our nation's premier news-gathering organizations. Enlightened philanthropists must act now or watch a vital component of American democracy fade into irrelevance.

Responding to Reading

1. Why do Swensen and Schmidt believe that "newspapers must be saved" (2)? According to the authors, why isn't the Internet a satisfactory substitute for newspapers? Do you agree?
2. How do the authors propose to avoid the problem of "a government without newspapers" (2)? What advantages do they see in their proposal? Do they acknowledge any drawbacks?
3. The authors' argument rests in part on the notion that newspapers have a "place in society" that is similar to that of "America's colleges and universities" (11). How is the role of newspapers in American society analogous to the role of institutions of higher learning? Are there any differences between the two that might challenge Swensen and Schmidt's position?

Responding in Writing

Imagine that you are a professional fund-raiser who is appealing for funds to support a particular local or national newspaper. Write a letter to potential donors explaining why their financial support is needed and what it might accomplish.

THE UNIVERSE OF MEANING
Stephen Roxburgh
1950–

*Stephen Roxburgh is the president and founder of namelos, a group of inde-
pendent publishing specialists who produce books for children and young
adults. Previously, he published children's and young adult books for Boyds
Mills Press; Front Street Books; and Farrar, Straus and Giroux. In the following short essay, Roxburgh considers traditional print books alongside the
Kindle, Amazon's handheld wireless reading device.*

I love my Kindle (and most other mechanical and digital gadgets), but let's
step away from the hardware. And, for the moment, let's not engage in
the "death of the book as we know it" debate. Technology is the means to
an end, and not necessarily the end of a means. Think about the fact that
people still walk, bicycle, ride horses, drive cars, take trains, and fly to get
where they are going. When we read, we have a goal in mind. We are going
somewhere. One model of reading suggests that it is a process of decoding the surface structure of words to get to their deep semantic structure—
i.e., their meaning. The more experienced we are as readers, the more
transparent that process becomes. We lose our awareness of the process
and immediately engage the meaning. In other words, we just go there. In
*Star Trek*ian terms, we are instantly transported, "beaming up" from one
place to emerge in another. Once you enter J. R. R. Tolkien's Middle-earth,
or Daphne du Maurier's Manderley, or Anthony Trollope's Barchester, or
T. S. Eliot's Waste Land, you are unconscious of the mechanism that got you
there. Once you know the stock price of Microsoft, or the definition of
peregrination, or the atomic weight of molybdenum, or Genghis Khan's
birth date, you know it. How you got it is incidental. So, the crux of the matter is where you want to go. Why are you going there? How quickly do you
need to get there? Are you going to hang around for a while? Will you be
going back? What's the cost of the trip? I'll hang on to my Folio Club edition of *Middlemarch,* my tattered paperback of *Four Quartets,* my Uncle
Scrooge comic books, my laptop, my iTouch, and my Kindle. If you think
about it, all media and all mechanisms have a place in the universe of
meaning—and isn't it neat that we have so many ways to get around in it?

Responding to Reading

1. Paraphrase Roxburgh's basic premise. Do you agree with him, or do you
   think he is oversimplifying a complex issue?
2. Does Roxburgh's analogy between methods of transportation and methods
   of reading make sense to you? Why or why not?
3. Do you think print books have a future? Explain your conclusion.

Responding in Writing

Write a paragraph about some of the worlds to which you have been "instantly transported" in books. Do you believe, as Roxburgh does, that all that matters is that you got to those places, or do you believe *how* you got there also matters?

DEAR JOHN WAYNE
Louise Erdrich
1954–

*A poet and novelist who belongs to the Turtle Mountain Band of Chippewa,
Louise Erdrich writes about the Native American experience. She has published numerous books, including, most recently,* The Game of Silence
(2005), The Painted Drum *(2005),* The Plague of Doves *(2008), and* The
Porcupine Year *(2008). The following poem explores the meaning of a popular American cultural icon.*

August and the drive-in picture is packed.
We lounge on the hood of the Pontiac
surrounded by the slow-burning spirals they sell
at the window, to vanquish the hordes of mosquitoes.
5   Nothing works. They break through the smoke-screen for blood.

Always the look-out spots the Indians first,
spread north to south, barring progress.
The Sioux, or Cheyenne, or some bunch
in spectacular columns, arranged like SAC missiles,[1]
10   their feathers bristling in the meaningful sunset.

The drum breaks. There will be no parlance.
Only the arrows whining, a death-cloud of nerves
swarming down on the settlers
who die beautifully, tumbling like dust weeds
15   into the history that brought us all here
together: this wide screen beneath the sign of the bear.

The sky fills, acres of blue squint and eye
that the crowd cheers. His face moves over us,
a thick cloud of vengeance, pitted
20   like the land that was once flesh. Each rut,
each scar makes a promise: *It is
not over, this fight, not as long as you resist.*

Everything we see belongs to us.
A few laughing Indians fall over the hood
25   slipping in the hot spilled butter.

---

[1]Ballistic missles used by the United States Strategic Air Command (SAC). [Eds.]

The eye sees a lot, John, but the heart is so blind.
How will you know what you own?
He smiles, a horizon of teeth
the credits reel over, and then the white fields
again blowing in the true-to-life dark.   30
The dark films over everything.
We get into the car
scratching our mosquito bites, speechless and small
as people are when the movie is done.
We are back in ourselves.   35

How can we help but keep hearing his voice,
the flip side of the sound-track, still playing:
Come on, boys, we've got them
where we want them, drunk, running.
They will give us what we want, what we need: 40
The heart is a strange wood inside of everything
we see, burning, doubling, splitting out of its skin.

Responding to Reading

1. How are Native Americans portrayed in the film the speaker discusses? What image is presented of the Native Americans who watch the film (and other films like it)? Why do you think the audience is laughing at what they see onscreen?
2. Do you think this poem's central focus is on how movies portray the conflict between whites and Native Americans or on Native Americans' reactions to the images they see? Explain your reasoning.
3. Look online for general information about John Wayne and his roles in Western films. What kind of roles did he play? How do these roles explain why Erdrich's speaker addresses her comments to him?

Responding in Writing

Write a "Dear _____" email to a movie actor whose typical roles you object to for some reason—for example, because they stereotype or demean a group of people or because they are overly violent.

——————————— FOCUS ———————————

Does Social Networking Connect Us or Keep Us Apart?

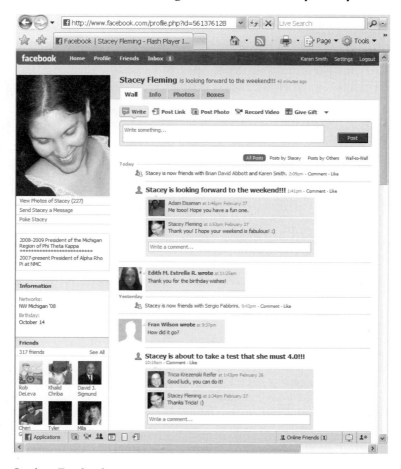

Student Facebook page

Responding to the Image

1. What information does this student supply about herself on her Facebook page? What additional information can you infer about her? How? What do you suppose Alice Mathias (p. 239) would say about this page?

2. This student has 317 friends, some of whom are pictured, and visitors to her page are able to see the names of Stacey's newest friends. Look carefully at the posted comments. Which sound as if they were written by friends? Which sound like the voices of acquaintances? Is there a difference?

THE FAKEBOOK GENERATION
Alice Mathias

Formerly a columnist for the Dartmouth Mirror, *Dartmouth College's weekly magazine, Alice Mathias graduated from Dartmouth in 2007 with a degree in creative writing and film and television. She has contributed to the* New York Times *blog the* Graduates, *which focuses on students' experiences and challenges as they prepare to graduate from college. In the following essay, Mathias discusses the Facebook phenomenon.*

The time-chugging Web site Facebook.com first appeared during my freshman year as the exclusive domain of college students. This spring, Facebook opened its pearly gates, enabling myself and other members of the class of '07 to graduate from our college networks into those of the real world.

In no time at all, the Web site has convinced its rapidly assembling adult population that it is a forum for genuine personal and professional connections. Its founder, Mark Zuckerberg, has even declared his quest to chart a "social graph" of human relationships the way that cartographers once charted the world.

Just a warning: if you're planning on following the corner of this map that's been digitally doodled by my 659 Facebook friends, you are going to end up in the middle of nowhere. All the rhetoric about human connectivity misses the real reason this popular online study buddy has so distracted college students for the past four years.

Facebook did not become popular because it was a functional tool— after all, most college students live in close quarters with the majority of their Facebook friends and have no need for social networking. Instead, we log into the Web site because it's entertaining to watch a constantly evolving narrative starring the other people in the library.

I've always thought of Facebook as online community theater. In costumes we customize in a backstage makeup room—the Edit Profile page, where we can add a few Favorite Books or touch up our About Me section—we deliver our lines on the very public stage of friends' walls or photo albums. And because every time we join a network, post a link or make another friend it's immediately made visible to others via the News Feed, every Facebook act is a soliloquy to our anonymous audience.

It's all comedy: making one another laugh matters more than providing useful updates about ourselves, which is why entirely phony profiles were all the rage before the grown-ups signed in. One friend announced her status as In a Relationship with Chinese Food, whose profile picture was a carry-out box and whose personal information personified the cuisine of China.

5

CHAPTER 4 FOCUS

We even make a joke out of how we know one another—claiming to have met in "Intro to Super Mario Re-enactments," which I seriously doubt is a real course at Wesleyan, or to have lived together in a "spay and neuter clinic" instead of the dorm. Still, these humor bits often reveal more about our personalities and interests than any honest answers.

Facebook administrators have since exiled at least the flagrantly fake profiles, the Greta Garbos and the I Can't Believe It's Not Butters, in an effort to have the site grow up from a farce into the serious social networking tool promised to its new adult users, who earnestly type in their actual personal information and precisely label everyone they know as former co-workers or current colleagues, family members or former lovers.

But does this more reverent incarnation of Facebook actually enrich adult relationships? What do these constellations of work colleagues and long-lost friends amount to? An online office mixer? A reunion with that one other guy from your high school who has a Facebook profile? Oh! You get to see pictures of your former college sweetheart's family! (Only depressing possibilities are coming to mind for some reason.)

10   My generation has long been bizarrely comfortable with being looked at, and as performers on the Facebook stage, we upload pictures of ourselves cooking dinner for our parents or doing keg stands at last night's party; we are reckless with our personal information. But there is one area of privacy that we won't surrender: the secrecy of how and whom we search.

A friend of mine was recently in a panic over rumors of a hacker application that would allow Facebook users to see who's been visiting their profiles. She'd spent the day ogling a love interest's page and was horrified at the idea that he knew she'd been looking at him. But there's no way Facebook would allow such a program to exist: the site is popular largely because it enables us to indulge our gazes anonymously. (We might feel invulnerable in the spotlight, but we don't want to be caught sitting in someone else's audience.) If our ability to privately search is ever jeopardized, Facebook will turn into a ghost town.

Facebook purports to be a place for human connectivity, but it's made us more wary of real human confrontation. When I was in college, people always warned against the dangers of "Facebook stalking" at a library computer—the person whose profile you're perusing might be right behind you. Dwelling online is a cowardly and utterly enjoyable alternative to real interaction.

So even though Facebook offers an elaborate menu of privacy settings, many of my friends admit that the only setting they use is the one that prevents people from seeing that they are Currently Logged In. Perhaps we fear that the Currently Logged In feature advertises to everyone else that we (too!) are Currently Bored, Lustful, Socially Unfulfilled or Generally Avoiding Real Life.

For young people, Facebook is yet another form of escapism; we can turn our lives into stage dramas and relationships into comedy routines. Make believe is not part of the postgraduate Facebook user's agenda. As more and more older users try to turn Facebook into a legitimate social reference guide, younger people may follow suit and stop treating it as a circus ring. But let's hope not.

Responding to Reading

1. Why does Mathias refer to Facebook as "Fakebook" in her essay's title? In what sense are she and her friends part of the "Fakebook Generation"? For example, do you think she sees herself and her friends as creative? As narcissistic?
2. What, according to Mathias, is "the real reason" Facebook has become so popular (3)? In what respects is Facebook a kind of "online community theater" (5)?
3. In paragraph 12, Mathias says, "Facebook purports to be a place for human connectivity, but it's made us more wary of real human confrontation." What does she mean? Can you think of examples besides the one she supplies to illustrate her statement? Which examples cited by Brent Staples (p. 241) would also support her statement?

Responding in Writing

In paragraph 9, Mathias asks, "But does . . . Facebook actually enrich adult relationships?" Write a paragraph arguing that it does.

WHAT ADOLESCENTS MISS WHEN WE LET THEM GROW UP IN CYBERSPACE

Brent Staples

1951–

After earning a Ph.D. in psychology from the University of Chicago in 1977, Brent Staples turned to journalism, writing for the Chicago Sun-Times *and the* New York Times. *In 1990, he joined the editorial board of the* New York Times, *where his columns now appear regularly. In the following* Times *column, Staples argues that so-called online communities isolate adolescents and hinder their social development.*

My 10th-grade heartthrob was the daughter of a fearsome steel-worker who struck terror into the hearts of 15-year-old boys. He made it his business to answer the telephone—and so always knew who was calling—and grumbled in the background when the conversation went on too long. Unable to make time by phone, the boy either gave up or appeared at the front door. This meant submitting to the intense scrutiny that the girl's father soon became known for.

He greeted me with a crushing handshake, then leaned in close in a transparent attempt to find out whether I was one of those *bad* boys who smoked. He retired to the den during the visit, but cruised by the living room now and then to let me know he was watching. He let up after some weeks, but only after getting across what he expected of a boy who spent time with his daughter and how upset he'd be if I disappointed him.

This was my first sustained encounter with an adult outside my family who needed to be convinced of my worth as a person. This, of course, is a crucial part of growing up. Faced with same challenge to day, however, I would probably pass on meeting the girl's father—and outflank him on the Internet.

Thanks to e-mail, online chat rooms and instant messages—which permit private, real-time conservations—adolescents have at last succeeded in shielding their social lives from adult scrutiny. But this comes at a cost: teenagers nowadays are both more connected to the world at large than ever, and more cut off from the social encounters that have historically prepared young people for the move into adulthood.

5   The Internet was billed as a revolutionary way to enrich our social lives and expand our civic connections. This seems to have worked well for elderly people and others who were isolated before they got access to the World Wide Web. But a growing body of research is showing that heavy use of the Net can actually isolate younger socially connected people who unwittingly allow time online to replace face-to-face interactions with their families and friends.

Online shopping, checking e-mail and Web surfing—mainly solitary activities—have turned out to be more isolating than watching television, which friends and family often do in groups. Researchers have found that the time spent in direct contact with family members drops by as much as half for every hour we use the Net at home.

This should come as no surprise to the two-career couples who have seen their domestic lives taken over by e-mail and wireless tethers that keep people working around the clock. But a startling body of research from the Human-Computer Interaction Institute at Carnegie Mellon has shown that heavy Internet use can have stunting effect outside the home as well.

Studies show that gregarious, well-connected people actually lost friends, and experienced symptoms of loneliness and depression, after joining discussion groups and other activities. People who communicated with disembodied strangers online found the experience empty and emotionally frustrating but were nonetheless seduced by the novelty of the new medium. As Prof. Robert Kraut, a Carnegie Mellon researcher, told me recently, such people allowed low-quality relationships developed in virtual reality to replace higher-quality relationships in the real world.

No group has embraced this socially impoverishing trade-off more enthusiastically than adolescents, many of whom spend most of their free hours cruising the Net in sunless rooms. This hermetic existence has left many of these teenagers with nonexistent social skills—a point widely noted in stories about the computer geeks who rose to prominence in the early days of Silicon Valley.

Adolescents are drawn to cyberspace for different reasons than 10 adults. As the writer Michael Lewis observed in his book "Next: The Future Just Happened," children see the Net as a transformational device that lets them discard quotidian identities for more glamorous ones. Mr. Lewis illustrated the point with Marcus Arnold, who, as a 15-year-old, adopted a pseudonym a few years ago and posed as a 25-year-old legal expert for an Internet information service. Marcus did not feel the least bit guilty, and wasn't deterred, when real-world lawyers discovered his secret and accused him of being a fraud. When asked whether he had actually read the law, Marcus responded that he found books "boring," leaving us to conclude that he had learned all he needed to know from his family's big-screen TV.

Marcus is a child of the Net, where everyone has a pseudonym, telling a story makes it true, and adolescents create older, cooler, more socially powerful selves any time they wish. The ability to slip easily into a new, false self is tailor-made for emotionally fragile adolescents, who can consider a bout of acne or a few excess pounds an unbearable tragedy.

But teenagers who spend much of their lives hunched over computer screens miss the socializing, the real-world experience that would allow them to leave adolescence behind and grow into adulthood. These vital experiences, like much else, are simply not available in a virtual form.

Responding to Reading

1. In paragraph 4, Staples says that "teenagers nowadays are both more connected to the world at large than ever, and more cut off from the social encounters that have historically prepared young people for the move into adulthood." What does he mean? Do you think he is right?
2. Staples believes that the Internet essentially isolates adolescents, who "unwittingly allow time online to replace face-to-face interactions" (5); in paragraph 9, he refers to this replacement as a "socially impoverishing trade-off." How might Reid Goldsborough (p. 250) respond to the notion of the Internet as a "replacement" for social interaction?
3. Throughout his essay, Staples refers to "a growing body of research" (5) that supports his position. What research does he cite? Do you find it convincing? Why or why not?

Responding in Writing

Write a paragraph with the title, "What Adolescents Gain When We Let Them Grow Up in Cyberspace."

TO TWITTER OR NOT TO TWITTER?

Robert W. Lucky

1936–

Robert W. Lucky is the corporate vice president of applied research at Telcordia Technologies, a fellow of the Institute of Electrical and Electronics Engineers (IEEE), and a member of the National Academy of Engineering as well as the American and European Academies of Arts and Sciences. An engineer who writes and speaks on issues related to technology, Lucky is the author of Silicon Dreams: Information, Man, and Machine *(1989) and* Lucky Strikes . . . Again *(1993). In the following essay, Lucky examines the popularity of Twitter.*

Twitter, the social-networking Web site that allows users to broadcast short text messages to a group of friends, has burst into popularity with millions of subscribers. I'm a confirmed e-mail user, but that's so 20th century. I feel a certain pressure to get with it. So, to Twitter or not to Twitter? I view it as a question for the ages—the ages of the users, that is.

It was my generation of engineers that created the Internet, but it is largely today's youth who are molding the social connectedness that is coming to characterize cyberspace. These are the so-called digital natives, who grew up with the Internet already a part of everyday life. They're always online, inhabiting multiple identities, living a culture of sharing and peer collaboration. For them, multitasking is just the way it is. We older engineers built cyberspace, but our kids live in it, and for many of them the technology is transparent and almost irrelevant.

So as a digital immigrant, already an adult as the new culture was forming, I am amazed at what I see. At a recent meeting a young speaker casually mentioned that every morning he Twitters that he has just woken up. Alarm bells went off in my head. I thought about the fact that several scores of people are going to read a message that this guy has awakened. Isn't this is an incredible waste of time for everyone involved? But a more unpleasant thought also formed in the back of my head—the worry that no one would care that I myself had just arisen. There must be some social consequence that I'm missing. An older acquaintance told me that he had been using Twitter and that after a week he had begun to feel a sense of connectedness.

At this same meeting, another young speaker berated the whole audience of industry leaders. "I was told this was a conference of executives, so I'm going to talk slow and use big slides," he began. "You are living in a bubble. You come here to find out what kids do. You guys are pencil pushers. You're forced to make money." I shrank in my seat, blanking out the rest of this tirade while testing unspoken counterarguments. And I wonder: years from now will this young person adopt the ways of us older workers, or are we seeing the rise of an entirely new social fabric?

Later, I discussed a forthcoming meeting with other organizers. 5 Should we encourage the audience to Twitter during the next meeting? On the one hand, we felt this would distract from our speakers. Moreover, we had reviewed the unsolicited Twitters during a previous meeting and concluded that they were largely vacuous. On the other hand, perhaps the Twitters encouraged engagement. And anyway, how could we deny a growing use of that technology in a technology meeting? Alas, we could draw no rational conclusion other than to designate a "tag" for that particular meeting for Twitters to congregate around. We're in the middle of something happening around us, and we don't really understand the consequences.

I am constantly fascinated with the development of the sociology of the Web. Perhaps two insightful cartoons from *The New Yorker* illustrate the evolution. In 1993, the magazine published Peter Steiner's famous cartoon of two dogs at a computer, one saying to the other, "On the Internet,

"On the Internet, nobody knows you're a dog."

CHAPTER 4 FOCUS

nobody knows you're a dog." At that time the Internet was relatively young, and we all rejoiced in the unbridled freedom the cartoon embraced.

By 2005, in the same magazine, Alex Gregory had a cartoon with two dogs (I'm thinking the same dogs!) at a computer. One says to the other, "I had my own blog for a while, but I decided to go back to just pointless, incessant barking."

So is the networking phenomenon a great revolution in social consciousness, or is this just a lot of pointless, incessant barking? If you get a message that I've just awakened, you'll know what I've decided.

"I had my own blog for a while, but I decided to go back to just pointless, incessant barking."

Responding to Reading

1. According to Lucky, what is a "digital native" (2)? Why does Lucky see himself as a "digital immigrant" (3)? How do these terms help you understand the distinction he is making?
2. What do you think Lucky means when he says that for young people "the technology [of cyberspace] is transparent and almost irrelevant" (2)? Do you think he is correct?
3. Look carefully at the two cartoons in this essay. How do they illustrate the evolution of the culture of the Web? How do you think the other writers in this Focus section would respond to the cartoons?

Responding in Writing

Do you see Twitter and other social networking sites as "a great revolution in social consciousness" or as "just a lot of pointless, incessant barking" (8)?

DOES SOCIAL NETWORKING REALLY CONNECT YOU TO HUMANITY?

Dave Taylor

1962–

Dave Taylor is an author of numerous books on computer technology, including The Complete Idiot's Guide to Growing Your Business with Google *(2005). Coauthored with Linda S. Sanford, his most recent book,* Let Go to Grow: Escaping the Commodity Trap *(2006), examines issues related to business and technology. In the following essay, Taylor examines the ways in which several social networking sites succeed or fail in helping to create and support meaningful relationships.*

Let me start out with a confession. I'm about as plugged in to the computer networks as anyone you're likely to meet. I first connected to the Internet back in 1980, when it was the ARPAnet and commercial use was completely verboten. Yes, it's come a long way, and so has our society.

Nowadays, professionals are just as likely to have their Facebook or LinkedIn URL on their business cards as a phone number, and entire conferences seem to be run simultaneously in both the physical world and as a running, often snarky, stream-of-consciousness dialog on the microblogging service Twitter.

But all of this begs the question: are we really more connected? Do computer and social networks *really make us more connected as human beings?*

MySpace Redefined Friendship

One of the first phenomena you notice when you start to connect with people through web sites that are designed to memorialize connections is that the word "friend" takes on a different meaning. In the physical world—what people in the virtual reality world of Second Life call "RL," or real life—friends are generally defined as those people you have a personal relationship with, not anyone you happen to encounter, anyone at your college, company, or other organizations. The latter are colleagues or acquaintances or just people with whom you have something in common.

The first popular sites to delve into the world of friendship, of letting you quantify and identify your circle of friends, were Friendster, which is now essentially defunct, having long-since fallen out of the zeitgeist, and MySpace. On these sites every connection you made had a similar strength, so your best friend Mike is considered just as important in your life as Aunt Flo, with whom you've connected to stop her complaining at family gatherings.

5

In real life, of course, we all have close, important friends, intimates who are privy to the highs and lows of our lives, a larger circle of what we can call "pretty good" friends who can help out in a crunch but with whom we don't interact regularly and, finally, "almost friends" who are people with whom we feel an affinity but geography, time, or other logistical issues prevent us from becoming closer. And then there are the ever more nebulous circles of acquaintances, colleagues, and so on.

The Kevin Bacon Effect

Very little research in sociology has caught the public fancy as much as the early work by Harvard social psychologist Stanley Milgram, in which he posited that we all are far more connected than we realize. His famous 1967 Small World Experiment, in which randomly-chosen Midwesterners hand-delivered letters to Bostonians they didn't know through a chain of friends, produced the conclusion that people in the United States are separated by about six people on average.

A variety of flaws have been found with Milgram's research, but whether we're connected through six hops, eight hops, or 17, the basic idea that social chains are sufficiently all-encompassing that you and I can find a sequence of friends or acquaintances to connect us is fascinating. Make the end point well-known actor Kevin Bacon and you have a party game: "Six Degrees of Kevin Bacon," or "the Kevin Bacon Effect."

It was this question of how to gain access to your friends' friends, or, more accurately, the connections of your connections, that has become the basis of LinkedIn, a social network that lets you answer the question, "I wonder if any of my friends know someone who . . ."

10   The numbers quickly grow at an extraordinary rate. For instance, I have 705 connections on LinkedIn. Take one further step out onto that social network and that gives me more than 330,000 people in my immediate network. Take an additional step out—we'd call these friends of friends of friends, I suppose—and the number is a staggering 8,392,600 connections.

What does that mean? Am I obligated to send holiday cards to them all or keep track of their birthdays? I sure hope not!

Because they're not friends. While they offer up a tremendous professional resource, they don't in any fundamental way expand my social or personal network. They don't connect me with the greater humanity.

In case you're wondering, Facebook isn't any better. You can certainly join many, many different circles of common interests through mailing lists, applications, and other tools, but it's still a very abstract, intellectual world. Of my 358 Facebook friends, I wouldn't recognize at least 25 percent if we bumped into each other at the local Starbucks.

Do Any Social Networking Sites Really Make a Human Connection?

So if we're trying to determine what sites help us become less socially isolated, rather than gaining the appearance of more friends while still leaving us as disconnected as before, perhaps the answer lies in dating sites? After all, those are sites where we connect with others because of either an existing or desired personal connection. But that's still not right because, with the exception of novel sites like Ignighter.com, they are focused on whom you *want* to know, not whom you already know.

Other possibilities are lightweight social networks like Twitter. The 15 idea behind sites like Twitter is that it would be useful and interesting to be able to keep tabs on your friends as you all go through your day. Spontaneous meet-ups, collaboration, and mutual support all easily flow from this sort of connectivity.

Twitter indeed fulfills some of peoples' desire to be connected, especially with its great strength as a mobile application. It's interesting to see how this will evolve too, however, particularly in light of our quest for online tools that help us truly connect with humanity. Case in point: I keep track of slightly more than 100 friends, all of whom I *would* recognize at a party, but more than 2,000 people keep track of what I am saying and doing. I'm connected, and yet I'm not . . . at least not really, and certainly not to the degree you might infer from those numbers.

Is Social Media About Measuring Friendships?

As we explore the landscape of social media and social networks, whether it's the immediacy of Twitter or the businesslike utility of LinkedIn, what has become clear is that these tools need to let us differentiate between close friends and acquaintances and to rate the strength of our connection. Without that capability, everyone's in the same proverbial pool; my connection with my close friend Richard is identical to my new connection with members of Phi Kappa Phi's editorial staff.

That being the case, you need to make a decision, preferably before you proceed to enmesh yourself in a social network, as to whether it will capture everyone you know and have more than a passing acquaintance with, or whether you will restrict it to only your closest friends.

In the social network world we refer to this as *quality versus quantity,* and there are strong arguments for each approach. To wit: a quality approach ensures that every single person on your list will help you move or offer up their couch when times are tough, while a quantity approach means you always have a large circle of people to invite to parties and solicit for business opportunities. But what I want, predictably, is both. Quality gets you the connection with humanity, the ability to stay in closer touch with intimate friends. Quantity offers all the benefits of our modern, highly connected world.

Chapter 4 Focus

20   How to attain both? Well, we're still at the veritable infancy of social networks so I'm pushing their edges and watching it all evolve on a weekly basis.

So which tool connects us more? I could waffle at this point and say that any tool can connect you more with your fellow human beings, depending on how you use it, but instead I'll state directly that it's the small, high-interaction tools like Twitter (and, by extension, the short status updates that a small percentage of Facebook users can utilize for a similar purpose) that let you gain insight into the lives of your digital friends and nurture those relationships into full-blown friendship.

Responding to Reading

1. In paragraph 1, Taylor establishes himself as "about as plugged in . . . as anyone [readers are] likely to meet." Why does he think this statement is necessary?
2. Taylor discusses MySpace, LinkedIn, and Twitter. Does he have the same reservations about all three of these sites, or does he seem to believe one is more effective at making connections than the others? Do you think one of these sites is better than the others at forging connections? Why?
3. How does Milgram's "Small World Experiment" (7) help to explain the appeal of today's social networking sites?

Responding in Writing

One point Taylor makes in this essay is that social networking sites "need to let us differentiate between close friends and acquaintances and to rate the strength of our connection" (17). How do people you know make these distinctions in face-to-face communication? What might social networking sites do to make it easier for their members to make such distinctions?

SOCIAL NETWORKING: CROSSING DIGITAL DIVIDE CAN PAY DIVIDENDS

Reid Goldsborough

1955–

Reid Goldsborough is the author of the syndicated column Personal Computing, *which appears in more than twenty publications, as well as the book* Straight Talk about the Information Superhighway *(1994). His articles have appeared in such publications as* PC World, Internet World, Yahoo Internet Life, *and* MSNBC Interactive. *In the following essay, Goldsborough examines the generation gap in relation to social networking sites.*

There's always been a generation gap, more or less, with the younger generation trying to improve on the latter. Seeing things differently and trying for new solutions to old problems can be seen as agents of progress.

Today's generation gap manifests itself perhaps most with digital social networking. Unlike in the 1960s, when those younger than 30 couldn't trust those older about politics, lifestyles and other issues, today's young people are more likely to heavily use digital social networks whereas those older are less likely.

Whether the digital device used for social networking is a cell phone, MP3 player or personal computer connected to such Web-based social networking services as MySpace (www.myspace.com) and Facebook (www.facebook.com), the imperative is to stay connected. Social scientists call it "ambient awareness."

It can get taken to an absurd extreme. For instance, when you're waiting in line as an 18-year-old clerk texts his buddy about the moron he just waited on—the customer standing in front of you—it can elicit the same annoyance in you, for the very same reason, as that previous customer experienced.

Are other people really interested in the mundane minute-by-minute minutiae of your existence?   5

Apparently the answer is "yes," judging by the popularity of such newer offerings as Twitter (www.twitter.com), which promotes itself as a "microblogging" service where you can stay "hyper-connected" to your friends.

People use Twitter, a free advertising-supported service, by sending and receiving short text messages, 140 words or less, using a PC or cell phone, about what they're doing. It even includes the question, "What are you doing?" after its name in the title line of its web site. As of this writing, more than two million people have signed up to use Twitter to broadcast, you guessed it, what they're doing.

The absurdity, or fun, of spending your time this way gets hotly debated online, as does just about everything else. The sometimes nonverbal context of the debate relates to age, with many older folks regarding digital social networking as narcissistic and many younger folks contending their elders just don't get it.

The fact is that new techniques have always been adopted more readily by young people.

Computer-phobia has been around since the inception of computers, and it afflicts those who came of age using typewriters and slide rules much more than those weaned on PCs.   10

The adage about old dogs and new tricks is partially true here. Older folks tend to get complacent, finding what works and sticking to it, which can sometimes land them in a rut. Young people, with minds more malleable, have an easier time learning new ways. Trying out the new, however, takes not only intellectual curiosity but also time, which younger people typically have more of than those with jobs, families to support and other responsibilities.

Still, even with people pressed for time, digital social networks can be useful. Many people, both young and mature, have reported using these services to find jobs, an online extension and improvement of traditional networking using the phone, the mail and the visit. Those who travel a lot through their jobs or are self-employed use digital social networks as a weapon against solitude.

Just as with other forms of online communication, digital social networking can be a good way to get consumer advice when making a purchase and point you in the right direction or provide support when confronting a health problem.

No matter what your age, social networking works best socially when it brings people together in real life. It can be a great way, for instance, to quickly organize a social event among your friends, from a dinner party to a meeting at a local club.

15   Despite its reliance on cutting-edge technology, digital social networking can take you back in time, adding a small-town flavor to your life, where your circle knows everything about everybody, for better or worse. Frequently updating others on what you're up to can also increase your self-awareness, helping you take stock and make better choices in the future.

As with many things, balance here is key. Digital social networks used judiciously can improve the quality of life. But they shouldn't replace face time—contact of the genuine kind. One of the negative consequences of the computer revolution is the digital shut-in.

In Isaac Asimov's 1957 novel *The Naked Sun*, people avoid personal contact in the flesh and relate to one another through holographic projection. That's one computer-aided future best relegated to science fiction.

Responding to Reading

1. What is the nature of the "generation gap" Goldsborough identifies (2)? How does it apply to digital social networks? Do your own observations support or challenge the existence of this generation gap?
2. In what sense does Goldsborough see social networking as useful? Can you suggest additional advantages of social networking?
3. Why does Goldsborough refer to Asimov's *The Naked Sun* in his conclusion? Is this conclusion necessary, or would the essay make its point just as effectively without this paragraph?

Responding in Writing

In paragraph 16, Goldsborough says, "Digital social networks used judiciously can improve the quality of life. But they shouldn't replace face time—contact of the genuine kind." Given your own experience, do you think the balance he advocates is possible?

WIDENING THE FOCUS

For Critical Reading and Writing

Do you think social networking sites bring people together, or do you think they ultimately make it possible for them to avoid face-to-face communication? Write an essay that answers this question, referring to the selections by Alice Mathias ("The Fakebook Generation"), Brent Staples ("What Adolescents Miss When We Let Them Grow Up in Cyberspace"), Robert W. Lucky ("To Twitter or Not to Twitter?"), Dave Taylor ("Does Social Networking Really Connect You to Humanity?"), and Reid Goldsborough ("Social Networking: Crossing Digital Divide Can Pay Dividends").

For Further Reading

The following readings can suggest additional perspectives for reading and writing about the kinds of communities created online—and how they are different from face-to-face communities.

- Amy Ma, "My Grandmother's Dumpling" (p. 18)
- Lynda Barry, "The Sanctuary of School" (p. 61)
- William C. Symonds, Brian Grow, and John Cady, "Earthly Empires" (p. 544)

For Focused Research

The question of whether social networking helps to foster meaningful connections or whether it creates new levels of isolation is a complicated one. One thing is certain: online social networking sites abound, and more and more Web space is being devoted to services and resources that allow users to interact online. In 2009, Google started its Social Web Blog "for anyone interested or involved in helping to make the web more social." Its introductory post asks users to "Tell us about what you've been doing to make the web more social, what you've seen others successfully do, or simply what you think about our posts." Visit Google's Social Web Blog http://googlesocialweb.blogspot.com/ and read the introductory blog posting as well as several user responses. Then, post an entry in which you assess the value of an online space such as this one for connecting people online.

CHAPTER 4   FOCUS

─────────────── **WRITING** ───────────────

Media and Society

1. What do you think the impact of the various media discussed in this chapter will be in the years to come? What trends do you see emerging that you believe will change the way you think or the way you live? Write an essay in which you speculate about future trends and their impact, using the essays in this chapter by Robert W. Lucky (p. 244) and Michael Hirschorn (p. 218) to support the points you make.

2. Write an essay in which you consider the representation of a particular ethnic or racial group (or the portrayal of women, the elderly, or people with disabilities) in movies, on television, or in magazine ads. Do you believe the group you have chosen to write about is adequately represented? Do you think its members are portrayed fairly and accurately, or do you think they are stereotyped? Support your conclusions with specific examples. Before you begin, read "Dear John Wayne" (p. 236).

3. Should the government continue to support public television and radio? What, if anything, do public radio and television provide that commercial programming does not offer? (Before beginning this essay, compare newspaper listings of public and commercial programming, and try to spend a few hours screening public television and radio programs if you are not familiar with them.)

4. Do you think newspapers will survive in their present form, or do you believe that the Internet threatens their survival? Do you believe newspapers *should* survive—that is, that they are necessary? Read "Goodbye, Colorado" (p. 230) and "News You Can Endow" (p. 231) before you write your essay.

5. What kind of "family values" are promoted on television? Would you say that TV is largely "profamily" or "antifamily"? Using the essays in this chapter by Winn (p. 207) and Rushdie (p. 215) for background, choose several films and television programs that support your position. Then, write an essay that takes a strong stand on this issue. (Be sure to define exactly what you mean by *family* and *family values*.)

6. To what extent, if any, should explicitly sexual or violent images in magazine ads, on TV, or on the Internet be censored? Write an essay in which you take a stand on this issue and explain why you believe such censorship is (or is not) necessary.

7. What danger, if any, do you see for young people in the seductive messages of the music they listen to? Do you believe that parents and educators are right to be concerned about the effect the messages in

rock and rap music have on teenagers and young adults, or do you think they are overreacting? Support your position with quotations from popular music lyrics. If you like, you can also interview friends and relatives and use their responses to help you develop your argument. Before you begin, read Mary Eberstadt's "Eminem Is Right" (p. 223).

8. What qualities, if any, do printed books have that their electronic counterparts lack—and vice versa? After reading "The Universe of Meaning" in this chapter, "Learning to Read and Write" in Chapter 3, and "The Library Card" in Chapter 6, write an essay in which you assess the relative merits of print and electronic books.

9. Write an analysis of a Web site or a blog, considering the techniques it uses to appeal to its target audience. Who is being addressed, what message is conveyed, and how successfully is this message communicated?

5

GENDER AND IDENTITY

Attitudes about gender have changed dramatically over the past forty years, and they continue to change. For some, these changes have resulted in confusion as well as liberation. One reason for this confusion is that people can no longer rely on fixed gender roles to tell them how to behave in public and how to function within their families. Still, many men and women—uncomfortable with the demands of confining gender roles and unhappy with the expectations those roles create—yearn for even less rigidity, for an escape from stereotypes into a society where roles are not strictly defined by gender.

In spite of these changes, many people still see men and women in terms of outdated or unrealistic stereotypes. Men are strong, tough, and brave, and women are weak, passive, and in need of protection. Men

Two young boys fighting with toy swords

understand mathematics and science and have a natural aptitude for mechanical tasks. They also have the drive, the aggressiveness, the competitive edge, and the power to succeed. They are never sentimental and never cry. Women are better at small, repetitive tasks and shy away from taking bold, decisive actions. They enjoy, and are good at, domestic activities, and they have a natural aptitude for nurturing. Although women may like their jobs, they will leave them to devote themselves to husband and children.

As you read the preceding list of stereotypes, you may react neutrally (or even favorably), or you may react with annoyance; how we react tells us something about our society and something about ourselves. As a number of writers in this chapter point out, however, stereotypes can limit the way people think, the roles they chose to assume, and, ultimately, the positions they occupy in society.

As the Focus section of this chapter, "Who Has It Harder, Girls or Boys?" (p. 300) illustrates, both men and women have problems living up to the images they believe they should conform to and filling the roles that have been set for them. Some believe that it is boys who have suffered more because, as parents and teachers have focused on the girls, they have ignored the needs of boys. Others say that, before the problems boys and girls face can be addressed, society—especially educators—must stop spreading ideas about gender differences that are either misleading or incorrect. Still others assert that, in today's society, young women are presented with an impossible set of expectations that make it difficult, if not impossible, for

Two young girls playing with dolls

them to function. Only by broadening the dialogue, and by challenging conventional wisdom, will our society be able to ensure that both males and females are able to realize their full potential.

—————— PREPARING TO READ AND WRITE ——————

As you read and prepare to write about the essays in this chapter, you may consider the following questions:

- Is the writer male or female? Can you determine the writer's gender without reading his or her name or the headnote? Does the writer's gender matter?

- Does the writer focus on males, on females, or on both?

- Does the essay's date of publication affect its content?

- Does the essay seem fair? Balanced?

- Does the writer discuss gender as a sexual, political, economic, or social issue?

- What does the writer suggest are the specific advantages or disadvantages of being male? Of being female? Of being gay or straight?

- Does the writer support the status quo, or does he or she suggest that change is necessary? That change is possible? That change is inevitable?

- Does the writer recommend specific societal changes? What are they?

- Does the writer think that men and women are fundamentally different? If so, does he or she suggest that these differences can (or should) be overcome, or at least lessened?

- Does the writer think gender differences are the result of environment, heredity, or both?

- Does the essay challenge any of your ideas about male or female roles?

- In what ways is the essay like other essays in this chapter?

BARBIE DOLL

Marge Piercy

1936–

Marge Piercy's work includes the novels Small Changes *(1972),* He, She, and It *(1991),* Three Women *(1999), and* Sex Wars: A Novel of Gilded Age New York *(2005) and the poetry collections* The Art of Blessing the Day *(1999) and* The Crooked Inheritance *(2006). According to Piercy, who has been active in the women's movement since 1969, the movement "has been a great source (as well as energy sink!) and healer of the psyche for me." The following poem from* Circles in the Water *(1988) is an ironic look at the influence of the doll that has become a controversial icon.*

This girlchild was born as usual
and presented dolls that did pee-pee
and miniature GE stoves and irons
and wee lipsticks the color of cherry candy.
Then in the magic of puberty, a classmate said: 5
You have a great big nose and fat legs.

She was healthy, tested intelligent,
possessed strong arms and back,
abundant sexual drive and manual dexterity.
She went to and fro apologizing.   10
Everyone saw a fat nose on thick legs.
She was advised to play coy,
exhorted to come on hearty,
exercise, diet, smile and wheedle.
Her good nature wore out   15
like a fan belt.
So she cut off her nose and her legs
and offered them up.

In the casket displayed on satin she lay
with the undertaker's cosmetics painted on,   20
a turned-up putty nose,
dressed in a pink and white nightie.
Doesn't she look pretty? everyone said.
Consummation at last.
To every woman a happy ending.   25

Responding to Reading

1. What is the significance of the poem's title? To whom or what does it refer? What toys was the "girlchild" (1) given after she was born? What effect does Piercy imply that these toys had on the child?
2. What happens to the "girlchild" when she reaches "the magic of puberty" (5)? Do you think this change is inevitable? Explain.
3. Piercy ends on a cynical note. Is this an effective conclusion? What does she gain (or lose) with this kind of ending?

Responding in Writing

What toy (or toys) did you have as a child that defined your "femaleness" or "maleness"? Do you think Piercy accurately portrays the impact of such toys on children, or do you think she exaggerates?

RITE OF PASSAGE

Sharon Olds

1942–

Sharon Olds was thirty-seven years old when she published her first book of poems. Her collections include The Gold Cell *(1987),* The Wellspring *(1996),* Blood, Tin, Straw *(1999),* The Unswept Room *(2002),* Strike Sparks: Selected Poems 1980–2002 *(2004), and* One Secret Thing *(2008). Much of her poetry focuses on family relationships. Olds is active in community outreach programs, such as the writing workshop at Goldwater Hospital in New York City. In her poetry, Olds often dwells on family and relationships among parents and children, using plain language that reveals surprising emotional depths. In the following poem, Olds implies that her young son and his male friends already possess the violent tendencies of adult men.*

As the guests arrive at my son's party
they gather in the living room—
short men, men in first grade
with smooth jaws and chins.
5   Hands in pockets, they stand around
jostling, jockeying for place, small fights

breaking out and calming. One says to another
How old are you? Six. I'm seven. So?
They eye each other, seeing themselves
tiny in the other's pupils. They clear their   10
throats a lot, a room of small bankers,
they fold their arms and frown. *I could beat you*
up, a seven says to a six,
the dark cake, round and heavy as a
turret, behind them on the table. My son,   15
freckles like specks of nutmeg on his cheeks,
chest narrow as the balsa keel[1] of a
model boat, long hands
cool and thin as the day they guided him
out of me, speaks up as a host   20
for the sake of the group.
We could easily kill a two-year-old,
he says in his clear voice. The other
men agree, they clear their throats
like Generals, they relax and get down to   25
playing war, celebrating my son's life.

Responding to Reading

1. Look up the definition of "rite of passage." Why do you think Olds gives her poem this title?
2. Why does Olds refer to the children at her son's birthday party as "men"?
3. What comment do you think Olds is making about what it means to be male in contemporary American society?

Responding in Writing

Do you think that Olds's portrayal of boys is accurate, or do you think it is exaggerated? Why do you think that she characterizes boys as she does?

---

[1]The long, narrow bottom of a wooden ship. [Eds.]

GARDENLAND, SACRAMENTO, CALIFORNIA

Michael Nava

1954–

Currently working as an attorney for the California Supreme Court, Michael Nava has written seven mystery novels, and won Lambda Literary Awards for LGBT (lesbian, gay, bisexual, and transgendered) literary achievement. Coauthor of Created Equal: Why Gay Rights Matter to America *(1994), Nava often writes about outsider perspectives, the subject of the following essay.*

I grew up in a neighborhood of Sacramento called Gardenland, a poor community, almost entirely Mexican, where my maternal family, the Acunas, had lived since the 1920s. Sacramento's only distinction used to be that it was the state capital. Today, because it frequently appears on lists of the country's most livable cities, weary big-town urbanites have turned it into a boomtown rapidly becoming unlivable. But when I was a child, in the late fifties and early sixties, the only people who lived in Sacramento were the people who'd been born there.

Downtown the wide residential neighborhoods were lined with oaks shading turreted, run-down Victorian mansions, some partitioned into apartments, others still of a piece, but all of them exuding a shadowy small-town melancholy. The commercial district was block after block of shabby brick buildings housing small businesses. The city's skyline was dominated by the gold-domed capitol, a confectioner's spun-sugar dream of a building. It was set in a shady park whose grass seemed always to glisten magically, as if hidden under each blade of grass were an Easter egg.

Sacramento's only other landmarks of note were its two rivers, the American and the Sacramento. They came together in muddy confluence beneath the slender iron joints of railroad bridges. Broad and shallow, the rivers passed as slowly as thought between the thick and tumble of their banks.

A system of levees fed into the rivers. One of these tributaries was called the Bannon Slough. Gardenland was a series of streets carved out of farmland backed up against the slough. It flowed south, curving east behind a street called Columbus Avenue, creating Gardenland's southern and eastern boundaries. The northern boundary was a street called El Camino. Beyond El Camino was middle-class tract housing. To the west, beyond Bowman Street, were fields and then another neighborhood that may just as well have existed on another planet for all I knew of it.

5   What I knew were the nine streets of Gardenland: Columbus, Jefferson, Harding, Cleveland, El Camino, Peralta, Wilson, Haggin, and

Bowman; an explorer, an odd lot of presidents, an unimaginative Spanish phrase, and three inexplicable proper names, one in Spanish, two in English. It was as if the streets had been named out of a haphazard perusal of a child's history text. There were two other significant facts about the streets in Gardenland; they all dead-ended into the levee and their names were not continued across El Camino Boulevard into the Anglo suburb, called Northgate. Gardenland's streets led, literally, nowhere.

Unlike El Camino, where little square houses sat on little square lots, Gardenland had not been subdivided to maximum utility. Broad uncultivated fields stretched between and behind the ramshackle houses. Someone's "front yard" might consist of a quarter acre of tall grass and the remnants of an almond orchard. The fields were littered with abandoned farming implements and the foundations of long-gone houses. For a dreamy boy like me, these artifacts were magical. Finding my own world often harsh, I could imagine from these rusted pieces of metal and fragments of walls a world in which I would have been a prince.

But princes were hard to come by in Gardenland. Almost everyone was poor, and most residents continued to farm after a fashion, keeping vegetable gardens and flocks of chickens. There were neither sidewalks nor streetlights, and the roads, cheaply paved, were always crumbling and narrow as country lanes. At night, the streets and fields were lit by moonlight and the stars burned with millennial intensity above the low roofs of our houses.

The best way to think of Gardenland is not as an American suburb at all, but rather as a Mexican village, transported perhaps from Guanajuato, where my grandmother's family originated, and set down lock, stock, and chicken coop in the middle of California.

My cousin Josephine Robles had divided her tiny house in half and ran a beauty shop from one side. Above her porch was a wooden sign that said in big blue letters GARDENLAND and, in smaller print below, BEAUTY SALON. Over the years the weather took its toll and the bottom half faded completely, leaving only the word GARDENLAND in that celestial blue, like a road sign to a cut-rate Eden.

By the time I was born, in 1954, my family had lived in Gardenland for 10 at least twenty-five years. Virtually all I know of my grandfather's family, the Acunas, was that they were Yaqui Indians living in northern Mexico near the American border at Yuma, Arizona. My grandmother's family, the Trujillos, had come out of central Mexico in 1920, escaping the displacements caused by the Mexican Revolution of 1910. I have dim memories of my great-grandparents, Ygnacio and Phillipa Trujillo, doll-like, white-haired figures living in a big, dark two-story house in east Sacramento.

My grandparents settled on Haggin Avenue in a house they built themselves. My cousins, the Robles, lived two doors down. My family also eventually lived on Haggin Avenue, next door to my grandparents. Our house was the pastel plaster box that became standard suburban architecture in California in the fifties and sixties but it was the exception in Gardenland.

Most houses seemed to have begun as shacks to which rooms were added to accommodate expanding families. They were not built with privacy in mind but simply as shelter. We lived in a series of such houses until our final move to Haggin Avenue. In one of them, the living room was separated from the kitchen by the narrow rectangular bedroom in which my brothers and sisters and I slept. Adults were always walking through it while we were trying to sleep. This made for jittery children, but no one had patience for our complaints. It was enough that we had a place to live.

By the standards of these places, my grandparents' house was luxurious. It was a four-bedroom, L-shaped building that they had built themselves. My grandmother put up the original three rooms while my grandfather was in the navy during World War II. My aunt Socorro told me that my grandmother measured the rooms by having her children lie head to toe across a plot of ground. She bought the cement for the foundations, mixed and troweled it, and even installed pipes for plumbing. Later, when my grandfather returned, they added a series of long, narrow rooms paneled in slats of dark-stained pine, solid and thick walled.

Massive, dusty couches upholstered in a heavy maroon fabric, oversize beds soft as sponges, and a leather-topped dining room table furnished the house. Like the rusted combines in the field, these things seemed magical in their antiquity. I would slip into the house while my grandparents were both at work and wander through it, opening drawers and inspecting whatever presented itself to my attention. It was in this fashion that I opened a little-used closet and found it full of men's clothes that obviously were not my grandfather's. Later I learned that they had belonged to my uncle Raymond who had been killed in a car accident. In a subsequent exploration I found pictures of his funeral, including a picture taken of him in his casket, a smooth-faced, dark-skinned, pretty boy of fifteen.

15   Another time, I found a voluminous red petticoat in a cedar chest. Without much hesitation, I put it on and went into my grandmother's bedroom where I took out her face powder and lipstick. I applied these in the careful manner of my grandmother, transforming myself in the dressing mirror beneath the grim gaze of a crucified Christ. Looking back, I don't think I was trying to transform myself into a girl, but only emulating the one adult in my family who loved me

without condition. Because she was the soul of kindness, it never occurred to me, as a child, that my grandmother might be unhappy. Only looking back do I see it.

She and my grandfather slept in separate rooms at opposite ends of their house. In the evening, my grandfather would sit on a couch in front of the television quietly drinking himself into a stupor while my grandmother did needlework at the kitchen table. They barely spoke. I would sit with my grandmother, looking at pictures in the *Encyclopedia Americana*, comfortable with the silence, which, to her, must have been a deafening indictment of a failed marriage.

In my parents' house, the marriage of my mother and stepfather was as noisily unhappy as my grandparents' was quietly miserable. In each shabby house where we lived I would be awakened by their fights. I learned to turn myself into a stone, or become part of the bed or the walls so as to abate the terror I felt. No one ever spoke of it. There was only one house in which my family lived together peaceably but it only existed as a blueprint that had come somehow into my stepfather's possession.

In the evening, he would take it down from a shelf and unroll it on the kitchen table. Together we would study it, laying claim to rooms, planning alterations. At the time, we lived in a tiny one-bedroom cinder-block house. My brother and I slept on a bunk bed in an alcove off the kitchen. At night, I could hear mice scampering across the cement floor, terrifying me when I woke up having to pee and pick my way through the darkness to the bathroom.

When we finally moved from the cinder-block house, it was to another, bigger version of that house rather than to the dream house of the blueprint. One night, my mother's screaming woke me. I hurried into the bedroom she and my stepfather occupied and found him beating her. When I tried to stop him, he threw me across the room. The next morning my mother told me he was sorry, but it was too late. Where I lived no longer mattered to me because I learned to live completely within myself in rooms of rage and grief. Now I think these rooms were not so different from the rooms we all occupied, my unhappy family and I.

Although not literally cut off from the outside world, Gardenland was 20 little touched by it. We were tribal in our outlook and our practices. Anglos were generically called "paddies," whether or not they were Irish. All fair-skinned people were mysterious but also alike. Even TV, that great equalizer, only emphasized our isolation since we never saw anyone who looked remotely like us, or lived as we did, on any of the popular shows of the day. At school, the same homogeneity prevailed. Until I was nine I attended a neighborhood grade school where virtually every other child was like me, dark eyed and dark skinned, answering to names like Juarez, Delgadillo, Robles, Martinez. My own name, Michael Angel, was but an Anglicized version of Miguel Angel, a name I shared with at least three other of my classmates.

I had a remarkable amount of freedom as a child. As I said, we eventually lived on the same street as other members of my maternal family and I roamed their houses as unself-consciously as a Bedouin child might move among the tents of his people. I ate in whatever house I found myself at mealtime and the meals were the same in each of my relatives' houses—rice, beans, lettuce and tomato salad, stewed or fried meat, tortillas, salsa. My grandparents did not lock their doors at night—who did? what was there to steal?—so that I could slip into their house quietly and make my bed on their sofa when my parents were fighting.

But most of the time I spent outdoors, alone or with my friends. In spring, the field behind my house was overrun with thistles. We neighborhood kids put in long days cutting trails through them and hacking out clearings that became our forts. Tiring of the fields, we'd lurk in abandoned houses, empty barns, and chicken coops. When all other amusements failed, there was always Bannon Slough, a muddy brown creek that flowed between thickly wooded banks. It was too filthy to swim in. Instead, in the steep shadows of bridges and railroad trestles we taught each other how to smoke and to swear.

Just as often I would be off by myself. Early on, I looked for ways to escape my family. I found it in the stillness of the grass and the slap of the slough's brown water against the shore. There I discovered my own capacity for stillness. Lying on the slope of the levee, I could hear my own breath in the wind and feel my skin in the warm blades of grass that pressed against my neck. In those moments, Gardenland *was* Eden, and I felt the wonder and loneliness of the first being.

For, like Adam, I was lonely. Being everyone's child, I was no one's child. I could disappear in the morning and stay out until dusk and my absence went unnoticed. Children barely counted as humans in our tribe. We were more like livestock and our parents' main concern was that the head count at night matched the head count in the morning.

25   My loneliness became as much a part of me as my brown hair and the mole above my lip, something unremarkable. When I came out, I missed that sense of joining a community of others like me that so many of my friends describe. My habits of secrecy and loneliness were too deeply ingrained. I had become like my grandfather, who, in a rare moment of self-revelation, told me he was a "lone wolf"; the most unsociable of an unsociable tribe. Though I've changed as I've grown older, I still sometimes wonder if one reason I write is because I am filled with all the words I never spoke as a child.

Two things opened up for me the narrow passage through which I finally escaped Gardenland for good. The first was books. I learned to read early and, once started, could not get enough of books. In this affinity, I was neither encouraged nor discouraged by my family. Education beyond its most basic functions, learning how to read and write, to do sums, had absolutely no interest for them. My love of reading became simply another secret part of me.

There wasn't a library in Gardenland. Instead, a big white van pulled up to the corner of Wilson and El Camino, the city Bookmobile. Inside, patrons squeezed into a narrow passageway between tall shelves of books. The children's books occupied the bottom shelves. At the exit, a woman checked out books from a standing desk. The Bookmobile came once a week and I was a regular customer, always taking my limit of books.

Everything about the process pleased me. I was proud of my library card, a yellow piece of cardboard with my name typed on it, which I carried in a cowhide wallet that was otherwise empty. I liked taking books from the shelves, noting their heft and volume, the kind of type, whether they were illustrated, and I studied the record of their circulation, the checkout dates stamped in blue on stiff white cards in paper pockets on the inside covers. I loved the books as much as I loved reading. To me, they were organic things, as alive in their way as I was.

Like so many other bright children growing up in the inarticulate world of the poor, books fueled my imagination, answered my questions, led me to new ones, and helped me conceive of a world in which I would not feel so set apart. Yet I do not believe that my brains alone, even aided by my bookish fantasies, would have been enough to escape Gardenland. For this, I needed the kind of courage that arises out of desperation.

I found this courage in my homosexuality. Early on, I acquired a 30 taste for reading history, particularly ancient history. I suppose that pictures of ruined Greek cities reminded me of the crumbling, abandoned houses in the fields of Gardenland. But I was also fascinated by pictures of the nude male statues. There was something about the smooth, headless torsos, the irisless eyes of ephebes that made me stop my idle flipping through pages and touch the paper where these things were depicted. By the time I was twelve I understood that my fascination was rooted in my sexual nature. One day, walking to school, clutching my books to my chest, girl-style, I heard myself say, "I'm a queer."

It was absolutely clear to me that Gardenland could not accommodate this revelation. Gardenland provided the barest of existences for its people. What made it palatable was the knowledge that everyone was about the same, united in ethnicity and poverty and passivity.

The only rituals were the rituals of family, and family was everything there. But I knew that I was not the same as everyone else. And I was certain that my family, already puzzled by my silent devotion to books, would reject me entirely if it became known exactly what thoughts occupied my silence.

Had I been a different child I would have run away from home. Instead, I ran away without leaving home. I escaped to books, to sexual fantasy, to painful, unrequited crushes on male classmates. No one ever knew. I turned myself into an outsider, someone at the margins of a community that was itself outcast. Paradoxically, by doing this, I learned the peasant virtues of my hometown, endurance and survival. As a member of yet another embattled community, those virtues I absorbed as a child continue to serve me.

Responding to Reading

1. In his conclusion, Nava says that he was an outsider living in a community that was itself an outcast; he sees Gardenland as a Mexican village set down in the middle of California. What are the disadvantages of such cultural isolation? What, if any, are the advantages?
2. Nava grew up both Chicano and gay. Which of these two cultures do you think defined his childhood identity more clearly?
3. What did Nava learn in Gardenland that prepared him for the outside world? Did his experiences ultimately help him or hurt him?

Responding in Writing

Nava says that the fact that he read books marked him as different. How did his reading separate him from his community?

The M/F Boxes

E. J. Graff

1958–

Associate director and senior researcher at the Brandeis Institute for Investigative Journalism and resident scholar at the Brandeis Women's Studies Research Center, E. J. Graff is a widely published author of articles on gender equality and family issues. She is a senior correspondent at the American Prospect; *a contributor to* Out *magazine, TPMCafe.com, and Slate.com; and the author of two books—*What Is Marriage For? The Strange History of Our Most Intimate Institution *(1999) and, with Evelyn F. Murphy,* Getting Even: Why Women Don't Get Paid Like Men—and What to Do about It *(2005). The following essay questions conventional male/female distinctions and argues that either/or labels falsely prepackage identity and gender.*

A 15-year-old girl is incarcerated in a Chicago mental hospital in 1981 and kept there for three years because she won't wear a dress. A Winn-Dixie truck driver is fired from a job he held for twenty years when his boss learns that he wears women's clothes at home. A small-time hustler in Falls City, Nebraska, is raped and then murdered when he's discovered to be physically female. A woman bleeds to death after a Washington, DC, hit-and-run accident when, after finding male genitals under her clothes, paramedics stand by laughing.

M or F? For most of us that's a simple question, decided while we were in utero. Checking off that box—at the doctor's, on the census, on a driver's license—takes scarcely a thought. But there's an emerging movement of increasingly vocal people whose bodies or behavior unsettle that clear division. They're calling themselves "transgendered": It's a spongy neologism that, at its broadest, absorbs everyone from medically reassigned transsexuals to cross-dressing men to women so masculine that security guards are called to eject them from women's restrooms. Fellow travelers include intersexuals (once called hermaphrodites), whose bodies are both/and rather than either/or. The slash between M/F cuts painfully through these lives.

And so they've started to organize. Brought together by the Internet, inspired by the successes of the gay rights movement, and with national sympathy gained from the movie *Boys Don't Cry,* intersex and transgender activists are starting to get a hearing in organizations ranging from college campuses to city councils, from lesbian and gay rights groups to pediatric conferences. And, like the feminist and gay rights movements before them, the new sex-and-gender activists may force us to rethink, in life and in law, how we define and interpret the basics of sex.

A first clue to how zealously the M/F border is guarded—to how sex is literally constructed—comes at birth. One in 2,000 infants is born with genitalia ambiguous enough to make doctors hem and haw when parents ask that first question: boy or girl? Since the late 1950s/early 1960s, standard medical procedure has been to lie and obfuscate. Rather than explain that the child is "a mixture of male and female," writes Anne Fausto-Sterling, author of *Sexing the Body*, medical manuals advise physicians to reassign the child surgically to one sex or another, telling parents only that "the gonads were incompletely developed . . . and therefore required removal." A large clitoris may be cut down; a micropenis may be removed and a vagina built; a testis or testes are sliced out—sometimes over the parents' explicit objections.

5   Now some of those children have come of age and are telling their stories: severe depression, sexual numbness and a long-time despair at having been folded, spindled and mutilated. The leader of this nascent movement is Cheryl Chase, who in 1993 organized the Intersex Society of North America. ISNA opposes reassignment surgery on intersex infants and advocates raising intersex children as social males or females, educating them about their bodies and letting them choose at puberty whether they'd like surgical assistance or a shift in social sex. ISNA's cause was helped when Johns Hopkins sex researcher and PhD John Money, who wrote the intersex silence-and-reassignment protocol, was profoundly discredited. After a child he called "John" was accidentally castrated soon after birth, Money advised his parents to have him undergo surgery to construct a vagina, raise him as "Joan" and give him female hormones at puberty. Money reported this involuntary sex reassignment as fully successful. But in 1997, both a medical journal report and a Rolling Stone article revealed that the reassignment had been a disaster. Despite the insistence of parents, doctors, psychologists and teachers, "Joan" had always insisted that she was "just a boy with long hair in girl's clothes." In adolescence, John took back his manhood.

        How did John "know" he was male—and by extension, how do any of us decide we're girls or boys? One theory is that, in utero, John had undergone the androgen bath that turns an undifferentiated fetus—which otherwise becomes female—male, giving him a male identity and masculine behavior. In the other rare cases where XY infants lose penises and are raised as girls, some insist on being boys—but others happily identify as (masculine, lesbian) women, which suggests that things aren't quite so simple. Scientists recognize that our brains and nervous systems are somewhat plastic, developing in response to environmental stimuli. Sexuality—all of it, from identity to presentation to sexual orientation—is no exception; it develops as a biological interaction between inborn capacities and outside influences. As a result, most of us have a narrow range in which we feel "natural" as we gender ourselves daily through clothes, stance, stride, tone. For most, that gendered behavior is consonant with biological sex: Girls present as female, if not feminine, and fall in love with boys; boys present as male or masculine and fall in love with girls. But those in whom gendered behavior is vice versa—feminine boys, highly masculine girls—get treated as unnatural, even though their gendering is just as biological as the rest of ours. What happens to these transgendered folks can be so brutal that the pediatric surgeons who cut off infant clitorises or penises look like merely the advance guard of the M/F border patrol.

Take, for instance, Daphne Scholinski, so masculine that at age 6, strangers chastised her when she tried to use women's restrooms. In her dry, pitiless memoir *The Last Time I Wore a Dress*, Scholinski tells the story of being committed to a mental hospital at 15 for some very real problems, including severe neglect, her father's violence and her own delinquency. The hospital ignored her shocking childhood and instead "treated" her masculinity. Scholinski got demerits if she didn't wear makeup. She was put on a boys' ward, where she was twice raped, to encourage her to be more feminine. Her confinement was so disturbing that she still gets posttraumatic stress flashbacks, including nightmares so terrifying that she wakes up and vomits. And so Scholinski is starting an organization dedicated to reforming the diagnosis of childhood GID, or gender identity disorder, under which she was treated.

Or consider the treatment of Darlene Jespersen and Peter Oiler. After working for Harrah's Reno casino for eighteen years, in the summer of 2000, Jespersen was fired from her bar-tending job when Harrah's launched a new policy requiring all its female employees to wear foundation, powder, eye-liner, lipstick and so on. "I tried it," says Jespersen in a plaintive voice, "but I felt so naked." The obverse happened to Peter Oiler, a weathered, middle-aged man with large aviator glasses, a pleasant drawl and a bit of an overbite. After twenty years of being rotated through progressively more responsible jobs in Winn-Dixie's shipping yards, in 1999 Oiler was driving a fifty-foot truck delivering grocery supplies throughout southeastern Louisiana—until Winn-Dixie learned that he called himself "transgendered." Oiler tried to explain that he simply wore women's clothes on the weekends: He wasn't going to become a woman; he didn't want to wear makeup and heels on company time. In January 2000 Oiler was fired.

Jespersen and Oiler are stunned. Jespersen is suing Harrah's. Says Oiler, "I was raised to believe that if you do an honest day's work, you'll get an honest day's pay." The ACLU Lesbian and Gay Rights Project has taken up his case, in part because of the sheer injustice—and in part to get courts to treat discrimination against people who violate sex stereotypes as illegal sex discrimination. If a woman can wear a dress, or if a man can refuse makeup, why not vice versa? In doing so; the ACLU, like the three national lesbian and gay legal organizations, would be building on the 1989 Supreme Court decision *Price Waterhouse v. Ann Hopkins*. Price Waterhouse had told Hopkins that she wasn't going to make partner because she was too masculine—and, in actual written memos, advised her to wear jewelry and makeup, to go to charm school, to be less aggressive. The Supreme Court declared such stereotyping to be sex discrimination.

10   Will judges see Peter Oiler's dismissal as illegal sex stereotyping? There have been some recent hints that they might. In Massachusetts, for instance, the US Court of Appeals for the First Circuit said Lucas Rosa could sue a bank that instructed feminine Rosa, who had shown up to apply for a loan wearing a dress, to go home and come back in men's clothes; a female, after all, would have been considered for the loan. Another Massachusetts judge said that a male student could come to school in a dress, since female students could. A Washington transsexual prisoner raped by a prison guard, and two New York municipal employees harassed for being gay, were allowed to sue when judges ruled they'd been attacked for violating stereotyped expectations of their sex.

Our society has learned to see why women would want masculine privileges like playing soccer and serving on the Supreme Court, but there's been no matching force expanding the world for males. Boys and men still patrol each other's masculinity with a Glengarry Glen Ross level of ridicule and violence that can seem, to women, nearly surreal. Those males who violate the M-box's limits on behavior are quite literally risking their lives.

Which means that, if you're a performing drag queen, a cross-dressing straight man like Peter Oiler, or a transsexual who still has some male ID, do not under any circumstances get stopped by a cop. In New York City, says Pauline Park, a co-founder of NYAGRA (New York Association for Gender Rights Advocacy), even if the police don't actually beat you, "you could be arrested and detained for days or weeks. They don't let people out until they plead guilty to prostitution. They put them in the men's cell, where they're often assaulted and sometimes raped, as a tactic to get people to plead guilty."

And don't turn to emergency medical personnel. In August 1995 Tyra Hunter's car crashed in Washington, DC. When firefighting paramedics cut away her dress and found male genitals, they laughed and mocked her. She bled to death in the hospital. In August 2000 a jury awarded Hunter's mother $1.75 million in a wrongful-death action. Hunter's experience, unfortunately, is not unusual. Once a month, someone transgendered is murdered, and those are just the documented cases. Transgender activists are beginning to mark November 28, the anniversary of another such death, as a Day of Remembrance, with candlelight vigils and a determination to slow the steady drumbeat of murder.

"We're despised. We're pariahs in this society," says Miranda Stevens-Miller, chair of the transgender rights organization It's Time, Illinois, about transsexuals and otherwise transgendered people. Many transsexuals are fired once they begin to transition. Others lose custody and visitation rights, houses, leases. Many are shut out of office and other public restrooms for years—an indignity that cuts to the very core of being human, since every living body needs to pee. And so the most urgent transgender organizing is happening locally, in organizations such as TGNet Arizona, NYAGRA and It's Time, Oregon. They're teaching Trans 101 to local employers, doctors, city councils, lesbian and gay organizations, judges, families, landlords, friends. They're attempting to collect statistics on firings, beatings, murders, bathroom harassment, police abuse. Often these groups are driven by the energy and determination of one or two people who spend their own time and pennies writing and photocopying leaflets, giving workshops for corporate and college groups, and lobbying city councils and lesbian and gay organizations for inclusion in hate-crimes and antidiscrimination laws. Lately, they're having remarkable success at adding "gender identity and expression" to the protected categories in local and state employment nondiscrimination and hate-crimes laws; they've won in locales ranging from Portland, Oregon, to DeKalb, Illinois, to the state of Rhode Island.

Nationally, trans groups are still in the skirmishing phase faced by 15 any new movement, with the inevitable splits over strategy and personality. The group with the most name recognition, GenderPAC, angers some transgender activists by avoiding the "T" word in its advocacy, saying that it aims at gender freedom for everyone; it acts on behalf of such people as Darlene Jespersen and Peter Oiler, or boys called "faggot" for not being noticeably masculine. Currently the most significant transgender organizations nationally are IFGE (International Foundation for Gender Education), GEA (Gender Education and Advocacy) and the Working Group on Trans Equality, a loose network of grass-roots trans activists aiming at a coordinated national presence. Perhaps the biggest success so far is that all the major lesbian and gay organizations and many smaller ones have added transgendered folks to their mission statements as folks who are equally, if differently, queer.

Or is it so different? All of us deviate from what's expected from our sex. While the relationship between transgender activists and lesbian and gay groups has at times been contentious, some lesbian and gay activists, notably Chai Feldblum, Georgetown law professor, are starting to urge that we all organize around our common deviance from sex stereotypes. The differences between homosexual, transgender and transsexual experiences are not that great: All are natural variations on the brain's gendered development that have cropped up throughout human history, from Tiresias to Radclyffe Hall, from Billy Tipton to Quentin Crisp. For the most part, the mainstream sees us on one sliding scale of queerness. And occasionally our struggles and goals intersect quite neatly. For instance, homos can't always tell whether we're harassed at work because someone figures out that we date others of the same sex, or simply because we're too butch or too fey.

And none of us can rely on having our marriages recognized by the institutions around us when we need them—because marriage is one of the last laws on the books that discriminate based on sex. Recently, Joe Gardiner asked a Kansas court to invalidate his dead father's marriage to transwoman (born male, medically and legally reassigned as female) J'Noel Gardiner, saying J'Noel was "really" a man—and therefore could not have legally married a man. The lower court agreed with the son that XY = man, which meant the son would inherit his father's fat estate. But the Kansas appeals judge remanded the case back down for a new trial. Sex, the appeals court declared, isn't decided simply by a chromosome test. Rather, sex is a complex constellation of characteristics that includes not only chromosomes but also "gonadal sex, internal morphologic sex, external morphologic sex, hormonal sex, phenotypic sex, assigned sex and gender of rearing, and sexual identity." The court approvingly quoted Johns Hopkins researcher and medical doctor William Reiner, who wrote, "The organ that appears to be critical to psychosexual development and adaptation is not the external genitalia, but the brain."

Responding to Reading

1. How does Graff define the term *transgendered?* What does she mean when she says, "The slash between M/F cuts painfully through these lives" (2)?
2. In paragraph 4, Graff says that the border between male and female is "zealously . . . guarded." What does she mean by this statement? How effectively does her essay support it?
3. Graff says that boys and men "patrol each other's masculinity with a . . . level of ridicule and violence that can seem, to women, nearly surreal" (11). Do agree with this contention? Do you believe that "males who violate the M-box's limits on behavior are quite literally risking their lives" (11)?

Responding in Writing

In paragraph 3, Graff says, "like the feminist and gay rights movements before them, the new sex-and-gender activists may force us to rethink, in life and in law, how we define and interpret the basics of sex." Do you agree with this statement? How is the situation of transgendered individuals similar to and different from that of women and gays?

WHY I WANT A WIFE

Judy Brady

1937–

Judy Brady studied art before getting married, having a family, and starting her writing career. A breast cancer survivor, Brady cofounded the Toxic Links Coalition, an environmental advocacy group based in California. She has edited two books about cancer, including Women and Cancer *(1980) and a collection of essays and poems written by cancer victims,* One in Three: Women with Cancer Confront an Epidemic *(1991). The following essay, "Why I Want a Wife," appeared in the first issue of* Ms. *magazine in 1972. In this essay, Brady takes a satirical look at what it means to be a wife and mother.*

I belong to that classification of people known as wives. I am A Wife. And, not altogether incidentally, I am a mother.

Not too long ago a male friend of mine appeared on the scene fresh from a recent divorce. He had one child, who is, of course, with his ex-wife. He is looking for another wife. As I thought about him while I was ironing one evening, it suddenly occurred to me that I, too, would like to have a wife. Why do I want a wife?

I would like to go back to school so that I can become economically independent, support myself, and, if need be, support those dependent upon me. I want a wife who will work and send me to school. And while I am going to school I want a wife to take care of my children. I want a wife to keep track of the children's doctor and dentist appointments. And to keep track of mine, too. I want a wife to make sure my children eat properly and are kept clean. I want a wife who will wash the children's clothes and keep them mended. I want a wife who is a good nurturant attendant to my children, who arranges for their schooling, makes sure that they have an adequate social life with their peers, takes them to the park, the zoo, etc. I want a wife who takes care of the children when they are sick, a wife who arranges to be around when the children need special care, because, of course, I cannot miss classes at school. My wife must arrange to lose time at work and not lose the job. It may mean a small cut in my wife's income from time to time, but I guess I can tolerate that. Needless to say, my wife will arrange and pay for the care of the children while my wife is working.

I want a wife who will take care of *my* physical needs. I want a wife who will keep my house clean. A wife who will pick up after me. I want a wife who will keep my clothes clean, ironed, mended, replaced when need be, and who will see to it that my personal things are kept in their proper place so that I can find what I need the minute I need it. I want a wife who cooks the meals, a wife who is a *good* cook. I want a wife who will plan the menus, do the necessary grocery shopping, prepare the meals, serve them pleasantly, and then do the cleaning up while I do my studying. I want a wife who will care for me when I am sick and sympathize with my pain and loss of time from school. I want a wife to go along when our family takes a vacation so that someone can continue to care for me and my children when I need a rest and change of scene.

5   I want a wife who will not bother me with rambling complaints about a wife's duties. But I want a wife who will listen to me when I feel the need to explain a rather difficult point I have come across in my course of studies. And I want a wife who will type my papers for me when I have written them.

I want a wife who will take care of the details of my social life. When my wife and I are invited out by friends, I want a wife who will take care of the babysitting arrangements. When I meet people at school that I like and want to entertain, I want a wife who will have the house clean, will prepare a special meal, serve it to me and my friends, and not interrupt when I talk about the things that interest me and my friends. I want a wife who will have arranged that the children are fed and ready for bed before my guests arrive so that the children do not bother us. I want a wife who takes care of the needs of my guests so that they feel comfortable, who makes sure that they have an ashtray, that they are passed the hors d'oeuvres, that they are offered a second helping of the food, that their wine glasses are replenished when necessary, that their coffee is served to them as they like it. And I want a wife who knows that sometimes I need a night out by myself.

I want a wife who is sensitive to my sexual needs, a wife who makes love passionately and eagerly when I feel like it, a wife who makes sure that I am satisfied. And, of course, I want a wife who will not demand sexual attention when I am not in the mood for it. I want a wife who assumes the complete responsibility for birth control, because I do not want more children. I want a wife who will remain sexually faithful to me so that I do not have to clutter up my intellectual life with jealousies. And I want a wife who understands that *my* sexual needs may entail more than strict adherence to monogamy. I must, after all, be able to relate to people as fully as possible.

If, by chance, I find another person more suitable as a wife than the wife I already have, I want the liberty to replace my present wife with another one. Naturally, I will expect a fresh, new life; my wife will take the children and be solely responsible for them so that I am left free.

When I am through with school and have a job, I want my wife to quit working and remain at home so that my wife can more fully and completely take care of a wife's duties.

10   My God, who *wouldn't* want a wife?

Responding to Reading

1. Why does Brady begin her essay by saying that she is both a wife and a mother? How does her encounter with a male friend lead her to decide that she would like to have a wife?
2. This essay, written more than thirty years ago, has been anthologized many times. To what do you attribute its continued popularity? In what ways, if any, is the essay dated? In what ways is it still relevant?
3. Brady wrote her essay to address a stereotype and a set of social conventions that she thought were harmful to women. Could you make the case that Brady's characterization of a "wife" is harmful both to women and to feminism?

Responding in Writing

What is your definition of a wife? How is it different from (or similar to) Brady's?

Stay-at-Home Dads

Glenn Sacks

1964–

Glenn Sacks is a columnist who writes about men's and fathers' issues and hosts the radio talk show His Side *in Los Angeles. His columns have appeared in the* Chicago Tribune, *the* Los Angeles Times, Newsday, *the* Philadelphia Inquirer, Insight Magazine, *and other publications. Before embarking on a career as a columnist and radio personality, Sacks taught high school, elementary school, and adult education courses in Los Angeles and Miami. In the following essay, Sacks discusses the difficulties men (as well as their wives) face if they want to devote themselves to childrearing and housework.*

The subtext to the wave of concern over the recently announced epidemic of childlessness in successful career women is that women can't have it all after all—and it's men's fault. Why? Because men interfere with their wives' career aspirations by their refusal to become their children's primary caregivers, forcing women to sidetrack their careers if they want children.

Despite the criticism, men generally focus on their careers not out of selfishness but because most women still expect men to be their family's primary breadwinners. For women willing to shoulder this burden themselves, replacing the two-earner couple with a female breadwinner and a stay-at-home dad (SAHD) can be an attractive option. I became a SAHD with the birth of my daughter four years ago, and the arrangement has benefited my family immensely.

My wife and I sometimes remark that if we had met in the era before women had real career opportunities, we'd both be pretty unhappy. As a lone breadwinner I would feel deprived of time with my children. My wife, an ambitious woman who loves her career, would feel stifled as a stay-at-home mom. Since each of us would want to be doing what the other is doing, we would probably resent each other. Instead, the freedom to switch gender roles has allowed each of us to gravitate towards what we really want in life.

Men need not fear a loss of power when they become a SAHD. While SAHDs are sometimes stereotyped as being at the mercy of their stronger wives' commands, in reality, I have more power in the family now than I ever did when I was the family breadwinner. The most important issue in any marriage is deciding how to raise the children. While my wife is an equal partner in any major decision regarding the children, I supervise the children on a day to day basis and I make sure that things are done the way I want them done.

5   Women also benefit from SAHDs because, with reduced familial responsibilities, they can compete on a level playing field with career-oriented men. For men, it is an opportunity to witness the countless magical, irreplaceable moments of a young child's life, and to enjoy some of the subtle pleasures our fathers never knew, like making dinner with a three year-old's "help," or putting the baby down for a mid-day nap in a hammock.

Still, there are adjustments that both men and women will need to make. Women will need to discard the popular yet misguided notion that men "have it all," and understand that being the breadwinner comes with disadvantages as well as advantages.

One disadvantage can be the loss of their primary status with their young children. Mom is #1 not because of biology or God's law but because mom is the one who does most of the child care. This can change when dad becomes the primary caregiver. When my young daughter has a nightmare and cries at 2 AM, my wife is relieved that she's not the one who has to get up and comfort her. The price that my wife has had to accept is that her child insists on being comforted not by her but by "yaddy."

Another disadvantage is that taking on the main breadwinner role reduces a woman's ability to cut back her work schedule or look for a more rewarding job if her career disappoints her. This is one of the reasons many women prefer life as a frazzled two-earner couple—keeping the man on career track as the main breadwinner helps to preserve women's options.

Men will also have to make adjustments. For one, they will have to endure the unconscious hypocrisy of a society which often wrings its hands over the lot of the housewife yet at the same time views SAHDs as freeloaders who have left their working wives holding the bag.

SAHDs also have to contend with the societal perception that being 10 a househusband is unmanly. The idea is so pervasive that even I still tend to think "wimp" when I first hear about a SAHD.

Working women sometimes complain that men in the workplace don't take them as seriously as they take men. As a SAHD I have the same complaint. For example, last year I attended a school meeting with my wife, my son's elementary school teacher, and some school officials, most of whom knew that I drove my son to and from school, met with his teachers, and did his spelling words with him every day. Yet the woman who chaired the meeting introduced herself to my wife, began the meeting, and then, only as an afterthought, looked at me and said "and who might you be?"

In addition, while many stay-at-home parents face boredom and social isolation, it can be particularly acute for SAHDs, since there are few other men at home, and connections with stay-at-home moms can be difficult to cultivate.

None of these hurdles are insurmountable, and they pale in comparison to the benefits children derive from having a parent as a primary caregiver—particularly a parent grateful for the once-in-a-lifetime opportunity that he never knew he wanted, and never thought he would have.

Responding to Reading

1. According to Sacks, what is the "subtext to the wave of concern over the recently announced epidemic of childlessness in successful career women" (1)? Why does he think most men concentrate on their careers? What does he think is a good alternative to this situation?
2. What are the advantages of being a stay-at-home dad? What does Sacks see as the disadvantages? How practical do you think his solution is?
3. Could you make the argument that Sacks and his wife are simply switching traditional male/female roles? Are there any other models for work and childcare that Sacks and his wife could emulate? Do any of these seem preferable to the one they currently employ?

Responding in Writing

Would you want your husband to be (or would you want to be) a stay-at-home dad? Why or why not?

MAN BASHING: TRIVIAL PURSUIT
OR A TRUTH WITH CONSEQUENCES?

Warren Farrell

1943–

Warren Farrell was born in New York City and earned a B.A. degree from Montclair State College (1965), an M.A. from the University of California, Los Angeles (1966), and a Ph.D. from New York University (1974). He has taught at the School of Medicine at the University of California, San Diego, as well as at Georgetown University, Rutgers University, and American University. Farrell has been described as "the Gloria Steinem of Men's Liberation." His books include Women Can't Hear What Men Don't Say *(1999), from which the following selection has been excerpted;* Father and Child Reunion: How to Bring the Dads We Need to the Children We Love *(2001);* Why Men Earn More: The Startling Truth behind the Pay Gap— and What Women Can Do about It *(2005); and* Does Feminism Discriminate against Men? A Debate *(2008).*

Man bashers focus on the problems *with* men and ignore the problems *of* men. They usually become man bashers by focusing on the problems of women and blaming those problems on men. The combination is misandry.

Misandry—or man hating—is the equivalent of misogyny. If you are unaware of misandry, welcome to the club. Our failure to see it is so complete that even the most careful observer of the human vocabulary, *Webster's Unabridged Dictionary*, is blind to it. One writer calls misandry "the hate that dares us to breathe its name."

Is misandry not acknowledged because it does not exist? A week after you read this chapter, misandry will become apparent in commercials, in films, in everyday conversations. But the bias that is hardest to see is the bias we share. Even allegedly gender-neutral words like "sexist" imply slights only against women.

Man bashing is *not* a problem per se. A person who cannot laugh at her- or himself has a serious problem. But when one group gets singled out far more often than others—whether it be "dumb Poles," "dumb blondes," or "corrupt lawyers"—then a red flag is sent up. And I find man bashing now runs about 9 to 1 over woman bashing. As *Time* magazine puts it, it's as if "masculinity were a bad smell in the room."

5   The lopsided objectification of a group as the devil always makes us callous to its deaths. Men's life expectancy was one year less than women's in 1920; today, it is seven years less, yet the federal government has only an Office of Research on Women's Health. It's part of what leads us to our blindness toward domestic violence against men and to caring more about saving whales than males.

On a personal level, man bashing hurts women because it under-mines the one thing that has most motivated men to work for women and die for women throughout history: appreciation. **I've never seen a greeting card for thanking mentors, or for thanking volunteer firemen.**

The Double Standard and Its Consequences

Today, misandry is also in the double standard of our response: **Woman bashing is a lawsuit; man bashing is a Hallmark card.** Public woman bashing is illegal; public man bashing is institutionalized.

Is man bashing less damaging than woman bashing because boys spend a lifetime putting each other down? The two are different. When boys put each other down, there is an unwritten rule that *it goes both ways*. Not true when women put men down. If she implies he's inept, it's a joke; if he implies she's inept, it might be a joke, or it might be a "hostile work environment." If she considers it a joke at the time, but a year later fails to get promoted, yesterday's joke can become tomor-row's lawsuit. And an end to the "joker's" career.

A man whose career ends in shame is often a man whose marriage ends, which often leads to his children calling him visitor (as in "she has the children . . . he has visitation"). When the U.S. Coast Guard's top spokesperson, Captain Ernie Blanchard, told much less offensive jokes than the ones we'll see below, Coast Guard feminists complained. Cap-tain Blanchard apologized. The apologies weren't good enough. He was subjected to a *criminal* probe. He offered to resign to spare his family— on the condition the probe would stop. The Coast Guard refused. Beside himself, he took his grandfather's Smith & Wesson revolver, pointed it to his head, and shot a bullet through his brains.

Why would the Coast Guard refuse to stop a criminal probe for a 10 joke? Once the machinery of a sexual harassment complaint is set into motion, few officers or corporate executives have the guts to stop the machinery for fear they'll become part of the complaint.

This double standard ultimately violates women. Mentors have proven crucial to female success, and women consistently seek male mentors—the higher up, the better. But the higher up the man, the far-ther he has to fall. Sexual harassment legislation has left potential men-tors increasingly feeling there is a thin line between helping a woman advance her career and helping himself hurt his career. Mentoring requires intimacy that includes joking, criticism, and time alone. A joke that seems safe during the intimacy of mentoring can become a law-suit when the woman being mentored begins to want to create an iden-tity independent of the mentor. Then she often goes through a period of rebellion similar to any adolescent trying to create identity. The jokes and intimacies can come back to haunt him. Once a man sees this happen to someone in the company, or a friend, he thinks twice about being a mentor. Which is why the double standard hurts women.

Misandry's double standard is also in our language.

Doublespeak

When we make positive references, it is politically correct to include women: chairman becomes chairperson; spokesman becomes spokesperson; yet when the reference is negative, no one cries, "Don't say gunman, say gunperson."

When a wealthy older man marries a younger woman, we say, "He's robbing the cradle." We don't say "She's robbing the bank." When Warren Beatty was single, he was called a "womanizer," as if his women friends were victims; when Madonna was single, she was never called a "manizer." She was called either liberated or promiscuous. The difference? Neither liberated nor promiscuous suggests her men friends were victims. The old double standard of labeling women promiscuous while suggesting men were sowing their wild oats has reversed itself: Women with many partners are now liberated; their male counterparts, womanizers.

15   Even self-help writers voice only women's complaint that men leave the toilet seat up. No one suggests thanking the man for putting it up so he gets nothing on it. **And no one asks why a woman expects the toilet to always be as it is in women's rooms, and never as half the toilets are in men's rooms: urinals.** Why, when a woman enters the picture, do her rules prevail? When she doesn't prevail, why is *he* criticized—why don't *they* compromise? When self-help writers help only her, are they really just helping themselves?

Unfortunately, the strongest opponents of misogyny are often the greatest misandrists. Feminists rightly ask us to reconsider references to women as "baby," "honey," "doll," and "spinster," but are often the first to call men dead-beats, jerks, perverts, macho, rapists, and womanizers. And should a man protest, he risks being labeled a wimp, whiner, chauvinist, or misogynist....

Haven't Men Always Dished It Out? Why Can't They Take It?

When man bashing first appears on someone's radar screen, it is almost always dismissed as a function of the pendulum swinging too far—from woman bashing to man bashing. Not true. Comics like *Dagwood* have portrayed man-as-fool since the 1920s. Prior to the women's movement, shows like *The Three Stooges* made a joke of both verbal and physical man bashing. In *The Honeymooners,* the louder Ralph Kramden said "One of these days, *pow,* right in the kisser," or "To the moon, Alice," the farther *he* would fall. Every *Honeymooners* episode followed this formula—or Ralph's fall from man-as-boastful-jerk to the redis-covery of the greater superiority and wisdom of his wife. Only *he* was wrong; only *he* apologized.

On the other hand, shows like *I Love Lucy* mocked both sexes for the excesses of their sex role. And still others idealized both sexes' role (from the *Father Knows Best* image of masculinity to the "motherhood-and-apple-pie" image of *I Remember Mama*).

In the past, when *either* sex deviated from its role, it was a target of epithets. A woman was cheap, easy, promiscuous, a bitch; a man was a jerk, asshole, bastard, motherfucker, faggot. I am not aware of any time in the past in which men were not also the subject of ridicule. Femi-nists, though, have specialized in uncovering only the ridicule against women, making the pendulum appear to have been off balance, thus justifying man bashing as returning to balance.

Now the pendulum *is* off to one side. While epithets against women 20 can end a man's career track, epithets against men can begin a career track for writers of cards, comedies, cartoons, and commercials.

Are Men *Called* Jerks Because Men *Are* Jerks?

A study of thousands of commercials found that if both sexes appeared in the commercial but only one was portrayed as a jerk, *it was the man who was the jerk 100 percent of the time.*

Would men be called jerks less often if they were jerks less often? Yes and no. Men are jerks more often in part because they take risks more often. A woman who doesn't receive a call from a man for a long time after a date often calls her woman friend and they both label him a "jerk." **No one asks why she's expecting *him* to make the call.** He doesn't call her a jerk if she doesn't call *him*.

Suppose he promised to call? That's part of their lopsided expectations—that he will make the promise to do something, not she. Those expected to take most of the risks, make most of the promises, do most of the performing, are most often called a jerk when they fail. When they do it perfectly, they're a hero. **A jerk is a potential hero who messes it up along the way.** Women who repeatedly fall in love with jerks have usually fallen in love with risk-takers rather than take the risks themselves.

Does man bashing make women believe men are getting worse even in areas in which they are improving? Yes. Remember how we saw in the chapter on housework that even though men were doing much more housework, women believed they were doing less? The only thing consistent with that belief was the male-bashing headlines about men and housework.

Obviously, something deeper is going on to generate this anger.   25

Why Are Women So Angry at Men?

The anger from women to men . . . can easily make us feel angry toward women. But understanding what creates that anger, and what can be done to change what creates it provides more compassion toward women, and is far more productive to loving each other. Both for ourselves and our children.

Are women angry because they're powerless, and anger is the way the powerless are heard? Yes and no. Never in history has any large single group of people had, on the surface, more options, wealth, education, personal power, privilege, and respect than women in middle- and upper-middle-class industrialized societies today. And never has such a large group been so angry. Why?

Until recently, there was no social permission for divorce. Marriage guaranteed for a lifetime meant economic security guaranteed for a lifetime. Any man who didn't provide that was ostracized, ridiculed, or ignored. Black men, Indian men, homeless men, and gay men have the toughest time among American males. *And they all have something in common: They do not provide an economic security blanket for women.*

Divorce altered the economic relationship between men and women, and, therefore, the psychological relationship between men and women. When divorce was not permitted, men's addiction to sex and the twenty-year-old woman worked for her—the addiction made him agree to support her for a lifetime; the taboo on divorce made him stick to his agreement. When the taboo on divorce weakened and she was forty, his addiction to the twenties worked against her. She felt disposable.

30   While this was true for all divorced women, the more beautiful the woman was when she was younger, the more she had been treated like a celebrity—what I call a "genetic celebrity." The more she had been a genetic celebrity, the more likely, she was to feel anger as age brought feelings of invisibility in the beauty contest of everyday life in which she used to be the winner.

Many divorced women with children feel they are not being treated as a woman, but as a package deal: a woman with children. A woman friend of mine deeply loved a man, but he was supporting his ex and their children and was already working more than he wanted. When he saw my woman friend's guilt about not spending more time with her children, he became afraid marriage would lead to her quitting work as his previous wife had. Thus he would never commit. My woman friend broke up with him and, after that, I noticed she would often make digs at men—digs that never quite disappeared.

Feminism had a powerful effect on helping women become stronger, more independent. But it had almost no impact on the type of man a woman would find suitable if she did marry. In workshops, **when**

I ask women, "On your wedding day, did you believe the man you married would consistently earn less than you?" almost no woman says "yes." That is, almost every woman who *marries* still believes her future husband will earn equal to or more than she. If she feels he doesn't "have potential," she might have sex with him, might even live with him, but rarely marries him. Why?

This evolved as part of women's historic and biological obligation to find a good provider and protector, not just for themselves, but for their children. Her search for a successful man was her first step to becoming a responsible mother. But women's biology, like men's, created a barrier to our struggle not to treat each other as objects. Men treated women as sex objects; women treated men as success objects. Feminism confronted men's addiction to women as "sex objects," but no one confronted women's addiction to men as "success objects."

So worldwide, women are still set up with "The Princess Diana Fantasy." President Clinton made clear the problem with the male fantasy, but no one asked Monica to re-examine the problem with the female fantasy. Which is . . . ?

When two-and-a-half-billion people, mostly women, are comparing their own lives to that of the future Princess Diana as they watch the TV broadcast of her marrying the prince, more than a few are likely to find their own lives disappointing. When 25 million American women read an average of twelve romance novels per month, often with *Bridges of Madison County*–type themes of married moms being swept away by roving Clint Eastwoods, again, more than a few are likely to find their own lives disappointing.

Even in the late '60s, the National Longitudinal Survey found that 70 percent of younger women believed they would not be working at age thirty-five, yet when they actually reached age thirty-five, more than 70 percent of them *were* working. *These women's dreams, of being swept away, had been swept away.* This created disappointment and anger.

Then, when women like Diana, who do marry the prince, are themselves disappointed, and that disappointment resonates with her own, and men are not offering their perspective, *marital* problems become interpreted as problems of women, *with* men.

Women's greater-than-ever wealth and power fails to predict happiness, then, because it fails to consider disappointed expectations, the hurt and pain of being rejected, and the hopelessness many women feel when they have less beauty power and more children than they did when they were twenty—thus making the princes who were interested in her when she had external beauty be less interested in her now that she has more internal beauty.

The degree to which we help our daughters resist the temptation to feel entitled to a prince is the degree to which they will feel less angry when the prince they marry is half prince and half frog . . . a bit like themselves. When I have seen, in my workshops, women without these expectations, or women who can see the world from men's perspectives without denying their own, I see the anger soften, and openings for love be created.

Responding to Reading

1. What is "man bashing"? According to Farrell, when does it become a problem? What harm does it do?
2. What does Farrell mean when he says that when it comes to bashing, there is a double standard? What form does this double standard take? In what way does man bashing hurt women?
3. Why does Farrell think that women are so angry with men? What does he think should be done to lessen this anger?

Responding in Writing

Make a list of examples of man bashing that you encounter every day—in movies, commercials, and conversation. Do you agree with Farrell that man bashing can have negative consequences?

WITHOUT APOLOGY: GIRLS, WOMEN, AND THE DESIRE TO FIGHT

Leah Hager Cohen

1967–

Leah Hager Cohen has published seven books, including four works of nonfiction and three novels. Her book Without Apology: Girls, Women, and the Desire to Fight *(2005), from which the following essay is drawn, explores the link between female aggression and desire.*

My first impulse was to dismiss her. Whatever my idea of how a boxing coach should look, it was nothing like this woman standing above me on the ring apron, elbows on the ropes, calling out to her boxer in the ring. She wore a pink tank top, red shorts, white socks, and black boxing shoes, and her hair, wavy and fine and light brown, was held back with a pink scrunchie, and her limbs looked tender and ungainly and very white. She was little, Raphaëlla Johnson, five-four and not much over a hundred pounds. But it wasn't just her physical size, it was her voice, too, a girl's voice, indelibly gentle and light.

"You're dropping your hands!" she yelled. "Jab! Keep firing the jab! Work!"

In the ring, a teenage Latina girl was sparring with a white man in his thirties. The girl wore red headgear and gloves, and a thick white mouthguard that made it look as if she couldn't suppress a smile. Her tank top said DON'T EVEN DON'T EVEN DON'T EVEN DON'T EVEN DON'T EVEN DON'T EVEN THINK ABOUT IT. Her sparring partner, broadly muscular, wore black headgear and gloves. His bare torso was a gallery of sweat-glazed tattoos, the most magnificent of which—an American flag in the shape of the United States, with portraits of a woman and three children set inside the borders—rippled across his trapezius muscles and caught the light as he danced. Whenever the girl seemed to tire, the man would yell at her, provoke her, hit her in the face.

"C'mon, *move!*" yelled the coach. "Thirty seconds!" Clustered around her on the ring apron, variously standing or kneeling, were three other girls and a woman, all drinking in the spectacle with unchecked merriment, erupting in bursts of excited laughter, hoots of encouragement, and sharp exhortations that echoed those of the coach. Their obvious pleasure in the event seemed to me incongruous and complicated. But no more so than the sheer physical presence of the coach, to whom my gaze kept returning, even as the action in the ring commanded my attention. She was thirty-two, I would later learn, but she looked half that. She was so small, that was the thing. She was the size of me.

I'd never before been in a boxing gym. It was late October, late in the day, when I first pulled up, just a few minutes earlier, in the shabby lot behind the building. Through the windshield I could see a feeble growth of weeds, then cement steps leading to a wide metal door, with a sign forbidding its use. ONLY ENTRANCE TO BOXING CLUB GYM, it said, above a long arrow pointing off to the left. Below that a second sign read NO PARKING AT ALL OUT BACK. Beside me, a couple of other cars and a pickup truck had been left on the chewed-up asphalt in apparent disregard of the warning. It had begun to drizzle. I considered the other vehicles for a long moment, and turned off my engine.

The windows had been boarded up and painted over, and save for the two rather stern signs, the whole side of the building was feature-less. From the other side of the concrete exterior came a sort of pumping sound, impressively rhythmic, like machinery operating beyond a factory wall. I'd followed the arrow to an unmarked door, yanked it open. Smells of leather and sweat, a short flight up, then into a musty, unpopulated office with an open door at the other end, and I'd found myself quickening my steps toward the noise beyond that door, my timorousness overtaken by a building curiosity until I stood where I was now, astonished by what I was seeing.

I had come prepared to meet this woman boxer and the girls she coached, but I was expecting to find them—I don't know, doing drills, stretching, throwing punches in the air, maybe, not actually sparring in the ring, battling, getting hit in the face, pounding their own gloved fists against another sweating body. When the time clock blared three times, signaling the end of the round, the girl fell to the floor for comic effect and when her headgear and mouthguard were removed, she was grinning. But the next girl who climbed through the ropes and sparred with the man had something wild about her. She was frightening to watch and at the same time I felt frightened for her; her pupils were dilated, and the force of her blows seemed fueled by something uncontrolled. Her gloves crashed against the man's headgear with a wrecking sound. When her headgear came off at the end of sparring, it seemed the coach had to speak with her for a minute, touch her hair and make eye contact, rub her shoulders and hug her, before the girl resurfaced, like a small child returning to waking life by degrees from a night terror.

With the sparring finished, for the first time I took a look around the room beyond the ring. Everyone else in the gym was male. A handful of men and not-really-yet-men worked out in pairs or solo along the periphery of the gym, signaling with their inattention the relative normality of what had just happened in the ring. But it had my heart pounding, my breath shallow. I knew I had entered a foreign land.

The Somerville Boxing Club had been around for over twenty years but on that first evening it had been in its current location, the back of a large stone church built in 1917, for only two weeks. Filling the rear sanctuary of what had most recently housed a Brazilian evangelical ministry, it looked more lived-in than that. The space projected a heady confusion of functions, a few sheets of plywood having transformed the altar into locker rooms of unequal size, one for each gender, with a weight-lifting area sandwiched between them. Three flags—Irish, Puerto Rican, and Italian—provided vertical drapes above the dais and evoked a certain theatricality. A couple of old pews, covered in blue velvet and leaking stuffing out the back, bordered, respectively, the weight area and the bloodstained ring, behind which hung a huge American flag and a dozen fight posters. The rest was equipment: heavy bags and speed bags, a double-end bag, a hook for jump ropes; some mats, medicine balls, cracked mirrors for shadow boxing propped against the walls; Vaseline, paper towels, water bottles; a greenish doctor's-office scale; spit buckets rigged with plastic funnels and tubing and duct tape. The time clock beeped at clear, dispassionate intervals, and skin and leather connected soundly, beating out their own, more complex counterpoint. The boom box played salsa or hip-hop or techno or pop, or static when the dial slipped between stations and no one bothered to go tune it for a while. When I got there that evening, it was playing, of all things, "Calling All Angels."

10   Now the coach was squirting water into the white girl's mouth, which was tipped open in the manner of a baby bird's beak. The girl's hands, still gloved, hung limp at her sides. The coach spoke to her, too

softly for me to hear the words, but in a tone that was tender and intimate. The girl, looking down, listened with all her being, nodding occasionally, panting a little. Their heads were almost touching. I got a better look at the coach's face, which—even though what I had witnessed her boxers doing made it impossible to be dismissive—only completed my idea of an unboxerly persona: open, guileless, undefended. Raphaëlla's features don't seem set or sleek; there is a haphazard quality to them, an artlessness, which is her beauty. When she smiles at you, the smile floods her face, every muscle giving itself over to the action, and you feel yourself the recipient of something tangible, an actual object with heft.

Later I would learn that she was the first female New England Golden Gloves champion, that she was a painter as well as a fighter, that she was working toward a master's degree in education, not with the intent of getting a teaching job but for the sole purpose of becoming a better coach, that she'd been to five funerals in the past year, that she had been harmed, that she believed everyone who made his or her way into the gym was in some way broken inside. That night it seemed all I knew was her size, and the knowledge was profound.

I was impatient to meet her and the four girls with whom she was obviously so intensely engaged. But even as the tattooed man stepped out of the ring (a former pro boxer, I later learned, he sometimes sparred with the girls as a personal favor to Raphaëlla), one of the younger girls stepped into the ring to work one-on-one with her coach. The other three girls moved onto the mats for push-ups and sit-ups. So I bided my time, waiting for them to finish.

As the dinner hour ended, more bodies came through the gym doors, from wiry boys to grizzled men, and outside the heavy fire door, which was eventually propped open in defiance of a handwritten sign taped on it, a wedge of sky showed blue-black, throwing into high relief the light, the heat, the fleshly congregation within. Everybody, as he entered, fell wordlessly into the shifting landscape of activity. A boy with an orange bandanna around his head, one foot up on a velvet pew, wrapped his hands. A tall white man worked the speed bag, shifting his weight from one hip to the other with unlikely grace. A barrel-chested man in glasses, arms folded across his formidable girth, scrutinized a lithesome kid on the double-end bag. A couple of brothers jumped rope with the finesse and footwork of circus acrobats. Someone fed the boom box a techno CD and cranked the volume. A trainer greased up a guy's face with fine, utilitarian speed: the nose, the chin, the cheek, the cheek. None of them betrayed the slightest interest in the presence of the girls training among them.

I turned 360 degrees, reading the motivational slogans tacked to the walls: VICTORY GOES TO THOSE WILLING TO PAY THE PRICE; THE WILL TO WIN IS NOT NEARLY IMPORTANT AS THE WILL TO PREPARE TO WIN! I tried to eavesdrop on the bits of conversation between trainers and boxers, but the room was too loud. I cut wide swaths around the multiplying numbers of men working out on the main floor of the gym, so as not to get slapped by anyone's jump rope. It was plain to me that I didn't belong yet the boxers' attitude toward me seemed one of easy indifference.

15   At last the girls finished their workout and came tumbling down like cubs from the ring and the free-weight area. I met them then: Jacinta and Josefina and Candida Rodriguez, three sisters, ages fifteen, twelve, and ten, respectively; Nikki Silvano, also fifteen and Jacinta's best friend; and Maria, mother to the Rodriguezes. Five people, and they seemed like a dozen that night, talking in bursts, reaching out to slap or pinch or muss one another even as they chatted with me. Maria talked to me as though well accustomed to speaking with reporters, which she was not, but she was roundly and assertively expressive, an agent for her daughters at all times. We were standing over by one of the speed bags, the one by the door to the parking lot, and she and some of the girls took turns swatting at it. Josefina, the middle daughter (known as Sefina), swung herself up on the recently erected wooden supports from which the gym equipment hung, and Maria interrupted herself to snap at the girl to get her butt *down*. She was telling me the story of the Women's Nationals that August, how Raphaëlla had taken the two big girls down to Augusta, Georgia, and how Jacinta had come home with a silver medal and left her opponent a bloody nose and two black eyes.

Candida—Candi—at ten the littlest, and too short to hit the speed bag even at its lowest adjustment without standing on something, burst out, "I want to hit a boy!" She'd been training with Raphaëlla for eight months and hadn't even had a proper sparring session yet: tough to find anyone her size.

Maria regarded her with proud amusement. "You want to fight a boy?"

"Hit. I said hit. Hit is different than fight."

Jacinta calmly grabbed her little sister and turned her upside down. Candi, her knees hooked at Jacinta's middle, her hands folded behind her head, began to do sit-ups from that vertical position.

20   "A moth!" cried Sefina. It fluttered on the floor. "Kill it! Step on it!"

"Don't kill it," said Maria, sucking her teeth derisively.

Sefina got down on her knees and poked at the quivering body.

Nikki told me she'd come home from Augusta with a bronze, that her legs were wobbling in the ring because she hadn't been training that long, that the ref stopped her fight and gave it to the other girl, and that she'd been mad. She explained that she and Jacinta had known each other since attending the same day-care program as little kids, and that Maria had given them matching cornrows for their bouts in Augusta. "I'm five things," said Nikki, ticking them off for me on her fingers: "Irish, Italian, Dutch, Cherokee, French." She had a lightness of presentation and demeanor that made her seem deceptively uncomplicated.

Sefina came over, bawling hoarsely. Jacinta had given her a fat lip, playing. Maria rolled her eyes. "This one cries a lot," she said.

"Sorry," said Jacinta, laughter quivering all about her dark eyes and dimples.

"Shut up!" Sefina lunged for the older girl, who yelped in mock fright and darted out of range. "*Mira, mira, Mami!*" Gingerly she lifted back the injured lip.

"*Callete,*" shushed Maria, pretending to slap her with the back of her hand. Then, to me, "This one's better at gymnastics. She can do flips and everything. Go, show her a cartwheel." But Sefina had drifted over to one of the full-length mirrors propped against the wall to examine her wound.

Someone had switched the music from Top Forty to hip-hop, something with a lot of *fuck you, bitch* in it and a solid, galvanizing bass line, and the outside air sifted chilly and pinpricked with rain through the doorway, and inside the sweat ran and ran and the time clock rode on, insistent, above everything else, dictating intervals of work and rest. Jacinta hit Nikki in the back with a medicine ball, and Nikki pretended, halfheartedly, to be mad. I tried to keep up with Maria's amiable, expansive narration of her own childhood, in Puerto Rico and Boston, and her own adolescent wish to fight, to box, to work out with the boys. Around us, the girls fought and played and finally retreated to the locker room to change.

Raphaëlla emerged in jeans and a jacket, a gym bag slung over her shoulder, car keys out. I'd been eager to shake her hand and introduce myself properly. I asked whether I could be in touch for an interview. She asked how long it would take, and recited her number at work. She was not impolite. But her manner contrasted sharply with the easy accessibility offered by Maria and the girls. I felt chastened by her aloofness, all the more so because it felt deserved.

The unsettled feeling I'd had out in the parking lot earlier, the anxiety I'd needed to stuff aside in order to make myself go into the building, had not been based on anything so literal as the fear of coming to harm from the boxers within. It wasn't that I was intimidated by the thought of mingling with people who inflict pain for sport. I think it was the product of my own barely acknowledged scorn for the idea of boxing and for those who choose to identify themselves with it. I was about to enter a club whose members I had never met but whom I secretly held in a measure of contempt. How fitting, then, that I had felt nervous about coming inside. And now it was as though Raphaëlla had seen through me.

I had come expecting to find something alien, and found instead, in the person before me, an eerie and shocking resemblance. We might have been sisters, this woman and I. I watched her bid the others farewell with all the warmth and openness she'd kept from her contact with me, and then she was gone, out the side door into the wedge of darkness. The girls left soon after, but I stayed awhile. I was reeling, embarrassed at all that I was feeling.

What *was* this place? I prowled around a bit, unable to go home just yet. The church's main sanctuary was locked up tight, but its lights were on. Peeking through the crack between the doors, I could catch stained-glass silvers of high, arched windows: This was where the Masons, who owned the building, convened. The basement held a social hall with a large adjacent kitchen that smelled of age and damp. That was all, really. Some bathrooms, a boiler room. And the great incongruity of its upstairs tenant, the boxing club.

Going back through the office, I found a man sitting behind the desk. He was short and stocky, with a cleft chin and a toothpick in his mouth and a backward baseball cap. He had dark pebble eyes that didn't hold my gaze. A grandmotherly woman in a green suit sat on the other side of the desk, on which had been laid wads of hundred-dollar bills. Her name was Ann Cooper, and she was recently back from Las Vegas, where the gym's star fighter had just relocated. Her hand was soft and cool, and she smelled like face powder. She seemed something like a den mother, but when I tried to get her actual title, she waved her hand modestly. "Oh, we're all just volunteers. Aren't we, Vinny?" The man with the pebble eyes shrugged and worked his toothpick to the other side of his mouth.

The money, apparently, had come from the boxer in Las Vegas, John "The Quiet Man" Ruiz, who had won the World Boxing Association heavyweight title from Evander Holyfield some seven months earlier— the first Latino ever to hold a world heavyweight title. His portrait hung, several times over, around the shabby little room. (Later I would learn that Raphaëlla had contributed one; she often painted portraits of the boxers she loved.) Ann Cooper's eyes teared up when she talked about John Ruiz. "'Cause we've struggled, you know," she said. "Everybody always said we'd never have a world champion out of our club. Not that that's the most important thing—we're here for the kids, first. But it doesn't hurt." She touched a wad of bills with her long polished fingernails. Rent. Gym fees were twenty-five dollars a month for kids who could afford to pay. As it happened, almost none of them could.

35   The warmth of this woman, and the sorrow shimmering about her, intrigued me. As did the gross unease of the toothpick man. And the man who emerged pink-skinned from the gym's single bathroom, wearing a little white towel around his waist and concern for no one's gaze as he trod past us on his way to the locker room. And the noble-warrior image of the Quiet Man in the pictures, somber-eyed, naked to the waist, girded by a championship belt of almost burdensome dimensions. And

the live-fuse beat of the music inside the gym, and the sharp percussion of fists at their own nonmusical purpose. The idea of all these young boxers bent on being here because they loved—what? Fighting? Hitting? Survival? The odd—*absurd*—impression of wholesomeness about the club, of something nurturing, nourishing, as though this were still a sanctuary, a place of healing instead of hurting. And above all: the fact that girls and women had dug out a place here.

I went back inside the gym proper, sat on a pew, and watched the men. What I am used to, when I report on a story, is disappearing inside it. I could feel that happening now, but only imperfectly. Something unfamiliar was getting in the way, asserting itself amid the rhythms and sweat and brewing questions. This unfamiliar thing was my awareness of *me*. It was as though I'd had ten cups of coffee before coming, as though I'd swallowed some sort of radioactive dye that made my physical presence irrefutable. It was as though, on some cellular level, my body knew what was to come, that this would not be a place where I could lose myself inside the story. That the opposite would prove true.

I sat there, watching the boxers, and floated in the din and the kinesthetic swirl. After a while I became aware of something specific leaping and burning within me, and when I went to put a name to it, it was jealousy.

Responding to Reading

1. What does Cohen mean when she says, "I knew I had entered a foreign land"(8)? What is "foreign" about the Somerville Boxing Club? What does this statement indicate about Cohen?
2. What were Cohen's preconceptions about female boxers? How do the people she meets conform (or not conform) to these stereotypes?
3. Cohen sees the Somerville Boxing Club as a place of contradictions. On the one hand, it is devoted to fighting and hitting. On the other hand, it is "something . . . nourishing . . . a sanctuary" (35). Does she ever come to terms with these differences? Why, at the end of the essay, does she feel jealousy?

Responding in Writing

In her 1987 book *On Boxing,* Joyce Carol Oates observes, "Boxing is a purely masculine activity and it inhabits a purely male world." The female boxer, she says, "cannot be taken seriously—she is a parody, she is cartoon, she is monstrous." Would Cohen agree with this sentiment? Do you?

MARKED WOMEN

Deborah Tannen

1945–

Deborah Tannen, a professor of linguistics at Georgetown University, has written books for both scholarly and popular audiences, with most of her work focusing on communication between men and women. Tannen is best known for her bestseller You Just Don't Understand: Women and Men in Conversation *(1990); her most recent book is* You're Wearing That? Mothers and Daughters in Conversation *(2006). The following essay, written in 1993, is a departure from Tannen's usual work. Here she focuses not on different communication styles but on the contrast she finds between the neutral way men in our culture present themselves to the world and the more message-laden way women present themselves.*

Some years ago I was at a small working conference of four women and eight men. Instead of concentrating on the discussion I found myself looking at the three other women at the table, thinking how each had a different style and how each style was coherent.

One woman had dark brown hair in a classic style, a cross between Cleopatra and Plain Jane. The severity of her straight hair was softened by wavy bangs and ends that turned under. Because she was beautiful, the effect was more Cleopatra than plain.

The second woman was older, full of dignity and composure. Her hair was cut in a fashionable style that left her with only one eye, thanks to a side part that let a curtain of hair fall across half her face. As she looked down to read her prepared paper, the hair robbed her of bifocal vision and created a barrier between her and the listeners.

The third woman's hair was wild, a frosted blond avalanche falling over and beyond her shoulders. When she spoke she frequently tossed her head, calling attention to her hair and away from her lecture.

5   Then there was makeup. The first woman wore facial cover that made her skin smooth and pale, a black line under each eye and mascara that darkened already dark lashes. The second wore only a light gloss on her lips and a hint of shadow on her eyes. The third had blue bands under her eyes, dark blue shadow, mascara, bright red lipstick and rouge; her fingernails flashed red.

I considered the clothes each woman had worn during the three days of the conference: In the first case, man-tailored suits in primary colors with solid-color blouses. In the second, casual but stylish black T-shirts, a floppy collarless jacket and baggy slacks or a skirt in neutral colors. The third wore a sexy jump suit; tight sleeveless jersey and tight yellow slacks; a dress with gaping armholes and an indulged tendency to fall off one shoulder.

Shoes? No. 1 wore string sandals with medium heels; No. 2, sensible, comfortable walking shoes; No. 3, pumps with spike heels. You can fill in the jewelry, scarves, shawls, sweaters—or lack of them.

As I amused myself finding coherence in these styles, I suddenly wondered why I was scrutinizing only the women. I scanned the eight men at the table. And then I knew why I wasn't studying them. The men's styles were unmarked.

The term "marked" is a staple of linguistic theory. It refers to the way language alters the base meaning of a word by adding a linguistic particle that has no meaning on its own. The unmarked form of a word carries the meaning that goes without saying—what you think of when you're not thinking anything special.

The unmarked tense of verbs in English is the present—for example, *visit*. To indicate past, you mark the verb by adding *ed* to yield *visited*. For future, you add a word: *will visit*. Nouns are presumed to be singular until marked for plural, typically by adding *s* or *es*, so *visit* becomes *visits* and *dish* becomes *dishes*. 10

The unmarked forms of most English words also convey "male." Being male is the unmarked case. Endings like *ess* and *ette* mark words as "female." Unfortunately, they also tend to mark them for frivolousness. Would you feel safe entrusting your life to a doctorette? Alfre Woodard, who was an Oscar nominee for best supporting actress, says she identifies herself as an actor because "actresses worry about eyelashes and cellulite, and women who are actors worry about the characters we are playing." Gender markers pick up extra meanings that reflect common associations with the female gender: not quite serious, often sexual.

Each of the women at the conference had to make decisions about hair, clothing, makeup and accessories, and each decision carried meaning. Every style available to us was marked. The men in our group had made decisions, too, but the range from which they chose was incomparably narrower. Men can choose styles that are marked, but they don't have to, and in this group none did. Unlike the women, they had the option of being unmarked.

Take the men's hair styles. There was no marine crew cut or oily longish hair falling into eyes, no asymmetrical, two-tiered construction to swirl over a bald top. One man was unabashedly bald; the others had hair of standard length, parted on one side, in natural shades of brown or gray or graying. Their hair obstructed no views, left little to toss or push back or run fingers through and, consequently, needed and attracted no attention. A few men had beards. In a business setting, beards might be marked. In this academic gathering, they weren't.

There could have been a cowboy shirt with string tie or a three-piece suit or a necklaced hippie in jeans. But there wasn't. All eight men wore brown or blue slacks and nondescript shirts of light colors. No man wore sandals or boots; their shoes were dark, closed, comfortable and flat. In short, unmarked.

15 Although no man wore makeup, you couldn't say the men didn't wear makeup in the sense that you could say a woman didn't wear makeup. For men, no makeup is unmarked.

I asked myself what style we women could have adopted that would have been unmarked, like the men's. The answer was none. There is no unmarked woman.

There is no woman's hair style that can be called standard, that says nothing about her. The range of women's hair styles is staggering, but a woman whose hair has no particular style is perceived as not caring about how she looks, which can disqualify her for many positions, and will subtly diminish her as a person in the eyes of some.

Women must choose between attractive shoes and comfortable shoes. When our group made an unexpected trek, the woman who wore flat, laced shoes arrived first. Last to arrive was the woman in spike heels, shoes in hand and a handful of men around her.

If a woman's clothing is tight or revealing (in other words, sexy), it sends a message—an intended one of wanting to be attractive, but also a possibly unintended one of availability. If her clothes are not sexy, that too sends a message, lent meaning by the knowledge that they could have been. There are thousands of cosmetic products from which women can choose and myriad ways of applying them. Yet no makeup at all is anything but unmarked. Some men see it as a hostile refusal to please them.

20 Women can't even fill out a form without telling stories about themselves. Most forms give four titles to choose from. "Mr." carries no meaning other than that the respondent is male. But a woman who checks "Mrs." or "Miss" communicates not only whether she has been married but also whether she has conservative tastes in forms of address—and probably other conservative values as well. Checking "Ms." declines to let on about marriage (checking "Mr." declines nothing since nothing was asked), but it also marks her as either liberated or rebellious, depending on the observer's attitudes and assumptions.

I sometimes try to duck these variously marked choices by giving my title as "Dr."—and in so doing risk marking myself as either uppity (hence sarcastic responses like *Excuse me!*) or an overachiever (hence reactions of congratulatory surprise like "Good for you!").

All married women's surnames are marked. If a woman takes her husband's name, she announces to the world that she is married and has traditional values. To some it will indicate that she is less herself, more identified by her husband's identity. If she does not take her husband's name, this too is marked, seen as worthy of comment: she has done something; she has "kept her own name." A man is never said to have "kept his own name" because it never occurs to anyone that he might have given it up. For him using his own name is unmarked.

A married woman who wants to have her cake and eat it too may use her surname plus his, with or without a hyphen. But this too announces her marital status and often results in a tongue-tying string. In a list (Harvey O'Donovan, Jonathan Feldman, Stephanie Woodbury McGillicutty), the woman's multiple name stands out. It is marked.

I have never been inclined toward biological explanations of gender differences in language, but I was intrigued to see Ralph Fasold bring biological phenomena to bear on the question of linguistic marking in his book "The Sociolinguistics of Language." Fasold stresses that language and culture are particularly unfair in treating women as the marked case because biologically it is the male that is marked. While two X chromosomes make a female, two Y chromosomes make nothing. Like the linguistic markers *s, es* or *ess,* the Y chromosome doesn't "mean" anything unless it is attached to a root form—an X chromosome.

Developing this idea elsewhere, Fasold points out that girls are born 25 with fully female bodies, while boys are born with modified female bodies. He invites men who doubt this to lift up their shirts and contemplate why they have nipples.

In his book, Fasold notes "a wide range of facts which demonstrates that female is the unmarked sex." For example, he observes that there are a few species that produce only females, like the whiptail lizard. Thanks to parthenogenesis, they have no trouble having as many daughters as they like. There are no species, however, that produce only males. This is no surprise, since any such species would become extinct in its first generation.

Fasold is also intrigued by species that produce individuals not involved in reproduction, like honeybees and leaf-cutter ants. Reproduction is handled by the queen and a relatively few males; the workers are sterile females. "Since they do not reproduce," Fasold says, "there is no reason for them to be one sex or the other, so they default, so to speak, to female."

Fasold ends his discussion of these matters by pointing out that if language reflected biology, grammar books would direct us to use "she" to include males and females and "he" only for specifically male referents. But they don't. They tell us that "he" means "he or she," and that "she" is used only if the referent is specifically female. This use of "he" as the sex-indefinite pronoun is an innovation introduced into English by grammarians in the 18th and 19th centuries, according to Peter Mühlhäusler and Rom Harré in "Pronouns and People." From at least about 1500, the correct sex-indefinite pronoun was "they," as it still is in casual spoken English. In other words, the female was declared by grammarians to be the marked case.

Writing this article may mark me not as a writer, not as a linguist, not as an analyst of human behavior, but as a feminist—which will have positive or negative, but in any case powerful, connotations for readers. Yet I doubt that anyone reading Ralph Fasold's book would put that label on him.

30   I discovered the markedness inherent in the very topic of gender after writing a book on differences in conversational style based on geographical region, ethnicity, class, age and gender. When I was interviewed, the vast majority of journalists wanted to talk about the differences between women and men. While I thought I was simply describing what I observed—something I had learned to do as a researcher—merely mentioning women and men marked me as a feminist for some.

When I wrote a book devoted to gender differences, in ways of speaking, I sent the manuscript to five male colleagues, asking them to alert me to any interpretation, phrasing or wording that might seem unfairly negative toward men. Even so, when the book came out, I encountered responses like that of the television talk show host who, after interviewing me, turned to the audience and asked if they thought I was male-bashing.

Leaping upon a poor fellow who affably nodded in agreement, she made him stand and asked, "Did what she said accurately describe you?" "Oh, yes," he answered. "That's me exactly." "And what she said about women—does that sound like your wife?" "Oh yes," he responded. "That's her exactly." "Then why do you think she's male-bashing?" He answered, with disarming honesty, "Because she's a woman and she's saying things about men."

To say anything about women and men without marking oneself as either feminist or anti-feminist, male-basher or apologist for men seems as impossible for a woman as trying to get dressed in the morning without inviting interpretations of her character.

Sitting at the conference table musing on these matters, I felt sad to think that we women didn't have the freedom to be unmarked that the men sitting next to us had. Some days you just want to get dressed and go about your business. But if you're a woman, you can't, because there is no unmarked woman.

Responding to Reading

1. Tannen notes that men "can choose styles that are marked, but they don't have to" (12); however, she believes that women do not have "the option of being unmarked" (12). What does she mean? Can you give some examples of women's styles that you believe are unmarked? (Note that in paragraph 16, Tannen says there are no such styles.)

2. In paragraph 33, Tannen says, "To say anything about women and men without marking oneself as either feminist or anti-feminist, male-basher or

apologist for men seems as impossible for a woman as trying to get dressed in the morning without inviting interpretations of her character." Do you agree?

3. In paragraphs 24–28, Tannen discusses Ralph Fasold's book *The Sociolinguistics of Language.* Why does she include this material? Could she have made her point just as effectively without it?

Responding in Writing

Consider the men and women you see every day at school or in your neighborhood. Does their appearance support Tannen's thesis?

FOCUS

Who Has It Harder, Girls or Boys?

Advertisement showing girl in museum looking at dinosaur skull

Responding to the Image

1. The advertisement above is designed to encourage girls to study math and science. What elements in the picture emphasize these subjects? In what way do they reinforce the message, "See the world through math and science"?
2. How does this ad attempt to reach its target audience—girls below the age of twelve? Do you think it is successful? What changes, if any, would you make to the ad?

WHAT IS THE TRIPLE BIND?
Stephen Hinshaw
1952–

Stephen Hinshaw is the chair of the psychology department and professor of psychology at the University of California at Berkeley. He researches behavior disorders in children and attention-deficit/hyperactivity disorder (ADHD), among other topics related to child psychology. His books include The Mark of Shame: Stigma of Mental Illness and an Agenda for Change *(2007),* Breaking the Silence: Mental Health Professionals Disclose Their Personal and Family Experiences of Mental Illness *(2008), and* Child and Adolescent Psychopathology *(2008). The following essay is excerpted from Hinshaw's most recent book,* The Triple Bind: Saving Our Teenage Girls from Today's Pressures *(2009).*

The original notion of a double bind came from social scientists in the 1950s who studied children growing up with contradictory, impossible demands. For example, a child might be told, "Tell me everything that's going on with you," and then told (either with or without words), "Don't bother me with so much information." Trying ever more frantically to do the impossible, the double-bind child was thought to be at risk of mental illness.

Of course, mental illness has more complex origins than this picture indicates, nearly always including biological and genetic underpinnings. And the types of family messages most associated with serious disorders aren't necessarily those of the double bind. But even if double-bind-style messages don't produce clinical conditions, they certainly produce distress. When we're asked to do two contradictory things, and especially when we fear being punished for not doing them, we're in a bind: confused, frustrated, and likely to blame ourselves. Our feelings might turn into anger, despair, resignation, or an ever more desperate attempt to go in two directions at once.

Today's girl faces not only a double but actually a Triple Bind: a set of impossible, contradictory expectations. Our teenage girls are baffled, distressed, and overwhelmed as they try ever harder to meet these ever more punishing demands. They've responded with a lower age of onset of depression, increases in aggression and violence, and skyrocketing rates of self-mutilation, binge eating, and suicide. They've also responded by sacrificing key portions of their identities, developing feelings of self-hatred, and becoming overwhelmed with a general sense of pressured confusion. The Triple Bind is possibly the greatest current threat to our daughters' health and well-being, an enormous obstacle to their becoming healthy, happy, and successful adults.

CHAPTER 5 FOCUS

Each portion of the Triple Bind is challenging enough. But it's the combination of all three aspects that makes it deadly:

1. Be good at all of the traditional girl stuff.
2. Be good at most of the traditional guy stuff.
3. Conform to a narrow, unrealistic set of standards that allows for no alternative.

5   Let's take a closer look.

1. **Be good at all of the traditional girl stuff.** Today's girl knows she's supposed to fulfill all the traditional "girl" expectations—look pretty, be nice, get a boyfriend—while excelling at the "girl skills" of empathy, cooperation, and relationship building. Any girl who wants to feel normal knows the drill: bond with your girlfriends, support your boyfriend, and make your family proud. The essence of these girl skills is maintaining relationships: doing what others expect of you while putting their needs first. It's the quality that leads a girl to spend all evening talking a friend through a crisis rather than using those hours to write her own A-level paper. It's also the quality that might lead her to suppress her own abilities or desires in order to boost a boyfriend's ego or reassure an anxious parent.

2. **Be good at most of the traditional guy stuff.** Female skills might once have been all a girl needed—but no longer. Today, a girl isn't just looking for marriage and family; she expects to succeed at what were once traditionally considered "boy" goals, such as getting straight As and being a super-athlete. Girls, especially those from the middle- or upper-income brackets, are often expected to win acceptance to a top college. A poor or working-class girl's family may also look to her for the kind of financial support or upward mobility, through school, sports, or entertainment, that was once expected only of her brother.

So in today's competitive environment, girl skills are not enough. A successful girl must also master the ultimate boy skills of assertion, maybe even aggression: the commitment to becoming a winner at anything you undertake, regardless of your own or others' feelings. It's the quality that leads the star football player to charge through the line, suppressing any fear he might feel, ignoring both the pain he experiences and the pain he causes. It's also the quality that might lead a boy to promise himself, "Someday, I'm going to discover a cure for cancer, no matter how hard I have to work, no matter how many hours I miss with my family, no matter how many people think I can't do it."

As you can see, there are pluses and minuses to both approaches, but what's really difficult, if not impossible, is to master both of them at the same time. How do "best friends

4ever" fight each other over a diminishing number of college slots? What if the empowered basketball star doesn't fit into the size-2 miniskirt or can't stand letting her boyfriend win at ping-pong? What about the girl who wants to get off the merry-go-round and explore an alternative identity that allows a little more breathing room?

3. **Conform to a narrow, unrealistic set of standards that allows for no alternative.** Enter the third component of the Triple Bind: the way that alternatives of all types—different ways of becoming a woman, relating to society, or constructing an authentic self—have been virtually erased by the culture. This is the truly insidious aspect of the Triple Bind, which seems to offer choices with one hand only to take them away with the other.

At first glance, you might think that a girl was free to become anything she chooses. Look a little closer, though, and you'll see that whatever *else* she may decide, she must also always be sexy, thin, and pretty; have either a great boyfriend or a husband and kids, and be wildly successful at her career.

Girls used to be able to escape the narrow demands of femininity through such alternative roles as beatnik, tomboy, intellectual, hippie, punk, or goth. They'd embrace the ideals of feminism to proclaim that women didn't always have to be pretty, nice, and thin; that they didn't always have to have boyfriends; and that not all women wanted to become mothers. Or girls might follow a counterculture that challenged the notion of ascending the corporate ladder or fulfilling men's notions of the ideal woman. They'd imitate pop stars who presented alternate looks and styles of femininity: Janis Joplin, Patti Smith, Tina Turner, Cyndi Lauper. They'd take up basketball or hockey; they'd turn into bookworms or dream of being president. All of these alternatives to traditional female roles gave independent girls a little breathing room, the space to insist that they didn't necessarily have to fit into skimpy clothes or learn how to flirt at age eleven. Other types of alternatives—bohemianism, the counterculture, activism, art, humanitarian ideals—helped girls challenge the achievement-oriented culture that insisted on straight As, elite colleges, and seven-figure incomes as the only prizes worth having. A free-spirited girl might even find a way of being sexy that wasn't about how she looked, a sexual style that was uniquely her own.

Now virtually all of these possibilities have been co-opted, consumerized, and forced into an increasingly narrow, unrealistic set of roles. Standards have become narrower and less realistic for both looks ("girl stuff") and achievement ("boy stuff"), even as the cultural alternatives that might have helped girls resist these standards have been erased.

First, the definitions of "sexy" and "pretty" have narrowed enormously in recent years, with an ever-escalating demand that girls turn themselves into sexual objects. For a girl to fit the acceptable look now requires an almost superhuman commitment to dieting, waxing, applying makeup, and shopping; for some girls, plastic surgery has also come to seem like a minimum requirement. These trends begin at frighteningly young ages. Even many lesbian girls, whose choice once seemed to free them from the "male gaze" of conventional beauty, are now also expected to present themselves in sexually objectified terms, sporting the same lipstick and lingerie as their heterosexual sisters.

10   At the same time, girls face increasingly unrealistic standards for achievement. Only the top grades and test scores, combined with the most impressive extracurriculars, will fit a girl for a top college, a destination that is becoming virtually a requirement for more and more middle-class girls. Poor and working-class girls now dream of becoming superstar athletes, top models, or self-made entrepreneurs—and attending the Ivies as well. I'm all for dreaming, but girls are being given the message that anything less than the absolute best counts as failure.

So both the "girl" and "boy" requirements have become harder to meet, even as the alternatives that might have freed girls from either set of demands—feminism, bohemianism, political activism, community spirit—have all but disappeared from the cultural landscape. Our girls are truly trapped, and the crisis-level statistics I have shared with you are a key consequence.

This third aspect of the Triple Bind is particularly insidious because it's so deceptive. On the surface, all jobs, all activities, indeed all possibilities are open to every teenage girl. Look a little deeper, though and you can see the constraining need for girls to objectify themselves in order to fit the feminine mold. Yes, you might be able to do something "alternative" and unique—you can become the first female Indy driver, like Danica Patrick, or the first female presidential contender, like Hillary Clinton—but you still have to pose in a sexy outfit for *Playboy* or obsess publicly about your weight. Instead of Chrissie Hynde, we have Britney Spears; instead of Annie Lennox, we have Lindsay Lohan; instead of Queen Latifah, we have Beyoncé Knowles. Political pundits toss their hair and sport short skirts; women are told to exhibit empowerment, originality, and pride even as they don swimsuits to become the next top model. Our daughters might admire a whole roster of female athletes, but they, too, are expected to look skinny and "hot." (A colleague of mine, a sports psychologist, tells me that this is a recurring worry among the top female athletes he treats each week.) The 24/7 barrage of media images contributes to the sense that the walls are closing in. Skinny, sexy, scantily dressed teens and preteens appear everywhere, an airtight world that seems to offer no way out, reinforcing the notion that the only possible way to become a woman is to turn oneself into an object. Even the pioneering Nancy Pelosi, who will go down in history as the first female Speaker of the House, seems polite and ultrafeminine compared to such forebears as the hefty, abrasive congresswoman Bella Abzug.

Despite the apparent wealth of choices, our girls are ultimately presented with a very narrow, unrealistic set of standards that allow for no alternative. A seemingly boundless and hermetic culture insists on every female looking thin, pretty, and sexually available, whether she's a political pundit, a professional athlete, or a ten-year-old girl, even as it also demands that every girl aspire to being a wife (lesbian or straight) and mother—and all while climbing to the top of her career ladder, becoming a millionaire, and triumphing over every possible competitor. No wonder our girls are increasingly becoming depressed, expressing their anguish through binge eating, self-mutilation, acts of violence, and even suicide.

As I lay out the elements of the Triple Bind, they sound neat and discrete, easy-to-separate qualities that are clearly at odds with one another. But for the teenage girl caught in the middle of that bind, the contradictions seem to blend seamlessly together. If you want to understand how this works, just watch a few episodes of *America's Next Top Model.* The show is wildly popular with teenage girls: nearly every one of the girls I spoke with told me she loved the show, including feminists, lesbians, and girls who wouldn't be caught dead wearing makeup, let alone prancing down a runway or posing for a swimsuit ad.

The show's format is simple: it gathers a group of thirteen young 15 women of various shapes, backgrounds, and sizes, and asks them to compete for a top modeling spot. Every week, one more contestant is eliminated as the women are put through the complicated demands of photo shoots, runway modeling, and extreme athleticism. They might have to don mermaids' tails and dangle in fishing nets suspended above a canal or pose, shivering in skimpy clothing, upon ice sculptures. They also have to endure twenty-four-hour surveillance from the show's cameras and find some way to get along with the other women they're competing against. And they have to learn how to make it all seem effortless, keeping a smiling, pretty face constantly on display in case some photographer snaps an unflattering "casual" shot and sells it to the tabloids. As the show's press release puts it, "Participants are asked to demonstrate both inner and outer beauty as they learn to master complicated catwalks, intense physical fitness, fashion photo shoots, and perfect publicity skills."

Looks count: a model has to have a lovely face and body, and usually she needs to be thin, though the show almost always includes a voluptuous woman or someone with unusual looks. (In fact, on the Spring 2008 cycle, a "plus-size" model won the competition for the first time.) However, a model can't be *just* a pretty face; the judges speak contemptuously of "beauty queens" and "ordinary" pretty girls. A model, especially a top model, has to have something extra—an unusual face, a signature walk. She must both fit the mold and break the mold, and of course, no one can ever quite tell her when she must do which.

CHAPTER 5 FOCUS

One contestant is told to leave the show because she refuses to cut her hair in the style that the judges have decided is best for her. Another is informed that if she doesn't let the show's dentist fix the gap in her front teeth, she won't be eligible for the Cover Girl contract that is part of the prize package.

Both girls agonize over their decisions: they see their hair, their gap-toothed smile, as aspects of who they are, their own sort of signature. No, the judges insist, those parts of their body are the wrong ground on which to take a stand. Get rid of those elements—and then find another way to be unique. "Confidence," "personality," and "being yourself" are probably the words most often spoken on *America's Next Top Model,* but unquestioning obedience is also a requirement.

The show's creator and producer is Tyra Banks, herself a ground-breaking African American model who clearly cares deeply for her young charges. But like many caring parents of today's girls, Banks has to teach the next generation how to fit into a system that she readily acknowledges is often unfair. Accordingly, she urges the girls to "be themselves" even as she demands that they conform.

In one episode. Banks explains to one young woman that her "country" accent is getting in her way. You shouldn't cut yourself off from your roots, Banks says firmly, but you can't be bound by them, either. Learn to turn your accent on and off, or you'll never be able to sell makeup on TV. Then Banks demonstrates how to play with a non-mainstream accent, teasing the model in her own childhood "street" speech and then reverting immediately to a more cultured voice.

20   No one minds where you actually came from: on one episode, the runway coach talked about himself as someone who had grown up in the projects, and fashion icon Twiggy, who was one of the judges for several seasons, referred frequently to her own working-class background. (Significantly, Twiggy herself started the fashion for thin models; before she came on the scene, models were full-figured.) But your background has to be incorporated into the larger ideal of an infinitely malleable woman who is nevertheless always unique. We should be able to identify your signature walk even in silhouette, says Tyra, but you also need to speak without an accent.

Imagine, for a moment, being one of the millions of teenage girls who watch this show. What message is she supposed to derive from this? *Be yourself—but not too much yourself. Be proud of who you are—but cover it up the moment someone else says it's offensive. Be unique—but unique in the right way, not in the wrong way. And if you want to know how to follow these contradictory instructions, well, we can't tell you exactly how, but don't worry, we'll know it when we see it. So just keep trying and trying and trying. If you're lucky, you'll figure it out. If not, well, you're off the program!*

On another episode, Tyra confronts a voluptuous young woman whose body doesn't fit the model stereotype. "Being a big girl is almost harder than being a black girl," Tyra says, pointing out that, like any minority, the "big girl" will have to work harder and present herself more cheerfully than her mainstream counterparts. The judges see no problem with giving the girl contradictory advice: she is encouraged both to glory in her unusual body (unusual by models' standards) and to compensate for it.

Clearly, looks aren't all that matter: ambition counts, too. Girls don't see their families or their boyfriends for several weeks as they remain shut up in the "model house" or travel to some exotic location, all the while working around the clock on each week's task. Any girl who loses focus is reprimanded, by the judges and by her fellow models; everyone agrees that boyfriends must come second if you expect to win. The show's theme song drives the point home: "Wanna be on top?" it asks, again and again and again.

Accordingly, Danielle, the model with the gap-toothed smile and "country" accent, drags herself out of a hospital bed, fighting the aftereffects of dehydration, exhaustion, and food poisoning to pose for a photo shoot on top of an elephant. She seems haggard and frail as she climbs on the beast's back, but the moment the cameras start to click, she looks dreamy and beautiful. She overcomes her physical weakness like a man but offers herself up to the camera like a woman, all in the service of a unique identity that is nevertheless ultrafeminized and overly sexualized.

To her credit, Banks wants to send a positive message about body image and race: the show always includes several African American and Latina models, as well as one or two girls who don't fit the mold. One season, that girl is Kim, a self-avowed lesbian who openly agonizes over her gender presentation: does she want to come across as a boy or a girl? The judges praise her androgyny and are obviously reluctant to cut her from the show. Clearly, Kim's no traditional girl; she even has a mini-affair with one of the other contestants. (Significantly, the other models object not to the homosexual activity but to the way the affair seems to distract both girls from the contest.)

Still, like all the women on the show, Kim is *also* ultrafeminine and overly sexualized: made up, dressed up, obediently allowing herself to be styled and posed however the client wants. Sometimes the judges want her to keep her boyish air; at other times, she's expected to look girlishly cute and sexy. Her unconventional qualities—androgyny, sexual difference—don't free her from traditional femininity so much as give her a unique spin on it. Even a gender-bending lesbian doesn't get a free pass: she has to retain her own style *and* be a "girly girl," sometimes switching back and forth, sometimes doing both at once.

Learning to be America's Next Top Model is clearly a balancing act even more demanding than staying on the back of an elephant. In true girl style, the models seek to please, to obey, to look good. In true boy style, they seek to prove their physical prowess and to reach the top. ("Suck it up," say the judges when the models complain about working in the cold or dangling upside down in the heat. "I'm here to win, not to make friends," say the models when asked about their competitors.) And any alternative identity or personal style they might develop, no matter how unique or apparently transgressive, is always cycled back into the demand to be ultrafeminized and overly sexualized, to make money for whatever corporate client has sponsored the photo shoot, to do whatever it takes to reach the top. Being a proud black woman, Danielle nonetheless accepts a long, silky hairstyle; being a boyish lesbian doesn't keep Kim from wanting to sell makeup. They don't see any contradictions, and perhaps girls watch the show so eagerly because they, too, need to reconcile so many conflicting demands.

"I like the show while I watch it, but it makes me feel bad afterwards," says fifteen-year-old Madeleine, a junior at a public high school in a small midwestern college town. When I ask her why, she explains, "Well, it's intriguing, but it's sort of sad. I feel bad about myself, because I don't look that way. And I feel bad for them, because they want to reach the top but you know most of them aren't going to. They're never going to get what they dream about—but they just don't realize it."

Yet Madeleine watches the show every week, riveted by the balancing act that is her own struggle writ large. Like the contestants she watches, she needs to be herself—and to please others; to radiate confidence—but not to be arrogant; to look sexy—but not slutty; to be ambitious—but not mean. And if she stumbles on her own private runway or falters at her personal judge's latest demand, she at least has the comfort of knowing that thinner, prettier, more famous girls are also struggling with the impossible contradictions posed by the Triple Bind.

Responding to Reading

1. What is the "triple bind"? According to Hinshaw, in what sense is the triple bind "the greatest current threat to our daughters' health and well being" (3)?
2. Hinshaw points out that at one time girls used to be able to escape from the narrow demands of femininity. How, according to Hinshaw, has this situation changed? How does he account for this change?
3. What does Hinshaw mean when he says, "Despite the apparent wealth of choices, our girls are ultimately presented with a very narrow, unrealistic set of standards that allow for no alternative" (13)? According to Hinshaw, how does the show *America's Next Top Model* illustrate this contradiction? What do teenage female viewers take away from this show?

Responding in Writing

Do you think men suffer from a version of the triple bind? Write a few paragraphs in which you discuss this possibility.

THE WAR AGAINST BOYS

Christina Hoff Sommers

1950–

Christina Hoff Sommers is a resident scholar at the American Enterprise Insti-
tute in Washington, D.C. A frequent television commentator, Sommers is also
the author of essays in a wide variety of periodicals and has published several
books, including Who Stole Feminism? How Women Have Betrayed
Women *(1994) and* The War against Boys: How Misguided Feminism Is
Harming Our Young Men *(2000). Her latest book is* One Nation under
Therapy: How the Helping Culture Is Eroding Self-Reliance *(2005). In*
the following, the opening section of a long essay that appeared in the Atlantic
Monthly, *Sommers examines what she calls "the myth of girls in crisis" and*
demonstrates that, contrary to popular opinion, boys, not girls, are short-
changed by today's educational establishment.

It's a bad time to be a boy in America. The triumphant victory of the U.S.
women's soccer team at the World Cup last summer has come to symbolize the spirit of American girls. The shooting at Columbine High last
spring might be said to symbolize the spirit of American boys.

That boys are in disrepute is not accidental. For many years
women's groups have complained that boys benefit from a school system that favors them and is biased against girls. "Schools shortchange
girls," declares the *American Association of University Women*. Girls are
"undergoing a kind of psychological foot-binding," two prominent educational psychologists say. A stream of books and pamphlets cite
research showing not only that boys are classroom favorites but also
that they are given to schoolyard violence and sexual harassment.

In the view that has prevailed in American education over the past
decade, boys are resented, both as unfairly privileged sex and as obstacles on the path to gender justice for girls. This perspective is promoted
in schools of education, and many a teacher now feels that girls need
and deserve special indemnifying consideration. "It is really clear that
boys are Number One in this society and in most of the world," says
Patricia O'Reilly, a professor of education and the director of the Gender Equity Center, at the University of Cincinnati.

The idea that schools and society grind girls down has given rise to
an array of laws and policies intended to curtail the advantage boys
have and to redress the harm done to girls. That girls are treated as the
second sex in school and consequently suffer, that boys are accorded
privileges and consequently benefit—these are things everyone is presumed to know. But they are not true.

The research commonly cited to support claims of male privilege 5
and male sinfulness is riddled with errors. Almost none of it has been

published in peer-reviewed professional journals. Some of the data turn out to be mysteriously missing. A review of the facts shows boys, not girls, on the weak side of an education gender gap. The typical boy is a year and a half behind the typical girl in reading and writing; he is less committed to school and less likely to go to college. In 1997 college full-time enrollments were 45 percent male and 55 percent female. The Department of Education predicts that the proportion of boys in college classes will continue to shrink.

Data from the U.S. Department of Education and from several recent university studies show that far from being shy and demoralized, today's girls outshine boys. They get better grades. They have higher educational aspirations. They follow more rigorous academic programs and participate in advanced-placement classes at higher rates. According to the National Center for Education Statistics, slightly more girls than boys enroll in high-level math and science courses. Girls, allegedly timorous and lacking in confidence, now outnumber boys in student government, in honor societies, on school newspapers, and in debating clubs. Only in sports are boys ahead, and women's groups are targeting the sports gap with a vengeance. Girls read more books. They outperform boys on tests for artistic and musical ability. More girls than boys study abroad. More join the Peace Corps. At the same time, more boys than girls are suspended from school. More are held back and more drop out. Boys are three times as likely to receive a diagnosis of attention-deficit hyperactivity disorder. More boys than girls are involved in crime, alcohol, and drugs. Girls attempt suicide more often than boys, but it is boys who more often succeed. In 1997, a typical year, 4,483 young people aged five to twenty-four committed suicide: 701 females and 3,782 males.

In the technical language of education experts, girls are academically more "engaged." Last year an article in *The CQ Researcher* about male and female academic achievement described a common parental observation: "Daughters want to please their teachers by spending extra time on projects, doing extra credit, making homework as neat as possible. Sons rush through homework assignments and run outside to play, unconcerned about how the teacher will regard the sloppy work."

School engagement is a critical measure of student success. The U.S. Department of Education gauges student commitment by the following criteria: "How much time do students devote to homework each night?" and "Do students come to class prepared and ready to learn? (Do they bring, books and pencils? Have they completed their homework?)" According to surveys of fourth, eighth, and twelfth graders, girls consistently do more homework than boys. By the twelfth grade boys are four times as likely as girls not to do homework. Similarly, more boys than girls report that they "usually" or "often" come to school without supplies or without having done their homework.

The performance gap between boys and girls in high school leads directly to the growing gap between male and female admissions to college. The Department of Education reports that in 1996 there were 8.4 million women but only 6.7 million men enrolled in college. It predicts that women will hold on to and increase their lead well into the next decade, and that by 2007 the numbers will be 9.2 million women and 6.9 million men.

Deconstructing the Test-Score Gap

Feminists cannot deny that girls get better grades, are more engaged   10
academically, and are now the majority sex in higher education. They argue, however, that these advantages are hardly decisive. Boys, they point out, get higher scores than girls on almost every significant standardized test—especially the Scholastic Assessment Test and law school, medical school, and graduate school admissions tests.

In 1996 I wrote an article for *Education Week* about the many ways in which girl students were moving ahead of boys. Seizing on the test-score data that suggest boys are doing better than girls, David Sadker, a professor of education at American University and a co-author with his wife, Myra, of *Failing at Fairness: How America's Schools Cheat Girls* (1994), wrote, "If females are soaring in school, as Christina Hoff Sommers writes, then these tests are blind to their flight." On the 1998 SAT boys were thirty-five points (out of 800) ahead of girls in math and seven points ahead in English. These results seem to run counter to all other measurements of achievement in school. In almost all other areas boys lag behind girls. Why do they test better? Is Sadker right in suggesting that this is a manifestation of boys' privileged status?

The answer is no. A careful look at the pool of students who take the SAT and similar tests shows that the girls' lower scores have little or nothing to do with bias or unfairness. Indeed, the scores do not even signify lower achievement by girls. First of all, according to *College Bound Seniors*, an annual report on standardized-test takers published by the College Board, many more "at risk" girls than "at risk" boys take the SAT—girls from lower-income homes or with parents who never graduated from high school or never attended college. "These characteristics," the report says, "are associated with lower than average SAT scores." Instead of wrongly using SAT scores as evidence of bias against girls, scholars should be concerned about the boys who never show up for the tests they need if they are to move on to higher education.

Another factor skews test results so that they appear to favor boys. Nancy Cole, the president of the Educational Testing Service, calls it the "spread" phenomenon. Scores on almost any intelligence or achievement test are more spread out for boys than for girls—boys include more prodigies and more students of marginal ability. Or, as the political scientist James Q. Wilson once put it, "There are more male geniuses and more male idiots."

Boys also dominate dropout lists, failure lists, and learning-disability lists. Students in these groups rarely take college-admissions tests. On the other hand, exceptional boys who take school seriously show up in disproportionately high numbers for standardized tests. Gender-equity activists like Sadker ought to apply their logic consistently: if the shortage of girls at the high end of the ability distribution is evidence of unfairness to girls, then the excess of boys at the low end should be deemed evidence of unfairness to boys.

15   Suppose we were to turn our attention away from the highly motivated, self-selected two fifths of high school students who take the SAT and consider instead a truly representative sample of American schoolchildren. How would girls and boys then compare? Well, we have the answer. The National Assessment of Educational Progress started in 1969 and mandated by Congress, offers the best and most comprehensive measure of achievement among students at all levels of ability. Under the NAEP program 70,000 to 100,000 students, drawn from forty-four states, are tested in reading, writing, math, and science at ages nine, thirteen, and seventeen. In 1996, seventeen-year-old boys outperformed seventeen-year-old girls by five points in math and eight points in science, whereas the girls outperformed the boys by fourteen points in reading and seventeen points in writing. In the past few years girls have been catching up in math and science while boys have continued to lag far behind in reading and writing.

In the July, 1995, issue of *Science,* Larry V. Hedges and Amy Nowell, researchers at the University of Chicago, observed that girls' deficits in math were small but not insignificant. These deficits, they noted, could adversely affect the number of women who "excel in scientific and technical occupations." Of the deficits in boys' writing skills they wrote, "The large sex differences in writing . . . are alarming. . . . The data imply that males are, on average, at a rather profound disadvantage in the performance of this basic skill." They went on to warn,

> The generally larger numbers of males who perform near the bottom of the distribution on reading comprehension and writing also have policy implications. It seems likely that individuals with such poor literacy skills will have difficulty finding employment in an increasingly information-driven economy. Thus, some intervention may be required to enable them to participate constructively.

Hedges and Nowell were describing a serious problem of national scope, but because the focus elsewhere has been on girls' deficits, few Americans know much about the problem or even suspect that it exists.

Indeed, so accepted has the myth of girls in crisis become that even teachers who work daily with male and female students tend to reflexively dismiss any challenge to the myth, or any evidence pointing to the very real crisis among boys. Three years ago Scarsdale High School, in New York, held a gender-equity workshop for faculty members. It was the standard girls-are-being-shortchanged fare, with one notable difference. A male student gave a presentation in which he pointed to evidence suggesting that girls at Scarsdale High were well ahead of boys. David Greene, a social-studies teacher, thought the student must be mistaken, but when he and some colleagues analyzed department grading patterns, they discovered that the student was right. They found little or no difference in the grades of boys and girls in advanced-placement social-studies classes. But in standard classes the girls were doing a lot better.

And Greene discovered one other thing: few wanted to hear about his startling findings. Like schools everywhere, Scarsdale High has been strongly influenced by the belief that girls are systematically deprived. That belief prevails among the school's gender-equity committee and has led the school to offer a special senior elective on gender equity. Greene has tried to broach the subject of male underperformance with his colleagues. Many of them concede that in the classes they teach, the girls seem to be doing better than the boys, but they do not see this as part of a larger pattern. After so many years of hearing about silenced, diminished girls, teachers do not take seriously the suggestion that boys are not doing as well as girls even if they see it with their own eyes in their own classrooms.

Responding to Reading

1. In paragraph 4, Sommers states her essay's thesis: "That girls are treated as the second sex in school and consequently suffer, that boys are accorded privileges and consequently benefit—these are things everyone is presumed to know. But they are not true." Do you agree that the supposed privileged position of boys is something "everyone is presumed to know"?
2. Paragraph 6 of this essay presents a long list of areas in which "girls outshine boys." Do you find this list convincing? What other information could Sommers have provided to support her case?
3. Sommers believes that "the myth of girls in crisis" is so entrenched that "even teachers who work daily with male and female students tend to reflexively dismiss any challenge to the myth" (17). If what she says is true, would you expect this belief among teachers to benefit boys or girls in the long run? Why?

Responding in Writing

Based on your experience, who is more successful in school—girls or boys?

MEN ARE FROM EARTH, AND SO ARE WOMEN: IT'S FAULTY RESEARCH THAT SETS THEM APART

Rosalind C. Barnett

1937–

Caryl Rivers

1937–

Research director at Brandeis University's Women's Studies Research Center's Community, Families, and Work Program, Rosalind C. Barnett is a widely published author on gender-related issues. Caryl Rivers, professor of journalism at Boston University, has written numerous books and articles exploring the nature of gender, family, work, and religion. Like Barnett and Rivers's most recent book, Same Difference: How Gender Myths Are Hurting Our Relationships, Our Children, and Our Jobs *(2004), the following essay reexamines popular (and damaging) beliefs about gender difference.*

Are American college professors unwittingly misleading their students by teaching widely accepted ideas about men and women that are scientifically unsubstantiated?

Why is the dominant narrative about the sexes one of difference, even though it receives little support from carefully designed peer-reviewed studies?

One reason is that findings from a handful of small studies with nonrepresentative samples have often reported wildly overgeneralized but headline-grabbing findings about gender differences. Those findings have then been picked up by the news media—and found their way back into the academy, where they are taught as fact. At the same time, research that tends to debunk popular ideas is often ignored by the news media.

Even worse, many researchers have taken untested hypotheses at face value and used them to plan their studies. Many have also relied exclusively on statistical tests that are designed to find difference, without using tests that would show the degree of overlap between men and women. As a result, findings often suggest—erroneously—that the sexes are categorically different with respect to some specific variable or other.

5   Yet in the latest edition of its publications manual, the American Psychological Association explicitly asks researchers to consider and report the degree of overlap in statistical studies. For good reason: Even if the mean difference between groups being compared is statistically significant, it may be of trivial consequence if the distributions show a

high degree of overlap. Indeed, most studies that do report the size of effects indicate that the differences between the sexes are trivial or slight on a host of personality traits and cognitive and social behaviors.

Because of such serious and pervasive problems, we believe that college students get a distorted picture about the sexes, one that over-states differences while minimizing the more accurate picture—that of enormous overlap and similarity.

It is easy to understand why college professors might spread myths about gender differences. Many of the original studies on which such find-ings were based have been embraced by both the academy and the wider culture. As Martha T. Mednick, an emerita professor of psychology at Howard University, pointed out in an article some years ago, popular ideas that are intuitively appealing, even if inadequately documented, all too often take on lives of their own. They may have shaky research founda-tions; they may be largely disproved by later—and better—studies. But bandwagon concepts that have become unhitched from research moor-ings are rampant in academe, particularly in the classroom. For example:

Women Are Inherently More Caring and More "Relational" than Men

The chief architect of this essentialist idea is Carol Gilligan, the longtime Harvard University psychologist who is now at New York University. In the early 1980s, she laid out a new narrative for women's lives that theorized that women have a unique, caring nature not shared by men. Her ideas have revolutionized the psychology of women and revamped curricula to an unprecedented degree, some observers say. Certainly, almost every student in women's studies and the psychology of women is familiar with Gilligan. But how many are aware of the critics of her theories about women's moral development and the relational self?

Many scholarly reviews of Gilligan's research contend that it does not back up her claims, that she simply created an intriguing hypothe-sis that needs testing. But the relational self has become near-sacred writ, cited in textbooks, classrooms, and the news media.

Anne Alonso, a Harvard psychology professor and director of the 10 Center for Psychoanalytic Studies at Massachusetts General Hospital, told us recently that she is dismayed by the lightning speed at which Gilligan's ideas, based on slender evidence, have been absorbed into psychotherapy. Usually new theories go through a long and rigorous process of publication in peer-reviewed journals before they are accepted by the field. "None of this work has been published in such journals. It's hard to take seriously a whole corpus of work that hasn't been peer-reviewed," Alonso said. The idea of a relational self, she charged, is simply an "idea du jour," one that she called "penis scorn."

CHAPTER 5 FOCUS

Men Don't Value Personal Relations

According to essentialist theorists, men are uncomfortable with any kind of communication that has to do with personal conflicts. They avoid talking about their problems. They avoid responding too deeply to other people's problems, instead giving advice, changing the subject, making a joke, or giving no response. Unlike women, they don't react to troubles talk by empathizing with others and expressing sympathy. These ideas are often cited in textbooks and in popular manuals, like those written by John Gray, a therapist, and Deborah Tannen, a linguistics professor at Georgetown University. Men are from Mars, women are from Venus, we are told. They just don't understand each other. But systematic research does not support those ideas.

An important article, "The Myth of Gender Cultures: Similarities Outweigh Differences in Men's and Women's Provision of and Responses to Supportive Communication," was published this year in *Sex Roles: A Journal of Research.* Erina L. MacGeorge, of Purdue University, and her colleagues at the University of Pennsylvania find no support for the idea that women and men constitute different "communication cultures." Their article, based on three studies that used questionnaires and interviews, sampled 738 people—417 women and 321 men.

In fact, the authors find, the sexes are very much alike in the way they communicate: "Both men and women view the provision of support as a central element of close personal relationships; both value the supportive communication skills of their friends, lovers, and family members; both make similar judgments about what counts as sensitive, helpful support; and both respond quite similarly to various support efforts."

Yet, MacGeorge and her colleagues point out, we still read in textbooks that:

- "Men's and women's communication styles are startlingly dissimilar"—*The Interpersonal Communication Reader,* edited by Joseph A. DeVito (Allyn and Bacon, 2002).

- "American men and women come from different sociolinguistic subcultures, having learned to do different things with words in a conversation"—a chapter by Daniel N. Maltz and Ruth A. Borker in *Language and Social Identity* (Cambridge University Press, 1982), edited by John J. Gumperz.

- "Husbands and wives, especially in Western societies, come from two different cultures with different learned behaviors and communication styles"—a chapter by Carol J. S. Bruess and Judy C. Pearson in *Gendered Relationships* (Mayfield, 1996), edited by Julia T. Wood.

Gender differences in mate selection are pervasive and well established.

Evolutionary psychologists like David M. Buss, a professor at the   15
University of Texas at Austin, tell us in such books as *The Evolution of
Desire: Strategies of Human Mating* (Basic Books, 1994) that men and
women differ widely with respect to the traits they look for in a potential mate. Men, such writers claim, lust after pretty, young, presumably fertile women. Pop culture revels in this notion: Men want young
and beautiful mates. There is, it is presumed, a universal female type
beloved by men—young, unlined, with features that are close to those
of an infant—that signals fertility. If there were a universal male preference for beautiful young women, it would have to be based on a
strong correlation between beauty and reproductive success. Sure,
Richard Gere chose Julia Roberts in Pretty Woman because of her
beauty and youth. But would those qualities have assured enhanced
fertility?

The answer, according to empirical research, seems to be no. Having a pretty face as a young adult has no relationship to the number of
children a woman produces or to her health across the life span. Among
married women, physical attractiveness is unrelated to the number of
children they produce. If beauty has little to do with reproductive success, why would nature insist that men select for it? It seems more likely
that having a young beauty on his arm indicates, instead, that a man is
living up to certain cultural and social norms.

According to some who take what we call an ultra-Darwinist stance,
there is no mystery about whom women prefer as a mate: The man with
resources to feed and protect her future children. The combination of
wealth, status, and power (which usually implies an older man) makes
"an attractive package in the eyes of the average woman," as Robert
Wright, a journalist and author of *The Moral Animal: The New Science of
Evolutionary Psychology* (Pantheon, 1994), sums up the argument.

But those who believe that gender roles are shaped at least as much
by culture and environment as by biology point out that women's preference for older good providers fits perfectly with the rise of the Industrial state. That system, which often called for a male breadwinner and
a female working at home, arose in the United States in the 1830s, was
dominant until the 1970s, and then declined.

If that is correct, then we should see a declining preference for older
men who are good providers, particularly among women with
resources. In fact, a study by Alice Eagley, a psychologist at North-
western University, and Wendy Wood, of Duke University, suggests
that as gender equality in society has increased, women have expressed
less of a preference for older men with greater earning potential. The
researchers have found that when women have access to their own
resources, they do not look for age in mates, but prefer qualities like
empathy, understanding, and the ability to bond with children. The

desire for an older "provider" is evidently not in women's genes. Terri D. Fisher, a psychologist at Ohio State University, told a reporter last year that whenever she teaches her college students the ultra-Darwinian take on the power of youth and beauty, the young men smile and nod and the young women look appalled.

For Girls, Self-Esteem Plummets at Early Adolescence

20   Girls face an inevitable crisis of self-esteem as they approach adolescence. They are in danger of losing their voices, drowning, and facing a devastating dip in self-regard that boys don't experience. This is the picture that Carol Gilligan presented on the basis of her research at the Emma Willard School, a private girls' school in Troy, N.Y. While Gilligan did not refer to genes in her analysis of girls' vulnerability, she did cite both the "wall of Western culture" and deep early childhood socialization as reasons.

Her theme was echoed in 1994 by the clinical psychologist Mary Pipher's surprise best seller, *Reviving Ophelia* (Putnam, 1994), which spent three years on *The New York Times* best-seller list. Drawing on case studies rather than systematic research, Pipher observed how naturally outgoing, confident girls get worn down by sexist cultural expectations. Gilligan's and Pipher's ideas have also been supported by a widely cited study in 1990 by the American Association of University Women. That report, published in 1991, claimed that teenage girls experience a "free-fall in self-esteem from which some will never recover."

The idea that girls have low self-esteem has by now become part of the academic canon as well as fodder for the popular media. But is it true? No.

Critics have found many faults with the influential AAUW study. When children were asked about their self-confidence and academic plans, the report said 60 percent of girls and 67 percent of boys in elementary school responded, "I am happy the way I am." But by high school, the percentage of girls happy with themselves fell to 29 percent. Could it be that 71 percent of the country's teenage girls were low in self-esteem? Not necessarily. The AAUW counted as happy only those girls who checked "always true" to the question about happiness. Girls who said they were "sometimes" happy with themselves or "sort of" happy with themselves were counted as unhappy.

A sophisticated look at the self-esteem data is far more reassuring than the headlines. A new analysis of all of the AAUW data, and a meta-analysis of hundreds of studies, done by Janet Hyde, a psychologist at the University of Wisconsin at Madison, showed no huge gap between boys and girls. Indeed, Hyde found that the self-esteem scores of boys and girls were virtually identical. In particular there was no plunge in scores for girls during the early teen years—the supposed basis for the idea that girls "lost their voices" in that period. Parents, understandably concerned about noxious, hypersexual media images, may gaze in horror at those images while underestimating the resilience of their daughters, who are able to thrive in spite of them.

Boys Have a Mathematics Gene, or at Least a Biological Tendency to Excel in Math, That Girls Do Not Possess

Do boys have a mathematics gene—or at least a biological tendency to   25 excel in math—that girls lack, as a popular stereotype has it? Suffice it to say that, despite being discouraged from pursing math at almost every level of school, girls and women today are managing to perform in math at high levels.

Do data support arguments for hard-wired gender differences? No. In 2001 Erin Leahey and Guang Guo, then a graduate student and an assistant professor of sociology, respectively, at the University of North Carolina at Chapel Hill, looked at some 20,000 math scores of children ages 4 to 18 and found no differences of any magnitude, even in areas that are supposedly male domains, such as reasoning skills and geometry.

The bandwagon concepts that we have discussed here are strongly held and dangerous. Even though they have been seriously challenged, they continue to be taught by authority figures in the classroom. These ideas are embedded in the curricula of courses in child and adolescent development, moral development, education, moral philosophy, feminist pedagogy, evolutionary psychology, gender studies, and the psychology of women.

Few students have the ability to investigate the accuracy of the claims on their own. And since these ideas resonate with the cultural zeitgeist, students would have little reason to do so in any case. The essentialist perspective has so colored the dialogue about the sexes that there is scant room for any narrative other than difference.

Obviously the difference rhetoric can create harm for both men and women. Men are taught to believe that they are deficient in caring and empathy, while women are led to believe that they are inherently unsuited for competition, leadership, and technological professions. Given how little empirical support exists for essentialist ideas, it's crucial that professors broaden the dialogue, challenging the conventional wisdom and encouraging their students to do so as well.

Responding to Reading

1. According to Barnett and Rivers, what problems cause college students to "get a distorted picture about the sexes . . ." (6)? In what sense is the view distorted?
2. What specific misleading ideas do Barnett and Rivers identify? How do they challenge these ideas? How effective are their responses to these ideas?

Chapter 5   Focus

3. Why do Barnett and Rivers see the "bandwagon concepts" they discuss as dangerous (27)? Why do teachers continue to spread these ideas? What do Barnett and Rivers think should be done about this situation?

Responding in Writing

Barnett and Rivers do not specifically address the issue of academic performance in their essay. Do you think they should have? How do you think they would respond to the discussion of academic performance in Christina Hoff Sommers's essay "The War Against Boys" (p. 309)?

WIDENING THE FOCUS

For Critical Thinking and Writing

After reading the three essays in the Focus section of this chapter—Stephen Hinshaw's "The Triple Bind," Christina Hoff Sommers's "The War Against Boys," and Rosalind C. Barnett and Caryl Rivers's "Men Are from Earth, and So Are Women"—write an essay in which you answer the question, "Who has it harder, girls or boys?" You may use your own ideas as well as those in the three essays.

For Further Reading

The following readings can suggest additional perspectives for thinking and writing about the roles of men and women:

- Alleen Pace Nilsen, "Sexism in English: Embodiment and Language" (p. 150)

- Judith Ortiz Cofer, "The Myth of the Latin Woman: I Just Met a Girl Named Maria" (p. 346)

- Arlie Hochschild, "The Second Shift" (p. 415)

For Focused Research

Differences in the ways men and women are treated in school remain a contentious discussion topic. In preparation for writing an essay about the gender gap in education, open one of the popular Web search engines that compiles news stories—http://news.google.com or http://news.yahoo.com—and enter the search terms *gender gap and education.* From the search results, select readings about your topic, and use information from these sources to support your essay. You can begin by reading one or all of the following readings, which were found through the Google news site:

- Conlin, Michelle. "The New Gender Gap." Business Week Online. May 26, 2003. http://www.businessweek.com/magazine/content/03_21/b3834001_mz001.htm.

- "Girls Get Extra School Help while Boys Get Ritalin." USA Today. Aug. 29, 2003. http://www.usatoday.com/news/opinion/editorials/2003-08-28-our-view_x.htm.

- Wyer, Kathy. "Grads of All-Girls Schools Show Stronger Academic Orientations than Coed Grads." UCLA Newsroom. Mar. 19, 2009. http://www.newsroom.ucla.edu/portal/ucla/graduates-of-all-girls-schools-85038.aspx.

CHAPTER 5   FOCUS

--- **Writing** ---

Gender and Identity

1. In her well-known work *A Room of One's Own,* novelist and critic Virginia Woolf observes that "any woman born with a great gift in the sixteenth century would certainly have gone crazed, shot herself, or ended her days in some lonely cottage outside the village, half witch, half wizard, feared and mocked at." Write an essay in which you discuss in what respects this statement may still apply to gifted women of your own generation or of your parents' generation. You may want to read Marge Piercy's poem "Barbie Doll" (p. 259) and Deborah Tannen's "Marked Women" (p. 294) before you plan your paper.

2. List all the stereotypes of women—and of men—identified in the selections you read in this chapter. Then, write an essay in which you discuss those that you think have had the most negative effects. Do you consider these stereotypes just annoying, or actually dangerous? Refer to one or two essays in this chapter to support your points.

3. Several of the selections in this chapter—for example, "Stay-at-Home Dads" (p. 277) and "Why I Want a Wife" (p. 275)—draw distinctions, implicitly or explicitly, between "men's work" and "women's work." Write an essay in which you consider the extent to which such distinctions exist today, and explain how they have affected your professional goals.

4. The title of a best-selling self-help book by John Gray, *Men Are from Mars, Women Are from Venus,* suggests that men and women are so completely different that they may as well be from different planets. Write an essay in which you support or contradict this title's claim. You may focus on men's and women's actions, tastes, values, preferences, or behavior.

5. Write a letter to Judy Brady in which you update (or challenge) her characterization of a wife in "Why I Want a Wife" (p. 275).

6. Could all-male (or all-female) schools solve the problems encountered by boys and girls in school? Write an essay in which you present your views on this issue.

7. In her essay "Marked Women" (p. 294), Deborah Tannen discusses the distinction between the terms *marked* and *unmarked.* Study the men and women around you, or those you see in films or on television, and determine whether or not your observations support Tannen's point that, unlike women, men have "the option of being unmarked" (12). Write an essay in which you agree or disagree with Tannen's conclusion, citing her essay as well as your own observations. (Be sure to define the terms *marked* and *unmarked* in your introduction.)

8. A number of the writers in this chapter examine current ideas about what it means to be male and what it means to be female. Write an essay in which you develop your own definitions of these terms. You may want to consider Sharon Olds's "Rite of Passage" (p. 260), Michael Nava's "Gardenland, Sacramento, California" (p. 262), E. J. Graff's "The M/F Boxes" (p. 269), Glenn Sacks's "Stay-at-Home Dads" (p. 277), and Warren Farrell's "Man Bashing" (p. 280).

9. In "Without Apology" (p. 286), Leah Hager Cohen describes her visit to a gym where female boxers train. Throughout her essay, she keeps trying to deal with the fact that the women she sees want to hit and to be hit. Choose two or three traditionally male sports that have female participants—basketball, tennis, and soccer, for example. Then, discuss how the female players challenge (or possibly reinforce) traditional stereotypes.

6

THE AMERICAN DREAM

The American Dream—of political and religious freedom, equal access to education, equal opportunity in the workplace, and ultimately, success and wealth—is often elusive. In the process of working toward the dream, people struggle to overcome their status as newcomers or outsiders—to fit in, to belong, to be accepted. As they work toward their goals, however, some must make painful decisions, for full participation in American society may mean assimilating: giving up language, custom, and culture and becoming more like others. Thus, although the American Dream may ultimately mean winning something, it can often mean losing something—a vital part of oneself—as well.

For many people, an important part of the American Dream is the chance to reinvent themselves—the opportunity to become someone

African-American man at "colored" drinking fountain, Oklahoma City, OK, 1939

different, someone better. From Benjamin Franklin to Malcolm X, Americans have a long tradition of reinvention, which can involve anything from undertaking a program of self-improvement to undergoing a complete change of social identity.

In a free and mobile society, people can (theoretically, at least) become whatever they want to be. In the United States, reinvention has often come about through education and hard work, but Americans have also been able to change who they are and how they are perceived by changing their professions, their associations, or their places of residence. Along with this process of reinvention comes a constant self-analysis, as we Americans continue to question who we are and what we can become.

Many of the essays in this chapter are written from the point of view of outsiders looking in. These writers want to be accepted, to belong. Still, while some of these outsiders eagerly anticipate full acceptance, with all the rights and responsibilities that this entails, others are more cautious, afraid of the personal or cultural price they will have to pay for full acceptance into the American mainstream.

In "What Is the American Dream?" (p. 374), the Focus section that concludes this chapter, Thomas Jefferson, Abraham Lincoln, John F. Kennedy, Martin Luther King, Jr., and Elizabeth Cady Stanton explore the political, historical, and emotional ties that bind Americans to their country and to one another. These readings showcase the idealism with which Americans approach their dream, reminding us that achieving this dream is worth the struggle.

President-elect Barack Obama saluted by U.S. Capitol Police guards at his inauguration in January 2009

———————— PREPARING TO READ AND WRITE ————————

As you read and prepare to write about the essays in this chapter, you may consider the following questions:

- What does the American Dream mean to the writer?

- Is the essay a personal narrative? an analysis of a problem facing a group? both of these?

- Is the writer's purpose to explain his or her dream to others? to explore his or her place in American society? to persuade others to take action?

- Has the writer been able to achieve the American Dream? If so, by what means? If not, why not?

- What are the greatest obstacles that stand between the writer and the American Dream? Would you characterize these obstacles as primarily cultural, social, political, racial, economic, religious, or educational?

- Who has the easiest access to the American Dream? For whom is access most difficult? Why?

- Is the writer looking at the United States from the point of view of an insider or an outsider?

- Does the writer want to change his or her status? To change the status of others? What steps, if any, does he or she take to do so? What additional steps could he or she take?

- With what ethnic, racial, geographic, or economic group does the writer most identify? What is the writer's attitude toward this group? What is the writer's attitude toward what he or she identifies as mainstream American culture?

- Does the writer speak as an individual or as a representative of a particular group?

- Which writers' views of the American Dream are most similar? Most different? Most like your own?

THE NEW COLOSSUS

Emma Lazarus

1849–1887

Born to a wealthy family in New York City and educated by private tutors, Emma Lazarus became one of the foremost poets of her day. Today, she is remembered solely for her poem "The New Colossus," a sonnet written in 1883 as part of an effort to raise funds for the Statue of Liberty. The poem was later inscribed on the statue's base, and it remains a vivid reminder of the immigrant's American dream.

Not like the brazen giant of Greek fame,
With conquering limbs astride from land to land;
Here at our sea-washed, sunset gates shall stand
A mighty woman with a torch, whose flame
Is the imprisoned lightning, and her name   5
Mother of Exiles. From her beacon-hand
Glows world-wide welcome; her mild eyes command
The air-bridged harbor that twin cities frame.
"Keep, ancient lands, your storied pomp!" cries she
With silent lips. "Give me your tired, your poor,   10
Your huddled masses yearning to breathe free,
The wretched refuse of your teeming shore.
Send these, the homeless, tempest-tost to me,
I lift my lamp beside the golden door!"

Responding to Reading

1. The Colossus of Rhodes, an enormous statue of the Greek god Apollo, was considered one of the seven wonders of the ancient world. It stood at the mouth of the harbor at Rhodes. Why do you think this poem is called "The New Colossus"?
2. Who is the poem's speaker? Who is being addressed?
3. What is the "golden door" to which the poem's last line refers? What aspects of the American Dream does this poem express?

Responding in Writing

Look at the photograph on page 374. What elements of the Statue of Liberty has Lazarus captured in this poem? What characteristics, if any, has she failed to capture?

WHAT SACAGAWEA MEANS TO ME
(AND PERHAPS TO YOU)

Sherman Alexie

1966–

*Sherman Alexie grew up on an Indian reservation in Wellpinit, Washington,
about fifty miles northwest of Spokane. Alexie is a Spokane/Coeur d'Alene
Indian whose works focus on tribal connections and draw upon the oral and religious traditions of his heritage. Although he began his writing career as a poet,
Alexie has also written stories and novels. A story from his first collection,* The
Lone Ranger and Tonto Fistfight in Heaven *(1993), became the basis for the
screenplay and film* Smoke Signals *(1998). Alexie has published seventeen
books, most recently* Face *(2009). In the following essay, he explores the cultural significance of Sacagawea, the Shoshone Indian who traveled as an inter-
preter with the Lewis and Clark expedition in the early nineteenth century.*

In the future, every U.S. citizen will get to be Sacagawea for 15 minutes. For the low price of admission, every American, regardless of race,
religion, gender and age, will climb through the portal into Sacagawea's
Shoshone Indian brain. In the multicultural theme park called Sacagawea Land, you will be kidnapped as a child by the Hidatsa tribe and
sold to Toussaint Charbonneau, the French-Canadian trader who will
take you as one of his wives and father two of your children. Your first
child, Jean-Baptiste, will be only a few months old as you carry him
during your long journey with Lewis and Clark. The two captains will
lead the adventure, fighting rivers, animals, weather and diseases for
thousands of miles, and you will march right beside them. But you, the
aboriginal multitasker, will also breast-feed. And at the end of your
Sacagawea journey, you will be shown the exit and given a souvenir
T-shirt that reads, IF THE U.S. IS EDEN, THEN SACAGAWEA IS EVE.

Sacagawea is our mother. She is the first gene pair of the American
DNA. In the beginning, she was the word, and the word was possibility. I revel in the wondrous possibilities of Sacagawea. It is good to be
joyous in the presence of her spirit, because I hope she had moments of
joy in what must have been a grueling life. This much is true: Sacagawea died of some mysterious illness when she was only in her 20s.
Most illnesses were mysterious in the 19th century, but I suspect that
Sacagawea's indigenous immune system was defenseless against an
immigrant virus. Perhaps Lewis and Clark infected Sacagawea. If true,
then certain postcolonial historians would argue that she was murdered
not by germs but by colonists who carried those germs. I don't know
much about the science of disease and immunities, but I know enough
poetry to recognize that individual human beings are invaded and

colonized by foreign bodies, just as individual civilizations are invaded and colonized by foreign bodies. In that sense, colonization might be a natural process, tragic and violent to be sure, but predictable and ordinary as well, and possibly necessary for the advance, however constructive and destructive, of all civilizations.

After all, Lewis and Clark's story has never been just the triumphant tale of two white men, no matter what the white historians might need to believe. Sacagawea was not the primary hero of this story either, no matter what the Native American historians and I might want to believe. The story of Lewis and Clark is also the story of the approximately 45 nameless and faceless first- and second-generation European Americans who joined the journey, then left or completed it, often without monetary or historical compensation. Considering the time and place, I imagine those 45 were illiterate, low-skilled laborers subject to managerial whims and 19th century downsizing. And it is most certainly the story of the black slave York, who also cast votes during this allegedly democratic adventure. It's even the story of Seaman, the domesticated Newfoundland dog who must have been a welcome and friendly presence and who survived the risk of becoming supper during one lean time or another. The Lewis and Clark Expedition was exactly the kind of multicultural, trigenerational, bigendered, animal-friendly, government-supported, partly French-Canadian project that should rightly be celebrated by liberals and castigated by conservatives.

In the end, I wonder if colonization might somehow be magical. After all, Miles Davis is the direct descendant of slaves and slave owners. Hank Williams is the direct descendant of poor whites and poorer Indians. In 1876 Emily Dickinson was writing her poems in an Amherst attic while Crazy Horse was killing Custer on the banks of the Little Big Horn. I remain stunned by these contradictions, by the successive generations of social, political and artistic mutations that can be so beautiful and painful. How did we get from there to here? This country somehow gave life to Maria Tallchief and Ted Bundy, to Geronimo and Joe McCarthy, to Nathan Bedford Forrest and Toni Morrison, to the Declaration of Independence and Executive Order No. 1066, to Cesar Chavez and Richard Nixon, to theme parks and national parks, to smallpox and the vaccine for smallpox.

As a Native American, I want to hate this country and its contra-   5
dictions. I want to believe that Sacagawea hated this country and its contradictions. But this country exists, in whole and in part, because Sacagawea helped Lewis and Clark. In the land that came to be called Idaho, she acted as diplomat between her long-lost brother and the Lewis and Clark party. Why wouldn't she ask her brother and her tribe to take revenge against the men who had enslaved her? Sacagawea is a contradiction. Here in Seattle, I exist, in whole and in part, because a half-white man named James Cox fell in love with a Spokane Indian

woman named Etta Adams and gave birth to my mother. I am a contradiction; I am Sacagawea.

Responding to Reading

1. The tone of Alexie's first paragraph is very different from the tone of the rest
    of his essay. How would you characterize this paragraph's tone? Why do
    you suppose Alexie begins this way? Is this an effective opening strategy?
2. Consider the meanings (both denotations and connotations) of the words
    possibility (2), *triumphant* (3), and *magical* (4). What do you think Alexie means
    to suggest by using each of these words? How might each word be applied
    to Sacagawea and her journey?
3. In paragraph 2, Alexie writes that "colonization" is a "natural" process that
    may well be "necessary for the advance, however constructive and destruc-
    tive, of all civilizations." What does he mean by "colonization"? Why does
    he see it as both a natural and a necessary process?

Responding in Writing

Alexie's essay explores America's "contradictions," and, in paragraph 4, he lists
some of these. Make two lists of your own: one of people who have made positive contributions to American life and one of people whose actions have threatened to corrupt, or even destroy, our nation. In one sentence, summarize the basic
contradictions your two lists reveal.

THE LIBRARY CARD

Richard Wright

1908–1960

*Born on a former plantation near Natchez, Mississippi, Richard Wright spent
much of his childhood in an orphanage or with various relatives. He attended
schools in Jackson and in 1934 moved to Chicago, where he worked at a number of unskilled jobs before joining the Federal Writers' Project. When his politics became radical, he wrote poetry for leftist publications. In 1938, he published
his first book,* Uncle Tom's Children: Four Novellas; *two years later, his novel*
Native Son *made him famous. After World War II, Wright lived as an expatriate
in Paris, where he wrote* Black Boy (1945), *an autobiography that celebrates
African American resilience and courage much as nineteenth-century slave narratives do. In this excerpt from* Black Boy, *Wright tells how he took advantage
of an opportunity to feed his hunger for an intellectual life.*

One morning I arrived early at work and went into the bank lobby
where the Negro porter was mopping. I stood at a counter and picked
up the Memphis *Commercial Appeal* and began my free reading of the

press. I came finally to the editorial page and saw an article dealing with one H. L. Mencken.[1] I knew by hearsay that he was the editor of the *American Mercury,* but aside from that I knew nothing about him. The article was a furious denunciation of Mencken, concluding with one hot, short sentence: Mencken is a fool.

I wondered what on earth this Mencken had done to call down upon him the scorn of the South. The only people I had ever heard denounced in the South were Negroes, and this man was not a Negro. Then what ideas did Mencken hold that made a newspaper like the *Commercial Appeal* castigate him publicly? Undoubtedly he must be advocating ideas that the South did not like. Were there, then, people other than Negroes who criticized the South? I knew that during the Civil War the South had hated northern whites, but I had not encountered such hate during my life. Knowing no more of Mencken than I did at that moment, I felt a vague sympathy for him. Had not the South, which had assigned me the role of a non-man, cast at him its hardest words?

Now, how could I find out about this Mencken? There was a huge library near the riverfront, but I knew that Negroes were not allowed to patronize its shelves any more than they were the parks and playgrounds of the city. I had gone into the library several times to get books for the white men on the job. Which of them would now help me to get books? And how could I read them without causing concern to the white men with whom I worked? I had so far been successful in hiding my thoughts and feelings from them, but I knew that I would create hostility if I went about this business of reading in a clumsy way.

I weighed the personalities of the men on the job. There was Don, a Jew; but I distrusted him. His position was not much better than mine and I knew that he was uneasy and insecure; he had always treated me in an offhand, bantering way that barely concealed his contempt. I was afraid to ask him to help me to get books; his frantic desire to demonstrate a racial solidarity with the whites against Negroes might make him betray me.

Then how about the boss? No, he was a Baptist and I had the suspicion that he would not be quite able to comprehend why a black boy would want to read Mencken. There were other white men on the job whose attitudes showed clearly that they were Kluxers or sympathizers, and they were out of the question. 5

There remained only one man whose attitude did not fit into an anti-Negro category, for I had heard the white men refer to him as a "Pope lover." He was an Irish Catholic and was hated by the white

---

[1]Henry Louis Mencken (1880–1956), journalist, critic, and essayist, who was known for his pointed, outspoken, and satirical comments about the blunders and imperfections of democracy and the cultural awkwardness of Americans. [Eds.]

Southerners. I knew that he read books, because I had got him volumes from the library several times. Since he, too, was an object of hatred, I felt that he might refuse me but would hardly betray me. I hesitated, weighing and balancing the imponderable realities.

One morning I paused before the Catholic fellow's desk.

"I want to ask you a favor," I whispered to him.

"What is it?"

"I want to read. I can't get books from the library. I wonder if you'd let me use your card?"

He looked at me suspiciously.

"My card is full most of the time," he said.

"I see," I said and waited, posing my question silently.

"You're not trying to get me into trouble, are you, boy?" he asked, staring at me.

"Oh, no, sir."

"What book do you want?"

"A book by H. L. Mencken."

"Which one?"

"I don't know. Has he written more than one?"

"He has written several."

"I didn't know that."

"What makes you want to read Mencken?"

"Oh, I just saw his name in the newspaper," I said.

"It's good of you to want to read," he said. "But you ought to read the right things."

I said nothing. Would he want to supervise my reading?

"Let me think," he said. "I'll figure out something."

I turned from him and he called me back. He stared at me quizzically.

"Richard, don't mention this to the other white men," he said.

"I understand," I said. "I won't say a word."

A few days later he called me to him.

"I've got a card in my wife's name," he said. "Here's mine."

"Thank you, sir."

"Do you think you can manage it?"

"I'll manage fine," I said.

"If they suspect you, you'll get in trouble," he said.

"I'll write the same kind of notes to the library that you wrote when you sent me for books," I told him. "I'll sign your name."

He laughed.

"Go ahead. Let me see what you get," he said.

That afternoon I addressed myself to forging a note. Now, what were the names of books written by H. L. Mencken? I did not know any of them. I finally wrote what I thought would be a foolproof note: *Dear Madam: Will you please let this nigger boy*—I used the word "nigger" to make the librarian feel that I could not possibly be the author of the note—*have some books by H. L. Mencken?* I forged the white man's name.

I entered the library as I had always done when on errands for whites, but I felt that I would somehow slip up and betray myself. I doffed my hat, stood a respectful distance from the desk, looked as unbookish as possible, and waited for the white patrons to be taken care of. When the desk was clear of people, I still waited. The white librarian looked at me.

"What do you want, boy?"

As though I did not possess the power of speech, I stepped forward and simply handed her the forged note, not parting my lips.

"What books by Mencken does he want?" she asked.

"I don't know, ma'am," I said, avoiding her eyes.

"Who gave you this card?"

"Mr. Falk," I said.

"Where is he?"

"He's at work, at the M——— Optical Company," I said. "I've been in here for him before."

"I remember," the woman said. "But he never wrote notes like this."

Oh, God, she's suspicious. Perhaps she would not let me have the books? If she had turned her back at that moment, I would have ducked out the door and never gone back. Then I thought of a bold idea.

"You can call him up, ma'am," I said, my heart pounding.

"You're not using these books, are you?" she asked pointedly.

"Oh, no, ma'am. I can't read."

"I don't know what he wants by Mencken," she said under her breath.

I knew now that I had won; she was thinking of other things and the race question had gone out of her mind. She went to the shelves. Once or twice she looked over her shoulder at me, as though she was still doubtful. Finally she came forward with two books in her hand.

"I'm sending him two books," she said. "But tell Mr. Falk to come in next time, or send me the names of the books he wants. I don't know what he wants to read."

I said nothing. She stamped the card and handed me the books. Not daring to glance at them, I went out of the library, fearing that the woman would call me back for further questioning. A block away from the library I opened one of the books and read a title: *A Book of Prefaces.* I was nearing my nineteenth birthday and I did not know how to pronounce the word "preface." I thumbed the pages and saw strange words and strange names. I shook my head, disappointed. I looked at the other book; it was called *Prejudices.* I knew what that word meant; I had heard it all my life. And right off I was on guard against Mencken's books. Why would a man want to call a book *Prejudices?* The word was so stained with all my memories of racial hate that I could not conceive of anybody using it for a title. Perhaps I had made a mistake about Mencken? A man who had prejudices must be wrong.

When I showed the books to Mr. Falk, he looked at me and frowned.

"That librarian might telephone you," I warned him.

60   "That's all right," he said. "But when you're through reading those books, I want you to tell me what you get out of them."

That night in my rented room, while letting the hot water run over my can of pork and beans in the sink, I opened *A Book of Prefaces* and began to read. I was jarred and shocked by the style, the clear, clean, sweeping sentences. Why did he write like that? And how did one write like that? I pictured the man as a raging demon, slashing with his pen, consumed with hate, denouncing everything American, extolling everything European or German, laughing at the weaknesses of people, mocking God, authority. What was this? I stood up, trying to realize what reality lay behind the meaning of the words.... Yes, this man was fighting, fighting with words. He was using words as a weapon, using them as one would use a club. Could words be weapons? Well, yes, for here they were. Then, maybe, perhaps, I could use them as a weapon? No. It frightened me. I read on and what amazed me was not what he said, but how on earth anybody had the courage to say it.

Occasionally I glanced up to reassure myself that I was alone in the room. Who were these men about whom Mencken was talking so passionately? Who was Anatole France? Joseph Conrad? Sinclair Lewis, Sherwood Anderson, Dostoevski, George Moore, Gustave Flaubert, Maupassant, Tolstoy, Frank Harris, Mark Twain, Thomas Hardy, Arnold Bennett, Stephen Crane, Zola, Norris, Gorky, Bergson, Ibsen, Balzac, Bernard Shaw, Dumas, Poe, Thomas Mann, O. Henry, Dreiser, H. G. Wells, Gogol, T. S. Eliot, Gide, Baudelaire, Edgar Lee Masters, Stendhal, Turgenev, Huneker, Nietzsche, and scores of others? Were these men real? Did they exist or had they existed? And how did one pronounce their names?

I ran across many words whose meanings I did not know, and I either looked them up in a dictionary or, before I had a chance to do that, encountered the word in a context that made its meaning clear. But what strange world was this? I concluded the book with the conviction that I had somehow overlooked something terribly important in life. I had once tried to write, had once reveled in feeling, had let my crude imagination roam, but the impulse to dream had been slowly beaten out of me by experience. Now it surged up again and I hungered for books, new ways of looking and seeing. It was not a matter of believing or disbelieving what I read, but of feeling something new, of being affected by something that made the look of the world different.

As dawn broke I ate my pork and beans, feeling dopey, sleepy. I went to work, but the mood of the book would not die; it lingered, coloring everything I saw, heard, did. I now felt that I knew what the white men were feeling. Merely because I had read a book that had spoken of how they lived and thought, I identified myself with that book. I felt vaguely guilty. Would I, filled with bookish notions, act in a manner that would make the whites dislike me?

I forged more notes and my trips to the library became frequent. 65 Reading grew into a passion. My first serious novel was Sinclair Lewis's *Main Street*.[2] It made me see my boss, Mr. Gerald, and identify him as an American type. I would smile when I saw him lugging his golf bags into the office. I had always felt a vast distance separating me from the boss, and now I felt closer to him, though still distant. I felt now that I knew him, that I could feel the very limits of his narrow life. And this had happened because I had read a novel about a mythical man called George F. Babbitt.[3]

The plots and stories in the novels did not interest me so much as the point of view revealed. I gave myself over to each novel without reserve, without trying to criticize it; it was enough for me to see and feel something different. And for me, everything was something different. Reading was like a drug, a dope. The novels created moods in which I lived for days. But I could not conquer my sense of guilt, my feeling that the white men around me knew that I was changing, that I had begun to regard them differently.

Whenever I brought a book to the job, I wrapped it in newspaper—a habit that was to persist for years in other cities and under other circumstances. But some of the white men pried into my packages when I was absent and they questioned me.

"Boy, what are you reading those books for?"

"Oh, I don't know, sir."

"That's deep stuff you're reading, boy."   70

"I'm just killing time, sir."

"You'll addle your brains if you don't watch out."

I read Dreiser's *Jennie Gerhardt* and *Sister Carrie*[4] and they revived in me a vivid sense of my mother's suffering; I was overwhelmed. I grew silent, wondering about the life around me. It would have been impossible for me to have told anyone what I derived from these novels, for it was nothing less than a sense of life itself. All my life had

---

[2]*Main Street*, published in 1920, examines the smugness, intolerance, and lack of imagination that characterize small-town American life. [Eds.]

[3]The central character in Sinclair Lewis's *Babbit* (1922), who believed in the virtues of home, the Republican Party, and middle-class conventions. To Wright, Babbitt symbolizes the mindless complacency of white middle-class America. [Eds.]

[4]Both *Jennie Gerhardt* (1911) and *Sister Carrie* (1900), by Theodore Dreiser, tell the stories of working women who struggle against poverty and social injustice. [Eds.]

shaped me for the realism, the naturalism of the modern novel, and I could not read enough of them.

Steeped in new moods and ideas, I bought a ream of paper and tried to write; but nothing would come, or what did come was flat beyond telling. I discovered that more than desire and feeling were necessary to write and I dropped the idea. Yet I still wondered how it was possible to know people sufficiently to write about them. Could I ever learn about life and people? To me, with my vast ignorance, my Jim Crow station in life, it seemed a task impossible of achievement. I now knew what being a Negro meant. I could endure the hunger. I had learned to live with hate. But to feel that there were feelings denied me, that the very breath of life itself was beyond my reach, that more than anything else hurt, wounded me. I had a new hunger.

75   In buoying me up, reading also cast me down, made me see what was possible, what I had missed. My tension returned, new, terrible, bitter, surging, almost too great to be contained. I no longer *felt* that the world about me was hostile, killing; I *knew* it. A million times I asked myself what I could do to save myself, and there were no answers. I seemed forever condemned, ringed by walls.

I did not discuss my reading with Mr. Falk, who had lent me his library card; it would have meant talking about myself and that would have been too painful. I smiled each day, fighting desperately to maintain my old behavior, to keep my disposition seemingly sunny. But some of the white men discerned that I had begun to brood.

"Wake up there, boy!" Mr. Olin said one day.

"Sir!" I answered for the lack of a better word.

"You act like you've stolen something," he said.

80   I laughed in the way I knew he expected me to laugh, but I resolved to be more conscious of myself, to watch my every act, to guard and hide the new knowledge that was dawning within me.

If I went north, would it be possible for me to build a new life then? But how could a man build a life upon vague, unformed yearnings? I wanted to write and I did not even know the English language. I bought English grammars and found them dull. I felt that I was getting a better sense of the language from novels than from grammars. I read hard, discarding a writer as soon as I felt that I had grasped his point of view. At night the printed page stood before my eyes in sleep.

Mrs. Moss, my landlady, asked me one Sunday morning: "Son, what is this you keep on reading?"

"Oh, nothing. Just novels."

"What you get out of 'em?"

85   "I'm just killing time," I said.

"I hope you know your own mind," she said in a tone which implied that she doubted if I had a mind.

I knew of no Negroes who read the books I liked and I wondered if any Negroes ever thought of them. I knew that there were Negro doctors, lawyers, newspapermen, but I never saw any of them. When I read a Negro newspaper I never caught the faintest echo of my preoccupation in its pages. I felt trapped and occasionally, for a few days, I would stop reading. But a vague hunger would come over me for books, books that opened up new avenues of feeling and seeing, and again I would forge another note to the white librarian. Again I would read and wonder as only the naïve and unlettered can read and wonder, feeling that I carried a secret, criminal burden about with me each day.

That winter my mother and brother came and we set up housekeeping, buying furniture on the installment plan, being cheated and yet knowing no way to avoid it. I began to eat warm food and to my surprise found that regular meals enabled me to read faster. I may have lived through many illnesses and survived them, never suspecting that I was ill. My brother obtained a job and we began to save toward the trip north, plotting our time, setting tentative dates for departure. I told none of the white men on the job that I was planning to go north; I knew that the moment they felt I was thinking of the North they would change toward me. It would have made them feel that I did not like the life I was living, and because my life was completely conditioned by what they said or did, it would have been tantamount to challenging them.

I could calculate my chances for life in the South as a Negro fairly clearly now.

I could fight the southern whites by organizing with other Negroes, 90 as my grandfather had done. But I knew that I could never win that way; there were many whites and there were but few blacks. They were strong and we were weak. Outright black rebellion could never win. If I fought openly I would die and I did not want to die. News of lynchings were frequent.

I could submit and live the life of a genial slave, but that was impossible. All of my life had shaped me to live by my own feelings and thoughts. I could make up to Bess and marry her and inherit the house. But that, too, would be the life of a slave; if I did that, I would crush to death something within me, and I would hate myself as much as I knew the whites already hated those who had submitted. Neither could I ever willingly present myself to be kicked, as Shorty had done. I would rather have died than do that.

I could drain off my restlessness by fighting with Shorty and Harrison. I had seen many Negroes solve the problem of being black by transferring their hatred of themselves to others with a black skin and fighting them. I would have to be cold to do that, and I was not cold and I could never be.

I could, of course, forget what I had read, thrust the whites out of my mind, forget them; and find release from anxiety and longing in sex and alcohol. But the memory of how my father had conducted himself made that course repugnant. If I did not want others to violate my life, how could I voluntarily violate it myself?

I had no hope whatever of being a professional man. Not only had I been so conditioned that I did not desire it, but the fulfillment of such an ambition was beyond my capabilities. Well-to-do Negroes lived in a world that was almost as alien to me as the world inhabited by whites.

95   What, then, was there? I held my life in my mind, in my consciousness each day, feeling at times that I would stumble and drop it, spill it forever. My reading had created a vast sense of distance between me and the world in which I lived and tried to make a living, and that sense of distance was increasing each day. My days and nights were one long, quiet, continuously contained dream of terror, tension, and anxiety. I wondered how long I could bear it.

Responding to Reading

1. In what sense did access to books bring Wright closer to achieving the American Dream? What new obstacles did books introduce?
2. In paragraph 74, Wright mentions his "Jim Crow station in life." The term *Jim Crow,* derived from a character in a minstrel show, refers to laws enacted in Southern states that legalized racial segregation. What is Wright's "station in life"? In what ways does he adapt his behavior to accommodate this Jim Crow image? In what ways does he defy this stereotype?
3. After World War II, Wright left the United States to live in Paris. Given what you have read in this essay, does his decision surprise you? Do you think he made the right choice? What other options did he have?

Responding in Writing

If Wright were alive today, what books, magazines, newspapers, and Web sites would you recommend he look at? Why?

BECOMING AMERICAN

Dinesh D'Souza

1961–

Dinesh D'Souza was born in Bombay, India, and immigrated to the United States with his family in 1978. He now works as a fellow at the Hoover Institution of Stanford University and writes articles on culture and politics. D'Souza's books include the bestseller Illiberal Education *(1991),* The Virtue of Prosperity: Finding Values in an Age of Techno-Affluence *(2000), the bestseller* What's So Great About America *(2002), from which the following essay is taken, and* The Enemy at Home: The Cultural Left and Its Responsibility for 9/11 *(2007). Here he tries to explain exactly why America is so appealing to immigrants like himself.*

Critics of America, both at home and abroad, have an easy explanation for why the American idea is so captivating, and why immigrants want to come here. The reason, they say, is money. America represents "the bitch goddess of success." That is why poor people reach out for the American idea: they want to touch some of that lucre. As for immigrants, they allegedly flock to the United States for the sole purpose of getting rich. This view, which represents the appeal of America as the appeal of the almighty dollar, is disseminated on Arab streets and in multicultural textbooks taught in U.S. schools. It is a way of demeaning the United States by associating it with what is selfish, base, and crass: an unquenchable appetite for gain.

It is not hard to see why this view of America has gained a wide currency. When people in foreign countries turn on American TV shows, they are stupefied by the lavish displays of affluence: the sumptuous homes, the bejeweled women, the fountains and pools, and so on. Whether reruns of *Dallas* and *Dynasty* are true to the American experience is irrelevant here; the point is that this is how the United States appears to outsiders who have not had the chance to come here. And even for those who do, it is hard to deny that America represents the chance to live better, even to become fantastically wealthy. For instance, there are several people of Indian descent on the *Forbes* 400 list. And over the years I have heard many Indians now living in the United States say, "We want to live an Indian lifestyle, but at an American standard of living."

If this seems like a crass motive for immigration, it must be evaluated in the context of the harsh fate that poor people endure in much of the Third World. The lives of many of these people are defined by an ongoing struggle to exist. It is not that they don't work hard. On the contrary, they labor incessantly and endure hardships that are almost unimaginable to people in the West. In the villages of Asia and Africa, for example, a common sight is a farmer beating a pickax into the ground, women wobbling under heavy loads, children carrying stones. These people are performing very hard labor, but they are getting nowhere. The best they can hope for is to survive for another day. Their clothes are tattered, their teeth are rotted, and disease and death constantly loom over their horizon. For the poor of the Third World, life is characterized by squalor, indignity, and brevity.

I emphasize the plight of the poor, but I recognize, of course, that there are substantial middle classes even in the underdeveloped world. For these people basic survival may not be an issue, but still, they endure hardships that make everyday life a strain. One problem is that the basic infrastructure of the Third World is abysmal: the roads are not properly paved, the water is not safe to drink, pollution in the cities has reached hazardous levels, public transportation is overcrowded and unreliable, and there is a two-year waiting period to get a telephone. Government officials, who are very poorly paid, are inevitably corrupt, which means that you must pay bribes on a regular basis to get things done. Most important, there are limited prospects for the children's future.

5   In America, the immigrant immediately recognizes, things are different. The newcomer who sees America for the first time typically experiences emotions that alternate between wonder and delight. Here is a country where *everything works:* the roads are clean and paper smooth, the highway signs are clear and accurate, the public toilets function properly, when you pick up the telephone you get a dial tone, you can even buy things from the store and then take them back. For the Third World visitor, the American supermarket is a thing to behold: endless aisles of every imaginable product, fifty different types of cereal, multiple flavors of ice cream. The place is full of countless unappreciated inventions: quilted toilet paper, fabric softener, cordless telephones, disposable diapers, roll-on luggage, deodorant. Most countries even today do not have these benefits: deodorant, for example, is unavailable in much of the Third World and unused in much of Europe.

What the immigrant cannot help noticing is that America is a country where the poor live comparatively well. This fact was dramatized in the 1980s, when CBS television broadcast an anti-Reagan documentary, "People Like Us," which was intended to show the miseries of the poor during an American recession. The Soviet Union also broadcast the documentary, with a view to embarrassing the Reagan administration. But by the testimony of former Soviet leaders, it had the opposite effect. Ordinary people across the Soviet Union saw that the poorest Americans have television sets and microwave ovens and cars. They arrived at the same perception of America that I witnessed in a friend of mine from Bombay who has been unsuccessfully trying to move to the United States for nearly a decade. Finally I asked him, "Why are you so eager to come to America?" He replied, "Because I really want to live in a country where the poor people are fat."

The point is that the United States is a country where the ordinary guy has a good life. This is what distinguishes America from so many other countries. Everywhere in the world, the rich person lives well. Indeed, a good case can be made that if you are rich, you live better in countries other than America. The reason is that you enjoy the pleasures of aristocracy. This is the pleasure of being treated as a superior person. Its gratification derives from subservience: in India, for example, the wealthy enjoy the satisfaction of seeing innumerable servants and toadies grovel before them and attend to their every need.

In the United States the social ethic is egalitarian, and this is unaffected by the inequalities of wealth in the country. Tocqueville noticed this egalitarianism a century and a half ago, but it is, if anything, more prevalent today. For all his riches, Bill Gates could not approach a homeless person and say, "Here's a $100 bill. I'll give it to you if you kiss my feet." Most likely the homeless guy would tell Gates to go to hell! The American view is that the rich guy may have more money, but he isn't in any fundamental sense better than you are. The American janitor or waiter sees himself as performing a service, but he doesn't see himself as inferior to those he serves. And neither do the customers see him that way: they are generally happy to show him respect and appreciation on a plane of equality. America is the only country in the world where we call the waiter "Sir," as if he were a knight.

The moral triumph of America is that it has extended the benefits of comfort and affluence, traditionally enjoyed by very few, to a large segment of society. Very few people in America have to wonder where their next meal is coming from. Even sick people who don't have proper insurance can receive medical care at hospital emergency rooms. The poorest American girls are not humiliated by having to wear torn clothes. Every child is given an education, and most have the chance to go on to college. The common man can expect to live long enough and have free time to play with his grandchildren.

Ordinary Americans enjoy not only security and dignity, but also 10 comforts that other societies reserve for the elite. We now live in a country where construction workers regularly pay $4 for a nonfat latte, where maids drive very nice cars, where plumbers take their families on vacation to Europe. As Irving Kristol once observed, there is virtually no restaurant in America to which a CEO can go to lunch with the absolute assurance that he will not find his secretary also dining there. Given the standard of living of the ordinary American, it is no wonder that socialist or revolutionary schemes have never found a wide constituency in the United States. As sociologist Werner Sombart observed, all socialist utopias in America have come to grief on roast beef and apple pie.*

Thus it is entirely understandable that people would associate the idea of America with a better life. For them, money is not an end in itself; money is the means to a longer, healthier, and fuller life. Money allows them to purchase a level of security, dignity, and comfort that they could not have hoped to enjoy in their native countries. Money also frees up time for family life, community involvement, and spiritual pursuits: thus it produces not just material, but also moral, gains. All of this is true, and yet in my view it offers an incomplete picture of why America is so appealing to so many. Let me illustrate with the example of my own life.

Not long ago, I asked myself: what would my life have been like if I had never come to the United States, if I had stayed in India? Materially, my life has improved, but not in a fundamental sense. I grew up in a middle-class family in Bombay. My father was a chemical engineer; my mother, an office secretary. I was raised without great luxury, but neither did I lack for anything. My standard of living in America is higher, but it is not a radical difference. My life has changed far more dramatically in other ways.

If I had remained in India, I would probably have lived my entire existence within a one-mile radius of where I was born. I would undoubtedly have married a woman of my identical religious, socio-economic, and cultural background. I would almost certainly have become a medical doctor, an engineer, or a software programmer. I would have socialized within my ethnic community and had cordial relations, but few friends, outside that group. I would have a whole set of opinions that could be predicted in advance; indeed, they would not be very different from what my father believed, or his father before him. In sum, my destiny would to a large degree have been given to me.

This is not to say that I would have no choice; I would have choice, but within narrowly confined parameters. Let me illustrate with the example of my sister, who got married several years ago. My parents began the process by conducting a comprehensive survey of all the eligible families in our neighborhood. First they examined primary criteria, such as religion, socioeconomic position, and educational background. Then my parents investigated subtler issues: the social reputation of the family, reports of a lunatic uncle, the character of the son, and so on. Finally my parents were down to a dozen or so eligible families, and they were invited to our house for dinner with suspicious

---

*Werner Sombart, *Why Is There No Socialism in the United States?* (White Plains: International Arts and Sciences Press, 1976), 109–10.

regularity. My sister was, in the words of Milton Friedman, "free to choose." My sister knew about, and accepted, the arrangement; she is now happily married with two children. I am not quarreling with the outcome, but clearly my sister's destiny was, to a considerable extent, choreographed by my parents.

By coming to America, I have seen my life break free of these tra- 15 ditional confines. I came to Arizona as an exchange student, but a year later I was enrolled at Dartmouth College. There I fell in with a group of students who were actively involved in politics; soon I had switched my major from economics to English literature. My reading included books like Plutarch's *Moralia*; Hamilton, Madison, and Jay's *Federalist Papers*; and Evelyn Waugh's *Brideshead Revisited*. They transported me to places a long way from home and implanted in my mind ideas that I had never previously considered. By the time I graduated, I decided that I should become a writer, which is something you can do in this country. America permits many strange careers: this is a place where you can become, say, a comedian. I would not like to go to my father and tell him that I was thinking of becoming a comedian. I do not think he would have found it funny.

Soon after graduation I became the managing editor of a policy magazine and began to write freelance articles in the *Washington Post*. Someone in the Reagan White House was apparently impressed by my work, because I was called in for an interview and promptly hired as a senior domestic policy analyst. I found it strange to be working at the White House, because at the time I was not a United States citizen. I am sure that such a thing would not happen in India or anywhere else in the world. But Reagan and his people didn't seem to mind; for them, ideology counted more than nationality. I also met my future wife in the Reagan administration, where she was at the time a White House intern. (She has since deleted it from her résumé.) My wife was born in Louisiana and grew up in San Diego; her ancestry is English, French, Scotch-Irish, German, and American Indian.

I notice that Americans marry in a rather peculiar way: by falling in love. You may think that I am being ironic, or putting you on, so let me hasten to inform you that in many parts of the world, romantic love is considered a mild form of insanity. Consider a typical situation: Anjali is in love with Arjun. She considers Arjun the best-looking man in the world, the most intelligent, virtually without fault, a paragon of humanity! But everybody else can see that Arjun is none of these things. What, then, persuades Anjali that Arjun possesses qualities that are nowhere in evidence? There is only one explanation: Anjali is deeply deluded. It does not follow that her romantic impulses should be ruthlessly crushed. But, in the view of many people and many traditions around the world, they should be steered and directed and prevented from ruining Anjali's life. This is the job of parents and the community, to help Anjali see beyond her delusions and to make decisions that are based on practical considerations and common sense.

If there is a single phrase that encapsulates life in the Third World, it is that "birth is destiny." I remember an incident years ago when my grandfather called in my brother, my sister, and me, and asked us if we knew how lucky we were. We asked him why he felt this way: was it because we were intelligent, or had lots of friends, or were blessed with a loving family? Each time he shook his head and said, "No." Finally we pressed him: why did he consider us so lucky? Then he revealed the answer: "Because you are Brahmins!"

The Brahmin, who is the highest ranking in the Hindu caste system, is traditionally a member of the priestly class. As a matter of fact, my family had nothing to do with the priesthood. Nor are we Hindu: my ancestors converted to Christianity many generations ago. Even so, my grandfather's point was that before we converted, hundreds of years ago, our family used to be Brahmins. How he knew this remains a mystery. But he was serious in his insistence that nothing that the three of us achieved in life could possibly mean more than the fact that we were Brahmins.

20   This may seem like an extreme example, revealing my grandfather to be a very narrow fellow indeed, but the broader point is that traditional cultures attach a great deal of importance to data such as what tribe you come from, whether you are male or female, and whether you are the eldest son. Your destiny and your happiness hinge on these things. If you are a Bengali, you can count on other Bengalis to help you, and on others to discriminate against you; if you are female, then certain forms of society and several professions are closed to you; and if you are the eldest son, you inherit the family house and your siblings are expected to follow your direction. What this means is that once your tribe, caste, sex, and family position have been established at birth, your life takes a course that is largely determined for you.

In America, by contrast, you get to write the script of your own life. When your parents say to you, "What do you want to be when you grow up?" the question is open-ended; it is you who supply the answer. Your parents can advise you: "Have you considered law school?" "Why not become the first doctor in the family?" It is considered very improper, however, for them to try and force your decision. Indeed, American parents typically send their teenage children away to college, where they live on their own and learn independence. This is part of the process of forming your mind and choosing a field of interest for yourself and developing your identity. It is not uncommon in the United States for two brothers who come from the same gene pool and were raised in similar circumstances to do quite different things: the eldest becomes a gas station attendant, the younger moves up to be vice president at Oracle; the eldest marries his high-school sweetheart and raises four kids, the youngest refuses to settle down, or comes out of the closet as a homosexual; one is the Methodist that he was raised to be, the other becomes a Christian Scientist or a Buddhist. What to be, where to live, whom to love, whom to marry, what to believe, what religion to practice—these are all decisions that Americans make for themselves.

In most parts of the world your identity and your fate are to a large extent handed to you; in America, you determine them for yourself. In America your destiny is not prescribed; it is constructed. Your life is like a blank sheet of paper, and you are the artist. This notion of you being the architect of your own destiny is the incredibly powerful idea that is behind the worldwide appeal of America. Young people especially find irresistible the prospect of being in the driver's seat, of authoring the narrative of their own lives. So too the immigrant discovers that America permits him to break free of the constraints that have held him captive, so that the future becomes a landscape of his own choosing.

Responding to Reading

1. D'Souza seems to agree with those who claim that many immigrants come to the United States "for the sole purpose of getting rich" (1), but he does not criticize these immigrants who are motivated by dreams of wealth. How does he justify their motivation?
2. What is D'Souza's purpose in telling the story of his own life? Does he achieve this purpose? Would this essay have the same impact without his personal story? Why or why not?
3. What specific differences does D'Souza observe between life in America and life in Third World nations? Between his own life in the United States and the life he would have led in India?

Responding in Writing

In paragraph 21, D'Souza says, "In America,...you get to write the script of your own life." Do you think this is true, or do you think D'Souza is too optimistic about what his adopted country has to offer?

THE MYTH OF THE LATIN WOMAN: I JUST MET A GIRL NAMED MARIA

Judith Ortiz Cofer

1952–

Born in Hormigueros, Puerto Rico, and raised in Paterson, New Jersey, Judith Ortiz Cofer teaches creative writing at the University of Georgia. She is an award-winning poet and novelist whose books include the novels The Line of the Sun *(1989) and* Silent Dancing *(1990) as well as a collection of biographical essays. Her most recent work is* A Love Story Beginning in Spanish: Poems *(2005). In the following essay from her collection* The Latin Deli: Prose and Poetry *(1993), Cofer describes the stereotypes she has confronted as a Latina.*

On a bus trip to London from Oxford University where I was earning some graduate credits one summer, a young man, obviously fresh from a pub, spotted me and as if struck by inspiration went down on his knees in the aisle. With both hands over his heart he broke into an Irish tenor's rendition of "Maria" from *West Side Story*.[1] My politely amused fellow passengers gave his lovely voice the round of gentle applause it deserved. Though I was not quite as amused, I managed my version of an English smile: no show of teeth, no extreme contortions of the facial muscles—I was at this time of my life practicing reserve and cool. Oh, that British control, how I coveted it. But "Maria" had followed me to London, reminding me of a prime fact of my life: you can leave the island, master the English language, and travel as far as you can, but if you are a Latina, especially one like me who so obviously belongs to Rita Moreno's[2] gene pool, the island travels with you.

This is sometimes a very good thing—it may win you that extra minute of someone's attention. But with some people, the same things can make *you* an island—not a tropical paradise but an Alcatraz, a place nobody wants to visit. As a Puerto Rican girl living in the United States[3] and wanting like most children to "belong," I resented the stereotype that my Hispanic appearance called forth from many people I met.

Growing up in a large urban center in New Jersey during the 1960s, I suffered from what I think of as "cultural schizophrenia." Our life was designed by my parents as a microcosm of their *casas*[4] on the island.

---

[1]A popular Broadway musical, loosely based on *Romeo and Juliet*, about two rival street gangs, one Anglo and one Puerto Rican, in New York City. [Eds.]

[2]Puerto Rico–born actress who won an Oscar for her role in the 1960 movie version of *West Side Story*. [Eds.]

[3]Although it is an island, Puerto Rico is part of the United States (it is a self-governing commonwealth). [Eds.]

[4]Homes. [Eds.]

We spoke in Spanish, ate Puerto Rican food bought at the *bodega*,[5] and practiced strict Catholicism at a church that allotted us a one-hour slot each week for mass, performed in Spanish by a Chinese priest trained as a missionary for Latin America.

As a girl I was kept under strict surveillance by my parents, since my virtue and modesty were, by their cultural equation, the same as their honor. As a teenager I was lectured constantly on how to behave as a proper *senorita*. But it was a conflicting message I received, since the Puerto Rican mothers also encouraged their daughters to look and act like women and to dress in clothes our Anglo friends and their mothers found too "mature" and flashy. The difference was, and is, cultural; yet I often felt humiliated when I appeared at an American friend's party wearing a dress more suitable to a semi-formal than to a playroom birthday celebration. At Puerto Rican festivities, neither the music nor the colors we wore could be too loud.

I remember Career Day in our high school, when teachers told us to come dressed as if for a job interview. It quickly became obvious that to the Puerto Rican girls "dressing up" meant wearing their mother's ornate jewelry and clothing, more appropriate (by mainstream standards) for the company Christmas party than as daily office attire. That morning I had agonized in front of my closet, trying to figure out what a "career girl" would wear. I knew how to dress for school (at the Catholic school I attended, we all wore uniforms), I knew how to dress for Sunday mass, and I knew what dresses to wear for parties at my relatives' homes. Though I do not recall the precise details of my Career Day outfit, it must have been a composite of these choices. But I remember a comment my friend (an Italian American) made in later years that coalesced my impressions of that day. She said that at the business school she was attending, the Puerto Rican girls always stood out for wearing "everything at once." She meant, of course, too much jewelry, too many accessories. On that day at school we were simply made the negative models by the nuns, who were themselves not credible fashion experts to any of us. But it was painfully obvious to me that to the others, in their tailored skirts and silk blouses, we must have seemed "hopeless" and "vulgar." Though I now know that most adolescents feel out of step much of the time, I also know that for the Puerto Rican girls of my generation that sense was intensified. The way our teachers and classmates looked at us that day in school was just a taste of the cultural clash that awaited us in the real world, where prospective employers and men on the street would often misinterpret our tight skirts and jingling bracelets as a "come-on."

5

---

[5]Small grocery store. [Eds.]

Mixed cultural signals have perpetuated certain stereotypes—for example, that of the Hispanic woman as the "hot tamale" or sexual firebrand. It is a one-dimensional view that the media have found easy to promote. In their special vocabulary, advertisers have designated "sizzling" and "smoldering" as the adjectives of choice for describing not only the foods but also the women of Latin America. From conversations in my house I recall hearing about the harassment that Puerto Rican women endured in factories where the "boss-men" talked to them as if sexual innuendo was all they understood, and worse, often gave them the choice of submitting to their advances or being fired.

It is custom, however, not chromosomes, that leads us to choose scarlet over pale pink. As young girls, it was our mothers who influenced our decisions about clothes and colors—mothers who had grown up on a tropical island where the natural environment was a riot of primary colors, where showing your skin was one way to keep cool as well as to look sexy. Most important of all, on the island, women perhaps felt freer to dress and move more provocatively since, in most cases, they were protected by the traditions, mores, and laws of a Spanish/Catholic system of morality and machismo whose main rule was: *You may look at my sister, but if you touch her I will kill you.* The extended family and church structure could provide a young woman with a circle of safety in her small pueblo on the island; if a man "wronged" a girl, everyone would close in to save her family honor.

My mother has told me about dressing in her best party clothes on Saturday nights and going to the town's plaza to promenade with her girlfriends in front of the boys they liked. The males were thus given an opportunity to admire the women and to express their admiration in the form of *piropos*: erotically charged street poems they composed on the spot. (I have myself been subjected to a few *piropos* while visiting the island, and they can be outrageous, although custom dictates that they must never cross into obscenity.) This ritual, as I understand it, also entails a show of studied indifference on the woman's part; if she is "decent," she must not acknowledge the man's impassioned words. So I do understand how things can be lost in translation. When a Puerto Rican girl dressed in her idea of what is attractive meets a man from the mainstream culture who has been trained to react to certain types of clothing as a sexual signal, a clash is likely to take place. I remember the boy who took me to my first formal dance leaning over to plant a sloppy, over-eager kiss painfully on my mouth; when I didn't respond with sufficient passion, he remarked resentfully: "I thought you Latin girls were supposed to mature early," as if I were expected to *ripen* like a fruit or vegetable, not just grow into womanhood like other girls.

It is surprising to my professional friends that even today some people, including those who should know better, still put others "in their place." It happened to me most recently during a stay at a classy

metropolitan hotel favored by young professional couples for weddings. Late one evening after the theater, as I walked toward my room
with a colleague (a woman with whom I was coordinating an arts program), a middle-aged man in a tuxedo, with a young girl in satin and
lace on his arm, stepped directly into our path. With his champagne
glass extended toward me, he exclaimed "Evita!"[6]

Our way blocked, my companion and I listened as the man half-   10
recited, half-bellowed "Don't Cry for Me, Argentina." When he finished, the young girl said: "How about a round of applause for my
daddy?" We complied, hoping this would bring the silly spectacle to a
close. I was becoming aware that our little group was attracting the
attention of the other guests. "Daddy" must have perceived this too,
and he once more barred the way as we tried to walk past him. He
began to shout-sing a ditty to the tune of "La Bamba"—except the lyrics
were about a girl named Maria whose exploits rhymed with her name
and gonorrhea. The girl kept saying "Oh, Daddy" and looking at me
with pleading eyes. She wanted me to laugh along with the others. My
companion and I stood silently waiting for the man to end his offensive
song. When he finished, I looked not at him but at his daughter. I
advised her calmly never to ask her father what he had done in the
army. Then I walked between them and to my room. My friend com-
plimented me on my cool handling of the situation, but I confessed that
I had really wanted to push the jerk into the swimming pool. This same
man—probably a corporate executive, well-educated, even worldly by
most standards—would not have been likely to regale an Anglo woman
with a dirty song in public. He might have checked his impulse by
assuming that she could be somebody's wife or mother, or at least
somebody who might take offense. But, to him, I was just an Evita or a
Maria: merely a character in his cartoon-populated universe.

Another facet of the myth of the Latin woman in the United States
is the menial, the domestic—Maria the housemaid or countergirl. It's
true that work as domestics, as waitresses, and in factories is all that's
available to women with little English and few skills. But the myth of
the Hispanic menial—the funny maid, mispronouncing words and
cooking up a spicy storm in a shiny California kitchen—has been per-
petuated by the media in the same way that "Mammy" from *Gone with
the Wind* became America's idea of the black woman for generations.
Since I do not wear my diplomas around my neck for all to see, I have
on occasion been sent to that "kitchen" where some think I obviously
belong.

One incident has stayed with me, though I recognize it as a minor
offense. My first public poetry reading took place in Miami, at a restaurant

---

[6]A Broadway musical, later made into a movie, about Eva Duarte de Perón, the former first lady of
Argentina. [Eds.]

where a luncheon was being held before the event. I was nervous and excited as I walked in with notebook in hand. An older woman motioned me to her table, and thinking (foolish me) that she wanted me to auto-graph a copy of my newly published slender volume of verse, I went over. She ordered a cup of coffee from me, assuming that I was the waitress. (Easy enough to mistake my poems for menus, I suppose.) I know it wasn't an intentional act of cruelty. Yet of all the good things that hap-pened later, I remember that scene most clearly, because it reminded me of what I had to overcome before anyone would take me seriously. In ret-rospect I understand that my anger gave my reading fire. In fact, I have almost always taken any doubt in my abilities as a challenge, the result most often being the satisfaction of winning a convert, of seeing the cold, appraising eyes warm to my words, the body language change, the smile that indicates I have opened some avenue for communication. So that day as I read, I looked directly at that woman. Her lowered eyes told me she was embarrassed at her faux pas, and when I willed her to look up at me, she graciously allowed me to punish her with my full attention. We shook hands at the end of the reading and I never saw her again. She has prob-ably forgotten the entire incident, but maybe not.

Yet I am one of the lucky ones. There are thousands of Latinas with-out the privilege of an education or the entrees into society that I have. For them life is a constant struggle against the misconceptions per-petuated by the myth of the Latina. My goal is to try to replace the old stereotypes with a much more interesting set of realities. Every time I give a reading, I hope the stories I tell, the dreams and fears I examine in my work, can achieve some universal truth that will get my audience past the particulars of my skin color, my accent, or my clothes.

I once wrote a poem in which I called all Latinas "God's brown daughters." This poem is really a prayer of sorts, offered upward, but also, through the human-to-human channel of art, outward. It is a prayer for communication and for respect. In it, Latin women pray "in Spanish to an Anglo God/with a Jewish heritage," and they are "fer-vently hoping/that if not omnipotent,/at least He be bilingual."

Responding to Reading

1. What exactly is the "myth of the Latin woman"? According to Cofer, what has perpetuated this stereotype? Do you see this "myth" as simply demeaning, or as potentially dangerous? Why?
2. In paragraph 1, Cofer says, "you can leave [Puerto Rico], master the English language, and travel as far as you can, but if you are a Latina,... the island travels with you." What does she mean? Do you think this is also true of people from other ethnic groups (and other nations)? Can you think of any groups whose culture and ethnicity is *not* likely to travel with them?
3. Throughout this essay, Cofer speaks of the "cultural schizophrenia" (3) she felt, describing the "conflicting message" (4), the "cultural clash" (5), and the

"mixed cultural signals" (6) she received from the two worlds she inhabited. Do you see this kind of "schizophrenia" as inevitable? Do you see it as an obstacle to the American Dream? Explain.

Responding in Writing

What stereotypes are associated with your own ethnic group? Do you see these stereotypes as benign or harmful?

COMING INTO THE COUNTRY
Gish Jen
1956–

Gish Jen is the author of a short-story collection and three novels, most recently The Love Wife *(2004). Her work is frequently anthologized and published in the* New York Times Magazine, *the* New Yorker, *and the* New Republic. *Jen, born to Chinese immigrants, writes primarily about the challenges of cultural assimilation faced by American immigrants and descendants of recent immigrants. The following essay explores the immigrant's process of shaping a distinctly American identity.*

In the Old World, there was one way of life, or 2, maybe 10. Here there are dozens, hundreds, all jammed in together, cheek by jowl, especially in the dizzying cities. Everywhere has a somewhere else just around the corner. We newish Americans leap-frog from world to world, reinventing ourselves en route. We perform our college selves, our waitress selves, our dot-com selves, our parent selves, our downtown selves, our Muslim, Greek, Hindi, South African selves. Even into the second or third generation, we speak different languages—more languages, often, than we know we know. We sport different names. I am Gish, Geesh, Jen, Lillian, Lil, Bilien, Ms. Jen, Miss Ren, Mrs. O'Connor. Or maybe we insist on one name. The filmmaker Mira Nair, for example, will be called *NIGH-ear*, please; she is not a depilatory product.

Of course, there are places where she does not have to insist, and places that don't get the joke, that need—that get—other jokes. It's a kind of high, switching spiels, eating Ethiopian, French, Thai, getting around. And the inventing! The moments of grand inspiration: *I think I will call myself Houdini.* Who could give up even the quotidian luxury of choosing, that small swell of power: to walk or to drive? The soup or the salad? The green or the blue? We bubble with pleasure. *It's me. I'm taking the plane. I'll take the sofa, the chair, the whole shebang—why not?*

Why not, indeed? A most American question, a question that comes to dominate our most private self-talk. In therapy-speak, we Americans like *to give ourselves permission.* To do what? To take care of ourselves, to express ourselves, to listen to ourselves. We tune out the loudspeaker of duty, tune in to the whisper of desire. This is faint at first, but soon proves easily audible; indeed, irresistible. *Why not go to town? Why not move away? Why not marry out? Why not? Why not? Why not?*

To come to America is to be greatly disoriented for many a day. The smell of the air is wrong, the taste of the water, the strength of the sun, the rate the trees grow. The rituals are strange—the spring setting out of mulch, the summer setting out of barbecues. How willingly the men heat themselves with burgers! Nobody eats the wildlife, certainly not the bugs or leaves. And beware, beware the rules about smoking. Your skin feels tight, your body fat or thin, your children stranger than they were already. Your sensations are exhausting.

5   Yet one day a moment comes—often, strangely, abroad—when we find ourselves missing things. Our choice of restaurants, perhaps, or our cheap gas and good roads; or, more tellingly, our rights. To be without freedom of movement, to be without freedom of speech—these things pain everyone. But to be without *our* freedom of movement, without *our* freedom of speech is an American affliction; and in this, as in many facets of American life, possession matters. The moment we feel certain rights to be inalienable, when we feel them to be ours as our lungs are ours, so that their loss is an excision and a death, we have become American.

It's not always a happy feeling. For the more at home we become with our freedom, the more we become aware of its limits. There's much true opportunity in the land of opportunity, but between freedom in theory and freedom in practice gapes a grand canyon. As often as not, what we feel is the burn of injustice. A rise of anger, perhaps followed by a quick check on our impulse to act rashly; perhaps followed by a decision to act courageously. *We gather here today to make known our grievance. For is this not America?*

We wonder who we are—what does it mean to be Irish-American, Cuban-American, Armenian-American?—and are amazed to discover that others wonder, too. Indeed, nothing seems more typically American than to obsess about identity. Can so many people truly be so greatly confused? We feel very much a part of the contemporary gestalt.

Yet two or three generations later, we still may not be insiders. Recently, I heard about a basketball game starring a boy from the Cochiti pueblo in Santa Fe. The kids on his team, a friend reported, had one water bottle, which they passed around, whereas the kids on the other team each had his own. This was a heartening story, signaling the survival of a communal culture against the pressures of individualism. But did the Cochiti boy notice the other team? I couldn't help wondering. Did he feel the glass pane between himself and the mainstream, so familiar, so tangible, so bittersweet? *Nobody has been here longer than we; how come our ways need protecting?* Later a member of the pueblo told me that the Cochiti have started a language-immersion program for the younger generation, and that it has been a success. They are saving their language from extinction.

Hooray! The rest of us cheer. How awed we feel in the presence of tradition, of authenticity. How avidly we will surf to such sites, some of us, and what we will pay to do so! We will pay for bits of the Southwest the way we will pay handsomely, in this generation or the next, for a home. Whatever that looks like; we find ourselves longing for some combination of Martha Stewart and what we can imagine, say, of our family seat in Brazil. At any rate, we can say this much: the home of our dreams is a safe place, a still place. A communal place, to which we contribute; to which we have real ties; a place that feels more stable, perhaps, than ourselves. How American this is—to long, at day's end, for a place where we belong more, invent less; for a heartland with more heart.

Responding to Reading

1. In paragraph 1, Jen says, "We newish Americans leap-frog from world to world, reinventing ourselves en route." Is the concept of reinvention as she describes it limited to "newish Americans," or could it also apply to more assimilated Americans? Explain.
2. Jen says, "the more at home we become with our freedom, the more we become aware of its limits" (6). What does she mean? Do you think she is correct?
3. In paragraph 7, Jen observes, "nothing seems more typically American than to obsess about identity." Why, according to Jen, is this obsession "typically American"?

Responding in Writing

Do you consider yourself an American (in Jen's terms, an "insider"), a "hyphen-ated American" (for example, Irish-American or Cuban-American), or something else?

JUST WALK ON BY
Brent Staples
1951–

*After earning a Ph.D. in psychology from the University of Chicago (1977),
Brent Staples turned to journalism, writing for the* Chicago Sun-Times *and
the* New York Times. *In 1990, he joined the editorial board of the* Times,
where his columns now appear regularly. His memoir Parallel Time *(1994),
which was sparked by his brother's murder in a dispute over a cocaine deal,
describes Staples's own internal struggles as he straddled the black and white
worlds. Originally published in* Ms. *in 1986, the following essay conveys
Staples's reactions to white people's images of black men.*

My first victim was a woman—white, well dressed, probably in her early
twenties. I came upon her late one evening on a deserted street in Hyde
Park, a relatively affluent neighborhood in an otherwise mean, impoverished section of Chicago. As I swung onto the avenue behind her, there
seemed to be a discreet, uninflammatory distance between us. Not so.
She cast back a worried glance. To her, the youngish black man—a broad
six feet two inches with a beard and billowing hair, both hands shoved
into the pockets of a bulky military jacket—seemed menacingly close.
After a few more quick glimpses, she picked up her pace and was soon
running in earnest. Within seconds she disappeared into a cross street.

That was more than a decade ago. I was 22 years old, a graduate student newly arrived at the University of Chicago. It was in the echo of
that terrified woman's footfalls that I first began to know the unwieldy
inheritance I'd come into—the ability to alter public space in ugly ways.
It was clear that she thought herself the quarry of a mugger, a rapist, or
worse. Suffering a bout of insomnia, however, I was stalking sleep, not
defenseless wayfarers. As a softy who is scarcely able to take a knife to
a raw chicken—let alone hold it to a person's throat—I was surprised,
embarrassed, and dismayed all at once. Her flight made me feel like an
accomplice in tyranny. It also made it clear that I was indistinguishable
from the muggers who occasionally seeped into the area from the surrounding ghetto. That first encounter, and those that followed, signified
that a vast, unnerving gulf lay between nighttime pedestrians—particularly women—and me. And I soon gathered that being perceived as
dangerous is a hazard in itself. I only needed to turn a corner into a
dicey situation, or crowd some frightened, armed person in a foyer
somewhere, or make an errant move after being pulled over by a police-
man. Where fear and weapons meet—and they often do in urban America—there is always the possibility of death.

In that first year, my first away from my hometown, I was to
become thoroughly familiar with the language of fear. At dark, shadowy

intersections in Chicago, I could cross in front of a car stopped at a traffic light and elicit the *thunk, thunk, thunk, thunk* of the driver—black, white, male, or female—hammering down the door locks. On less traveled streets after dark, I grew accustomed to but never comfortable with people who crossed to the other side of the street rather than pass me. Then there were the standard unpleasantries with police, doormen, bouncers, cab drivers, and others whose business it is to screen out troublesome individuals *before* there is any nastiness.

I moved to New York nearly two years ago and I have remained an avid night walker. In central Manhattan, the near-constant crowd cover minimizes tense one-on-one street encounters. Elsewhere—visiting friends in SoHo, where sidewalks are narrow and tightly spaced buildings shut out the sky—things can get very taut indeed.

Black men have a firm place in New York mugging literature.   5
Norman Podhoretz in his famed (or infamous) 1963 essay, "My Negro Problem—And Ours," recalls growing up in terror of black males; they "were tougher than we were, more ruthless," he writes—and as an adult on the Upper West Side of Manhattan, he continues, he cannot constrain his nervousness when he meets black men on certain streets. Similarly, a decade later, the essayist and novelist Edward Hoagland extols a New York where once "Negro bitterness bore down mainly on other Negroes." Where some see mere panhandlers, Hoagland sees "a mugger who is clearly screwing up his nerve to do more than just *ask* for money." But Hoagland has "the New Yorker's quickhunch posture for broken-field maneuvering," and the bad guy swerves away.

I often witness that "hunch posture," from women after dark on the warrenlike streets of Brooklyn where I live. They seem to set their faces on neutral and, with their purse straps strung across their chests bandolier style, they forge ahead as though bracing themselves against being tackled. I understand, of course, that the danger they perceive is not a hallucination. Women are particularly vulnerable to street violence, and young black males are drastically overrepresented among the perpetrators of that violence. Yet these truths are no solace against the kind of alienation that comes of being ever the suspect, against being set apart, a fearsome entity with whom pedestrians avoid making eye contact.

It is not altogether clear to me how I reached the ripe old age of 22 without being conscious of the lethality nighttime pedestrians attributed to me. Perhaps it was because in Chester, Pennsylvania, the small, angry industrial town where I came of age in the 1960s, I was scarcely noticeable against a backdrop of gang warfare, street knifings, and murders. I grew up one of the good boys, had perhaps a half-dozen fist fights. In retrospect, my shyness of combat has clear sources.

Many things go into the making of a young thug. One of those things is the consummation of the male romance with the power to

intimidate. An infant discovers that random flailings send the baby bottle flying out of the crib and crashing to the floor. Delighted, the joyful
babe repeats those motions again and again, seeking to duplicate the
feat. Just so, I recall the points at which some of my boyhood friends
were finally seduced by the perception of themselves as tough guys.
When a mark cowered and surrendered his money without resistance,
myth and reality merged—and paid off. It is, after all, only manly to
embrace the power to frighten and intimidate. We, as men, are not supposed to give an inch of our lane on the highway; we are to seize the
fighter's edge in work and in play and even in love; we are to be valiant
in the face of hostile forces.

Unfortunately, poor and powerless young men seem to take all this
nonsense literally. As a boy, I saw countless tough guys locked away; I
have since buried several, too. They were babies, really—a teenage
cousin, a brother of 22, a childhood friend in his mid-twenties—all gone
down in episodes of bravado played out in the streets. I came to doubt
the virtues of intimidation early on. I chose, perhaps even unconsciously, to remain a shadow—timid, but a survivor.

10   The fearsomeness mistakenly attributed to me in public places often
has a perilous flavor. The most frightening of these confusions occurred
in the late 1970s and early 1980s when I worked as a journalist in
Chicago. One day, rushing into the office of a magazine I was writing
for with a deadline story in hand, I was mistaken for a burglar. The
office manager called security and, with an ad hoc posse, pursued me
through the labyrinthine halls, nearly to my editor's door. I had no way
of proving who I was. I could only move briskly toward the company
of someone who knew me.

Another time I was on assignment for a local paper and killing time
before an interview. I entered a jewelry store on the city's affluent Near
North Side. The proprietor excused herself and returned with an enormous red Doberman pinscher straining at the end of a leash. She stood,
the dog extended toward me, silent to my questions, her eyes bulging
nearly out of her head. I took a cursory look around, nodded, and bade
her good night. Relatively speaking, however, I never fared as badly as
another black male journalist. He went to nearby Waukegan, Illinois, a
couple of summers ago to work on a story about a murderer who was
born there. Mistaking the reporter for the killer, police hauled him from
his car at gunpoint and but for his press credentials would probably
have tried to book him. Such episodes are not uncommon. Black men
trade tales like this all the time.

In "My Negro Problem—And Ours," Podhoretz writes that the
hatred he feels for blacks makes itself known to him through a variety
of avenues—one being his discomfort with that "special brand of paranoid touchiness" to which he says blacks are prone. No doubt he is
speaking here of black men. In time, I learned to smother the rage I felt

at so often being taken for a criminal. Not to do so would surely have led to madness—via that special "paranoid touchiness" that so annoyed Podhoretz at the time he wrote the essay.

I began to take precautions to make myself less threatening. I move about with care, particularly late in the evening. I give a wide berth to nervous people on subway platforms during the wee hours, particularly when I have exchanged business clothes for jeans. If I happen to be entering a building behind some people who appear skittish, I may walk by, letting them clear the lobby before I return, so as not to seem to be following them. I have been calm and extremely congenial on those rare occasions when I've been pulled over by the police.

And on late-evening constitutionals along streets less traveled by, I employ what has proved to be an excellent tension-reducing measure: I whistle melodies from Beethoven and Vivaldi and the more popular classical composers. Even steely New Yorkers hunching toward night-time destinations seem to relax, and occasionally they even join in the tune. Virtually everybody seems to sense that a mugger wouldn't be warbling bright, sunny selections from Vivaldi's *Four Seasons.* It is my equivalent of the cowbell that hikers wear when they know they are in bear country.

Responding to Reading

1. Staples speaks quite matter-of-factly about the fear he inspires. Does your experience support his assumption that black men have the "ability to alter public space" (2)? Why or why not? Do you believe white men also have this ability?
2. In paragraph 13, Staples suggests some strategies that he believes make him "less threatening." What else, if anything, do you think he could do? Do you believe he *should* adopt such strategies?
3. Although Staples says he arouses fear in others, he also admits that he himself feels fearful. Why? Do you think he has reason to be fearful? What does this sense of fear say about his access to the American Dream?

Responding in Writing

Imagine you are the woman Staples describes in paragraph 1. Send an email to Staples in which you explain why you reacted as you did.

ON DUMPSTER DIVING

Lars Eighner
1948–

When Lars Eighner was eighteen years old, his mother threw him out of her house after she learned he was gay. Then a student at the University of Texas at Austin (1966–1969), Eighner began a series of part-time and dead-end jobs that ended in 1988, when he was fired from his position at an Austin mental hospital and soon after was evicted from his apartment. At that point, he headed for Los Angeles and spent three years homeless on the streets, shuttling between California and Texas with Lizbeth, his Labrador retriever. During his travels, he kept a journal and later published these entries, along with letters he wrote to a friend, as Travels with Lizbeth: Three Years on the Road and on the Streets *(1993), portions of which had been published previously in several different magazines and journals. The essay that follows, a chapter from this book, describes the steps he took to survive on the streets. Eighner's most recent book is the novel* Pawn to Queen Four *(1995).*

This chapter was composed while the author was homeless. The present tense has been preserved.

Long before I began Dumpster diving I was impressed with Dumpsters, enough so that I wrote the Merriam-Webster research service to discover what I could about the word *Dumpster.* I learned from them that it is a proprietary word belonging to the Dempsey Dumpster company. Since then I have dutifully capitalized the word, although it was lowercased in almost all the citations Merriam-Webster photocopied for me. Dempsey's word is too apt. I have never heard these things called anything but Dumpsters. I do not know anyone who knows the generic name for these objects. From time to time I have heard a wino or hobo give some corrupted credit to the original and call them Dipsy Dumpsters.

I began Dumpster diving about a year before I became homeless.

I prefer the word *scavenging* and use the word *scrounging* when I mean to be obscure. I have heard people, evidently meaning to be polite, use the word *foraging,* but I prefer to reserve that word for gathering nuts and berries and such which I do also according to the season and the opportunity. *Dumpster diving* seems to me to be a little too cute and, in my case, inaccurate because I lack the athletic ability to lower myself into the Dumpsters as the true divers do, much to their increased profit.

I like the frankness of the word *scavenging,* which I can hardly think of without picturing a big black snail on an aquarium wall. I live from the refuse of others. I am a scavenger. I think it a sound and honorable niche, although if I could I would naturally prefer to live the comfortable consumer life, perhaps—and only perhaps—as a slightly less wasteful consumer, owing to what I have learned as a scavenger.

While Lizbeth and I were still living in the shack on Avenue B as   5
my savings ran out, I put almost all my sporadic income into rent. The
necessities of daily life I began to extract from Dumpsters. Yes, we ate
from them. Except for jeans, all my clothes came from Dumpsters.
Boom boxes, candles, bedding, toilet paper, a virgin male love doll,
medicine, books, a typewriter, dishes, furnishings, and change, sometimes amounting to many dollars—I acquired many things from the
Dumpsters.

I have learned much as a scavenger. I mean to put some of what I
have learned down here, beginning with the practical art of Dumpster
diving and proceeding to the abstract.

What is safe to eat?

After all, the finding of objects is becoming something of an urban
art. Even respectable employed people will sometimes find something
tempting sticking out of a Dumpster or standing beside one. Quite a
number of people, not all of them of the bohemian type, are willing to
brag that they found this or that piece in the trash. But eating from
Dumpsters is what separates the dilettanti from the professionals. Eating safely from the Dumpsters involves three principles: using the senses
and common sense to evaluate the conditions of the found materials,
knowing the Dumpsters of a given area and checking them regularly,
and seeking always to answer the question "Why was this discarded?"

Perhaps everyone who has a kitchen and a regular supply of groceries has, at one time or another, made a sandwich and eaten half of it
before discovering mold on the bread or got a mouthful of milk before
realizing the milk had turned. Nothing of the sort is likely to happen to
a Dumpster diver because he is constantly reminded that most food is
discarded for a reason. Yet a lot of perfectly good food can be found in
Dumpsters.

Canned goods, for example, turn up fairly often in the Dumpsters   10
I frequent. All except the most phobic people would be willing to eat
from a can, even if it came from a Dumpster. Canned goods are among
the safest of foods to be found in Dumpsters but are not utterly foolproof.

Although very rare with modern canning methods, botulism is a
possibility. Most other forms of food poisoning seldom do lasting harm
to a healthy person, but botulism is most certainly fatal and often the
first symptom is death. Except for carbonated beverages, all canned
goods should contain a slight vacuum and suck air when first punc-
tured. Bulging, rusty, and dented cans and cans that spew when punc-
tured should be avoided, especially when the contents are not very
acidic or syrupy.

Heat can break down the botulin, but this requires much more cooking than most people do to canned goods. To the extent that botulism
occurs at all, of course, it can occur in cans on pantry shelves as well as

in cans from Dumpsters. Need I say that home-canned goods are simply too risky to be recommended.

From time to time one of my companions, aware of the source of my provisions, will ask, "Do you think these crackers are really safe to eat?" For some reason it is most often the crackers they ask about.

This question has always made me angry. Of course I would not offer my companion anything I had doubts about. But more than that, I wonder why he cannot evaluate the condition of the crackers for himself. I have no special knowledge and I have been wrong before. Since he knows where the food comes from, it seems to me he ought to assume some of the responsibility for deciding what he will put in his mouth. For myself I have few qualms about dry foods such as crackers, cookies, cereal, chips, and pasta if they are free of visible contaminants and still dry and crisp. Most often such things are found in the original packaging, which is not so much a positive sign as it is the absence of a negative one.

15   Raw fruits and vegetables with intact skins seem perfectly safe to me, excluding of course the obviously rotten. Many are discarded for minor imperfections that can be pared away. Leafy vegetables, grapes, cauliflower, broccoli, and similar things may be contaminated by liquids and may be impractical to wash.

Candy, especially hard candy, is usually safe if it has not drawn ants. Chocolate is often discarded only because it has become discolored as the cocoa butter de-emulsified. Candying, after all, is one method of food preservation because pathogens do not like very sugary substances.

All of these foods might be found in any Dumpster and can be evaluated with some confidence largely on the basis of appearance. Beyond these are foods that cannot be correctly evaluated without additional information.

I began scavenging by pulling pizzas out of the Dumpster behind a pizza delivery shop. In general, prepared food requires caution, but in this case I knew when the shop closed and went to the Dumpster as soon as the last of the help left.

Such shops often get prank orders; both the orders and the products made to fill them are called *bogus*. Because help seldom stays long at these places, pizzas are often made with the wrong topping, refused on delivery for being cold, or baked incorrectly. The products to be discarded are boxed up because inventory is kept by counting boxes: A boxed pizza can be written off; an unboxed pizza does not exist.

20   I never placed a bogus order to increase the supply of pizzas and I believe no one else was scavenging in this Dumpster. But the people in the shop became suspicious and began to retain their garbage in the shop overnight. While it lasted I had a steady supply of fresh, sometimes warm pizza. Because I knew the Dumpster I knew the source of

the pizza, and because I visited the Dumpster regularly I knew what was fresh and what was yesterday's.

The area I frequent is inhabited by many affluent college students. I am not here by chance; the Dumpsters in this area are very rich. Students throw out many good things, including food. In particular they tend to throw everything out when they move at the end of a semester, before and after breaks, and around midterm, when many of them despair of college. So I find it advantageous to keep an eye on the academic calendar.

Students throw food away around breaks because they do not know whether it has spoiled or will spoil before they return. A typical discard is a half jar of peanut butter. In fact, nonorganic peanut butter does not require refrigeration and is unlikely to spoil in any reasonable time. The student does not know that, and since it is Daddy's money, the student decides not to take a chance. Opened containers require caution and some attention to the question "Why was this discarded?" But in the case of discards from student apartments, the answer may be that the item was thrown out through carelessness, ignorance, or wastefulness. This can sometimes be deduced when the item is found with many others, including some that are obviously perfectly good.

Some students, and others, approach defrosting a freezer by chucking out the whole lot. Not only do the circumstances of such a find tell the story, but also the mass of frozen goods stays cold for a long time and items may be found still frozen or freshly thawed.

Yogurt, cheese, and sour cream are items that are often thrown out while they are still good. Occasionally I find a cheese with a spot of mold, which of course I just pare off, and because it is obvious why such a cheese was discarded, I treat it with less suspicion than an apparently perfect cheese found in similar circumstances. Yogurt is often discarded, still sealed, only because the expiration date on the carton had passed. This is one of my favorite finds because yogurt will keep for several days, even in warm weather.

Students throw out canned goods and staples at the end of semesters and when they give up college at midterm. Drugs, pornography, spirits, and the like are often discarded when parents are expected— Dad's day, for example. And spirits also turn up after big party weekends, presumably discarded by the newly reformed. Wine and spirits, of course, keep perfectly well even once opened, but the same cannot be said of beer. 25

My test for carbonated soft drinks is whether they still fizz vigorously. Many juices or other beverages are too acidic or too syrupy to cause much concern, provided they are not visibly contaminated. I have discovered nasty molds in vegetable juices, even when the product was found under its original seal; I recommend that such products be decanted slowly into a clear glass. Liquids always require some care. One hot day I found a large jug of Pat O'Brien's Hurricane mix. The jug had been opened, but it was still ice cold. I drank three large glasses before it became apparent to me that someone had added the rum to the mix, and not a little rum. I never tasted the rum, and by the time I began to feel the effects I had already ingested a very large quantity of the beverage. Some divers would have considered this a boon, but being suddenly intoxicated in a public place in the early afternoon is not my idea of a good time.

I have heard of people maliciously contaminating discarded food and even handouts, but mostly I have heard of this from people with vivid imaginations who have had no experience with Dumpsters themselves. Just before the pizza shop stopped discarding its garbage at night, jalapeños began showing up on most of the discarded pizzas. If indeed this was meant to discourage me it was a wasted effort because I am native Texan.

For myself, I avoid game, poultry, pork, and egg-based foods, whether I find them raw or cooked. I seldom have the means to cook what I find, but when I do I avail myself of plentiful supplies of beef, which is often in very good condition. I suppose fish becomes disagreeable before it becomes dangerous. Lizbeth is happy to have any such thing that is past its prime and, in fact, does not recognize fish as food until it is quite strong.

Home leftovers, as opposed to surpluses from restaurants, are very often bad. Evidently, especially among students, there is a common type of personality that carefully wraps up even the smallest leftover and shoves it into the back of the refrigerator for six months or so before discarding it. Characteristic of this type are the reused jars and margarine tubs to which the remains are committed. I avoid ethnic foods I am unfamiliar with. If I do not know what it is supposed to look like when it is good, I cannot be certain I will be able to tell if it is bad.

30   No matter how careful I am I still get dysentery at least once a month, oftener in warm weather. I do not want to paint too romantic a picture. Dumpster diving has serious drawbacks as a way of life.

I learned to scavenge gradually, on my own. Since then I have initiated several companions into the trade. I have learned that there is a predictable series of stages a person goes through in learning to scavenge.

At first the new scavenger is filled with disgust and self-loathing. He is ashamed of being seen and may lurk around, trying to duck behind things, or he may try to dive at night. (In fact, most people instinctively look away from a scavenger. By skulking around, the novice calls attention to himself and arouses suspicion. Diving at night is ineffective and needlessly messy.)

Every grain of rice seems to be a maggot. Everything seems to stink. He can wipe the egg yolk off the found can, but he cannot erase from his mind the stigma of eating garbage.

That stage passes with experience. The scavenger finds a pair of running shoes that fit and look and smell brand-new. He finds a pocket calculator in perfect working order. He finds pristine ice cream, still frozen, more than he can eat or keep. He begins to understand: People throw away perfectly good stuff, a lot of perfectly good stuff.

At this stage, Dumpster shyness begins to dissipate. The diver, after 35 all, has the last laugh. He is finding all manner of good things that are his for the taking. Those who disparage his profession are the fools, not he.

He may begin to hang on to some perfectly good things for which he has neither a use nor a market. Then he begins to take note of the things that are not perfectly good but are nearly so. He mates a Walkman with broken earphones and one that is missing a battery cover. He picks up things that he can repair.

At this stage he may become lost and never recover. Dumpsters are full of things of some potential value to someone and also of things that never have much intrinsic value but are interesting. All the Dumpster divers I have known come to the point of trying to acquire everything they touch. Why not take it, they reason, since it is all free? This is, of course, hopeless. Most divers come to realize that they must restrict themselves to items of relatively immediate utility. But in some cases the diver simply cannot control himself. I have met several of these pack-rat types. Their ideas of the values of various pieces of junk verge on the psychotic. Every bit of glass may be a diamond, they think, and all that glistens, gold.

I tend to gain weight when I am scavenging. Partly this is because I always find far more pizza and doughnuts than water-packed tuna, nonfat yogurt, and fresh vegetables. Also I have not developed much faith in the reliability of Dumpsters as a food source, although it has been proven to me many times. I tend to eat as if I have no idea where my next meal is coming from. But mostly I just hate to see food go to waste and so I eat much more than I should. Something like this drives the obsession to collect junk.

As for collecting objects, I usually restrict myself to collecting one kind of small object at a time, such as pocket calculators, sunglasses, or campaign buttons. To live on the street I must anticipate my needs to a certain extent: I must pick up and save warm bedding I find in August because it will not be found in Dumpsters in November. As I have no access to health care, I often hoard essential drugs, such as antibiotics and antihistamines. (This course can be recommended only to those with some grounding in pharmacology. Antibiotics, for example, even when indicated are worse than useless if taken in insufficient amounts.) But even if I had a home with extensive storage space, I could not save everything that might be valuable in some contingency.

I have proprietary feelings about my Dumpsters. As I have men- 40 tioned, it is no accident that I scavenge from ones where good finds are common. But my limited experience with Dumpsters in other areas suggests to me that even in poorer areas, Dumpsters, if attended with sufficient diligence, can be made to yield a livelihood. The rich students discard perfectly good kiwi fruit; poorer people discard perfectly good apples. Slacks and Polo shirts are found in the one place; jeans and T-shirts in the other. The population of competitors rather than the affluence of the dumpers most affects the feasibility of survival by scavenging. The large number of competitors is what puts me off the idea of trying to scavenge in places like Los Angeles.

Curiously, I do not mind my direct competition, other scavengers, so much as I hate the can scroungers.

People scrounge cans because they have to have a little cash. I have tried scrounging cans with an able-bodied companion. Afoot a can scrounger simply cannot make more than a few dollars a day. One can extract the necessities of life from the Dumpsters directly with far less effort than would be required to accumulate the equivalent value in cans. (These observations may not hold in places with container redemption laws.)

Can scroungers, then, are people who must have small amounts of cash. These are drug addicts and winos, mostly the latter because the amounts of cash are so small. Spirits and drugs do, like all other commodities, turn up in Dumpsters and the scavenger will from time to time have a half bottle of a rather good wine with his dinner. But the wino cannot survive on these occasional finds; he must have his daily dose to stave off the DTs. All the cans he can carry will buy about three bottles of Wild Irish Rose.

I do not begrudge them the cans, but can scroungers tend to tear up the Dumpsters, mixing the contents and littering the area. They become so specialized that they can see only cans. They earn my contempt by passing up change, canned goods, and readily hockable items.

45   There are precious few courtesies among scavengers. But it is common practice to set aside surplus items: pairs of shoes, clothing, canned goods, and such. A true scavenger hates to see good stuff go to waste, and what he cannot use he leaves in good condition in plain sight.

Can scroungers lay waste to everything in their path and will stir one of a pair of good shoes to the bottom of a Dumpster, to be lost or ruined in the muck. Can scroungers will even go through individual garbage cans, something I have never seen a scavenger do.

Individual garbage cans are set out on the public easement only on garbage days. On other days going through them requires trespassing close to a dwelling. Going through individual garbage cans without scattering litter is almost impossible. Litter is likely to reduce the public's tolerance of scavenging. Individual cans are simply not as productive as Dumpsters; people in houses and duplexes do not move so often and for some reason do not tend to discard as much useful material. Moreover, the time required to go through one garbage can that serves one household is not much less than the time required to go through a Dumpster that contains the refuse of twenty apartments.

But my strongest reservation about going through individual garbage cans is that this seems to me a very personal kind of invasion to which I would object if I were a householder. Although many things in Dumpsters are obviously meant never to come to light, a Dumpster is somehow less personal.

I avoid trying to draw conclusions about the people who dump in the Dumpsters I frequent. I think it would be unethical to do so, although I know many people will find the idea of scavenger ethics too funny for words.

Dumpsters contain bank statements, correspondence, and other documents, just as anyone might expect. But there are also less obvious sources of information. Pill bottles, for example. The labels bear the name of the patient, the name of the doctor, and the name of the drug. AIDS drugs and antipsychotic medicines, to name but two groups, are specific and are seldom prescribed for any other disorders. The plastic compacts for birth-control pills usually have complete label information. 50

Despite all of this sensitive information, I have had only one apartment resident object to my going through the Dumpster. In that case it turned out the resident was a university athlete who was taking bets and who was afraid I would turn up his wager slips.

Occasionally a find tells a story. I once found a small paper bag containing some unused condoms, several partial tubes of flavored sexual lubricants, a partially used compact of birth-control pills, and the torn pieces of a picture of a young man. Clearly she was through with him and planning to give up sex altogether.

Dumpster things are often sad—abandoned teddy bears, shredded wedding books, despaired-of sales kits. I find many pets lying in state in Dumpsters. Although I hope to get off the streets so that Lizbeth can have a long and comfortable old age, I know this hope is not very realistic. So I suppose when her time comes she too will go into a Dumpster. I will have no better place for her. And after all, it is fitting, since for most of her life her livelihood has come from the Dumpster. When she finds something I think is safe that has been spilled from a Dumpster, I let her have it. She already knows the route around the best ones. I like to think that if she survives me she will have a chance of evading the dog catcher and of finding her sustenance on the route.

Silly vanities also come to rest in the Dumpsters. I am a rather accomplished needleworker. I get a lot of material from the Dumpsters. Evidently sorority girls, hoping to impress someone, perhaps themselves, with their mastery of a womanly art, buy a lot of embroider-by-number kits, work a few stitches horribly, and eventually discard the whole mess. I pull out their stitches, turn the canvas over, and work an original design. Do not think I refrain from chuckling as I make gifts from these kits.

55   I find diaries and journals. I have often thought of compiling a book of literary found objects. And perhaps I will one day. But what I find is hopelessly commonplace and bad without being, even unconsciously, camp. College students also discard their papers. I am horrified to discover the kind of paper that now merits an A in an undergraduate course. I am grateful, however, for the number of good books and magazines the students throw out.

In the area I know best I have never discovered vermin in the Dumpsters, but there are two kinds of kitty surprise. One is alley cats whom I meet as they leap, claws first, out of Dumpsters. This is especially thrilling when I have Lizbeth in tow. The other kind of kitty surprise is a plastic garbage bag filled with some ponderous, amorphous mass. This always proves to be used cat litter.

City bees harvest doughnut glaze and this makes the Dumpster at the doughnut shop more interesting. My faith in the instinctive wisdom of animals is always shaken whenever I see Lizbeth attempt to catch a bee in her mouth, which she does whenever bees are present. Evidently some birds find Dumpsters profitable, for birdie surprise is almost as common as kitty surprise of the first kind. In hunting season all kinds of small game turn up in Dumpsters, some of it, sadly, not entirely dead. Curiously, summer and winter, maggots are uncommon.

The worst of the living and near-living hazards of the Dumpsters are the fire ants. The food they claim is not much of a loss, but they are vicious and aggressive. It is very easy to brush against some surface of the Dumpster and pick up half a dozen or more fire ants, usually in some sensitive area such as the underarm. One advantage of bringing Lizbeth along as I make Dumpster rounds is that, for obvious reasons, she is very alert to ground-based fire ants. When Lizbeth recognizes a fire-ant infestation around our feet, she does the Dance of the Zillion Fire Ants. I have learned not to ignore this warning from Lizbeth, whether I perceive the tiny ants or not, but to remove ourselves at Lizbeth's first pas de bourrée.[1] All the more so because the ants are the worst in the summer months when I wear flip-flops if I have them. (Perhaps someone will misunderstand this. Lizbeth does the Dance of the Zillion Fire Ants when she recognizes more fire ants than she cares to eat, not when she is being bitten. Since I have learned to react promptly, she does not get bitten at all. It is the isolated patrol of fire ants that falls in Lizbeth's range that deserves pity. She finds them quite tasty.)

---

[1]A short walking or running step in ballet. [Eds.]

By far the best way to go through a Dumpster is to lower yourself into it. Most of the good stuff tends to settle at the bottom because it is usually weightier than the rubbish. My more athletic companions have often demonstrated to me that they can extract much good material from a Dumpster I have already been over.

To those psychologically or physically unprepared to enter a Dumpster, I recommend a stout stick, preferably with some barb or hook at one end. The hook can be used to grab plastic garbage bags. When I find canned goods or other objects loose at the bottom of a Dumpster, I lower a bag into it, roll the desired object into the bag, and then hoist the bag out—a procedure more easily described than executed. Much Dumpster diving is a matter of experience for which nothing will do except practice.

Dumpster diving is outdoor work, often surprisingly pleasant. It is not entirely predictable; things of interest turn up every day and some days there are finds of great value. I am always very pleased when I can turn up exactly the thing I most wanted to find. Yet in spite of the element of chance, scavenging more than most other pursuits tends to yield returns in some proportion to the effort and intelligence brought to bear. It is very sweet to turn up a few dollars in change from a Dumpster that has just been gone over by a wino.

The land is now covered with cities. The cities are full of Dumpsters. If a member of the canine race is ever able to know what it is doing, then Lizbeth knows that when we go around to the Dumpsters, we are hunting. I think of scavenging as a modern form of self-reliance. In any event, after having survived nearly ten years of government service, where everything is geared to the lowest common denominator, I find it refreshing to have work that rewards initiative and effort. Certainly I would be happy to have a sinecure again, but I am no longer heartbroken that I left one.

I find from the experience of scavenging two rather deep lessons. The first is to take what you can use and let the rest go by. I have come to think that there is no value in the abstract. A thing I cannot use or make useful, perhaps by trading, has no value however rare or fine it may be. I mean useful in a broad sense—some art I would find useful and some otherwise.

I was shocked to realize that some things are not worth acquiring, but now I think it is so. Some material things are white elephants that eat up the possessor's substance. The second lesson is the transience of material being. This has not quite converted me to a dualist,[2] but it has made some headway in that direction. I do not suppose that ideas are immortal, but certainly mental things are longer lived than other material things.

---

[2]One who believes that material things also exist as spiritual ideals or abstractions. [Eds.]

65 Once I was the sort of person who invests objects with sentimental value. Now I no longer have those objects, but I have the sentiments yet.

Many times in our travels I have lost everything but the clothes I was wearing and Lizbeth. The things I find in Dumpsters, the love letters and rag dolls of so many lives, remind me of this lesson. Now I hardly pick up a thing without envisioning the time I will cast it aside. This I think is a healthy state of mind. Almost everything I have now has already been cast out at least once, proving that what I own is valueless to someone.

Anyway, I find my desire to grab for the gaudy bauble has been largely sated. I think this is an attitude I share with the very wealthy— we both know there is plenty more where what we have came from. Between us are the rat-race millions who nightly scavenge the cable channels looking for they know not what.

I am sorry for them.

Responding to Reading

1. In paragraph 6, Eighner explains, "I have learned much as a scavenger. I mean to put some of what I have learned down here, beginning with the practical art of Dumpster diving and proceeding to the abstract." Do you think Eighner's purpose goes beyond educating his readers? What other purpose do you think he might have?
2. What surprised you most about Eighner's essay? Did any information disturb you? repulse you? make you feel guilty? arouse your sympathy? arouse your pity? Do you think Eighner intended you to feel the way you do?
3. How do you suppose Eighner would define the American Dream? What do you think he might have to say about its limits?

Responding in Writing

Assuming that Eighner wished to continue living on the streets, what could he do to make his life easier? Write a flyer, to be distributed to the homeless, advising them of resources available to them in your community (for example, public rest rooms).

WHERE EVIL DWELLS: REFLECTIONS ON THE COLUMBINE SCHOOL MASSACRE

James Howard Kunstler

1948–

James Howard Kunstler is a novelist, essayist, and lecturer whose work centers on social, urban, economic, and environmental concerns. A contributing writer for the New York Times, *Kunstler has published numerous books, including* The City in Mind: Meditations on the Urban Condition *(2001),* Maggie Darling: A Modern Romance *(2004), and* The Long Emergency: Surviving the Converging Catastrophes of the Twenty-First Century *(2005). The following remarks were presented to the Congress for the New Urbanism (CNU) in 1999.*

When we set aside all the technical considerations and all the familiar economic arguments and tedious political angles that swirl around this enormous and momentous field of human ecology,[1] we're left with the question of how it affects our souls. That this question gets such spectacularly short shrift in the public discussion is itself a powerful indictment of our idiot contemporary culture, because what could be of more profound importance to each and every one of us than how we feel about our literal place in the world?

How do we even account for such a fabulous failure of moral imagination?

I believe that there is such a thing as mainstream culture, which changes, mutates, and readapts itself over time in an organic process akin to the way other living systems grow and change. I believe that in the past and up into our time, American culture has admitted a notion of the human spirit, that such a thing exists and is worthy of our attention. We know this from reading Emerson, Thoreau, Lincoln, Whitman, Santayana, Mumford, Flannery O'Conner, Alan Ginsburg, Annie Dillard, Wendell Berry, and scores of others who were moved to express themselves on the subject. Is there a more potent phrase in our national letters than "the better angels of our nature" invoked by Lincoln.

I don't think there can be any doubt that the issues of the human spirit have been embedded in our national habits of thinking and that, at one time or another, they occupied a broad band in the mainstream. But what is it about the particular nature of our time that appears to have suppressed them, tried to vanquish them, or driven them to the margins of our collective psychology?

---

[1]Academic discipline that considers people's relationships to and interactions with their environments. [Eds.]

5   My sense is that American culture has an unfortunate tendency toward abstraction, and where the idea of the human spirit meets the issues of place, this tendency becomes very troublesome because this is exactly where the abstract collides with the concrete. The situation is badly aggravated by those professional agents of untruth, the corporate advertisers, marketers, and spin-doctors who bombard the populace with so many deliberately false messages that language itself loses its vested authority as the best medium for an honest understanding of the real world. Professional intellectuals (especially academics) have ceded the moral ground as defenders of reality by adopting the same despicable tactics as the advertisers and spin doctors in trying to advance a wishful politically leveling view of the world that does not comport with organizing principles of nature, which tend to be hierarchical. Abstraction, therefore, becomes a refuge for those who fear the actual nature of things. (That it is tragic when intellectuals surrender this ground is another matter.)

What we've gotten in America the past several generations is some very very bad, very untruthful ideas about the nature of reality, among them: that there may not indeed be any such thing as objective reality, that the virtual is an adequate substitute for the authentic; that the abstract is identical to the particular (i.e. that the idea of something counts as much as the thing itself); that wishing is the same as doing; that nothing is inherently better than any other thing; that all behaviors, values, attitudes, undertakings, and aspirations are equally valid (and equally provisional).

But what could be more concrete than a particular spot on the planet, its specific quality and character in relation to our experience of that place, including our memories of the past there and our hopes and expectations about the future there? For most of modern history—that is, since men gave up a nomadic existence for a settled one—this complex of ideas and emotions has been bundled into the notion of a place called home. Of course, in contemporary American culture, where every mass-produced vinyl box is called a "home"—whether it possesses any of the real qualities that define the nature of a home—it becomes impossible to endow any place with meaning, or conduct an intelligible conversation about it.

The deliberate, relentless perversion of truth and truthfulness in our culture has prompted us to give ourselves permission to create a human ecology that is, for practical purposes, the anti-place. It is the dwelling place of untruth. We call it suburbia. A cartoon of rural life, with none of the qualities of it. I believe we in the CNU recognize its profound culturally toxic nature, and yet it has become as commonplace as the fog of lies and propaganda that envelopes us, and we cannot quite believe that something so ubiquitous can be so deeply, thoroughly evil.

The school massacre at Littleton, Colorado, just over a month ago is a case in point. Notice how the nation went through a highly ritualized act of national handwringing while evincing a shocking inability to examine the nature of the place where the deed occurred in relation to the deed itself, or the relation of the place, the deed, and the spirits of the young people who lived in the place and carried out the deed. None of this was difficult to understand, either. We just didn't want to look.

I've been to Littleton, and this is what you get there: a place with no   10 sense of a past, no hope of a future, and a spiritually degrading present. The common complaint about these brand-new mega-suburbs is that "everything looks the same." This is only the most superficial symptom of their evil nature. Not only is everything the same in Littleton as in thousands of other anti-places created in the name of prosperity and economic expansion, but the components of this massive sameness have in common their nature as a massive cultural swindle, resulting in an ecology of lies. The chief lie concerns our relation to the passage of time.

There is nothing more fundamental to the nature of reality, and to the role of humans within it, than the continuity of life through time; that things, events, and personalities came before us and made way for us, as we will have to make way for new things, events, and personalities, with the expectation that across time we will all—the dead, the living, and the unborn—contribute to a chain of being (as Jefferson's generation called it), in a process of dynamic disequilibrium that adds up to more than the sum of each thing, event, and personality, and supports a unifying quest toward a state of grace.

This is exactly what suburbia, the anti-place, lacks. It is easy to see that there is no past. It might take a little reflection—but not much—to perceive that it has no future. Its present is a dangerously provisional collective hallucination, nourished by a sado-masochistic idiot pop culture, which can fall apart at the slightest provocation. (We have a name for this collective hallucination, by the way: The American Dream, a sort of mega-lie stating that this sort of ghastly provisional collective hallucination is the ultimate state of being worth aspiring to.) I maintain that the provisional order of the anti-place is continually being subverted by an array of logical human responses. Most are self-defense mechanisms of one sort or another. For instance, teen drug use as a social phenomenon exists because the ecology of the anti-place is so deeply unrewarding, corrosive, and degrading that the spirit demands analgesia. Teen drug abuse is really self-medication gone awry. Likewise, teen violence is a logical response to the deep sense of purposelessness generated by the American Dream. Just as young adults begin to acquire some inkling of their physical and mental power as human beings, and lacking any notion as to how these might be used to construct a purposeful life, the kids squander their poorly understood personal power to act in a single reckless act intended to destroy the legitimacy of their everyday environment and everything that it represents.

I doubt that there is anything more malign about the anti-place than its failure to furnish any sense of a future for young people. If anyone needs the signifiers of a hopeful future it is children and teenagers. Since the anti-place is the home of untruth, however, it is perfectly logical that it fails most those young persons which it pretends to serve best. It is especially shameful that adults and professionals insist despite all evidence to the contrary that suburbia, the anti-place is "a great place for kids." Supporting this lie contributes directly to the slaughter of their own children.

(By the way, wasn't it horrifyingly embarrassing when, at the start of our air war against the Serbians, American children carried out an effective act of war against their own culture? Fifteen dead, many wounded. How could we explain this to ourselves? We couldn't. We failed to. We stopped trying eventually because the truth was too painful.)

15   When I say "signifiers," by the way, I mean that combination of physical artifacts, institutions, and the ideas and feelings invested in them, that traditionally inform people who and where they are in the world, where they've come from and where they might be going. For instance, the organic system of authentic village, town, neighborhood, or city contains the requisite organs for assuring the continuity of human life—the civic organs, the commercial organs, the cultural organs, the family organs, and so on. One of the chief characteristics of the anti-place, suburbia, is that it lacks these organs, and therefore is not a living organism existing within a hierarchy of other living organisms—the person, the family, the group, the village, the region, the biosphere, and so on.

The anti-place fails to signify to young people that such a thing as a plausible future exists, so that by utilizing one's powers of personal sovereignty, one might create a life worth living in a place worth living in. Clearly, the two young men who shot up Columbine high school came from circumstances that seemed to furnish all the requisite advantages for a positive development to adulthood. And what they just as clearly lacked was enough of a sense of a hopeful future to chose any other path besides their own deliberate self-destruction following an orgy of wrathful bloodletting. I don't think we can over-estimate the depth and degree of anomie breeding in the thousands of anti-places that are designed to the specifications of Littleton, Colorado. By anomie, I mean, according to the dictionary:

1. Social instability caused by steady erosion of standards and values.

2. Alienation and purposelessness experienced by a person or a class as a result of a lack of standards and values.
3. Personal disorganization resulting in unsociable behavior.

If we were truthful and realistic about the way we were living in America, we would expect tragic outbursts like the Columbine massacre at regular intervals, and not be the least bit surprised, nor go through the disingenuous rituals of shock and disbelief. (And, in fact, we have been getting school massacres at regular intervals.) Because we know that we have created a vast and evil setting for American life to take place in.

I often joke that we are a wicked people who deserve to be punished. But the joke is, it's no joke. I believe it with all my heart. I also often remark in my public utterances that when we succeed in creating enough places that are not worth caring about, that we will succeed in becoming a nation that is not worth defending, and a way of life that is not worth carrying on. We are guilty of foreclosing our own future, and we are evil because we don't care.

If this is seems like a pessimistic view of the current situation than I congratulate you on your powers of perception.

Responding to Reading

1. This speech addresses the 1999 Littleton shootings, suburbia, and the American Dream. Which of these three topics do you think is Kunstler's true focus? What makes you think so?
2. According to Kunstler, what is wrong with the suburbs? In what respects does he blame "suburbia, the anti-place" (12) for the Littleton shootings? Do you think his arguments have merit? What (or whom) do you blame?
3. In paragraph 12, Kunstler calls the American Dream "a sort of mega-lie," a "collective hallucination" that Americans share. What exactly does he mean?

Responding in Writing

Unlike the other readings in this chapter, Kunstler's essay is very pessimistic and very critical of the American Dream. (Note that Kunstler was born and brought up in the United States.) Consider how other writers in this chapter might respond to his characterization of the American Dream. Then, write an email to Kunstler from one of these writers.

——————————— FOCUS ———————————

What Is the American Dream?

Immigrant families on board ship approaching Statue of Liberty, c. 1900

Responding to the Image

1. What does this photograph suggest to you about the power of the American Dream? How might the immigrants pictured here define the American Dream?
2. What do you think the Statue of Liberty symbolizes to the people in the picture? Do you think the statue means something different to today's Americans? (Note that most immigrants no longer come to the United States by ship.)

CHAPTER 6   FOCUS

THE DECLARATION OF INDEPENDENCE

Thomas Jefferson

1743–1826

Thomas Jefferson—lawyer, statesman, diplomat, architect, scientist, politician, writer, education theorist, and musician—graduated from William and Mary College in 1762 and went on to lead an impressive political life. Jefferson served as a member of the Continental Congress, governor of Virginia, secretary of state to George Washington, and vice president to John Adams and also served two terms as the U.S. president (1801–1809), during which he oversaw the Louisiana Purchase. After retiring from public office, Jefferson founded the University of Virginia in 1819. He was an avid collector of books and owned nearly ten thousand, which later became the foundation of the Library of Congress. A firm believer in reason and the natural rights of individuals, Jefferson drafted the Declaration of Independence, which was later amended by the Continental Congress. In this document, he presents the colonists' grievances in order to justify their decision to declare their independence from England.

In Congress, July 4, 1776: The Unanimous Declaration of the Thirteen United States of America

When in the Course of human events it becomes necessary for one people to dissolve the political bands which have connected them with another, and to assume among the powers of the earth, the separate and equal station to which the Laws of Nature and of Nature's God entitle them, a decent respect to the opinions of mankind requires that they should declare the causes which impel them to the separation.

We hold these truths to be self-evident, that all men are created equal, that they are endowed by their Creator with certain unalienable Rights, that among these are Life, Liberty and the pursuit of Happiness. That to secure these rights, Governments are instituted among Men, deriving their just powers from the consent of the governed. That whenever any Form of Government becomes destructive of these ends, it is the Right of the People to alter or to abolish it, and to institute new Government, laying its foundation on such principles and organizing its powers in such form, as to them shall seem most likely to effect their Safety and Happiness. Prudence, indeed, will dictate that Governments long established should not be changed for light and transient causes; and accordingly all experience hath shewn, that mankind are more disposed to suffer, while evils are sufferable, than to right themselves by abolishing the forms to which they are accustomed. But when a long train of abuses and usurpations, pursuing invariably the same Object, evinces a design to reduce them under absolute Despotism, it is their right, it is their duty, to throw off such Government, and to provide new Guards for their

CHAPTER 6 FOCUS

future security. Such has been the patient sufferance of these Colonies; and such is now the necessity which constrains them to alter their former Systems of Governors. The history of the present King of Great Britain is a history of repeated injuries and usurpations, all having in direct object the establishment of an absolute Tyranny over these States. To prove this, let Facts be submitted to a candid world.

He has refused his Assent to Laws, the most wholesome and necessary for the public good.

He has forbidden his Governors to pass laws of immediate and pressing importance, unless suspended in their operation till his Assent should be obtained; and when so suspended, he has utterly neglected to attend to them.

5   He has refused to pass other Laws for the accommodation of large districts of people, unless those people would relinquish the right of Representation in the Legislature, a right inestimable to them and formidable to tyrants only.

He has called together legislative bodies at places unusual, uncomfortable, and distant from the depository of their Public Records, for the sole purpose of fatiguing them into compliance with his measures.

He has dissolved Representative Houses repeatedly, for opposing with manly firmness his invasions on the rights of the people.

He has refused for a long time, after such dissolutions, to cause others to be elected; whereby the Legislative Powers, incapable of Annihilation, have returned to the People at large for their exercise; the State remaining in the mean time exposed to all the dangers of invasion from without, and convulsions within.

He has endeavored to prevent the population of these States; for that purpose obstructing the Laws for Naturalization of Foreigners; refusing to pass others to encourage their migration hither, and raising the conditions of new Appropriations of Lands.

10   He has obstructed the Administration of Justice, by refusing his Assent to Laws for establishing Judiciary Powers.

He has made Judges dependent on his Will alone, for the tenure of their offices, and the amount and payment of their salaries.

He has erected a multitude of New Offices, and sent hither swarms of Officers to harass our people, and eat out their substance.

He has kept among us, in times of peace, Standing Armies without the Consent of our legislatures.

He has affected to render the Military independent of and superior to the Civil Power.

15   He has combined with others to subject us to a jurisdiction foreign to our constitution, and unacknowledged by our laws; giving his Assent to their Acts of pretended Legislation: For quartering large bodies of armed troops among us: For protecting them, by a mock Trial, from punishment for any Murders which they should commit on the Inhabitants

of these States: For cutting off our Trade with all parts of the world: For imposing Taxes on us without our Consent: For depriving us in many cases, of the benefits of Trial by Jury; For transporting us beyond Seas to be tried for pretended offenses: For abolishing the free System of English Laws in a neighboring Province, establishing therein an Arbitrary government, and enlarging its Boundaries so as to render it at once an example and fit instrument for introducing the same absolute rule into these Colonies: For taking away our Charters, abolishing our most valuable Laws and altering fundamentally the Forms of our Governments: For suspending our own Legislatures, and declaring themselves invested with power to legislate for us in all cases whatsoever.

He has abdicated Government here, by declaring us out of his Protection and waging War against us.

He has plundered our seas, ravaged our Coasts, burnt our towns, and destroyed the lives of our people.

He is at this time transporting large Armies of foreign Mercenaries to complete the works of death, desolation and tyranny, already begun with circumstances of Cruelty & Perfidy scarcely paralleled in the most barbarous ages, and totally unworthy the Head of a civilized nation.

He has constrained our fellow Citizens taken Captive on the high Seas to bear Arms against their Country, to become the executioners of their friends and Brethren, or to fall themselves by their Hands.

He has excited domestic insurrections amongst us, and has endeavored to bring on the inhabitants of our frontiers, the merciless Indian Savages, whose known rule of warfare, is an undistinguished destruction of all ages, sexes, and conditions.

In every stage of these Oppressions We have Petitioned for Redress in the most humble terms: Our repeated Petitions have been answered only by repeated injury. A Prince, whose character is thus marked by every act which may define a Tyrant, is unfit to be the ruler of a free people.

Nor have We been wanting in attention to our British brethren. We have warned them from time to time of attempts by their legislature to extend an unwarrantable jurisdiction over us. We have reminded them of the circumstances of our emigration and settlement here. We have appealed to their native justice and magnanimity, and we have conjured them by the ties of our common kindred to disavow these usurpations, which would inevitably interrupt our connections and correspondence. They too have been deaf to the voice of justice and of consanguinity. We must, therefore, acquiesce in the necessity, which denounces our Separation, and hold them, as we hold the rest of mankind, Enemies in War, in Peace Friends.

We, THEREFORE, the Representatives of the UNITED STATES OF AMERICA, in General Congress, Assembled, appealing to the Supreme Judge of the world for the rectitude of our intentions, do, in the Name, and by Authority of the good People of these Colonies, solemnly publish and

20

CHAPTER 6   FOCUS

declare, That these United Colonies are, and of Right ought to be FREE AND INDEPENDENT STATES; that they are Absolved from all Allegiance to the British Crown, and that all political connection between them and the State of Great Britain, is and ought to be totally dissolved; and that as Free and Independent States, they have full Power to levy War, conclude Peace, contract Alliances, establish Commerce, and to do all other Acts and Things which Independent States may of right do. And for the support of this Declaration, with a firm reliance on the protection of Divine Providence, we mutually pledge to each other our Lives, our Fortunes, and our sacred Honor.

Responding to Reading

1. The Declaration of Independence was written in the eighteenth century, a time when logic and reason were thought to be the supreme achievements of human beings. Do you think this document appeals just to reason, or does it also appeal to the emotions?
2. Paragraphs 3–20 consist of a litany of grievances, expressed in forceful parallel language. How is this use of parallelism similar to (or different from) the language used by Kennedy (p. 380) and King (p. 383)?
3. Do you think it is fair, as some have done, to accuse the framers of the Declaration of Independence of being racist? of being sexist? Do you think Stanton (p. 387) would see them as sexist?

Responding in Writing

Rewrite five or six sentences from paragraphs 3–20 of the Declaration of Independence in modern English, substituting contemporary examples for the injustices Jefferson enumerates.

THE GETTYSBURG ADDRESS

Abraham Lincoln

1809–1865

The sixteenth president of the United States, Abraham Lincoln led the Union to victory in the American Civil War. Known as the "Great Emancipator," Lincoln freed the slaves of the Confederacy with the Emancipation Proclamation, which was issued on January 1, 1863. On November 19, 1863, Lincoln delivered the Gettysburg Address during the dedication of the National Cemetery at Gettysburg, Pennsylvania, where the Battle of Gettysburg had claimed more than 40,000 Union and Confederate lives in July of that year.

Four score and seven years ago our fathers brought forth on this continent, a new nation, conceived in Liberty, and dedicated to the proposition that all men are created equal.

Now we are engaged in a great civil war, testing whether that nation, or any nation so conceived and so dedicated, can long endure. We are met on a great battle-field of that war. We have come to dedicate a portion of that field, as a final resting place for those who here gave their lives that that nation might live. It is altogether fitting and proper that we should do this.

But, in a larger sense, we can not dedicate—we can not consecrate—we can not hallow—this ground. The brave men, living and dead, who struggled here, have consecrated it, far above our poor power to add or detract. The world will little note, nor long remember what we say here, but it can never forget what they did here. It is for us the living, rather, to be dedicated here to the unfinished work which they who fought here have thus far so nobly advanced. It is rather for us to be here dedicated to the great task remaining before us—that from these honored dead we take increased devotion to that cause for which they gave the last full measure of devotion—that we here highly resolve that these dead shall not have died in vain—that this nation, under God, shall have a new birth of freedom—and that government of the people, by the people, for the people, shall not perish from the earth.

Responding to Reading

1. To Lincoln and his audience, what is the "great task remaining before us" (3)?
2. The first paragraph of this speech looks back, the second paragraph describes the present, and the third paragraph looks ahead. Using contemporary conversational style, write a one-sentence summary of each of these paragraphs.
3. In paragraph 3, Lincoln says, "The world will little note, nor long remember what we say here, but it can never forget what they [the brave soldiers] did here." In what sense, if any, does this statement apply to the other four readings in this Focus section?

Responding in Writing

What "great tasks" do you believe still face our nation's leaders? Which of these do you think will still be a challenge in fifty years? Why?

CHAPTER 6 FOCUS

INAUGURAL ADDRESS

John F. Kennedy

1917–1963

Born in Brookline, Massachusetts, John Fitzgerald Kennedy received a bachelor's degree from Harvard University and served in the navy as a PT boat commander in the South Pacific. A highly charismatic politician, he was elected to the United States House of Representatives in 1947 and to the Senate in 1953. In 1960, defeating Republican candidate (and later president) Richard Nixon, Kennedy became the youngest man and the first Catholic to be elected president. During his tenure, he supported policies promoting racial equality, aid to the poor and to education, and increased availability of medical care; he also conceived of the idea of the Peace Corps. However, Kennedy was also responsible for involving the country further in the doomed Vietnam conflict. He was assassinated in November of 1963, a year before the end of his first term.

Vice President Johnson, Mr. Speaker, Mr. Chief Justice, President Eisenhower, Vice President Nixon, President Truman, Reverend Clergy, fellow citizens:

We observe today not a victory of party but a celebration of freedom—symbolizing an end as well as a beginning—signifying renewal as well as change. For I have sworn before you and Almighty God the same solemn oath our forebears prescribed nearly a century and three-quarters ago.

The world is very different now. For man holds in his mortal hands the power to abolish all forms of human poverty and all forms of human life. And yet the same revolutionary beliefs for which our forebears fought are still at issue around the globe—the belief that the rights of man come not from the generosity of the state but from the hand of God.

We dare not forget today that we are the heirs of that first revolution. Let the word go forth from this time and place, to friend and foe alike, that the torch has been passed to a new generation of Americans—born in this century, tempered by war, disciplined by a hard and bitter peace, proud of our ancient heritage—and unwilling to witness or permit the slow undoing of those human rights to which this nation has always been committed, and to which we are committed today at home and around the world.

5   Let every nation know, whether it wishes us well or ill, that we shall pay any price, bear any burden, meet any hardship, support any friend, oppose any foe to assure the survival and the success of liberty.

This much we pledge—and more.

To those old allies whose cultural and spiritual origins we share, we pledge the loyalty of faithful friends. United there is little we cannot do in a host of cooperative ventures. Divided there is little we can do—for we dare not meet a powerful challenge at odds and split asunder.

To those new states whom we welcome to the ranks of the free, we pledge our word that one form of colonial control shall not have passed away merely to be replaced by a far more iron tyranny. We shall not always expect to find them supporting our view. But we shall always hope to find them strongly supporting their own freedom—and to remember that, in the past, those who foolishly sought power by riding the back of the tiger ended up inside. To those people in the huts and villages of half the globe struggling to break the bonds of mass misery, we pledge our best efforts to help them help themselves, for whatever period is required—not because the communists may be doing it, not because we seek their votes, but because it is right. If a free society cannot help the many who are poor, it cannot save the few who are rich.

To our sister republics south of our border, we offer a special pledge—to convert our good words into good deeds—in a new alliance for progress—to assist free men and free governments in casting off the chains of poverty. But this peaceful revolution of hope cannot become the prey of hostile powers. Let all our neighbors know that we shall join with them to oppose aggression or subversion anywhere in the Americas. And let every other power know that this Hemisphere intends to remain the master of its own house.

To that world assembly of sovereign states, the United Nations, 10 our last best hope in an age where the instruments of war have far outpaced the instruments of peace, we renew our pledge of support—to prevent it from becoming merely a forum for invective—to strengthen its shield of the new and the weak—and to enlarge the area in which its writ may run.

Finally, to those nations who would make themselves our adversary, we offer not a pledge but a request: that both sides begin anew the quest for peace, before the dark powers of destruction unleashed by science engulf all humanity in planned or accidental self-destruction.

We dare not tempt them with weakness. For only when our arms are sufficient beyond doubt can we be certain beyond doubt that they will never be employed.

But neither can two great and powerful groups of nations take comfort from our present course—both sides overburdened by the cost of modern weapons, both rightly alarmed by the steady spread of the deadly atom, yet both racing to alter that uncertain balance of terror that stays the hand of mankind's final war.

So let us begin anew—remembering on both sides that civility is not a sign of weakness, and sincerity is always subject to proof. Let us never negotiate out of fear. But let us never fear to negotiate.

Let both sides explore what problems unite us instead of belabor- 15 ing those problems which divide us.

Let both sides, for the first time, formulate serious and precise proposals for the inspection and control of arms and bring the absolute power to destroy other nations under the absolute control of all nations.

Let both sides seek to invoke the wonders of science instead of its terrors. Together let us explore the stars, conquer the deserts, eradicate disease, tap the ocean depths and encourage the arts and commerce.

Let both sides unite to heed in all corners of the earth the command of Isaiah—to "undo the heavy burdens...(and) let the oppressed go free."

And if a beachhead of cooperation may push back the jungle of suspicion, let both sides join in creating a new endeavor, not a new balance of power, but a new world of law, where the strong are just and the weak secure and the peace preserved.

20   All this will not be finished in the first one hundred days. Nor will it be finished in the first one thousand days, nor in the life of this Administration, nor even perhaps in our lifetime on this planet. But let us begin.

In your hands, my fellow citizens, more than mine, will rest the final success or failure of our course. Since this country was founded, each generation of Americans has been summoned to give testimony to its national loyalty. The graves of young Americans who answered the call to service surround the globe.

Now the trumpet summons us—again not as a call to bear arms, though arms we need—not as a call to battle, though embattled we are—but a call to bear the burden of a long twilight struggle, year in and year out, "rejoicing in hope, patient in tribulation"—a struggle against the common enemies of man: tyranny, poverty, disease and war itself. Can we forge against these enemies a grand and global alliance, North and South, East and West, that can assure a more fruitful life for all mankind? Will you join in that historic effort?

In the long history of the world, only a few generations have been granted the role of defending freedom in its hour of maximum danger. I do not shrink from this responsibility—I welcome it. I do not believe that any of us would exchange places with any other people or any other generation. The energy, the faith, the devotion which we bring to this endeavor will light our country and all who serve it—and the glow from that fire can truly light the world. And so, my fellow Americans: ask not what your country can do for you—ask what you can do for your country. My fellow citizens of the world: ask not what America will do for you, but what together we can do for the freedom of man.

Finally, whether you are citizens of America or citizens of the world, ask of us here the same high standards of strength and sacrifice which we ask of you. With a good conscience our only sure reward, with history the final judge of our deeds, let us go forth to lead the land we love, asking His blessing and His help, but knowing that here on earth God's work must truly be our own.

Responding to Reading

1. At the beginning of his speech, Kennedy alludes to the "revolutionary beliefs" of Jefferson (p. 375) and asserts, "We are the heirs of that first revolution" (3–4). What does he mean? Do you think his speech offers adequate support for this statement?
2. What, according to Kennedy, must we still achieve in order to fulfill Jefferson's dreams? What other problems do you believe must still be solved before we can consider the American Dream a reality?
3. Near the end of his speech, Kennedy says, "And so, my fellow Americans: ask not what your country can do for you—ask what you can do for your country" (23). What does this famous, often-quoted passage actually mean in practical terms? Do you think this exhortation is realistic? Do you think it is fair? Explain.

Responding in Writing

Exactly what do you expect America to do for you, and what do you expect to do for your country?

I HAVE A DREAM
Martin Luther King, Jr.
1929–1968

One of the greatest civil rights leaders and orators of this century, Baptist minister Martin Luther King, Jr., earned a B.A. degree from Morehouse College (1948), a B.D. degree from Crozer Theological Seminary in Pennsylvania (1951), and a Ph.D. from Boston University (1955). Influenced by Thoreau and Gandhi, King altered the spirit of African American protest in the United States by advocating nonviolent civil disobedience to achieve racial equality. King was arrested more than twenty times and assaulted at least four times for his activities, but he also was awarded five honorary degrees, was named Man of the Year by Time *magazine in 1963, and the following year was awarded the Nobel Peace Prize. King was assassinated on April 4, 1968, in Memphis, Tennessee. He delivered the following speech from the steps of the Lincoln Memorial on August 28, 1963, during the March on Washington in support of civil rights.*

I am happy to join with you today in what will go down in history as the greatest demonstration for freedom in the history of our nation.

Fivescore years ago, a great American, in whose symbolic shadow we stand today, signed the Emancipation Proclamation. This momentous decree came as a great beacon light of hope to millions of Negro slaves who had been seared in the flames of withering injustice. It came as a joyous daybreak to end the long night of their captivity.

But one hundred years later, the Negro still is not free; one hundred years later, the life of the Negro is still sadly crippled by the manacles of segregation and the chains of discrimination; one hundred years later, the Negro lives on a lonely island of poverty in the midst of a vast ocean of material prosperity; one hundred years later, the Negro is still languishing in the corners of American society and finds himself in exile in his own land.

So we've come here today to dramatize a shameful condition. In a sense we've come to our nation's capital to cash a check. When the architects of our republic wrote the magnificent words of the Constitution and the Declaration of Independence, they were signing a promissory note to which every American was to fall heir. This note was the promise that all men, yes, black men as well as white men, would be guaranteed the unalienable rights of life, liberty, and the pursuit of happiness.

5   It is obvious today that America has defaulted on this promissory note in so far as her citizens of color are concerned. Instead of honoring this sacred obligation, America has given the Negro people a bad check; a check which has come back marked "insufficient funds." We refuse to believe that there are insufficient funds in the great vaults of opportunity of this nation. And so we've come to cash this check, a check that will give us upon demand the riches of freedom and the security of justice.

We have also come to this hallowed spot to remind America of the fierce urgency of now. This is no time to engage in the luxury of cooling off or to take the tranquilizing drug of gradualism. Now is the time to make real the promises of democracy; now is the time to rise from the dark and desolate valley of segregation to the sunlit path of racial justice; now is the time to lift our nation from the quicksands of racial injustice to the solid rock of brotherhood; now is the time to make justice a reality for all God's children. It would be fatal for the nation to overlook the urgency of the moment. This sweltering summer of the Negro's legitimate discontent will not pass until there is an invigorating autumn of freedom and equality.

Nineteen sixty-three is not an end, but a beginning. And those who hope that the Negro needed to blow off steam and will now be content, will have a rude awakening if the nation returns to business as usual.

There will be neither rest nor tranquility in America until the Negro is granted his citizenship rights. The whirlwinds of revolt will continue to shake the foundations of our nation until the bright day of justice emerges.

But there is something that I must say to my people who stand on the warm threshold which leads into the palace of justice. In the process of gaining our rightful place we must not be guilty of wrongful deeds.

Let us not seek to satisfy our thirst for freedom by drinking from the cup of bitterness and hatred. We must forever conduct our struggle on the high plane of dignity and discipline. We must not allow our creative protest to degenerate into physical violence. Again and again we must rise to the majestic heights of meeting physical force with soul force.

The marvelous new militancy which has engulfed the Negro community must not lead us to a distrust of all white people, for many of our white brothers, as evidenced by their presence here today, have come to realize that their destiny is tied up with our destiny and they have come to realize that their freedom is inextricably bound to our freedom. This offense we share mounted to storm the battlements of injustice must be carried forth by a biracial army. We cannot walk alone.

And as we walk, we must make the pledge that we shall always march ahead. We cannot turn back. There are those who are asking the devotees of civil rights, "When will you be satisfied?" We can never be satisfied as long as the Negro is the victim of the unspeakable horrors of police brutality.

We can never be satisfied as long as our bodies, heavy with fatigue of travel, cannot gain lodging in the motels of the highways and the hotels of the cities. We cannot be satisfied as long as the Negro's basic mobility is from a smaller ghetto to a larger one.

We can never be satisfied as long as our children are stripped of their selfhood and robbed of their dignity by signs stating "for whites only." We cannot be satisfied as long as a Negro in Mississippi cannot vote and a Negro in New York believes he has nothing for which to vote. No, we are not satisfied, and we will not be satisfied until justice rolls down like waters and righteousness like a mighty stream.

I am not unmindful that some of you have come here out of excessive trials and tribulation. Some of you have come fresh from narrow jail cells. Some of you have come from areas where your quest for freedom left you battered by the storms of persecution and staggered by the winds of police brutality. You have been the veterans of creative suffering. Continue to work with the faith that unearned suffering is redemptive.

Go back to Mississippi; go back to Alabama; go back to South Carolina; go back to Georgia; go back to Louisiana; go back to the slums and ghettos of the northern cities, knowing that somehow this situation can, and will be changed. Let us not wallow in the valley of despair.

So I say to you, my friends, that even though we must face the difficulties of today and tomorrow, I still have a dream. It is a dream deeply rooted in the American dream that one day this nation will rise up and live out the true meaning of its creed—we hold these truths to be self-evident, that all men are created equal.

I have a dream that one day on the red hills of Georgia, sons of former slaves and sons of former slave-owners will be able to sit down together at the table of brotherhood.

CHAPTER 6 FOCUS

I have a dream that one day, even the state of Mississippi, a state sweltering with the heat of injustice, sweltering with the heat of oppression, will be transformed into an oasis of freedom and justice.

20   I have a dream my four little children will one day live in a nation where they will not be judged by the color of their skin but by the content of their character. I have a dream today!

I have a dream that one day, down in Alabama, with its vicious racists, with its governor having his lips dripping with the words of interposition and nullification, that one day, right there in Alabama, little black boys and black girls will be able to join hands with little white boys and white girls as sisters and brothers. I have a dream today!

I have a dream that one day every valley shall be exalted, every hill and mountain shall be made low, the rough places shall be made plain, and the crooked places shall be made straight and the glory of the Lord will be revealed and all flesh shall see it together.

This is our hope. This is the faith that I go back to the South with.

With this faith we will be able to hew out of the mountain of despair a stone of hope. With this faith we will be able to transform the jangling discords of our nation into a beautiful symphony of brotherhood.

25   With this faith we will be able to work together, to pray together, to struggle together, to go to jail together, to stand up for freedom together, knowing that we will be free one day. This will be the day when all of God's children will be able to sing with new meaning— "my country 'tis of thee; sweet land of liberty; of thee I sing; land where my fathers died, land of the pilgrim's pride; from every mountain side, let freedom ring"—and if America is to be a great nation, this must become true.

So let freedom ring from the prodigious hilltops of New Hampshire.
Let freedom ring from the mighty mountains of New York.
Let freedom ring from the heightening Alleghenies of Pennsylvania.
Let freedom ring from the snow-capped Rockies of Colorado.
30   Let freedom ring from the curvaceous slopes of California.
But not only that.
Let freedom ring from Stone Mountain of Georgia.
Let freedom ring from Lookout Mountain of Tennessee.
Let freedom ring from every hill and molehill of Mississippi, from every mountainside, let freedom ring.

35   And when we allow freedom to ring, when we let it ring from every village and hamlet, from every state and city, we will be able to speed up that day when all of God's children—black men and white men, Jews and Gentiles, Catholics and Protestants—will be able to join hands and to sing in the words of the old Negro spiritual, "Free at last, free at last; thank God Almighty, we are free at last."

Responding to Reading

1. What exactly is King's dream? Do you believe it has come true? If he were alive today, do you think he would believe his dream had been realized?
2. Speaking as a representative of his fellow African-American citizens, King tells his audience that African Americans find themselves "in exile in [their] own land" (3). Do you believe this is still true of African Americans? Of members of other minority groups? Which groups? Why?
3. Jefferson (p. 375) wrote in the eighteenth century; King, in the twentieth. Jefferson wrote as an insider, a man of privilege; King, as an outsider. What do their dreams have in common? How did each man intend to achieve his dream?

Responding in Writing

What dreams do you have for yourself and for your family? What dreams do you have for your country? Do you expect these dreams to be realized?

DECLARATION OF SENTIMENTS
AND RESOLUTIONS
Elizabeth Cady Stanton
1815–1902

A pivotal figure in the women's rights movement, Elizabeth Cady Stanton campaigned for equal rights and women's suffrage in the United States. In 1848, she and Lucretia Mott, an influential social reformer, organized and held the Seneca Falls Convention "to discuss the social, civil, and religious rights of women." At the convention, Stanton delivered her Declaration of Sentiments, which, based on the Declaration of Independence, enumerates the social inequalities between women and men in the nineteenth century. Stanton also presented twelve resolutions, including women's right to vote, all of which were passed at the convention. Stanton's relentless advocacy of women's rights helped to usher in a new era in U.S. history in which women began to experience civil liberties previously available only to men.

When, in the course of human events, it becomes necessary for one portion of the family of man to assume among the people of the earth a position different from that which they have hitherto occupied, but one to which the laws of nature and of nature's God entitle them, a decent respect to the opinions of mankind requires that they should declare the causes that impel them to such a course.

We hold these truths to be self-evident: that all men and women are created equal; that they are endowed by their Creator with certain inalienable rights; that among these are life, liberty, and the pursuit of happiness; that to secure these rights governments are instituted,

CHAPTER 6   FOCUS

deriving their just powers from the consent of the governed. Whenever any form of government becomes destructive of these ends, it is the right of those who suffer from it to refuse allegiance to it, and to insist upon the institution of a new government, laying its foundation on such principles, and organizing its powers in such form, as to them shall seem most likely to effect their safety and happiness.

Prudence, indeed, will dictate that governments long established should not be changed for light and transient causes; and, accordingly, all experience has shown that mankind are more disposed to suffer, while evils are sufferable, than to right themselves by abolishing the forms to which they were accustomed. But when a long train of abuses and usurpations, pursuing invariably the same object, evinces a design to reduce them under absolute despotism, it is their duty to throw off such government and to provide new guards for their future security. Such has been the patient sufferance of the women under this government, and such is now the necessity which constrains them to demand the equal station to which they are entitled.

The history of mankind is a history of repeated injuries and usurpations on the part of man toward woman, having in direct object the establishment of an absolute tyranny over her. To prove this, let facts be submitted to a candid world.

5   He has never permitted her to exercise her inalienable right to the elective franchise.

He has compelled her to submit to law in the formation of which she had no voice.

He has withheld from her rights which are given to the most ignorant and degraded men, both natives and foreigners.

Having deprived her of this first right as a citizen, the elective franchise, thereby leaving her without representation in the halls of legislation, he has oppressed her on all sides.

He has made her, if married, in the eye of the law, civilly dead.

10   He has taken from her all right in property, even to the wages she earns.

He has made her morally, an irresponsible being, as she can commit many crimes with impunity, provided they be done in the presence of her husband. In the covenant of marriage, she is compelled to promise obedience to her husband, he becoming, to all intents and purposes, her master—the law giving him power to deprive her of her liberty and to administer chastisement.

He has so framed the laws of divorce, as to what shall be the proper causes and, in case of separation, to whom the guardianship of the children shall be given, as to be wholly regardless of the happiness of the women—the law, in all cases, going upon a false supposition of the supremacy of man and giving all power into his hands.

After depriving her of all rights as a married woman, if single and the owner of property, he has taxed her to support a government which recognizes her only when her property can be made profitable to it.

He has monopolized nearly all the profitable employments, and from those she is permitted to follow, she receives but a scanty remuneration. He closes against her all the avenues to wealth and distinction which he considers most honorable to himself. As a teacher of theology, medicine, or law, she is not known.

He has denied her the facilities for obtaining a thorough education, 15 all colleges being closed against her.

He allows her in church, as well as state, but a subordinate position, claiming apostolic authority for her exclusion from the ministry, and, with some exceptions, from any public participation in the affairs of the church.

He has created a false public sentiment by giving to the world a different code of morals for men and women, by which moral delinquencies which exclude women from society are not only tolerated but deemed of little account in man.

He has usurped the prerogative of Jehovah himself, claiming it as his right to assign for her a sphere of action, when that belongs to her conscience and to her God.

He has endeavored, in every way that he could, to destroy her confidence in her own powers, to lessen her self-respect, and to make her willing to lead a dependent and abject life.

Now, in view of this entire disfranchisement of one-half the peo- 20 ple of this country, their social and religious degradation, in view of the unjust laws above mentioned, and because women do feel themselves aggrieved, oppressed, and fraudulently deprived of their most sacred rights, we insist that they have immediate admission to all the rights and privileges which belong to them as citizens of the United States.

In entering upon the great work before us, we anticipate no small amount of misconception, misrepresentation, and ridicule; but we shall use every instrumentality within our power to effect our object. We shall employ agents, circulate tracts, petition the state and national legislatures, and endeavor to enlist the pulpit and the press in our behalf. We hope this Convention will be followed by a series of conventions embracing every part of the country.

Resolutions

Whereas, the great precept of nature is conceded to be that "man shall pursue his own true and substantial happiness." Blackstone[1] in his Commentaries remarks that this law of nature, being coeval with mankind and dictated by God himself, is, of course, superior in obligation to any other. It is binding over all the globe, in all countries and at all times; no human laws are of any validity if contrary to this, and such of them as are valid derive all their force, and all their validity, and all their authority, mediately and immediately, from this original; therefore,

---

[1]Sir William Blackstone (1723–1780), English jurist whose *Commentaries on the Laws of England* informed early American law. [Eds.]

Resolved, That such laws as conflict, in any way, with the true and substantial happiness of woman, are contrary to the great precept of nature and of no validity, for this is "superior in obligation to any other."

Resolved, that all laws which prevent woman from occupying such a station in society as her conscience shall dictate, or which place her in a position inferior to that of man, are contrary to the great precept of nature and therefore of no force or authority.

25   Resolved, that woman is man's equal, was intended to be so by the Creator, and the highest good of the race demands that she should be recognized as such.

Resolved, that the women of this country ought to be enlightened in regard to the laws under which they live, that they may no longer publish their degradation by declaring themselves satisfied with their present position, nor their ignorance, by asserting that they have all the rights they want.

Resolved, that inasmuch as man, while claiming for himself intellectual superiority, does accord to woman moral superiority, it is pre-eminently his duty to encourage her to speak and teach, as she has an opportunity, in all religious assemblies.

Resolved, that the same amount of virtue, delicacy, and refinement of behavior that is required of woman in the social state also be required of man, and the same transgressions should be visited with equal severity on both man and woman.

Resolved, that the objection of indelicacy and impropriety, which is so often brought against woman when she addresses a public audience, comes with a very ill grace from those who encourage, by their attendance, her appearance on the stage, in the concert, or in feats of the circus.

30   Resolved, that woman has too long rested satisfied in the circumscribed limits which corrupt customs and a perverted application of the Scriptures have marked out for her, and that it is time she should move in the enlarged sphere which her great Creator has assigned her.

Resolved, that it is the duty of the women of this country to secure to themselves their sacred right to the elective franchise.

Resolved, that the equality of human rights results necessarily from the fact of the identity of the race in capabilities and responsibilities.

Resolved, that the speedy success of our cause depends upon the zealous and untiring efforts of both men and women for the overthrow of the monopoly of the pulpit, and for the securing to woman an equal participation with men in the various trades, professions, and commerce.

Resolved, therefore, that, being invested by the Creator with the same capabilities and same consciousness of responsibility for their exercise, it is demonstrably the right and duty of woman, equally with man, to promote every righteous cause by every righteous means; and especially in regard to the great subjects of morals and religion, it is self-evidently her right to participate with her brother in teaching them,

both in private and in public, by writing and by speaking, by any instru-
mentalities proper to be used, and in any assemblies proper to be held;
and this being a self-evident truth growing out of the divinely implanted
principles of human nature, any custom or authority adverse to it,
whether modern or wearing the hoary sanction of antiquity, is to be
regarded as a self-evident falsehood, and at war with mankind.

Responding to Reading

1. In developing the Declaration of Sentiments, Stanton reframed the Declaration of Independence (p. 375) to apply specifically to women's rights. Compare the language and organization of these two historical documents. Where
   does Stanton follow the model established by the Declaration of Independence, and where does she break from it? Can you explain these decisions?
2. Stanton uses the metaphor of "an absolute tyranny" to describe men's social
   superiority over women (4). Do you think this metaphor accurately describes
   women's status during Stanton's time? Why or why not?
3. What is Stanton's vision of the American Dream? If Stanton were alive today,
   do you think she would believe her vision had been realized? Do you believe
   it has been realized? Explain.

Responding in Writing

List three or four social injustices that you believe women continue to face in the
United States today, using paragraphs 5–19 of the Declaration of Sentiments as a
model. Then, propose a "resolution" for each of the injustices you list.

WIDENING THE FOCUS

For Critical Thinking and Writing

Read the selections by Jefferson, Lincoln, Kennedy, King, and Stanton in this chapter's Focus section. Then, try to answer the question, "What is the American Dream?"

For Further Reading

The following readings can suggest additional perspectives for thinking and writing about the American Dream:

- Gary Shteyngart, "Sixty-Nine Cents" (p. 47)
- Bich Minh Nguyen, "The Good Immigrant Student" (p. 79)
- Jonathan Kozol, "The Human Cost of an Illiterate Society" (p. 164)
- Martin Luther King, Jr., "Letter from Birmingham Jail" (p. 608)

For Focused Research

The American Dream was first defined more than two centuries ago, and over the years it has changed along with our society. How would you define today's American Dream? For example, does it include access for all to education, employment, healthcare, and home ownership? Visit some Web sites that offer their visions of the American Dream, such as the following:

- Bill Moyers Journal: Deepening the American Dream, http://www .pbs.org/moyers/journal/americandream/text.html
- The American Dream Group, http://www.achieve-the-dream.net/
- America's Promise Alliance, http://www.americaspromise.org/
- The "I Have a Dream" Foundation, http://www.ihad.org/

Or, use a search engine to find discussion of the American Dream in online political magazines listed on the Yahoo! Directory, http://dir.yahoo.com/News_and_Media/Magazines/.

Then, write an essay in which you define what you think the American Dream should be for the twenty-first century.

WRITING

The American Dream

1. In an excerpt from his book *The Audacity of Hope,* President Barack Obama writes, "I believe that part of America's genius has always been its ability to absorb newcomers, to forge a national identity out of the disparate lot that arrived on our shores." Write an essay in which you support the idea that the strength of the United States comes from its ability to assimilate many different groups. In your essay, discuss specific contributions your own ethnic group and others have made to American society.

2. Both "The Library Card" (p. 330) and "Becoming American" (p. 339) deal with the uniquely American concept of reinventing oneself, taking on a new identity. Some Americans reinvent themselves through education; others do so simply by changing their appearance. Write an essay in which you outline the options available to newcomers to the United States who wish to achieve this kind of transformation. Whenever possible, give examples from the readings in this chapter.

3. Interview a first-generation American, a second-generation American, and a third-generation American. How are their views of the American Dream different? How are they like and unlike the dreams of various writers represented in this chapter?

4. In "Becoming American" (p. 339), Dinesh D'Souza says, "In America your destiny is not prescribed; it is constructed. Your life is like a blank sheet of paper, and you are the artist" (22). Similarly, Gish Jen identifies the ability to make choices—what she calls the "luxury of choosing"—as a distinctly American advantage (2). Do you think the United States is really a place in which, as D'Souza says, "you get to write the script of your own life" (21)? Support your position on this issue with references to readings in this book.

5. Using the readings in this chapter as source material, write a manifesto that sets forth the rights and responsibilities of all Americans. (Begin by reading Kennedy's inaugural address, p. 380.)

6. Some of the writers in this chapter—for example, Judith Ortiz Cofer—feel pulled in two directions, torn between their own culture and the "American" society in which they live. Do you believe this conflict can ever be resolved, or do you think first-generation (and even second-generation) Americans will always feel torn?

7. Discouraged by the racism he experienced in the United States, Richard Wright (p. 330) left his country in 1947 and lived the rest of his life as an expatriate in Paris. Under what circumstances could you imagine leaving the United States and becoming a citizen of another country?

7

WHY WE WORK

Although work has always been a part of the human experience, the nature of work has evolved considerably—especially over the last two hundred years. During the Middle Ages and the Renaissance, work was often done by family units. Whether it involved planting and harvesting crops, tending livestock, or engaging in the manufacture of goods, parents, grandparents, and children (and possibly an apprentice or two) worked together, at home. With the Industrial Revolution, however, the nature of work changed. Manufacturing became centralized in factories, and tasks that were formerly divided among various members of a family were now carried out more efficiently by machines. People worked long hours—in many cases twelve to fifteen hours a day, six and sometimes seven days a week—and could be fired for any reason. By the middle of the nineteenth century, most of the great manufacturing cities of Europe were overcrowded and polluted, teeming with unskilled factory

Auto workers making car radiators on assembly line, circa 1915

workers. It is no wonder that labor unions became increasingly popular as they organized workers to fight for job security, shorter workdays, and minimum safety standards

Thanks to the labor struggles of the past, many workers today have pension plans, health insurance, sick leave, paid vacations, life insurance, and other benefits. In spite of these advances, however, there is a dark side to this situation. American workers—like all workers—are subject to unpredictable changes in both the national and the global economies. As a result, during good times workers experience low unemployment and receive high wages, and during economic downturns— such as the one that began in 2008—workers experience higher unemployment and receive lower wages. Add to this situation the tendency of American companies to move manufacturing and high-tech jobs overseas and to see employees as entities whose jobs can be phased out as the need arises, and it is no surprise that workers are often stressed, insecure, and unhappy. The result is that many of today's workers question the role that work plays in their lives and wonder if it is in their best interest to invest so much time and energy in their jobs.

The essays in the Focus section of this chapter (p. 444) address the question, "Is Outsourcing Bad for America?" These essays examine outsourcing and the effect it has on the U.S. economy. For example, businesses that engage in this practice say that by shifting jobs to countries that have lower wages, they are able to remain competitive in a global business environment. In addition, they say that outsourcing not only benefits American consumers, but it also benefits countries

Welding robots on a Volkswagen assembly line in Germany, 2004

in the developing world by giving them desperately needed capital. The essays in this section ask important questions. Is the United States becoming a nation of outsourcers, shifting the responsibility for everything from education to healthcare to others? Does outsourcing really represent a danger to the American economy, or is its effect being exaggerated? How should we as a society respond to the plight of workers whose jobs are lost to outsourcing? Finally, what moral responsibility do both U.S. companies and the U.S. government have to the poor in nations of the world who could benefit from outsourcing?

——————— PREPARING TO READ AND WRITE ———————

As you read and prepare to write about the essays in this chapter, you may consider the following questions:

- What do you know about the writer? In what way does the writer's economic and social position affect his or her definition of work?

- Is the writer male or female? Does the writer's gender affect his or her attitude toward work?

- When was the essay written? Does the date of publication affect its content?

- Does the essay seem fair? Balanced? Does the writer have any preconceived ideas about work and its importance?

- Is the writer generally sympathetic or unsympathetic toward workers?

- Does the writer have a realistic or unrealistic view of work?

- On what specific problems does the writer focus?

- What specific solutions does the writer suggest? Are these solutions practical?

- Is your interpretation of the problem the same as or different from the interpretation presented in the essay?

- Are there any aspects of the problem that the writer ignores?

- Does the essay challenge any of your ideas about work?

- In what ways is the essay like other essays in this chapter?

WHY WE WORK
Andrew Curry
1976–

Andrew Curry writes and reports for U.S. News and World Report. *"Why We Work" was the cover story of the February 24, 2003, issue. In this essay, Curry examines the nature of work and explains why many workers today feel unfulfilled.*

In 1930, W. K. Kellogg made what he thought was a sensible decision, grounded in the best economic, social, and management theories of the time. Workers at his cereal plant in Battle Creek, Mich., were told to go home two hours early. Every day. For good.

The Depression-era move was hailed in Factory and Industrial Management magazine as the "biggest piece of industrial news since [Henry] Ford announced his five-dollar-a-day policy." President Herbert Hoover summoned the eccentric cereal magnate to the White House and said the plan was "very worthwhile." The belief: Industry and machines would lead to a workers' paradise where all would have less work, more free time, and yet still produce enough to meet their needs.

So what happened? Today, work dominates Americans' lives as never before, as workers pile on hours at a rate not seen since the Industrial Revolution. Technology has offered increasing productivity and a higher standard of living while bank tellers and typists are replaced by machines. The mismatch between available work and those available to do it continues, as jobs go begging while people beg for jobs. Though Kellogg's six-hour day lasted until 1985, Battle Creek's grand industrial experiment has been nearly forgotten. Instead of working less, our hours have stayed steady or risen—and today many more women work so that families can afford the trappings of suburbia. In effect, workers chose the path of consumption over leisure.

But as today's job market shows so starkly, that road is full of potholes. With unemployment at a nine-year high and many workers worried about losing their jobs—or forced to accept cutbacks in pay and benefits—work is hardly the paradise economists once envisioned.

Instead, the job market is as precarious today as it was in the early 1980s, when business began a wave of restructurings and layoffs to maintain its competitiveness. Many workers are left feeling insecure, unfulfilled, and underappreciated. It's no wonder surveys of today's workers show a steady decline in job satisfaction. "People are very emotional about work, and they're very negative about it," says David Rhodes, a principal at human resource consultants Towers Perrin. "The biggest issue is clearly workload. People are feeling crushed."

The backlash comes after years of people boasting about how hard they work and tying their identities to how indispensable they are. Ringing cellphones, whirring faxes, and ever present E-mail have blurred the lines between work and home. The job penetrates every aspect of life. Americans don't exercise, they work out. We manage our time and work on our relationships. "In reaching the affluent society, we're working longer and harder than anyone could have imagined," says Rutgers University historian John Gillis. "The work ethic and identifying ourselves with work and through work is not only alive and well but more present now than at any time in history."

Stressed Out

It's all beginning to take a toll. Fully one third of American workers— who work longer hours than their counterparts in any industrialized country—felt overwhelmed by the amount of work they had to do, according to a 2001 Families and Work Institute survey. "Both men and women wish they were working about 11 hours [a week] less," says Ellen Galinsky, the institute's president. "A lot of people believe if they do work less they'll be seen as less committed, and in a shaky economy no one wants that."

The modern environment would seem alien to pre-industrial laborers. For centuries, the household—from farms to "cottage" craftsmen— was the unit of production. The whole family was part of the enterprise, be it farming, blacksmithing, or baking. "In pre-industrial society, work and family were practically the same thing," says Gillis.

The Industrial Revolution changed all that. Mills and massive iron smelters required ample labor and constant attendance. "The factory took men, women and children out of the workshops and homes and put them under one roof and timed their movements to machines," writes Sebastian de Grazia in *Of Time, Work and Leisure.* For the first time, work and family were split. Instead of selling what they produced, workers sold their time. With more people leaving farms to move to cities and factories, labor became a commodity, placed on the market like any other.

10   Innovation gave rise to an industrial process based on machinery and mass production. This new age called for a new worker. "The only safeguard of order and discipline in the modern world is a standardized worker with interchangeable parts," mused one turn-of-the-century writer.

Business couldn't have that, so instead it came up with the science of management. The theories of Frederick Taylor, a Philadelphia factory foreman with deep Puritan roots, led to work being broken down into component parts, with each step timed to coldly quantify jobs that skilled craftsmen had worked a lifetime to learn. Workers resented Taylor and his stopwatch, complaining that his focus on process stripped their jobs of creativity and pride, making them irritable. Long before anyone knew what "stress" was, Taylor brought it to the workplace—and without sympathy. "I have you for your strength and mechanical ability, and we have other men paid for thinking," he told workers.

Long Hours

The division of work into components that could be measured and easily taught reached its apex in Ford's River Rouge plant in Dearborn, Mich., where the assembly line came of age. "It was this combination of a simplification of tasks...with moving assembly that created a manufacturing revolution while at the same time laying waste human potential on a massive scale," author Richard Donkin writes in *Blood, Sweat and Tears*.

To maximize the production lines, businesses needed long hours from their workers. But it was no easy sell. "Convincing people to work 9 to 5 took a tremendous amount of propaganda and discipline," says the University of Richmond's Joanne Ciulla, author of *The Working Life: The Promise and Betrayal of Modern Work*. Entrepreneurs, religious leaders, and writers like Horatio Alger created whole bodies of literature to glorify the work ethic.

Labor leaders fought back with their own propaganda. For more than a century, a key struggle for the labor movement was reducing the amount of time workers had to spend on the job. "They were pursuing shorter hours and increased leisure. In effect, they were buying their time," says University of Iowa Prof. Benjamin Hunnicutt, author of *Work Without End: Abandoning Shorter Hours for the Right to Work.*

The first labor unions were organized in response to the threat of 15 technology, as skilled workers sought to protect their jobs from mechanization. Later, semi- and unskilled workers began to organize as well, agitating successfully for reduced hours, higher wages, and better work conditions. Unions enjoyed great influence in the early 20th century, and at their height in the 1950s, 35 percent of U.S. workers belonged to one.

Union persistence and the mechanization of factories gradually made shorter hours more realistic. Between 1830 and 1930, work hours were cut nearly in half, with economist John Maynard Keynes famously predicting in 1930 that by 2030 a 15-hour workweek would be standard. The Great Depression pressed the issue, with job sharing proposed as a serious solution to widespread unemployment. Despite business and religious opposition over worries of an idle populace, the Senate passed a bill that would have mandated a 30-hour week in 1933; it was narrowly defeated in the House.

Franklin Delano Roosevelt struck back with a new gospel that lives to this very day: consumption. "The aim...is to restore our rich domestic market by raising its vast consuming capacity," he said. "Our first purpose is to create employment as fast as we can." And so began the modern work world. "Instead of accepting work's continuing decline and imminent fall from its dominant social position, businessmen, economists, advertisers, and politicians preached that there would never be 'enough,'" Hunnicutt writes in *Kellogg's Six-Hour Day*. "The entrepreneur and industry could invent new things for advertising to sell and for people to want and work for indefinitely."

The New Deal dumped government money into job creation, in turn encouraging consumption. World War II fueled the fire, and American workers soon found themselves in a "golden age"—40-hour workweeks, plenty of jobs, and plenty to buy. Leisure was the road not taken, a path quickly forgotten in the postwar boom of the 1950s and 1960s.

Discontent

Decades of abundance, however, did not bring satisfaction. "A significant number of Americans are dissatisfied with the quality of their working lives," said the 1973 report "Work in America" from the Department of Health, Education and Welfare. "Dull, repetitive, seemingly meaningless tasks, offering little challenge or autonomy, are causing discontent among workers at all occupational levels." Underlying the dissatisfaction was a very gradual change in what the "Protestant work ethic" meant. Always a source of pride, the idea that hard work was a calling from God dated to the Reformation and the teachings of Martin Luther. While work had once been a means to serve God, two centuries of choices and industrialization had turned work into an end in itself, stripped of the spiritual meaning that sustained the Puritans who came ready to tame the wilderness.

20   By the end of the '70s, companies were reaching out to spiritually drained workers by offering more engagement while withdrawing the promise of a job for life, as the American economy faced a stiff challenge from cheaper workers abroad. "Corporations introduced feel-good programs to stimulate jaded employees with one hand while taking away the elements of a 'just' workplace with the other," says Andrew Ross, author of *No Collar: The Humane Workplace and Its Hidden Costs*. Employees were given more control over their work and schedules, and "human relations" consultants and motivational speakers did a booming business. By the 1990s, technology made working from home possible for a growing number of people. Seen as a boon at first, telecommuting and the rapidly proliferating "electronic leash" of cellphones made work inescapable, as employees found themselves on call 24/7. Today, almost half of American workers use computers, cellphones, E-mail, and faxes for work during what is supposed to be non-work time, according to the Families and Work Institute. Home is no longer a refuge but a cozier extension of the office.

The shift coincided with a shortage of highly skilled and educated workers, some of whom were induced with such benefits as stock options in exchange for their putting the company first all the time. But some see a different explanation for the rise in the amount of time devoted to work. "Hours have crept up partly as a consequence of the declining power of the trade-union movement," says Cornell University labor historian Clete Daniel. "Many employers find it more economical to require mandatory overtime than hire new workers and pay their benefits." Indeed, the trend has coincided with the steady decline in the percentage of workers represented by unions, as the labor movement failed to keep pace with the increasing rise of white-collar jobs in the economy. Today fewer than 15 percent of American workers belong to unions.

Nirvana?

The Internet economy of the '90s gave rise to an entirely new corporate climate. The "knowledge worker" was wooed with games, gourmet chefs, and unprecedented freedom over his schedule and environment. Employees at Intuit didn't have to leave their desks for massages; Sun Microsystems offered in-house laundry, and Netscape workers were offered an on-site dentist. At first glance, this new corporate world seemed like nirvana. But "for every attractive feature, workers found there was a cost," says Ross. "It was both a worker's paradise and a con game."

When the stock market bubble burst and the economy fell into its recent recession, workers were forced to re-evaluate their priorities. "There used to be fat bonuses and back rubs, free bagels and foosball tables—it didn't really feel like work," says Allison Hemming, who organizes "pink-slip parties" for laid-off workers around the country and has written *Work It! How to Get Ahead, Save Your Ass, and Land a Job in Any Economy.* "I think people are a lot wiser about their choices now. They want a better quality of life; they're asking for more flextime to spend with their families."

In a study of Silicon Valley culture over the past decade, San Jose State University anthropologist Jan English-Lueck found that skills learned on the job were often brought home. Researchers talked to families with mission statements, mothers used conflict-resolution buzzwords with their squabbling kids, and engineers used flowcharts to organize Thanksgiving dinner. Said one participant: "I don't live life; I manage it."

In some ways, we have come full circle. "Now we're seeing the return of work to the home in terms of telecommuting," says Gillis. "We may be seeing the return of households where work is the central element again."

But there's still the question of fulfillment. In a recent study, human resources consultants Towers Perrin tried to measure workers' emotions about their jobs. More than half of the emotion was negative, with the biggest single factor being workload but also a sense that work doesn't satisfy their deeper needs. "We expect more and more out of our jobs," says Hunnicutt. "We expect to find wonderful people and experiences all around us. What we find is Dilbert."

Responding to Reading

1. Why is it that "work dominates Americans' lives as never before" (3)? According to Curry, what toll does this situation take on American workers?
2. How did the Industrial Revolution change the nature of work? What effect did Fredrick Taylor have on work? According to Curry, why were the first labor unions formed? Why was the New Deal the "golden age" for workers (18)?
3. Why does Curry think that workers today are unfulfilled? What evidence does he offer to support this contention? What view of work do you think he has? Do you agree or disagree with his assessment?

Responding in Writing

Why do the people you know work? Do their motives support or challenge Curry's conclusion?

ONE LAST TIME

Gary Soto

1952–

Gary Soto grew up working along with his family as a migrant laborer in California's San Joaquin Valley. Soto often writes of the struggles of Mexican Americans, as he does in the following autobiographical essay, in which he describes his experiences picking grapes and cotton. This essay is taken from Living Up the Street: Narrative Recollections, *for which he won the American Book Award in 1985. The author of numerous poetry collections, Soto has also published short story collections, novels, and picture books for children. He is also involved with two organizations that work for justice for migrant workers: California Rural Legal Assistance (CRLA) and the United Farm Workers of America (UFWA).*

Yesterday I saw the movie *Gandhi*[1] and recognized a few of the people— not in the theater but in the film. I saw my relatives, dusty and thin as sparrows, returning from the fields with hoes balanced on their shoulders. The workers were squinting, eyes small and veined, and

---

[1]The 1982 film biography of the nonviolent revolutionary Mohandas Gandhi (known as Mahatma), which was set in part among the peasants of India. [Eds.]

were using their hands to say what there was to say to those in the audience with popcorn and Cokes. I didn't have anything, though. I sat thinking of my family and their years in the fields, beginning with Grandmother who came to the United States after the Mexican revolution to settle in Fresno where she met her husband and bore children, many of them. She worked in the fields around Fresno, picking grapes, oranges, plums, peaches, and cotton, dragging a large white sack like a sled. She worked in the packing houses, Bonner and Sun-Maid Raisin, where she stood at a conveyor belt passing her hand over streams of raisins to pluck out leaves and pebbles. For over twenty years she worked at a machine that boxed raisins until she retired at sixty-five.

Grandfather worked in the fields, as did his children. Mother also found herself out there when she separated from Father for three weeks. I remember her coming home, dusty and so tired that she had to rest on the porch before she trudged inside to wash and start dinner. I didn't understand the complaints about her ankles or the small of her back, even though I had been in the grape fields watching her work. With my brother and sister I ran in and out of the rows; we enjoyed ourselves and pretended not to hear Mother scolding us to sit down and behave ourselves. A few years later, however, I caught on when I went to pick grapes rather than play in the rows.

Mother and I got up before dawn and ate quick bowls of cereal. She drove in silence while I rambled on how everything was now solved, how I was going to make enough money to end our misery and even buy her a beautiful copper tea pot, the one I had shown her in Long's Drugs. When we arrived I was frisky and ready to go, self-consciously aware of my grape knife dangling at my wrist. I almost ran to the row the foreman had pointed out, but I returned to help Mother with the grape pans and jug of water. She told me to settle down and reminded me not to lose my knife. I walked at her side and listened to her explain how to cut grapes; bent down, hands on knees, I watched her demonstrate by cutting a few bunches into my pan. She stood over me as I tried it myself, tugging at a bunch of grapes that pulled loose like beads from a necklace. "Cut the stem all the way," she told me as last advice before she walked away, her shoes sinking in the loose dirt, to begin work on her own row.

I cut another bunch, then another, fighting the snap and whip of vines. After ten minutes of groping for grapes, my first pan brimmed with bunches. I poured them on the paper tray, which was bordered by a wooden frame that kept the grapes from rolling off, and they spilled like jewels from a pirate's chest. The tray was only half filled, so I hurried to jump under the vines and begin groping, cutting, and tugging at the grapes again. I emptied the pan, raked the grapes with my hands to make them look like they filled the tray, and jumped back under the vine on my knees. I tried to cut faster because Mother, in the next row, was slowly moving ahead. I peeked into her row and saw five trays gleaming in the early morning. I cut, pulled hard, and stopped to gather the grapes that missed the pan; already bored, I spat on a few to wash them before tossing them like popcorn into my mouth.

5   So it went. Two pans equaled one tray—or six cents. By lunchtime I had a trail of thirty-seven trays behind me while mother had sixty or more. We met about halfway from our last trays, and I sat down with a grunt, knees wet from kneeling on dropped grapes. I washed my hands with the water from the jug, drying them on the inside of my shirt sleeve before I opened the paper bag for the first sandwich, which I gave to Mother. I dipped my hand in again to unwrap a sandwich without looking at it. I took a first bite and chewed it slowly for the tang of mustard. Eating in silence I looked straight ahead at the vines, and only when we were finished with cookies did we talk.

"Are you tired?" she asked.

"No, but I got a sliver from the frame," I told her. I showed her the web of skin between my thumb and index finger. She wrinkled her forehead but said it was nothing.

"How many trays did you do?"

I looked straight ahead, not answering at first. I recounted in my mind the whole morning of bend, cut, pour again and again, before answering a feeble "thirty-seven." No elaboration, no detail. Without looking at me she told me how she had done field work in Texas and Michigan as a child. But I had a difficult time listening to her stories. I played with my grape knife, stabbing it into the ground, but stopped when Mother reminded me that I had better not lose it. I left the knife sticking up like a small, leafless plant. She then talked about school, the junior high I would be going to that fall, and then about Rick and Debra, how sorry they would be that they hadn't come out to pick grapes because they'd have no new clothes for the school year. She stopped talking when she peeked at her watch, a bandless one she kept in her pocket. She got up with an "*Ay, Dios,*" and told me that we'd work until three, leaving me cutting figures in the sand with my knife and dreading the return to work.

10   Finally I rose and walked slowly back to where I had left off, again kneeling under the vine and fixing the pan under bunches of grapes. By that time, 11:30, the sun was over my shoulder and made me squint and think of the pool at the Y.M.C.A. where I was a summer member. I saw myself diving face first into the water and loving it. I saw myself gleaming like something new, at the edge of the pool. I had to daydream and keep my mind busy because boredom was a terror almost as awful as the work itself. My mind went dumb with stupid things, and I had to keep it moving with dreams of baseball and would-be girlfriends. I even sang, however softly, to keep my mind moving, my hands moving.

I worked less hurriedly and with less vision. I no longer saw that copper pot sitting squat on our stove or Mother waiting for it to whistle. The wardrobe that I imagined, crisp and bright in the closet, numbered only one pair of jeans and two shirts because, in half a day, six cents times thirty-seven trays was two dollars and twenty-two cents. It became clear to me. If I worked eight hours, I might make four dollars. I'd take this, even gladly, and walk downtown to look into store windows on the mall and long for the bright madras shirts from Walter Smith or Coffee's, but settling for two imitation ones from Penney's.

That first day I laid down seventy-three trays while Mother had a hundred and twenty behind her. On the back of an old envelope, she wrote out our numbers and hours. We washed at the pump behind the farm house and walked slowly to our car for the drive back to town in the afternoon heat. That evening after dinner I sat in a lawn chair listening to music from a transistor radio while Rick and David King played catch. I joined them in a game of pickle, but there was little joy in trying to avoid their tags because I couldn't get the fields out of my mind: I saw myself dropping on my knees under a vine to tug at a branch that wouldn't come off. In bed, when I closed my eyes, I saw the fields, yellow with kicked up dust, and a crooked trail of trays rotting behind me.

The next day I woke tired and started picking tired. The grapes rained into the pan, slowly filling like a belly, until I had my first tray and started my second. So it went all day, and the next, and all through the following week, so that by the end of thirteen days the foreman counted out, in tens mostly, my pay of fifty-three dollars. Mother earned one hundred and forty-eight dollars. She wrote this on her envelope, with a message I didn't bother to ask her about.

The next day I walked with my friend Scott to the downtown mall where we drooled over the clothes behind fancy windows, bought popcorn, and sat at a tier of outdoor fountains to talk about girls. Finally we went into Penney's for more popcorn, which we ate walking around, before we returned home without buying anything. It wasn't until a few days before school that I let my fifty-three dollars slip quietly from my hands, buying a pair of pants, two shirts, and a maroon T-shirt, the kind that was in style. At home I tried them on while Rick looked on enviously; later, the day before school started, I tried them on again wondering not so much if they were worth it as who would see me first in those clothes.

Along with my brother and sister I picked grapes until I was fif- 15 teen, before giving up and saying that I'd rather wear old clothes than stoop like a Mexican. Mother thought I was being stuck-up, even stupid, because there would be no clothes for me in the fall. I told her I didn't care, but when Rick and Debra rose at five in the morning, I lay awake in bed feeling that perhaps I had made a mistake but unwilling to change my mind. That fall Mother bought me two pairs of socks, a packet of colored T-shirts, and underwear. The T-shirts would help, I thought, but who would see that I had new underwear and socks? I wore a new T-shirt on the first day of school, then an old shirt on Tuesday, then another T-shirt on Wednesday, and on Thursday an old Nehru shirt that was embarrassingly out of style. On Friday I changed into the corduroy pants my brother had handed down to me and slipped into my last new T-shirt. I worked like a magician, blinding my classmates, who were all clothes conscious and small-time social climbers, by arranging my wardrobe to make it seem larger than it really was. But by spring I had to do something—my blue jeans were almost silver and my shoes had lost their form, puddling like black ice around my feet. That spring of my sixteenth year, Rick and I decided to take a labor bus to chop cotton. In his old Volkswagen, which was more noise than power, we drove on a Saturday morning to West Fresno—or Chinatown as some call it—parked, walked slowly toward a bus, and stood gawking at the winos, toothy blacks, Okies, *Tejanos*[2] with gold teeth, whores, Mexican families, and labor contractors shouting "Cotton" or "Beets," the work of spring.

We boarded the "Cotton" bus without looking at the contractor who stood almost blocking the entrance because he didn't want winos. We boarded scared and then were more scared because two blacks in the rear were drunk and arguing loudly about what was better, a two-barrel or four-barrel Ford carburetor. We sat far from them, looking straight ahead, and only glanced briefly at the others who boarded, almost all of them broken and poorly dressed in loudly mismatched clothes. Finally when the contractor banged his palm against the side of the bus, the young man at the wheel, smiling and talking in Spanish, started the engine, idled it for a moment while he adjusted the mirrors, and started off in slow chugs. Except for the windshield there was no glass in the windows, so as soon as we were on the rural roads outside Fresno, the dust and sand began to be sucked into the bus, whipping about like irate wasps as the gravel ticked about us. We closed our eyes, clotted up our mouths that wanted to open with embarrassed laughter because we couldn't believe we were on that bus with those people and the dust attacking us for no reason.

When we arrived at a field we followed the others to a pickup where we each took a hoe and marched to stand before a row. Rick and I, self-conscious and unsure, looked around at the others who leaned on their hoes or squatted in front of the rows, almost all talking in Spanish, joking, lighting cigarettes—all waiting for the foreman's whistle to begin work. Mother had explained how to chop cotton by showing us with a broom in the backyard.

---

[2]Descendants of early Mexican settlers in Texas. [Eds.]

"Like this," she said, her broom swishing down weeds. "Leave one plant and cut four—and cut them! Don't leave them standing or the foreman will get mad."

The foreman whistled and we started up the row stealing glances at other workers to see if we were doing it right. But after awhile we worked like we knew what we were doing, neither of us hurrying or falling behind. But slowly the clot of men, women, and kids began to spread and loosen. Even Rick pulled away. I didn't hurry, though. I cut smoothly and cleanly as I walked at a slow pace, in a sort of funeral march. My eyes measured each space of cotton plants before I cut. If I missed the plants, I swished again. I worked intently, seldom looking up, so when I did I was amazed to see the sun, like a broken orange coin, in the east. It looked blurry, unbelievable, like something not of this world. I looked around in amazement, scanning the eastern horizon that was a taut line jutted with an occasional mountain. The horizon was beautiful, like a snapshot of the moon, in the early light of morning, in the quiet of no cars and few people.

The foreman trudged in boots in my direction, stepping awkwardly over the plants, to inspect the work. No one around me looked up. We all worked steadily while we waited for him to leave. When he did leave, with a feeble complaint addressed to no one in particular, we looked up smiling under straw hats and bandanas. 20

By 11:00, our lunch time, my ankles were hurting from walking on clods the size of hardballs. My arms ached and my face was dusted by a wind that was perpetual, always busy whipping about. But the work was not bad, I thought. It was better, so much better, than picking grapes, especially with the hourly wage of a dollar twenty-five instead of piece work. Rick and I walked sorely toward the bus where we washed and drank water. Instead of eating in the bus or in the shade of the bus, we kept to ourselves by walking down to the irrigation canal that ran the length of the field, to open our lunch of sandwiches and crackers. We laughed at the crackers, which seemed like a cruel joke from our Mother, because we were working under the sun and the last thing we wanted was a salty dessert. We ate them anyway and drank more water before we returned to the field, both of us limping in exaggeration. Working side by side, we talked and laughed at our predicament because our Mother had warned us year after year that if we didn't get on track in school we'd have to work in the fields and then we would see. We mimicked Mother's whining voice and smirked at her smoky view of the future in which we'd be trapped by marriage and screaming kids. We'd eat beans and then we'd see.

Rick pulled slowly away to the rhythm of his hoe falling faster and smoother. It was better that way, to work alone. I could hum made-up songs or songs from the radio and think to myself about school and friends. At the time I was doing badly in my classes, mainly because of a difficult stepfather, but also because I didn't care anymore. All through junior high and into my first year of high school there were those who said I would never do anything, be anyone. They said I'd work like a donkey and marry the first Mexican girl that came along. I was reminded so often, verbally and in the way I was treated at home, that I began to believe that chopping cotton might be a lifetime job for me. If not chopping cotton, then I might get lucky and find myself in a car wash or restaurant or junkyard. But it was clear; I'd work, and work hard.

I cleared my mind by humming and looking about. The sun was directly above with a few soft blades of clouds against a sky that seemed bluer and more beautiful than our sky in the city. Occasionally the breeze flurried and picked up dust so that I had to cover my eyes and screw up my face. The workers were hunched, brown as the clods under our feet, and spread across the field that ran without end—fields that were owned by corporations, not families.

I hoed, trying to keep my mind busy with scenes from school and pretend girlfriends until finally my brain turned off and my thinking went fuzzy with boredom. I looked about, no longer mesmerized by the beauty of the landscape, no longer wondering if the winos in the fields could hold out for eight hours, no longer dreaming of the clothes I'd buy with my pay. My eyes followed my chopping as the plants, thin as their shadows, fell with each strike. I worked slowly with ankles and arms hurting, neck stiff, and eyes stinging from the dust and the sun that glanced off the field like a mirror.

25   By quitting time, 3:00, there was such an excruciating pain in my ankles that I walked as if I were wearing snowshoes. Rick laughed at me and I laughed too, embarrassed that most of the men were walking normally and I was among the first timers who had to get used to this work. "And what about you, wino," I came back at Rick. His eyes were meshed red and his long hippie hair was flecked with dust and gnats and bits of leaves. We placed our hoes in the back of a pickup and stood in line for our pay, which was twelve fifty. I was amazed at the pay, which was the most I had ever earned in one day, and thought that I'd come back the next day, Sunday. This was too good.

Instead of joining the others in the labor bus, we jumped in the back of a pickup when the driver said we'd get to town sooner and were welcome to join him. We scrambled into the truck bed to be joined by a heavy-set and laughing *Tejano* whose head was shaped like an egg, particularly so because the bandana he wore ended in a point on the top of his head. He laughed almost demonically as the pickup roared up the dirt path, a gray cape of dust rising behind us. On the highway, with the wind in our faces, we squinted at the fields as if we were looking for someone. The *Tejano* had quit laughing but was smiling broadly, occasionally chortling tunes he never finished. I was scared of him, though

Rick, two years older and five inches taller, wasn't. If the *Tejano* looked at him, Rick stared back for a second or two before he looked away to the fields.

I felt like a soldier coming home from war when we rattled into Chinatown. People leaning against car hoods stared, their necks following us, owl-like; prostitutes chewed gum more ferociously and showed us their teeth; Chinese grocers stopped brooming their storefronts to raise their cadaverous faces at us. We stopped in front of the Chi Chi Club where Mexican music blared from the juke box and cue balls cracked like dull ice. The *Tejano,* who was dirty as we were, stepped awkwardly over the side rail, dusted himself off with his bandana, and sauntered into the club.

Rick and I jumped from the back, thanked the driver who said *de nada* and popped his clutch, so that the pickup jerked and coughed blue smoke. We returned smiling to our car, happy with the money we had made and pleased that we had, in a small way, proved ourselves to be tough; that we worked as well as other men and earned the same pay.

We returned the next day and the next week until the season was over and there was nothing to do. I told myself that I wouldn't pick grapes that summer, saying all through June and July that it was for Mexicans, not me. When August came around and I still had not found a summer job, I ate my words, sharpened my knife, and joined Mother, Rick, and Debra for one last time.

Responding to Reading

1. What types of work did Soto's relatives do? What does he mean when he says that they reminded him of some of the characters in the film *Gandhi*?
2. What is Soto's attitude toward picking grapes? How is his attitude different from his mother's? What does he mean when he says, "I'd rather wear old clothes than stoop like a Mexican" (15)?
3. What do you think Soto learned about work by picking grapes and cotton? What did he learn about his mother? about himself? about Mexicans?

Responding in Writing

Write about a difficult (and possibly unpleasant) job that you had. What did you learn from doing this job?

PROFESSIONS FOR WOMEN
Virginia Woolf
1882–1941

Virginia Woolf was born into a literary family in London, England. Largely self-educated, she began writing criticism for the Times Literary Supplement *when she was in her early twenties and published her first novel,* The Voyage Out, *in 1915. In later novels, including* Mrs. Dalloway *(1925),* To the Lighthouse *(1927), and* The Waves *(1931), she experimented with stream of consciousness and other stylistic and narrative innovations. She published two collections of her essays under the title* The Common Reader *(1925, 1932) and two feminist tracts,* A Room of One's Own *(1929) and* Three Guineas *(1938). The following essay was originally composed as a speech delivered in 1931 to a British women's organization, the Women's League of Service. In her remarks, Woolf discusses employment opportunities for women, focusing on the experience of women writers.*

When your secretary invited me to come here, she told me that your Society is concerned with the employment of women and she suggested that I might tell you something about my own professional experiences. It is true I am a woman; it is true I am employed, but what professional experiences have I had? It is difficult to say. My profession is literature; and in that profession there are fewer experiences for women than in any other, with the exception of the stage—fewer, I mean, that are peculiar to women. For the road was cut many years ago—by Fanny Burney, by Aphra Behn, by Harriet Martineau, by Jane Austen, by George Eliot—many famous women, and many more unknown and forgotten, have been before me, making the path smooth, and regulating my steps. Thus, when I came to write, there were very few material obstacles in my way. Writing was a reputable and harmless occupation. The family peace was not broken by the scratching of a pen. No demand was made upon the family purse. For ten and sixpence one can buy paper enough to write all the plays of Shakespeare—if one has a mind that way. Pianos and models, Paris, Vienna and Berlin, masters and mistresses, are not needed by a writer. The cheapness of writing paper is, of course, the reason why women have succeeded as writers before they have succeeded in the other professions.

But to tell you my story—it is a simple one. You have only got to figure to yourselves a girl in a bedroom with a pen in her hand. She had only to move that pen from left to right—from ten o'clock to one. Then it occurred to her to do what is simple and cheap enough after all—to slip a few of those pages into an envelope, fix a penny stamp in the corner, and drop the envelope in the red box at the corner. It was thus that I became a journalist; and my effort was rewarded on the first day of the following month—a very glorious day it was for me—by a letter from an editor containing a check for one pound ten shillings and sixpence. But to show you how little I deserve to be called a professional woman, how little I know of the struggles and difficulties of such lives, I have to admit that instead of spending that sum upon bread and butter, rent, shoes and stockings, or butcher's bills, I went out and bought a cat—a beautiful cat, a Persian cat, which very soon involved me in bitter disputes with my neighbors.

What could be easier than to write articles and to buy Persian cats with the profits? But wait a moment. Articles have to be about something. Mine, I seem to remember, was about a novel by a famous man. And while I was writing this review, I discovered that if I were going to review books I should need to do battle with a certain phantom. And the phantom was a woman, and when I came to know her better I called her after the heroine of a famous poem, The Angel in the House. It was she who used to come between me and my paper when I was writing reviews. It was she who bothered me and wasted my time and so tormented me that at last I killed her. You who come of a younger and happier generation may not have heard of her—you may not know what I mean by the Angel in the House. I will describe her as shortly as I can. She was intensely sympathetic. She was immensely charming. She was utterly unselfish. She excelled in the difficult arts of family life. She sacrificed herself daily. If there was chicken, she took the leg; if there was a draught she sat in it—in short she was so constituted that she never had a mind or a wish of her own but preferred to sympathize always with the minds and wishes of others. Above all—I need not say it—she was pure. Her purity was supposed to be her chief beauty—her blushes, her great grace. In those days—the last of Queen Victoria— every house had its Angel. And when I came to write I encountered her with the very first words. The shadow of her wings fell on my page; I heard the rustling of her skirts in the room. Directly, that is to say, I took my pen in hand to review that novel by a famous man, she slipped behind me and whispered: "My dear, you are a young woman. You are writing about a book that has been written by a man. Be sympathetic; be tender; flatter; deceive; use all the arts and wiles of our sex. Never let anybody guess that you have a mind of your own. Above all, be pure." And she made as if to guide my pen. I now record the one act for which I take some credit to myself, though the credit rightly belongs to some excellent ancestors of mine who left me a certain sum of money— shall we say five hundred pounds a year?—so that it was not necessary for me to depend solely on charm for my living. I turned upon her and caught her by the throat. I did my best to kill her. My excuse, if I were to be had up in a court of law, would be that I acted in self-defense. Had I not killed her she would have killed me. She would have plucked the heart out of my writing. For, as I found, directly I put pen to paper, you cannot review even a novel without having a mind of your own, without expressing what you think to be the truth about human relations, morality, sex. And all these questions, according to the Angel in the House, cannot be dealt with freely and openly by women; they must charm, they must conciliate, they must—to put it bluntly—tell lies if they are to succeed. Thus, whenever I felt the shadow of her wing or the radiance of her halo upon my page, I took up the inkpot and flung it at her. She died hard. Her fictitious nature was of great assistance to her. It is far harder to kill a phantom than a reality. She was always creeping back when I thought I had dispatched her. Though I flatter myself that I killed her in the end, the struggle was severe; it took much time that had better have been spent upon learning Greek grammar; or in roaming the world in search of adventures. But it was a real experience; it was an experience that was bound to befall all women writers at that time. Killing the Angel in the House was part of the occupation of a woman writer.

But to continue my story. The Angel was dead; what then remained? You may say that what remained was a simple and common object—a young woman in a bedroom with an inkpot. In other words, now that she had rid herself of falsehood, that young woman had only to be herself. Ah, but what is "herself"? I mean, what is a woman? I assure you, I do not know. I do not believe that you know. I do not believe that anybody can know until she has expressed herself in all the arts and professions open to human skill. That indeed is one of the reasons why I have come here—out of respect for you, who are in process of showing us by your experiments what a woman is, who are in process of providing us, by your failures and successes, with that extremely important piece of information.

5   But to continue the story of my professional experiences. I made one pound ten and six by my first review; and I bought a Persian cat with the proceeds. Then I grew ambitious. A Persian cat is all very well, I said; but a Persian cat is not enough. I must have a motor car. And it was thus that I became a novelist—for it is a very strange thing that people will give you a motor car if you will tell them a story. It is a still stranger thing that there is nothing so delightful in the world as telling stories. It is far pleasanter than writing reviews of famous novels. And yet, if I am to obey your secretary and tell you my professional experiences as a novelist, I must tell you about a very strange experience that befell me as a novelist. And to understand it you must try first to imagine a novelist's state of mind. I hope I am not giving away professional secrets if I say that a novelist's chief desire is to be as unconscious as possible. He has to induce in himself a state of perpetual lethargy. He wants life to proceed with the utmost quiet and regularity. He wants to see the same faces, to read the same books, to do the same things day after day, month after month, while he is writing, so

that nothing may break the illusion in which he is living—so that nothing may disturb or disquiet the mysterious nosings about, feelings round, darts, dashes and sudden discoveries of that very shy and illusive spirit, the imagination. I suspect that this state is the same both for men and women. Be that as it may, I want you to imagine me writing a novel in a state of trance. I want you to figure to yourselves a girl sitting with a pen in her hand, which for minutes, and indeed for hours, she never dips into the inkpot. The image that comes to my mind when I think of this girl is the image of a fisherman lying sunk in dreams on the verge of a deep lake with a rod held out over the water. She was letting her imagination sweep unchecked round every rock and cranny of the world that lies submerged in the depths of our unconscious being. Now came the experience, the experience that I believe to be far commoner with women writers than with men. The line raced through the girl's fingers. Her imagination had rushed away. It had sought the pools, the depths, the dark places where the largest fish slumber. And then there was a smash. There was an explosion. There was foam and confusion. The imagination had dashed itself against something hard. The girl was roused from her dream. She was indeed in a state of the most acute and difficult distress. To speak without figure she had thought of something, something about the body, about the passions which it was unfitting for her as a woman to say. Men, her reason told her, would be shocked. The consciousness of what men will say of a woman who speaks the truth about her passions had roused her from her artist's state of unconsciousness. She could write no more. The trance was over. Her imagination could work no longer. This I believe to be a very common experience with women writers—they are impeded by the extreme conventionality of the other sex. For though men sensibly allow themselves great freedom in these respects, I doubt that they realize or can control the extreme severity with which they condemn such freedom in women.

These then were two very genuine experiences of my own. These were two of the adventures of my professional life. The first—killing the Angel in the House—I think I solved. She died. But the second, telling the truth about my own experiences as a body, I do not think I solved. I doubt that any woman has solved it yet. The obstacles against her are still immensely powerful—and yet they are very difficult to define. Outwardly, what is simpler than to write books? Outwardly, what obstacles are there for a woman rather than for a man? Inwardly, I think the case is very different; she has still many ghosts to fight, many prejudices to overcome. Indeed it will be a long time still, I think, before a woman can sit down to write a book without finding a phantom to be slain, a rock to be dashed against. And if this is so in literature, the freest of all professions for women, how is it in the new professions which you are now for the first time entering?

Those are the questions that I should like, had I time, to ask you. And indeed, if I have laid stress upon these professional experiences of mine, it is because I believe that they are, though in different forms, yours also. Even when the path is nominally open—when there is nothing to prevent a woman from being a doctor, a lawyer, a civil servant—there are many phantoms and obstacles, as I believe, looming in her way. To discuss and define them is I think of great value and importance; for thus only can the labor be shared, the difficulties be solved. But besides this, it is necessary also to discuss the ends and the aims for which we are fighting, for which we are doing battle with these formidable obstacles. Those aims cannot be taken for granted; they must be perpetually questioned and examined. The whole position, as I see it—here in this hall surrounded by women practising for the first time in history I know not how many different professions—is one of extraordinary interest and importance. You have won rooms of your own in the house hitherto exclusively owned by men. You are able, though not without great labor and effort, to pay the rent. You are earning your five hundred pounds a year. But this freedom is only a beginning; the room is your own, but it is still bare. It has to be furnished; it has to be decorated; it has to be shared. How are you going to furnish it, how are you going to decorate it? With whom are you going to share it, and upon what terms? These, I think, are questions of the utmost importance and interest. For the first time in history you are able to ask them; for the first time you are able to decide for yourselves what the answers should be. Willingly would I stay and discuss those questions and answers—but not tonight. My time is up; and I must cease.

Responding to Reading

1. According to Woolf, why have women found success in writing? How does Woolf's explanation shed light on the fact that there were few female doctors, lawyers, or corporate executives in 1931—the year she delivered her address?
2. What does Woolf mean in paragraph 3 when she says that if she were going to review books, she would have to "do battle with a...phantom"? Why does she call this phantom "The Angel in the House"? What does Woolf mean when she says, "Killing the Angel in the House was part of the occupation of a woman writer" (3)?
3. In paragraph 7, Woolf says that women writers now have a room in a house that was once "exclusively owned by men." What must women do to make the room their own? What does Woolf mean when she says, "It has to be furnished; it has to be decorated; it has to be shared" (7)?

Responding in Writing

In what ways would Woolf's speech be different if she were delivering it today to a graduating class at your college or university?

The Second Shift
Arlie Hochschild
1940–

Arlie Hochschild was co-director of the Center for Working Families and has done extensive research into the role of work in personal and family life. Hochschild has published The Second Shift: Working Parents and the Revolution at Home *(1989) and* The Time Bind: When Work Becomes Home and Home Becomes Work *(1997). Her latest book,* The Commercialization of Intimate Life *(2003), is a collection of essays written over the last thirty years. The following essay, taken from* The Second Shift, *makes the point that most working women have two jobs: one that lasts from nine to five and another that begins the moment they return home.*

Every American household bears the footprints of economic and cultural trends that originate far outside its walls. A rise in inflation eroding the earning power of the male wage, an expanding service sector opening for women, and the inroads made by women into many professions—all these changes do not simply go on around the American family. They occur *within* a marriage or living-together arrangement and transform it. Problems between couples, problems that seem "unique" or "marital," are often the individual ripples of powerful economic and cultural shock waves. Quarrels between husbands and wives in households across the nation result mainly from a friction between faster-changing women and slower-changing men.

The exodus of women from the home to the workplace has not been accompanied by a new view of marriage and work that would make this transition smooth. Most workplaces have remained inflexible in the face of the changing needs of workers with families, and most men have yet to really adapt to the changes in women. I call the strain caused by the disparity between the change in women and the absence of change elsewhere the "stalled revolution."

If women begin to do less at home because they have less time, if men do little more, and if the work of raising children and tending a home requires roughly the same effort, then the questions of who does what at home and of what "needs doing" become a source of deep tension in a marriage.

Over the past 30 years in the United States, more and more women have begun to work outside the home, and more have divorced. While some commentators conclude that women's work *causes* divorce, my research into changes in the American family suggests something else. Since all the wives in the families I studied (over an eight-year period) worked outside the home, the fact that they worked did not account for why some marriages were happy and others were not. What *did* contribute to happiness was the husband's willingness to do the work at home. Whether they were traditional or more egalitarian in their relationship, couples were happier when the men did a sizable share of housework and child care.

5   In one study of 600 couples filing for divorce, researcher George Levinger found that the second most common reason women cited for wanting to divorce—after "mental cruelty"—was their husbands' "neglect of home or children." Women mentioned this reason more often than financial problems, physical abuse, drinking, or infidelity.

A happy marriage is supported by a couple's being economically secure, by their enjoying a supportive community, and by their having compatible needs and values. But these days it may also depend on a shared appreciation of the work it takes to nurture others. As the role of the homemaker is being abandoned by many women, the homemaker's work has been continually devalued and passed on to low-paid house-keepers, baby-sitters, or day-care workers. Long devalued by men, the contribution of cooking, cleaning, and care-giving is now being devalued as mere drudgery by many women, too.

In the era of the stalled revolution, one way to make housework and child care more valued is for men to share in that work. Many working mothers are already doing all they can at home. Now it's time for men to make the move.

If more mothers of young children are working at full-time jobs outside the home, and if most couples can't afford household help, who's doing the work at home? Adding together the time it takes to do a paid job and to do housework and child care and using estimates from major studies on time use done in the 1960s and 1970s, I found that women worked roughly 15 more hours each week than men. Over a year, they worked an extra month of 24-hour days. Over a dozen years, it was an extra year of 24-hour days. Most women without children spend much more time than men on housework. Women with children devote more time to both housework and child care. Just as there is a wage gap between men and women in the workplace, there is a "leisure gap" between them at home. Most women work one shift at the office or factory and a "second shift" at home.

In my research, I interviewed and observed 52 couples over an eight-year period as they cooked dinner, shopped, bathed their children, and in general struggled to find enough time to make their complex lives work. The women I interviewed seemed to be far more deeply torn between the demands of work and family than were their husbands. They talked more about the abiding conflict between work and family. They felt the second shift was *their* issue, and most of their husbands agreed. When I telephoned one husband to arrange an interview with him, explaining that I wanted to ask him how he managed work and family life, he replied genially, "Oh, this will *really* interest my *wife*."

Men who shared the load at home seemed just as pressed for time 10 as their wives, and as torn between the demands of career and small children. But of the men I surveyed, the majority did not share the load at home. Some refused outright. Others refused more passively, often offering a loving shoulder to lean on, or an understanding ear, as their working wife faced the conflict they both saw as hers. At first it seemed to me that the problem of the second shift *was* hers. But I came to realize that those husbands who helped very little at home were often just as deeply affected as their wives—through the resentment their wives felt toward them and through their own need to steel themselves against that resentment.

A clear example of this phenomenon is Evan Holt, a warehouse furniture salesman who did very little housework and played with his four-year-old son, Joey, only at his convenience. His wife, Nancy, did the second shift, but she resented it keenly and half-consciously expressed her frustration and rage by losing interest in sex and becoming overly absorbed in Joey.

Even when husbands happily shared the work, their wives *felt* more responsible for home and children. More women than men kept track of doctor's appointments and arranged for kids playmates to come over. More mothers than fathers worried about a child's Halloween costume or a birthday present for a school friend. They were more likely to think about their children while at work and to check in by phone with the baby-sitter.

Partly because of this, more women felt torn between two kinds of urgency, between the need to soothe a child's fear of being left at day-care and the need to show the boss she's "serious" at work. Twenty percent of the men in my study shared housework equally. Seventy percent did a substantial amount (less than half of it, but more than a third), and 10 percent did less than a third. But even when couples more equitably share the work at home, women do two thirds of the daily jobs at home, such as cooking and cleaning up—jobs that fix them into a rigid routine. Most women cook dinner, for instance, while men change the oil in the family car. But, as one mother pointed out, dinner needs to be prepared every evening around six o'clock, whereas the car oil needs to be changed every six months, with no particular deadline. Women do more child care than men, and men repair more household appliances. A child needs to be tended to daily, whereas the repair of household appliances can often wait, said the men, "until I have time." Men thus have more control over when they make their contributions than women do. They may be very busy with family chores, but, like the executive who tells his secretary to "hold my calls," the man has more control over his time.

Another reason why women may feel under more strain than men is that women more often do two things at once—for example, write checks and return phone calls, vacuum and keep an eye on a three-year-old, fold laundry and think out the shopping list. Men more often will either cook dinner *or* watch the kids. Women more often do both at the same time.

15   Beyond doing more at home, women also devote proportionately, more of their time at home to housework than men and proportionately less of it to child care. Of all the time men spend working at home, a growing amount of it goes to child care. Since most parents prefer to tend to their children than to clean house, men do more of what they'd rather do. More men than women take their children on "fun" outings to the park, the zoo, the movies. Women spend more time on maintenance, such as feeding and bathing children—enjoyable activities, to be sure, but often less leisurely or "special" than going to the zoo. Men also do fewer of the most undesirable household chores, such as scrubbing the toilet.

As a result, women tend to talk more intensely about being overtired, sick, and emotionally drained. Many women interviewed were fixated on the topic of sleep. They talked about how much they could "get by on" six and a half, seven, seven and a half, less, more. They talked about who they knew who needed more or less. Some apologized for how much sleep they needed—"I'm afraid I need eight hours of sleep"—as if eight was "too much." They talked about how to avoid fully waking up when a child called them at night, and how to get back to sleep. These women talked about sleep the way a hungry person talks about food.

If, all in all, the two-job family is suffering from a speedup of work and family life, working mothers are its primary victims. It is ironic, then, that often it falls to women to be the time-and-motion experts of family life. As I observed families inside their homes, I noticed it was often the mother who rushed children, saying, "Hurry up! It's time to go." "Finish your cereal now," "You can do that later," or "Let's go!" When a bath needed to be crammed into a slot between 7:45 and 8:00, it was often the mother who called out "Let's see who can take their bath the quickest." Often a younger child would rush out, scurrying to be first in bed, while the older and wiser one stalled, resistant, sometimes resentful: "Mother is always rushing us." Sadly, women are more often the lightning rods for family tensions aroused by this speedup of work and family life. They are the villains in a process in which they are also the primary victims. More than the longer hours and the lack of sleep, this is the saddest cost to women of their extra month of work each year.

Raising children in a nuclear family is still the overwhelming preference of most people. Yet in the face of new problems for this family mode we have not created an adequate support system so that the nuclear family can do its job well in the era of the two-career couple. Corporations have done little to accommodate the needs of working parents, and the government has done little to prod them.

We really need, as sociologist Frank Furstenberg has suggested, a Marshall Plan for the family. After World War II we saw that it was in our best interests to aid the war-torn nations of Europe. Now—it seems obvious in an era of growing concern over drugs, crime, and family instability—is in our best interests to aid the overworked two-job families right here at home. We should look to other nations for a model of what could be done. In Sweden, for example, upon the birth of a child every working couple is entitled to 12 months of paid parental leave— nine months at 90 percent of the worker's salary, plus an additional three months at about three hundred dollars a month. The mother and father are free to divide this year off between them as they wish. Working parents of a child under eight have the opportunity to work no more than six hours a day, at six hours' pay. Parental insurance offers parents money for work time lost while visiting a child's school or caring for a sick child. That's a true pro-family policy.

A pro-family policy in the United States could give tax breaks to   20 companies that encourage job sharing, part-time work, flex time, and family leave for new parents. By implementing comparable worth policies we could increase pay scales for "women's" jobs. Another key element of a pro-family policy would be instituting, fewer-hour, more flexible options—called "family phases"—for all regular jobs filled by parents of young children.

Day-care centers could be made more warm and creative through generous public and private funding. If the best form of day-care comes from the attention of elderly neighbors, students, or grandparents, these people could be paid to care for children through social programs.

In these ways, the American government would create a safer environment for the two-job family. If the government encouraged corporations to consider the long-ranged interests of workers and their families, they would save on long-range costs caused by absenteeism, turnover, juvenile delinquency, mental illness, and welfare support for single mothers.

These are real pro-family reforms. If they seem utopian today, we should remember that in the past the eight-hour day, the abolition of child labor, and the vote for women seemed utopian, too. Among top rated employers listed in *The 100 Best Companies to Work for in America* are many offering country-club memberships, first-class air travel, and million-dollar fitness centers. But only a handful offer job sharing, flex time, or part-time work. Not one provides on-site day-care, and only three offer child-care deductions: Control Data, Polaroid, and Honeywell. In his book *Megatrends*, John Naisbitt reports that 83 percent of corporate executives believed that more men feel the need to share the responsibilities of parenting; yet only 9 percent of corporations offer paternity leave.

Public strategies are linked to private ones. Economic and cultural trends bear on family relations in ways it would be useful for all of us to understand. The happiest two-job marriages I saw during my research were ones in which men and women shared the housework and parenting. What couples called good communication often meant that they were good at saying thanks to one another for small aspects of taking care of the family. Making it to the school play, helping a child read, cooking dinner in good spirit, remembering the grocery list, taking responsibility for cleaning up the bedrooms—these were the silver and gold of the marital exchange. Until now, couples committed to an equal sharing of house-work and child care have been rare. But, if we as a culture come to see the urgent need of meeting the new problems posed by the second shift, and if society and government begin to shape new policies that allow working parents more flexibility then we will be making some progress toward happier times at home and work. And as the young learn by example, many more women and men will be able to enjoy the pleasure that arises when family life is family life, and not a second shift.

Responding to Reading

1. Hochschild coined the terms "second shift" and "stalled revolution." Define each of these terms. Are they appropriate for what they denote? Would other terms—for example, *late shift* or *swing shift* and *postponed revolution* or *failed revolution*—be more appropriate? Explain.
2. According to Hochschild, women *think* that they are "under more strain than men" (14), even when their husbands do their share of housework and child-care. How does Hochschild account for this impression?
3. Beginning with paragraph 18, Hochschild recommends changes that she believes will ease the strain on working families—because, as she says in paragraph 24, "public strategies are linked to private ones." Given what Hochschild has said about the basic differences in men's and women's approaches to family roles, do you believe that government and corporations can solve the problem she identifies?

Responding in Writing

Would you say that your parents are committed to equal sharing of housework and childcare? What changes, if any, would you suggest?

Behind the Counter
Eric Schlosser
1960–

Eric Schlosser became a full-time journalist after writing a two-part article for
Rolling Stone *magazine, which was later expanded into the book* Fast Food
Nation *(2001). Schlosser is a correspondent for the* Atlantic Monthly *and
has written about the families of homicide victims and the "prison-industrial
complex." His latest book, coauthored with Charles Wilson, is* Chew on This:
Everything You Don't Want to Know about Fast Food *(2006). In the following essay, Schlosser examines the working conditions of those who prepare
and serve the food at fast-food restaurants.*

Every Saturday Elisa Zamot gets up at 5:15 in the morning. It's a struggle, and her head feels groggy as she steps into the shower. Her little sisters, Cookie and Sabrina, are fast asleep in their beds. By 5:30, Elisa's
showered, done her hair, and put on her McDonald's uniform. She's
sixteen, bright-eyed and olive-skinned, pretty and petite, ready for
another day of work. Elisa's mother usually drives her the half-mile or
so to the restaurant, but sometimes Elisa walks, leaving home before
the sun rises. Her family's modest townhouse sits beside a busy highway
on the south side of Colorado Springs, in a largely poor and working-
class neighborhood. Throughout the day, sounds of traffic fill the house,
the steady whoosh of passing cars. But when Elisa heads for work, the
streets are quiet, the sky's still dark, and the lights are out in the small
houses and rental apartments along the road.

When Elisa arrives at McDonald's, the manager unlocks the door
and lets her in. Sometimes the husband-and-wife cleaning crew are just
finishing up. More often, it's just Elisa and the manager in the restaurant, surrounded by an empty parking lot. For the next hour or so, the
two of them get everything ready. They turn on the ovens and grills.
They go downstairs into the basement and get food and supplies for
the morning shift. They get the paper cups, wrappers, cardboard containers, and packets of condiments. They step into the big freezer and
get the frozen bacon, the frozen pancakes, and the frozen cinnamon
rolls. They get the frozen hash browns, the frozen biscuits, the frozen
McMuffins. They get the cartons of scrambled egg mix and orange juice
mix. They bring the food upstairs and start preparing it before any customers appear, thawing some things in the microwave and cooking
other things on the grill. They put the cooked food in special cabinets
to keep it warm.

The restaurant opens for business at seven o'clock, and for the next
hour or so, Elisa and the manager hold down the fort, handling all the
orders. As the place starts to get busy, other employees arrive. Elisa

works behind the counter. She takes orders and hands food to customers from breakfast through lunch. When she finally walks home, after seven hours of standing at a cash register, her feet hurt. She's wiped out. She comes through the front door, flops onto the living room couch, and turns on the TV. And the next morning she gets up at 5:15 again and starts the same routine.

Up and down Academy Boulevard, along South Nevada, Circle Drive, and Woodman Road, teenagers like Elisa run the fast food restaurants of Colorado Springs. Fast food kitchens often seem like a scene from *Bugsy Malone,* a film in which all the actors are children pretending to be adults. No other industry in the United States has a workforce so dominated by adolescents. About two-thirds of the nation's fast food workers are under the age of twenty. Teenagers open the fast food outlets in the morning, close them at night, and keep them going at all hours in between. Even the managers and assistant managers are sometimes in their late teens. Unlike Olympic gymnastics—an activity in which teenagers consistently perform at a higher level than adults—there's nothing about the work in a fast food kitchen that requires young employees. Instead of relying upon a small, stable, well-paid, and well-trained workforce, the fast food industry seeks out part-time, unskilled workers who are willing to accept low pay. Teenagers have been the perfect candidates for these jobs, not only because they are less expensive to hire than adults, but also because their youthful inexperience makes them easier to control.

5   The labor practices of the fast food industry have their origins in the assembly line systems adopted by American manufacturers in the early twentieth century. Business historian Alfred D. Chandler has argued that a high rate of "throughput" was the most important aspect of these mass production systems. A factory's throughput is the speed and volume of its flow—a much more crucial measurement, according to Chandler, than the number of workers it employs or the value of its machinery. With innovative technology and the proper organization, a small number of workers can produce an enormous amount of goods cheaply. Throughput is all about increasing the speed of assembly, about doing things faster in order to make more.

Although the McDonald brothers had never encountered the term "throughput" or studied "scientific management," they instinctively grasped the underlying principles and applied them in the Speedee Service System. The restaurant operating scheme they developed has been widely adopted and refined over the past half century. The ethos of the assembly line remains at its core. The fast food industry's obsession with throughput has altered the way millions of Americans work, turned commercial kitchens into small factories, and changed familiar foods into commodities that are manufactured.

At Burger King restaurants, frozen hamburger patties are placed on a conveyor belt and emerge from a broiler ninety seconds later fully cooked. The ovens at Pizza Hut and at Domino's also use conveyer belts to ensure standardized cooking times. The ovens at McDonald's look like commercial laundry presses, with big steel hoods that swing down and grill hamburgers on both sides at once. The burgers, chicken, french fries, and buns are all frozen when they arrive at a McDonald's. The shakes and sodas begin as syrup. At Taco Bell restaurants the food is "assembled," not prepared. The guacamole isn't made by workers in the kitchen; it's made at a factory in Michoàcán, Mexico, then frozen and shipped north. The chain's taco meat arrives frozen and precooked in vacuum-sealed plastic bags. The beans are dehydrated and look like brownish corn flakes. The cooking process is fairly simple. "Everything's add water," a Taco Bell employee told me. "Just add hot water."

Although Richard and Mac McDonald introduced the division of labor to the restaurant business, it was a McDonald's executive named Fred Turner who created a production system of unusual thoroughness and attention to detail. In 1958, Turner put together an operations and training manual for the company that was seventy-five pages long, specifying how almost everything should be done. Hamburgers were always to be placed on the grill in six neat rows; french fries had to be exactly 0.28 inches thick. The McDonald's operations manual today has ten times the number of pages and weighs about four pounds. Known within the company as "the Bible," it contains precise instructions on how various appliances should be used, how each item on the menu should look, and how employees should greet customers. Operators who disobey these rules can lose their franchises. Cooking instructions are not only printed in the manual, they are often designed into the machines. A McDonald's kitchen is full of buzzers and flashing lights that tell employees what to do.

At the front counter, computerized cash registers issue their own commands. Once an order has been placed, buttons light up and suggest other menu items that can be added. Workers at the counter are told to increase the size of an order by recommending special promotions, pushing dessert, pointing out the financial logic behind the purchase of a larger drink. While doing so, they are instructed to be upbeat and friendly. "Smile with a greeting and make a positive first impression," a Burger King training manual suggests. "Show them you are GLAD TO SEE THEM. Include eye contact with the cheerful greeting."

The strict regimentation at fast food restaurants creates standard- 10
ized products. It increases the throughput. And it gives fast food companies an enormous amount of power over their employees. "When management determines exactly how every task is to be done … and can impose its own rules about pace, output, quality, and technique," the sociologist Robin Leidner has noted, "[it] makes workers increasingly interchangeable." The management no longer depends upon the talents or skills of its workers—those things are built into the operating

system and machines. Jobs that have been "de-skilled" can be filled cheaply. The need to retain any individual worker is greatly reduced by the ease with which he or she can be replaced.

Teenagers have long provided the fast food industry with the bulk of its workforce. The industry's rapid growth coincided with the baby-boom expansion of that age group. Teenagers were in many ways the ideal candidates for these low-paying jobs. Since most teenagers still lived at home, they could afford to work for wages too low to support an adult, and until recently, their limited skills attracted few other employers. A job at a fast food restaurant became an American rite of passage, a first job soon left behind for better things. The flexible terms of employment in the fast food industry also attracted housewives who needed extra income. As the number of baby-boom teenagers declined, the fast food chains began to hire other marginalized workers: recent immigrants, the elderly, and the handicapped.

English is now the second language of at least one-sixth of the nation's restaurant workers, and about one-third of that group speaks no English at all. The proportion of fast food workers who cannot speak English is even higher. Many know only the names of the items on the menu; they speak "McDonald's English."

The fast food industry now employs some of the most disadvantaged members of American society. It often teaches basic job skills—such as getting to work on time—to people who can barely read, whose lives have been chaotic or shut off from the mainstream. Many individual franchisees are genuinely concerned about the well-being of their workers. But the stance of the fast food industry on issues involving employee training, the minimum wage, labor unions, and overtime pay strongly suggests that its motives in hiring the young, the poor, and the handicapped are hardly altruistic.

At a 1999 conference on foodservice equipment, top American executives from Burger King, McDonald's, and Tricon Global Restaurants, Inc. (the owner of Taco Bell, Pizza Hut, and KFC) appeared together on a panel to discuss labor shortages, employee training, computerization, and the latest kitchen technology. The three corporations now employ about 3.7 million people worldwide, operate about 60,000 restaurants, and open a new fast food restaurant every two hours. Putting aside their intense rivalry for customers, the executives had realized at a gathering the previous evening that when it came to labor issues, they were in complete agreement. "We've come to the conclusion that we're in support of each other," Dave Brewer, the vice president of engineering at KFC, explained. "We are aligned as a team to support this industry." One of the most important goals they held in common was the redesign of kitchen equipment so that less money needed to be spent training workers. "Make the equipment intuitive, make it so that the job is easier to do right than to do wrong," advised Jerry Sus, the leading equipment systems engineer at McDonald's. "The easier it is for him [the worker] to use, the easier it is for us not to have to train him." John Reckert—director of strategic operations and of research and development at Burger King—felt optimistic about the benefits that new technology would bring the industry. "We can develop equipment that only works one way," Reckert said. "There are many different ways today that employees can abuse our product, mess up the flow … If the equipment only allows one process, there's very little to train." Instead of giving written instructions to crew members, another panelist suggested, rely as much as possible on photographs of menu items, and "if there are instructions, make them very simple, write them at a fifth-grade level, and write them in Spanish and English." All of the executives agreed that "zero training" was the fast food industry's ideal, though it might not ever be attained.

While quietly spending enormous sums on research and technology   15 to eliminate employee training, the fast food chains have accepted hundreds of millions of dollars in government subsidies for "training" their workers. Through federal programs such as the Targeted Jobs Tax Credit and its successor, the Work Opportunity Tax Credit, the chains have for years claimed tax credits of up to $2,400 for each new low-income worker they hired. In 1996 an investigation by the U.S. Department of Labor concluded that 92 percent of these workers would have been hired by the companies anyway—and that their new jobs were part-time, provided little training, and came with no benefits. These federal subsidy programs were created to reward American companies that gave job training to the poor.

Attempts to end these federal subsidies have been strenuously opposed by the National Council of Chain Restaurants and its allies in Congress. The Work Opportunity Tax Credit program was renewed in 1996. It offered as much as $385 million in subsidies the following year. Fast food restaurants had to employ a worker for only four hundred hours to receive the federal money—and then could get more money as soon as that worker quit and was replaced. American taxpayers have in effect subsidized the industry's high turnover rate, providing company tax breaks for workers who are employed for just a few months and receive no training. The industry front group formed to defend these government subsidies is called the "Committee for Employment Opportunities." Its chief lobbyist, Bill Signer, told the *Houston Chronicle* there was nothing wrong with the use of federal subsidies to create low-paying, low-skilled, short-term jobs for the poor. Trying to justify the minimal amount of training given to these workers, Signer said, "They've got to crawl before they can walk."

The employees whom the fast food industry expects to crawl are by far the biggest group of low-wage workers in the United States today. The nation has about 1 million migrant farm workers and about 3.5 million fast food workers. Although picking strawberries is orders of magnitude more difficult than cooking hamburgers, both jobs are now filled by people who are generally young, unskilled, and willing to work long hours for low pay. Moreover, the turnover rates for both jobs are among the highest in the American economy. The annual turnover rate in the fast food industry is now about 300 to 400 percent. The typical fast food worker quits or is fired every three to four months.

The fast food industry pays the minimum wage to a higher proportion of its workers than any other American industry. Consequently, a low minimum wage has long been a crucial part of the fast food industry's business plan. Between 1968 and 1990, the years when the fast food chains expanded at their fastest rate, the real value of the U.S. minimum wage fell by almost 40 percent. In the late 1990s, the real value of the U.S. minimum wage still remained about 27 percent lower than it was in the late 1960s. Nevertheless, the National Restaurant Association (NRA) has vehemently opposed any rise in the minimum wage at the federal, state, or local level. About sixty large food-service companies—including Jack in the Box, Wendy's, Chevy's, and Red Lobster—have backed congressional legislation that would essentially eliminate the federal minimum wage by allowing states to disregard it. Pete Meersman, the president of the Colorado Restaurant Association, advocates creating a federal guest worker program to import low-wage foodservice workers from overseas.

While the real value of the wages paid to restaurant workers has declined for the past three decades, the earnings of restaurant company executives have risen considerably. According to a 1997 survey in *Nation's Restaurant News,* the average corporate executive bonus was $131,000, an increase of 20 percent over the previous year. Increasing the federal minimum wage by a dollar would add about two cents to the cost of a fast food hamburger.

20   In 1938, at the height of the Great Depression, Congress passed legislation to prevent employers from exploiting the nation's most vulnerable workers. The Fair Labor Standards Act established the first federal minimum wage. It also imposed limitations on child labor. And it mandated that employees who work more than forty hours a week be paid overtime wages for each additional hour. The overtime wage was set at a minimum of one and a half times the regular wage.

Today few employees in the fast food industry qualify for overtime—and even fewer are paid it. Roughly 90 percent of the nation's fast food workers are paid an hourly wage, provided no benefits, and scheduled to work only as needed. Crew members are employed "at will." If the restaurant's busy, they're kept longer than usual. If business is slow, they're sent home early. Managers try to make sure that each worker is employed less than forty hours a week, thereby avoiding any overtime payments. A typical McDonald's or Burger King restaurant has about fifty crew members. They work an average of thirty hours a week. By hiring a large number of crew members for each restaurant, sending them home as soon as possible, and employing them for fewer than forty hours a week whenever possible, the chains keep their labor costs to a bare minimum.

A handful of fast food workers are paid regular salaries. A fast food restaurant that employs fifty crew members has four or five managers and assistant managers. They earn about $23,000 a year and usually receive medical benefits, as well as some form of bonus or profit sharing. They have an opportunity to rise up the corporate ladder. But they also work long hours without overtime—fifty, sixty, seventy hours a week. The turnover rate among assistant managers is extremely high. The job offers little opportunity for independent decision-making. Computer programs, training manuals, and the machines in the kitchen determine how just about everything must be done.

Fast food managers do have the power to hire, fire, and schedule workers. Much of their time is spent motivating their crew members. In the absence of good wages and secure employment, the chains try to inculcate "team spirit" in their young crews. Workers who fail to work hard, who arrive late, or who are reluctant to stay extra hours are made to feel that they're making life harder for everyone else, letting their friends and coworkers down. For years the McDonald's Corporation has provided its managers with training in "transactional analysis," a set of psychological techniques popularized in the book *I'm OK—You're OK* (1969). One of these techniques is called "stroking"—a form of positive reinforcement, deliberate praise, and recognition that many teenagers don't get at home. Stroking can make a worker feel that his or her contribution is sincerely valued. And it's much less expensive than raising wages or paying overtime.

The fast food chains often reward managers who keep their labor costs low, a practice that often leads to abuses. In 1997 a jury in Washington State found that Taco Bell had systematically coerced its crew members into working off the clock in order to avoid paying them overtime. The bonuses of Taco Bell restaurant managers were tied to their success at cutting labor costs. The managers had devised a number of creative ways to do so. Workers were forced to wait until things got busy at a restaurant before officially starting their shifts. They were forced to work without pay after their shifts ended. They were forced to clean restaurants on their own time. And they were sometimes compensated with food, not wages. Many of the workers involved were minors and recent immigrants. Before the penalty phase of the Washington lawsuit, the two sides reached a settlement; Taco Bell agreed to pay millions of dollars in back wages, but admitted no wrongdoing. As many as 16,000 current and former employees were owed money by the company. One employee, a high school dropout named Regina

Jones, regularly worked seventy to eighty hours a week but was paid for only forty. In 2001, Taco Bell settled a class-action lawsuit in California, agreeing to pay $9 million in back wages for overtime and an Oregon jury found that Taco Bell managers had falsified the time cards of thousands of workers in order to get productivity bonuses.

Responding to Reading

1. Why does Schlosser begin his essay with a description of Eliza Zamot's daily routine? What does Schlosser mean when he says, "Fast food kitchens often seem like a scene from *Bugsy Malone,* a film in which all the actors are children pretending to be adults" (4)?
2. In what way do the labor practices of the Speedee Service System resemble those of an assembly line? What are the advantages of this system? What are the disadvantages?
3. Why are teenagers the ideal candidates for the fast-food workforce? What other types of worker does this industry employ? Overall, would you say that Schlosser presents a positive picture of the fast-food industry?

Responding in Writing

Have you (or has anyone you have known) worked in a fast-food restaurant? Do your experiences (or the experiences of someone you know) support Schlosser's conclusions?

SELLING IN MINNESOTA

Barbara Ehrenreich

1941–

Barbara Ehrenreich labels herself an unabashed "feminist, populist, socialist, and secular humanist." Ehrenreich has written about social, political, and economic issues for Mother Jones *magazine,* Time *magazine, and the* Guardian. *Her books of social criticism include* Fear of Falling: The Inner Life of the Middle Class *(1989);* The Worst Years of Our Lives: Irreverent Notes on a Decade of Greed *(1990);* Nickel and Dimed: On (Not) Getting by in America *(2001);* Global Woman: Nannies, Maids, and Sex Workers in the New Economy *(2003),* Bait and Switch: The (Futile) Pursuit of the American Dream *(2005), and* Bright-Sided: How the Relentless Promotion of Positive Thinking Has Undermined America *(2009). The following essay, taken from* Nickel and Dimed, *describes a Wal-Mart corporate orientation that Ehrenreich took part in when she was hired as a sales associate.*

For sheer grandeur, scale, and intimidation value, I doubt if any corporate orientation exceeds that of Wal-Mart. I have been told that the process will take eight hours, which will include two fifteen-minute breaks and one half-hour break for a meal, and will be paid for like a regular shift. When I arrive, dressed neatly in khakis and clean T-shirt, as befits a potential Wal-Mart "associate," I find there are ten new hires besides myself, mostly young and Caucasian, and a team of three, headed by Roberta, to do the "orientating." We sit around a long table in the same windowless room where I was interviewed, each with a thick folder of paperwork in front of us, and hear Roberta tell once again about raising six children, being a "people person," discovering that the three principles of Wal-Mart philosophy were the same as her own, and so on. We begin with a video, about fifteen minutes long, on the history and philosophy of Wal-Mart, or, as an anthropological observer might call it, the Cult of Sam. First young Sam Walton, in uniform, comes back from the war. He starts a store, a sort of five-and-dime; he marries and fathers four attractive children; he receives a Medal of Freedom from President Bush, after which he promptly dies, making way for the eulogies. But the company goes on, yes indeed. Here the arc of the story soars upward unstoppably, pausing only to mark some fresh milestone of corporate expansion. 1992: Wal-Mart becomes the largest retailer in the world. 1997: Sales top $100 billion. 1998: The number of Wal-Mart associates hits 825,000, making Wal-Mart the largest private employer in the nation. Each landmark date is accompanied by a clip showing throngs of shoppers, swarms of associates, or scenes of handsome new stores and their adjoining parking lots. Over and over we hear in voiceover or see in graphic display the "three principles," which are maddeningly, even defiantly, nonparallel: "respect for the individual, exceeding customers' expectations, strive for excellence."

"Respect for the individual" is where we, the associates, come in, because vast as Wal-Mart is, and tiny as we may be as individuals, everything depends on us. Sam always said, and is shown saying, that "the best ideas come from the associates"—for example, the idea of having a "people greeter," an elderly employee (excuse me, associate) who welcomes each customer as he or she enters the store. Three times during the orientation, which began at three and stretches to nearly eleven, we are reminded that this brainstorm originated in a mere associate, and who knows what revolutions in retailing each one of us may propose? Because our ideas are welcome, more than welcome, and we are to think of our managers not as bosses but as "servant leaders," serving us as well as the customers. Of course, all is not total harmony, in every instance, between associates and their servant-leaders. A video on "associate honesty" shows a cashier being caught on videotape as he pockets some bills from the cash register. Drums beat ominously as he is led away in handcuffs and sentenced to four years.

The theme of covert tensions, overcome by right thinking and positive attitude, continues in the twelve-minute video entitled *You've Picked a Great Place to Work*. Here various associates testify to the "essential feeling of family for which Wal-Mart is so well-known," leading up to the conclusion that we don't need a union. Once, long ago, unions had a place in American society, but they "no longer have much to offer workers," which is why people are leaving them "by the droves." Wal-Mart is booming; unions are declining: judge for yourself. But we are warned that "unions have been targeting Wal-Mart for years." Why? For the dues money of course. Think of what you would lose with a union: first, your dues money, which could be $20 a month "and sometimes much more." Second, you would lose "your voice" because the union would insist on doing your talking for you. Finally, you might lose even your wages and benefits because they would all be "at risk on the bargaining table." You have to wonder—and I imagine some of my teenage fellow orientees may be doing so—why such fiends as these union organizers, such outright extortionists, are allowed to roam free in the land.

There is more, much more than I could ever absorb, even if it were spread out over a semester-long course. On the reasonable assumption that none of us is planning to go home and curl up with the "Wal-Mart Associate Handbook," our trainers start reading it out loud to us, pausing every few paragraphs to ask, "Any questions?" There never are. Barry, the seventeen-year-old to my left, mutters that his "butt hurts." Sonya, the tiny African American woman across from me, seems frozen in terror. I have given up on looking perky and am fighting to keep my eyes open. No nose or other facial jewelry, we learn; earrings must be small and discreet, not dangling; no blue jeans except on Friday, and then you have to pay $1 for the privilege of wearing them. No "grazing," that is, eating from food packages that somehow become open; no "time theft." This last sends me drifting off in a sci-fi direction: *And as the time thieves headed back to the year 3420, loaded with weekends and days off looted from the twenty-first century*...Finally, a question. The old guy who is being hired as a people greeter wants to know, "What is time theft?" Answer: Doing anything other than working during company time, anything at all. Theft of *our* time is not, however, an issue. There are stretches amounting to many minutes when all three of our trainers wander off, leaving us to sit there in silence or take the opportunity to squirm. Or our junior trainers go through a section of the handbook, and then Roberta, returning from some other business, goes over the same section again. My eyelids droop and I consider walking out. I have seen time move more swiftly during seven-hour airline delays. In fact, I am getting nostalgic about seven-hour airline delays. At least you can read a book or get up and walk around, take a leak.

5   On breaks, I drink coffee purchased at the Radio Grill, as the inhouse fast-food place is called, the real stuff with caffeine, more because I'm concerned about being alert for the late-night drive home than out of any need to absorb all the Wal-Mart trivia coming my way. Now, here's a drug the drug warriors ought to take a little more interest in.

Since I don't normally drink it at all—iced tea can usually be counted on for enough of a kick—the coffee has an effect like reagent-grade Dexedrine: my pulse races, my brain overheats, and the result in this instance is a kind of delirium. I find myself overly challenged by the little kindergarten-level tasks we are now given to do, such as affixing my personal bar code to my ID card, then sticking on the punch-out letters to spell my name. The letters keep curling up and sticking to my fingers, so I stop at "Barb," or more precisely, "B*ARB*," drifting off to think of all the people I know who have gentrified their names in recent years—Patsy to Patricia, Dick to Richard, and so forth—while I am going in the other direction. Now we start taking turns going to the computers to begin our CBL, or Computer-Based Learning, and I become transfixed by the HIV-inspired module entitled "Bloodborne Pathogens," on what to do in the event that pools of human blood should show up on the sales floor. All right, you put warning cones around the puddles, don protective gloves, etc., but I can't stop trying to envision the circumstances in which these pools might arise: an associate uprising? a guest riot? I have gone through six modules, three more than we are supposed to do tonight—the rest are to be done in our spare moments over the next few weeks—when one of the trainers gently pries me away from the computer. We are allowed now to leave.

Responding to Reading

1. Ehrenreich begins her essay with the statement, "For sheer grandeur, scale, and intimidation value, I doubt if any corporate orientation exceeds that of Wal-Mart" (1). Do you think Ehrenreich wants her readers to take this statement seriously? In what way do these opening remarks set the tone for the rest of the essay?
2. Why does Ehrenreich describe the orientation process in such detail? What does she hope to accomplish with this strategy?
3. How would you describe Ehrenreich's attitude toward the orientation process? toward Wal-Mart? toward her coworkers? What words and phrases in the essay convey these attitudes?

Responding in Writing

Assume you are one of the trainers at Wal-Mart's orientation section. Write a one- or two-paragraph memo that explains the orientation process and its goals.

DON'T BLAME WAL-MART
Robert B. Reich
1946–

A professor of public policy at the University of California at Berkeley, Robert B. Reich was the United States secretary of labor from 1993 to 1997. He is the author of numerous books, including, most recently, Reason: Why Liberals Will Win the Battle for America *(2004) and* Supercapitalism: The Transformation of Business, Democracy, and Everyday Life *(2007). He has published articles in the* New York Times, *the* New Yorker, *the* Atlantic Monthly, *the* Washington Post, *and the* Wall Street Journal. *In the following essay, Reich considers the economic and cultural influence of the mega-store Wal-Mart.*

Bowing to intense pressure from neighborhood and labor groups, a real estate developer has just given up plans to include a Wal-Mart store in a mall in Queens, thereby blocking Wal-Mart's plan to open its first store in New York City. In the eyes of Wal-Mart's detractors, the Arkansas-based chain embodies the worst kind of economic exploitation: it pays its 1.2 million American workers an average of only $9.68 an hour, doesn't provide most of them with health insurance, keeps out unions, has a checkered history on labor law and turns main streets into ghost towns by sucking business away from small retailers.

But isn't Wal-Mart really being punished for our sins? After all, it's not as if Wal-Mart's founder, Sam Walton, and his successors created the world's largest retailer by putting a gun to our heads and forcing us to shop there.

Instead, Wal-Mart has lured customers with low prices. "We expect our suppliers to drive the costs out of the supply chain," a spokeswoman for Wal-Mart said. "It's good for us and good for them."

Wal-Mart may have perfected this technique, but you can find it almost everywhere these days. Corporations are in fierce competition to get and keep customers, so they pass the bulk of their cost cuts through to consumers as lower prices. Products are manufactured in China at a fraction of the cost of making them here, and American consumers get great deals. Back-office work, along with computer programming and data crunching, is "offshored" to India, so our dollars go even further.

5   Meanwhile, many of us pressure companies to give us even better bargains. I look on the Internet to find the lowest price I can and buy airline tickets, books, merchandise from just about anywhere with a click of a mouse. Don't you?

The fact is, today's economy offers us a Faustian bargain:[1] it can give consumers deals largely because it hammers workers and communities.

We can blame big corporations, but we're mostly making this bargain with ourselves. The easier it is for us to get great deals, the stronger the downward pressure on wages and benefits. Last year, the real wages of hourly workers, who make up about 80 percent of the work force, actually dropped for the first time in more than a decade; hourly workers' health and pension benefits are in free fall. The easier it is for us to find better professional services, the harder professionals have to hustle to attract and keep clients. The more efficiently we can summon products from anywhere on the globe, the more stress we put on our own communities.

But you and I aren't just consumers. We're also workers and citizens. How do we strike the right balance? To claim that people shouldn't have access to Wal-Mart or to cut-rate airfares or services from India or to Internet shopping, because these somehow reduce their quality of life, is paternalistic tripe. No one is a better judge of what people want than they themselves.

The problem is, the choices we make in the market don't fully reflect our values as workers or as citizens. I didn't want our community bookstore in Cambridge, Mass., to close (as it did last fall) yet I still bought lots of books from Amazon.com. In addition, we may not see the larger bargain when our own job or community isn't directly at stake. I don't like what's happening to airline workers, but I still try for the cheapest fare I can get.

The only way for the workers or citizens in us to trump the consumers in us is through laws and regulations that make our purchases a social choice as well as a personal one. A requirement that companies with more than 50 employees offer their workers affordable health insurance, for example, might increase slightly the price of their goods and services. My inner consumer won't like that very much, but the worker in me thinks it a fair price to pay. Same with an increase in the minimum wage or a change in labor laws making it easier for employees to organize and negotiate better terms.

I wouldn't go so far as to re-regulate the airline industry or hobble free trade with China and India—that would cost me as a consumer far too much—but I'd like the government to offer wage insurance to ease the pain of sudden losses of pay. And I'd support labor standards that make trade agreements a bit more fair.

These provisions might end up costing me some money, but the citizen in me thinks they are worth the price. You might think differently, but as a nation we aren't even having this sort of discussion. Instead, our

10

---

[1]Reference to a legendary German magician who makes a deal with the devil. [Eds.]

debates about economic change take place between two warring camps: those who want the best consumer deals, and those who want to preserve jobs and communities much as they are. Instead of finding ways to soften the blows, compensate the losers or slow the pace of change— so the consumers in us can enjoy lower prices and better products without wreaking too much damage on us in our role as workers and citizens—we go to battle.

I don't know if Wal-Mart will ever make it into New York City. I do know that New Yorkers, like most other Americans, want the great deals that can be had in a rapidly globalizing high-tech economy. Yet the prices on sales tags don't reflect the full prices we have to pay as workers and citizens. A sensible public debate would focus on how to make that total price as low as possible.

Responding to Reading

1. According to Reich, why do some people oppose Wal-Mart? What does he mean when he says that Wal-Mart is "really being punished for our sins" (2)?
2. What does Reich mean when he says that today's economy "offers us a Faustian bargain" (6)? Do you think this Faustian bargain is fair? Do you think it is inevitable?
3. What does Reich think should be done to address the problem he identifies? Why does he think his "inner consumer" (10) will not like the suggestions he proposes?

Responding in Writing

How do the interests of "workers," "citizens," and "consumers" differ? Which interests do you see as most important, and why?

DELUSIONS OF GRANDEUR
Henry Louis Gates, Jr.
1950–

Henry Louis Gates, Jr., earned a Ph.D. (1979) in English literature from Clare College at the University of Cambridge, where he was the first African American to do so. At age thirty, he received a MacArthur Foundation Genius Grant (1980). He has taught at Yale, Cornell, Duke, and Harvard. One of Gates's best-known works is Loose Canons: Notes on the Culture Wars *(1992), in which he discusses gender, literature, and multiculturalism in American arts and letters. His latest book is* In Search of Our Roots: How Nineteen Extraordinary African Americans Reclaimed Their Past *(2009). He is general editor of* The Norton Anthology of African-American Literature, *second edition (2003); a staff writer for the* New Yorker; *and the author of essays, reviews, and profiles in many other publications. In the following essay, Gates points out how few African Americans actually succeed as professional athletes and argues that the schools should do more to encourage young black men to pursue more realistic goals.*

Standing at the bar of an all-black VFW post in my hometown of Piedmont, W.Va., I offered five dollars to anyone who could tell me how many African-American professional athletes were at work today. There are 35 million African-Americans, I said.

"Ten million!" yelled one intrepid soul, too far into his cups.

"No way...more like 500,000," said another.

"You mean *all* professional sports," someone interjected, "including golf and tennis, but not counting the brothers from Puerto Rico?" Everyone laughed.

"Fifty thousand, minimum," was another guess.   5

Here are the facts:

There are 1,200 black professional athletes in the U.S.
There are 12 times more black lawyers than black athletes.
There are $2\frac{1}{2}$ times more black dentists than black athletes.
There are 15 times more black doctors than black athletes.

Nobody in my local VFW believed these statistics; in fact, few people would believe them if they weren't reading them in the pages of *Sports Illustrated*. In spite of these statistics, too many African-American youngsters still believe that they have a much better chance of becoming another Magic Johnson or Michael Jordan than they do of matching the achievements of Baltimore Mayor Kurt Schmoke or neurosurgeon Dr. Benjamin Carson, both of whom, like Johnson and Jordan, are black.

In reality, an African-American youngster has about as much chance of becoming a professional athlete as he or she does of winning the lottery. The tragedy for our people, however, is that few of us accept that truth.

Let me confess that I love sports. Like most black people of my generation—I'm 40—I was raised to revere the great black athletic heroes, and I never tired of listening to the stories of triumph and defeat that, for blacks, amount to a collective epic much like those of the ancient Greeks: Joe Louis's demolition of Max Schmeling; Satchel Paige's dazzling repertoire of pitches; Jesse Owens's in-your-face performance in Hitler's 1936 Olympics; Willie Mays's over-the-shoulder basket catch; Jackie Robinson's quiet strength when assaulted by racist taunts; and a thousand other grand tales.

10   Nevertheless, the blind pursuit of attainment in sports is having a devastating effect on our people. Imbued with a belief that our principal avenue to fame and profit is through sport, and seduced by a win-at-any-cost system that corrupts even elementary school students, far too many black kids treat basketball courts and football fields as if they were classrooms in an alternative school system. "O.K., I flunked English," a young athlete will say. "But I got an A plus in slamdunking."

The failure of our public schools to educate athletes is part and parcel of the schools' failure to educate almost everyone. A recent survey of the Philadelphia school system, for example, stated that "more than half of all students in the third, fifth and eighth grades cannot perform minimum math and language tasks." One in four middle school students in that city fails to pass to the next grade each year. It is a sad truth that such statistics are repeated in cities throughout the nation. Young athletes—particularly young black athletes—are especially ill-served. Many of them are functionally illiterate, yet they are passed along from year to year for the greater glory of good old Hometown High. We should not be surprised to learn, then, that only 26.6% of black athletes at the collegiate level earn their degrees. For every successful educated black professional athlete, there are thousands of dead and wounded. Yet young blacks continue to aspire to careers as athletes, and it's no wonder why; when the University of North Carolina recently commissioned a sculptor to create archetypes of its student body, guess which ethnic group was selected to represent athletes?

Those relatively few black athletes who do make it in the professional ranks must be prevailed upon to play a significant role in the education of all of our young people, athlete and nonathlete alike. While some have done so, many others have shirked their social obligations: to earmark small percentages of their incomes for the United Negro College Fund; to appear on television for educational purposes rather than merely to sell sneakers; to let children know the message that becoming a lawyer, a teacher or a doctor does more good for our people than winning the Super Bowl; and to form productive liaisons with educators to help forge solutions to the many ills that beset the black community. These are merely a few modest proposals.

A similar burden falls upon successful blacks in all walks of life. Each of us must strive to make our young people understand the realities. Tell them to cheer Bo Jackson but to emulate novelist Toni Morrison or businessman Reginald Lewis or historian John Hope Franklin or Spelman College president Johnetta Cole—the list is long.

Of course, society as a whole bears responsibility as well. Until colleges stop using young blacks as cannon fodder in the big-business wars of so-called nonprofessional sports, until training a young black's mind becomes as important as training his or her body, we will continue to perpetuate a system akin to that of the Roman gladiators, sacrificing a class of people for the entertainment of the mob.

Responding to Reading

1. Why does Gates begin his essay with an anecdote? What does this story reveal about African Americans' assumptions about sports? According to Gates, what harm do these assumptions do?
2. What does Gates mean when he says, "The failure of our public schools to educate athletes is part and parcel of the schools' failure to educate almost everyone" (11)? Do you agree? In addition to the public schools, who or what else could be responsible for the situation Gates describes?
3. What does Gates mean when he says that colleges are using young blacks as "cannon fodder" (14)? According to Gates, how are young black athletes like Roman gladiators? Do you think that this comparison is accurate? fair?

Responding in Writing

What were your reactions to the statistics presented in paragraph 6? Write the text of a children's picture book designed to convey this information accurately to preschoolers.

FICTION

A & P

John Updike

1932–2009

One of the most influential and prolific American authors of the twentieth century, John Updike was a fiction writer, poet, playwright, and essayist. He published numerous novels, poetry collections, and essay collections, and his work frequently appeared in the New Yorker *and the* New York Review of Books, *among other publications. His last books, both published posthumously in 2009, are* Endpoint and Other Poems *and* My Father's Tears and Other Stories. *In the following 1961 short story, Updike captures the experience of a young man working in a New England supermarket.*

In walks these three girls in nothing but bathing suits. I'm in the third check-out slot, with my back to the door, so I don't see them until they're over by the bread. The one that caught my eye first was the one in the plaid green two-piece. She was a chunky kid, with a good tan and a sweet broad soft-looking can with those two crescents of white just under it, where the sun never seems to hit, at the top of the backs of her legs. I stood there with my hand on a box of HiHo crackers trying to remember if I rang it up or not. I ring it up again and the customer starts giving me hell. She's one of these cash-register-watchers, a witch about fifty with rouge on her cheekbones and no eyebrows, and I know it made her day to trip me up. She'd been watching cash registers forty years and probably never seen a mistake before.

By the time I got her feathers smoothed and her goodies into a bag—she gives me a little snort in passing, if she'd been born at the right time they would have burned her over in Salem—by the time I get her on her way the girls had circled around the bread and were coming back, without a pushcart, back my way along the counters, in the aisle between the check-outs and the Special bins. They didn't even have shoes on. There was this chunky one, with the two-piece—it was bright green and the seams on the bra were still sharp and her belly was still pretty pale so I guessed she just got it (the suit)—there was this one, with one of those chubby berry-faces, the lips all bunched together under her nose, this one, and a tall one, with black hair that hadn't quite frizzed right, and one of these sunburns right across under the eyes, and a chin that was too long—you know, the kind of girl other girls think is very "striking" and "attractive" but never quite makes it, as they very well know, which is why they like her so much—and then the third one, that wasn't quite so tall. She was the queen. She kind of led them, the other two peeking around and making their shoulders round. She didn't look around, not this queen, she just walked straight on slowly, on these long white prima donna legs. She came down a little hard on her heels, as if she didn't walk in her bare feet that much, putting down her heels and then letting the weight move along to her toes as if she was testing the floor with every step, putting a little deliberate extra action into it. You never know for sure how girls' minds work (do you really think it's a mind in there or just a little buzz like a bee in a glass jar?) but you got the idea she had talked the other two into coming in here with her, and now she was showing them how to do it, walk slow and hold yourself straight.

She had on a kind of dirty-pink—beige maybe, I don't know— bathing suit with a little nubble all over it and, what got me, the straps were down. They were off her shoulders looped loose around the cool tops of her arms, and I guess as a result the suit had slipped a little on her, so all around the top of the cloth there was this shining rim. If it hadn't been there you wouldn't have known there could have been anything whiter than those shoulders. With the straps pushed off, there was nothing between the top of the suit and the top of her head except just her, this clean bare plane of the top of her chest down from the shoulder bones like a dented sheet of metal tilted in the light. I mean, it was more than pretty.

She had sort of oaky hair that the sun and salt had bleached, done up in a bun that was unravelling, and a kind of prim face. Walking into the A & P with your straps down, I suppose it's the only kind of face you *can* have. She held her head so high her neck, coming up out of those white shoulders, looked kind of stretched, but I didn't mind. The longer her neck was, the more of her there was.

She must have felt in the corner of her eye me and over my shoul- 5 der Stokesie in the second slot watching, but she didn't tip. Not this queen. She kept her eyes moving across the racks, and stopped, and turned so slow it made my stomach rub the inside of my apron, and buzzed to the other two, who kind of huddled against her for relief, and they all three of them went up the cat-and-dog-food-breakfast-cereal-macaroni-rice-raisins-seasonings-spreads-spaghetti-soft drinks-crackers-and-cookies aisle. From the third slot I look straight up this aisle to the meat counter, and I watched them all the way. The fat one with the tan sort of fumbled with the cookies, but on second thought she put the packages back. The sheep pushing their carts down the aisle— the girls were walking against the usual traffic (not that we have one-way signs or anything)—were pretty hilarious. You could see them, when Queenie's white shoulders dawned on them, kind of jerk, or hop, or hiccup, but their eyes snapped back to their own baskets and on they pushed. I bet you could set off dynamite in an A & P and the people would by and large keep reaching and checking oatmeal off their lists and muttering "Let me see, there was a third thing, began with A, asparagus, no, ah, yes, applesauce!" or whatever it is they do mutter. But there was no doubt, this jiggled them. A few house-slaves in pin curlers even looked around after pushing their carts past to make sure what they had seen was correct.

You know, it's one thing to have a girl in a bathing suit down on the beach, where what with the glare nobody can look at each other much anyway, and another thing in the cool of the A & P, under the fluorescent lights, against all those stacked packages, with her feet paddling along naked over our checkerboard green-and-cream rubber-tile floor.

"Oh Daddy," Stokesie said beside me. "I feel so faint."

"Darling," I said. "Hold me tight." Stokesie's married, with two babies chalked up on his fuselage already, but as far as I can tell that's the only difference. He's twenty-two, and I was nineteen this April.

"Is it done?" he asks, the responsible married man finding his voice. I forgot to say he thinks he's going to be manager some sunny day, maybe in 1990 when it's called the Great Alexandrov and Petrooshki Tea Company or something.

10   What he meant was, our town is five miles from a beach, with a big summer colony out on the Point, but we're right in the middle of town, and the women generally put on a shirt or shorts or something before they get out of the car into the street. And anyway these are usually women with six children and varicose veins mapping their legs and nobody, including them, could care less. As I say, we're right in the middle of town, and if you stand at our front doors you can see two banks and the Congregational church and the newspaper store and three real-estate offices and about twenty-seven old free-loaders tearing up Central Street because the sewer broke again. It's not as if we're on the Cape; we're north of Boston and there's people in this town haven't seen the ocean for twenty years.

The girls had reached the meat counter and were asking McMahon something. He pointed, they pointed, and they shuffled out of sight behind a pyramid of Diet Delight peaches. All that was left for us to see was old McMahon patting his mouth and looking after them sizing up their joints. Poor kids, I began to feel sorry for them, they couldn't help it.

Now here comes the sad part of the story, at least my family says it's sad but I don't think it's sad myself. The store's pretty empty, it being Thursday afternoon, so there was nothing much to do except lean on the register and wait for the girls to show up again. The whole store was like a pinball machine and I didn't know which tunnel they'd come out of. After a while they come around out of the far aisle, around the light bulbs, records at discount of the Caribbean Six or Tony Martin Sings or some such gunk you wonder they waste the wax on, sixpacks of candy bars, and plastic toys done up in cellophane that fall apart when a kid looks at them anyway. Around they come, Queenie still leading the way, and holding a little gray jar in her hand. Slots Three through Seven are unmanned and I could see her wondering between Stokes and me, but Stokesie with his usual luck draws an old party in baggy gray pants who stumbles up with four giant cans of pineapple juice (what do these bums *do* with all that pineapple juice? I've often asked myself) so the girls come to me. Queenie puts down the jar and I take it into my fingers icy cold. Kingfish Fancy Herring Snacks in Pure Sour Cream: 49¢. Now her hands are empty, not a ring or a bracelet, bare as God made them, and I wonder where the money's coming from. Still with that prim look she lifts a folded dollar bill out of the hollow at the center of her nubbled pink top. The jar went heavy in my hand. Really, I thought that was so cute.

Then everybody's luck begins to run out. Lengel comes in from haggling with a truck full of cabbages on the lot and is about to scuttle into that door marked MANAGER behind which he hides all day when the girls touch his eye. Lengel's pretty dreary, teaches Sunday school and the rest, but he doesn't miss that much. He comes over and says, "Girls, this isn't the beach."

Queenie blushes, though maybe it's just a brush of sunburn I was noticing for the first time, now that she was so close. "My mother asked me to pick up a jar of herring snacks." Her voice kind of startled me, the way voices do when you see the people first, coming out so flat and dumb yet kind of tony, too, the way it ticked over "pick up" and "snacks." All of a sudden I slid right down her voice into her living room. Her father and the other men were standing around in ice-cream coats and bow ties and the women were in sandals picking up herring snacks on toothpicks off a big plate and they were all holding drinks the color of water with olives and sprigs of mint in them. When my parents have somebody over they get lemonade and if it's a real racy affair Schlitz in tall glasses with "They'll Do It Every Time" cartoons stencilled on.

"That's all right," Lengel said. "But this isn't the beach." His repeating this struck me as funny, as if it had just occurred to him, and he had been thinking all these years the A & P was a great big dune and he was the head lifeguard. He didn't like my smiling—as I say he doesn't miss much—but he concentrates on giving the girls that sad Sunday-school-superintendent stare.

Queenie's blush is no sunburn now, and the plump one in plaid, that I liked better from the back—a really sweet can—pipes up, "We weren't doing any shopping. We just came in for the one thing." 15

"That makes no difference," Lengel tells her, and I could see from the way his eyes went that he hadn't noticed she was wearing a two-piece before. "We want you decently dressed when you come in here."

"We are decent," Queenie says suddenly, her lower lip pushing, getting sore now that she remembers her place, a place from which the crowd that runs the A & P must look pretty crummy. Fancy Herring Snacks flashed in her very blue eyes.

"Girls, I don't want to argue with you. After this come in here with your shoulders covered. It's our policy." He turns his back. That's policy for you. Policy is what the kingpins want. What the others want is juvenile delinquency.

All this while, the customers had been showing up with their carts but, you know, sheep, seeing a scene, they had all bunched up on Stokesie, who shook open a paper bag as gently as peeling a peach, not wanting to miss a word. I could feel in the silence everybody getting nervous, most of all Lengel, who asks me, "Sammy, have you rung up this purchase?"

20   I thought and said "No" but it wasn't about that I was thinking. I go through the punches, 4, 9, GROC, TOT—it's more complicated than you think, and after you do it often enough, it begins to make a little song, that you hear words to, in my case "Hello (*bing*) there, you (*gung*) hap-py pee-pul (*splat*)"—the splat being the drawer flying out. I uncrease the bill, tenderly as you may imagine, it just having come from between the two smoothest scoops of vanilla I had ever known were there, and pass a half and a penny into her narrow pink palm, and nestle the herrings in a bag and twist its neck and hand it over, all the time thinking.

The girls, and who'd blame them, are in a hurry to get out, so I say "I quit" to Lengel quick enough for them to hear, hoping they'll stop and watch me, their unsuspected hero. They keep right on going, into the electric eye; the door flies open and they flicker across the lot to their car, Queenie and Plaid and Big Tall Goony-Goony (not that as raw material she was so bad), leaving me with Lengel and a kink in his eyebrow.

"Did you say something, Sammy?"

"I said I quit."

"I thought you did."

25   "You didn't have to embarrass them."

"It was they who were embarrassing us."

I started to say something that came out "Fiddle-de-doo." It's a saying of my grandmother's, and I know she would have been pleased.

"I don't think you know what you're saying," Lengel said.

"I know you don't," I said. "But I do." I pull the bow at the back of my apron and start shrugging it off my shoulders. A couple customers that had been heading for my slot begin to knock against each other, like scared pigs in a chute.

30   Lengel sighs and begins to look very patient and old and gray. He's been a friend of my parents for years. "Sammy, you don't want to do this to your Mom and Dad," he tells me. It's true, I don't. But it seems to me

that once you begin a gesture it's fatal not to go through with it. I fold the apron, "Sammy" stitched in red on the pocket, and put it on the counter, and drop the bow tie on top of it. The bow tie is theirs, if you've ever wondered. "You'll feel this for the rest of your life," Lengel says, and I know that's true, too, but remembering how he made that pretty girl blush makes me so scrunchy inside I punch the No Sale tab and the machine whirs "pee-pul" and the drawer splats out. One advantage to this scene taking place in summer, I can follow this up with a clean exit, there's no fumbling around getting your coat and galoshes, I just saunter into the electric eye in my white shirt that my mother ironed the night before, and the door heaves itself open, and outside the sunshine is skating around on the asphalt.

I look around for my girls, but they're gone, of course. There wasn't anybody but some young married screaming with her children about some candy they didn't get by the door of a powder-blue Falcon station wagon. Looking back in the big windows, over the bags of peat moss and aluminum lawn furniture stacked on the pavement, I could see Lengel in my place in the slot, checking the sheep through. His face was dark gray and his back stiff, as if he'd just had an injection of iron, and my stomach kind of fell as I felt how hard the world was going to be to me hereafter.

Responding to Reading

1. What is Sammy's attitude toward his job? toward Lengel, the store manager? toward the customers of the A&P? What words and phrases in the story lead you to your conclusions?
2. How accurate are Sammy's judgments about Queenie and her friends? How would these characters be described if Lengel were telling the story?
3. Why does Sammy quit his job? Is his quitting some form of rebellion, or does he do it for some other reason? What do you think Sammy is trying to accomplish with this action? (Consider all possible motives.)

Responding in Writing

If you were in Sammy's place, would you have made the same choice he did? Why or why not?

———————————— FOCUS ————————————

Is Outsourcing Bad for America?

Workers at computers in an outsourcing center in Rangreth, on the outskirts of Srinagar

Responding to the Image

1. What is your initial response to this photograph? After reading the essays in this Focus section, has your response changed in any way?
2. Do you think outsourcing is good for the United States? For the people of Kashmir? What impression of outsourcing does the photo convey?

Let Someone Else Do It: The Impulse Behind Everything

Cullen Murphy

1952–

Managing editor at the Atlantic Monthly *magazine, Cullen Murphy has written numerous articles on political, linguistic, and religious issues. He has published four books, most recently* Are We Rome? The Fall of an Empire and the Fate of America *(2007). In the following essay, Murphy examines the social, political, and religious implications of outsourcing.*

The terminology of economics—"marginal utility," "vertical equity," "asymmetric information"—is not, by and large, the stuff of deep public passion. But in recent years one economic term has become hot to the touch. The term is "outsourcing," which refers to the spinning off of job functions from one place to another, and especially to the export of jobs from high-wage America to low-wage countries such as India and China. Both presidential candidates have expressed concern about outsourcing, which has devastated some of the most vigorously contested swing states, even as economists debate the overall pluses and minuses of outsourcing in the long run. What nobody disputes is that outsourcing has been occurring, that the pace is picking up, and that it affects all economic sectors and levels of management. Indeed, much of the job of President of the United States seems to have been outsourced to a lower-wage Vice President.

But it would be a mistake to think of outsourcing as simply an economic transaction; it is a universal tendency, like gravity, that exerts a pull on everything. It may be helpful to think in terms of a fourth law of thermodynamics. The first law, you'll recall, holds that the amount of matter and energy in the universe is constant. The second holds that the default direction of everything is toward entropy. The third law … well, never mind. The fourth law, newly postulated, holds that outsourcing—getting others to do things for you—is the intrinsic vector of all human activity.

National governments, for instance, once cherished their vaunted "monopoly on violence"; this was among the chief attributes of sovereignty. The war in Iraq has made Americans aware of the extent to which military functions have been outsourced to corporations like Halliburton, Bechtel, and DynCorp. Of course, armies never provided everything for themselves (the toilet paper inside meals-ready-to-eat, for example, comes from a $1.4 million contract to the Rose Resnick Lighthouse for the Blind and Visually Impaired, in Oakland), but core military functions such as building bases, guarding depots, and conducting surveillance are increasingly private-sector affairs. So, too, sometimes, is torture, as the Abu Ghraib scandal reveals, although the more common practice is for squeamish governments (i.e., ours) to outsource problematic interrogations to less squeamish governments (Cairo, Manila)—a practice that goes by the artfully bland term "rendition." Even the political task of educating Iraqis about the virtues of democracy has been outsourced—in this instance not to an American company but to a British public-relations firm, Bell Pottinger, which received a $5.6 million contract to produce promotional commercials for use on Iraqi television. (Bell Pottinger's chairman, Lord Tim Bell, previously oversaw publicity for Margaret Thatcher.)

Outsourcing extends into areas one might never have expected. The United States, seemingly self-sufficient in its own territory, has been outsourcing itself for years, at least when it comes to movie and television locales. New York is often played by (cheap) Toronto. The Appalachian settings in the movie Cold Mountain were played by (even cheaper) Romania. It used to be that standing in line for a driver's license or a government hearing, or to buy tickets, was the sort of thing one pretty much had to do for oneself. This function, too, is outsourceable. Today the "service expediter" industry provides human substitutes (for up to $30 an hour) who will save a place until your turn arrives. It's hard to see how this industry could ever be moved offshore to people in Thailand or Indonesia, but God help anyone needing a license if it is.

5   According to the *Chronicle of Higher Education*, the diploma-mill industry is being outsourced. There have long been unaccredited educational institutions in America willing for a fee to offer fast-track doctorates, and fly-by-night companies willing to send out handsome facsimile transcripts ("for amusement purposes only"), but the nation's homegrown diploma mills are now being undermined by competition from abroad. The Jerusalem-based University Degree Program has sold more than 30,000 advanced degrees of various kinds, from nonexistent institutions such as Ashbourne University and the University of Palmers Green. (There is even a phone number employers can call to confirm a job applicant's claims.) A China-based company called BackAlleyPress.com sells official-looking fake transcripts from real universities, custom-made to suit every educational need.

Demographic realities create urgent outsourcing needs. The shortage of Catholic priests in America has resulted in a grave backlog of prayers and masses. When the devout request special prayers of thanksgiving or remembrance, often to be said for years at a time, the requests (and monetary offerings) are increasingly outsourced to India, whose Catholic priests are giving the notion of service expediter a whole new dimension. Asked about this by *The New York Times,* a spokesman for the Catholic Church commented, "The prayer is heartfelt, and every prayer is treated as the same whether it is paid for in dollars, euros, or rupees."

If spiritual succor can be outsourced, so, presumably, can other ineffable qualities and pursuits. A bit of a fuss was caused some years ago when it was revealed that clergymen in the United States had been outsourcing their sermons—buying them from an online "sermon mill." But the entire range of human expression, from toasts by a best man to eulogies by a grieving friend, can now be acquired at a factory outlet. InstantWeddingToasts.com sells fill-in-the-blank templates to help clients create a memorable wedding speech. "In about five painless minutes, you'll have a wedding speech ready to go…without writing!"

In America we've been outsourcing the idea of personal responsibility for years. The old-fashioned moral stance is the one articulated in Julius Caesar: "The fault, dear Brutus, is not in the stars but in ourselves." That was before the "Twinkie defense," which attributed a murderer's actions to elevated blood-sugar levels brought on by vigorous snacking on junk food. The dispositions of diet, the lash of upbringing, the twist of genetics—targets of other-directed blame have become only more plentiful. A killer in Eustis, Florida, cited the fantasy role-playing game Vampire: The Masquerade as the catalyst of the alleged mental illness that formed the basis of his defense. In another case, according to a newspaper account, a man in Panama City, Florida, "claimed drinking jasmine tea caused him to go temporarily insane before he smashed his way into a neighbor's house and chased the woman with a large dagger." The charges against him were dropped.

Outsourcing has been with us from the very beginning. Think of slavery, a fundamental form of outsourcing. On a macro scale, the great imperial systems of history have been exercises in outsourcing. No doubt one of the earliest forms of outsourcing was the delegation of one's intellectual chores to a support staff of consultants.

Middle-class Americans today have typically outsourced a vast pro- 10 portion of child care, food preparation, and money handling. With the help of personal concierges, many higher-end Americans also have outsourced the great bulk of their interpersonal relationships. Reproduction itself is often outsourced (by means of sperm and egg donors and in vitro fertilization), and people needing various kinds of human tissue for purposes of repair increasingly seek outsourced components in the developing world, where life is cheap and so are kidneys.

And I must confess that much of this column was in fact outsourced to subcontracting facilities in Bangalore and Nogales, where I've been told that quality control is adequate and language issues should present no cause for concern. To be sure, there are glitches still to be worked out (for instance, the previous sentence originally came off the assembly line as "where I've been told that quality control is jolly good and language issues should present no problema"). But I can assure you that the sentiments expressed herein remain heartfelt, whether paid for in dollars, euros, or rupees.

CHAPTER 7 FOCUS

Responding to Reading

1. What is the meaning of the term *outsourcing?* What does Murphy mean when he says that outsourcing "is a universal tendency, like gravity, that exerts a pull on everything" (2)?
2. Murphy applies the concept of outsourcing to areas such as politics, the war in Iraq, education, religion, and childcare. Are these applications of the term justified? Convincing?
3. Murphy makes several references to contemporary politics. Do these references strengthen or weaken his case? What do these remarks tell you about how he views his audience?

Responding in Writing

Do you think the government should act to limit outsourcing? Or, do you believe that the decision to outsource should be left up to individual businesses?

MISSED TARGET: IS OUTSOURCING REALLY SO BAD?

Clay Risen

1976–

Clay Risen is managing editor at Democracy: A Journal of Ideas, *opinion editor at* Flak *magazine, and a contributing writer for* Morning News *magazine. His work includes articles about various political and economic issues as well as film, television, book, and music reviews. In the following essay, Risen considers the problem of outsourcing and attempts to allay Americans' fears about its scope and its impact.*

Ask folks in Silicon Valley these days about their biggest fear, and you likely won't hear about Osama bin Laden, global warming, or failing schools. These days, everyone's afraid of offshore outsourcing—the movement of white-collar jobs, especially in the high-tech sector, from the United States to foreign countries, where the labor is cheap, plentiful, and, increasingly, well-educated. "There's an increased level of anxiety about what the economy's going to be like," says Marcus Courtney, president of the Washington Alliance of Technology Workers. "People who entered this field thought it was going to be a career for twenty years, and now their jobs are gone." And they may not be coming back. "America is short of jobs as never before, and the major candidates for our offshore outsourcing are ramping up employment as never before," Stephen Roach, chief economist at Morgan Stanley, recently told the *New York Times*. "[T]hese jobs are, by [and] large, lost forever."

Predictably, politicians and the media have been quick to pick up on these fears. "tech workers struggle to answer overseas threat," noted a *New York Times* headline in November. And United Press International claimed recently that the financial benefits of offshoring would "come with a hefty price tag, with significant economic as well as social consequences." In turn, a growing number in Congress have called for a raft of anti-offshoring measures, from tax incentives to keep jobs offshore to bans on using foreign labor for government projects; Senators George Voinovich and Craig Thomas, for example, added an amendment to the 2004 Transportation and Treasury appropriations bill that would prevent contractors from using overseas labor to complete some federal contracts. And, on the op-ed page of the *New York Times,* Senator Charles Schumer recently asked "whether the case for free trade…is undermined by the changes now evident in the modern global economy," particularly offshore outsourcing. His answer? A resounding "yes." Offshore outsourcing, especially to developing powerhouses like China and India, has become this decade's "giant sucking sound."

But, like the fears that surrounded NAFTA, those around offshoring are mostly baseless. While offshoring is definitely an economic trend, there is no statistical evidence pointing to the massive employment drain activists call the "coring out" of America's best jobs. In fact, recent studies show that the opposite is true: While offshoring may displace some workers in the short term, in the medium and long terms it represents a net benefit for both domestic businesses and their workers. In fact, the greatest threat from outsourcing is that its opponents will use it to force a new wave of protectionism.

The frenzy over offshoring got going in late 2002, when Forrester Research released a startling study showing that 3.3 million white-collar jobs would move overseas by 2015. Then, in July of last year, the research firm Gartner trotted out its own study saying that as many as 5 percent of all information technology (I.T.) jobs could move abroad between mid-2003 and the end of 2004. And a 2003 report from Deloitte Research said that the top 100 financial-services firms plan to move $356 billion in operations and two million jobs overseas in the next five years.

But those numbers aren't as scary as they sound. For one thing, 5 while offshore outsourcing is definitely occurring, it's difficult to say just how large a trend it is at present. The Forrester research is based primarily on surveys of business leaders who are merely speculating about future offshoring decisions they might make: "There is no objective data to prove all these jobs are going overseas," says Michaela Platzer of the AeA (formerly the American Electronics Association). "There's just a lot of anecdotal evidence." Some point to the jobless recovery as evidence of offshoring's impact, but the lack of jobs is just as likely the result of booming productivity and the economy's (until recently)

CHAPTER 7   FOCUS

anemic pace. "I think people are confusing the business cycle with long-term trends," says Daniel Griswold, an economist at the Cato Institute. "People are looking for someone to blame. They say, 'Aha, it's because our jobs are moving to India.' If you look at the late 1990s, though, all these globalizing phenomena were going on." In other words, it wasn't that offshoring practices changed; it was that the economy slowed.

What's more, economists don't even agree on how such data could be collected—for example, many offshoring moves represent not a direct shift of a given job overseas but rather its restructuring, which in turn might create a new job overseas as well as a new job, with a new job description, in the United States. Such restructuring is particularly prevalent in high-tech fields like software and data management—for example, an America employee might be tasked with the design, implementation, and testing of a software program; under restructuring, his employer might hire an Indian, at one-tenth the cost, to do the implementation and testing and then hire an American to do the design work. IBM for example, plans to offshore 3,000 programming jobs this year. But, at the same time, it will also create 5,000 jobs in the United States. Does that count as jobs lost, jobs gained, or both? "[Offshoring is] going to lead to individual job loss," says Gary Burtless, an economist at Brookings, "but that does not mean it will lead to aggregate loss of employment in the United States."

Even if there were a short-term loss of jobs, the losses would likely have a more muted effect on the economy than the factory flight of the 1980s and '90s, when most factory workers had to undergo intensive retraining in order to find new jobs. White-collar workers tend to be, both in terms of skills and career perspective, more capable of moving on to other jobs. Another mitigating factor is the wide dispersal of high-tech jobs throughout the country; unlike manufacturing, which tends to clump hundreds or thousands of jobs in the same factory or town, high-tech work can be done anywhere. For example, one of the job sectors frequently cited as "offshoring prone" is medical transcription. Although it's a $15 billion industry, medical-transcription work is almost always farmed out to small firms around the country; even if all of them closed, the impact on any one community would be small.

And, while Forrester's 3.3 million jobs estimate may sound like a lot, keep in mind that it's a loss spread out over 15 years (2000–2015)—just 220,000 jobs annually. Furthermore, Forrester isn't talking about net job loss, but rather gross loss. In fact, even during periods of fast job growth, the U.S. economy sheds hundreds of thousands of jobs each year; it's simply robust enough to make up for the loss. In 1999, a year the economy produced a net 1.13 million jobs, it shed 2.5 million. But few argued that those job cuts were bad for the economy; in fact, most economists would argue they were beneficial, because they allowed companies to structure their operations more efficiently.

Offshoring is no different. In a sense, offshoring is simply the radical extension of the "creative destruction" processes that many credit as a driving force behind the '90s boom. Under the mantra "focus on what you do best," companies have been outsourcing non-core operations (such as human resources and call centers) for years; it is only with the emergence of high-quality telecommunications links that those operations have begun to move offshore. Unburdened by such ancillary concerns, companies are free to focus on—and innovate within—their core businesses, in turn creating new jobs, even new industries. "The standard arguments for free trade exist in this case," says Josh Bivens, an economist at the Economy Policy Institute. "I think the United States could see a productivity gain through this kind of trade." Meanwhile, the bulk of jobs that the Forrester survey claims will be outsourced are hardly the sorts of jobs on which the U.S. economy depends. "The lower-level jobs, the programming jobs, a lot of them will not be done in this country," says Stephanie Moore, an outsourcing expert at Giga, an economic research firm. In their place, she says, "New jobs are going to be created. Citibank will never let an Indian vendor manage its retail-banking operations."

Indeed, recent studies delving beyond the Forrester and Gartner 10 numbers indicate that, despite the impact of short-term job loss, offshore outsourcing represents a net economic benefit for the United States. According to the McKinsey Global Institute, for every dollar a U.S. company spends on offshoring to India, the U.S. economy gains $1.14, thanks to a number of factors: savings from the increased operational efficiency, equipment sales to Indian outsourcers, the value of American labor reemployed to higher-wage jobs, and repatriated earnings by U.S. companies that own Indian outsourcing firms. "The recent changes driving offshoring are not that different or radical from the changes that dynamic, competitive, technologically evolving economies have experienced for the last few decades," the report concludes.

None of this, of course, has stopped antioffshoring critics from calling for restrictions. In 2002, after Shirley Turner, a New Jersey state representative, learned that calls to the state's welfare and food-stamps programs were being routed to a call center in Mumbai, she introduced a bill that would block foreign firms from working on state-funded projects. The bill created a firestorm in the I.T. community, with most workers supporting Turner. "I've been in the legislature now for ten years, and I have never received as much correspondence from people as I have with this bill," she told *USA Today*. Similar legislation has popped up in six other states. And, though none of those bills have been approved, observers say they'll likely pick up steam as the November elections approach. "I would expect that those bills will reemerge," says Information Technology Association of America President Harris Miller. "And, given it's an election year in most states, the likelihood of passage will be much higher." Anti-outsourcing fever is also growing in Congress, where a raft of bills has been introduced to limit the number of visas available for skilled laborers. The USA Jobs Protection Act, introduced by Senator Chris Dodd and Representative Nancy Johnson, would prevent U.S. companies from hiring foreign workers when American workers are available for the same job.

But there's little reason to believe these sorts of plans could stanch job contractions, even if they did manage to prevent jobs from going offshore. Particularly during rough economic times, the need to cut costs is an absolute priority, and, if offshoring weren't a possibility, domestic jobs would still likely be cut. "The choice isn't outsourcing or keeping jobs here," says Griswold. "It's outsourcing or going out of business. Which isn't good for jobs. This is an absolute necessity for many companies." If companies were somehow prevented from shipping jobs offshore, they would likely turn to other methods of reducing labor costs, such as technological upgrades—a process that has resulted in job loss since the birth of capitalism. "It's striking that people have less sympathy if those people are replaced by machines than if they are replaced by foreign workers," says Burtless. "It's all part of the same phenomenon of trying to squeeze value out of the same resources."

But, while offshoring-related protectionism may stifle economic development and unnecessarily force business closures, its biggest impact may be longer term. That's because, as the baby-boomers move into retirement, the size of the working population will decline precipitously, by 5 percent by 2015, according to the McKinsey report. Without a readily available source of high-quality, young labor—i.e., the sort provided by offshore outsourcing—the country could find itself in a sort of economic sclerosis. Growth could be permanently hamstrung by the high labor costs and booming social spending that have turned Germany, where it's extraordinarily difficult for companies to lay off employees, from an economic engine into a plodding giant. As Carl Steidtmann, chief economist for Deloitte Research, wrote recently, "Restrictive employment laws in Europe go a long way toward explaining why Europe consistently runs a higher rate of unemployment when contrasted with the U.S. or Britain."

Nevertheless, the fact that there are benefits to offshore outsourcing doesn't mean we should sit back and let it ride. At the individual level, job loss is a painful process, and there is no guarantee that even a relatively mobile white-collar worker whose job is outsourced will be able to find a new one, let alone at the same wage. The response, however, isn't to fight against offshoring but to find ways to alleviate its negative effects. One approach—advocated by Lori Kletzer, a senior fellow at the Institute for International Economics, and Robert Litan of the Brookings Institution—is to require companies to purchase "outsourcing insurance," which would cover a portion of displaced employees' salaries for a fixed period of time in the event their jobs are outsourced. Not only would this help alleviate the pain of layoffs, but it would force companies to internalize the economic cost of their outsourcing decisions. The McKinsey report, which also favors this approach, argues that, "as offshoring volumes rise, the insurance premiums will increase, cutting into the gains from offshoring and, thereby, making offshoring less attractive to companies in periods of high unemployment."

The most obvious and, in the global economy, most necessary solution, however, is worker training. The Trade Adjustment Assistance program already provides assistance to workers displaced by NAFTA-related factory closings; a similar program could easily be crafted to respond to offshore outsourcing. Indeed, requiring companies that outsource to contribute a portion of their savings to training programs would both internalize the cost and provide the necessary funds. And job training would not only alleviate periods of protracted unemployment; by making workers more agile, it would also make the U.S. economy more efficient and productive. Indeed, thanks to its combination of high job mobility and a highly educated work force, one of the U.S. economy's greatest strengths is its ability to redeploy workers quickly without dramatic cuts in their wages. And, thanks to that flexibility, notes the McKinsey report, "Over the past 10 years, the U.S. economy has created a total of 35 million new private sector jobs." It would be ironic if, in an effort to protect jobs, we closed off one of the most powerful means by which they are created. 15

Responding to Reading

1. According to Risen, why are workers concerned about outsourcing? How have politicians responded to these fears?
2. Why does Risen think that the fears surrounding outsourcing are "mostly baseless" (3)? What evidence does he present to support this opinion?
3. According to Risen, what is the best way to respond to outsourcing? Why is he against protectionism? What does he mean when he says, "It would be ironic if, in an effort to protect jobs, we closed off one of the most powerful means by which they are created" (15)?

Responding in Writing

Are people who lose their jobs because of outsourcing different from other unemployed Americans? Do you think they should get special help from the government?

FAIR EXCHANGE: WHO BENEFITS FROM OUTSOURCING?

Albino Barrera

Professor of economics and theology at Providence College, Albino Barrera often writes about the religious implications of economic policy. He has written four books, most recently Globalization and Economic Ethics: Distributive Justice in the Knowledge Economy *(2007). The following essay makes a moral argument about the nature of outsourcing.*

The outsourcing of U.S. jobs overseas, the subject of much discussion in this year's presidential campaign, is part of an economic movement that promises a better life—indeed, a new beginning—for many people in developing countries. It gives technologically savvy young people in countries like India livelihoods that move them into the ranks of the middle class. On the other hand, workers in industrialized nations are being displaced in large numbers. Comparably well-paying jobs are not being created fast enough to make up for the positions headed offshore.

How does one morally evaluate this complex situation? Since international trade by its nature entails shifting resources for comparative advantage, the phenomenon of international outsourcing is not really new. The U.S. imports goods that would have cost more to produce domestically, and it manufactures and sells to other countries commodities that would have been more expensive for them to supply themselves. It is a win-win situation for nations, providing gains in consumption, production and exchange.

Cheaper imports mean that incomes can be stretched to buy more goods and services. Trade increases real income because it improves people's purchasing power. It also brings gains in production, since it allows countries to manufacture only those commodities that provide them the best possible earnings.

It makes sense for the U.S. to use its scarce natural and human resources to manufacture airplanes, high-end computer chips and advanced software—products that command better prices than do less complex things like shoes or textiles. Why produce something ourselves that we can get more cheaply elsewhere? Why use our resources to manufacture something of lesser value when we could use them to make something of greater value?

5   The world reaps enormous benefits from letting countries specialize in what they do best and most cheaply. Not only does this system increase efficiency and achieve economies of scale (both of which lead

to a drop in costs), but it lays the groundwork for even more path-breaking technological changes in processes and products.

Economic history makes clear that openness to the global market-place is a significant determiner of a nation's economic well-being. Thus, the promotion of trade liberalization has been a perennial part of the World Bank's and the International Monetary Fund's assistance packages.

Yet assertions about the advantages of international trade (and, by extension, international outsourcing) must be heavily qualified. They refer only to overall gains and do not acknowledge how benefits are disbursed. One error in economic reasoning is the fallacy of division: the assumption that what is good for the whole is necessarily good for its individual parts. Not everybody gains from trade. The benefits of inter-national trade come at the price of creating an economic life in constant flux and even disequilibrium.

Concern over the deleterious impact of trade (or technological change) is also not new. Tensions arising from market innovations and expansion began with the onset of the Industrial Revolution. British master weavers' hard-won and highly paid skills were rendered obsolete overnight by the introduction of machinery that quickly and abundantly produced textiles of comparable and uniform quality. Some of these disaffected weavers (eventually known as the Luddites) rioted, destroyed textile machinery and heavily lobbied parliament to ban or regulate the use of labor-displacing equipment (all to no avail).

Earlier, through contentious, drawn-out debates, "free-traders" succeeded in convincing the British parliament to repeal the Corn Laws and allow the unrestricted entry of cheaper grains from abroad. Industrialists asserted that this approach kept food prices (and wages) low, thereby making British industrial products more competitive abroad. Urban workers and industrialists benefited from the liberal-ization of the food market, but at the expense of farmers and landowners.

Technological change and market expansion can precipitate radical 10 overnight changes in income distribution. They can produce a profound reallocation of burdens and benefits across local communities and even nations. No wonder international trade has always been a contentious issue.

Outsourcing has gained notoriety in recent months because of the accelerating volume of job transfers overseas and the sudden vulnerability of high-tech and service occupations that were once thought immune to trade displacement. Services that used to be nontradable (back-office operations, call centers, data management and accounting sectors) have now been made fully tradable because of advances in

CHAPTER 7 FOCUS

communications and computational technologies. Location is increasingly insignificant in the provision of these services. Moreover, the ready availability of large pools of technically capable and computer-savvy workers overseas has eroded what traditionally had been considered the distinct preserve of the U.S. and other developed countries: sophisticated, high-end technologies.

Many people have come to expect that blue-collar workers will sometimes be displaced as a consequence of trade. The fact that the same fate can descend on highly skilled and educated professionals is a new concern. Developed countries are torn between the steady call to stay the course with international trade and the ever-growing clamor to slow down or even ban outsourcing.

According to the standards of procedural justice, which calls for treating similar cases in a similar fashion, nations should not be selective in implementing trade rules but should simply let mutually agreed-upon processes and procedures run their course. Since World War II, developed countries, especially the U.S., have championed trade liberalization, having learned from the ill effects of trade protectionism during the interwar years. The spectacular economic growth in the second half of the 20th century reflects the enormous benefits reaped from the free trade of goods and services. The Asian Tigers (South Korea, Taiwan, Hong Kong and Singapore) and Japan became economic powerhouses. China owes its current economic boom to the open Western markets for its products and services.

Developed countries, too, have been major beneficiaries, since their comparative advantage lies in the trade of manufactures, services, intellectual property and capital. Industrialized countries have been vocal in promoting trade openness in these areas and have fiercely defended the need to respect and enforce intellectual property rights (e.g., pharmaceutical patents and software). There are, of course, adjustment costs that accompany trade, since segments of local populations are hurt by open markets. Despite these costs, poor countries have subscribed to international trade rules and have slowly but steadily opened their markets in those economic sectors (especially manufactures and services) where industrialized countries have much to gain.

15   Having reaped enormous profits from free trade in those areas where they enjoy a distinct comparative advantage, developed countries violate procedural justice whenever they curtail or suppress the liberalization of markets in which they have a comparative disadvantage. This is exactly what the European Union, Japan and the U.S. have done in food markets, making poor countries unable fully to reap the gains of their comparative advantage (agricultural crops). The industrialized nations have steadfastly refused to open up trade

in farm goods in an effort to protect farmers from being displaced by global trade. This is the proverbial case of wanting to have one's cake and eat it too.

A second conception of justice, justice as mutual advantage, calls for an equitable disposition of costs and benefits for all involved. Relationships should not be one-sided; gains and liabilities should be shared according to some mutually approved criteria. There are many variants of this school of thought, one of the best known being John Rawls's conception of justice as fairness: every person has the maximum freedoms consistent with others' enjoyment of the same liberties; and inequalities are permitted only to the extent that such disparities benefit the most disadvantaged.

The quickest and easiest way to understand the second condition is to use its theological analog, the preferential option for the poor: the more disadvantage are, the greater should be the assistance and solicitude extended to them by those in a position to help.

The promise that outsourcing holds for many impoverished people is vividly seen in India. Computer-related industries around Bangalore have spavined a wide and beneficial ripple effect across the nation. Human capital has replaced physical capital and natural resources as the primary creator of wealth in this postindustrial era. This augurs well for many nations poor in financial capital and natural resources but richly endowed with an educated workforce. They can leapfrog the traditional process of industrial development and parlay their human capital into much-needed foreign exchange. In other words, the technological advances that have made outsourcing possible have created a new global market for what used to be "nontradable" services.

In assessing mutual advantage in economic exchange, second-order effects should also be considered. U.S. consumers benefit from outsourcing through their gains in consumption. Moreover, a leaner cost structure makes U.S. producers more competitive in global markets, which should create more jobs. Blocking outsourcing thus imposes hidden costs ("taxes") on other Americans.

Future generations are the biggest beneficiaries of the dynamic 20 gains from trade brought on by technological advances. Innovation is price-sensitive and responds to incentives and increased earnings. Trade distortions would erode future gains from efficiency, and succeeding generations would be adversely affected if outsourcing were impeded. The efficient use of finite resources benefits not only contemporary market participants but future economic agents as well. Justice requires mutual advantages across different generations.

Despite these arguments against obstructing outsourcing, a laissez-faire approach is also not right. Justice calls for remedial action for the negative unintended consequences of market operations. Those who map the benefits of international trade have duties toward those who bear the costs of making such market exchanges possible.

The claim that trade is ultimately beneficial because it creates new jobs even as it destroys old ones runs into two problems. First, disparities in skills or in geographic location may make for a bad fit between displaced workers and new jobs. Finding a new job, getting retrained, shifting to a new field or securing age-appropriate employment can be difficult and costly. A second problem is the time lag between job destruction and job creation.

Who should bear these unavoidable and significant costs? A laissez-faire approach to outsourcing simply leaves people to fend for themselves. Justice as mutual advantage requires a transfer of resources and assistance between beneficiaries and losers in market exchange. Relief cannot be limited to unemployment payments, food stamps or other stopgap measures, but must be substantive and geared toward reintegrating displaced workers back into the economy. This can take many forms, such as the provision of trade adjustment assistance grants, retraining, tuition assistance, extended health care benefits and career counseling.

Funding these programs will be a contentious issue because of the difficulty of identifying and then compelling beneficiaries (e.g., firms and consumers) to give up some of their gains from outsourcing. Government should not be viewed as the sole provider of these measures. Unions and local communities have an obligation to do whatever they can for themselves. Higher bodies should not arrogate functions that lower bodies can provide for themselves. Involving nongovernmental organizations can elicit new and creative ways of providing assistance to those who have been hurt by outsourcing.

25   Theological ethics arrives at the same conclusion as philosophical ethics: though outsourcing must take its course as part of the normal workings of international trade, the beneficiaries of this market exchange must help displaced workers make the transition to a new place in the economy. We have a dual obligation to be efficient in our use of the goods of the earth and to cooperate with one another in our economic work. God entrusted the earth to our care as we use it to fill our needs. International trade fulfils these twin duties by satisfying human needs in the most effective way while eliciting collaborative work through the division of labor.

The formation of ancient Israel provides insights into how the global economy ought to approach the dilemmas posed by outsourcing. Yahweh not only liberates the oppressed He brews from their slavery in Egypt but also brings them into a land "flowing with milk and honey."

God offers his people a life both free and abundant, but only if they live up to their covenantal responsibility. The covenant code (Exod. 20:22–23:33), the Deuteronomic law (Deut. 12–26) and the code of holiness (Lev. 17–26) present a formidable array of statutes governing economic life: mandatory lending, interest-free loans, sabbatical rest and festivals, jubilee releases and land tenure, gleaning restrictions, tithing, debt remission, slave manumission, and the preferential treatment of widows, orphans and strangers.

We can draw various insights from these divine initiatives. Divine providence fills our needs; God intended us to have a bounteous life. But this abundant life is possible only if we truly care for each other. Our mutual solicitude is God's channel for providing us with plenty. Consequently, we must take responsibility for those who are in economic distress, reintegrating them into the community's economic life. Globalization affords us unique opportunities to take responsibility for each other's welfare. We are on the cusp of a global economy that requires humans to function as a single interdependent family. If we embrace the claim that we are all brothers and sisters in Christ, then national borders cannot limit our solicitude for others.

We cannot end outsourcing simply because local jobs are lost; outsourcing has an immense upside in its effect on the lives of poor people. It presents a unique opportunity to assist people mired in poverty. Economists and policymakers know that the best and most enduring form of assistance developed countries can give to poor nations is not in direct grants but in open markets. The global economy can be the "land flowing with milk and honey" entrusted to us all. Nevertheless, neither outsourcing nor trade should be completely unfettered. The moral obligations that tell us to assist the poor of the world by opening our markets also call us to help displaced workers find another place in the economy. Our duties toward poor nations and displaced domestic workers are not mutually exclusive. They can be satisfied simultaneously, but only if people are willing to sacrifice for each other's well-being.

Responding to Reading

1. What is "procedural justice" (13)? What does Barrera mean when he says, "developed countries violate procedural justice whenever they curtail or suppress the liberalization of markets in which they have a comparative disadvantage" (15)?
2. What is "justice as mutual advantage" (16)? What promise does outsourcing hold for impoverished people? Why does Barrera believe that despite the arguments in favor of outsourcing, "a laissez-faire approach is also not right" (21)?

3. According to Barrera, how does globalization offer us "unique opportunities to take responsibility for each other's welfare" (27)? What does he mean when he says, "Our duties toward poor nations and displaced domestic workers are not mutually exclusive" (28)?

Responding in Writing

What moral argument does Barrera make? Do you think his allusions to the Bible and his appeals to divine providence strengthen or weaken his case?

WIDENING THE FOCUS

For Critical Thinking and Writing

Write an essay in which you answer the Focus question, "Is outsourcing bad for America?" In your essay, refer to the ideas in Cullen Murphy's "Let Someone Else Do It: The Impulse Behind Everything," Clay Risen's "Missed Target: Is Outsourcing Really so Bad?" and Albino Barrera's "Fair Exchange: Who Benefits from Outsourcing?"

For Further Reading

The following readings can suggest additional perspectives for thinking and writing about how to address outsourcing and its effects:

- Daniel H. Pink, "School's Out" (p. 87)

- Jonathan Kozol, "The Human Cost of an Illiterate Society" (p. 164)

- Andrew Curry, "Why We Work" (p. 397)

For Focused Research

As the essays in the Focus section indicate, outsourcing is a source of debate. Proponents see outsourcing as a way of increasing productivity while at the same time reducing costs. In addition, they see outsourcing as a way of helping developing countries gain desperately needed capital. Opponents see outsourcing as an insidious activity that damages the American economy by permanently transferring jobs to other countries, where workers are exploited and underpaid. To gain greater insight into the issue of outsourcing, read the information on the following Web sites:

- www.blogsource.org, Outsourcing Times, a site that promotes outsourcing

- http://www.topix.net/business/outsourcing, a site that provides updated outsourcing news from various sources on the Web

Then, write an essay in which you discuss the advantages and disadvantages of outsourcing. As you do so, consider these questions: Is outsourcing really a less expensive alternative to domestic labor? Are there hidden costs that make outsourcing less desirable than it appears to be? Do companies that try outsourcing actually achieve the benefits that they expected?

CHAPTER 7 FOCUS

——————————— WRITING ———————————

Why We Work

1. In "Professions for Women" (p. 410), Virginia Woolf speaks of the obstacles women must overcome to have careers in fields dominated by men; in "The Second Shift" (p. 415), Arlie Hochschild makes the point that most working women have two jobs: the one they do at work and the one that begins when they get home. Write an essay in which you consider the obstacles that women face when they work. Make sure you refer to the ideas of both Woolf and Hochschild in your essay.

2. What do young people learn by having a job—even a bad job? Look at two of the works in this chapter that show young people in jobs—for example, "One Last Time" by Gary Soto (p. 402) and "A & P" by John Updike (p. 438). Then, discuss what the young Soto and Updike's character Sammy learned about work.

3. Write an essay in which you describe the worst job you ever had.

4. Considering the essays in this chapter—especially "Why We Work" (p. 397), "One Last Time" (p. 402), "Behind the Counter," (p. 421), and "The Second Shift" (p. 415)—write an essay in which you discuss what you believe the purpose of work should be. For example, should it be to earn money, or should it be to gain personal satisfaction and fulfillment? Are these two goals mutually exclusive? Does the way we work in this country help people achieve these goals? Would alternative arrangements—such as working fewer days with longer hours or having two people share one job—be better? Given the challenges of the global economy, are these changes in the way we work possible?

5. In "The Second Shift" (p. 415), Arlie Hochschild says that both society and the government should institute new policies that would allow workers to have more time at home. Write an essay in which you briefly summarize Hochschild's ideas and then go on to explain in detail why people need more time with their families.

6. In "Professions for Women" (p. 410), Virginia Woolf sees work as a way to achieve her full potential as a human being. In "Why We Work" (p. 397), however, Andrew Curry makes the point that most workers dislike their jobs. Which of these two views of work do you hold? Write an essay in which you give the reasons for your belief. Illustrate your points with your own experiences as well as with references to the essays by Woolf and Curry.

7. Imagine that you have been asked by your former high school to address students in this year's graduating class about how to get part-time and summer jobs to offset the high cost of college. Write a speech that is inspirational but also offers specific advice.

8. Do you agree with Henry Louis Gates's contention in "Delusions of Grandeur" that colleges place too much emphasis on sports—especially when it concerns the African American athlete? If you agree with Gates, present specific suggestions for rectifying the situation. If you do not agree, show where in the essay he is in error.

9. In "Selling in Minnesota," Barbara Ehrenreich attends an orientation session for new employees and is told about all the positive qualities of Wal-Mart. In "Don't Blame Wal-Mart," Robert B. Reich discusses the harm that people do by shopping at Wal-Mart. Write an essay in which you present your view of Wal-Mart. Make sure you refer to both essays as well as to any other material you find to support your points. Document all ideas that are not your own and include a Works-Cited page at the end of your essay.

8

SAVING THE PLANET

The environmental movement had its beginnings in the United States with the publication of Henry David Thoreau's *Walden* in 1854. At the same time that Thoreau was retreating into the woods, his friend Ralph Waldo Emerson (as well as others in the movement that came to be called Transcendentalism) saw a return to nature as a way of communing with God. Then, in 1868, the naturalist John Muir moved to the Yosemite Valley in California and became convinced that parts of the natural environment should be conserved—protected from the destructive influence of human beings. As a result of Muir's writing and lobbying, Congress created Yosemite National Park in 1890. Later, along with Robert Underwood Johnson, Muir founded the Sierra Club, one of the first groups dedicated to the preservation of the environment.

Open trash dump

The modern environmental movement began in the 1960s when Rachel Carson published *Silent Spring,* which captured wide public attention. (As a result of the uproar caused by the book, the Environmental Protection Agency eventually banned the use of DDT.) In 1969, the public was further aroused when an oil spill occurred off the coast of Santa Barbara, and then, several months later, when chemicals floating on the polluted Ohio River caught fire. In response to these and other events, the first Earth Day was celebrated on March 21, 1970.

Since these beginnings, the modern environmental movement has taken many forms. For example, environmentalists have lobbied Congress to pass laws that protect endangered species and their habitats. They also have taken steps to address issues such as global warming and atmospheric pollution. As a result, terms like *climate change* and *carbon footprint* have become part of our vocabulary. In addition, the organic-food movement has had an impact on the way we think about food. By encouraging people to buy food produced in an environmentally friendly way—without the use of pesticides and artificial fertilizers—this movement has encouraged the production of healthy, natural foods. Going a step further, the ethical-food movement has encouraged people to reduce the use of fossil fuels by buying and eating only food produced by local organic farmers. What most of these groups have in common is a commitment to sustainability—that is, to consuming resources at a rate at which they can be replenished.

Bales of trash at recycling center

The Focus section of this chapter asks the question, "How Can We Create a More Sustainable Environment?" As the essays in this section suggest, one of the major challenges today is living in a way that does not deplete the planet's resources. In order to accomplish this end, concepts such as renewable energy and green design have become increasingly important. Critics of environmentalism say that its adherents go too far, sacrificing the progress offered by technology in favor of an impossible utopian dream. Environmentalists counter by charging that our consumer-based society is squandering the earth's limited resources, and, in the process, is upsetting the earth's fragile ecosystems. Only by creating a sustainable environment, say environmentalists, will this generation leave the next generation with the food, energy, and climate it will need to survive.

PREPARING TO READ AND WRITE

As you read and prepare to write about the selections in this chapter, you may consider the following questions:

- Is the writer a scientist? a layperson? a journalist? Does the writer's background make you more or less receptive to his or her ideas?

- On what environmental issue does the writer focus?

- What position does the writer take on the issue? Do you agree or disagree with this position?

- Is the writer's emphasis theoretical or practical?

- What preconceptions do you have about the issue? Does the essay reinforce or challenge these preconceptions?

- What background in science does the writer assume readers have?

- Does the writer think science alone will be able to solve the problems he or she mentions? Does the writer believe other kinds of solutions are necessary? Is the writer optimistic or pessimistic about the future?

- What is the writer's purpose? Is it to make readers think about a controversial idea? to persuade readers? to educate them? to warn them?

- In what ways is the essay similar or different from the others in its Focus section?

FROM "THROUGH THE STORIES WE HEAR WHO WE ARE"

Leslie Marmon Silko

1948–

Leslie Marmon Silko grew up on the Laguna Pueblo Indian reservation in New Mexico. A novelist, poet, and essayist, Silko writes about issues relating to her Native American heritage, such as storytelling and colonization, as well as current political issues, such as women's rights. Her works include Laguna Woman: Poems *(1974),* Ceremony *(1977),* Storyteller *(1981),* Almanac of the Dead: A Novel *(1991), and* Gardens in the Dunes: A Novel *(1999). In the following essay, Silko explores the nature of human survival in an unforgiving environment.*

A high dark mesa rises dramatically from a grassy plain fifteen miles southeast of Laguna, in an area known as Swanee. On the grassy plain one hundred and forty years ago, my great-grandmother's uncle and his brother-in-law were grazing their herd of sheep. Because visibility on the plain extends for over twenty miles, it wasn't until the two sheep-herders came near the high dark mesa that the Apaches were able to stalk them. Using the mesa to obscure their approach, the raiders swept around from both ends of the mesa. My great-grandmother's relatives were killed, and the herd lost. The high dark mesa played a critical role: the mesa has compromised the safety which the openness of the plains had seemed to assure. Pueblo and Apache alike relied upon the terrain, the very earth herself, to give them protection and aid. Human activities or needs were maneuvered to fit the existing surroundings and conditions. I imagine the last afternoon of my distant ancestors as warm and sunny for late September. They might have been traveling slowly, bringing the sheep closer to Laguna in preparation for the approach of colder weather. The grass was tall and only beginning to change from green to a yellow which matched the late-afternoon sun shining off it. There might have been comfort in the warmth and the sight of the sheep fattening on good pasture which lulled my ancestors into their fatal inattention. They might have had a rifle whereas the Apaches had only bows and arrows. But there would have been four or five Apache raiders, and the surprise attack would have canceled any advantage the rifles gave them.

Survival in any landscape comes down to making the best use of all available resources. On that particular September afternoon, the raiders made better use of the Swanee terrain than my poor ancestors did. Thus the high dark mesa and the story of the two lost Laguna herders became inextricably linked. The memory of them and their story resides in part with the high black mesa. For as long as the mesa stands, people within the family and clan will be reminded of the story of that afternoon long ago. Thus the continuity and accuracy of the oral narratives are reinforced by the landscape—and the Pueblo interpretation of that landscape is maintained.

Responding to Reading

1. Why does Silko tell the story of her great-grandmother's uncle and his brother-in-law? What point does their story make about the mesa?
2. What does Silko mean when she says, "Human activities or needs were maneuvered to fit the existing surroundings and conditions" (1)?
3. What point is Silko making about the relationship of human beings to the environment? What is the "Pueblo interpretation" of the landscape she describes (2)?

Responding in Writing

What is Silko implying about the relationship between contemporary American culture and the environment? Do you agree with her view?

THE AMERICAN FORESTS

John Muir

1838–1914

A naturalist, conservationist, and farmer, John Muir fought for the protection of forests in the United States. He published hundreds of articles in the major magazines of his time: Atlantic Monthly, Century, Harper's, *and* Scribner's. *He also wrote several books, including* The Mountains of California *(1894),* Our National Parks *(1901),* Stickeen: The Story of a Dog *(1909),* My First Summer in the Sierra *(1911), and* Steep Trails *(1918). Muir's writing explores the spirituality inherent in nature. Through his writing and his conservationist work, Muir helped to establish several national parks, including California's Sequoia and Yosemite national parks. He also cofounded the Sierra Club in 1892. In the following 1897 essay, Muir calls for a governmental response to the destruction of U.S. forests.*

The forests of America, however slighted by man, must have been a great delight to God; for they were the best he ever planted. The whole continent was a garden, and from the beginning it seemed to be favored above all the other wild parks and gardens of the globe. To prepare the ground, it was rolled and sifted in seas with infinite loving deliberation and forethought, lifted into the light, submerged and warmed over and over again, pressed and crumpled into folds and ridges, mountains and hills, subsoiled with heaving volcanic fires, ploughed and ground and sculptured into scenery and soil with glaciers and rivers—every feature growing and changing from beauty to beauty, higher and higher. And in the fullness of time it was planted in groves, and belts, and broad, exuberant, mantling forests, with the largest, most varied, most fruitful, and most beautiful trees in the world ...

So [the forests] appeared a few centuries ago when they were rejoicing in wildness. The Indians with stone axes could do them no more harm than could gnawing beavers and browsing moose. Even the fires of the Indians and the fierce shattering lightning seemed to work together only for good in clearing spots here and there for smooth garden prairies, and openings for sunflowers seeking the light. But when the steel axe of the white man rang out in the startled air their doom was sealed. Every tree heard the bodeful sound, and pillars of smoke gave the sign in the sky...

Many of nature's five hundred kinds of wild trees had to make way for orchards and cornfields. In the settlement and civilization of the country, bread more than timber or beauty was wanted; and in the blindness of hunger, the early settlers, claiming Heaven as their guide, regarded God's trees as only a larger kind of pernicious weeds, extremely hard to get rid of. Accordingly, with no eye to the future, these pious destroyers waged interminable forest wars; chips flew thick and fast; trees in their beauty fell crashing by millions, smashed to confusion, and the smoke of their burning has been rising to heaven more than two hundred years...

Surely, then, it should not be wondered at that lovers of their country, bewailing its baldness, are now crying aloud, "Save what is left of the forests!" Clearing has surely now gone far enough; soon timber will be scarce, and not a grove will be left to rest in or pray in ...

So far our government has done nothing effective with its forests,   5 though the best in the world, but is like a rich and foolish spendthrift who has inherited a magnificent estate in perfect order, and then has left his rich fields and meadows, forests and parks, to be sold and plundered and wasted at will...

Any fool can destroy trees. They cannot run away; and if they could, they would still be destroyed,—chased and hunted down as long as fun or a dollar could be got out of their bark hides, branching horns, or magnificent bole backbones. Few that fell trees plant them; nor would planting avail much towards getting back anything like the noble primeval forests. During a man's life only saplings can be grown, in the place of the old trees—tens of centuries old—that have been destroyed. It took more than three thousand years to make some of the trees in these Western woods,—trees that are still standing in perfect strength and beauty, waving and singing in the mighty forests of the Sierra.

Through all the wonderful, eventful centuries since Christ's time—and long before that—God has cared for these trees, saved them from drought, disease, avalanches, and a thousand straining leveling tempests and floods; but he cannot save them from fools,—only Uncle Sam can do that.

Responding to Reading

1. How does Muir picture the forests of America? Do you think his view of them is accurate or overly idealistic? Why do you think he portrays the forests as he does?
2. Why doesn't Muir think the Indians are a threat to the American forests? How, according to him, are the white settlers different?
3. What does Muir think should be done to save the forests? Why does he think that only government action can save them from destruction?

Responding in Writing

Muir wrote this essay in 1897. Is it still relevant? Is it perhaps even *more* relevant? Explain your reasoning.

BEING KIND TO THE LAND
Wendell Berry
1934–

An essayist, novelist, poet, and farmer, Wendell Berry explores themes of nature, spirituality, farming, and traveling in his writing. He has written numerous articles for publications such as the Progressive, *the* New York Times, Harper's *magazine, the* Christian Century, Christianity and Literature, Sojourners *magazine, and* Sierra. *Berry's recent works include* Blessed Are the Peacemakers: Christ's Teachings of Love, Compassion, and Forgiveness *(2005),* Given: New Poems *(2005),* The Way of Ignorance: And Other Essays *(2005),* Andy Catlett: Early Travels: A Novel *(2006), and* Whitefoot: A Story from the Center of the World *(2009). In the following essay, Berry contrasts traditional farming methods with large-scale factory farming.*

My father devoted much of his life to the politics of tobacco, which was the staple crop of small farmers here in Kentucky, but he was not a promoter of tobacco. What he promoted, in passionate speeches to me and others during the fifty-odd years I knew him, was grass and grazing. His reason for this was sound, and it was urgent. We lived and farmed in a landscape of slopes, varying from gentle to steep, but everywhere vulnerable to erosion. In our country, a plow quickly could become a weapon. And so the kind of farming my father subscribed to, which was fairly well established here during the years of my growing up, involved cattle, sheep, hogs, and (until the middle of the last century) work horses and mules on pasture.

And so I am—for all I know, genetically—a lover of grass. Or, to be more precise, I am a lover of sod, a compound organism consisting of topsoil covered by growing plants and held together by perennial roots, populated by grasses, legumes, weeds (many of which are palatable, or inoffensive, and beautiful), birds, animals, bugs, worms, and tons of invisible soil organisms. A good sod, healthy and not overgrazed, is a sponge, gathering the rain, holding it, releasing it slowly. It is kind to the land it grows on, kind to the local watershed, kind to the people and other creatures downstream. Land under a healthy, well-kept sod is safe; it will grow richer and healthier year after year; it is not going to wash away. A farmer whose fields are well sodded will wake in the night, hear the hard rain coming down, and go comfortably back to sleep.

When the rain strikes sod, it does not loosen the soil and run off as a muddy slurry. It clings in droplets to the standing plants. It soaks into the thatch of dead foliage. It seeps into the open pores of the ground. Nature's way, which ought to be the human way, is to retain the maximum amount of the rainfall, and then to release the surplus as slowly as possible. Thus the good health of a watershed becomes the good fortune of downstream farms and towns.

By the time I was experienced enough to understand the wisdom of my father's advocacy of grass, I had also traveled enough to know that it applied far beyond our own countryside. I have seen shocking plowland erosion here in my home neighborhood, but I have seen it just as bad in Iowa. As a rule—and this is a rule we have ignored at tremendous cost—all farmland needs to lie under perennial cover for a significant fraction of its time in use. The length of time will vary from place to place, but the need is everywhere and it cannot safely be ignored. Under a grass sod the land restores and renews itself in ways we humans should not expect ever to understand completely. Returning cropland to grass for a year or two in every rotation should be regarded as an act of humility and courtesy toward the world, which after all we did not make. On many farms there are places that ought to stay under perennial cover, either pasture or woodland.

I once asked a neighbor of mine, a good farmer now dead, "Do you think we can safely plow in any year as much as ten percent of this country?" 5

He said, "More like five."

He refused to use his vulnerable land to grow grain for the market. He grew only the grain he needed for his own livestock. When it left his place, as the saying went, "it would walk off." And then he would go from sod to sod as directly as possible.

That man was a true farmer. He was not an industrial producer of agricultural commodities. At present, and temporarily, the so-called agricultural economy and our rural landscapes are dominated by the agri-industrialist, who stands exactly in opposition to my friend. Agri-industrialists run cotton factories or sugar factories or grain factories or meat factories or milk factories or egg factories. These factories have four outstanding characteristics:

1. They depend entirely on industrial machinery and chemicals.
2. They depend entirely on cheap fossil fuel, which is why they are temporary. While we still depend upon them, they are already relics.
3. They treat organisms (that is to say creatures: plants and animals, living beings) as machines.
4. They are highly specialized.

Animal factories do not grow plants. Plant factories have no animals. Animal factories produce, in addition to meat, manure—which, far from the cropland where the feed is produced, becomes a dangerous pollutant. Plant factories, having no animals and therefore no manure and therefore lacking in health, are dependent on large quantities of fertilizers and other chemicals, which are dangerous pollutants.

10   But the most dangerous pollutant issuing from the agri-industrial enterprise is the radically oversimplified agri-industrial mind. This mind assumes that it is all right to produce stuff by using up stuff, that it is all right to "externalize" all ecological and social costs, that health is never an issue except when and if regulations are enforced by government, and that all relationships and connections, causes and effects, are somebody else's business.

True farmers, on the other hand, have minds that are complex and responsible. They understand that their fundamental resource is not acreage or capital, but a home place that is healthful and fertile. They want to conserve their land and improve it. They farm with both plants and animals. They understand and honor their debts to nature. They understand and honor their obligations to neighbors and consumers. They understand and respect the land's need to be protected from washing. They are friends of trees and grass. Their thinking is all about conserving and connecting, husbandry and artistry.

It cannot be too much insisted upon that good farming involves both plants and animals in the right relationship or balance on every farm. At present, and for understandable reasons, including the cruelties of confinement feeding and the destructive fashion of "finishing" most animals predominantly on grain, some people would like to remove animals from agriculture altogether. This "solution" is characteristic of so-called environmentalism, which has tended to operate between the poles of abuse and prohibition, overlooking entirely any middle ground of good use. But whatever the dictates of ignorant idealism, it remains true that good farming has always involved pasture, grazing animals, and animal manure for fertilization. This farming is good because it preserves the land and the people. If we want to produce food from vulnerable land without destroying it, we must do so by growing grass on it, harvesting the grass by pasturing animals, and then eating the animals. (I only wish that the animals could be slaughtered humanely in small local facilities, which would be better for the animals, the consumers, and the rural economy than the present system.)

We still have some true farmers who have survived so far the damages and discouragements of agri-industrialism. Some of them believe, and I believe, that they have survived by remaining true to their land and their good agricultural practices. In the time that is coming, we are going to need many more such farmers than we have, and we will need them much sooner than we can expect to get them. We will get them only to the extent that young people come along who are willing to fit their farming to the nature of their farms and their home landscapes, who recognize the paramount importance of grass and grazing animals to good farming everywhere.

The reason for this is plain. On a factory farm, nature is too likely to be an adversary of the farmer, because such a farm is too much an adversary of nature. Nature responds with diseases, weeds, pests, and gullies which, in the process of damaging or destroying the farmer, enrich the suppliers of chemicals, machinery, fuel, and credit. Only with grass, with pastures, can nature enter farming fairly dependably as an ally of the farmer.

In an era of expensive fuels, nature will continue to work cheap, as 15 she always has, for those who befriend her. Henry Besuden, the great farmer and Southdown breeder of Clark County, Kentucky, restored his inherited rundown farm with grass, and he then made good pasture the basis and standard of his farming. He wanted "a way of farming compatible with nature," and he applied all his work and his remarkable intelligence to that end. "It's good to have Nature working for you," he said. "She works for a minimum wage."

Responding to Reading

1. What does Berry mean when he says, "In our country, a plow quickly could become a weapon" (1)? Why was his father an advocate of grass?
2. What is the difference between "a true farmer" and "an industrial producer of agricultural commodities" (8)? According to Berry, what harm do people in the second category do?
3. Why does Berry think that environmentalism misses the point? How does he think farmers can produce food without destroying the land?

Responding in Writing

Do you see Berry's definition of "good farming" as realistic? Do you think it is possible to farm in a way that is compatible with nature and still manage to feed over 300 million people?

THE OBLIGATION TO ENDURE
Rachel Carson
1907–1964

Naturalist and environmentalist Rachel Carson was a specialist in marine biology. She won the National Book Award for The Sea Around Us *(1951), which, like her other books, appeals to scientists and laypeople alike. While working as an aquatic biologist for the U.S. Fish and Wildlife Service, Carson became concerned with ecological hazards and wrote* Silent Spring *(1962), in which she warned readers about the indiscriminate use of pesticides. This book influenced President John F. Kennedy to begin investigations into this and other environmental problems. In the selection from* Silent Spring *that follows, Carson urges readers to question the use of chemical pesticides.*

The history of life on earth has been a history of interaction between living things and their surroundings. To a large extent, the physical form and the habits of the earth's vegetation and its animal life have been molded by the environment. Considering the whole span of earthly time, the opposite effect, in which life actually modifies its surroundings, has been relatively slight. Only within the moment of time represented by the present century has one species—man—acquired significant power to alter the nature of his world.

During the past quarter century this power has not only increased to one of disturbing magnitude but it has changed in character. The most alarming of all man's assaults upon the environment is the contamination of air, earth, rivers, and sea with dangerous and even lethal materials. This pollution is for the most part irrecoverable; the chain of evil it initiates not only in the world that must support life but in living tissues is for the most part irreversible. In this now universal contamination of the environment, chemicals are the sinister and little-recognized partners of radiation in changing the very nature of the world—the very nature of its life. Strontium 90, released through nuclear explosions into the air, comes to earth in rain or drifts down in fallout, lodges in soil, enters into the grass or corn or wheat grown there, and in time takes up its abode in the bones of a human being, there to remain until his death. Similarly, chemicals sprayed on croplands or forests or gardens lie long in soil, entering into living organisms, passing from one to another in a chain of poisoning and death. Or they pass mysteriously by underground streams until they emerge and, through the alchemy of air and sunlight, combine into new forms that kill vegetation, sicken cattle, and work unknown harm on those who drink from once pure wells. As Albert Schweitzer[1] has said, "Man can hardly even recognize the devils of his own creation."

It took hundreds of millions of years to produce the life that now inhabits the earth—eons of time in which that developing and evolving and diversifying life reached a state of adjustment and balance with its surroundings. The environment, rigorously shaping and directing the life it supported, contained elements that were hostile as well as supporting. Certain rocks gave out dangerous radiation; even within the light of the sun, from which all life draws its energy, there were short-wave radiations with power to injure. Given time—time not in years but in millennia—life adjusts, and a balance has been reached. For time is the essential ingredient; but in the modern world there is no time.

The rapidity of change and the speed with which new situations are created follow the impetuous and heedless pace of man rather than the deliberate pace of nature. Radiation is no longer merely the background radiation of rocks, the bombardment of cosmic rays, the ultra-violet of the sun that have existed before there was any life on earth; radiation is now the unnatural creation of man's tampering with the atom. The chemicals to which life is asked to make its adjustment are no longer merely the calcium and silica and copper and all the rest of the minerals washed out of the rocks and carried in rivers to the sea; they are the synthetic creations of man's inventive mind, brewed in his laboratories, and having no counterparts in nature.

To adjust to these chemicals would require time on the scale that is   5 nature's; it would require not merely the years of a man's life but the life of generations. And even this, were it by some miracle possible, would be futile, for the new chemicals come from our laboratories in an endless stream; almost five hundred annually find their way into actual use in the United States alone. The figure is staggering and its implications are not easily grasped—500 new chemicals to which the bodies of men and animals are required somehow to adapt each year, chemicals totally outside the limits of biologic experience.

Among them are many that are used in man's war against nature. Since the mid-1940s over 200 basic chemicals have been created for use in killing insects, weeds, rodents, and other organisms described in the

---

[1]French theologian (1875–1965) honored for his work as a scientist, humanitarian, musician, and religious thinker. In 1952, he was awarded the Nobel Peace Prize. [Eds.]

modern vernacular as "pests"; and they are sold under several thousand different brand names.

These sprays, dusts, and aerosols are now applied almost universally to farms, gardens, forests, and homes—nonselective chemicals that have the power to kill every insect, the "good" and the "bad," to still the songs of birds and the leaping of fish in the streams, to coat the leaves with a deadly film, and to linger on in soil—all this though the intended target may be only a few weeds or insects. Can anyone believe it is possible to lay down such a barrage of poisons on the surface of the earth without making it unfit for all life? They should not be called "insecticides," but "biocides."

The whole process of spraying seems caught up in an endless spiral. Since DDT was released for civilian use, a process of escalation has been going on in which ever more toxic materials must be found. This has happened because insects, in a triumphant vindication of Darwin's principle of the survival of the fittest, have evolved super races immune to the particular insecticide used, hence a deadlier one has always to be developed—and than a deadlier one than that. It has happened also because, for reasons to be described later, destructive insects often undergo a "flare-back" or resurgence, after spraying in numbers greater than before. Thus the chemical war is never won, and all life is caught in its violent crossfire.

Along with the possibility of the extinction of mankind by nuclear war, the central problem of our age has therefore become the contamination of man's total environment with such substances of incredible potential for harm—substances that accumulate in the tissues of plants and animals and even penetrate the germ cells to shatter or alter the very material of heredity upon which the shape of the future depends.

10   Some would-be architects of our future look toward a time when it will be possible to alter the human germ plasm by design. But we may easily be doing so now by inadvertence, for many chemicals, like radiation, bring about gene mutations. It is ironic to think that man might determine his own future by something so seemingly trivial as the choice of an insect spray.

All this has been risked—for what? Future historians may well be amazed by our distorted sense of proportion. How could intelligent beings seek to control a few unwanted species by a method that contaminated the entire environment and brought the threat of disease and death even to their own kind? Yet this is precisely what we have done. We have done it, moreover, for reasons that collapse the moment we examine them. We are told that the enormous and expanding use of pesticides is necessary to maintain farm production. Yet is our real problem not one of *overproduction*? Our farms, despite measures to remove acreages from production and to pay farmers *not* to produce, have yielded such a staggering excess of crops that the American taxpayer in

1962 in payout out more than one billion dollars a year as the total carrying cost of the surplus-food storage program. And is the situation helped when one branch of the Agriculture Department tries to reduce production while another states, as it did in 1958, "It is believed generally that reduction of crop acreages under provisions of the Soil Bank will stimulate interest in use of chemicals to obtain maximum production on the land retained in crops."

All this is not to say there is no insect problem and no need of control. I am saying, rather, that control must be geared to realities, not to mythical situations, and that the methods employed must be such that they do not destroy us along with the insects.

The problem whose attempted solution has brought such a train of disaster in its wake is an accomplishment of our modern way of life. Long before the age of man, insects inhabited the earth—a group of extraordinarily varied and adaptable beings. Over the course of time since man's advent, a small percentage of the more than half a million species of insects have come into conflict with human welfare in two principal ways: as competitors for the food supply and as carriers of human disease.

Disease-carrying insects become important where human beings are crowded together, especially under conditions where sanitation is poor, as in time of natural disaster or war or in situations of extreme poverty and deprivation. Then control of some sort becomes necessary. It is a sobering fact, however, as we shall presently see, that the method of massive chemical control has had only limited success, and also threatens to worsen the very conditions it is intended to curb.

Under primitive agricultural conditions the farmer had few insect 15 problems. These arose with the intensification of agriculture—the devotion of immense acreages to a single crop. Such a system set the stage for explosive increases in specific insect populations. Single-crop farming does not take advantage of the principles by which nature works; it is agriculture as an engineer might conceive it to be. Nature has introduced great variety into the landscape, but man has displayed a passion for simplifying it. Thus he undoes the built-in checks and balances by which nature holds the species within bounds. One important natural check is a limit on the amount of suitable habitat for each species. Obviously then, an insect that lives on wheat can build up its population to much higher levels on a farm devoted to wheat than on one in which wheat is intermingled with other crops to which the insect is not adapted.

The same thing happens in other situations. A generation or more ago, the towns of large areas of the United States lined their streets with the noble elm tree. Now the beauty they hopefully created is threatened with complete destruction as disease sweeps through the elms, carried by a beetle that would have only limited chance to build up large populations and to spread from tree to tree if the elms were only occasional trees in a richly diversified planting.

Another factor in the modern insect problem is one that must be viewed against a background of geologic and human history: the spreading of thousands of different kinds of organisms from their native homes to invade new territories. This worldwide migration has been studied and graphically described by the British ecologist Charles Elton in his recent book *The Ecology of Invasions*. During the Cretaceous Period, some hundred million years ago, flooding seas cut many land bridges between continents and living things found themselves confined in what Elton calls "colossal separate nature reserves." There, isolated from others of their kind, they developed many new species. When some of the land masses were joined again, about 15 million years ago, these species began to move out into new territories—a movement that is not only still in progress but is now receiving considerable assistance from man.

The importation of plants is the primary agent in the modern spread of species, for animals have almost invariably gone along with the plants, quarantine being a comparatively recent and not completely effective innovation. The United States Office of Plant Introduction alone has introduced almost 200,000 species and varieties of plants from all over the world. Nearly half of the 180 or so major insect enemies of plants in the United States are accidental imports from abroad, and most of them have come as hitchhikers on plants.

In new territory, out of reach of the restraining hand of the natural enemies that kept down its numbers in its native land, an invading plant or animal is able to become enormously abundant. Thus it is no accident that our most troublesome insects are introduced species.

20   These invasions, both the naturally occurring and those dependent on human assistance, are likely to continue indefinitely. Quarantine and massive chemical campaigns are only extremely expensive ways of buying time. We are faced, according to Dr. Elton, "with a life-and-death need not just to find new technological means of suppressing this plant or that animal"; instead we need the basic knowledge of animal populations and their relations to their surroundings that will "promote an even balance and damp down the explosive power of outbreaks and new invasions."

Much of the necessary knowledge is now available but we do not use it. We train ecologists in our universities and even employ them in our governmental agencies but we seldom take their advice. We allow the chemical death rain to fall as though there were no alternative, whereas in fact there are many, and our ingenuity could soon discover many more if given opportunity.

Have we fallen into a mesmerized state that makes us accept as inevitable that which is inferior or detrimental, as though having lost the will or the vision to demand that which is good? Such thinking, in the words of the ecologist Paul Shepard, "idealizes life with only its head out of water, inches above the limits of toleration of the corruption of its own environment...Why should we tolerate a diet of weak poisons, a home in insipid surroundings, a circle of acquaintances who are not quite our enemies, the noise of motors with just enough relief to prevent insanity? Who would want to live in a world which is just not quite fatal?"

Yet such a world is pressed upon us. The crusade to create a chemically sterile, insect-free world seems to have engendered a fanatic zeal on the part of many specialists and most of the so-called control agencies. On every hand there is evidence that those engaged in spraying operations exercise a ruthless power. "The regulatory entomologists... function as prosecutor, judge and jury, tax assessor and collector and sheriff to enforce their own orders," said Connecticut entomologist Neely Turner. The most flagrant abuses go unchecked in both state and federal agencies.

It is not my contention that chemical insecticides must never be used. I do contend that we have put poisonous and biologically potent chemicals indiscriminately into the hands of persons largely or wholly ignorant of their potentials for harm. We have subjected enormous numbers of people to contact with these poisons, without their consent and often without their knowledge. If the Bill of Rights contains no guarantee that a citizen shall be secure against lethal poisons distributed either by private individuals or by public officials, it is surely only because our forefathers, despite their considerable wisdom and foresight, could conceive of no such problem.

I contend, furthermore, that we have allowed these chemicals to be 25 used with little or no advance investigation of their effect on soil, water, wildlife, and man himself. Future generations are unlikely to condone our lack of prudent concern for the integrity of the natural world that supports all life.

There is still very limited awareness of the nature of the threat. This is an era of specialists, each of whom sees his own problem and is unaware of or intolerant of the larger frame into which it fits. It is also an era dominated by industry, in which the right to make a dollar at whatever cost is seldom challenged. When the public protests, confronted with some obvious evidence of damaging results of pesticide applications, it is fed little tranquilizing pills of half truth. We urgently need an end to these false assurances, to the sugar coating of unpalatable facts. It is the public that is being asked to assume the risks that the insect controllers calculate. The public must decide whether it wishes to continue on the present road, and it can do so only when in full possession of the facts. In the words of Jean Rostand, "The obligation to endure gives us the right to know."

Responding to Reading

1. In paragraph 9, Carson says, "Along with the possibility of the extinction of mankind by nuclear war, the central problem of our age has…become the contamination of man's total environment with such substances of incredible potential for harm…." Do you think she makes a good point, or do you think she overstates her case?
2. In paragraph 7, Carson says that the chemicals that people spray to control insects should be called "biocides" instead of "insecticides." What does she mean? Does she provide enough evidence to support her point? Explain.
3. In paragraph 24, Carson attempts to address critics' objections by saying that she does not believe insecticides "must never be used." Is she successful? Do you think she should have discussed the problems that could result if the use of insecticides such as DDT were reduced or eliminated?

Responding in Writing

Since Carson wrote her book, DDT has been banned. Recently, however, some scientists have said that it should be reintroduced on a limited basis because some insects have developed resistance to safer insecticides. Do you think this information strengthens or weakens Carson's position?

FATEFUL VOICE OF A GENERATION STILL DROWNS OUT REAL SCIENCE

John Tierney

1953–

A columnist for the New York Times, *John Tierney writes about issues related to the environment, technology, and the economy. His articles have appeared in such publications as the* Atlantic, *the* Chicago Tribune, Esquire, National Geographic Traveler, Newsweek, New York *magazine,* Reason, Rolling Stone, Vogue, *the* Wall Street Journal, Washington Monthly, *and the* Washington Post. *He is the author of* The Best-Case Scenario Handbook *(2002) and coauthor of the comic novel* God Is My Broker: A Monk-Tycoon Reveals the 7½ Laws of Spiritual and Financial Growth *(1998). In the following essay, Tierney challenges the arguments made by Rachel Carson in* Silent Spring.

For Rachel Carson admirers, it has not been a silent spring. They've been celebrating the centennial of her birthday with paeans to her saintliness. A new generation is reading her book in school—and mostly learning the wrong lesson from it.

If students are going to read "Silent Spring" in science classes, I wish it were paired with another work from that same year, 1962, titled

"Chemicals and Pests." It was a review of "Silent Spring" in the journal Science written by I. L. Baldwin, a professor of agricultural bacteriology at the University of Wisconsin.

He didn't have Ms. Carson's literary flair, but his science has held up much better. He didn't make Ms. Carson's fundamental mistake, which is evident in the opening sentence of her book: "There was once a town in the heart of America where all life seemed to live in harmony with its surroundings," she wrote, extolling the peace that had reigned "since the first settlers raised their houses." Lately, though, a "strange blight" had cast an "evil spell" that killed the flora and fauna, sickened humans and "silenced the rebirth of new life."

This "Fable for Tomorrow," as she called it, set the tone for the hodgepodge of science and junk science in the rest of the book. Nature was good; traditional agriculture was all right; modern pesticides were an unprecedented evil. It was a Disneyfied version of Eden.

Ms. Carson used dubious statistics and anecdotes (like the improbable story of a woman who instantly developed cancer after spraying her basement with DDT) to warn of a cancer epidemic that never came to pass. She rightly noted threats to some birds, like eagles and other raptors, but she wildly imagined a mass "biocide." She warned that one of the most common American birds, the robin, was "on the verge of extinction"—an especially odd claim given the large numbers of robins recorded in Audubon bird counts before her book. 5

Ms. Carson's many defenders, ecologists as well as other scientists, often excuse her errors by pointing to the primitive state of environmental and cancer research in her day. They argue that she got the big picture right: without her passion and pioneering work, people wouldn't have recognized the perils of pesticides. But those arguments are hard to square with Dr. Baldwin's review.

Dr. Baldwin led a committee at the National Academy of Sciences studying the impact of pesticides on wildlife. (Yes, scientists were worrying about pesticide dangers long before "Silent Spring.") In his review, he praised Ms. Carsons's literary skills and her desire to protect nature. But, he wrote, "Mankind has been engaged in the process of upsetting the balance of nature since the dawn of civilization."

While Ms. Carson imagined life in harmony before DDT, Dr. Baldwin saw that civilization depended on farmers and doctors fighting "an unrelenting war" against insects, parasites and disease. He complained that "Silent Spring" was not a scientific balancing of costs and benefits but rather a "prosecuting attorney's impassioned plea for action."

Ms. Carson presented DDT as a dangerous human carcinogen, but Dr. Baldwin said the question was open and noted that most scientists "feel that the danger of damage is slight." He acknowledged that pesticides were sometimes badly misused, but he also quoted an adage: "There are no harmless chemicals, only harmless use of chemicals."

10   Ms. Carson, though, considered new chemicals to be inherently different. "For the first time in the history of the world," she wrote, "every human being is now subjected to contact with dangerous chemicals, from the moment of conception until death."

She briefly acknowledged that nature manufactured its own carcinogens, but she said they were "few in number and they belong to that ancient array of forces to which life has been accustomed from the beginning." The new pesticides, by contrast, were "elixirs of death," dangerous even in tiny quantities because humans had evolved "no protection" against them and there was "no 'safe' dose."

She cited scary figures showing a recent rise in deaths from cancer, but she didn't consider one of the chief causes: fewer people were dying at young ages from other diseases (including the malaria that persisted in the American South until DDT). When that longevity factor as well as the impact of smoking are removed, the cancer death rate was falling in the decade before "Silent Spring," and it kept falling in the rest of the century.

Why weren't all of the new poisons killing people? An important clue emerged in the 1980s when the biochemist Bruce Ames tested thousands of chemicals and found that natural compounds were as likely to be carcinogenic as synthetic ones. Dr. Ames found that 99.99 percent of the carcinogens in our diet were natural, which doesn't mean that we are being poisoned by the natural pesticides in spinach and lettuce. We ingest most carcinogens, natural or synthetic, in such small quantities that they don't hurt us. Dosage matters, not whether a chemical is natural, just as Dr. Baldwin realized.

But scientists like him were no match for Ms. Carson's rhetoric. DDT became taboo even though there wasn't evidence that it was carcinogenic (and subsequent studies repeatedly failed to prove harm to humans).

15   It's often asserted that the severe restrictions on DDT and other pesticides were justified in rich countries like America simply to protect wildlife. But even that is debatable (see www.tierneylab.com), and in any case, the chemophobia inspired by Ms. Carson's book has been harmful in various ways. The obsession with eliminating minute risks from synthetic chemicals has wasted vast sums of money: environmental experts complain that the billions spent cleaning up Superfund sites[1] would be better spent on more serious dangers.

The human costs have been horrific in the poor countries where malaria returned after DDT spraying was abandoned. Malariologists have made a little headway recently in restoring this weapon against the disease, but they've had to fight against Ms. Carson's disciples who still

---

[1]Hazardous waste sites identified by the U.S. Environmental Protection Agency. [Eds.]

divide the world into good and bad chemicals, with DDT in their fearsome "dirty dozen."

Ms. Carson didn't urge an outright ban on DDT, but she tried to downplay its effectiveness against malaria and refused to acknowledge what it had accomplished. As Dr. Baldwin wrote, "No estimates are made of the countless lives that have been saved because of the destruction of insect vectors of disease." He predicted correctly that people in poor countries would suffer from hunger and disease if they were denied the pesticides that had enabled wealthy nations to increase food production and eliminate scourges.

But Dr. Baldwin did make one mistake. After expressing the hope "that someone with Rachel Carson's ability will write a companion volume dramatizing the improvements in human health and welfare derived from the use of pesticides," he predicted that "such a story would be far more dramatic than the one told by Miss Carson in 'Silent Spring.' "

That never happened, and I can't imagine any writer turning such good news into a story more dramatic than Ms. Carson's apocalypse in Eden. A best-seller titled "Happy Spring"? I don't think so.

Responding to Reading

1. According to Tierney, what is the "wrong lesson" that a new generation of students is learning from Rachael Carson's *Silent Spring* (1)? Exactly why is the lesson "wrong"?
2. In his essay, Tierney refers to I. L. Baldwin, a professor of agricultural bacteriology at the University of Wisconsin. In a 1962 review of *Silent Spring,* Baldwin claimed that the book was not a scientific examination of the issues but a "prosecuting attorney's impassioned plea for action" (8). What does Baldwin mean? Why does Tierney think Baldwin's distinction is important?
3. Why, according to Tierney, was DDT banned even though there was little scientific evidence to indicate it caused cancer? How did banning DDT affect people in poor countries? What facts does Tierney claim that people who want to continue the ban ignore?

Responding in Writing

Do you think that the benefits of DDT outweigh its drawbacks? Why or why not?

THE CONQUEST OF GARBAGE

Heather Rogers

1970–

Journalist Heather Rogers researches and writes about the environmental impact of garbage. Her 2002 documentary film about garbage, Gone Tomorrow, *was shown at numerous international film festivals. She has published articles in the* Nation, Utne Reader, Z *magazine,* Art and Design, *the* Brooklyn Rail, *and* Punk Planet. *Rogers is the author of* Gone Tomorrow: The Hidden Life of Garbage *(2005), from which the following essay is taken.*

> *A society in which consumption has to be artificially stimulated*
> *in order to keep production going is a society founded on trash and*
> *waste, and such a society is a house built upon sand.*
> Dorothy L. Sayers, "Why Work?" 1942

From outer space several human-made objects are visible on earth: the Great Wall of China, the pyramids, and, on the southwestern tip of New York City, another monument to civilization, Fresh Kills Landfill. Briefly a depository for the gory debris of 9/11, this colossal waste heap looks rather like a misplaced Western butte. Its fifty-three years' worth of refuse are mostly covered by graded dirt and grasses, and not far off one can see what looks like a functioning estuary. On a bad day the methane stench of consumption past wafts up from the guts of the hill, and when storms hit, toxic leachate flows into the surrounding surface and groundwater. If garbage were a nation, this would be its capital. It's an astounding place, but apart from its size, not so unusual.

In 2003 Americans threw out almost 500 billion pounds of paper, glass, plastic, wood, food, metal, clothing, dead electronics and other refuse. Every day a phantasmagoric rush of spent, used and broken riches flows through our homes, offices and cars, and from there is burned, dumped at sea, or more often buried under a civilized veil of dirt and grass seed. The United States is the world's number one producer of garbage: we consume 30 percent of the planet's resources and produce 30 percent of all its wastes. But we are home to just 4 percent of the global population. Recent figures show that every American discards over 1,600 pounds of rubbish a year—more than 4.5 pounds per person per day. And over the past generation our mountains of waste have doubled.

Eat a take-out meal, buy a pair of shoes, read a newspaper, and you're soon faced with a bewildering amount of trash. And forget trying to fix a broken toaster, malfunctioning cell phone or frozen VCR—nowadays it's less expensive to toss the old one and purchase a brand-new replacement. Many people feel guilty about their waste and helpless over how to avoid it. This angst intensifies if our discards aren't promptly hauled away. Consider this tortured passage from a Chicago journalist writing during a 2003 garbage strike:

> I want to improve the environment. I do. But looking at an extra week's worth of Lucky Charms With New Larger Marshmallows boxes and Conair packaging and empty water bottles and ripped-up Instyle magazines and dried-out nail polish in Bus Stop Crimson and Gap bags... I wonder if maybe I'm not doing my part.
>
> The mounting trash is a constant reminder of how much we spend. How much we consume. How much we waste.
>
> Won't someone please come take it away?

Disruptions in the channeling of trash out of our immediate lives are infrequent; most often the rubbish gets collected on time. But even when the system works well, a nagging feeling can linger: Where does it all go? The opening lines of the popular 1989 film *Sex, Lies, and Videotape* bring these repressed anxieties to the surface. Andie MacDowell's character confesses to her therapist: "Garbage. All I've been thinking about all week is garbage....I mean, we've got so much of it. You know, I mean, we have to run out of places to put this stuff, eventually." Many people today feel at least a little uneasy about the profusion of garbage that our society produces. But while its fate most often lies hidden, trash remains a distressing element of daily life, linked to much larger questions that never really go away.

Garbage is the text in which abundance is overwritten by decay and filth: natural substances rot next to art images on discarded plastic packaging; objects of superb design—the spent lightbulb or battery—lie among sanitary napkins and rancid meat scraps. Rubbish is also a border separating the clean and useful from the unclean and dangerous. And trash is the visible interface between everyday life and the deep, often abstract horrors of ecological crisis. Through waste we can read the logic of industrial society's relationship to nature and human labor. Here it is, all at once, all mixed together: work, nature, land, production, consumption, the past and the future. And in garbage we find material proof that there is no plan for stewarding the earth, that resources are not being conserved, that waste and destruction are the necessary analogues of consumer society.

This book focuses on household waste, or what is often referred to as "municipal solid waste," which includes rejectamenta from kitchens, bathrooms, hotels, schools, local shops and offices, and small construction sites. Even though over seventy tons of industrial debris from mining, agriculture, manufacturing, and petrochemical production are created for every ton of household discards, it is the slough of daily life that affects average people most directly because it is the waste we make.

Trash Ecology

The direct environmental impacts of garbage are sobering. Increased amounts of trash mean more collection trucks on the road spewing diesel exhaust into the atmosphere. Incinerators release toxics into the air and spawn ash that can contaminate soil and water. Landfills metastasize like cancer across the countryside, leaching their hazardous brew into nearby groundwater, unleashing untold environmental problems for future generations.

Garbage graveyards have met stricter environmental controls for only the past two decades, with a national set of standards being implemented just over ten years ago. This means that there are scores of dumps across the country still struggling to meet newer, tougher regulations. Meanwhile, they pollute local aquifers, soil and air.

In addition to leaching liquid wastes, landfills also erupt "landfill gas," the emissions of decomposing waste. This wretched vapor consists mostly of highly flammable methane, which is a major contributor to global climate change. According to the Environmental Protection Agency (EPA), "Methane is of particular concern because it is 21 times more effective at trapping heat in the atmosphere than carbon dioxide." Landfill gas also includes the air-borne wastes from things like adhesives, household cleaners, plastics and paints, including carbon dioxide, hazardous air pollutants (HAP) and volatile organic compounds (VOC). One EPA assessment reads: "Emissions of VOC contribute to ground-level ozone formation (smog). Ozone is capable of reducing or damaging vegetation growth as well as causing respiratory problems in humans... exposure to HAP can cause a variety of health problems such as cancerous illnesses, respiratory irritation, and central nervous system damage."

10   Incinerators are just as onerous. As of the year 2000, according to the United Nations Environment Programme, municipal waste incinerators were responsible for creating 69 percent of worldwide dioxin emissions. Dioxins are a group of chemicals identified as among the most toxic in existence. Even if a facility is outfitted with all the latest filtration gear, dioxin cannot be destroyed or neutralized because it is generated through the very process of incineration. When everyday substances like paper and plastic are burned together they form dioxin, which either takes to the air or lingers in the remaining ash. Incinerators also spew acidic gases (which cause acid rain), particulate matter, carbon monoxide and mercury. Leftover ash can also contain heavy metals like lead, mercury, cadmium and other toxic substances that can leach once buried in landfills.

Packaging comprises the largest, and most rapidly growing, category of discards. More than 30 percent of municipal waste is packaging, and 40 percent of that is plastic. Polymers are now ubiquitous in the country's incinerators and landfills as they overflow with televisions, computers, cell phones, medical waste, soda bottles and cellophane wrappers. But because they are resilient and toxic, synthetics cannot be safely returned to the environment. On average, plastics are predicted to stay intact for 200, 400, maybe 1,000 years, and these are only guesses. For their life span, plastics kept above ground will abrade and "off-gas" malignant releases into the air. When buried, plastic resins can leach hazardous materials into the water and soil, and during production polymers are notoriously dangerous, poisoning workers and the environment. Regardless of these problems, the U.S. plastics industry has boomed over the last fifty years, growing at twice the annual rate of all other manufacturing combined. Perhaps that's why the middle of the Pacific Ocean is now six times more abundant with plastic waste than with zooplankton.

Recycling was presented as a solution to the garbage crisis, but it can't keep pace with the staggering output of throwaways. About 80 percent of U.S. products are used once and then discarded. Although there are more than 9,000 curbside recycling programs in the country, many towns do not collect the stuff. And even if the dutiful separate their metal from glass, much of it still ends up at the landfill or incinerator, having found no buyer on the other end. If substances sent to recovery centers can't compete with lower-priced "virgin" materials, they get dumped. And, further limiting the expansion of recycling, U.S. producers are not required to use reprocessed materials even though most manufacturers now stamp their containers with the eco-friendly recycling symbol.

Perhaps surprisingly, 50 percent of all paper ends up as garbage (in fact, paper accounts for fully half of the discards in U.S. landfills). Today, only 5 percent of all plastic is recycled, while almost two-thirds of all glass containers and half of aluminum beverage cans get trashed. Tossed as soon as it is empty, sometimes within minutes of purchase, packaging is garbage waiting to happen.

There are other catastrophic environmental consequences of a mass consumption society. While they may not appear explicitly connected to garbage, these effects are unmistakably bound with a system that produces so much trash. Just as manufacturing creates the bulk of all refuse, the mass production that creates the torrent of cans, bottles, and electronics we throw away wreaks havoc on nature due to the insatiable need for raw materials. Extraction of timber, natural gas, oil and coal, along with massive water and power usage, all speed the destruction of the earth's natural systems.

Forecast: Extreme Conditions

The rate of climate change is perhaps the broadest barometer of environmental health and is closely linked to trash; the more that gets thrown out, the more pollution-causing processes are relied on to make replacement goods. According to the latest reports, global warming is increasing at a far faster rate than previously predicted. In contravention of the Kyoto Protocol[1] (which the U.S. refuses to sign), America's carbon emissions from burning fossil fuels—a major contributor to heat-trapping greenhouse gases—increased almost 20 percent between 1990 and 2000.

Most likely the result of these emissions, extreme weather has already caused a series of apocalyptic scenarios. A 2003 heat wave in France killed 15,000. A quartet of hurricanes in 2004 slammed into the Caribbean and Florida, slaying hundreds, displacing thousands and causing an estimated $25 billion in damages in Florida alone. On the other side of the planet, Bangladesh suffered the most violent flooding in a half-century during the summer of 2004. Almost 800 people drowned, 30 million were left homeless and countless crops were ruined. The storms left behind more than $6 billion in damages to roads, agriculture and industry.

Not only are the knock-on environmental effects exported from developed countries to the global South, so are mass production, consumption and wasting patterns. As factories move overseas seeking ever-cheaper armies of labor, they disseminate manufacturing practices that churn out epic amounts of trash and pollution, beyond the reach of the global North's tighter environmental controls.

Consumption has been transformed in places like India, where ceramic throwaway teacups are being replaced by disposable plastic cups and bottles. Instead of getting harmlessly ground into the roadside, polluting plastic must be buried or burned. Plastic shopping bags are unleashing their wrath across developing countries as well. In China they're known as the "white pollution," while South Africans call trashed polymer bags the "national flower." India is flocked with the soft, thin material; it hangs from trees, litters streets, ruins rivers and chokes sacred cows that consume it while grazing. And in Bangladesh, plastic bags have clogged and destroyed drainage systems, causing such major flooding that the government outlawed the manufacture of disposable synthetic totes in 2002.

Adding still more to these new and growing wellsprings of trash, much of America's discards get shipped overseas for recycling and disposal. These encompass used plastic bottles, scrap metal, spent chemicals, and a virulent new category of refuse that includes trashed televisions, computers, cell phones and other electronics, known as "e-waste." And foreign processing firms are buying rubbish from the United States—the world's largest consumer—at a rapidly expanding rate. Exporting wastes from the United States, an industry worth just under $200 million in 1997, grew to over $1 billion in revenues in 2002.

---

[1]International treaty whose aim is to decrease greenhouse gas emissions that influence climate change. [Eds.]

Container ships from Asia that bring brand-new sneakers, Teflon kitchenware and CD players to the United States now return home packed with American rubbish.

How did we get into this mess? Consumption lies at the heart of 20 American life and economic health, and intrinsic to consumption is garbage. Such high levels of waste are the product not of any natural law or strange primordial impulse but of history, of social forces.

The world of trash did not always exist as it does today. In the nineteenth century refuse was sorted, municipal waste was composted, and all kinds of materials that left the home as discards were extensively reused. But with industrialization and two massive world wars the production system was radically transformed, and so too was garbage. Increasingly, what gets thrown away is shaped by monopolistic corporate power: at one end manufacturers, marketers and ad men, at the other giant corporations like Waste Management Inc. With annual consumer spending in the United States now accounting for about two-thirds of the nation's $11 trillion economy while outlays on discard handling and disposal approaches $50 billion, it's no wonder there's so much trash—garbage is good for business.

Responding to Reading

1. Why does the United States produce so much garbage? What does Rogers imply could be done to reduce the amount of garbage we produce? What does she mean when she says, "waste and destruction are the necessary analogues of consumer society" (5)?
2. What are the "direct environmental impacts of garbage" (7)? What, if anything, does Rogers think can be done to lessen these impacts?
3. What facts and figures does Rogers use to support her claims? Do you think she includes the right kind of support? Does she include enough support?

Responding in Writing

In her essay, Rogers uses adjectives like *toxic, malignant,* and *apocalyptic* to describe the effects of garbage on the environment. Are such adjectives appropriate, or do you think they exaggerate the severity of the problem?

BUILT TO LAST

Alan Weisman

1947–

A journalist as well as an associate professor of journalism and Latin American studies at the University of Arizona, Alan Weisman reports on topics related to the environment and Latin America. His articles have appeared in such publications as Wilson Quarterly, *the* New York Times Magazine, *the* Los Angeles Times Magazine, Harper's, *the* Atlantic Monthly, Orion, Audubon, Discover, *and* Mother Jones. *His most recent books, both published in 2007, are* Prince of Darkness: Richard Perle: The Kingdom, the Power and the End of Empire in America *and* The World without Us. *In the following essay, Weisman considers the long-term consequences of designing and building our industrial infrastructure the way we do.*

The fire station where Erin Moore and I have paused in our stroll through downtown Tucson won't fall apart anytime soon. Its bottom half is walled in 18-inch-thick concrete, which surrounds massive I-beams that frame tall, wooden double doors. The steel-clad upper two stories are faced in slabs of pale stone. "Now *that* one," Moore says, nodding approvingly, "will leave a very nice skeleton." A tall, light-haired architect in her early thirties, Moore has wide, alert eyes that absorb copious amounts of information in a glance. Through them she sees architecture in four dimensions, not the usual three.

"I don't see a structure as beautiful unless it has a graceful way to break down built into its future," she says, shading her eyes against the autumnal desert glare. Solid as this fire station is, she can envision how, if its destiny is left to time, the sun will loosen the grout and caulking that secure its facing, sending the stone crashing someday. The big doors will succumb as gravity and moisture undo their hinges, and its floors of concrete, poured over corrugated decking, will crack and flake apart. Slowly but inexorably, the building's base will disintegrate to sand and lime, eventually leaving only a rusting matrix of rebar and steel beams. Finally, that too will corrode, to iron oxide dust. Aesthetically, Moore says, the deterioration of this building will be far more interesting and pleasing than the fate of the tinted-glass-and-steel downtown boxes we've passed, doomed to collapse one day into messy piles.

"We live and build within a cyclical ecosystem, in which things mean as much in death as in life. When we show clients an architectural rendering, it's like when an OB-GYN shows expectant parents an ultrasound image—that's not what their kid will always look like. It's not just how something looks now, but how it *will* look. Architects should think of ourselves as choreographers. What we make will always be interacting with time, weather, chemistry, and with people's touch."

Across the street is a venerable example: one of Tucson's few remaining blocks of flat-roofed adobe houses. Replastered every few years, they last indefinitely; neglected, they melt attractively until all that remains is a pile of reusable window frames. Once, such natural mud constructions defined the entire city. Then railroads arrived, bringing sheet metal that could form low-maintenance pitched roofs. But that was only the beginning. Most of the Tucson of today won't dissolve charmingly back into the earth from which its walls rose. Instead, its legacy will be heaps of aluminum shower-stall parts; sun-cracked, faux-clay vinyl roofing tiles; cement-and-polymer hybrid siding advertised not to weather, but which does anyway as water infiltrates its nail holes; plastic and brass- or chrome-plated debris that once adorned façades and swimming pools; and lumps of polymer glop used to bind these items, that won't break down for thousands of years.

Yet even if our cities were filled with totally biodegradable and recy- 5 clable architecture, we would still be faced with clutter that won't disappear in any reasonably human span of time, because every edifice and dwelling is linked by infrastructure intended to be resilient. Unlike buildings, whose durability isn't always a virtue—"You want a McDonald's to be ultrapermanent?" Erin Moore asks students at the University of Arizona, where she teaches—we get into trouble when entropy shreds the connective tissues of our civilization. We want our roads, bridges, tunnels, mass-transit rails, dams, pipelines, sewers, canals, and transmission cables to last. When they don't, the consequences range from irritation and anxiety to panic and disaster. But if we design infrastructure to endure forever, have we only created another kind of problem?

On August 1, 2007, a Minneapolis bridge that forms part of our interstate highway system dropped into the Mississippi River—"without warning," newscasters said repeatedly. Though their shock was genuine, their analysis was mistaken. While I was researching my book *The World Without Us,* a bridge expert named Jerry Del Tufo had explained to me exactly why such events were predictable, if not inevitable.

Del Tufo, a structural engineer with the Port Authority of New York and New Jersey, has at various times been in charge of several bridges linking New York's boroughs. One snowy February afternoon in 2005 he drove me to the Bayonne Bridge, which connects Staten Island to New Jersey. As we gazed up at the Bayonne's colossal underside matrix of steel bracing, Del Tufo explained that New York bridges such as the George Washington and this one, both more than 70 years old, were built before computers were around to calculate the minimum amount of materials budget-crunched contractors could get away with. Back then, cautious engineers simply heaped excess mass onto the bridges they imagined.

"These bridges are so overbuilt, traffic's like an ant on an elephant," Del Tufo said. "The GW alone has enough galvanized steel wire in its three-inch suspension cables to wrap the earth four times. We're living off the over-capacity of our forefathers."

By contrast, the Minneapolis bridge, half the age of these robust older spans, was already known to be crumbling before it failed. At the time of its collapse, four of its eight lanes were closed for repairs to the roadway deck and to several weakened steel joints, the extent of their deterioration hidden from public view behind tarpaulins. Although no official cause of the calamity has been identified by the National Transportation Safety Board, the added weight of construction materials and cement trucks to evening rush hour traffic was apparently enough to break the I-35W bridge's back. That only 13 people died was considered miraculous.

10   A year earlier, just one car was crushed when a three-ton slab of concrete held in place by epoxy became unglued and fell from the ceiling of an enclosed ramp in Boston's recently completed Big Dig, a massive public-works project that rerouted snarled downtown traffic over a new bridge and through two tunnels—one of which is more than three miles long. Thousands who'd traveled the same route that day were stunned by the random good fortune of their near miss.

The dilemma of modern construction is summed up in an anecdote that Wernher von Braun, the scientist who developed the U.S. space program, used to tell about John Glenn, the first American to orbit the earth: "Seconds before lift-off, with Glenn strapped into that rocket we built for him and man's best efforts all focused on that moment, you know what he said to himself? 'My God! I'm sitting on a pile of low bids!' "

And we've been driving over and under them. One obvious remedy is to spend more public funds to shore up our underpinnings. Yet this logic collides with an invisible obstacle—invisible because it lies beyond the horizon, that is, in the future: How can we know what kind of infrastructure will be necessary five or 15 years from now? Can we risk building something enormously costly that might soon become obsolete? And when it eventually does outlive its service, will we be able to afford to dismantle it without leaving huge, indelible gashes in the landscape, and reuse the stuff for which we paid so much to construct it?

Two hundred miles west of Tucson, 300-year-old wagon wheel ruts marking the passage of Jesuit explorer Padre Eusebio Kino are still traceable in the desert caliche, just above the Mexican border. To the north, paralleling Kino's route, the 10-inch-thick, four-lane band of poured concrete ending at San Diego known as Interstate 8 will last far longer. But what if our search for energy-efficient, next-generation transportation were to produce a vehicle—say, a hovercraft—that rendered unnecessary not only energy-gobbling transmissions and friction-prone rubber tires but possibly even roads themselves—and for that matter, tunnels and bridges?

What would we do then with the four million miles of pavement cross-hatching the United States alone? What would China do with its own ever-thickening, mostly brand-new weave of highways, already half the size of ours and spreading fast? Although concrete and asphalt can be recycled, their main application is to build more roads. Either way, reusing or removing implies vast, possibly prohibitive energy expenditures. Even leaving them intact for bicycles would become extravagant once maintenance costs were factored in. Nature would eventually overgrow them—in a few centuries to a few millennia, depending on climate—but until then, they would bear accusing witness to how our century of motorized vehicular addiction scarred formerly sublime land.

Hovercraft may seem an unlikely scenario to us now (though at 15 Chicago's 1893 World's Columbian Exposition, technology exhibits for the next century failed to predict airplanes, television, and personal computers). But another potential innovation that could supersede a significant part of our infrastructural legacy isn't so far-fetched. During the 20th century, we wrapped much of the earth's landmasses in wire: electrical and communications lines that, if the United States' grids alone were strung in a single strand, would reach the moon and back, and nearly back again. Whenever storms or accidents sever their copper, aluminum, or optical-fiber lengths, we lose money and, temporarily, our sanity, as we wait helplessly for repairs to restore power or re-establish contact.

Yet increasingly we communicate wirelessly, with devices that require far fewer cables and antennae. With no small envy, we encourage developing nations to seize the chance to leapfrog our stage of technological advancement, with its unsightly tangle of overhead cables, and beam their telephony, voice and data alike, via radio bands. Although we can't yet substitute pulsing lasers for high-voltage power lines that require 150-foot steel-lattice towers every thousand feet to bear their ponderous weight, we already have technologies that could drastically reduce the sheer mileage of metal we've draped across continents, simply by generating electricity locally—possibly on every rooftop. All that copper and aluminum, if salvaged, might even slake our need to uproot entire mountain ranges and everything that lives on them just to rip more minerals from the ground.

Less easy to dismember, let alone recycle, would be the tons of concrete poured into forms spanning river canyons to create dams. Among the most immense and costly of all human creations, dams are an instant mix of blessings, which in time often become greater liabilities than assets. China's soon-to-be-completed Three Gorges Dam, the world's biggest, is but the latest such structure to provoke predictions that the havoc it wreaks on land, people, and ecology may only be resolved by dismantling it.

It wouldn't be the first. Along North America's coastlines, dams meant to electrify and irrigate so that people and crops might flourish have also clogged arteries through which irreplaceable organisms such as salmon flow. Not only are they commercially precious, but their disappearance causes such cascading losses of life (or livelihood, in the case of fishermen) that dams that obstruct salmon spawning routes lately have been torn down at an expensive clip. Similarly, in the wake of catastrophes such as Hurricane Katrina, the wisdom of channeling rivers through concrete chutes so that cities can occupy their deltas is being reassessed. Once freed, a river heals surprisingly quickly, burying under great loads of silt whatever unsightly scrabble remains after we try to put nature back the way we found it.

As the massive cost of clearing the way for Boston's Big Dig suggests, should large numbers of roads ever become unwanted, it would simply be too expensive to do much other than bury them. In fact, in urban centers destined to be abandoned (or abandoned already, such as parts of Detroit), that job will probably be left to nature. As sewers become clogged with plastic bags and other debris, deserted streets are colonized by germinating weeds and trees, whose roots crack through the pavement as it disappears beneath leaf litter. Like sewers themselves, the cement and asphalt paths that formerly connected our lives to homes and workplaces will gradually sink out of sight, overlain by a spreading cap of new soil.

20   Given enough time, nature will also inter any other infrastructure still standing—most likely our oldest, built from large stones hewn directly from the earth, which will long outlast our more economical but far more vulnerable assemblages of concrete and steel. The ghost of a Mayan pyramid builder would be amazed to see his once monumental, seemingly indomitable kingdom swallowed by forests. So would we.

Responding to Reading

1. Why is Weisman concerned with how architectural structures will break down? What problem is created when we "design infrastructure to endure forever" (5)?
2. Why do bridges built over seventy years ago last longer than newer ones built with the help of computers? According to Weisman, what is the "dilemma of modern construction" (11)?
3. In paragraph 15, Weisman points out that the 1893 World's Columbian Exposition failed to predict many of the technological advances of the next century. What does this observation have to do with the way we design and build our infrastructure?

Responding in Writing

What problems are created when our roads and bridges deteriorate? What problems are created when they don't?

THE INVASION FROM OUTER SPACE
Steven Millhauser
1943–

A professor of English at Skidmore College and a Pulitzer Prize–winning author, Steven Millhauser writes novels, novellas, and short stories. His most recent works include Enchanted Night: A Novella *(1999),* The King in the Tree: Three Novellas *(2003), and* Dangerous Laughter: Thirteen Stories *(2008). A story from his collection* The Barnum Museum *(1990) became the basis for the feature film* The Illusionist *(2006). The following story, "The Invasion from Outer Space," describes a mysterious natural phenomenon.*

From the beginning we were prepared, we knew just what to do, for hadn't we seen it all a hundred times?—the good people of the town going about their business, the suddenly interrupted TV programs, the faces in the crowd looking up, the little girl pointing in the air, the mouths opening, the dog yapping, the traffic stopped, the shopping bag falling to the sidewalk, and there, in the sky, coming closer…And so, when it finally happened, because it was bound to happen, we all knew it was only a matter of time, we felt, in the midst of our curiosity and terror, a certain calm, the calm of familiarity, we knew what was expected of us, at such a moment. The story broke a little after ten in the morning. The TV anchors looked exactly the way we knew they'd look, their faces urgent, their hair neat, their shoulders tense, they were filling us with alarm but also assuring us that everything was under control, for they, too, had been prepared for this, in a sense had been waiting for it, already they were looking back at themselves during their great moment. The sighting was indisputable but, at the same time, inconclusive: something from out there had been detected, it appeared to be approaching our atmosphere at great speed, the Pentagon was monitoring the situation closely. We were urged to remain calm, to stay inside, to await further instructions. Some of us left work immediately and hurried home to our families, others stayed close to the TV, the radio, the computer, we were all talking into our cells. Through our windows we could see people at their windows, looking up at the sky. All that morning we followed the news fiercely, like children listening to a thunderstorm in the dark. Whatever was out there was still unknown, scientists had not yet been able to determine its nature, caution was advised but there was no reason for panic, our job was to stay tuned and sit tight and await further developments. And though we were anxious, though quivers of nervousness ran along our bodies like mice, we wanted to see whatever it was, we wanted to be there, since after all it was coming toward *us,* it was ours to witness, as if we were the ones they'd chosen, out there on the other side of the sky. For already it was being said that our town was the likely landing place, already the TV crews were rolling in. We wondered where it would land: between the duck pond and the seesaws in the public park, or deep in the woods at the north end of town, or maybe in the field out by the mall, where a new excavation was already under way, or maybe it would glide over the old department store on Main Street and crash through the second-floor apartments above Mangione's Pizza and Café, with a great shattering of brick and glass, maybe it would land on the throughway and we'd see eighteen-wheelers turn over, great chunks of pavement rise up at sharp angles, and car after car swerve into the guardrail and roll down the embankment.

Something appeared in the sky shortly before one o'clock. Many of us were still at lunch, others were already outside, standing motionless on the streets and sidewalks, gazing up. There were shouts and cries, arms in the air, a wildness of gesturing, pointing. And, sure enough, something was glittering, up there in the sky, something was shimmering, in the blue air of summer—we saw it clearly, whatever it was. Secretaries in offices rushed to windows, storekeepers abandoned their cash registers and hurried outdoors, road workers in orange hard hats looked up from the asphalt, shaded their eyes. It must have lasted—that faraway glow, that spot of shimmer—some three or four minutes. Then it began to grow larger, until it was the size of a dime, a quarter. Suddenly the entire sky seemed to be filled with points of gold. Then it was coming down on us, like fine pollen, like yellow dust. It lay on our roof slopes, it sifted down onto our sidewalks, covered our shirtsleeves and the tops of our cars. We did not know what to make of it.

It continued to come down, that yellow dust, for nearly thirteen minutes. During that time we could not see the sky. Then it was over. The sun shone, the sky was blue. Throughout the downpour, we'd been warned to stay inside, to be careful, to avoid touching the substance from outer space, but it had happened so quickly that most of us had streaks of yellow on our clothes and in our hair. Soon after the warnings, we heard cautious reassurances: preliminary tests revealed nothing toxic, though the nature of the yellow dust remained unknown. Animals that had eaten it revealed no symptoms. We were urged to keep out of its way and await further test results. Meanwhile it lay over our lawns and sidewalks and front steps, it coated our maple trees and telephone poles. We were reminded of waking in the morning after the first snow. From our porches we watched the three-wheeled sweepers move slowly along our streets, carrying it off in big hoppers. We hosed down our grass, our front walks, our porch furniture. We looked up at the sky, we waited for more news—already we were hearing reports that the substance was composed of one-celled organisms—and through it all we could sense the swell of our disappointment.

We had wanted, we had wanted—oh, who knew what we'd been looking for? We had wanted blood, crushed bones, howls of agony. We had wanted buildings crumbling onto streets, cars bursting into flame. We had wanted monstrous versions of ourselves with enlarged heads on stalklike necks, merciless polished robots armed with death rays. We had wanted noble lords of the universe with kind, soft eyes, who would usher in a glorious new era. We had wanted terror and ecstasy— anything but this yellow dust. Had it even been an invasion? Later that afternoon, we learned that scientists all agreed: the dust was a living thing. Samples had been flown to Boston, Chicago, Washington, D.C. The single-celled organisms appeared to be harmless, though we were cautioned not to touch anything, to keep the windows shut, to wash our hands. The cells reproduced by binary fission. They appeared to do nothing but multiply.

In the morning, we woke to a world covered in yellow dust. It lay on the tops of our fences, on the crossbars of telephone poles. Black tire tracks showed in the yellow streets. Birds, shaking their wings, threw up sprays of yellow powder. Again the street-sweepers came, the hoses splashed on driveways and lawns, making a yellow mist and revealing the black and the green underneath. Within an hour the driveways and lawns resembled yellow fields. Lines of yellow ran along cables and telephone wires. 5

According to the news, the unicellular microorganisms are rod-shaped and nourish themselves by photosynthesis. A single cell, placed in a brightly illuminated test tube, divides at such a rate that the tube will fill in about forty minutes. An entire room, in strong light, will fill in six hours. The organisms do not fit easily into our classification schemes, though in some respects they resemble blue-green algae. There is no evidence that they are harmful to human or animal life.

We have been invaded by nothing, by emptiness, by animate dust. The invader appears to have no characteristic other than the ability to reproduce rapidly. It doesn't hate us. It doesn't seek our annihilation, our subjection and humiliation. Nor does it desire to protect us from danger, to save us, to teach us the secret of immortal life. What it wishes to do is replicate. It is possible that we will find a way of limiting the spread of this primitive intruder, or of eliminating it altogether; it's also possible that we will fail and that our town will gradually disappear under a fatal accumulation. As we follow the reports from day to day, the feeling grows in us that we deserved something else, something bolder, something grander, something more thrilling, something bristling or fiery or fierce, something that might have represented a revelation or a destiny. We imagine ourselves surrounding the tilted spaceship, waiting for the door to open. We imagine ourselves protecting our children, slashing the tentacles that thrust in through the smashed cellar windows. Instead, we sweep our front walks, hose off our porches, shake out our shoes and sneakers. The invader has entered our homes. Despite our drawn shades and closed curtains, it lies in thick layers on our end tables and windowsills. It lies along the tops of our flat-screen televisions and the narrow edges of our shelved DVDs. Through our windows we can see the yellow dust covering everything, forming gentle undulations. We can almost see it rising slowly, like bread. Here and there it catches the sunlight and reminds us, for a moment, of fields of wheat.

It is really quite peaceful, in its way.

Responding to Reading

1. What is the yellow "animate dust" (7)? Does it pose a danger to earth? Although the dust is described as being "quite peaceful," might its appearance suggest just the opposite (8)?
2. How do the people react to the dust? Is their reaction surprising to you in any way?
3. Do you think this story is about human nature? about the environment? about American culture?

Responding in Writing

Several critics have said that the dust in this story is a symbol. Do you agree? What do you think the dust could represent?

—————————— FOCUS ——————————

How Can We Create a More Sustainable Environment?

Community gardeners displaying organic vegetables

Responding to the Image

1. What is your initial response to this photograph? After reading the essays in this Focus section, does your response change in any way?
2. Other than planting gardens, what else can people do to create a more sustainable environment? Do you think that changing the way we live can have a significant effect on the earth's climate?

THE CHALLENGE TO ENVIRONMENTALISM

Bill McKibben

1960–

A scholar in environmental studies at Middlebury College, Bill McKibben writes about social and environmental issues, including the dangers of global warming and climate change. His numerous articles have appeared in such publications as Daedalus, the Atlantic, National Geographic, Christianity Today, Tikkun, Forbes, Mother Jones, *and the* Christian Century. *His recent books include* Wandering Home: A Long Walk across America's Most Hopeful Landscape, Vermont's Champlain Valley and New York's Adirondacks *(2005),* Deep Economy: The Wealth of Communities and the Durable Future *(2007), and* Fight Global Warming Now: The Handbook for Taking Action in Your Community *(2007). In the following essay, McKibben argues for a new understanding of environmentalism.*

Quantity can redefine quality: meaning can and does change if something gets big enough to pass some invisible but real threshold.

Consider, for instance, how the atom bomb redefined the ways we thought about conflict and war. The old ideas—particularly that warfare was a kind of natural extension of statecraft—had survived a great deal of scaling up, from Agincourt to Antietam, from Thermopylae to Tarawa. But the explosion of the first nuclear weapon, though in some sense just a much larger version of things we'd been doing for years, clearly made us reconsider the idea of war. Oppenheimer, watching the first desert test, quoted from the Gita: "We are become as gods, destroyers of worlds." We've managed to fight plenty of nasty wars since, but we've always made sure to keep them relatively small and manageable. The intellectual edifice we'd built around battle—from just war theory to Clausewitz—no longer works very well. When you could postulate a war that could not just kill millions but poison the soil with radioactivity, potentially trigger an endless nuclear winter, and generally raise the whole concept of return to the Stone Age, sheer quantity redefined meaning.

Now, too, with the environment. The relationship between people and the natural world has been largely taken for granted for most of human history—our impact upon the physical world was small enough not to raise deep conceptual problems. We had great effect on particular places around us—our fields, our forests—but those effects seemed to stop at the edge of our settlements. It was a long time indeed before we began even to suspect that we were putting much larger forces into play. George Perkins Marsh, in the mid-nineteenth century, was among the first to posit the possibility that, say, cutting down whole woodlands was changing hydrological cycles. Rachel Carson, in the mid-twentieth century, was among the first to suggest that our effects, albeit on an invisible level, could now be felt across the whole of creation (a suggestion that took the first real shine off the idea of technical progress for most Americans). But it's only in recent years, with the dawning understanding of how massively we have altered the earth's climate, that we really reach a sea change in our understanding of nature.

We are forced, for the first time, to understand that we are a truly titanic force, capable of affecting and altering the operation of the planetary whole. It's a startling revelation—we seem set to raise sea levels, change the seasons, determine the range of most every other species. You can measure our impact already, in drought and flood and melt. That means that we as a species, and even as individuals, mean something different: like Alice on her first pill, we've gone small to large in short order, earned a kind of unwanted agency.

We can see the practical effects of this shift already in the environ-   5
mental movement, which in the last few years has morphed into the global warming movement. That's where the money and the politics are concentrated: if you're a land conservationist, you're busy trying to figure out some theory of carbon sequestration that will allow you to go on, say, protecting forests or farmland. But as the environmental movement is quickly learning, it's not scaled for this kind of work. The panoply of organizations that saved various watersheds, built national parks, staved off oil drilling in the Arctic National Wildlife Refuge, and even passed the kind of legislation that forced automakers to install catalytic converters are heroic—but they are not up to the task of reshaping our economic life, which is what global warming demands. Forget filters—we're talking about the wholesale decarbonization of our country, about removing the fossil fuel base on which our prosperity has so far rested, and about doing it in the space of a decade or two. That's too much heavy lifting for the heirs of John Muir.

Instead, as its scale changes so dramatically, the problem of 'the environment' needs to go from 'a problem' to some other category. Instead of being one issue on a checklist, it will become a lens through which we survey the world. That's the role economic growth currently plays, and indeed has played for two centuries now. If something made the economy—our private ones, but especially our national ones— larger, then we generally assented; by now it feels inevitable and obvious. But as we start to see the effects of that endless expansion writ large, its continued virtue becomes a little less clear. Instead, the need for durability and resiliency (or to use the inelegant jargon of the movement, 'sustainability') is starting to compete. We see proposals for green GNP,[1] for carbon pricing to reflect the 'true cost' of oil and gas, and so

---

[1]An interpretation of Gross National Product (GNP) that takes environmental concerns into account. [Eds.]

on. More and more this will be the lens through which we measure progress, and one effect will be to make some form of environmentalism so pervasive that the 'movement' itself is somewhat swallowed up. We don't, after all, have an 'economic growth' movement because for the moment all agree (though we arguably have political parties that cater more to the demand for expansion).

These are largely pragmatic considerations; they involve our continued prosperity and perhaps our continued survival. (And they involve, crucially, some new conception of justice across both geography and time, as it becomes clear that most of the world is not going to be able to follow our extravagant example. Nothing will shake our moral sense, our foreign policy, even our theology, as much as the understanding that we've eaten all of the world's cake, and are now making it hard to put even bread on the table.) But as these shifts transform our sense of how carefully we need to tread on the natural world, they will also usher in a new possibility for a different kind of environmentalism that dates at least to Thoreau: the deep concern with where as humans we find meaning.

In a consumer society we've entrusted this concern mostly to the economy (just as in the theocratic one that preceded it we looked mostly to the church). But the economy can't do the job anymore, in part because excessive consumption is precisely what drives the environmental crisis we find ourselves in. And in part as well because we're finally starting to sense the limits of consumption to provide meaning and pleasure in a sated, even glutted, society. The countercultural critique that began with the first Earth Day and then abated somewhat seems now to be returning, albeit in gentler form: farmers' markets are the fastest growing part of the food economy in America, for instance. That's partly because they provide more ecologically sensible (and tasty and healthy) food, and partly because they help re-create the dense web of connections between people that were swept away in a centralizing, globalizing economy. The average shopper at a farmers' market has ten times as many conversations as the average shopper at a supermarket— that order of magnitude is a sign of the world we might be able to build, of the pleasures we might be able to substitute for stuff.

I predict that environmentalism will find itself increasingly interested in promoting this kind of reconnection: that 'wildness,' since Muir the animating force of environmentalism, will become relatively less important than 'community.' (My guess is that the most committed environmentalists now read more Wendell Berry than they do Muir or anyone else.) Both wildness and community continue in short supply, but the key to preserving any of the former may lie in building far more of the latter. The data shows, for instance, that even (or especially) among committed environmentalists, the imperative to build windmills now outranks the imperative to protect birds from their blades—largely because we've grown to understand that climate change will cause endlessly more avian carnage. You can't make a wilderness any more by drawing a line on the map—carbon dioxide is uninterested in lines. But you might be able to slow down the great warming with a farmers' market here and a solar panel there (and there, and there, and there as well), and in the process save some species and some habitats. The vastly increased scale of our damage, that is, may lead to an at least slightly decreased scale of our economic life. The twenty-first century, at least in the rich world, may be about trying to become smaller again.

Responding to Reading

1. McKibben compares the effect the atomic bomb had on warfare to the effect climate change has had on our understanding of the planet. Do you think this comparison is justified?
2. In what sense have human beings become "a truly titanic force" (4) in terms of their effect on the environment? What impact has this concept had on the environmental movement?
3. What is the "different kind of environmentalism" (7) that McKibben asks readers to consider? How does he think this new kind of environmentalism will change the way we live?

Responding in Writing

What does McKibben mean when he says, "the imperative to build windmills now outranks the imperative to protect birds from their blades" (9)? Do you agree with this statement?

GREEN, GREENER, GREENEST

Kate Zernike

A reporter for the New York Times, *Kate Zernike writes about various social and political issues, including college education and the economy. In the following essay, Zernike discusses how college campuses across the country are responding to the green movement.*

Higher education can't resist a ranking: best college, best cafeteria, biggest endowment, biggest party school. It says something about what's important on campus, then, that when the Princeton Review releases its annual guide to colleges this week, it will include a new metric: a "green rating," giving points for things like "environmentally preferable food," power from renewable sources and energy-efficient buildings.

CHAPTER 8   FOCUS

Green is good for the planet, but also for a college's public image. In a Princeton Review survey this year of 10,300 college applicants, 63 percent said that a college's commitment to the environment could affect their decision to go there.

And where there are application decisions to be made, there are rankings. The Association for the Advancement of Sustainability in Higher Education, with more than 660 members, is developing a rating for environmental friendliness; at least six other organizations rated campus greenness last year, according to the group. There are lists from, Forbes, Grist and Sierra magazines, and an annual report card from the Sustainable Endowments Institute, a research organization that assesses the greenness of an institution's investment portfolio. And the Princeton Review will give its top marks to—ta-da!—Arizona State, Bates, Binghamton University, the College of the Atlantic, Harvard, Emory, Georgia Institute of Technology, Yale and the Universities of New Hampshire, Oregon and Washington.

Campuses across the country are racing to be the greenest of them all. They are setting dates in the not too distant future for achieving carbon neutrality (the College of the Atlantic, an eco-college in Maine, already claims that distinction, as does Middlebury College's Snow Bowl ski area). They are hiring sustainability coordinators (the association's job board used to get one posting a month; now it often has five a week). And they are competing with one another in buying green power (in an Environmental Protection Agency contest among athletic conferences, the Ivies triumphed, with a combined 221.6 million kilowatt hours for the quarter ending in April).

5   "I don't think we've seen activism this strong since apartheid," says Cheryl Miller, vice president of Sightlines, a data company that helps campuses compare their operations, including environmental practices.

But as colleges and universities rush to declare themselves green, some higher education officials worry that campuses are taking easy steps to win the label rather than doing the kind of unglamorous work—replacing air exchange systems, for example—that would actually reduce their emissions of greenhouse gases. Some campuses are changing little more than their press releases. "I don't think we really have the tools to quantifiably test who's doing the best and who's not," says David W. Oxtoby, president of Pomona College. "It becomes a publicity hype type of thing."

Sustainability is far more than recycling and "Do It in the Dark" competitions to see which dorms use the least water and electricity. Sustainability is a complex concept, expensive and difficult to achieve. It involves an entirely new approach to day-to-day living and the reappraisal of the existing infrastructure.

Hail to the students demanding eating utensils made with cornstarch (they're biodegradable) for the dining halls. But the changes that make the most difference are not what Mary Gorman, an associate provost at Dartmouth, calls "the low-hanging fruit" of getting students to turn off their screensavers or take shorter showers. The big results come from projects that often sound less catchy and depend less on students than on those who manage the buildings.

She is thinking of the institutions that are vastly reshaping their campuses—converting to greener fuel and power sources, even building their own wind turbines; retrofitting buildings to make them more energy efficient; composting dining-hall waste; replacing fleets with hybrid cars and shuttles that run on oil recycled from French fry vats; and offering sustainability studies to grow a generation of environmental stewards.

"It's important that we focus on the significant rather than the sym- 10 bolic, or at least recognize the symbolic for what it is," says Sarah Hammond Creighton, the sustainability coordinator at Tufts. "I think the commitments are generally real, but I worry that the translation into the depth of the challenge hasn't hit people."

The most high-profile effort, and the most debated, is the American College and University Presidents Climate Commitment, signed over the last two years by more than 550 institutions representing about 30 percent of American students. Those who sign promise that within a year they will inventory their greenhouse gas emissions and within two will formulate a plan to arrive at carbon neutrality—that is, zero net CO_2 emissions—"as soon as possible." They also have to agree to at least two of seven measures, including buying 15 percent of their energy from renewable sources and building to LEED (Leadership in Energy and Environmental Design) standards, a certification developed by the nonprofit United States Green Building Council.

Anthony D. Cortese, who helped create the sustainability association in 2006 as well as the presidents pact, says the quest for carbon neutrality "is creating a real change in the culture."

"We're essentially telling people to put a bubble over their whole campus and say, 'We have to make sure the net greenhouse gases are zero someday,' " he says. "This is not going to be easy."

But to many people, carbon neutrality is a hollow concept, because the only way to get there currently is to buy offsets, credits sold by an entity pledging to, say, plant trees in another country or invest in renewable energy—the environmental equivalent of paying someone to eat broccoli so you can keep consuming ice cream. (For just $35.70 a year, students can feel guilt-free about their electronics-heavy dorm rooms, with an offset bought from Terrapass.)

Offsets can be meaningful. The College of the Atlantic weighed 15 options for a year before settling on a project in Portland, Ore., that manages traffic signals to reduce idling time. The changes are expected to cut carbon dioxide emissions by more than 189,000 tons over

10 years—the equivalent of taking more than 34,000 cars off the road for a year. For a contribution of $22,570, the college can offset 2,488 tons of its emissions.

But offset buyers can't always be sure the money goes to what it's supposed to, that the CO2 credit isn't being sold to someone else at the same time, or that the benefit to the environment is "additional," because the project would not happen without an offset payment.

Doubt about offsets was among the reasons Dartmouth declined to sign the pledge. "We were under a lot of pressure to sign, but we really said, 'How will Dartmouth be different if we're carbon neutral?' " says Ms. Gorman. "We decided we'd rather invest here and actually get real reductions." So while the college does not have a timetable for becoming carbon neutral, it completed an audit of the campus and is spending $12.5 million to make buildings more efficient.

Dr. Oxtoby signed the pledge for Pomona but argues that offsets create the wrong incentive. The college, in Claremont, Calif., is spending millions to install solar panels, though it could have achieved carbon neutrality with a mere $100,000 in offsets. "It's too cheap, it's too easy," Dr. Oxtoby says. "The actual hard work is more expensive, but it actually does something."

He tells of one college president who boasted that his campus was going green by spending about $20,000 to certify that the power it got from the grid was from a non-carbon-based source. "I'm sure the utility just sold the nasty electricity to someone else," Dr. Oxtoby says. "It doesn't change anything."

20   Some are choosing other models. The 23-campus City University of New York has aligned itself with Mayor Michael R. Bloomberg's call to reduce greenhouse emissions 30 percent in the next 10 years.

Instead of signing the presidents climate commitment, Tufts pledged to reduce its greenhouse gases by 75 percent by 2050, consistent with an agreement between New England states and Eastern Canadian provinces. It has already reduced its emissions level almost to that of 1990, in part by switching from oil to gas at its large animal hospital, installing photovoltaic and solar hot water systems on the roof of a new residence hall and installing super-efficient LED lights in a parking garage.

All this won it a spot on the Grist magazine "15 Green Campuses" list, but not on the Forbes top-10 greenest list. In the Princeton Review's forthcoming "Best 368 Colleges," it scored 94 on a scale of 60 to 99.

While the campuses deemed greenest have all taken serious steps to reduce their impact on the environment, the various comparisons rarely look the same and can disagree about what matters most.

Many consider how many buildings are LEED certified. (Purists point out that truly sustainable campuses would not be building at all—a LEED-certified building may use less energy than a conventional one, but it's still expanding the total energy used.) Some ask whether the institution has hired a sustainability coordinator, whether it has signed a carbon-neutrality pledge; there are attempts, even more open to "greenwashing," to gauge how well students are being prepared to make environmentally responsible decisions.

All this may be important, says Jennifer Andrews, the campus pro-   25 gram manager for Clean Air-Cool Planet, a nonprofit group that developed the Campus Carbon Calculator, which is used by many campuses to survey their emissions. But, she says, "A lot of it is measuring attitudes and values. Both are absolutely necessary, but there's a difference between looking at that broadly and looking at what we can quantify and track over time."

Even the quantifiable has its complications. Should we define greenness by how many tons of trash per student a campus recycles or how many kilowatt hours of electricity are supplied by green sources? What about the emissions produced to manufacture construction materials for a new dorm? The environmental cost of students flying in from distant homes or sports teams traveling to away games?

Ms. Andrews, like many others, fears that institutions are focused on where they stand rather than on making substantial changes that will reduce their carbon footprint. "They can lose sight of the fact that it's more important to think about where we need to go and what it's going to take to get us there than about what our peer school is doing," she says. "The natural thing to do is say, 'How does it compare to other schools?' "

Julian Dautremont-Smith, the associate director of the sustainability association, understands the ambivalence about rankings. "There is a suspicion that those lists are based on the strength of the P.R. office rather than the strength of actual efforts," he says. "There's a real fear people are responding to, because every time one of those rankings comes out, the sustainability officer has to go to their bosses and explain why we didn't perform well."

Indeed, campuses were eager to be rated by the Princeton Review. "We had a glorious response rate," reports Rob Franek, a vice president. "Generally speaking, when schools get on our 'reefer madness' list, I'm not their favorite person. For this, they were pretty great."

In fact, Mr. Dautremont-Smith and other sustainability advocates   30 advised the Princeton Review on its rating system. In rankings, they see a greater good. "It gets people's attention on the colleges and universities that might not have paid attention to these issues," says Mr. Cortese, the force behind the presidents commitment. "People are beginning to see that it is important to think about this. To me, that opens the door to more serious conversations about what people are really doing."

Responding to Reading

1. According to Zernike, why is green good for a college's image? What steps are colleges taking to project this image?
2. Why do some college officials worry about the rush to be green? What steps does Zernike think colleges should take to create a more sustainable environment?
3. What problems do colleges have defining *greenness* and *sustainability?* What are carbon "offsets" (14)? What special problems do offsets pose for environmental sustainability?

Responding in Writing

Look around your college campus. What steps is your college taking to create a "green" campus? Do you think your school is doing enough?

WHY BOTHER?

Michael Pollan

1955–

A professor of science and environmental journalism at the University of California at Berkeley, Michael Pollan writes about topics related to food and the environment. He has published numerous articles in publications such as the Saturday Evening Post, *the* New York Times Magazine, *the* New York Times, Time, *and* Mother Jones. *His essays have been anthologized in* Best American Essays, Best American Science Writing, *and the* Norton Book of Nature Writing. *Pollan's recent books include* The Botany of Desire: A Plant's Eye View of the World *(2001),* The Omnivore's Dilemma: A Natural History of Four Meals *(2006), and* In Defense of Food: An Eater's Manifesto *(2008). In the following essay, Pollan examines the role of individual efforts in addressing the global climate-change crisis.*

Why bother? That really is the big question facing us as individuals hoping to do something about climate change, and it's not an easy one to answer. I don't know about you, but for me the most upsetting moment in "An Inconvenient Truth" came long after Al Gore scared the hell out of me, constructing an utterly convincing case that the very survival of life on earth as we know it is threatened by climate change. No, the really dark moment came during the closing credits, when we are asked to…change our light bulbs. That's when it got really depressing. The immense disproportion between the magnitude of the problem Gore had described and the puniness of what he was asking us to do about it was enough to sink your heart.

But the drop-in-the-bucket issue is not the only problem lurking behind the "why bother" question. Let's say I do bother, big time. I turn my life upside-down, start biking to work, plant a big garden, turn down the thermostat so low I need the Jimmy Carter signature cardigan, forsake the clothes dryer for a laundry line across the yard, trade in the station wagon for a hybrid, get off the beef, go completely local. I could theoretically do all that, but what would be the point when I know full well that halfway around the world there lives my evil twin, some carbon-footprint doppelganger in Shanghai or Chongqing who has just bought his first car (Chinese car ownership is where ours was back in 1918), is eager to swallow every bite of meat I forswear and who's positively itching to replace every last pound of CO_2 I'm struggling no longer to emit. So what exactly would I have to show for all my trouble?

A sense of personal virtue, you might suggest, somewhat sheepishly. But what good is that when virtue itself is quickly becoming a term of derision? And not just on the editorial pages of The Wall Street Journal or on the lips of the vice president, who famously dismissed energy conservation as a "sign of personal virtue." No, even in the pages of The New York Times and The New Yorker, it seems the epithet "virtuous," when applied to an act of personal environmental responsibility, may be used only ironically. Tell me: How did it come to pass that virtue—a quality that for most of history has generally been deemed, well, a virtue—became a mark of liberal softheadedness? How peculiar, that doing the right thing by the environment—buying the hybrid, eating like a locavore—should now set you up for the Ed Begley Jr.[1] treatment.

And even if in the face of this derision I decide I am going to bother, there arises the whole vexed question of getting it right. Is eating local or walking to work really going to reduce my carbon footprint? According to one analysis, if walking to work increases your appetite and you consume more meat or milk as a result, walking might actually emit more carbon than driving. A handful of studies have recently suggested that in certain cases under certain conditions, produce from places as far away as New Zealand might account for less carbon than comparable domestic products. True, at least one of these studies was co-written by a representative of agribusiness interests in (surprise!) New Zealand, but even so, they make you wonder. If determining the carbon footprint of food is really this complicated, and I've got to consider not only "food miles" but also whether the food came by ship or truck and how lushly the grass grows in New Zealand, then maybe on second thought I'll just buy the imported chops at Costco, at least until the experts get their footprints sorted out.

There are so many stories we can tell ourselves to justify doing nothing, but perhaps the most insidious is that, whatever we do manage to do, it will be too little too late. Climate change is upon us, and it has arrived well ahead of schedule. Scientists' projections that seemed dire a decade ago turn out to have been unduly optimistic: the warming and

---

[1]American actor and environmental activist. [Eds.]

the melting is occurring much faster than the models predicted. Now truly terrifying feedback loops threaten to boost the rate of change exponentially, as the shift from white ice to blue water in the Arctic absorbs more sunlight and warming soils everywhere become more biologically active, causing them to release their vast stores of carbon into the air. Have you looked into the eyes of a climate scientist recently? They look really scared.

So do you still want to talk about planting gardens?

I do.

Whatever we can do as individuals to change the way we live at this suddenly very late date does seem utterly inadequate to the challenge. It's hard to argue with Michael Specter, in a recent New Yorker piece on carbon footprints, when he says: "Personal choices, no matter how virtuous [N.B.!], cannot do enough. It will also take laws and money." So it will. Yet it is no less accurate or hardheaded to say that laws and money cannot do enough, either; that it will also take profound changes in the way we live. Why? Because the climate-change crisis is at its very bottom a crisis of lifestyle— of character, even. The Big Problem is nothing more or less than the sum total of countless little everyday choices, most of them made by us (consumer spending represents 70 percent of our economy), and most of the rest of them made in the name of our needs and desires and preferences.

For us to wait for legislation or technology to solve the problem of how we're living our lives suggests we're not really serious about changing— something our politicians cannot fail to notice. They will not move until we do. Indeed, to look to leaders and experts, to laws and money and grand schemes, to save us from our predicament represents precisely the sort of thinking—passive, delegated, dependent for solutions on specialists— that helped get us into this mess in the first place. It's hard to believe that the same sort of thinking could now get us out of it.

10   Thirty years ago, Wendell Berry, the Kentucky farmer and writer, put forward a blunt analysis of precisely this mentality. He argued that the environmental crisis of the 1970s—an era innocent of climate change; what we would give to have back that environmental crisis!—was at its heart a crisis of character and would have to be addressed first at that level: at home, as it were. He was impatient with people who wrote checks to environmental organizations while thoughtlessly squandering fossil fuel in their everyday lives—the 1970s equivalent of people buying carbon offsets to atone for their Tahoes and Durangos. Nothing was likely to change until we healed the "split between what we think and what we do." For Berry, the "why bother" question came down to a moral imperative: "Once our personal connection to what is wrong becomes clear, then we have to choose: we can go on as before, recognizing our dishonesty and living with it the best we can, or we can begin the effort to change the way we think and live."

For Berry, the deep problem standing behind all the other problems of industrial civilization is "specialization," which he regards as the "disease of the modern character." Our society assigns us a tiny number of roles: we're producers (of one thing) at work, consumers of a great many other things the rest of the time, and then once a year or so we vote as citizens. Virtually all of our needs and desires we delegate to specialists of one kind or another—our meals to agribusiness, health to the doctor, education to the teacher, entertainment to the media, care for the environment to the environmentalist, political action to the politician.

As Adam Smith and many others have pointed out, this division of labor has given us many of the blessings of civilization. Specialization is what allows me to sit at a computer thinking about climate change. Yet this same division of labor obscures the lines of connection—and responsibility—linking our everyday acts to their real-world consequences, making it easy for me to overlook the coal-fired power plant that is lighting my screen, or the mountaintop in Kentucky that had to be destroyed to provide the coal to that plant, or the streams running crimson with heavy metals as a result.

Of course, what made this sort of specialization possible in the first place was cheap energy. Cheap fossil fuel allows us to pay distant others to process our food for us, to entertain us and to (try to) solve our problems, with the result that there is very little we know how to accomplish for ourselves. Think for a moment of all the things you suddenly need to do for yourself when the power goes out—up to and including entertaining yourself. Think, too, about how a power failure causes your neighbors—your community—to suddenly loom so much larger in your life. Cheap energy allowed us to leapfrog community by making it possible to sell our specialty over great distances as well as summon into our lives the specialties of countless distant others.

Here's the point: Cheap energy, which gives us climate change, fosters precisely the mentality that makes dealing with climate change in our own lives seem impossibly difficult. Specialists ourselves, we can no longer imagine anyone but an expert, or anything but a new technology or law, solving our problems. Al Gore asks us to change the light bulbs because he probably can't imagine us doing anything much more challenging, like, say, growing some portion of our own food. We can't imagine it, either, which is probably why we prefer to cross our fingers and talk about the promise of ethanol and nuclear power—new liquids and electrons to power the same old cars and houses and lives.

The "cheap-energy mind," as Wendell Berry called it, is the mind 15 that asks, "Why bother?" because it is helpless to imagine—much less attempt—a different sort of life, one less divided, less reliant. Since the cheap-energy mind translates everything into money, its proxy, it prefers to put its faith in market-based solutions—carbon taxes and pollution-trading schemes. If we could just get the incentives right, it believes, the economy will properly value everything that matters and nudge our self-interest down the proper channels. The best we can hope for is a greener version of the old invisible hand. Visible hands it has no use for.

But while some such grand scheme may well be necessary, it's doubtful that it will be sufficient or that it will be politically sustainable before we've demonstrated to ourselves that change is possible. Merely to give, to spend, even to vote, is not to do, and there is so much that needs to be done—without further delay. In the judgment of James Hansen, the NASA climate scientist who began sounding the alarm on global warming 20 years ago, we have only 10 years left to start cutting— not just slowing—the amount of carbon we're emitting or face a "different planet." Hansen said this more than two years ago, however; two years have gone by, and nothing of consequence has been done. So: eight years left to go and a great deal left to do.

Which brings us back to the "why bother" question and how we might better answer it. The reasons not to bother are many and compelling, at least to the cheap-energy mind. But let me offer a few admittedly tentative reasons that we might put on the other side of the scale:

If you do bother, you will set an example for other people. If enough other people bother, each one influencing yet another in a chain reaction of behavioral change, markets for all manner of green products and alternative technologies will prosper and expand. (Just look at the market for hybrid cars.) Consciousness will be raised, perhaps even changed: new moral imperatives and new taboos might take root in the culture. Driving an S.U.V. or eating a 24-ounce steak or illuminating your McMansion like an airport runway at night might come to be regarded as outrages to human conscience. Not having things might become cooler than having them. And those who did change the way they live would acquire the moral standing to demand changes in behavior from others—from other people, other corporations, even other countries.

All of this could, theoretically, happen. What I'm describing (imagining would probably be more accurate) is a process of viral social change, and change of this kind, which is nonlinear, is never something anyone can plan or predict or count on. Who knows, maybe the virus will reach all the way to Chongqing and infect my Chinese evil twin. Or not. Maybe going green will prove a passing fad and will lose steam after a few years, just as it did in the 1980s, when Ronald Reagan took down Jimmy Carter's solar panels from the roof of the White House.

20   Going personally green is a bet, nothing more or less, though it's one we probably all should make, even if the odds of it paying off aren't great. Sometimes you have to act as if acting will make a difference, even when you can't prove that it will. That, after all, was precisely what happened in Communist Czechoslovakia and Poland, when a handful of individuals like Vaclav Havel and Adam Michnik resolved that they would simply conduct their lives "as if" they lived in a free society. That improbable bet created a tiny space of liberty that, in time, expanded to take in, and then help take down, the whole of the Eastern bloc.

So what would be a comparable bet that the individual might make in the case of the environmental crisis? Havel himself has suggested that people begin to "conduct themselves as if they were to live on this earth forever and be answerable for its condition one day." Fair enough, but let me propose a slightly less abstract and daunting wager. The idea is to find one thing to do in your life that doesn't involve spending or voting, that may or may not virally rock the world but is real and particular (as well as symbolic) and that, come what may, will offer its own rewards. Maybe you decide to give up meat, an act that would reduce your carbon footprint by as much as a quarter. Or you could try this: determine to observe the Sabbath. For one day a week, abstain completely from economic activity: no shopping, no driving, no electronics.

But the act I want to talk about is growing some—even just a little— of your own food. Rip out your lawn, if you have one, and if you don't—if you live in a high-rise, or have a yard shrouded in shade—look into getting a plot in a community garden. Measured against the Problem We Face, planting a garden sounds pretty benign, I know, but in fact it's one of the most powerful things an individual can do—to reduce your carbon footprint, sure, but more important, to reduce your sense of dependence and dividedness: to change the cheap-energy mind.

A great many things happen when you plant a vegetable garden, some of them directly related to climate change, others indirect but related nevertheless. Growing food, we forget, comprises the original solar technology: calories produced by means of photosynthesis. Years ago the cheap-energy mind discovered that more food could be produced with less effort by replacing sunlight with fossil-fuel fertilizers and pesticides, with a result that the typical calorie of food energy in your diet now requires about 10 calories of fossil-fuel energy to produce. It's estimated that the way we feed ourselves (or rather, allow ourselves to be fed) accounts for about a fifth of the greenhouse gas for which each of us is responsible.

Yet the sun still shines down on your yard, and photosynthesis still works so abundantly that in a thoughtfully organized vegetable garden (one planted from seed, nourished by compost from the kitchen and involving not too many drives to the garden center), you can grow the proverbial free lunch—CO_2-free and dollar-free. This is the most-local food you can possibly eat (not to mention the freshest, tastiest and most nutritious), with a carbon footprint so faint that even the New Zealand lamb council dares not challenge it. And while we're counting carbon, consider too your compost pile, which shrinks the heap of garbage your household needs trucked away even as it feeds your vegetables and sequesters carbon in your soil. What else? Well, you will probably notice that you're getting a pretty good workout there in your garden, burning calories without having to get into the car to drive to the gym. (It is one of the absurdities of the modern division of labor that, having replaced physical labor with fossil fuel, we now have to burn even more fossil fuel to keep our unemployed bodies in shape.) Also, by engaging both body and mind, time spent in the garden is time (and energy) subtracted from electronic forms of entertainment.

25   You begin to see that growing even a little of your own food is, as Wendell Berry pointed out 30 years ago, one of those solutions that, instead of begetting a new set of problems—the way "solutions" like ethanol or nuclear power inevitably do—actually beget other solutions, and not only of the kind that save carbon. Still more valuable are the habits of mind that growing a little of your own food can yield. You quickly learn that you need not be dependent on specialists to provide for yourself—that your body is still good for something and may actually be enlisted in its own support. If the experts are right, if both oil and time are running out, these are skills and habits of mind we're all very soon going to need. We may also need the food. Could gardens provide it? Well, during World War II, victory gardens supplied as much as 40 percent of the produce Americans ate.

But there are sweeter reasons to plant that garden, to bother. At least in this one corner of your yard and life, you will have begun to heal the split between what you think and what you do, to commingle your identities as consumer and producer and citizen. Chances are, your garden will re-engage you with your neighbors, for you will have produce to give away and the need to borrow their tools. You will have reduced the power of the cheap-energy mind by personally overcoming its most debilitating weakness: its helplessness and the fact that it can't do much of anything that doesn't involve division or subtraction. The garden's season-long transit from seed to ripe fruit—will you get a load of that zucchini?!—suggests that the operations of addition and multiplication still obtain, that the abundance of nature is not exhausted. The single greatest lesson the garden teaches is that our relationship to the planet need not be zero-sum, and that as long as the sun still shines and people still can plan and plant, think and do, we can, if we bother to try, find ways to provide for ourselves without diminishing the world.

Responding to Reading

1. According to Pollan, why is personal virtue "quickly becoming a term of derision" (3)? In what sense is energy conservation an act of personal virtue?
2. What makes Pollan think that people are not serious about the climate-change crisis? Why does he think that "laws and money and grand schemes" will not be enough to get us out of our environmental crisis (9)?
3. What reasons does Pollan present for going green? Which do you think are the most compelling? Why does Pollan think that people should plant personal vegetable gardens even though these gardens will do little to affect climate change?

Responding in Writing

Do you think planting a vegetable garden teaches the lessons that Pollan thinks it does? What would motivate you to plant a vegetable garden?

WIDENING THE FOCUS

For Critical Thinking and Writing

Write an essay in which you answer the Focus question, "How can we create a more sustainable environment?" In your essay, refer to the ideas in Bill McKibben's "The Challenge to Environmentalism," Kate Zernike's "Green, Greener, Greenest," and Michael Pollan's "Why Bother?"

For Further Reading

The following readings can suggest additional perspectives for thinking and writing about how to address the issue of creating a sustainable environment:

- E. B. White, "Once More to the Lake" (p. 24)

- Lars Eighner, "On Dumpster Diving" (p. 358)

- Robert B. Reich, "Don't Blame Wal-Mart" (p. 432)

- Wendell Berry, "Being Kind to the Land" (p. 470)

For Focused Research

The issue of creating a sustainable environment is complex, with various kinds of efforts around the globe contributing to sustainability. In preparation for writing an essay about ways to create a more sustainable environment, visit the Web site for *Science Friday*, a weekly National Public Radio program that engages discussion on various scientific and environmental issues, at http://www.sciencefriday.com. Enter the search term *sustainable environment* and listen to archived radio coverage and watch archived video footage related to your topic. Use information from these resources to support your points.

CHAPTER 8   FOCUS

WRITING

Saving the Planet

1. In recent years, mosquitoes have spread diseases such as encephalitis and West Nile Fever to various parts of the United States. In an effort to control the spread of these diseases, state departments of public health have begun spraying pesticides formulated to kill both the adult mosquito and its larvae. As might be expected, various environmental groups have protested these mass sprayings, saying that other, more environmentally sound, methods for mosquito control should be used. Write an essay in which you present your views on this issue, considering how Rachel Carson (p. 474) and John Tierney (p. 480) would address this problem.

2. Rachel Carson (p. 474) and Heather Rogers (p. 484) discuss ways in which the environment can be preserved. Write an essay in which you discuss how specific changes in governmental policy, social behavior, or industrial policy could improve the environment.

3. Reread one of the essays in this chapter. Then, write an email to its author in which you argue against his or her position. Make sure you address the specific points the author makes, and support your position with references to your own observations and experiences. If you wish, you can also refer to other essays in this chapter.

4. According to Wendell Berry in "Being Kind to the Land" (p. 470), true farmers "want to conserve their land and improve it" (11). They understand the proper relationship between themselves and nature. In "Why Bother?" (p. 508), Michael Pollan says, "growing even a little of your own food" (25) will heal the split that exists between human beings and nature. What do you believe has caused this split between people and nature? Write an essay in which you discuss what you think you can do to address this problem. Make sure you refer to the ideas of both Berry and Pollan in your essay.

5. What responsibility do you think each person has for doing his or her part to save the planet? Consider what in particular is worth saving and what forces are working to destroy it. In your answer, refer to one or more of the following essays: the excerpt from Leslie Marmon Silko's "Through the Stories We Hear Who We Are" (p. 467), John Muir's "The American Forests" (p. 468), Wendell Berry's "Being Kind to the Land" (p. 470), and Michal Pollan's "Why Bother?" (p. 508).

6. Look around your college campus and decide what your school should do to help the environment. Then, write a proposal outlining your recommendations, referring to Kate Zernike's "Green, Greener, Greenest" (p. 503) and Alan Weisman's "Built to Last" (p. 490).

7. A number of writers in this chapter suggest steps that individuals can take to improve the environment. Focus on two essays that seem to take different positions—Rachel Carson's "The Obligation to Endure" (p. 474) and John Tierney's "Fateful Voice of a Generation Still Drowns Out Real Science" (p. 480), for example—and compare their ideas. What are the strengths and weaknesses of each writer's suggestions? Which writer makes the stronger case?

8. In his letter to President Franklin Pierce in 1855, Native American Chief Seattle said that eventually whites will "suffocate in [their] own waste." Write a letter from Heather Rogers (p. 484) to Chief Seattle supporting or challenging this statement. Before you begin, look at the text of Chief Seattle's letter at http://www.context.org/ICLIB/IC03/Seattle.htm.

9. Many writers, such as Leslie Marmon Silko (p. 467), John Muir (p. 468), and Wendell Berry (p. 470), believe that contact with nature can have a beneficial effect, serving as a refuge from the pressures of civilization or helping restore balance to our lives. Write an essay in which you describe the positive effects of nature on your life.

9

RELIGION IN AMERICA

Since its inception, the United States has been a country in which religion was important. Historical figures such as George Washington, Benjamin Franklin, and Abraham Lincoln routinely called on God for guidance, and many of our founding documents invoke the deity. As Alexis de Tocqueville, the nineteenth-century social philosopher, observed in 1830, "There is no country in the world where the Christian religion retains a greater influence over the souls of men than in America."

Although the United States has become a much more secular country since de Tocqueville wrote *Democracy in America,* we are still a nation in which religion is extremely influential. Even though the Constitution expressly forbids the establishment of a state religion, religion plays a significant role in our public life. For example, our currency carries the

A simple white church at Great Smoky Mountains National Park in Tennessee

phrase "In God we trust," the Pledge of Allegiance includes the words "One nation under God," and the president takes the oath of office with a hand on the Bible.

Moreover, organized religion plays a strong role in everyday American life. According to a survey conducted at the University of Michigan, the United States has a higher level of church attendance than any other country at a comparable level of development. Over 44 percent of Americans say they attend church, synagogue, or another house of worship once a week. This figure compares to 16 percent in Britain, 14 percent in France, and 13 percent in Germany. (In some areas of Sweden and The Netherlands, church attendance is less than 10 percent.) In addition, 53 percent of Americans say religion is very important in their lives, 80 percent say they pray regularly, and almost 80 percent believe God either created or guided the development of human beings. Over 60 percent of Americans say faith is critical to their lives, and almost 40 percent read the Bible at least once a week. Despite the fact that some scholars consider these figures somewhat inflated, they suggest the strength of religious belief in the United States. Even so, a secular view of the world also manifests itself in American thought, sometimes complementing religious interpretations and sometimes challenging them.

The Focus section of this chapter (p. 568) examines the conflicting claims of science and religion as they apply to Darwin's Theory of Evolution. Specifically, it asks the question, "Is There Intelligent Design in

The 7,000-seat Willow Creek Community Church in South Barrington, Illinois

Nature?" In "Finding Design in Nature," Christoph Schönborn argues that science alone cannot explain the complex design of nature. In "Why Intelligent Design Isn't," H. Allen Orr refutes two major critics of Darwinian evolution. Finally, in "Finding Darwin's God," Kenneth R. Miller attempts to bridge the gap between evolution and intelligent design.

PREPARING TO READ AND WRITE

- Is the writer examining religion or spirituality in general, or does he or she have a narrower focus?

- Is the writer's focus on morality? ethics? values?

- Does the writer focus on a particular social or political issue?

- Does the writer present opposing opinions fairly? Respectfully?

- Does the writer acknowledge the limitations of his or her own position?

- Is the writer discussing his or her own beliefs or considering the broader impact of religion on society?

- What role does the writer think religion should play in society?

- Does the writer see a conflict between science and religion?

- Does the writer think that the gap between science and religion can be bridged?

- Does the writer interpret religious doctrine literally or figuratively?

- In what way do the writer's beliefs affect his or her discussion?

- Which of the writers' ideas are most similar? Which are most like your own?

SALVATION

Langston Hughes

1902–1967

*Poet, novelist, dramatist, and nonfiction writer Langston Hughes was cen-
tral to the 1920s Harlem Renaissance, which helped to shape the genre of
African American literature. His work focuses largely on the social plight of
African Americans and their rich and vibrant culture, especially their contributions of jazz and blues to American music. In the following autobiographical essay, Hughes explores his own religious experience as a young boy.*

I was saved from sin when I was going on thirteen. But not really saved.
It happened like this. There was a big revival at my Auntie Reed's
church. Every night for weeks there had been much preaching, singing,
praying, and shouting, and some very hardened sinners had been
brought to Christ, and the membership of the church had grown by
leaps and bounds. Then just before the revival ended, they held a special meeting for children, "to bring the young lambs to the fold." My
aunt spoke of it for days ahead. That night I was escorted to the front
row and placed on the mourners' bench with all the other young sinners, who had not yet been brought to Jesus.

My aunt told me that when you were saved you saw a light, and
something happened to you inside! And Jesus came into your life!
And God was with you from then on! She said you could see and hear
and feel Jesus in your soul. I believed her. I had heard a great many old
people say the same thing and it seemed to me they ought to know. So
I sat there calmly in the hot, crowded church, waiting for Jesus to come
to me.

The preacher preached a wonderful rhythmical sermon, all moans
and shouts and lonely cries and dire pictures of hell, and then he sang
a song about the ninety and nine safe in the fold, but one little lamb
was left out in the cold. Then he said: "Won't you come? Won't you
come to Jesus? Young lambs, won't you come?" And he held out his
arms to all us young sinners there on the mourners' bench. And the little girls cried. And some of them jumped up and went to Jesus right
away. But most of us just sat there.

A great many old people came and knelt around us and prayed,
old women with jet-black faces and braided hair, old men with work-
gnarled hands. And the church sang a song about the lower lights are
burning, some poor sinners to be saved. And the whole building rocked
with prayer and song.

Still I kept waiting to *see* Jesus.

5

Finally all the young people had gone to the altar and were saved, but one boy and me. He was a rounder's[1] son named Westley. Westley and I were surrounded by sisters and deacons praying. It was very hot in the church, and getting late now. Finally Westley said to me in a whisper: "God damn! I'm tired o' sitting here. Let's get up and be saved." So he got up and was saved.

Then I was left all alone on the mourners' bench. My aunt came and knelt at my knees and cried, while prayers and song swirled all around me in the little church. The whole congregation prayed for me alone, in a mighty wail of moans and voices. And I kept waiting serenely for Jesus, waiting, waiting—but he didn't come. I wanted to see him, but nothing happened to me. Nothing! I wanted something to happen to me, but nothing happened.

I heard the songs and the minister saying: "Why don't you come? My dear child, why don't you come to Jesus? Jesus is waiting for you. He wants you. Why don't you come? Sister Reed, what is this child's name?"

"Langston," my aunt sobbed.

10   "Langston, why don't you come? Why don't you come and be saved? Oh, Lamb of God! Why don't you come?"

Now it was really getting late. I began to be ashamed of myself, holding everything up so long. I began to wonder what God thought about Westley, who certainly hadn't seen Jesus either, but who was now sitting proudly on the platform, swinging his knickerbockered[2] legs and grinning down at me, surrounded by deacons and old women on their knees praying. God had not struck Westley dead for taking his name in vain or for lying in the temple. So I decided that maybe to save further trouble, I'd better lie, too, and say that Jesus had come, and get up and be saved.

So I got up.

Suddenly the whole room broke into a sea of shouting, as they saw me rise. Waves of rejoicing swept the place. Women leaped in the air. My aunt threw her arms around me. The minister took me by the hand and led me to the platform.

When things quieted down, in a hushed silence, punctuated by a few ecstatic "Amens," all the new young lambs were blessed in the name of God. Then joyous singing filled the room.

15   That night, for the first time in my life but one for I was a big boy twelve years old—I cried. I cried, in bed alone, and couldn't stop. I buried my head under the quilts, but my aunt heard me. She woke up and told my uncle I was crying because the Holy Ghost had come into my life, and because I had seen Jesus. But I was really crying because I

---

[1]A dissolute person. [Eds.]

[2]Wearing short full trousers gathered at the knees. [Eds.]

couldn't bear to tell her that I had lied, that I had deceived everybody in the church, that I hadn't seen Jesus, and that now I didn't believe there was a Jesus anymore, since he didn't come to help me.

Responding to Reading

1. Hughes opens his essay by saying, "I was saved from sin when I was going on thirteen. But not really saved." What does he mean? Was he "saved" or not?
2. Paraphrase the explanation of salvation in paragraph 2. How is his aunt's description of this process different from what young Langston expects to experience?
3. Do you think Langston's motivation for accepting salvation is any different from Westley's? Explain.

Responding in Writing

The young Langston Hughes cries because he believes he has lied and "deceived everybody in the church" (15). Do you think he is being too hard on himself, or do you think he really has committed a sin?

NEW SUPERSTITIONS FOR OLD

Margaret Mead

1901–1978

The work of the American anthropologist Margaret Mead emphasized the importance of observation in scientific research, focusing on the human populations of Oceania, including Samoa and New Guinea. Mead wrote twenty-three books, including Coming of Age in Samoa *(1928),* Growing Up in New Guinea *(1930),* Sex and Temperament in Three Primitive Societies *(1935), and* Continuities in Cultural Evolution *(1964). A year after her death, Mead received the Presidential Medal of Freedom, the highest civilian award granted in the United States. In the following essay, Mead explores the relationship between superstition and religion.*

Once in a while there is a day when everything seems to run smoothly and even the riskiest venture comes out exactly right. You exclaim, "This is my lucky day!" Then as an afterthought you say, "Knock on wood!" Of course, you do not really believe that knocking on wood will ward off danger. Still, boasting about your own good luck gives you a slightly uneasy feeling—and you carry out the little protective ritual. If someone challenged you at that moment, you would probably say, "Oh, that's nothing. Just an old superstition."

But when you come to think about it, what is superstition?

In the contemporary world most people treat old folk beliefs as superstitions—the belief, for instance, that there are lucky and unlucky days or numbers, that future events can be read from omens, that there are protective charms or that what happens can be influenced by casting spells. We have excluded magic from our current world view, for we know that natural events have natural causes.

In a religious context, where truths cannot be demonstrated, we accept them as a matter of faith. Superstitions, however, belong to the category of beliefs, practices and ways of thinking that have been discarded because they are inconsistent with scientific knowledge. It is easy to say that other people are superstitious because they believe what we regard to be untrue. "Superstition" used in that sense is a derogatory term for the beliefs of other people that we do not share. But there is more to it than that. For superstitions lead a kind of half life in a twilight world where, sometimes, we partly suspend our disbelief and act as if magic worked.

5   Actually, almost every day, even in the most sophisticated home, something is likely to happen that evokes the memory of some old folk belief. The salt spills. A knife falls to the floor. Your nose tickles. Then perhaps, with a slightly embarrassed smile, the person who spilled the salt tosses a pinch over his left shoulder. Or someone recites the old rhyme, "Knife falls, gentleman calls." Or as you rub your nose you think, That means a letter. I wonder who's writing? No one takes these small responses very seriously or gives them more than a passing thought. Sometimes people will preface one of these ritual acts—walking around instead of under a ladder or hastily closing an umbrella that has been opened inside a house—with such remarks as "I remember my great-aunt used to..." or "Germans used to say you ought not..." And then, having placed the belief at some distance away in time or space, they carry out the ritual.

Everyone also remembers a few of the observances of childhood—wishing on the first star; looking at the new moon over the right shoulder; avoiding the cracks in the sidewalk on the way to school while chanting, "Step on a crack, break your mother's back"; wishing on white horses, on loads of hay, on covered bridges, on red cars; saying quickly, "Bread-and-butter" when a post or a tree separated you from the friend you were walking with. The adult may not actually recite the formula "Star light, star bright..." and may not quite turn to look at the new moon, but his mood is tempered by a little of the old thrill that came when the observance was still freighted with magic.

Superstition can also be used with another meaning. When I discuss the religious beliefs of other peoples, especially primitive peoples, I am often asked, "Do they really have a religion, or is it all just superstition?" The point of contrast here is not between a scientific and a magical view of the world but between the clear, theologically defensible religious beliefs of members of civilized societies and what we regard as the false and childish views of the heathen who "bow down to wood and stone." Within the civilized religions, however, where membership includes believers who are educated and urbane and others who are ignorant and simple, one always finds traditions and practices that the more sophisticated will dismiss offhand as "just superstition" but that guide the steps of those who live by older ways. Mostly these are very ancient beliefs, some handed on from one religion to another and carried from country to country around the world.

Very commonly, people associate superstition with the past, with very old ways of thinking that have been supplanted by modern knowledge. But new superstitions are continually coming into being and flourishing in our society. Listening to mothers in the park in the 1930s, one heard them say, "Now, don't you run out into the sun, or Polio will get you." In the 1940s elderly people explained to one another in tones of resignation, "It was the Virus that got him down." And every year the cosmetics industry offers us new magic—cures for baldness, lotions that will give every woman radiant skin, hair coloring that will restore to the middle-aged the charm and romance of youth—results that are promised if we will just follow the simple directions. Families and individuals also have their cherished, private superstitions. You must leave by the back door when you are going on a journey, or you must wear a green dress when you are taking an examination. It is a kind of joke, of course, but it makes you feel safe.

These old half-beliefs and new half-beliefs reflect the keenness of our wish to have something come true or to prevent something bad from happening. We do not always recognize new superstitions for what they are, and we still follow the old ones because someone's faith long ago matches our contemporary hopes and fears. In the past people "knew" that a black cat crossing one's path was a bad omen, and they turned back home. Today we are fearful of taking a journey and would give anything to turn back—and then we notice a black cat running across the road in front of us.

Child psychologists recognize the value of the toy a child holds in $_{10}$ his hand at bedtime. It is different from his thumb, with which he can close himself in from the rest of the world, and it is different from the real world to which he is learning to relate himself. Psychologists call these toys—these furry animals and old, cozy baby blankets—"transitional objects"; that is, objects that help the child move back and forth between the exactions of everyday life and the world of wish and dream.

Superstitions have some of the qualities of these transitional objects. They help people pass between the areas of life where what happens has to be accepted without proof and the areas where sequences of events are explicable in terms of cause and effect, based on knowledge. Bacteria and viruses that cause sickness have been identified; the cause of symptoms can be diagnosed and a rational course of treatment prescribed. Magical charms no longer are needed to treat the sick; modern medicine has brought the whole sequence of events into the secular world. But people often act as if this change had not taken place. Laymen still treat germs as if they were invisible, malign spirits, and physicians sometimes prescribe antibiotics as if they were magic substances.

Over time, more and more of life has become subject to the controls of knowledge. However, this is never a one-way process. Scientific investigation is continually increasing our knowledge. But if we are to make good use of this knowledge, we must not only rid our minds of old, superseded beliefs and fragments of magical practice, but also recognize new superstitions for what they are. Both are generated by our wishes, our fears and our feeling of helplessness in difficult situations.

Civilized peoples are not alone in having grasped the idea of superstitions—beliefs and practices that are superseded but that still may evoke the different worlds in which we live—the sacred, the secular and the scientific. They allow us to keep a private world also, where, smiling a little, we can banish danger with a gesture and summon luck with a rhyme, make the sun shine in spite of storm clouds, force the stranger to do our bidding, keep an enemy at bay and straighten the paths of those we love.

Responding to Reading

1. How does Mead define superstition? How does she explain why people cling to these "old half-beliefs and new half-beliefs" (9)?
2. According to Mead, how are superstitions similar to what psychologists call children's "transitional objects" (10)?
3. In general, does Mead see superstitions as valuable, with a useful place in modern life, or does she think superstitions limit people by creating a false belief system?

Responding in Writing

In what respects do you see your own religious beliefs as similar to the superstitions Mead discusses? In what respects are your religion's beliefs different from these superstitions?

OUR FAITH IN SCIENCE
Tenzin Gyatso, Dalai Lama XIV
1935–

The fourteenth Dalai Lama, Tenzin Gyatso is the spiritual and political leader of Tibetan Buddhism. In 1959, he was forced into exile when the Chinese military occupied Tibet. Literally the "Ocean of Wisdom," the Dalai Lama is a scholar, diplomat, politician, and civil servant who travels the world to foster peace and understanding among different cultures and religions. Gyatso has written numerous books, including The Universe in a Single Atom: The Controversy of Science and Spirituality *(2006), in which he explores the intersection of faith and science, also the topic of the following essay.*

Science has always fascinated me. As a child in Tibet, I was keenly curious about how things worked. When I got a toy I would play with it a bit, then take it apart to see how it was put together. As I became older, I applied the same scrutiny to a movie projector and an antique automobile.

At one point I became particularly intrigued by an old telescope, with which I would study the heavens. One night while looking at the moon I realized that there were shadows on its surface. I corralled my two main tutors to show them, because this was contrary to the ancient version of cosmology I had been taught, which held that the moon was a heavenly body that emitted its own light.

But through my telescope the moon was clearly just a barren rock, pocked with craters. If the author of that fourth-century treatise were writing today, I'm sure he would write the chapter on cosmology differently.

If science proves some belief of Buddhism wrong, then Buddhism will have to change. In my view, science and Buddhism share a search for the truth and for understanding reality. By learning from science about aspects of reality where its understanding may be more advanced, I believe that Buddhism enriches its own worldview.

For many years now, on my own and through the Mind and Life   5
Institute, which I helped found, I have had the opportunity to meet with scientists to discuss their work. World-class scientists have generously coached me in subatomic physics, cosmology, psychology, biology.

It is our discussions of neuroscience, however, that have proved particularly important. From these exchanges a vigorous research initiative has emerged, a collaboration between monks and neuroscientists, to explore how meditation might alter brain function.

The goal here is not to prove Buddhism right or wrong—or even to bring people to Buddhism—but rather to take these methods out of the traditional context, study their potential benefits, and share the findings with anyone who might find them helpful.

After all, if practices from my own tradition can be brought together with scientific methods, then we may be able to take another small step toward alleviating human suffering.

Already this collaboration has borne fruit. Dr. Richard Davidson, a neuroscientist at the University of Wisconsin, has published results from brain imaging studies of lamas meditating. He found that during meditation the regions of the brain thought to be related to happiness increase in activity. He also found that the longer a person has been a meditator, the greater the activity increase will be.

10   Other studies are under way. At Princeton University, Dr. Jonathan Cohen, a neuroscientist, is studying the effects of meditation on attention. At the University of California Medical School at San Francisco, Dr. Margaret Kemeny has been studying how meditation helps develop empathy in school teachers.

Whatever the results of this work, I am encouraged that it is taking place. You see, many people still consider science and religion to be in opposition. While I agree that certain religious concepts conflict with scientific facts and principles, I also feel that people from both worlds can have an intelligent discussion, one that has the power ultimately to generate a deeper understanding of challenges we face together in our interconnected world.

One of my first teachers of science was the German physicist Carl von Weizsäcker, who had been an apprentice to the quantum theorist Werner Heisenberg. Dr. Weizsäcker was kind enough to give me some formal tutorials on scientific topics. (I confess that while listening to him I would feel I could grasp the intricacies of the full argument, but when the sessions were over there was often not a great deal of his explanation left behind.)

What impressed me most deeply was how Dr. Weizsäcker worried about both the philosophical implications of quantum physics and the ethical consequences of science generally. He felt that science could benefit from exploring issues usually left to the humanities.

I believe that we must find a way to bring ethical considerations to bear upon the direction of scientific development, especially in the life sciences. By invoking fundamental ethical principles, I am not advocating a fusion of religious ethics and scientific inquiry.

15   Rather, I am speaking of what I call "secular ethics," which embrace the principles we share as human beings: compassion, tolerance, consideration of others, the responsible use of knowledge and power. These principles transcend the barriers between religious believers and nonbelievers; they belong not to one faith, but to all faiths.

Today, our knowledge of the human brain and body at the cellular and genetic level has reached a new level of sophistication. Advances in genetic manipulation, for example, mean scientists can create new genetic entities—like hybrid animal and plant species—whose long-term consequences are unknown.

Sometimes when scientists concentrate on their own narrow fields, their keen focus obscures the larger effect their work might have. In my conversations with scientists I try to remind them of the larger goal behind what they do in their daily work.

This is more important than ever. It is all too evident that our moral thinking simply has not been able to keep pace with the speed of scientific advancement. Yet the ramifications of this progress are such that it is no longer adequate to say that the choice of what to do with this knowledge should be left in the hands of individuals.

This is a point I intend to make when I speak at the annual meeting of the Society for Neuroscience today in Washington. I will suggest that how science relates to wider humanity is no longer of academic interest alone. This question must assume a sense of urgency for all those who are concerned about the fate of human existence.

A deeper dialogue between neuroscience and society—indeed 20 between all scientific fields and society—could help deepen our understanding of what it means to be human and our responsibilities for the natural world we share with other sentient beings.

Just as the world of business has been paying renewed attention to ethics, the world of science would benefit from more deeply considering the implications of its own work. Scientists should be more than merely technically adept; they should be mindful of their own motivation and the larger goal of what they do: the betterment of humanity.

Responding to Reading

1. The author of this essay, a Buddhist and the spiritual leader of the people of Tibet, makes the following statement: "If science proves some belief of Buddhism wrong, then Buddhism will have to change" (4). Do you accept this statement at face value, or do you find it insincere or unrealistic?
2. Do you think the primary purpose of this essay is to explain how religion might be influenced by science, to explain how science might be influenced by religion, or to explain how science and religion can work together to improve people's lives? Explain.
3. What does Gyatso mean by "'secular ethics'" (15)? Do you agree that the principles he mentions "transcend the barriers between religious believers and nonbelievers" (15)?

Responding in Writing

What specific values do you think "religious believers and nonbelievers" (15) might share? Why?

AMONG THE BELIEVERS

Tayari Jones

1970–

An assistant professor in the M.F.A. program at Rutgers University, Tayari Jones has written two novels, both of which explore coming of age, family, and identity. In the following essay, Jones describes the religious and irreligious transformation she experienced while she was growing up in the American South.

In elementary school, I spent a great deal of energy trying to explain the difference between atheism and devil worship. Until second grade I answered the commonplace query: "Where do you go to church?" with this: "My father says that we don't believe in God." Adults took this information with shocked silence, but children lack restraint. "You're a devil worshiper?" they asked. I didn't think I was but I asked Daddy who assured me that we were not. "Atheists," he explained, "don't believe in the devil either."

Though most of the other children found this argument to be convincing, they still demonstrated the difference between chilly tolerance and the warmth that came from actually fitting in. But I remained true to my faithlessness for the same reasons most children are true to a faith: because it is what their parents tell them.

My father, a preacher's son, had not been so obedient. When I visited his hometown, Oakdale, La., I was constantly aware that I was the daughter of the son who strayed.

During my summers in Oakdale, I understood what an outsider I really was. Unable to sing hymns from memory, not knowing when to stand or sit during the sermon—all of these things marked me as an infidel among believers. The most humiliating moment came at meals, when we all bowed our heads and one-by-one recited a Bible verse before starting to eat. My cousin Shunda—three years older, supremely disdainful and thus intimidatingly sophisticated—possessed a vast repertoire of premeal utterances. When my turn came, I could say only, "Jesus wept," which is like the tricycle of verses.

5   The summer before I entered fifth grade, my visit to Oakdale happened to coincide with vacation Bible school. At last, I could receive the remedial religious instruction I'd been longing for!

I looked forward to discussions in which I could ask some of the questions that I had previously posed to my father who gave the most unsatisfying responses:

Q. If God made the world, who made God?
A. God didn't make the world.

Q. Then why does it say so in the Bible?

A. Makes people feel better.

Q. How do the angels get their clothes on? Don't the wings get in the way?

A. The same way Santa gets down the chimney.

To my chagrin, there was little theological analysis in vacation Bible school. Mostly we used stumpy crayons to color bizarre pictures: line drawing of animals in pairs, dead giants, bread and fish. There weren't even captions saying who was who and what was what. We didn't learn any good hymns. By the third day of the five-day program, the only useful thing I had learned was that Job rhymed with "robe," not with "bob." On the fourth day, we used Popsicle sticks and yarn to make ornamental crucifixes called "God's Eyes." On the last day, the Bible school teacher pulled me aside and asked what was troubling me.

I blurted my most pressing question: "If God made the world, who made God?"

She squinted: "Are you trying to be funny?"

"No," I told her. I just wanted to understand religion and be like ₁₀ everyone else for a change. The teacher gave me a little smile and handed me a mimeographed sheet to read at home. It was the text of the 23rd Psalm. I read the opening line, "The Lord is my Shepherd; I shall not want." I knew this verse; it was Shunda's. Oh, the wonder of punctuation. When she quoted the verse, I thought it a bit rude, rejecting the Lord as one's shepherd, whatever that meant. But now I understood.

Feeling something akin to faith, I vowed to learn at least a verse or two. I imagined the adoring faces of my relatives as I surprised them at Sunday dinner. I smiled back at the teacher and she probably imagined that she had converted me, the daughter of Oakdale's best-known non-believing son.

The 23rd Psalm is not terribly long; before I knew it, I'd memorized the whole thing. Had I not won a prize the previous school year for reciting both "Hiawatha" and "Annabel Lee"? In Bible school we'd been told that God gives each person a special gift, a ministry. Perhaps dramatic recitation was mine.

At Grandmother's house the next Sunday, we all gathered around the table with our heads bowed. Beside me, my cousin said demurely, "Peace, be still." It was now my turn. Although most people pray with their eyes closed, I opened mine, wanting to see their expressions as I let loose with my Psalm.

"The Lord is my shepherd; I shall not want." Working my way through the first stanza, carefully pronouncing the "th" on "maketh," I felt something real. I pictured myself lying down in green pastures. In my mind's eye, I saw myself eating at the table prepared by the Lord. I'll never forget that moment of connection between myself and the glorious words; the comfort they described, was the warmth of well-being that I felt. By the time I got to the good part, I'd whipped myself into a fine crescendo: "Yea, though I walk through the valley of the shadow of death..."

15   At this instant, Shunda released a disapproving gasp-sigh. "Shut up," she said without saying. "The food is getting cold, you boring, annoying, little freak."

Chastened, I closed my eyes, but I continued my recitation, oblivious to the reaction of the others at the table, and the food cooling on the platters, riding the buoyancy of the words, filling my mind and heart with the lyrics of this strange and powerful song.

Now people think it charming when they find out that I grew up black, Southern and atheist. At a recent cocktail party, on hearing about my background, a woman said to me, "How idiosyncratic!" I suppose she is right. Left to find my own way in matters of religion, I have a quirky collection of experiences that have helped me sort out my relationship with the divine.

The 23rd Psalm mimeographed on cheap paper gave me my first glimpse into spirituality, but the moment was not marked by the speaking of tongues. That moment will be forever etched in my memory as the day that language revealed to me if not its full power, its awesome potential. Maybe this is the day it was decided that I would be a writer, when I saw in the beauty of a poem the true glory of God.

Responding to Reading

1. In paragraph 2, Jones says that she "remained true to [her] faithlessness for the same reasons most children are true to a faith: because it is what their parents tell them." In what other respects does Jones see atheism as similar to religious faith?
2. When she was a child, why did Jones want to learn more about religion? How satisfied was she with what she learned from her family? From Bible school?
3. What was it about the 23rd Psalm that enabled Jones to feel "something akin to faith" (11)? How did it give her her "first glimpse into spirituality" (18)?

Responding in Writing

Do you think Jones is an atheist today? Why or why not? Explain your conclusion.

KICKING THE SECULARIST HABIT
David Brooks
1961–

A New York Times *columnist and a radio and television political commentator, David Brooks has been an* Atlantic *correspondent, a* Weekly Standard *senior editor, and a* Newsweek *contributing editor. Widely published on various American political issues, he has written two books, most recently* On Paradise Drive: How We Live Now (and Always Have) in the Future Tense *(2004). In the following essay, Brooks considers America's burgeoning religiosity.*

Like a lot of people these days, I'm a recovering secularist. Until September 11 I accepted the notion that as the world becomes richer and better educated, it becomes less religious. Extrapolating from a tiny and unrepresentative sample of humanity (in Western Europe and parts of North America), this theory holds that as history moves forward, science displaces dogma and reason replaces unthinking obedience. A region that has not yet had a reformation and an enlightenment, such as the Arab world, sooner or later will.

It's now clear that the secularization theory is untrue. The human race does not necessarily get less religious as it grows richer and better educated. We are living through one of the great periods of scientific progress and the creation of wealth. At the same time, we are in the midst of a religious boom.

Islam is surging. Orthodox Judaism is growing among young people, and Israel has gotten more religious as it has become more affluent. The growth of Christianity surpasses that of all other faiths. In 1942 this magazine published an essay called "Will the Christian Church Survive?" Sixty years later there are two billion Christians in the world; by 2050, according to some estimates, there will be three billion. As Philip Jenkins, a Distinguished Professor of History and Religious Studies at Pennsylvania State University, has observed, perhaps the most successful social movement of our age is Pentecostalism (see "The Next Christianity," October *Atlantic*). Having gotten its start in Los Angeles about a century ago, it now embraces 400 million people—a number that, according to Jenkins, could reach a billion or more by the half-century mark.

Moreover, it is the denominations that refuse to adapt to secularism that are growing the fastest, while those that try to be "modern" and "relevant" are withering. Ecstatic forms of Christianity and "antimodern" Islam are thriving. The Christian population in Africa, which was about 10 million in 1900 and is currently about 360 million, is expected to grow to 633 million by 2025, with conservative, evangelical, and syncretistic groups dominating. In Africa churches are becoming more influential than many nations, with both good and bad effects.

5   Secularism is not the future; it is yesterday's incorrect vision of the future. This realization sends us recovering secularists to the bookstore or the library in a desperate attempt to figure out what is going on in the world. I suspect I am not the only one who since September 11 has found himself reading a paperback edition of the Koran that was bought a few years ago in a fit of high-mindedness but was never actually opened. I'm probably not the only one boning up on the teachings of Ahmad ibn Taymiyya, Sayyid Qutb, and Muhammad ibn Abd al-Wahhab.

There are six steps in the recovery process. First you have to accept the fact that you are not the norm. Western foundations and universities send out squads of researchers to study and explain religious movements. But as the sociologist Peter Berger has pointed out, the phenomenon that really needs explaining is the habits of the American professoriat: religious groups should be sending out researchers to try to understand why there are pockets of people in the world who do not feel the constant presence of God in their lives, who do not fill their days with rituals and prayers and garments that bring them into contact with the divine, and who do not believe that God's will should shape their public lives.

Once you accept this—which is like understanding that the earth revolves around the sun, not vice-versa—you can begin to see things in a new way.

The second step toward recovery involves confronting fear. For a few years it seemed that we were all heading toward a benign end of history, one in which our biggest worry would be boredom. Liberal democracy had won the day. Yes, we had to contend with globalization and inequality, but these were material and measurable concepts. Now we are looking at fundamental clashes of belief and a truly scary situation—at least in the Southern Hemisphere—that brings to mind the Middle Ages, with weak governments, missionary armies, and rampant religious conflict.

The third step is getting angry. I now get extremely annoyed by the secular fundamentalists who are content to remain smugly ignorant of enormous shifts occurring all around them. They haven't learned anything about religion, at home or abroad. They don't know who Tim LaHaye and Jerry B. Jenkins are, even though those co-authors have sold 42 million copies of their books. They still don't know what makes a Pentecostal a Pentecostal (you could walk through an American newsroom and ask that question, and the only people who might be able to answer would be the secretaries and the janitorial staff). They still don't know about Michel Aflaq, the mystical Arab nationalist who served as a guru to Saddam Hussein. A great Niagara of religious fervor is cascading down around them while they stand obtuse and dry in the little cave of their own parochialism—and many of them are journalists and policy analysts, who are paid to keep up with these things.

The fourth step toward recovery is to resist the impulse to find a materialistic explanation for everything. During the centuries when secularism seemed the wave of the future, Western intellectuals developed social-science models of extraordinary persuasiveness. Marx explained history through class struggle, other economists explained it through profit maximization. Professors of international affairs used conflict-of-interest doctrines and game theory to predict the dynamics between nation-states.

All these models are seductive and partly true. This country has built powerful institutions, such as the State Department and the CIA, that use them to try to develop sound policies. But none of the models can adequately account for religious ideas, impulses, and actions, because religious fervor can't be quantified and standardized. Religious motivations can't be explained by cost-benefit analysis.

Over the past twenty years domestic-policy analysts have thought hard about the roles that religion and character play in public life. Our foreign-policy elites are at least two decades behind. They go for months ignoring the force of religion; then, when confronted with something inescapably religious, such as the Iranian revolution or the Taliban, they begin talking of religious zealotry and fanaticism, which suddenly explains everything. After a few days of shaking their heads over the fanatics, they revert to their usual secular analyses. We do not yet have, and sorely need, a mode of analysis that attempts to merge the spiritual and the material.

The recovering secularist has to resist the temptation to treat religion as a mere conduit for thwarted economic impulses. For example, we often say that young Arab men who have no decent prospects turn to radical Islam. There's obviously some truth to this observation. But it's not the whole story: neither Mohammed Atta nor Osama bin Laden, for example, was poor or oppressed. And although it's possible to construct theories that explain their radicalism as the result of alienation or some other secular factor, it makes more sense to acknowledge that faith is its own force, independent of and perhaps greater than economic resentment.

Human beings yearn for righteous rule, for a just world or a world that reflects God's will—in many cases at least as strongly as they yearn for money or success. Thinking about that yearning means moving away from scientific analysis and into the realm of moral judgment. The crucial question is not What incentives does this yearning respond to? but Do individuals pursue a moral vision of righteous rule? And do they do so in virtuous ways, or are they, like Saddam Hussein and Osama bin Laden, evil in their vision and methods?

15   Fifth, the recovering secularist must acknowledge that he has been too easy on religion. Because he assumed that it was playing a diminishing role in public affairs, he patronized it. He condescendingly decided not to judge other creeds. They are all valid ways of approaching God, he told himself, and ultimately they fuse into one. After all, why stir up trouble by judging another's beliefs? It's not polite. The better option, when confronted by some nasty practice performed in the name of religion, is simply to avert one's eyes. Is Wahhabism a vicious sect that perverts Islam? Don't talk about it.

But in a world in which religion plays an ever larger role, this approach is no longer acceptable. One has to try to separate right from wrong. The problem is that once we start doing that, it's hard to say where we will end up. Consider Pim Fortuyn, a left-leaning Dutch politician and gay-rights advocate who criticized Muslim immigrants for their attitudes toward women and gays. When he was assassinated, last year, the press described him, on the basis of those criticisms, as a rightist in the manner of Jean-Marie Le Pen,[1] which was far from the truth. In the post-secular world today's categories of left and right will become inapt and obsolete.

The sixth and final step for recovering secularists is to understand that this country was never very secular anyway. We Americans long for righteous rule as fervently as anybody else. We are inculcated with the notion that, in Abraham Lincoln's words, we represent the "last, best hope of earth." Many Americans have always sensed that we have a transcendent mission, although, fortunately, it is not a theological one. We instinctively feel, in ways that people from other places do not, that history is unfulfilled as long as there are nations in which people are not free. It is this instinctive belief that has led George W. Bush to respond so ambitiously to the events of September 11, and that has led most Americans to support him.

Americans are as active as anyone else in the clash of eschatologies. Saddam Hussein sees history as ending with a united Arab nation globally dominant and with himself revered as the creator of a just world order. Osama bin Laden sees history as ending with the global imposition of sharia. Many Europeans see history as ending with the establishment of secular global institutions under which nationalism and religious passions will be quieted and nation-states will give way to international law and multilateral cooperation. Many Americans see history as ending in the triumph of freedom and constitutionalism, with religion not abandoned or suppressed but enriching democratic life.

We are inescapably caught in a world of conflicting visions of historical destiny. This is not the same as saying that we are caught in a

---

[1]1928–. French politician, founder of the far-right National Front Party. [Eds.]

world of conflicting religions. But understanding this world means beating the secularist prejudices out of our minds every day.

Responding to Reading

1. What does Brooks mean when he calls himself a "recovering secularist" (1)? What exactly is the habit he is trying to kick? Why?
2. What evidence does Brooks offer to support his claim that "we are in the midst of a religious boom" (2)? Can you offer examples of your own? Does Brooks see this rise of religion as a positive trend? Do you?
3. Summarize the six steps in Brooks's recovery program.

Responding in Writing

Adapt Brooks's "recovery program" for your fellow students, adding brief examples appropriate for your audience.

TURNING FAITH INTO ELEVATOR MUSIC

William J. Stuntz

1958–

Harvard Law School professor William J. Stuntz specializes in Christian legal theory and criminal justice. He coauthored the 1995 book Constitutional Criminal Procedure: An Examination of the Fourth, Fifth, and Sixth Amendments, and Related Areas. *In the following essay, Stuntz examines the legality of government-sanctioned religious displays.*

The Supreme Court has spoken, and then some: ten separate opinions in a pair of Ten Commandments cases, which seems nicely symmetrical. What all those opinions add up to, predictably, is a muddle. The Ten Commandments can stay on the Texas State Capitol grounds—but not in Kentucky's courthouses. Moses hangs in the balance. So does baby Jesus: Come December, you can bet on a raft of manger scenes on courthouse lawns across the South and Midwest, in all the places Michael Moore likes to call "Jesusland"—and a raft of lawsuits seeking to take them down.

I'm rooting for the lawsuits.

That's a little odd, since I'm part of the target audience, the constituency that is supposed to like these things. I live in Massachusetts (which Michael Moore likes to call "Canada"), but my natural sympathies belong to Jesusland. I'm a Christian. I believe the Bible is a true account of who God is and who we are. I believe the Ten Commandments lie at the core of wisdom. I believe the Incarnation, the event all those manger scenes celebrate, is incomparably the best and most important event in human history. If it matters, I even voted for George W. Bush, twice. So if anyone should want the Ten Commandments in state capitols and "in God we trust" on the coins and manger scenes on courthouse lawns, I should.

But I don't want any of those things. I'd much rather give them back.

5   Here's a thought experiment. Test the decision to put that monument on the Texas capitol grounds against another Biblical principle: the Golden Rule, the idea C. S. Lewis liked to call "do as you would be done by." Take the people who want symbols of their faith on government property, and put them in a society where passionate atheism is the majority view. Suppose all those passionate atheists want to put up monuments in every courthouse and state capitol saying that there is no God, that all good law consists of human wisdom and nothing more. Would my fellow believers like that state of affairs? I don't think so. I know I wouldn't like it. It would make me feel, just a little, like a stranger in my own home, someone who doesn't belong. It would be a tiny reminder that other people with beliefs hostile to mine own this country, and that I'm here at their sufferance. I wouldn't like that at all.

If that's right, then turning around and doing the same thing to people who don't believe what I do when my crowd is in the majority is wrong. Not wrong by the measure of the First Amendment or some legal theory or secular philosophy, but wrong by the measure of "do as you would be done by." That might be tolerable if the monuments and manger scenes satisfied some religious duty. If anything, though, duty cuts the other way. There is a passage in the book of Revelations that bears on this point. The risen Jesus is speaking of, and to, the church in Laodicea. He tells them: "I know your deeds, that you are neither cold nor hot. I wish you were either one or the other! So, because you are lukewarm—neither hot nor cold—I am about to spit you out of my mouth." Symbolic acknowledgments like the Texas monument and the Kentucky plaques, like religious mottoes on money or public manger scenes (usually accompanied by Santa and his reindeer), are quintessentially lukewarm. They do not so much honor God as try to buy him off, cheap. This was precisely the problem with most mandatory school prayers in the days when such things were allowed. The prayers were so vapid as to insult believers, yet still managed to offend non-believers. Just like baby Jesus with a stable full of reindeer.

Seeing the Ten Commandments in public spaces is a little like hearing the *Miranda* warnings on *Law and Order* which doesn't make anyone think about the real meaning of *Miranda* (whatever that is) because it doesn't make anyone think at all. It's the social equivalent of elevator music. Religious people shouldn't want their faith to be elevator music.

That leads to an even worse problem. Symbols like the ones the Supreme Court haggled about give the impression that Christianity and the government are somehow in cahoots with each other. That's a dangerous impression, and a false one. It's a small step from the idea that the government endorses Christianity to an idea that is much worse: that *Christianity* endorses the *government.* Christians are the big losers in that transaction. Western Europe is filled with Christian symbols—Christian Democrats are a leading political party in several countries—but almost entirely devoid of Christians. Christianity does not thrive when political parties take its name and capitol lawns showcase its precepts. On the contrary, it thrives when it stays as far from those things as possible.

The government thrives, too. Religious conservatives and secular liberals should be able to agree on this much: teaching good morals is not a job for the Texas legislature or the Kentucky courts—or any legislature or court. Making just laws is hard enough, and our government isn't so good at that. Teaching virtue is incomparably harder. Personally, I'd rather they stuck to the laws.

But the question shouldn't be what I'd rather. It shouldn't be what 10 is or isn't to my side's advantage. If the Golden Rule means anything in this context, the question should be, what is to the *other side's* advantage? Twenty-first century America is a land full of legal rights, and lawyers to make the most of them. The most Christian thing to do in a place like that is to make the *least* of them. Somewhere, sometime I'd like to hear that my fellow believers, when given the opportunity to erect some watered-down monument or display, said: "Thank you, but no. I don't want to exercise my rights." That would communicate more Christian faith than all the monuments and plaques and graduation prayers put together.

Then the Supreme Court could quit wasting its time on these cases (and, given the way the Supreme Court works, start wasting its time on something else). There are plenty of issues worth fighting about in America's courtrooms and legislative hallways. This isn't one of them.

Responding to Reading

1. Why is Stuntz, a self-described Christian, "rooting for the lawsuits" (2) that challenge the legality of public displays of religion on government property? Why does he go to the trouble of explaining his religious and political views in paragraph 3? Is this explanation necessary? Does it strengthen his arguments?
2. In paragraph 7, Stuntz says, "Religious people shouldn't want their faith to be elevator music." Explain this analogy. Do you think it is valid?
3. How does Stuntz use the Golden Rule to support his arguments? Do you find this strategy helpful? convincing? simplistic? condescending? Explain.

Responding in Writing

Stuntz believes that "symbols of ... faith on government property" (5) might make nonbelievers feel uncomfortable. Is there any government-sanctioned symbol, slogan, or practice that makes you feel like "someone who doesn't belong" (5)? If so, do you see this as something the government should change or as something you should adjust to?

MUSLIM IN AMERICA
Jeffery Sheler
Michael Betzold

Author of Is the Bible True? How Modern Debates and Discoveries Affirm the Essence of the Scriptures *(1999), Jeffery Sheler is a religion writer at* U.S. News & World Report *and a correspondent for PBS's* Religion & Ethics NewsWeekly *television news program. Freelance writer Michael Betzold has written several articles, three nonfiction books, and a novel. In the following essay, Sheler and Betzold explore what it means to be a Muslim in America.*

Inside a storefront on West Warren Avenue, a gritty Dearborn, Mich., neighborhood of modest shops with hand-painted Arabic signs, a handful of men respond to the high-pitched chant of the muezzin[1] and form a line facing Mecca. They bow, sit, and prostrate on colorful rugs in a mostly silent rendition of the salat, the daily prayers Muslims have recited for nearly 1,400 years. In a smaller room, a cluster of women with head coverings also recite the prayers in response to the voice of the imam, which they can hear from across the hall. Most of the worshipers are recent refugees from Iraq who want a link to the country they still consider home. "They thank God they are here" in America, says Imam Hushan Al-Husainy, the mosque leader. "But their heart is back home with their loved ones who are suffering."

Meanwhile, 68 miles away, beneath a gleaming white dome and twin minarets that tower over the Ohio cornfields southwest of Toledo, hundreds of families assemble for worship—a largely upper-middle-class flock that represents some 22 nationalities, most U.S. citizens and some second- or third-generation Americans. Few of the women wear head coverings outside of the prayer hall, where only a 3-foot-high partition separates men and women, side by side. After prayers, they all gather for a potluck. The Toledo center, says its president, Cherrefe

---

[1]At a mosque, the person who leads the call to prayer. [Eds.]

Kadri, represents a "progressive and middle-of-the-road" brand of Islam that, she says, is "very much at home in Middle America."

This, then, is American Islam: The modern Islamic Center of Greater Toledo and the traditionalist Karbala Islamic Education Center are but two examples of its wide-ranging diversity. And even though it is the nation's fastest-growing faith, with an estimated 7 million adherents here—nearly double from a decade ago—Islam remains widely misunderstood in this country. The religion of more than a fifth of the world's population is viewed by many Americans as foreign, mysterious, even threatening to the nation's "Judeo-Christian heritage"—certainly no less so since the events of September 11—despite the fact that it shares common roots with Christianity and Judaism and has been present in North America for centuries.

The rules. Indeed, Islam embraces the monotheism of Christianity and Judaism, accepts the Hebrew Bible, and venerates Jesus as a prophet. It is centered on the Koran—the Islamic scriptures, which Muslims believe were revealed to the prophet Mohammed—which commands five basic devotional duties, called the "Five Pillars": a declaration of belief that "there is no God but Allah [Arabic for "the God"] and Mohammed is his prophet"; prayers offered five times a day; daytime fasting during the month of Ramadan; charitable giving; and at least one pilgrimage to Mecca. Muslims are forbidden to consume alcohol, illicit drugs, pork, or any meat that is not halal—the Islamic equivalent of kosher. Premarital sex and extramarital sex are sternly prohibited, as are most forms of unchaperoned dating. Emphasis on public modesty prompts many Muslims to cover themselves from the wrists to the ankles. Muslims also may not gamble or pay or accept interest on loans or savings accounts. It is a regimen that often runs in conflict with the dominant culture. Most American Muslims have no choice but to break the prohibition on usury to buy homes and automobiles, for example.

But if the intense scrutiny focused on world Islam since September 11 has revealed anything, it is that the faith is no monolith. While there is much that binds the world's 1.2 billion Muslims together, there is no authoritative hierarchy—no pope, no central group of elders—that speaks to them or for them. And American Islam, it emerges, is its own special brand. A recent study sponsored by the Council on American-Islamic Relations [CAIR] in cooperation with the Hartford Institute for Religion Research found that American Muslims generally are more accepting of differences, less inclined to fundamentalism, and more at home in a secular society than most Muslims elsewhere. They are also ethnically diverse: Most are immigrants or their descendants from Islamic countries in Asia, Africa, and the Middle East. About a third are African-Americans, and a small number are whites of European descent.

Connections? But while diversity may naturally include the extremes, the question on many people's minds has been what exactly the relationship is between American Islam and the kind of terror and anti-Americanism that came so horribly into focus last month under the guise of religious zealotry. One moderate American Islamic leader, Sheik Muhammad Hisham Kabbani, told a State Department forum in 1999 that 80 percent of the nation's mosques are headed by clerics who espouse "extremist ideology"—which Kabbani associates with Wahhabism, an Islamic fundamentalist movement that began in Saudi Arabia in the 18th century. But Kabbani, head of the Islamic Supreme Council of America, a Washington, D.C.–based advocacy group, added that "a majority of American Muslims do not agree" with the extremist ideology.

Other American Muslim leaders say Kabbani's estimate of Wahhabi influence in U.S. mosques is exaggerated. "I don't know where he came up with that," says Ingrid Mattson, a Hartford Seminary professor and vice president of the Islamic Society of North America [ISNA]. African-Americans alone account for a third of the mosques, she notes, "and they clearly are not Wahhabis." The CAIR-Hartford study found that about 20 percent of mosques say they interpret the Koran literally, but 7 in 10 follow a more nuanced, nonfundamentalist approach.

Scholars say the democratic structure and autonomy of many American mosques protect them from extremist takeovers. Modern Islamic centers, like the one in Toledo, are "less likely to be dominated by a single teacher or viewpoint," says Frederick Denny, a scholar of Islam at the University of Colorado. That describes at least 60 percent of American mosques, according to the CAIR-Hartford study. Those that are more fundamentalist, he says, often are smaller, with transient members, such as those that "cater to foreign students who want something that feels like home." Even where fundamentalism exists, says Mattson, "there is a huge distinction between fundamentalist ideology and support of terrorism."

What divides American Muslims most often, says Denny, "is not liberal-versus-conservative ideology but how best to domesticate Islam in a Western society without doing violence to either." What, for example, are American Muslims to do with sharia, the Islamic legal and ethical codes that tradition says should undergird Islamic society? Radical clerics say it is a Muslim's duty to impose sharia throughout the world, by force if necessary. But moderates argue that Islamic law must be internalized. "It shouldn't be taken literally," says Imam Farooq Aboelzahab of the Toledo mosque. "The way sharia was applied 1,400 years ago may not always fit. It must be applied to the place and time where you live."

10   One indication that many Muslims are feeling more at home in America is their growing involvement in the nation's public life. During the past five years, Islamic leaders and groups have become increasingly outspoken on social- and foreign-policy issues. Groups like CAIR,

ISNA, the American Muslim Council, and the Islamic Institute maintain a high-visibility Washington presence, working to rally Muslim political activism and acting as media watchdogs. While American Islamic groups were virtually unanimous in condemning the terrorist attacks on New York and Washington, they remain vociferous critics of U.S. policy in the Middle East.

Stronger rhetoric, of course, has its price in this country. In late September, a prominent imam at a Cleveland mosque nearly lost his job over anti-Jewish remarks he had made in a speech 10 years ago. The board at the Islamic Center of Cleveland voted to keep Fawaz Damra after he apologized for the remarks, which appeared on a tape that surfaced recently, but local Jewish leaders are still upset. Incendiary rhetoric. Meanwhile, a leading Muslim teacher in Northern California has apologized for his own rhetorical excesses. Hamza Yusuf, who was invited to the White House to pray with President Bush after the attacks, later came under criticism for saying in a speech two days before the attacks that the United States "stands condemned" and faced "a terrible fate" because of rampant immorality and injustice in its treatment of minorities. While their causes may be just, says Yusuf, "the rhetoric of some Muslim leaders has been too incendiary—I myself have been guilty of it." September 11, he says, "was a wake-up call to me. I don't want to contribute to the hate in any shape or form."

A decade ago, Sulayman Nyang, professor of African studies at Howard University in Washington, D.C., warned in a speech that Islam will be accepted in America only when Muslims fully take their place alongside other citizens, participating in the nation's civic life, and when what the Islamic faith can offer Western culture is recognized widely as something of value. Neither, he says, will be easy to accomplish. But in times like these, such hard work is more important than ever.

Responding to Reading

1. This essay appeared in a newsmagazine on October 29, 2001, just weeks after the 9/11 terrorist attacks. What do you suppose the writers' purpose was? How can you tell?
2. According to Sheler and Betzold, how is Islam like other widely followed U.S. religions? How is it different?
3. In paragraph 5, the writers assert that the Muslim faith is "no monolith." What do they mean? What evidence do they offer to support this claim?

Responding in Writing

What do you think it would take for Muslims to truly feel "at home in America" (10)?

EARTHLY EMPIRES

William C. Symonds
1951–

Brian Grow
1969–

John Cady
1932–

Writers for BusinessWeek *magazine, William C. Symonds is Boston bureau chief, Brian Grow is Atlanta bureau correspondent, and John Cady is New York bureau correspondent. The following essay discusses the business aspects of the "megachurch" phenomenon.*

There's no shortage of churches in Houston, deep in the heart of the Bible Belt. So it's surprising that the largest one in the city—and in the entire country—is tucked away in a depressed corner most Houstonians would never dream of visiting. Yet 30,000 people endure punishing traffic on the narrow roads leading to Lakewood Church every weekend to hear Pastor Joel Osteen deliver upbeat messages of hope. A youthful-looking 42-year-old with a ready smile, he reassures the thousands who show up at each of his five weekend services that "God has a great future in store for you." His services are rousing affairs that often include his wife, Victoria, leading prayers and his mother, Dodie, discussing passages from the Bible.

Osteen is so popular that he has nearly quadrupled attendance since taking over the pulpit from his late father in 1999, winning over believers from other churches as well as throngs of the "unsaved." Many are drawn first by his ubiquitous presence on television. Each week 7 million people catch the slickly produced broadcast of his Sunday sermons on national cable and network channels, for which Lakewood shells out $15 million a year. Adherents often come clutching a copy of Osteen's best-seller, *Your Best Life Now,* which has sold 2.5 million copies since its publication last fall.

To keep them coming back, Lakewood offers free financial counseling, low-cost bulk food, even a "fidelity group" for men with "sexual addictions." Demand is brisk for the self-help sessions. Angie Mosqueda, 34, who was brought up a Catholic, says she and her husband, Mark, first went to Lakewood in 2000 when they were on the brink of a divorce. Mark even threw her out of the house after she confessed to infidelity. But over time, Lakewood counselors "really helped us to forgive one another and start all over again," she says.

Disney Look

Osteen's flourishing Lakewood enterprise brought in $55 million in contributions last year, four times the 1999 amount, church officials say. Flush with success, Osteen is laying out $90 million to transform the massive Compaq Center in downtown Houston—former home of the NBA's Houston Rockets—into a church that will seat 16,000, complete with a high-tech stage for his TV shows and Sunday School for 5,000 children. After it opens in July, he predicts weekend attendance will rocket to 100,000. Says Osteen: "Other churches have not kept up, and they lose people by not changing with the times."

Pastor Joel is one of a new generation of evangelical entrepreneurs [5] transforming their branch of Protestantism into one of the fastest-growing and most influential religious groups in America. Their runaway success is modeled unabashedly on business. They borrow tools ranging from niche marketing to MBA hiring to lift their share of U.S. churchgoers. Like Osteen, many evangelical pastors focus intently on a huge potential market—the millions of Americans who have drifted away from mainline Protestant denominations or simply never joined a church in the first place.

To reach these untapped masses, savvy leaders are creating Sunday Schools that look like Disney World and church cafes with the appeal of Starbucks. Although most hold strict religious views, they scrap staid hymns in favor of multimedia worship and tailor a panoply of services to meet all kinds of consumer needs, from divorce counseling to help for parents of autistic kids. Like Osteen, many offer an upbeat message intertwined with a religious one. To make newcomers feel at home, some do away with standard religious symbolism—even basics like crosses and pews—and design churches to look more like modern entertainment halls than traditional places of worship.

Branding Whiz

So successful are some evangelicals that they're opening up branches like so many new Home Depots or Subways. This year, the 16.4 million-member Southern Baptist Convention plans to "plant" 1,800 new churches using by-the-book niche-marketing tactics. "We have cowboy churches for people working on ranches, country music churches, even several motorcycle churches aimed at bikers," says Martin King, a spokesman for the Southern Baptists' North American Mission Board.

Branding whizzes that they are, the new church leaders are spreading their ideas through every available outlet. A line of "Biblezines" packages the New Testament in glossy magazines aimed at different market segments—there's a hip-hop version and one aimed at teen girls. Christian music appeals to millions of youths, some of whom otherwise might never give church a second thought, serving up everything from alternative rock to punk and even "screamo" (they scream religious lyrics). California megachurch pastor Rick Warren's 2002 book, *The Purpose-Driven Life,* has become the fastest-selling nonfiction book of all time, with more than 23 million copies sold, in part through a novel "pyro marketing" strategy. Then there's the Left Behind phenomenon, a series of action-packed, apocalyptic page-turners about those left on earth after Christ's second coming, selling more than 60 million copies since 1995.

Evangelicals' eager embrace of corporate-style growth strategies is giving them a tremendous advantage in the battle for religious market share, says Roger Finke, a Pennsylvania State University sociology professor and co-author of a new book, *The Churching of America, 1776–2005: Winners and Losers in Our Religious Economy.* A new Pope has given Catholicism a burst of global publicity, but its nominal membership growth in the U.S. stems largely from the influx of Mexican immigrants. Overall, the Catholic Church's long-term decline in U.S. attendance accelerated after the recent sex-abuse scandals, there's a severe priest shortage, and parish churches and schools are closing in the wake of a financial crisis.

10   Similarly, the so-called mainline Protestants who dominated 20th century America have become the religious equivalent of General Motors Corp. The large denominations—including the United Methodist Church and the Episcopal Church—have been shrinking for decades and have lost more than 1 million members in the past 10 years alone. Today, mainline Protestants account for just 16% of the U.S. population, says University of Akron political scientist John C. Green.

In contrast, evangelicalism's theological flexibility gives it the freedom to adapt to contemporary culture. With no overarching authority like the Vatican, leaders don't need to wrestle with a bureaucratic hierarchy that dictates acceptable behavior. "If you have a vision for ministry, you just do it, which makes it far easier to respond to market demand," says University of North Carolina at Chapel Hill sociology professor Christian Smith.

With such low barriers to entry, the number of evangelical megachurches—defined as those that attract at least 2,000 weekly worshippers—has shot up to 880 from 50 in 1980, figures John N. Vaughan, founder of research outfit Church Growth Today in Bolivar, Mo. He calculates that a new megachurch emerges in the U.S. an average of every two days. Overall, white evangelicals make up more than a quarter of Americans today, experts estimate. The figures are fuzzy because there's no common definition of evangelical, which typically refers to Christians who believe the Bible is the literal work of God. They may include many Southern Baptists, nondenominational churches, and some Lutherans and Methodists. There are also nearly 25 million black

Protestants who consider themselves evangelicals but largely don't share the conservative politics of most white ones. Says pollster George Gallup, who has studied religious trends for decades: "The evangelicals are the most vibrant branch of Christianity."

The triumph of evangelical Christianity is profoundly reshaping many aspects of American politics and society. Historically, much of the U.S. political and business elite has been mainline Protestant. Today, President George W. Bush and more than a dozen members of Congress, including House Speaker Dennis Hastert, are evangelicals. More important, the Republican Right has been fueled by the swelling ranks of evangelicals, whose leaders tend to be conservative politically despite their progressive marketing methods. In the 1960s and '70s, prominent evangelicals like Billy Graham kept a careful separation of pulpit and politics—even though he served as a spiritual adviser to President Richard M. Nixon. That began to change in the early 1980s, when Jerry Falwell formed the Moral Majority to express evangelicals' political views. Many of today's evangelicals hope to expand their clout even further. They're also gaining by taking their views into Corporate America. Exhibit A: the recent clash at software giant Microsoft.

As they thrive, though, there are growing tensions, with some mainline Protestants offended by their conservative politics and brazen marketing. "Jesus was not a capitalist; check out what [He] says about how hard it is to get into heaven if you're a rich man," says the Reverend Robert W. Edgar, general secretary of the liberal National Council of Churches.

Especially controversial are leaders like Osteen and the flamboy- 15 ant Creflo A. Dollar, pastor of World Changers Church International in College Park, Ga., who preach "the prosperity gospel." They endorse material wealth and tell followers that God wants them to be prosperous. In his book, Osteen talks about how his wife, Victoria, a striking blonde who dresses fashionably, wanted to buy a fancy house some years ago, before the money rolled in. He thought it wasn't possible. "But Victoria had more faith," he wrote. "She convinced me we could live in an elegant home . . . and several years later, it did come to pass." Dollar, too, defends materialistic success. Dubbed "Pass-the-Dollar" by critics, he owns two Rolls Royces and travels in a Gulfstream 3 jet. "I practice what I preach, and the Bible says . . . that God takes pleasure in the prosperity of his servants," says Dollar, 43, nattily attired in French cuffs and a pinstriped suit.

Hucksters?

Some evangelical leaders acknowledge that flagrant materialism can raise the specter of religious hucksterism à la Sinclair Lewis' fictional

Elmer Gantry[1] or Jim and Tammy Faye Bakker.[2] Our goal is not to turn the church into a business," insists Warren, the founder of Saddleback megachurch in Lake Forest, Calif. After *The Purpose-Driven Life* made him millions, he repaid Saddleback all the salary he had taken over the years and still lives modestly. Cautions Kurt Frederickson, a director of the Fuller Theological Seminary in Pasadena, Calif.: "We have to be careful when a pastor moves into the CEO mode and becomes too market-oriented, or there might be a reaction against megachurches just as there is against Wal-Mart."

Many evangelicals say they're just trying to satisfy demands not met by traditional churches. Craig Groeschel, who launched Life Church in Edmond, Okla., in 1996, started out doing market research with non-churchgoers in the area—and got an earful. "They said churches were full of hypocrites and were boring," he recalls. So he designed Life Church to counter those preconceptions, with lively, multimedia-filled services in a setting that's something between a rock concert and a coffee shop.

Once established, some ambitious churches are making a big business out of spreading their expertise. Willow Creek Community Church in South Barrington, Ill., formed a consulting arm called Willow Creek Assn. It earned $17 million last year, partly by selling marketing and management advice to 10,500 member churches from 90 denominations. Jim Mellado, the hard-charging Harvard MBA who runs it, last year brought an astonishing 110,000 church and lay leaders to conferences on topics such as effective leadership. "Our entrepreneurial impulse comes from the Biblical mandate to get the message out," says Willow Creek founder Bill Hybels, who hired Stanford MBA Greg Hawkins, a former McKinsey & Co. consultant, to handle the church's day-to-day management. Willow Creek's methods have even been lauded in a Harvard Business School case study.

Hybels's consumer-driven approach is evident at Willow Creek, where he shunned stained glass, Bibles, or even a cross for the 7,200-seat, $72 million sanctuary he recently built. The reason? Market research suggested that such traditional symbols would scare away non-churchgoers. He also gives practical advice. On a recent Wednesday evening, one of his four "teaching" pastors gave a service that started with 20 minutes of music, followed by a lengthy sermon about the Christian approach to personal finances. He told the 5,000 listeners about resisting advertising aimed at getting people to buy things they don't need and suggested they follow up at home by e-mailing questions. Like Osteen,

---

[1]Evangelical preacher and con man. [Eds.]

[2]Jim Bakker, Assemblies of God minister and former host (with his wife Tammy Faye Bakker) of the evangelical Christian TV program *The PTL Club.* Indicted on federal charges of fraud and tax evasion. [Eds.]

Hybels packages self-help programs with a positive message intended to make people feel good about themselves. "When I walk out of a service, I feel completely relieved of any stress I walked in with," says Phil Earnest, 38, a sales manager who in 2003 switched to Willow Creek from the Methodist Church he found too stodgy.

So adept at the sell are some evangelicals that it can be difficult to distinguish between their religious aims and the secular style they mimic. Last December, Prestonwood Baptist Church in Plano, Tex., staged a spectacular Christmas festival, including a 500-person choir, that attracted 70,000 people even though the cheapest ticket was $20. Throughout the year, some 16,000 people take part in its sports program, which uses eight playing fields and six gyms on its $100 million, 140-acre campus. The teams, coached by church members, bring in converts, many of them children, says Executive Pastor Mike Buster.

Gushers of Cash

Kids are often a prime target audience for megachurches. The main campus of Groeschel's Life Church in Edmond, Okla., includes a "Toon Town" of 3D buildings, a 16-foot high slide, and an animatronic police chief who recites rules. All the razzmatazz has helped Life Church quadruple its Sunday school attendance to more than 2,500 a week. "The kids are bringing their parents to church," says children's pastor Scott Werner.

Such marketing and services help to create brand loyalty any CEO would envy. Willow Creek ranks in the top 5% of 250 major brands, right up with Nike and John Deere, says Eric Arnson. He helped develop a consumer-brand practice that McKinsey then bought and recently did a pro bono study for Willow Creek using that methodology.

Other megachurches are franchising their good name. Life Church now has five campuses in Oklahoma and will expand into Phoenix this fall. Pastor Groeschel jumped the 1,000 miles to Arizona after market research pinpointed Phoenix as an area with a large population but few effective churches. Atlanta's Dollar, who is African American, has pushed into five countries, including Nigeria and South Africa.

All this growth, plus the tithing many evangelicals encourage, is generating gushers of cash. A traditional U.S. church typically has fewer than 200 members and an annual budget of around $100,000. The average megachurch pulls in $4.8 million, according to a 1999 study by the Hartford Seminary, one of the few surveys on the topic. The money is also fueling a megachurch building boom. First Baptist Church of Woodstock, near Atlanta, for example, has just finished a $62 million, 7,000-seat sanctuary.

Megachurch business ventures sometimes grow beyond the bounds of the church itself. In the mid-1990s, Kirbyjon Caldwell, a Wharton

MBA who sold bonds for First Boston before he enrolled in seminary, formed an economic development corporation that revived a depressed neighborhood near Houston's 14,000-member Windsor Village United Methodist Church, which he heads. A former Kmart now houses a mix of church and private businesses employing 270 people, including a Christian school and a bank. New plans call for a massive center with senior housing, retailing, and a public school.

For all their seemingly unstoppable success, evangelicals must contend with powerful forces in U.S. society. The ranks of Americans who express no religious preference have quadrupled since 1991, to 14%, according to a recent poll. Despite the megachurch surge, overall church attendance has remained fairly flat. And if anything, popular culture has become more vulgar in recent years. Still, experts like pollster Gallup see clear signs of a rising fascination with spirituality in the U.S. The September 11 attacks are one reason. So is the aging of the culturally influential Baby Boom, since spirituality tends to increase with age, he says. If so, no one is better poised than evangelicals to capitalize on the trend.

Responding to Reading

1. Is this essay's purpose essentially informative or persuasive? Can you tell whether the writers have a positive, negative, or neutral view of the evangelical churches they describe? Of those who worship there? Of Pastor Osteen? (Before you answer this question, look carefully at the essay's subject headings and at the analogies the writers make between religious institutions and businesses.)
2. What does Lakewood Church offer its parishioners? What do you think attracts worshippers to this church and to its pastor?
3. This essay appeared in *BusinessWeek,* and the writers use business terms and concepts to describe the rise of evangelical churches like Lakewood. Give some examples. Do you think such language is effective? Do you think it is appropriate?

Responding in Writing

What do you see as the advantages of a "megachurch" like Lakewood? What do you see as the disadvantages?

I BELIEVE IN AN AMERICA WHERE THE SEPARATION OF CHURCH AND STATE IS ABSOLUTE

John F. Kennedy

1917–1963

John F. Kennedy delivered the following speech to the Greater Houston Ministerial Association on September 12, 1960, just weeks before becoming the thirty-fifth president of the United States. (See page 380 for Kennedy's biography.)

While the so-called religious issue is necessarily and properly the chief topic here tonight, I want to emphasize from the outset that we have far more critical issues to face in the 1960 election; the spread of Communist influence, until it now festers 90 miles off the coast of Florida—the humiliating treatment of our President and Vice President by those who no longer respect our power—the hungry children I saw in West Virginia, the old people who cannot pay their doctor bills, the families forced to give up their farms—an America with too many slums, with too few schools, and too late to the moon and outer space.

These are the real issues which should decide this campaign. And they are not religious issues—for war and hunger and ignorance and despair know no religious barriers.

But because I am a Catholic, and no Catholic has ever been elected President, the real issues in this campaign have been obscured—perhaps deliberately, in some quarters less responsible than this. So it is apparently necessary for me to state once again—not what kind of church I believe in, for that should be important only to me—but what kind of America I believe in.

I believe in an America where the separation of church and state is absolute—where no Catholic prelate would tell the President (should he be Catholic) how to act, and no Protestant minister would tell his parishioners for whom to vote—where no church or church school is granted any public funds or political preference—and where no man is denied public office merely because his religion differs from the President who might appoint him or the people who might elect him.

I believe in an America that is officially neither Catholic, Protestant nor Jewish—where no public official either requests or accepts instructions on public policy from the Pope, the National Council of Churches or any other ecclesiastical source—where no religious body seeks to impose its will directly or indirectly upon the general populace or the public acts of its officials—and where religious liberty is so indivisible that an act against one church is treated as an act against all.   5

For while this year it may be a Catholic against whom the finger of suspicion is pointed, in other years it has been, and may someday be again, a Jew—or a Quaker—or a Unitarian—or a Baptist. It was Virginia's harassment of Baptist preachers, for example, that helped lead to Jefferson's statute of religious freedom. Today I may be the victim—but tomorrow it may be you—until the whole fabric of our harmonious society is ripped at a time of great national peril.

Finally, I believe in an America where religious intolerance will someday end—where all men and all churches are treated as equal—where every man has the same right to attend or not attend the church of his choice—where there is no Catholic vote, no anti-Catholic vote, no bloc voting of any kind—and where Catholics, Protestants and Jews, at both the lay and pastoral level, will refrain from those attitudes of disdain and division which have so often marred their works in the past, and promote instead the American ideal of brotherhood.

That is the kind of America in which I believe. And it represents the kind of Presidency in which I believe—a great office that must neither be humbled by making it the instrument of any one religious group nor tarnished by arbitrarily withholding its occupancy from the members of any one religious group. I believe in a President whose religious views are his own private affair, neither imposed by him upon the nation or imposed by the nation upon him as a condition to holding that office.

I would not look with favor upon a President working to subvert the first amendment's guarantees of religious liberty. Nor would our system of checks and balances permit him to do so—and neither do I look with favor upon those who would work to subvert Article VI of the Constitution by requiring a religious test—even by indirection—for it. If they disagree with that safeguard they should be out openly working to repeal it.

10   I want a Chief Executive whose public acts are responsible to all groups and obligated to none—who can attend any ceremony, service or dinner his office may appropriately require of him—and whose fulfillment of his Presidential oath is not limited or conditioned by any religious oath, ritual or obligation.

This is the kind of America I believe in—and this is the kind I fought for in the South Pacific, and the kind my brother died for in Europe. No one suggested then that we may have a "divided loyalty," that we did "not believe in liberty," or that we belonged to a disloyal group that threatened the "freedoms for which our forefathers died."

And in fact this is the kind of America for which our forefathers died—when they fled here to escape religious test oaths that denied office to members of less favored churches—when they fought for the Constitution, the Bill of Rights, and the Virginia Statute of Religious Freedom—and when they fought at the shrine I visited today, the

Alamo. For side by side with Bowie and Crockett died McCafferty and Bailey and Carey—but no one knows whether they were Catholic or not. For there was no religious test at the Alamo.

I ask you tonight to follow in that tradition—to judge me on the basis of my record of 14 years in Congress—on my declared stands against an Ambassador to the Vatican, against unconstitutional aid to parochial schools, and against any boycott of the public schools (which I have attended myself)—instead of judging me on the basis of these pamphlets and publications we all have seen that carefully select quotations out of context from the statements of Catholic church leaders, usually in other countries, frequently in other centuries, and always omitting, of course, the statement of the American Bishops in 1948 which strongly endorsed church–state separation, and which more nearly reflects the views of almost every American Catholic.

I do not consider these other quotations binding upon my public acts—why should you? But let me say, with respect to other countries, that I am wholly opposed to the state being used by any religious group, Catholic or Protestant, to compel, prohibit, or persecute the free exercise of any other religion. And I hope that you and I condemn with equal fervor those nations which deny their Presidency to Protestants and those which deny it to Catholics. And rather than cite the misdeeds of those who differ, I would cite the record of the Catholic Church in such nations as Ireland and France—and the independence of such statesmen as Adenauer and De Gaulle.

But let me stress again that these are my views—for contrary to common newspaper usage, I am not the Catholic candidate for President. I am the Democratic Party's candidate for President who happens also to be a Catholic. I do not speak for my church on public matters— and the church does not speak for me.   15

Whatever issue may come before me as President—on birth control, divorce, censorship, gambling or any other subject—I will make my decision in accordance with these views, in accordance with what my conscience tells me to be the national interest, and without regard to outside religious pressures or dictates. And no power or threat of punishment could cause me to decide otherwise.

But if the time should ever come—and I do not concede any conflict to be even remotely possible—when my office would require me to either violate my conscience or violate the national interest, then I would resign the office; and I hope any conscientious public servant would do the same.

But I do not intend to apologize for these views to my critics of either Catholic or Protestant faith—nor do I intend to disavow either my views or my church in order to win this election.

If I should lose on the real issues, I shall return to my seat in the Senate, satisfied that I had tried my best and was fairly judged. But if this election is decided on the basis that 40 million Americans lost their chance of being President on the day they were baptized, then it is the whole nation that will be the loser, in the eyes of Catholics and non-Catholics around the world, in the eyes of history, and in the eyes of our own people.

20   But if, on the other hand, I should win the election, then I shall devote every effort of mind and spirit to fulfilling the oath of the Presidency—practically identical, I might add, to the oath I have taken for 14 years in the Congress. For without reservation, I can "solemnly swear that I will faithfully execute the office of President of the United States, and will to the best of my ability preserve, protect, and defend the Constitution . . . so help me God."

Responding to Reading

1. Kennedy is addressing members of the clergy. How do you suppose he tailored the content and style of his remarks to this audience? How might his speech have been different if he were addressing a secular audience—for example, political leaders?
2. What purpose do you think Kennedy intended paragraphs 11 and 12 to serve? Are these paragraphs effective, or do you think they go too far?
3. In paragraph 16, Kennedy lists some issues that, given his personal religious views, voters might think present problems for him. What additional issues can you think of that might challenge a deeply religious president today? (Note that, in recent years, presidential hopefuls have included at least one Jew and one Mormon as well as several evangelical Protestants.)

Responding in Writing

In paragraph 7, Kennedy says, "I believe in an America where religious intolerance will someday end—where all men and all churches are treated as equal. . . . " Do you think we now live in the America Kennedy wished for? Why or why not?

CATHEDRAL

Raymond Carver

1938–1988

*A talented short story writer, Raymond Carver led a troubled life. Through-
out his adult life, Carver struggled with alcoholism and marital problems, but
he remained sober and productive during the last ten years of his life. His story
collections include* Will You Please Be Quiet, Please? *(1976),* What We
Talk About When We Talk About Love *(1981),* Short Cuts *(1984), and*
Cathedral *(1984), in which the following short story originally appeared.*

This blind man, an old friend of my wife's, he was on his way to spend
the night. His wife had died. So he was visiting the dead wife's relatives
in Connecticut. He called my wife from his in-laws'. Arrangements were
made. He would come by train, a five-hour trip, and my wife would
meet him at the station. She hadn't seen him since she worked for him
one summer in Seattle ten years ago. But she and the blind man had
kept in touch. They made tapes and mailed them back and forth. I wasn't
enthusiastic about his visit. He was no one I knew. And his being blind
bothered me. My idea of blindness came from the movies. In the movies,
the blind moved slowly and never laughed. Sometimes they were led
by seeing-eye dogs. A blind man in my house was not something I
looked forward to.

That summer in Seattle she had needed a job. She didn't have any
money. The man she was going to marry at the end of the summer
was in officers' training school. He didn't have any money, either. But
she was in love with the guy, and he was in love with her, etc. She'd
seen something in the paper: HELP WANTED—*Reading to Blind Man,* and
a telephone number. She phoned and went over, was hired on the spot.
She'd worked with this blind man all summer. She read stuff to him,
case studies, reports, that sort of thing. She helped him organize his
little office in the county social-service department. They'd become
good friends, my wife and the blind man. How do I know these
things? She told me. And she told me something else. On her last day
in the office, the blind man asked if he could touch her face. She agreed
to this. She told me he touched his fingers to every part of her face, her
nose—even her neck! She never forgot it. She even tried to write a
poem about it. She was always trying to write a poem. She wrote a
poem or two every year, usually after something really important had
happened to her.

When we first started going out together, she showed me the poem. In the poem, she recalled his fingers and the way they had moved around over her face. In the poem, she talked about what she had felt at the time, about what went through her mind when the blind man touched her nose and lips. I can remember I didn't think much of the poem. Of course, I didn't tell her that. Maybe I just don't understand poetry. I admit it's not the first thing I reach for when I pick up something to read.

Anyway, this man who'd first enjoyed her favors, the officer-to-be, he'd been her childhood sweetheart. So okay. I'm saying that at the end of the summer she let the blind man run his hands over her face, said goodbye to him, married her childhood etc., who was now a commissioned officer, and she moved away from Seattle. But they'd kept in touch, she and the blind man. She made the first contact after a year or so. She called him up one night from an Air Force base in Alabama. She wanted to talk. They talked. He asked her to send a tape and tell him about her life. She did this. She sent the tape. On the tape, she told the blind man about her husband and about their life together in the military. She told the blind man she loved her husband but she didn't like it where they lived and she didn't like it that he was part of the military-industrial thing. She told the blind man she'd written a poem and he was in it. She told him that she was writing a poem about what it was like to be an Air Force officer's wife. The poem wasn't finished yet. She was still writing it. The blind man made a tape. He sent her the tape. She made a tape. This went on for years. My wife's officer was posted to one base and then another. She sent tapes from Moody AFB, McGuire, McConnell, and finally Travis, near Sacramento, where one night she got to feeling lonely and cut off from people she kept losing in that moving-around life. She got to feeling she couldn't go it another step. She went in and swallowed all the pills and capsules in the medicine chest and washed them down with a bottle of gin. Then she got into a hot bath and passed out.

5   But instead of dying, she got sick. She threw up. Her officer—why should he have a name? he was the childhood sweetheart, and what more does he want?—came home from somewhere, found her, and called the ambulance. In time, she put it all on a tape and sent the tape to the blind man. Over the years, she put all kinds of stuff on tapes and sent the tapes off lickety-split. Next to writing a poem every year, I think it was her chief means of recreation. On one tape, she told the blind man she'd decided to live away from her officer for a time. On another tape, she told him about her divorce. She and I began going out, and of course she told her blind man about it. She told him everything, or so it seemed to me. Once she asked me if I'd like to hear the latest tape from the blind man. This was a year ago. I was on the tape, she said. So I said okay, I'd listen to it. I got us drinks and we settled down in

the living room. We made ready to listen. First she inserted the tape into the player and adjusted a couple of dials. Then she pushed a lever. The tape squeaked and someone began to talk in this loud voice. She lowered the volume. After a few minutes of harmless chitchat, I heard my own name in the mouth of this stranger, this blind man I didn't even know! And then this: "From all you've said about him, I can only conclude—" But we were interrupted, a knock at the door, something, and we didn't ever get back to the tape. Maybe it was just as well. I'd heard all I wanted to.

Now this same blind man was coming to sleep in my house.

"Maybe I could take him bowling," I said to my wife. She was at the draining board doing scalloped potatoes. She put down the knife she was using and turned around.

"If you love me," she said, "you can do this for me. If you don't love me, okay. But if you had a friend, any friend, and the friend came to visit, I'd make him feel comfortable." She wiped her hands with the dish towel.

"I don't have any blind friends," I said.

"You don't have *any* friends," she said. "Period. Besides," she said, "goddamn it, his wife's just died! Don't you understand that? The man's lost his wife!" 10

I didn't answer. She'd told me a little about the blind man's wife. Her name was Beulah. Beulah! That's a name for a colored woman.

"Was his wife a Negro?" I asked.

"Are you crazy?" my wife said. "Have you just flipped or something?" She picked up a potato. I saw it hit the floor, then roll under the stove. "What's wrong with you?" she said. "Are you drunk?"

"I'm just asking," I said.

Right then my wife filled me in with more detail than I cared to know. I made a drink and sat at the kitchen table to listen. Pieces of the story began to fall into place. 15

Beulah had gone to work for the blind man the summer after my wife had stopped working for him. Pretty soon Beulah and the blind man had themselves a church wedding. It was a little wedding—who'd want to go to such a wedding in the first place?—just the two of them, plus the minister and the minister's wife. But it was a church wedding just the same. It was what Beulah had wanted, he'd said. But even then Beulah must have been carrying the cancer in her glands. After they had been inseparable for eight years—my wife's word, *inseparable*—Beulah's health went into a rapid decline. She died in a Seattle hospital room, the blind man sitting beside the bed and holding on to her hand. They'd married, lived and worked together, slept together—had sex, sure—and then the blind man had to bury her. All this without his having ever seen what the goddamned woman looked like. It was beyond my understanding. Hearing this, I felt sorry for the blind man for a little bit. And then I found myself thinking what a pitiful life this woman must have led. Imagine a woman who could never see herself as she was seen in the eyes of her loved one. A woman who could go on day after day and never receive the smallest compliment from her beloved. A woman whose husband could never read the expression on her face, be it misery or something better. Someone who could wear makeup or not—what difference to him? She could, if she wanted, wear green eye-shadow around one eye, a straight pin in her nostril, yellow slacks, and purple shoes, no matter. And then to slip off into death, the blind man's hand on her hand, his blind eyes streaming tears—I'm imagining now—her last thought maybe this: that he never even knew what she looked like, and she on an express to the grave. Robert was left with a small insurance policy and a half of a twenty-peso Mexican coin. The other half of the coin went into the box with her. Pathetic.

So when the time rolled around, my wife went to the depot to pick him up. With nothing to do but wait—sure, I blamed him for that—I was having a drink and watching the TV when I heard the car pull into the drive. I got up from the sofa with my drink and went to the window to have a look.

I saw my wife laughing as she parked the car. I saw her get out of the car and shut the door. She was still wearing a smile. Just amazing. She went around to the other side of the car to where the blind man was already starting to get out. This blind man, feature this, he was wearing a full beard! A beard on a blind man! Too much, I say. The blind man reached into the backseat and dragged out a suitcase. My wife took his arm, shut the car door, and, talking all the way, moved him down the drive and then up the steps to the front porch. I turned off the TV. I finished my drink, rinsed the glass, dried my hands. Then I went to the door.

My wife said, "I want you to meet Robert. Robert, this is my husband. I've told you all about him." She was beaming. She had this blind man by his coat sleeve.

20   The blind man let go of his suitcase and up came his hand.

I took it. He squeezed hard, held my hand, and then he let it go.

"I feel like we've already met," he boomed.

"Likewise," I said. I didn't know what else to say. Then I said, "Welcome. I've heard a lot about you." We began to move then, a little group, from the porch into the living room, my wife guiding him by the arm. The blind man was carrying his suitcase in his other hand. My wife said things like, "To your left here, Robert. That's right. Now watch it, there's a chair. That's it. Sit down right here. This is the sofa. We just bought this sofa two weeks ago."

I started to say something about the old sofa. I'd liked that old sofa. But I didn't say anything. Then I wanted to say something else, small-talk, about the scenic ride along the Hudson. How going *to* New York, you should sit on the right-hand side of the train, and coming *from* New York, the left-hand side.

"Did you have a good train ride?" I said. "Which side of the train 25 did you sit on, by the way?"

"What a question, which side!" my wife said. "What's it matter which side?" she said.

"I just asked," I said.

"Right side," the blind man said. "I hadn't been on a train in nearly forty years. Not since I was a kid. With my folks. That's been a long time. I'd nearly forgotten the sensation. I have winter in my beard now," he said. "So I've been told, anyway. Do I look distinguished, my dear?" the blind man said to my wife.

"You look distinguished, Robert," she said. "Robert," she said. "Robert, it's just so good to see you."

My wife finally took her eyes off the blind man and looked at me. 30 I had the feeling she didn't like what she saw. I shrugged.

I've never met, or personally known, anyone who was blind. This blind man was late forties, a heavy-set, balding man with stooped shoulders, as if he carried a great weight there. He wore brown slacks, brown shoes, a light-brown shirt, a tie, a sports coat. Spiffy. He also had this full beard. But he didn't use a cane and he didn't wear dark glasses. I'd always thought dark glasses were a must for the blind. Fact was, I wished he had a pair. At first glance, his eyes looked like anyone else's eyes. But if you looked close, there was something different about them. Too much white in the iris, for one thing, and the pupils seemed to move around in the sockets without his knowing it or being able to stop it. Creepy. As I stared at his face, I saw the left pupil turn in toward his nose while the other made an effort to keep in one place. But it was only an effort, for that eye was on the roam without his knowing it or wanting it to be.

I said, "Let me get you a drink. What's your pleasure? We have a little of everything. It's one of our pastimes."

"Bub, I'm a Scotch man myself," he said fast enough in this big voice.

"Right," I said. Bub! "Sure you are. I knew it."

He let his fingers touch his suitcase, which was sitting alongside 35 the sofa. He was taking his bearings. I didn't blame him for that.

"I'll move that up to your room," my wife said.

"No, that's fine," the blind man said loudly. "It can go up when I go up."

"A little water with the Scotch?" I said.

"Very little," he said.

"I knew it," I said.   40

He said, "Just a tad. The Irish actor, Barry Fitzgerald? I'm like that fellow. When I drink water, Fitzgerald said, I drink water. When I drink whiskey, I drink whiskey." My wife laughed. The blind man brought his hand up under his beard. He lifted his beard slowly and let it drop.

I did the drinks, three big glasses of Scotch with a splash of water in each. Then we made ourselves comfortable and talked about Robert's travels. First the long flight from the West Coast to Connecticut, we covered that. Then from Connecticut up here by train. We had another drink concerning that leg of the trip.

I remembered having read somewhere that the blind didn't smoke because, as speculation had it, they couldn't see the smoke they exhaled. I thought I knew that much and that much only about blind people. But this blind man smoked his cigarette down to the nubbin and then lit another one. This blind man filled his ashtray and my wife emptied it.

When we sat down at the table for dinner, we had another drink. My wife heaped Robert's plate with cube steak, scalloped potatoes, green beans. I buttered him up two slices of bread. I said, "Here's bread and butter for you." I swallowed some of my drink. "Now let us pray," I said, and the blind man lowered his head. My wife looked at me, her mouth agape. "Pray the phone won't ring and the food doesn't get cold," I said.

45   We dug in. We ate everything there was to eat on the table. We ate like there was no tomorrow. We didn't talk. We ate. We scarfed. We grazed that table. We were into serious eating. The blind man had right away located his foods, he knew just where everything was on his plate. I watched with admiration as he used his knife and fork on the meat. He'd cut two pieces of meat, fork the meat into his mouth, and then go all out for the scalloped potatoes, the beans next, and then he'd tear off a hunk of buttered bread and eat that. He'd follow this up with a big drink of milk. It didn't seem to bother him to use his fingers once in a while, either.

We finished everything, including half a strawberry pie. For a few moments, we sat as if stunned. Sweat beaded on our faces. Finally, we got up from the table and left the dirty plates. We didn't look back. We took ourselves into the living room and sank into our places again. Robert and my wife sat on the sofa. I took the big chair. We had us two or three more drinks while they talked about the major things that had come to pass for them in the past ten years. For the most part, I just listened. Now and then I joined in. I didn't want him to think I'd left the room, and I didn't want her to think I was feeling left out. They talked of things that had happened to them—to them!—these past ten years. I waited in vain to hear my name on my wife's sweet lips: "And then my dear husband came into my life"—something like that. But I heard nothing of the sort. More talk of Robert. Robert had done a little of everything, it seemed, a regular blind jack-of-all-trades. But most recently he and his wife had had an Amway distributorship, from which, I gathered, they'd earned their living, such as it was. The blind man was also a ham radio operator.[1] He talked in his loud voice about conversations he'd had with fellow operators in Guam, in the Philippines, in Alaska,

---

[1]Amateur short-wave radio operator. [Eds.]

and even in Tahiti. He said he'd have a lot of friends there if he ever wanted to go visit those places. From time to time, he'd turn his blind face toward me, put his hand under his beard, ask me something. How long had I been in my present position? (Three years.) Did I like my work? (I didn't.) Was I going to stay with it? (What were the options?) Finally, when I thought he was beginning to run down, I got up and turned on the TV.

My wife looked at me with irritation. She was heading toward a boil. Then she looked at the blind man and said, "Robert, do you have a TV?"

The blind man said, "My dear, I have two TVs. I have a color set and a black-and-white thing, and old relic. It's funny, but if I turn the TV on, and I'm always turning it on, I turn on the color set. It's funny, don't you think?"

I didn't know what to say to that. I had absolutely nothing to say to that. No opinion. So I watched the news program and tried to listen to what the announcer was saying.

"This is a color TV," the blind man said. "Don't ask me how, but I can tell." 50

"We traded up a while ago," I said.

The blind man had another taste of his drink. He lifted his beard, sniffed it, and let it fall. He leaned forward on the sofa. He positioned his ashtray on the coffee table, then put the lighter to his cigarette. He leaned back on the sofa and crossed his legs at the ankles.

My wife covered her mouth, and then she yawned. She stretched. She said, "I think I'll go upstairs and put on my robe. I think I'll change into something else. Robert, you make yourself comfortable," she said.

"I'm comfortable," the blind man said.

"I want you to feel comfortable in this house," she said. 55

"I am comfortable," the blind man said.

After she'd left the room, he and I listened to the weather report and then to the sports roundup. By that time, she'd been gone so long I didn't know if she was going to come back. I thought she might have gone to bed. I wished she'd come back downstairs. I didn't want to be left alone with a blind man. I asked him if he wanted another drink, and he said sure. Then I asked if he wanted to smoke some dope with me. I said I'd just rolled a number. I hadn't, but I planned to do so in about two shakes.

"I'll try some with you," he said.

"Damn right," I said. "That's the stuff."

I got our drinks and sat down on the sofa with him. Then I rolled 60 us two fat numbers. I lit one and passed it. I brought it to his fingers. He took it and inhaled.

"Hold it as long as you can," I said. I could tell he didn't know the first thing.

My wife came back downstairs wearing her pink robe and her pink slippers.

"What do I smell?" she said.

"We thought we'd have us some cannabis," I said.

65   My wife gave me a savage look. Then she looked at the blind man and said, "Robert, I didn't know you smoked."

He said, "I do now, my dear. There's a first time for everything. But I don't feel anything yet."

"This stuff is pretty mellow," I said. "This stuff is mild. It's dope you can reason with," I said. "It doesn't mess you up."

"Not much it doesn't, bub," he said, and laughed.

My wife sat on the sofa between the blind man and me. I passed her the number. She took it and toked and then passed it back to me. "Which way is this going?" she said. Then she said, "I shouldn't be smoking this. I can hardly keep my eyes open as it is. That dinner did me in. I shouldn't have eaten so much."

70   "It was the strawberry pie," the blind man said. "That's what did it," he said, and he laughed his big laugh. Then he shook his head.

"There's more strawberry pie," I said.

"Do you want some more, Robert?" my wife said.

"Maybe in a little while," he said.

We gave our attention to the TV. My wife yawned again. She said, "Your bed is made up when you feel like going to bed, Robert. I know you must have had a long day. When you're ready to go to bed, say so." She pulled his arm. "Robert?"

75   He came to and said, "I've had a real nice time. This beats tapes, doesn't it?"

I said, "Coming at you," and I put the number between his fingers. He inhaled, held the smoke, and then let it go. It was like he'd been doing it since he was nine years old.

"Thanks, bub," he said. "But I think this is all for me. I think I'm beginning to feel it," he said. He held the burning roach out for my wife.

"Same here," she said. "Ditto. Me, too." She took the roach and passed it to me. "I may just sit here for a while between you two guys with my eyes closed. But don't let me bother you, okay? Either one of you. If it bothers you, say so. Otherwise, I may just sit here with my eyes closed until you're ready to go to bed," she said. "Your bed's made up, Robert, when you're ready. It's right next to our room at the top of the stairs. We'll show you up when you're ready. You wake me up now, you guys, if I fall asleep." She said that and then she closed her eyes and went to sleep.

The news program ended. I got up and changed the channel. I sat back down on the sofa. I wished my wife hadn't pooped out. Her head lay across the back of the sofa, her mouth open. She'd turned so that her robe slipped away from her legs, exposing a juicy thigh. I reached to

draw her robe back over her, and it was then that I glanced at the blind
man. What the hell! I flipped the robe open again.

"You say when you want some strawberry pie," I said.   80

"I will," he said.

I said, "Are you tired? Do you want me to take you up to your bed?
Are you ready to hit the hay?"

"Not yet," he said. "No, I'll stay up with you, bub. If that's all right.
I'll stay up until you're ready to turn in. We haven't had a chance to
talk. Know what I mean? I feel like me and her monopolized the
evening." He lifted his beard and he let it fall. He picked up his cigarettes and his lighter.

"That's all right," I said. Then I said, "I'm glad for the company."

And I guess I was. Every night I smoked dope and stayed up as   85
long as I could before I fell asleep. My wife and I hardly ever went to
bed at the same time. When I did go to sleep, I had these dreams. Sometimes I'd wake up from one of them, my heart going crazy.

Something about the church and the Middle Ages was on the TV.
Not your run-of-the-mill TV fare. I wanted to watch something else. I
turned to the other channels. But there was nothing on them, either. So
I turned back to the first channel and apologized.

"Bub, it's all right," the blind man said. "It's fine with me. Whatever you want to watch is okay. I'm always learning something. Learning
never ends. It won't hurt me to learn something tonight. I got ears,"
he said.

We didn't say anything for a time. He was leaning forward with his
head turned at me, his right ear aimed in the direction of the set. Very
disconcerting. Now and then his eyelids drooped and then they
snapped open again. Now and then he put his fingers into his beard
and tugged, like he was thinking about something he was hearing on
the television.

On the screen, a group of men wearing cowls was being set upon
and tormented by men dressed in skeleton costumes and men dressed
as devils. The men dressed as devils wore devil masks, horns, and long
tails. This pageant was part of a procession. The Englishman who was
narrating the thing said it took place in Spain once a year. I tried to
explain to the blind man what was happening.

"Skeletons," he said. "I know about skeletons," he said, and nodded.   90

The TV showed this one cathedral. Then there was a long, slow
look at another one. Finally, the picture switched to the famous one in
Paris, with its flying buttresses and its spires reaching up to the clouds.
The camera pulled away to show the whole of the cathedral rising above
the skyline.

There were times when the Englishman who was telling the thing
would shut up, would simply let the camera move around the cathedrals.
Or else the camera would tour the countryside, men in fields walking

behind oxen. I waited as long as I could. Then I felt I had to say something. I said, "They're showing the outside of this cathedral now. Gargoyles. Little statues carved to look like monsters. Now I guess they're in Italy. Yeah, they're in Italy. There's paintings on the walls of this one church."

"Are those fresco paintings,[2] bub?" he asked, and he sipped from his drink.

I reached for my glass. But it was empty. I tried to remember what I could remember. "You're asking me are those frescoes?" I said. "That's a good question. I don't know."

95   The camera moved to a cathedral outside Lisbon. The differences in the Portuguese cathedral compared with the French and Italian were not that great. But they were there. Mostly the interior stuff. Then something occurred to me, and I said, "Something has occurred to me. Do you have any idea what a cathedral is? What they look like, that is? Do you follow me? If somebody says cathedral to you, do you have any notion what they're talking about? Do you know the difference between that and a Baptist church, say?"

He let the smoke dribble from his mouth. "I know they took hundreds of workers fifty or a hundred years to build," he said. "I just heard the man say that, of course. I know generations of the same families worked on a cathedral. I heard him say that, too. The men who began their life's work on them, they never lived to see the completion of their work. In that wise, bub, they're no different from the rest of us, right?" He laughed. Then his eyelids drooped again. His head nodded. He seemed to be snoozing. Maybe he was imagining himself in Portugal. The TV was showing another cathedral now. This one was in Germany. The Englishman's voice droned on. "Cathedrals," the blind man said. He sat up and rolled his head back and forth. "If you want the truth, bub, that's about all I know. What I just said. What I heard him say. But maybe you could describe one to me? I wish you'd do it. I'd like that. If you want to know, I really don't have a good idea."

I stared hard at the shot of the cathedral on the TV. How could I even begin to describe it? But say my life depended on it. Say my life was being threatened by an insane guy who said I had to do it or else.

I stared some more at the cathedral before the picture flipped off into the countryside. There was no use. I turned to the blind man and said, "To begin with, they're very tall." I was looking around the room for clues. "They reach way up. Up and up. Toward the sky. They're so big, some of them, they have to have these supports. To help hold them up, so to speak. These supports are called buttresses. They remind me

---

[2]Paintings on plaster. [Eds.]

of viaducts,[3] for some reason. But maybe you don't know viaducts, either? Sometimes the cathedrals have devils and such carved into the front. Sometimes lords and ladies. Don't ask me why this is," I said.

He was nodding. The whole upper part of his body seemed to be moving back and forth.

"I'm not doing so good, am I?" I said.   100

He stopped nodding and leaned forward on the edge of the sofa. As he listened to me, he was running his fingers through his beard. I wasn't getting through to him, I could see that. But he waited for me to go on just the same. He nodded, like he was trying to encourage me. I tried to think what else to say. "They're really big," I said. "They're massive. They're built of stone. Marble, too, sometimes. In those olden days, when they built cathedrals, men wanted to be close to God. In those olden days, God was an important part of everyone's life. You could tell this from their cathedral-building. I'm sorry," I said, "but it looks like that's the best I can do for you. I'm just no good at it."

"That's all right, bub," the blind man said. "Hey, listen. I hope you don't mind my asking you. Can I ask you something? Let me ask you a simple question, yes or no. I'm just curious and there's no offense. You're my host. But let me ask if you are in any way religious? You don't mind my asking?"

I shook my head. He couldn't see that, though. A wink is the same as a nod to a blind man. "I guess I don't believe in it. In anything. Sometimes it's hard. You know what I'm saying?"

"Sure, I do," he said.

"Right," I said.   105

The Englishman was still holding forth. My wife sighed in her sleep. She drew a long breath and went on with her sleeping.

"You'll have to forgive me," I said. "But I can't tell you what a cathedral looks like. It just isn't in me to do it. I can't do any more than I've done."

The blind man sat very still, his head down, as he listened to me.

I said, "The truth is, cathedrals don't mean anything special to me. Nothing. Cathedrals. They're something to look at on late-night TV. That's all they are."

It was then that the blind man cleared his throat. He brought some- 110 thing up. He took a handkerchief from his back pocket. Then he said, "I get it, bub. It's okay. It happens. Don't worry about it," he said. "Hey, listen to me. Will you do me a favor? I got an idea. Why don't you find us some heavy paper? And a pen. We'll do something. We'll draw one together. Get us a pen and some heavy paper. Go on, bub, get the stuff," he said.

---

[3]Long elevated roadways. [Eds.]

So I went upstairs. My legs felt like they didn't have any strength in them. They felt like they did after I'd done some running. In my wife's room, I looked around. I found some ballpoints in a little basket on her table. And then I tried to think where to look for the kind of paper he was talking about.

Downstairs, in the kitchen, I found a shopping bag with onion skins in the bottom of the bag. I emptied the bag and shook it. I brought it into the living room and sat down with it near his legs. I moved some things, smoothed the wrinkles from the bag, spread it out on the coffee table.

The blind man got down from the sofa and sat next to me on the carpet.

He ran his fingers over the paper. He went up and down the sides of the paper. The edges, even the edges. He fingered the corners.

115   "All right," he said. "All right, let's do her."

He found my hand, the hand with the pen. He closed his hand over my hand. "Go ahead, bub, draw," he said. "Draw. You'll see. I'll follow along with you. It'll be okay. Just begin now like I'm telling you. You'll see. Draw," the blind man said.

So I began. First I drew a box that looked like a house. It could have been the house I lived in. Then I put a roof on it. At either end of the roof, I drew spires. Crazy.

"Swell," he said. "Terrific. You're doing fine," he said. "Never thought anything like this could happen in your lifetime, did you, bub? Well, it's a strange life, we all know that. Go on now. Keep it up."

I put in windows with arches. I drew flying buttresses. I hung great doors. I couldn't stop. The TV station went off the air. I put down the pen and closed and opened my fingers. The blind man felt around over the paper. He moved the tips of his fingers over the paper, all over what I had drawn, and he nodded.

120   "Doing fine," the blind man said.

I took up the pen again, and he found my hand. I kept at it. I'm no artist. But I kept drawing just the same.

My wife opened up her eyes and gazed at us. She sat up on the sofa, her robe hanging open. She said, "What are you doing? Tell me, I want to know."

I didn't answer her.

The blind man said, "We're drawing a cathedral. Me and him are working on it. Press hard," he said to me. "That's right. That's good," he said. "Sure. You got it, bub, I can tell. You didn't think you could. But you can, can't you? You're cooking with gas now. You know what I'm saying? We're going to really have us something here in a minute. How's the old arm?" he said. "Put some people in there now. What's a cathedral without people?"

125   My wife said, "What's going on? Robert, what are you doing? What's going on?"

"It's all right," he said to her. "Close your eyes now," the blind man said to me.

I did it. I closed them just like he said.

"Are they closed?" he said. "Don't fudge."

"They're closed," I said.

"Keep them that way," he said. He said, "Don't stop now. Draw." 130

So we kept on with it. His fingers rode my fingers as my hand went over the paper. It was like nothing else in my life up to now.

Then he said, "I think that's it. I think you got it," he said. "Take a look. What do you think?"

But I had my eyes closed. I thought I'd keep them that way for a little longer. I thought it was something I ought to do.

"Well?" he said. "Are you looking?"

My eyes were still closed. I was in my house. I knew that. But I 135 didn't feel like I was inside anything.

"It's really something," I said.

Responding to Reading

1. What is the narrator's first impression of the blind man? How does his attitude change? How do you account for this change?
2. Why do you think the blind man asks the narrator to draw a cathedral? Why does the blind man ask the narrator to close his eyes? What does the blind man hope to teach the narrator?
3. What is the significance of the story's title? In what sense is "Cathedral" a story about religious faith? In what sense is it *not* a story about religion?

Responding in Writing

How would you characterize the narrator's marriage? What effect do you think the blind man has on the marriage?

—————————————— FOCUS ——————————————

Is There Intelligent Design in Nature?

The "ascent" of man from simian through prehominid to Neanderthal
and finally to *Homo sapiens*

Responding to the Image

1. Do you think these figures accurately represent the theory of evolution? In
    what sense could the artist be accused of oversimplifying?
2. How is the last figure pictured above similar to the others? How is it different?

FINDING DESIGN IN NATURE
Christoph Schönborn
1945–

Roman Catholic Cardinal Archbishop of Vienna, Christoph Schönborn edited the 1992 Catechism of the Catholic Church, *contributing significantly to the works that have come to define Catholicism. In the following essay, Schönborn attempts to reconcile Catholic doctrine with theories of evolution.*

Ever since 1996, when Pope John Paul II said that evolution (a term he did not define) was "more than just a hypothesis," defenders of neo-Darwinian dogma have often invoked the supposed acceptance—or at least acquiescence—of the Roman Catholic Church when they defend their theory as somehow compatible with Christian faith.

But this is not true. The Catholic Church, while leaving to science many details about the history of life on earth, proclaims that by the light of reason the human intellect can readily and clearly discern purpose and design in the natural world, including the world of living things.

Evolution in the sense of common ancestry might be true, but evolution in the neo-Darwinian sense—an unguided, unplanned process of random variation and natural selection—is not. Any system of thought that denies or seeks to explain away the overwhelming evidence for design in biology is ideology, not science.

Consider the real teaching of our beloved John Paul. While his rather vague and unimportant 1996 letter about evolution is always and everywhere cited, we see no one discussing these comments from a 1985 general audience that represents his robust teaching on nature:

"All the observations concerning the development of life lead to a similar conclusion. The evolution of living beings, of which science seeks to determine the stages and to discern the mechanism, presents an internal finality which arouses admiration. This finality which directs beings in a direction for which they are not responsible or in charge, obliges one to suppose a Mind which is its inventor, its creator." 5

He went on: "To all these indications of the existence of God the Creator, some oppose the power of chance or of the proper mechanisms of matter. To speak of chance for a universe which presents such a complex organization in its elements and such marvelous finality in its life would be equivalent to giving up the search for an explanation of the world as it appears to us. In fact, this would be equivalent to admitting effects without a cause. It would be to abdicate human intelligence, which would thus refuse to think and to seek a solution for its problems."

CHAPTER 9   FOCUS

Note that in this quotation the word "finality" is a philosophical term synonymous with final cause, purpose or design. In comments at another general audience a year later, John Paul concludes, "It is clear that the truth of faith about creation is radically opposed to the theories of materialistic philosophy. These view the cosmos as the result of an evolution of matter reducible to pure chance and necessity."

Naturally, the authoritative Catechism of the Catholic Church agrees: "Human intelligence is surely already capable of finding a response to the question of origins. The existence of God the Creator can be known with certainty through his works, by the light of human reason." It adds: "We believe that God created the world according to his wisdom. It is not the product of any necessity whatever, nor of blind fate or chance."

In an unfortunate new twist on this old controversy, neo-Darwinists recently have sought to portray our new pope, Benedict XVI, as a satisfied evolutionist. They have quoted a sentence about common ancestry from a 2004 document of the International Theological Commission, pointed out that Benedict was at the time head of the commission, and concluded that the Catholic Church has no problem with the notion of "evolution" as used by mainstream biologists—that is, synonymous with neo-Darwinism.

10   The commission's document, however, reaffirms the perennial teaching of the Catholic Church about the reality of design in nature. Commenting on the widespread abuse of John Paul's 1996 letter on evolution, the commission cautions that "the letter cannot be read as a blanket approbation of all theories of evolution, including those of a neo-Darwinian provenance which explicitly deny to divine providence any truly causal role in the development of life in the universe."

Furthermore, according to the commission, "An unguided evolutionary process—one that falls outside the bounds of divine providence—simply cannot exist."

Indeed, in the homily at his installation just a few weeks ago, Benedict proclaimed: "We are not some casual and meaningless product of evolution. Each of us is the result of a thought of God. Each of us is willed, each of us is loved, each of us is necessary."

Throughout history the church has defended the truths of faith given by Jesus Christ. But in the modern era, the Catholic Church is in the odd position of standing in firm defense of reason as well. In the 19th century, the First Vatican Council taught a world newly enthralled by the "death of God" that by the use of reason alone mankind could come to know the reality of the Uncaused Cause, the First Mover, the God of the philosophers.

Now at the beginning of the 21st century, faced with scientific claims like neo-Darwinism and the multiverse hypothesis in cosmology invented to avoid the overwhelming evidence for purpose and design found in modern science, the Catholic Church will again defend human reason by proclaiming that the immanent design evident in nature is real. Scientific theories that try to explain away the appearance of design as the result of "chance and necessity" are not scientific at all, but, as John Paul put it, an abdication of human intelligence.

Responding to Reading

1. According to Schönborn, what is Pope John Paul's position on evolution? How is it different from that of neo-Darwinists?
2. Why do neo-Darwinists attempt to characterize Pope Benedict XVI as "a satisfied evolutionist" (9)? Why does Schönborn think this characterization is false?
3. How does the Catholic Church "defend human reason" (14)? In what sense is this defense antithetical to modern scientific theory?

Responding in Writing

Do you think it is possible, as Schönborn asserts, to defend human reason and at the same time to reject the neo-Darwinist view of the universe?

WHY INTELLIGENT DESIGN ISN'T

H. Allen Orr

1960–

A biology professor at the University of Rochester, H. Allen Orr studies genetic evolution and adaptation. A respected biologist, he has published numerous articles in various scientific journals. In the following New Yorker *essay, Orr characterizes intelligent design as "junk science."*

If you are in ninth grade and live in Dover, Pennsylvania, you are learning things in your biology class that differ considerably from what your peers just a few miles away are learning. In particular, you are learning that Darwin's theory of evolution provides just one possible explanation of life, and that another is provided by something called intelligent design. You are being taught this not because of a recent breakthrough in some scientist's laboratory but because the Dover Area School District's board mandates it. In October, 2004, the board decreed that "students will be made aware of gaps/problems in Darwin's theory and of other theories of evolution including, but not limited to, intelligent design."*

---

*In December 2005, a U.S. District Count barred the Dover schools from teaching intelligent design, saying the concept is creationism in disguise.

While the events in Dover have received a good deal of attention as a sign of the political times, there has been surprisingly little discussion of the science that's said to underlie the theory of intelligent design, often called I.D. Many scientists avoid discussing I.D. for strategic reasons. If a scientific claim can be loosely defined as one that scientists take seriously enough to debate, then engaging the intelligent-design movement on scientific grounds, they worry, cedes what it most desires: recognition that its claims are legitimate scientific ones.

Meanwhile, proposals hostile to evolution are being considered in more than twenty states; earlier this month, a bill was introduced into the New York State Assembly calling for instruction in intelligent design for all public-school students. The Kansas State Board of Education is weighing new standards, drafted by supporters of intelligent design, that would encourage schoolteachers to challenge Darwinism. Senator Rick Santorum, a Pennsylvania Republican, has argued that "intelligent design is a legitimate scientific theory that should be taught in science classes." An I.D.-friendly amendment that he sponsored to the No Child Left Behind Act—requiring public schools to help students understand why evolution "generates so much continuing controversy"—was overwhelmingly approved in the Senate. (The amendment was not included in the version of the bill that was signed into law, but similar language did appear in a conference report that accompanied it.) In the past few years, college students across the country have formed Intelligent Design and Evolution Awareness chapters. Clearly, a policy of limited scientific engagement has failed. So just what is this movement?

First of all, intelligent design is not what people often assume it is. For one thing, I.D. is not Biblical literalism. Unlike earlier generations of creationists—the so-called Young Earthers and scientific creationists—proponents of intelligent design do not believe that the universe was created in six days, that Earth is ten thousand years old, or that the fossil record was deposited during Noah's flood. (Indeed, they shun the label "creationism" altogether.) Nor does I.D. flatly reject evolution: adherents freely admit that some evolutionary change occurred during the history of life on Earth. Although the movement is loosely allied with, and heavily funded by, various conservative Christian groups—and although I.D. plainly maintains that life was created—it is generally silent about the identity of the creator.

5   The movement's main positive claim is that there are things in the world, most notably life, that cannot be accounted for by known natural causes and show features that, in any other context, we would attribute to intelligence. Living organisms are too complex to be explained by any natural—or, more precisely, by any mindless—process. Instead, the design inherent in organisms can be accounted for only by invoking a designer, and one who is very, very smart.

All of which puts I.D. squarely at odds with Darwin. Darwin's theory of evolution was meant to show how the fantastically complex features of organisms—eyes, beaks, brains—could arise without the intervention of a designing mind. According to Darwinism, evolution largely reflects the combined action of random mutation and natural selection. A random mutation in an organism, like a random change in any finely tuned machine, is almost always bad. That's why you don't, screwdriver in hand, make arbitrary changes to the insides of your television. But, once in a great while, a random mutation in the DNA that makes up an organism's genes slightly improves the function of some organ and thus the survival of the organism. In a species whose eye amounts to nothing more than a primitive patch of light-sensitive cells, a mutation that causes this patch to fold into a cup shape might have a survival advantage. While the old type of organism can tell only if the lights are on, the new type can detect the *direction* of any source of light or shadow. Since shadows sometimes mean predators, that can be valuable information. The new, improved type of organism will, therefore, be more common in the next generation. That's natural selection. Repeated over billions of years, this process of incremental improvement should allow for the gradual emergence of organisms that are exquisitely adapted to their environments and that look for all the world as though they were designed. By 1870, about a decade after *The Origin of Species* was published, nearly all biologists agreed that life had evolved, and by 1940 or so most agreed that natural selection was a key force driving this evolution.

Advocates of intelligent design point to two developments that in their view undermine Darwinism. The first is the molecular revolution in biology. Beginning in the nineteen-fifties, molecular biologists revealed a staggering and unsuspected degree of complexity within the cells that make up all life. This complexity, I.D.'s defenders argue, lies beyond the abilities of Darwinism to explain. Second, they claim that new mathematical findings cast doubt on the power of natural selection. Selection may play a role in evolution, but it cannot accomplish what biologists suppose it can.

These claims have been championed by a tireless group of writers, most of them associated with the Center for Science and Culture at the Discovery Institute, a Seattle-based think tank that sponsors projects in science, religion, and national defense, among other areas. The center's fellows and advisers—including the emeritus law professor Phillip E. Johnson, the philosopher Stephen C. Meyer, and the biologist Jonathan Wells—have published an astonishing number of articles and books that decry the ostensibly sad state of Darwinism and extoll the virtues of the design alternative. But Johnson, Meyer, and Wells, while highly visible, are mainly strategists and popularizers. The scientific leaders of the design movement are two scholars, one a biochemist and the other a mathematician. To assess intelligent design is to assess their arguments.

Chapter 9 Focus

Michael J. Behe, a professor of biological sciences at Lehigh University (and a senior fellow at the Discovery Institute), is a biochemist who writes technical papers on the structure of DNA. He is the most prominent of the small circle of scientists working on intelligent design, and his arguments are by far the best known. His book *Darwin's Black Box* (1996) was a surprise best-seller and was named by *National Review* as one of the hundred best nonfiction books of the twentieth century. (A little calibration may be useful here; *The Starr Report* also made the list.)

10   Not surprisingly, Behe's doubts about Darwinism begin with biochemistry. Fifty years ago, he says, any biologist could tell stories like the one about the eye's evolution. But such stories, Behe notes, invariably began with cells, whose own evolutionary origins were essentially left unexplained. This was harmless enough as long as cells weren't qualitatively more complex than the larger, more visible aspects of the eye. Yet when biochemists began to dissect the inner workings of the cell, what they found floored them. A cell is packed full of exceedingly complex structures—hundreds of microscopic machines, each performing a specific job. The "Give me a cell and I'll give you an eye" story told by Darwinists, he says, began to seem suspect: starting with a cell was starting ninety per cent of the way to the finish line.

Behe's main claim is that cells are complex not just in degree but in kind. Cells contain structures that are "irreducibly complex." This means that if you remove any single part from such a structure, the structure no longer functions. Behe offers a simple, nonbiological example of an irreducibly complex object: the mousetrap. A mousetrap has several parts—platform, spring, catch, hammer, and hold-down bar—and all of them have to be in place for the trap to work. If you remove the spring from a mousetrap, it isn't slightly worse at killing mice; it doesn't kill them at all. So, too, with the bacterial flagellum, Behe argues. This flagellum is a tiny propeller attached to the back of some bacteria. Spinning at more than twenty thousand r.p.m.s, it motors the bacterium through its aquatic world. The flagellum comprises roughly thirty different proteins, all precisely arranged, and if any one of them is removed the flagellum stops spinning.

In *Darwin's Black Box*, Behe maintained that irreducible complexity presents Darwinism with "unbridgeable chasms." How, after all, could a gradual process of incremental improvement build something like a flagellum, which needs *all* its parts in order to work? Scientists, he argued, must face up to the fact that "many biochemical systems cannot be built by natural selection working on mutations." In the end, Behe concluded that irreducibly complex cells arise the same way as irreducibly complex mousetraps—someone designs them. As he put it in a recent *Times* Op-Ed piece: "If it looks, walks,

CHAPTER 9   FOCUS

and quacks like a duck, then, absent compelling evidence to the contrary, we have warrant to conclude it's a duck. Design should not be overlooked simply because it's so obvious." In *Darwin's Black Box*, Behe speculated that the designer might have assembled the first cell, essentially solving the problem of irreducible complexity, after which evolution might well have proceeded by more or less conventional means. Under Behe's brand of creationism, you might still be an ape that evolved on the African savanna; it's just that your cells harbor micro-machines engineered by an unnamed intelligence some four billion years ago.

But Behe's principal argument soon ran into trouble. As biologists pointed out, there are several different ways that Darwinian evolution can build irreducibly complex systems. In one, elaborate structures may evolve for one reason and then get co-opted for some entirely different, irreducibly complex function. Who says those thirty flagellar proteins weren't present in bacteria long before bacteria sported flagella? They may have been performing other jobs in the cell and only later got drafted into flagellum-building. Indeed, there's now strong evidence that several flagellar proteins once played roles in a type of molecular pump found in the membranes of bacterial cells.

Behe doesn't consider this sort of "indirect" path to irreducible complexity—in which parts perform one function and then switch to another—terribly plausible. And he essentially rules out the alternative possibility of a direct Darwinian path: a path, that is, in which Darwinism builds an irreducibly complex structure while selecting all along for the same biological function. But biologists have shown that direct paths to irreducible complexity are possible, too. Suppose a part gets added to a system merely because the part improves the system's performance; the part is not, at this stage, essential for function. But, because subsequent evolution builds on this addition, a part that was at first just advantageous might *become* essential. As this process is repeated through evolutionary time, more and more parts that were once merely beneficial become necessary. This idea was first set forth by H. J. Muller, the Nobel Prize–winning geneticist, in 1939, but it's a familiar process in the development of human technologies. We add new parts like global-positioning systems to cars not because they're necessary but because they're nice. But no one would be surprised if, in fifty years, computers that rely on G.P.S. actually drove our cars. At that point, G.P.S. would no longer be an attractive option; it would be an essential piece of automotive technology. It's important to see that this process is thoroughly Darwinian: each change might well be small and each represents an improvement.

Design theorists have made some concessions to these criticisms. 15 Behe has confessed to "sloppy prose" and said he hadn't meant to imply that irreducibly complex systems "by definition" cannot evolve gradually. "I quite agree that my argument against Darwinism does not add up to a logical proof," he says—though he continues to believe that Darwinian paths to irreducible complexity are exceedingly unlikely. Behe and his followers now emphasize that, while irreducibly complex systems can in principle evolve, biologists can't reconstruct in convincing detail just how any such system did evolve.

What counts as a sufficiently detailed historical narrative, though, is altogether subjective. Biologists actually know a great deal about the evolution of biochemical systems, irreducibly complex or not. It's significant, for instance, that the proteins that typically make up the parts of these systems are often similar to one another. (Blood clotting—another of Behe's examples of irreducible complexity—involves at least twenty proteins, several of which are similar, and all of which are needed to make clots, to localize or remove clots, or to prevent the runaway clotting of all blood.) And biologists understand why these proteins are so similar. Each gene in an organism's genome encodes a particular protein. Occasionally, the stretch of DNA that makes up a particular gene will get accidentally copied, yielding a genome that includes two versions of the gene. Over many generations, one version of the gene will often keep its original function while the other one slowly changes by mutation and natural selection, picking up a new, though usually related, function. This process of "gene duplication" has given rise to entire families of proteins that have similar functions; they often act in the same biochemical pathway or sit in the same cellular structure. There's no doubt that gene duplication plays an extremely important role in the evolution of biological complexity.

It's true that when you confront biologists with a particular complex structure like the flagellum they sometimes have a hard time saying which part appeared before which other parts. But then it can be hard, with any complex historical process, to reconstruct the exact order in which events occurred, especially when, as in evolution, the addition of new parts encourages the modification of old ones. When you're looking at a bustling urban street, for example, you probably can't tell which shop went into business first. This is partly because many businesses now depend on each other and partly because new shops trigger changes in old ones (the new sushi place draws twenty-somethings who demand wireless Internet at the café next door). But it would be a little rash to conclude that all the shops must have begun business on the same day or that some Unseen Urban Planner had carefully determined just which business went where.

The other leading theorist of the new creationism, William A. Dembski, holds a Ph.D. in mathematics, another in philosophy, and a master of divinity in theology. He has been a research professor in the conceptual foundations of science at Baylor University, and was recently appointed to the new Center for Science and Theology at Southern Baptist Theological Seminary. (He is a longtime senior fellow at the Discovery Institute as well.) Dembski publishes at a staggering pace. His books—including *The Design Inference, Intelligent Design, No Free Lunch,* and *The Design Revolution*—are generally well written and packed with provocative ideas.

According to Dembski, a complex object must be the result of intelligence if it was the product neither of chance nor of necessity. The novel *Moby Dick,* for example, didn't arise by chance (Melville didn't scribble random letters), and it wasn't the necessary consequence of a physical law (unlike, say, the fall of an apple). It was, instead, the result of Melville's intelligence. Dembski argues that there is a reliable way to recognize such products of intelligence in the natural world. We can conclude that an object was intelligently designed, he says, if it shows "specified complexity"—complexity that matches an "independently given pattern." The sequence of letters "JKXVCJUDOPLVM" is certainly complex: if you randomly type thirteen letters, you are very unlikely to arrive at this particular sequence. But it isn't *specified:* it doesn't match any independently given sequence of letters. If, on the other hand, I ask you for the first sentence of "Moby Dick" and you type the letters "CALLMEISHMAEL," you have produced something that is both complex and specified. The sequence you typed is unlikely to arise by chance alone, and it matches an independent target sequence (the one written by Melville). Dembski argues that specified complexity, when expressed mathematically, provides an unmistakable signature of intelligence. Things like "CALLMEISHMAEL," he points out, just don't arise in the real world without acts of intelligence. If organisms show specified complexity, therefore, we can conclude that they are the handiwork of an intelligent agent.

For Dembski, it's telling that the sophisticated machines we find in 20 organisms match up in astonishingly precise ways with recognizable human technologies. The eye, for example, has a familiar, cameralike design, with recognizable parts—a pinhole opening for light, a lens, and a surface on which to project an image—all arranged just as a human engineer would arrange them. And the flagellum has a motor design, one that features recognizable O-rings, a rotor, and a drive shaft. Specified complexity, he says, is there for all to see.

Dembski's second major claim is that certain mathematical results cast doubt on Darwinism at the most basic conceptual level. In 2002, he focussed on so-called No Free Lunch, or N.F.L., theorems, which were derived in the late nineties by the physicists David H. Wolpert and William G. Macready. These theorems relate to the efficiency of different "search algorithms." Consider a search for high ground on some unfamiliar, hilly terrain. You're on foot and it's a moonless night; you've got two hours to reach the highest place you can. How to proceed? One sensible search algorithm might say, "Walk uphill in the steepest possible direction; if no direction uphill is available, take a couple of steps to the left and try again." This algorithm insures that you're generally moving upward. Another search algorithm—a so-called blind search algorithm—might say, "Walk in a random direction." This would sometimes take you uphill but sometimes down. Roughly, the N.F.L. theorems prove the surprising fact that, averaged over all possible terrains, no search algorithm is better than any other. In some landscapes, moving uphill gets you to higher ground in the allotted time, while in other landscapes moving randomly does, but on average neither outperforms the other.

Now, Darwinism can be thought of as a search algorithm. Given a problem—adapting to a new disease, for instance—a population uses the Darwinian algorithm of random mutation plus natural selection to search for a solution (in this case, disease resistance). But, according to Dembski, the N.F.L. theorems prove that this Darwinian algorithm is no better than any other when confronting all possible problems. It follows that, over all, Darwinism is no better than blind search, a process of utterly random change unaided by any guiding force like natural selection. Since we don't expect blind change to build elaborate machines showing an exquisite coordination of parts, we have no right to expect Darwinism to do so, either. Attempts to sidestep this problem by, say, carefully constraining the class of challenges faced by organisms inevitably involve sneaking in the very kind of order that we're trying to explain—something Dembski calls the displacement problem. In the end, he argues, the N.F.L. theorems and the displacement problem mean that there's only one plausible source for the design we find in organisms: intelligence. Although Dembski is somewhat noncommittal, he seems to favor a design theory in which an intelligent agent programmed design into early life, or even into the early universe. This design then unfolded through the long course of evolutionary time, as microbes slowly morphed into man.

Dembski's arguments have been met with tremendous enthusiasm in the I.D. movement. In part, that's because an innumerate public is easily impressed by a bit of mathematics. Also, when Dembski is wielding his equations, he gets to play the part of the hard scientist busily correcting the errors of those soft-headed biologists. (Evolutionary biology actually features an extraordinarily sophisticated body of mathematical theory, a fact not widely known because neither of evolution's great popularizers—Richard Dawkins and the late Stephen Jay Gould—did much math.) Despite all the attention, Dembski's mathematical claims about design and Darwin are almost entirely beside the point.

The most serious problem in Dembski's account involves specified complexity. Organisms aren't trying to match any "independently given pattern": evolution has no goal, and the history of life isn't try-ing to get anywhere. If building a sophisticated structure like an eye increases the number of children produced, evolution may well build an eye. But if destroying a sophisticated structure like the eye increases the number of children produced, evolution will just as happily destroy the eye. Species of fish and crustaceans that have moved into the total darkness of caves, where eyes are both unnecessary and costly, often have degenerate eyes, or eyes that begin to form only to be covered by skin—crazy contraptions that no intelligent agent would design. Despite all the loose talk about design and machines, organisms aren't striving to realize some engineer's blueprint; they're striving (if they can be said to strive at all) only to have more offspring than the next fellow.

Another problem with Dembski's arguments concerns the N.F.L. 25 theorems. Recent work shows that these theorems don't hold in the case of co-evolution, when two or more species evolve in response to one another. And most evolution is surely co-evolution. Organisms do not spend most of their time adapting to rocks; they are perpetually chal-lenged by, and adapting to, a rapidly changing suite of viruses, para-sites, predators, and prey. A theorem that doesn't apply to these situations is a theorem whose relevance to biology is unclear. As it hap-pens, David Wolpert, one of the authors of the N.F.L. theorems, recently denounced Dembski's use of those theorems as "fatally informal and imprecise." Dembski's apparent response has been a tactical retreat. In 2002, Dembski triumphantly proclaimed, "The No Free Lunch theo-rems dash any hope of generating specified complexity via evolution-ary algorithms." Now he says, "I certainly never argued that the N.F.L. theorems provide a direct refutation of Darwinism."

Those of us who have argued with I.D. in the past are used to such shifts of emphasis. But it's striking that Dembski's views on the history of life contradict Behe's. Dembski believes that Darwinism is incapable of building anything interesting; Behe seems to believe that, given a cell, Darwinism might well have built you and me. Although propo-nents of I.D. routinely inflate the significance of minor squabbles among evolutionary biologists (did the peppered moth evolve dark color as a defense against birds or for other reasons?), they seldom acknowledge their own, often major differences of opinion. In the end, it's hard to view intelligent design as a coherent movement in any but a political sense.

It's also hard to view it as a real research program. Though peo-ple often picture science as a collection of clever theories, scientists are generally staunch pragmatists: to scientists, a good theory is one that inspires new experiments and provides unexpected insights into familiar phenomena. By this standard, Darwinism is one of the best theories in the history of science: it has produced countless important

CHAPTER 9   FOCUS

experiments (let's re-create a natural species in the lab—yes, that's been done) and sudden insight into once puzzling patterns (*that's* why there are no native land mammals on oceanic islands). In the nearly ten years since the publication of Behe's book, by contrast, I.D. has inspired no nontrivial experiments and has provided no surprising insights into biology. As the years pass, intelligent design looks less and less like the science it claimed to be and more and more like an extended exercise in polemics.

In 1999, a document from the Discovery Institute was posted, anonymously, on the Internet. This Wedge Document, as it came to be called, described not only the institute's long-term goals but its strategies for accomplishing them. The document begins by labelling the idea that human beings are created in the image of God "one of the bedrock principles on which Western civilization was built." It goes on to decry the catastrophic legacy of Darwin, Marx, and Freud—the alleged fathers of a "materialistic conception of reality" that eventually "infected virtually every area of our culture." The mission of the Discovery Institute's scientific wing is then spelled out: "nothing less than the overthrow of materialism and its cultural legacies." It seems fair to conclude that the Discovery Institute has set its sights a bit higher than, say, reconstructing the origins of the bacterial flagellum.

The intelligent-design community is usually far more circumspect in its pronouncements. This is not to say that it eschews discussion of religion; indeed, the intelligent-design literature regularly insists that Darwinism represents a thinly veiled attempt to foist a secular religion—godless materialism—on Western culture. As it happens, the idea that Darwinism is yoked to atheism, though popular, is also wrong. Of the five founding fathers of twentieth-century evolutionary biology—Ronald Fisher, Sewall Wright, J. B. S. Haldane, Ernst Mayr, and Theodosius Dobzhansky—one was a devout Anglican who preached sermons and published articles in church magazines, one a practicing Unitarian, one a dabbler in Eastern mysticism, one an apparent atheist, and one a member of the Russian Orthodox Church and the author of a book on religion and science. Pope John Paul II himself acknowledged, in a 1996 address to the Pontifical Academy of Sciences, that new research "leads to the recognition of the theory of evolution as more than a hypothesis." Whatever larger conclusions one thinks *should* follow from Darwinism, the historical fact is that evolution and religion have often coexisted. As the philosopher Michael Ruse observes, "It is simply not the case that people take up evolution in the morning, and become atheists as an encore in the afternoon."

30   Biologists aren't alarmed by intelligent design's arrival in Dover and elsewhere because they have all sworn allegiance to atheistic materialism; they're alarmed because intelligent design is junk science.

Meanwhile, more than eighty per cent of Americans say that God either created human beings in their present form or guided their development. As a succession of intelligent-design proponents appeared before the Kansas State Board of Education earlier this month, it was possible to wonder whether the movement's scientific coherence was beside the point. Intelligent design has come this far by faith.

Responding to Reading

1. What is intelligent design? How is it different from creationism? How is it different from Darwinism?
2. What is Michael J. Behe's major argument against Darwinism? How does Orr counter this argument? How convincing is he?
3. What two points does William A. Dembski make to support intelligent design? What is Orr's response to these points? According to Orr, why are biologists alarmed by intelligent design?

Responding in Writing

Do you believe intelligent design is a legitimate scientific theory, or do you think it is simply a ploy to bring religion into public schools?

FINDING DARWIN'S GOD
Kenneth R. Miller
1948–

A biology professor at Brown University, Kenneth R. Miller is a widely published writer and expert on the intersection of religion and evolution. He has coauthored three biology textbooks and published the book Finding Darwin's God: A Scientist's Search for Common Ground between God and Evolution *(1999), from which the following essay is excerpted. His most recent book is* Only a Theory: Evolution and the Battle for America's Soul *(2008).*

The great hall of the Hynes Convention Center in Boston looks nothing like a church. And yet I sat there, smiling amid an audience of scientists, shaking my head and laughing to myself as I remembered another talk, given long ago, inside a church to an audience of children.

Without warning, I had experienced one of those moments in the present that connects with the scattered recollections of our past. Psychologists tell us that things happen all the time. Five thousand days of childhood are filed, not in chronological order, but as bits and pieces linked by words, or sounds, or even smells that cause us to retrieve

CHAPTER 9 FOCUS

them for no apparent reason when something "refreshes" our memory. And just like that, a few words in a symposium on developmental biology had brought me back to the day before my first communion. I was eight years old, sitting with the boys on the right side of our little church (the girls sat on the left), and our pastor was speaking.

Putting the finishing touches on a year of preparation for the sacrament, Father Murphy sought to impress us with the reality of God's power in the world. He pointed to the altar railing, its polished marble gleaming in sunlight, and firmly assured us that God himself had fashioned it. "Yeah, right," whispered the kid next to me. Worried that there might be the son or daughter of a stonecutter in the crowd, the good Father retreated a bit. "Now, he didn't carve the railing or bring it here or cement it in place…but God himself *made* the marble, long ago, and left it for someone to find and make into part of our church."

I don't know if our pastor sensed that his description of God as craftsman was meeting a certain tide of skepticism, but no matter. He had another trick up his sleeve, a can't-miss, sure-thing argument that, no doubt, had never failed him. He walked over to the altar and picked a flower from the vase.

5   "Look at the beauty of a flower," he began. "The Bible tells us that even Solomon in all his glory was never arrayed as one of these. And do you know what? Not a single person in the world can tell us what makes a flower bloom. All those scientists in their laboratories, the ones who can split the atom and build jet planes and televisions, well, not one of them can tell you how a plant makes flowers." And why should they be able to? "Flowers, just like you, are the work of God."

I was impressed. No one argued, no one wisecracked. We filed out of the church like good little boys and girls, ready for our first communion the next day. And I never thought of it again, until this symposium on developmental biology. Sandwiched between two speakers working on more fashionable topics in animal development was Elliot M. Meyerowitz, a plant scientist at Caltech. A few of my colleagues, uninterested in research dealing with plants, got up to stretch their legs before the final talk, but I sat there with an ear-to-ear grin on my face. I jotted notes furiously; I sketched the diagrams he projected on the screen and wrote additional speculations of my own in the margins. Meyerowitz, you see, had explained how plants make flowers.

The four principal parts of a flower—sepals, petals, stamens, and pistils—are actually modified leaves. This is one of the reasons why plants can produce reproductive cells just about anywhere, while animals are limited to a very specific set of reproductive organs. Your little finger isn't going to start shedding reproductive cells anytime soon. But in springtime, the tip of any branch on an apple tree may very well blossom and begin scattering pollen. Plants can produce new flowers anywhere they can grow new leaves. Somehow, however, the plant must find a way to "tell" an ordinary cluster of leaves that they should develop into floral parts. That's where Meyerowitz's lab took over.

Several years of patient genetic study had isolated a set of mutants that could only form two or three of the four parts. By crossing the various mutants, his team was able to identify four genes that had to be turned on or off in a specific pattern to produce a normal flower. Each of these genes, in turn, sets off a series of signals that "tell" the cells of a brand new bud to develop as sepals or petals rather than ordinary leaves. The details are remarkable, and the interactions between the genes are fascinating. To me, sitting in the crowd thirty-seven years after my first communion, the scientific details were just the icing on the cake. The real message was "Father Murphy, you were wrong." God doesn't make a flower. The floral induction genes do.

Our pastor's error, common and widely repeated, was to seek God in what science has not yet explained. His assumption was that God is best found in territory unknown, in the corners of darkness that have not yet seen the light of understanding. These, as it turns out, are exactly the wrong places to look.

Searching the Shadows

By pointing to the process of making a flower as proof of the reality of God, Father Murphy was embracing the idea that God finds it necessary to cripple nature. In his view, the blooming of a daffodil requires not a self-sufficient material universe, but direct intervention by God. We can find God, therefore, in the things around us that lack material, scientific explanations. In nature, elusive and unexplored, we will find the Creator at work. 10

The creationist opponents of evolution make similar arguments. They claim that the existence of life, the appearance of new species, and, most especially, the origins of mankind have not and cannot be explained by evolution or any other natural process. By denying the self-sufficiency of nature, they look for God (or at least a "designer") in the deficiencies of science. The trouble is that science, given enough time, generally explains even the most baffling things. As a matter of strategy, creationists would be well-advised to avoid telling scientists what they will never be able to figure out. History is against them. In a general way, we really do understand how nature works.

And evolution forms a critical part of that understanding. Evolution really does explain the very things that its critics say it does not. Claims disputing the antiquity of the earth, the validity of the fossil record, and the sufficiency of evolutionary mechanisms vanish upon close

CHAPTER 9 FOCUS

inspection. Even to the most fervent anti-evolutionists, the pattern should be clear—their favorite "gaps" are filling up: the molecular mechanisms of evolution are now well-understood, and the historical record of evolution becomes more compelling with each passing season. This means that science can answer their challenges to evolution in an obvious way. Show the historical record, provide the data, reveal the mechanism, and highlight the convergence of theory and fact.

There is, however, a deeper problem caused by the opponents of evolution, a problem for religion. Like our priest, they have based their search for God on the premise that nature is *not* self-sufficient. By such logic, only God can make a species, just as Father Murphy believed only God could make a flower. Both assertions support the existence of God *only* so long as these assertions are true, but serious problems for religion emerge when they are shown to be false.

If we accept a *lack* of scientific explanation as proof for God's existence, simple logic would dictate that we would have to regard a successful scientific explanation as an argument *against* God. That's why creationist reasoning, ultimately, is much more dangerous to religion than to science. Elliot Meyerowitz's fine work on floral induction suddenly becomes a threat to the divine, even though common sense tells us it should be nothing of the sort. By arguing, as creationists do, that nature cannot be self-sufficient in the formation of new species, the creationists forge a logical link between the limits of natural processes to accomplish biological change and the existence of a designer (God). In other words, they show the proponents of atheism exactly how to disprove the existence of God—show that evolution works, and it's time to tear down the temple. This is an offer that the enemies of religion are all too happy to accept.

15   Putting it bluntly, the creationists have sought God in darkness. What we have not found and do not yet understand becomes their best—indeed their only—evidence for the divine. As a Christian, I find the flow of this logic particularly depressing. Not only does it teach us to fear the acquisition of knowledge (which might at any time disprove belief), but it suggests that God dwells only in the shadows of our understanding. I suggest that, if God is real, we should be able to find him somewhere else—in the bright light of human knowledge, spiritual and scientific.

Faith and Reason

Each of the great Western monotheistic traditions sees God as truth, love, and knowledge. This should mean that each and every increase in our understanding of the natural world is a step toward God and not, as many people assume, a step away. If faith and reason are both gifts from God, then they should play complementary, not conflicting, roles in our struggle to understand the world around us. As a scientist and as a Christian, that is exactly what I believe. True knowledge comes only from a combination of faith and reason.

A nonbeliever, of course, puts his or her trust in science and finds no value in faith. And I certainly agree that science allows believer and nonbeliever alike to investigate the natural world through a common lens of observation, experiment, and theory. The ability of science to transcend cultural, political, and even religious differences is part of its genius, part of its value as a way of knowing. What science cannot do is assign either meaning or purpose to the world it explores. This leads some to conclude that the world as seen by science is devoid of meaning and absent of purpose. It is not. What it does mean, I would suggest, is that our human tendency to assign meaning and value must transcend science and, ultimately, must come from outside it. The science that results can thus be enriched and informed from its contact with the values and principles of faith. The God of Abraham does not tell us which proteins control the cell cycle. But he does give us a reason to care, a reason to cherish that understanding, and above all, a reason to prefer the light of knowledge to the darkness of ignorance.

As more than one scientist has said, the truly remarkable thing about the world is that it actually does make sense. The parts fit, the molecules interact, the darn thing works. To people of faith, what evolution says is that nature is complete. Their God fashioned a material world in which truly free and independent beings could evolve. He got it right the very first time.

To some, the murderous reality of human nature is proof that God is absent or dead. The same reasoning would find God missing from the unpredictable branchings of an evolutionary tree. But the truth is deeper. In each case, a deity determined to establish a world that was truly independent of his whims, a world in which intelligent creatures would face authentic choices between good and evil, would have to fashion a distinct, material reality and then let his creation run. Neither the self-sufficiency of nature nor the reality of evil in the world mean God is absent. To a religious person, both signify something quite different—the strength of God's love and the reality of our freedom as his creatures.

The Weapons of Disbelief

As a species, we like to see ourselves as the best and brightest. We are the intended, special, primary creatures of creation. We sit at the apex of the evolutionary tree as the ultimate products of nature, self-proclaimed and self-aware. We like to think that evolution's goal was to produce us.

20

In a purely biological sense, this comforting view of our own position in nature is false, a product of self-inflating distortion induced by the imperfect mirrors we hold up to life. Yes, we are objectively among the most complex of animals, but not in every sense. Among the systems of the body, we are the hands-down winners for physiological complexity in just one place—the nervous system—and even there, a nonprimate (the dolphin) can lay down a claim that rivals our own.

More to the point, any accurate assessment of the evolutionary process shows that the notion of one form of life being more highly evolved than another is incorrect. Every organism, every cell that lives today, is the descendant of a long line of winners, of ancestors who used successful evolutionary strategies time and time again, and therefore lived to tell about it—or, at least, to reproduce. The bacterium perched on the lip of my coffee cup has been through as much evolution as I have. I've got the advantage of size and consciousness, which matter when I write about evolution, but the bacterium has the advantage of numbers, of flexibility, and most especially, of reproductive speed. That single bacterium, given the right conditions, could literally fill the world with its descendants in a matter of days. No human, no vertebrate, no animal could boast of anything remotely as impressive.

What evolution tells us is that life spreads out along endless branching pathways from any starting point. One of those tiny branches eventually led to us. We think it remarkable and wonder how it could have happened, but any fair assessment of the tree of life shows that our tiny branch is crowded into insignificance by those that bolted off in a thousand different directions. Our species, *Homo sapiens,* has not "triumphed" in the evolutionary struggle any more than has a squirrel, a dandelion, or a mosquito. We are all here, now, and that's what matters. We have all followed different pathways to find ourselves in the present. We are all winners in the game of natural selection. *Current* winners, we should be careful to say.

That, in the minds of many, is exactly the problem. In a thousand branching pathways, how can we be sure that one of them, historically and unavoidably, would lead for sure to us? Consider this: we mammals now occupy, in most ecosystems, the roles of large, dominant land animals. But for much of their history, mammals were restricted to habitats in which only very small creatures could survive. Why? Because another group of vertebrates dominated the earth—until, as Stephen Jay Gould has pointed out, the cataclysmic impact of a comet or asteroid drove those giants to extinction. "In an entirely literal sense," Gould has written, "we owe our existence, as large and reasoning animals, to our lucky stars."

So, what if the comet had missed? What if our ancestors, and not 25 dinosaurs, had been the ones driven to extinction? What if, during the Devonian period, the small tribe of fish known as rhipidistians had been obliterated? Vanishing with them would have been the possibility of life for the first tetrapods. Vertebrates might never have struggled onto the land, leaving it, in Gould's words, forever "the unchallenged domain of insects and flowers."

Surely this means that mankind's appearance on this planet was *not* pre-ordained, that we are here not as the products of an inevitable procession of evolutionary success, but as an afterthought, a minor detail, a happenstance in a history that might just as well have left us out. What follows from this, to skeptic and true believer alike, is a conclusion whose logic is rarely challenged—that no God would ever have used such a process to fashion his prize creatures. How could he have been sure that leaving the job to evolution would lead things to working out the "right" way? If it was God's will to produce us, then by showing that we are the products of evolution, we would rule God as Creator. Therein lies the value or the danger of evolution.

Not so fast. The biological account of lucky historical contingencies that led to our own appearance on this planet is surely accurate. What does not follow is that a perceived lack of inevitability translates into something that we should regard as incompatibility with a divine will. To do so seriously underestimates God, even as this God is understood by the most conventional of Western religions.

Yes, the explosive diversification of life on this planet was an unpredictable process. But so were the rise of Western civilization, the collapse of the Roman Empire, and the winning number in last night's lottery. We do not regard the indeterminate nature of any of these events in human history as antithetical to the existence of a Creator; why should we regard similar events in natural history any differently? There is, I would submit, no reason at all. If we can view the contingent events in the families that produced our individual lives as consistent with a Creator, then certainly we can do the same for the chain of circumstances that produced our species.

The alternative is a world where all events have predictable outcomes, where the future is open neither to chance nor to independent human action. A world in which we would always evolve is a world in which we would never be free. To a believer, the particular history leading to us shows how truly remarkable we are, how rare is the gift of consciousness, and how precious is the chance to understand.

Certainty and Faith

One would like to think that all scientific ideas, including evolution, 30 would rise or fall purely on the basis of the evidence. If that were true, evolution would long since have passed, in the public mind, from controversy into common sense, which is exactly what has happened within the scientific community. This is, unfortunately, not the case—evolution remains, in the minds of much of the American public, a dangerous idea, and for biology educators, a source of never-ending strife.

I believe much of the problem is the fault of those in the scientific community who routinely enlist the findings of evolutionary biology in support of their own philosophical pronouncements. Sometimes these take the form of stern, dispassionate pronouncements about the meaninglessness of life. Other times we are lectured that the contingency of our presence on this planet invalidates any sense of human purpose. And very often we are told that the raw reality of nature strips the authority from any human system of morality.

As creatures fashioned by evolution, we are filled, as the biologist E. O. Wilson has said, with instinctive behaviors important to the survival of our genes. Some of these behaviors, though favored by natural selection, can get us into trouble. Our desires for food, water, reproduction, and status, our willingness to fight, and our tendencies to band together into social groups, can all be seen as behaviors that help ensure evolutionary success. Sociobiology, which studies the biological basis of social behaviors, tells us that in some circumstances natural selection will favor cooperative and nurturing instincts—"nice" genes that help us get along together. Some circumstances, on the other had, will favor aggressive self-centered behaviors, ranging all the way from friendly competition to outright homicide. Could such Darwinian ruthlessness be part of the plan of a loving God?

Yes, it could. To survive on this planet, the genes of our ancestors, like those of any other organism, had to produce behaviors that protected, nurtured, defended, and ensured the reproductive successes of the individuals that bore them. It should be no surprise that we carry such passions within us, and Darwinian biology cannot be faulted for giving their presence a biological explanation. Indeed, the Bible itself gives ample documentation of such human tendencies, including pride, selfishness, lust, anger, aggression, and murder.

Darwin can hardly be criticized for pinpointing the biological origins of these drives. All too often, in finding the sources of our "original sins," in fixing the reasons why our species displays the tendencies it does, evolution is misconstrued as providing a kind of justification for the worst aspects of human nature. At best, this is a misreading of the scientific lessons of sociobiology. At worst, it is an attempt to misuse biology to abolish any meaningful system of morality. Evolution may explain the existence of our most basic biological drives and desires, but that does not tell us that it is always proper to act on them.

CHAPTER 9   FOCUS

Evolution has provided me with a sense of hunger when my nutritional resources are running low, but evolution does not justify my clubbing you over the head to swipe your lunch. Evolution explains our biology, but it does not tell us what is good, or right, or moral. For those answers, however informed we may be by biology, we must look somewhere else.

What Kind of World?

Like it or not, the values that any of us apply to our daily lives have 35 been affected by the work of Charles Darwin. Religious people, however, have a special question to put to the reclusive naturalist of Down House. Did his work ultimately contribute to the greater glory of God, or did he deliver human nature and destiny into the hands of a professional scientific class, one profoundly hostile to religion? Does Darwin's work strengthen or weaken the idea of God?

The conventional wisdom is that whatever one may think of his science, having Mr. Darwin around certainly hasn't helped religion very much. The general thinking is that religion has been weakened by Darwinism and has been constrained to modify its view of the Creator in order to twist doctrine into conformity with the demands of evolution. As Stephen Jay Gould puts it, with obvious delight, "Now the conclusions of science must be accepted *a priori,* and religious interpretations must be finessed and adjusted to match unimpeachable results from the magisterium of natural knowledge!" Science calls the tune, and religion dances to its music.

This sad specter of a weakened and marginalized God drives the continuing opposition to evolution. This is why the God of the creationists requires, above all, that evolution be shown not to have functioned in the past and not to be working now. To free religion from the tyranny of Darwinism, creationists need a science that shows nature to be incomplete; they need a history of life whose events can only be explained as the result of supernatural processes. Put bluntly, the creationists are committed to finding permanent, intractable mystery in nature. To such minds, even the most perfect being we can imagine would not have been perfect enough to fashion a creation in which life would originate and evolve on its own. Nature must be flawed, static, and forever inadequate.

Science in general, and evolutionary science in particular, gives us something quite different. It reveals a universe that is dynamic, flexible, and logically complete. It presents a vision of life that spreads across the planet with endless variety and intricate beauty. It suggests a world in which our material existence is not an impossible illusion propped up by magic, but the genuine article, a world in which things are exactly what they seem. A world in which we were formed, as the Creator once told us, from the dust of the earth itself.

It is often said that a Darwinian universe is one whose randomness cannot be reconciled with meaning. I disagree. A world truly without meaning would be one in which a deity pulled the string of every human puppet, indeed of every material particle. In such a world, physical and biological events would be carefully controlled, evil and suffering could be minimized, and the outcome of historical processes strictly regulated. All things would move toward the Creator's clear, distinct, established goals. Such control and predictability, however, comes at the price of independence. Always in control, such a Creator would deny his creatures any real opportunity to know and worship him—authentic love requires freedom, not manipulation. Such freedom is best supplied by the open contingency of evolution.

40   One hundred and fifty years ago it might have been impossible not to couple Darwin to a grim and pointless determinism, but things look different today. Darwin's vision has expanded to encompass a new world of biology in which the links from molecule to cell and from cell to organism are becoming clear. Evolution prevails, but it does so with a richness and subtlety its original theorist may have found surprising and could not have anticipated.

We know from astronomy, for example, that the universe had a beginning, from physics that the future is both open and unpredictable, from geology and paleontology that the whole of life has been a process of change and transformation. From biology we know that our tissues are not impenetrable reservoirs of vital magic, but a stunning matrix of complex wonders, ultimately explicable in terms of biochemistry and molecular biology. With such knowledge we can see, perhaps for the first time, why a Creator would have allowed our species to be fashioned by the process of evolution.

If he so chose, the God whose presence is taught by most Western religions could have fashioned anything, ourselves included, *ex nihilo*, from his wish alone. In our childhood as a species, that might have been the only way in which we could imagine the fulfillment of a divine will. But we've grown up, and something remarkable has happened: we have begun to understand the physical basis of life itself. If a string of constant miracles were needed for each turn of the cell cycle or each flicker of a cilium, the hand of God would be written directly into every living thing—his presence at the edge of the human sandbox would be unmistakable. Such findings might confirm our faith, but they would also undermine our independence. How could we fairly choose between God and man when the presence and the power of the divine so obviously and so literally controlled our every breath? Our freedom as his creatures requires a little space and integrity. In the material world, it requires self-sufficiency and consistency with the laws of nature.

Evolution is neither more nor less than the result of respecting the reality and consistency of the physical world over time. To fashion material beings with an independent physical existence, any Creator would have had to produce an independent material universe in which our evolution over time was a contingent possibility. A believer in the divine accepts that God's love and gift of freedom are genuine—so genuine that they include the power to choose evil and, if we wish, to freely send ourselves to Hell. Not all believers will accept the stark conditions of that bargain, but our freedom to act has to have a physical and biological basis. Evolution and its sister sciences of genetics and molecular biology provide that basis. In biological terms, evolution is the only way a Creator could have made us the creatures we are— free beings in a world of authentic and meaningful moral and spiritual choices.

Those who ask from science a final argument, an ultimate proof, an unassailable position from which the issue of God may be decided will always be disappointed. As a scientist I claim no new proofs, no revolutionary data, no stunning insight into nature that can tip the balance in one direction or another. But I do claim that to a believer, even in the most traditional sense, evolutionary biology is not at all the obstacle we often believe it to be. In many respects, evolution is the key to understanding our relationship with God.

When I have the privilege of giving a series of lectures on evolu-   45
tionary biology to my freshman students, I usually conclude those lectures with a few remarks about the impact of evolutionary theory on other fields, from economics to politics to religion. I find a way to make clear that I do not regard evolution, properly understood, as either antireligious or antispiritual. Most students seem to appreciate those sentiments. They probably figure that Professor Miller, trying to be a nice guy and doubtlessly an agnostic, is trying to find a way to be unequivocal about evolution without offending the University chaplain.

There are always a few who find me after class and want to pin me down. They ask me point-blank: "Do you believe in God?"

And I tell each of them, "Yes."

Puzzled, they ask: "What kind of God?"

Over the years I have struggled to come up with a simple but precise answer to that question. And, eventually I found it. I believe in Darwin's God.

Responding to Reading

1. Why does Miller begin his essay with a story from his childhood? How does this story lead him to his larger point? What does Miller mean when he says, "By pointing to the process of making a flower as proof of the reality of God, Father Murphy was embracing the idea that God finds it necessary to cripple nature" (10)?

2. Why does Miller believe that scientists are to blame for the public's distrust of evolution? Why does Miller disagree with the idea that a "Darwinian universe is one whose randomness cannot be reconciled with meaning" (39)?
3. What does Miller mean when he says, "In many respects, evolution is the key to understanding our relationship with God" (44)?

Responding in Writing

Do you think it is possible both to believe in God and to accept evolution? Explain.

Widening the Focus

For Critical Thinking and Writing

Write an essay in which you answer the Focus question, "Is there intelligent design in nature?" In your essay, refer to the ideas in Christoph Schönborn's "Finding Design in Nature," H. Allen Orr's "Why Intelligent Design Isn't," and Kenneth R. Miller's "Finding Darwin's God."

For Further Reading

The following readings can suggest additional perspectives for thinking and writing about the issues surrounding the controversy over intelligent design.

- Albino Barrera, "Fair Exchange: Who Benefits from Outsourcing?" (p. 454)

- John Muir, "The American Forests" (p. 468)

- Tenzin Gyatso, "Our Faith in Science" (p. 527)

For Focused Research

The intelligent design debate has sparked heated discussion between scientists and philosophers on the questions, "Who are we?" and "Where do we come from?" Proponents of evolution, on the one hand, argue that life as we know it came to be through a series of random mutations and the process of natural selection; advocates of intelligent design, on the other hand, argue that organisms such as ourselves are not the result of chance occurrences, but rather the work of an intelligent creator. Read the 2002 *Natural History* magazine report *Intelligent Design?* at http://www.actionbioscience.org/evolution/nhmag.html, in which supporters of the intelligent design and evolution theories debate this important topic. Then, write a paper in which you evaluate this report. Is it effective in presenting the complexities of the issue? What arguments and evidence are presented? Which arguments do you find most convincing? Why?

Chapter 9 Focus

--------------------------------- WRITING ---------------------------------

RELIGION IN AMERICA

1. In Langston Hughes's "Salvation" (p. 521) and Tayari Jones's "Among the Believers" (p. 530), the writers recount childhood experiences in which they struggled to understand what religion and spirituality meant to them. Write an essay in which you trace your own efforts to come to terms with your family's faith (or lack of faith).

2. Do you see religion and science as compatible, or do you see them as inevitably in conflict? After reading "Our Faith in Science" (p. 527), try to answer this question, citing examples of specific moral and ethical issues.

3. Is there a place in American society for a strictly secular view of moral and social issues, or is this view somehow incomplete? Read "Kicking the Secularist Habit" (p. 533), and then write an essay in which you consider whether it is possible to live a moral life by following guidelines that are secular rather than religious.

4. Do you believe religious instruction and prayer—for example, Bible study groups or prayer among football players before a game—should be permitted in our nation's public schools? What advantages do you see in officially sanctioning such activities? What problems might they cause? Read "Turning Faith into Elevator Music" (p. 537) before you begin.

5. Do you think religious institutions should continue to be exempt from paying federal income tax? Why or why not? In your essay, consider the contributions religious organizations make to society and the services they provide—but also consider the fact that many religious groups take positions on social and political issues such as abortion, the death penalty, stem-cell research, and aiding undocumented immigrants.

6. Fewer and fewer young people are becoming priests and nuns; as a result, the Catholic Church is facing a crisis. What do you think might be done to attract more young people to consider devoting their lives to the Church?

7. In paragraph 6 of his speech (p. 551), John F. Kennedy says, "For while this year it may be a Catholic against whom the finger of suspicion is pointed, in other years it has been, and may someday be again, a Jew—or a Quaker—or a Unitarian—or a Baptist....Today I may be the victim—but tomorrow it may be you...." Do you believe that the religious tolerance Kennedy advocates should apply to atheists as well as to people of all different religions? (Note that in his 2009 inaugural address, President Obama urged religious tolerance, including tolerance for nonbelievers.)

8. Because more than 75 percent of the U.S. population is Christian, many people consider the United States to be a Christian nation—even though the population also includes significant numbers of Jews, Muslims, Buddhists, and Hindus (well over a million each), as well as people who follow numerous other religions. In what respects do you see the United States as a Christian nation? In what respects is it not a Christian nation? How do you think it *should* be perceived?

9. After reading "Earthly Empires" (p. 544), write a proposal for a new "megachurch" (or mosque or synagogue) that might attract worshippers in your community. What should this new institution offer in the way of religious services and instruction, facilities, social programs, and community outreach services? How would the programs you suggest help individual members of the community? How would they strengthen the institution? Be sure to explain *why* the programs and services you describe would be beneficial.

10. The title of Raymond Carver's short story "Cathedral" (p. 555) suggests that its focus is on religion. Is this actually the case? Is it about a religious experience, or is it about something else? Write an essay in which you explore the themes of this story.

10

MAKING CHOICES

As Robert Frost suggests in his poem "The Road Not Taken" (p. 599), making choices is fundamental to our lives. The ability—and, in fact, the need—to make complex decisions is part of what makes us human. On a practical level, we choose friends, mates, careers, and places to live. On a more abstract level, we struggle to make the moral and ethical choices that people have struggled with over the years.

Many times, complex questions have no easy answers; occasionally, they have no answers at all. For example, should we obey a law that we believe to be morally wrong? Should we stand up to authority even if our stand puts us at risk? Should we help less fortunate individuals if such help threatens our own social or economic status? Should we strive to do well or to do good? Should we tell the truth even if the truth may hurt us—or hurt someone else? Which road should we take, the easy one or the more difficult one?

Volunteers picking up litter in a park

Most of the time, the choice we (and the writers whose works appear in this chapter) face is the same: to act or not to act. To make a decision, we must understand both the long- and short-term consequences of acting in a particular way or of choosing not to act. We must struggle with the possibility of compromise—and with the possibility of making a morally or ethically objectionable decision. And, perhaps most important, we must learn to take responsibility for our decisions.

PREPARING TO READ AND WRITE

As you read and prepare to write about the selections in this chapter, you may consider the following questions:

- On what specific choice or choices does the essay focus? Is the decision to be made moral? ethical? political? theoretical?

- Does the writer introduce a **dilemma**, a choice between equally problematic alternatives?

- Does the choice the writer presents apply only to one specific situation or case, or does it also have a wider application?

- Is the writer emotionally involved with the issue he or she is discussing? Does this involvement (or lack of involvement) affect the writer's credibility?

- What social, political, or religious ideas influence the writer? How can you tell? Are these ideas similar to or different from your own views?

Business people meeting around a conference table

- Does the choice being considered lead the writer to examine his or her own values? The values of others? The values of the society at large? Does the writer lead you to examine your own values?

- Does the writer offer a solution to a problem? If so, do you find it reasonable?

- Does the choice the writer advocates require sacrifice? If so, does the sacrifice seem worth it?

- Which writers' views seem most alike? Which seem most different?

THE ROAD NOT TAKEN

Robert Frost

1874–1963

*Robert Frost, four-time Pulitzer Prize–winning poet of rural New England,
lived most of his life in New Hampshire and taught at Amherst College, Harvard University, and Dartmouth College. His subjects at first seem familiar
and comfortable, as does his language, but the symbols and allusions and
underlying meanings in many of his poems are quite complex. Some of Frost's
most famous poems are "Birches," "Mending Wall," and "Stopping by Woods
on a Snowy Evening." In the poem that follows, the speaker hesitates before
making a choice.*

Two roads diverged in a yellow wood,
And sorry I could not travel both
And be one traveller, long I stood
And looked down one as far as I could
To where it bent in the undergrowth;   5

Then took the other, as just as fair,
And having perhaps the better claim,
Because it was grassy and wanted wear;
Though as for that the passing there
Had worn them really about the same,   10

And both that morning equally lay
In leaves no step had trodden black.
Oh, I kept the first for another day!
Yet knowing how way leads on to way,
I doubted if I should ever come back.   15

I shall be telling this with a sigh
Somewhere ages and ages hence:
Two roads diverged in a wood, and I—
I took the one less travelled by,
And that has made all the difference.   20

Responding to Reading

1. What is the difference between the two paths Frost's speaker considers? Why
    does he make the choice he does?

2. Is "The Road Not Taken" simply about two paths in the wood, or does it suggest more? What makes you think so? To what larger choices might the speaker be alluding?
3. What does the speaker mean by "that has made all the difference" (line 20)?

Responding in Writing

In your own words, write a short prose summary of this poem. Use first person and past tense (as Frost does).

ETHICS

Linda Pastan

1932–

The winner of numerous prizes for her poetry, Linda Pastan often focuses on the complexity of domestic life, using intense imagery to bring a sense of mystery to everyday matters. She has been a lecturer at the Breadloaf Writers Conference in Vermont and an instructor at American University, and she has published numerous collections of poetry, including Waiting for My Life *(1981),* PM/AM: New and Selected Poems *(1983),* Carnival Evening: New and Selected Poems 1968–1998 *(1998),* The Last Uncle: Poems *(2002), and* Queen of a Rainy Country *(2006). In "Ethics," from* Waiting for My Life, *the speaker introduces an ethical dilemma.*

In ethics class so many years ago
our teacher asked this question every fall:
if there were a fire in a museum
which would you save, a Rembrandt painting
5   or an old woman who hadn't many
years left anyhow? Restless on hard chairs
caring little for pictures or old age
we'd opt one year for life, the next for art
and always half-heartedly. Sometimes
10   the woman borrowed my grandmother's face
leaving her usual kitchen to wander
some drafty, half imagined museum.
One year, feeling clever, I replied
why not let the woman decide herself?
15   Linda, the teacher would report, eschews
the burdens of responsibility.
This fall in a real museum I stand
before a real Rembrandt, old woman,

or nearly so, myself. The colors
within this frame are darker than autumn,   20
darker even than winter—the browns of earth,
though earth's most radiant elements burn
through the canvas. I know now that woman
and painting and season are almost one
and all beyond saving by children.   25

Responding to Reading

1. What choice actually confronts Pastan's speaker? What answer do you think
   the teacher expects the students to give?
2. Do you agree with the teacher that refusing to choose means avoiding responsibility? Does Frost's speaker (p. 599) have the option not to choose?
3. When the speaker says that "woman / and painting and season are almost
   one" (lines 23–24), what does she mean? Does she imply that the teacher's
   question really has no answer? that the children who would "opt one year
   for life, the next for art" (line 8) are right?

Responding in Writing

Confronted with the choice facing the speaker, would you save the Rembrandt
painting or the elderly woman? Why? Would you find this a difficult choice
to make?

Shooting an Elephant

George Orwell

1903–1950

*This detailed account of an incident with an elephant in Burma is George
Orwell's most powerful criticism of imperialism and the impossible position
of British police officers—himself among them—in the colonies. Orwell says
about the incident, "It was perfectly clear to me what I ought to do," but then
he thinks of "the watchful yellow faces from behind" and realizes that his choice
is not so simple. (Also see Orwell's essay "Politics and the English Language"
in Chapter 3.)*

In Moulmein, in lower Burma, I was hated by large numbers of people—
the only time in my life that I have been important enough for this to
happen to me. I was sub-divisional police officer of the town, and in an
aimless, petty kind of way anti-European feeling was very bitter. No one
had the guts to raise a riot, but if a European woman went through the

bazaars alone somebody would probably spit betel juice over her dress. As a police officer I was an obvious target and was baited whenever it seemed safe to do so. When a nimble Burman tripped me up on the football field and the referee (another Burman) looked the other way, the crowd yelled with hideous laughter. This happened more than once. In the end the sneering yellow faces of young men that met me everywhere, the insults hooted after me when I was at a safe distance, got badly on my nerves. The young Buddhist priests were the worst of all. There were several thousands of them in the town and none of them seemed to have anything to do except stand on street corners and jeer at Europeans.

All this was perplexing and upsetting. For at that time I had already made up my mind that imperialism was an evil thing and the sooner I chucked up my job and got out of it the better. Theoretically—and secretly, of course—I was all for the Burmese and all against their oppressors, the British. As for the job I was doing, I hated it more bitterly than I can perhaps make clear. In a job like that you see the dirty work of Empire at close quarters. The wretched prisoners huddling in the stinking cages of the lock-ups, the grey, cowed faces of the long-term convicts, the scarred buttocks of the men who had been flogged with bamboos—all these oppressed me with an intolerable sense of guilt. But I could get nothing into perspective. I was young and ill-educated and I had had to think out my problems in the utter silence that is imposed on every Englishman in the East. I did not even know that the British Empire is dying, still less did I know that it is a great deal better than the younger empires that are going to supplant it.[1] All I knew was that I was stuck between my hatred of the empire I served and my rage against the evil-spirited little beasts who tried to make my job impossible. With one part of my mind I thought of the British Raj[2] as an unbreakable tyranny, as something clamped down, in *saecula saeculorum*,[3] upon the will of prostrate peoples; with another part I thought that the greatest joy in the world would be to drive a bayonet into a Buddhist priest's guts. Feelings like these are the normal by-products of imperialism; ask any Anglo-Indian official, if you can catch him off duty.

One day something happened which in a roundabout way was enlightening. It was a tiny incident in itself, but it gave me a better glimpse than I had had before of the real nature of imperialism—the real motives for which despotic governments act. Early one morning the sub-inspector at a police station the other end of the town rang me up on the phone and said that an elephant was ravaging the bazaar. Would I please come and do something about it? I did not know what I could do, but I wanted to see what was happening and I got on to a

---

[1]This essay was written in 1936, three years before the start of World War II; Stalin and Hitler were in power. [Eds.]

[2]Sovereignty. [Eds.]

[3]From time immemorial. [Eds.]

pony and started out. I took my rifle, an old .44 Winchester and much too small to kill an elephant, but I thought the noise might be useful in *terrorem*. Various Burmans stopped me on the way and told me about the elephant's doings. It was not, of course, a wild elephant, but a tame one which had gone "must." It had been chained up, as tame elephants always are when their attack of "must"[4] is due, but on the previous night it had broken its chain and escaped. Its mahout,[5] the only person who could manage it when it was in that state, had set out in pursuit, but had taken the wrong direction and was now twelve hours' journey away, and in the morning the elephant had suddenly reappeared in the town. The Burmese population had no weapons and were quite helpless against it. It had already destroyed somebody's bamboo hut, killed a cow, and raided some fruit-stalls and devoured the stock; also it had met the municipal rubbish van and, when the driver jumped out and took to his heels, had turned the van over and inflicted violences upon it.

The Burmese sub-inspector and some Indian constables were waiting for me in the quarter where the elephant had been seen. It was a very poor quarter, a labyrinth of squalid bamboo huts, thatched with palm-leaf, winding all over a steep hillside. I remember that it was a cloudy, stuffy morning at the beginning of the rains. We began questioning the people as to where the elephant had gone and, as usual, failed to get any definite information. That is invariably the case in the East; a story always sounds clear enough at a distance, but the nearer you get to the scene of events the vaguer it becomes. Some of the people said that the elephant had gone in one direction, some said that he had gone in another, some professed not even to have heard of any elephant. I had almost made up my mind that the whole story was a pack of lies, when we heard yells a little distance away. There was a loud, scandalized cry of "Go away, child! Go away this instant!" and an old woman with a switch in her hand came round the corner of a hut, violently shooing away a crowd of naked children. Some more women followed, clicking their tongues and exclaiming; evidently there was something that the children ought not to have seen. I rounded the hut and saw a man's dead body sprawling in the mud. He was an Indian, a black Dravidian coolie,[6] almost naked, and he could not have been dead many minutes. The people said that the elephant had come suddenly upon him round the corner of the hut, caught him with its trunk, put its foot on his back, and ground him into the earth. This was the rainy season and the ground was soft, and his face had scored a trench a foot deep and a couple of yards long. He was lying on his belly with arms crucified and head sharply twisted to one side. His face was coated with mud, the eyes wide open, the teeth bared and grinning with an expression of unendurable

---

[4]Frenzy. [Eds.]

[5]Keeper. [Eds.]

[6]An unskilled laborer. [Eds.]

agony. (Never tell me, by the way, that the dead look peaceful. Most of the corpses I have seen looked devilish.) The friction of the great beast's foot had stripped the skin from his back as neatly as one skins a rabbit. As soon as I saw the dead man I sent an orderly to a friend's house nearby to borrow an elephant rifle. I had already sent back the pony, not wanting it to go mad with fright and throw me if it smelt the elephant.

5   The orderly came back in a few minutes with a rifle and five cartridges, and meanwhile some Burmans had arrived and told us that the elephant was in the paddy fields below, only a few hundred yards away. As I started forward practically the whole population of the quarter flocked out of the houses and followed me. They had seen the rifle and were all shouting excitedly that I was going to shoot the elephant. They had not shown much interest in the elephant when he was merely ravaging their homes, but it was different now that he was going to be shot. It was a bit of fun to them, as it would be to an English crowd; besides they wanted the meat. It made me vaguely uneasy. I had no intention of shooting the elephant—I had merely sent for the rifle to defend myself if necessary—and it is always unnerving to have a crowd following you. I marched down the hill, looking and feeling a fool, with the rifle over my shoulder and an ever-growing army of people jostling at my heels. At the bottom, when you got away from the huts, there was a metalled road and beyond that a miry waste of paddy fields a thousand yards across, not yet ploughed but soggy from the first rains and dotted with coarse grass. The elephant was standing eight yards from the road, his left side towards us. He took not the slightest notice of the crowd's approach. He was tearing up bunches of grass, beating them against his knees to clean them and stuffing them into his mouth.

I had halted on the road. As soon as I saw the elephant I knew with perfect certainty that I ought not to shoot him. It is a serious matter to shoot a working elephant—it is comparable to destroying a huge and costly piece of machinery—and obviously one ought not to do it if it can possibly be avoided. And at that distance, peacefully eating, the elephant looked no more dangerous than a cow. I thought then and I think now that his attack of "must" was already passing off; in which case he would merely wander harmlessly about until the mahout came back and caught him. Moreover, I did not in the least want to shoot him. I decided that I would watch him for a little while to make sure that he did not turn savage again, and then go home.

But at that moment I glanced round at the crowd that had followed me. It was an immense crowd, two thousand at the least and growing every minute. It blocked the road for a long distance on either side. I looked at the sea of yellow faces above the garish clothes—faces all happy and excited over this bit of fun, all certain that the elephant was going to be shot. They were watching me as they would watch a conjurer about to perform a trick. They did not like me, but with the magical rifle in my hands I was momentarily worth watching. And suddenly I realized that I should have to shoot the elephant after all. The people expected it of me and I had got to do it; I could feel their two thousand wills pressing me forward, irresistibly. And it was at this moment, as I stood there with the rifle in my hands, that I first grasped the hollowness, the futility of the white man's dominion in the East. Here was I, the white man with his gun, standing in front of the unarmed native crowd— seemingly the leading actor of the piece; but in reality I was only an absurd puppet pushed to and fro by the will of those yellow faces behind. I perceived in this moment that when the white man turns tyrant it is his own freedom that he destroys. He becomes a sort of hollow, posing dummy, the conventionalized figure of a sahib.[7] For it is the condition of his rule that he shall spend his life in trying to impress the "natives," and so in every crisis he has got to do what the "natives" expect of him. He wears a mask, and his face grows to fit it. I had got to shoot the elephant. I had committed myself to doing it when I sent for the rifle. A sahib has got to act like a sahib; he has got to appear resolute, to know his own mind and do definite things. To come all that way, rifle in hand, with two thousand people marching at my heels, and then to trail feebly away, having done nothing—no, that was impossible. The crowd would laugh at me. And my whole life, every white man's life in the East, was one long struggle not to be laughed at.

But I did not want to shoot the elephant. I watched him beating his bunch of grass against his knees, with that preoccupied grandmotherly air that elephants have. It seemed to me that it would be murder to shoot him. At that age I was not squeamish about killing animals, but I had never shot an elephant and never wanted to. (Somehow it always seems worse to kill a *large* animal.) Besides, there was the beast's owner to be considered. Alive, the elephant was worth at least a hundred pounds; dead, he would only be worth the value of his tusks, five pounds, possibly. But I had got to act quickly. I turned to some experienced looking Burmans who had been there when we arrived, and asked them how the elephant had been behaving. They all said the same thing: he took no notice of you if you left him alone, but he might charge if you went too close to him.

It was perfectly clear to me what I ought to do. I ought to walk up to within, say, twenty-five yards of the elephant and test his behavior. If he charged, I could shoot; if he took no notice of me, it would be safe to leave him until the mahout came back. But also I knew that I was going to do no such thing. I was a poor shot with a rifle and the ground was soft mud into which one would sink at every step. If the elephant charged and I missed him, I should have about as much chance as a toad under a steam-roller. But even then I was not thinking particularly

---

[7]Term used by natives of colonial India when referring to a European of rank. [Eds.]

of my own skin, only of the watchful yellow faces behind. For at that moment, with the crowd watching me, I was not afraid in the ordinary sense, as I would have been if I had been alone. A white man mustn't be frightened in front of "natives"; and so, in general, he isn't frightened. The sole thought in my mind was that if anything went wrong those two thousand Burmans would see me pursued, caught, trampled on, and reduced to a grinning corpse like that Indian up the hill. And if that happened it was quite probable that some of them would laugh. That would never do. There was only one alternative. I shoved the cartridges into the magazine and lay down on the road to get a better aim.

10   The crowd grew very still, and a deep, low, happy sigh, as of people who see the theatre curtain go up at last, breathed from innumerable throats. They were going to have their bit of fun after all. The rifle was a beautiful German thing with cross-hair sights. I did not then know that in shooting an elephant one would shoot to cut an imaginary bar running from ear-hole to ear-hole. I ought, therefore, as the elephant was sideways on, to have aimed straight at his ear-hole; actually I aimed several inches in front of this, thinking the brain would be further forward.

When I pulled the trigger I did not hear the bang or feel the kick—one never does when a shot goes home—but I heard the devilish roar of glee that went up from the crowd. In that instant, in too short a time, one would have thought, even for the bullet to get there, a mysterious, terrible change had come over the elephant. He neither stirred nor fell, but every line of his body had altered. He looked suddenly stricken, shrunken, immensely old, as though the frightful impact of the bullet had paralysed him without knocking him down. At last, after what seemed a long time—it might have been five seconds, I dare say—he sagged flabbily to his knees. His mouth slobbered. An enormous senility seemed to have settled upon him. One could have imagined him thousands of years old. I fired again into the same spot. At the second shot he did not collapse but climbed with desperate slowness to his feet and stood weakly upright, with legs sagging and head dropping. I fired a third time. That was the shot that did for him. You could see the agony of it jolt his whole body and knock the last remnant of strength from his legs. But in falling he seemed for a moment to rise, for as his hind legs collapsed beneath him he seemed to tower upward like a huge rock toppling, his trunk reaching skywards like a tree. He trumpeted, for the first and only time. And then down he came, his belly towards me, with a crash that seemed to shake the ground even where I lay.

I got up. The Burmans were already racing past me across the mud. It was obvious that the elephant would never rise again, but he was not dead. He was breathing very rhythmically with long rattling gasps, his great mound of a side painfully rising and falling. His mouth was wide open—I could see far down into caverns of pale pink throat. I waited a long time for him to die, but his breathing did not weaken. Finally I fired my two remaining shots into the spot where I thought his heart must be. The thick blood welled out of him like red velvet, but still he did not die. His body did not even jerk when the shots hit him, the tortured breathing continued without a pause. He was dying, very slowly and in great agony, but in some world remote from me where not even a bullet could damage him further. I felt that I had got to put an end to that dreadful noise. It seemed dreadful to see the great beast lying there, powerless to move and yet powerless to die, and not even to be able to finish him. I sent back for my small rifle and poured shot after shot into his heart and down his throat. They seemed to make no impression. The tortured gasps continued as steadily as the ticking of a clock.

In the end I could not stand it any longer and went away. I heard later that it took him half an hour to die. Burmans were bringing dahs[8] and baskets even before I left, and I was told they had stripped his body almost to the bones by the afternoon.

Afterwards, of course, there were endless discussions about the shooting of the elephant. The owner was furious, but he was only an Indian and could do nothing. Besides, legally I had done the right thing, for a mad elephant has to be killed, like a mad dog, if its owner fails to control it. Among the Europeans opinion was divided. The older men said I was right, the younger men said it was a damn shame to shoot an elephant for killing a coolie, because an elephant was worth more than any damn Coringhee coolie. And afterwards I was very glad that the coolie had been killed; it put me legally in the right and it gave me a sufficient pretext for shooting the elephant. I often wondered whether any of the others grasped that I had done it solely to avoid looking a fool.

Responding to Reading

1. The central focus of this essay is Orwell's struggle to decide how to control the elephant. Do you think he really has a choice?
2. Orwell says that his encounter with the elephant, although "a tiny incident in itself," gave him an understanding of "the real nature of imperialism—the real motives for which despotic governments act" (3). In light of this statement, do you think his purpose in this essay is to explore something about himself or something about the nature of British colonialism—or both?
3. In paragraphs 5–6, Orwell introduces the elephant as peaceful and innocent; in paragraphs 11–12, he describes the animal's misery. What do these paragraphs contribute to the essay?

Responding in Writing

Compare paragraphs 11–12 of Orwell's essay with paragraphs 27–33 of Claire McCarthy's essay (p. 632). How are the descriptions alike? How are they different?

---

[8]Large knives. [Eds.]

LETTER FROM BIRMINGHAM JAIL
Martin Luther King, Jr.
1929–1968

One of the greatest civil rights leaders and orators of this century, Martin Luther King, Jr., was a Baptist minister and winner of the 1964 Nobel Peace Prize. Influenced by Thoreau and Gandhi, King altered the spirit of African-American protest in the United States by advocating nonviolent civil disobedience to achieve racial equality. His books include Letter from Birmingham Jail *(1963) and* Where Do We Go from Here: Chaos or Community? *(1967). King was assassinated on April 4, 1968. The following letter, written in 1963, is his eloquent and impassioned response to a public statement by eight fellow clergymen in Birmingham, Alabama, who appealed to the citizenry of the city to "observe the principles of law and order and common sense" rather than join in the principled protests that King was leading. (Also see King's speech "I Have a Dream" in Chapter 6.)*

MY DEAR FELLOW CLERGYMEN:[1]

While confined here in the Birmingham city jail, I came across your recent statement calling my present activities "unwise and untimely." Seldom do I pause to answer criticism of my work and ideas. If I sought to answer all the criticisms that cross my desk, my secretaries would have little time for anything other than such correspondence in the course of the day, and I would have no time for constructive work. But since I feel that you are men of genuine good will and that your criticisms are sincerely set forth, I want to try to answer your statement in what I hope will be patient and reasonable terms.

I think I should indicate that I am here in Birmingham, since you have been influenced by the view which argues against "outsiders coming in." I have the honor of serving as president of the Southern Christian Leadership Conference, an organization operating in every southern state, with headquarters in Atlanta, Georgia. We have some eighty-five affiliated organizations across the South, and one of them is the Alabama Christian Movement for Human Rights. Frequently we share staff, educational, and financial resources with our affiliates. Several months ago the affiliate here in Birmingham asked us to be on call to engage in a non-violent direct-action program if such were deemed

---

[1]This response to a published statement by eight fellow clergymen from Alabama (Bishop C. C. J. Carpenter, Bishop Joseph A. Durick, Rabbi Milton L. Grafman, Bishop Paul Hardin, Bishop Holan B. Harmon, the Reverend George M. Murray, the Reverend Edward V. Ramage and the Reverend Earl Stallings) was composed under somewhat constricting circumstances. Begun on the margins of the newspaper in which the statement appeared while I was in jail, the letter was continued on scraps of writing paper supplied by a friendly Negro trusty, and concluded on a pad my attorneys were eventually permitted to leave me. Although the text remains in substance unaltered, I have indulged in the author's prerogative of polishing it for publication.

necessary. We readily consented, and when the hour came we lived up to our promise. So I, along with several members of my staff, am here because I was invited here. I am here because I have organizational ties here.

But more basically, I am in Birmingham because injustice is here. Just as the prophets of the eighth century B.C. left their villages and carried their "thus saith the Lord" far beyond the boundaries of their home towns, and just as the Apostle Paul left his village of Tarsus and carried the gospel of Jesus Christ to the far corners of the Greco-Roman world, so am I compelled to carry the gospel of freedom beyond my own home town. Like Paul, I must constantly respond to the Macedonian call for aid.

Moreover, I am cognizant of the interrelatedness of all communities and states. I cannot sit idly by in Atlanta and not be concerned about what happens in Birmingham. Injustice anywhere is a threat to justice everywhere. We are caught in an inescapable network of mutuality, tied in a single garment of destiny. Whatever affects one directly, affects all indirectly. Never again can we afford to live with the narrow, provincial "outside agitator" idea. Anyone who lives inside the United States can never be considered an outsider anywhere within its bounds.

You deplore the demonstrations taking place in Birmingham. But your statement, I am sorry to say, fails to express a similar concern for the conditions that brought about the demonstrations. I am sure that none of you would want to rest content with the superficial kind of social analysis that deals merely with effects and does not grapple with underlying causes. It is unfortunate that demonstrations are taking place in Birmingham, but it is even more unfortunate that the city's white power structure left the Negro community with no alternative.

In any nonviolent campaign there are four basic steps: collection of the facts to determine whether injustices exist; negotiation; self-purification; and direct action. We have gone through all these steps in Birmingham. There can be no gainsaying the fact that racial injustice engulfs this community. Birmingham is probably the most thoroughly segregated city in the United States. Its ugly record of brutality is widely known. Negroes have experienced grossly unjust treatment in the courts. There have been more unsolved bombings of Negro homes and churches in Birmingham than in any other city in the nation. These are the hard, brutal facts of the case. On the basis of these conditions, Negro leaders sought to negotiate with the city fathers. But the latter consistently refused to engage in good-faith negotiation.

Then, last September, came the opportunity to talk with leaders of Birmingham's economic community. In the course of the negotiations, certain promises were made by the merchants—for example, to remove the stores' humiliating racial signs. On the basis of these promises, the Reverend Fred Shuttlesworth and the leaders of the Alabama Christian

Movement for Human Rights agreed to a moratorium on all demonstrations. As the weeks and months went by, we realized that we were the victims of a broken promise. A few signs, briefly removed, returned; the others remained.

As in so many past experiences, our hopes had been blasted, and the shadow of deep disappointment settled upon us. We had no alternative except to prepare for direct action, whereby we would present our very bodies as a means of laying our case before the conscience of the local and the national community. Mindful of the difficulties involved, we decided to undertake a process of self-purification. We began a series of workshops on nonviolence, and we repeatedly asked ourselves: "Are you able to accept blows without retaliating?" "Are you able to endure the ordeal of jail?" We decided to schedule our direct-action program for the Easter season, realizing that except for Christmas, this is the main shopping period of the year. Knowing that a strong economic-withdrawal program would be the by-product of direct action, we felt that this would be the best time to bring pressure to bear on the merchants for the needed change.

Then it occurred to us that Birmingham's mayoral election was coming up in March, and we speedily decided to postpone action until after election day. When we discovered that the Commissioner of Public Safety, Eugene "Bull" Connor,[2] had piled up enough votes to be in the run-off, we decided again to postpone action until the day after the run-off so that the demonstrations could not be used to cloud the issues. Like many others, we wanted to see Mr. Connor defeated, and to this end we endured postponement after postponement. Having aided in this community need, we felt that our direct-action program could be delayed no longer.

10   You may well ask, "Why direct action? Why sit-ins, marches, and so forth? Isn't negotiation a better path?" You are quite right in calling for negotiation. Indeed, this is the very purpose of direct action. Nonviolent direct action seeks to create such a crisis and foster such a tension that a community which has constantly refused to negotiate is forced to confront the issue. It seeks so to dramatize the issue that it can no longer be ignored. My citing the creation of tension as part of the work of the nonviolent-resister may sound rather shocking. But I must confess that I am not afraid of the word "tension." I have earnestly opposed violent tension, but there is a type of constructive, nonviolent tension which is necessary for growth. Just as Socrates felt that it was necessary to create a tension in the mind so that individuals could rise from the bondage of myths and half-truths to the unfettered realm of creative analysis and objective appraisal, so must we see the need for

---

[2] An ardent segregationist, Connor ordered police officers to use police dogs and fire hoses to break up civil rights demonstrations. (Conner lost his bid for mayor.) [Eds.]

nonviolent gadflies to create the kind of tension in society that will help men rise from the dark depths of prejudice and racism to the majestic heights of understanding and brotherhood.

The purpose of our direct-action program is to create a situation so crisis-packed that it will inevitably open the door to negotiation. I therefore concur with you in your call for negotiation. Too long has our beloved Southland been bogged down in a tragic effort to live in monologue rather than dialogue.

One of the basic points in your statement is that the action that I and my associates have taken in Birmingham is untimely. Some have asked: "Why didn't you give the new city administration time to act?" The only answer that I can give to this query is that the new Birmingham administration must be prodded about as much as the outgoing one, before it will act. We are sadly mistaken if we feel that the election of Albert Boutwell as mayor will bring the millennium to Birmingham. While Mr. Boutwell is a much more gentle person than Mr. Connor, they are both segregationists, dedicated to maintenance of the status quo. I have hoped that Mr. Boutwell will be reasonable enough to see the futility of massive resistance to desegregation. But he will not see this without pressure from devotees of civil rights. My friends, I must say to you that we have not made a single gain in civil rights without determined legal and nonviolent pressure. Lamentably, it is an historical fact that privileged groups seldom give up their privileges voluntarily. Individuals may see the moral light and voluntarily give up their unjust posture; but, as Reinhold Niebuhr[3] has reminded us, groups tend to be more immoral than individuals.

We know through painful experience that freedom is never voluntarily given by the oppressor; it must be demanded by the oppressed. Frankly, I have yet to engage in a direct-action campaign that was "well timed" in the view of those who have not suffered unduly from the disease of segregation. For years now I have heard the word "Wait!" It rings in the ear of every Negro with piercing familiarity. This "Wait!" has almost always meant "Never." We must come to see, with one of our distinguished jurists, that "justice too long delayed is justice denied."[4]

We have waited for more than 340 years for our constitutional and God-given rights. The nations of Asia and Africa are moving with jet-like speed toward gaining political independence, but we still creep at horse-and-buggy pace toward gaining a cup of coffee at a lunch counter. Perhaps it is easy for those who have never felt the stinging darts of segregation to say, "Wait." But when you have seen vicious mobs lynch your mothers and fathers at will and drown your sisters and brothers

---

[3]American religious and social thinker (1892–1971). [Eds.]

[4]Attributed to British statesman William Ewart Gladstone (1809–1898), a stalwart of the Liberal Party who also said, "You cannot fight the future. Time is on our side." [Eds.]

at whim; when you have seen hate-filled policemen curse, kick, and even kill your black brothers and sisters; when you see the vast majority of your twenty million Negro brothers smothering in an airtight cage of poverty in the midst of an affluent society; when you suddenly find your tongue twisted and your speech stammering as you seek to explain to your six-year-old daughter why she can't go to the public amusement park that has just been advertised on television, and see tears welling up in her eyes when she is told that Funtown is closed to colored children, and see ominous clouds of inferiority beginning to form in her little mental sky, and see her beginning to distort her personality by developing an unconscious bitterness toward white people; when you have to concoct an answer for a five-year-old son who is asking, "Daddy, why do white people treat colored people so mean?"; when you take a cross-country drive and find it necessary to sleep night after night in the uncomfortable corners of your automobile because no motel will accept you; when you are humiliated day in and day out by nagging signs reading "white" and "colored"; when your first name becomes "nigger," your middle name becomes "boy" (however old you are) and your last name becomes "John," and your wife and mother are never given the respected title "Mrs."; when you are harried by day and haunted by night by the fact that you are a Negro, living constantly at tiptoe stance, never quite knowing what to expect next, and are plagued with inner fears and outer resentments; when you are forever fighting a degenerating sense of "nobodiness"—then you will understand why we find it difficult to wait. There comes a time when the cup of endurance runs over, and men are no longer willing to be plunged into the abyss of despair. I hope, sirs, you can understand our legitimate and unavoidable impatience.

15   You express a great deal of anxiety over our willingness to break laws. This is certainly a legitimate concern. Since we so diligently urge people to obey the Supreme Court's decision of 1954 outlawing segregation in the public schools, at first glance it may seem rather paradoxical for us consciously to break laws. One may well ask: "How can you advocate breaking some laws and obeying others?" The answer lies in the fact that there are two types of laws: just and unjust. I would be the first to advocate obeying just laws. One has not only a legal but a moral responsibility to obey just laws. Conversely, one has a moral responsibility to disobey unjust laws. I would agree with St. Augustine[5] that "an unjust law is no law at all."

Now, what is the difference between the two? How does one determine whether a law is just or unjust? A just law is a man-made code that squares with the moral law or the law of God. An unjust law is a

---

[5]Italian-born missionary and theologian (?–c. 604). [Eds.]

code this is out of harmony with the moral law. To put it in the terms of St. Thomas Aquinas:[6] An unjust law is a human law that is not rooted in eternal law and natural law. Any law that uplifts human personality is just. Any law that degrades human personality is unjust. All segregation statutes are unjust because segregation distorts the soul and damages the personality. It gives the segregator a false sense of superiority and the segregated a false sense of inferiority. Segregation, to use the terminology of the Jewish philosopher Martin Buber,[7] substitutes an "I-it" relationship for an "I-thou" relationship and ends up relegating persons to the status of things. Hence segregation is not only politically, economically, and sociologically unsound, it is morally wrong and sinful. Paul Tillich[8] has said that sin is separation. Is not segregation an existential expression of man's tragic separation, his awful estrangement, his terrible sinfulness? Thus it is that I can urge men to obey the 1954 decision of the Supreme Court, for it is morally right; and I can urge them to disobey segregation ordinances, for they are morally wrong.

Let us consider a more concrete example of just and unjust laws. An unjust law is a code that a numerical or power majority group compels a minority group to obey but does not make binding on itself. This is *difference* made legal. By the same token, a just law is a code that a majority compels a minority to follow and that it is willing to follow itself. This is *sameness* made legal.

Let me give another explanation. A law is unjust if it is inflicted on a minority that, as a result of being denied the right to vote, had no part in enacting or devising the law. Who can say that the legislature of Alabama which set up that state's segregation laws was democratically elected? Throughout Alabama all sorts of devious methods are used to prevent Negroes from becoming registered voters, and there are some counties in which, even though Negroes constitute a majority of the population, not a single Negro is registered. Can any law enacted under such circumstances be considered democratically structured?

Sometimes a law is just on its face and unjust in its application. For instance, I have been arrested on a charge of parading without a permit. Now, there is nothing wrong in having an ordinance which requires a permit for a parade. But such an ordinance becomes unjust when it is used to maintain segregation and to deny citizens the First-Amendment privilege of peaceful assembly and protest.

I hope you are able to see the distinction I am trying to point out. 20 In no sense do I advocate evading or defying the law, as would the rabid segregationist. That would lead to anarchy. One who breaks an unjust

---

[6]Italian philosopher and theologian (1225–1274). [Eds.]
[7]Austrian existentialist philosopher and Judaic scholar (1878–1965). [Eds.]
[8]American philosopher and theologian (1886–1965). [Eds.]

law must do so openly, lovingly, and with a willingness to accept the penalty. I submit that an individual who breaks a law that conscience tells him is unjust, and who willingly accepts the penalty of imprisonment in order to arouse the conscience of the community over its injustice, is in reality expressing the highest respect for law.

Of course, there is nothing new about this kind of civil disobedience. It was evidenced sublimely in the refusal of Shadrach, Meshach, and Abednego to obey the laws of Nebuchadnezzar, on the ground that a higher moral law was at stake.[9] It was practiced superbly by the early Christians, who were willing to face hungry lions and the excruciating pain of chopping blocks rather than submit to certain unjust laws of the Roman Empire. To a degree, academic freedom is a reality today because Socrates practiced civil disobedience.[10] In our own nation, the Boston Tea Party represented a massive act of civil disobedience.

We should never forget that everything Adolf Hitler did in Germany was "legal" and everything the Hungarian freedom fighters[11] did in Hungary was "illegal." It was "illegal" to aid and comfort a Jew in Hitler's Germany. Even so, I am sure that, had I lived in Germany at the time, I would have aided and comforted my Jewish brothers. If today I lived in a Communist country where certain principles dear to the Christian faith are suppressed, I would openly advocate disobeying that country's anti-religious laws.

I must make two honest confessions to you, my Christian and Jewish brothers. First, I must confess that over the past few years I have been gravely disappointed with the white moderate. I have almost reached the regrettable conclusion that the Negro's great stumbling block in his stride toward freedom is not the White Citizen's Counciler or the Ku Klux Klanner, but the white moderate, who is more devoted to "order" than to justice; who prefers a negative peace which is the absence of tension to a positive peace which is the presence of justice; who constantly says, "I agree with you in the goal you seek, but I cannot agree with your methods of direct action"; who paternalistically believes he can set the timetable for another man's freedom; who lives by a mythical concept of time and who constantly advises the Negro to wait for a "more convenient season." Shallow understanding from people of good will is more frustrating than absolute misunderstanding from people of ill will. Lukewarm acceptance is much more bewildering than outright rejection.

---

[9]In the book of Daniel, Nebuchadnezzar commanded the people to worship a golden statue or be thrown into a furnace of blazing fire. When Shadrach, Meshach, and Abednego refused to worship any god but their own, they were bound and thrown into a blazing furnace, but the fire had no effect on them. Their escape led Nebuchadnezzar to make a decree forbidding blasphemy against their god. [Eds.]

[10]The ancient Greek philosopher Socrates was tried by the Athenians for corrupting their youth through his use of questions to teach. When he refused to change his methods of teaching, he was condemned to death. [Eds.]

[11]The Hungarian anti-Communist uprising of 1956 was quickly crushed by the army of the USSR. [Eds.]

I had hoped that the white moderate would understand that law and order exist for the purpose of establishing justice and that when they fail in this purpose they become the dangerously structured dams that block the flow of social progress. I had hoped that the white moderate would understand that the present tension in the South is a necessary phase of the transition from an obnoxious negative peace, in which the Negro passively accepted his unjust plight, to a substantive and positive peace, in which all men will respect the dignity and worth of human personality. Actually, we who engage in nonviolent direct action are not the creators of tension. We merely bring to the surface the hidden tension that is already alive. We bring it out in the open, where it can be seen and dealt with. Like a boil that can never be cured so long as it is covered up but must be opened with all its ugliness to the natural medicines of air and light, injustice must be exposed, with all the tension its exposure creates, to the light of human conscience and the air of national opinion, before it can be cured.

In your statement you assert that our actions, even though peaceful, must be condemned because they precipitate violence. But is this a logical assertion? Isn't this like condemning a robbed man because his possession of money precipitated the evil act of robbery? Isn't this like condemning Socrates because his unswerving commitment to truth and his philosophical inquiries precipitated the act by the misguided populace in which they made him drink hemlock? Isn't this like condemning Jesus because his unique God-consciousness and never-ceasing devotion to God's will precipitated the evil act of crucifixion? We must come to see that, as the federal courts have consistently affirmed, it is wrong to urge an individual to cease his efforts to gain his basic constitutional rights because the quest may precipitate violence. Society must protect the robbed and punish the robber. 25

I had also hoped that the white moderate would reject the myth concerning time in relation to the struggle for freedom. I have just received a letter from a white brother in Texas. He writes: "All Christians know that the colored people will receive equal rights eventually, but it is possible that you are in too great a religious hurry. It has taken Christianity almost two thousand years to accomplish what it has. The teachings of Christ take time to come to earth." Such an attitude stems from a tragic misconception of time, from the strangely irrational notion that there is something in the very flow of time that will inevitably cure all ills. Actually, time itself is neutral; it can be used either destructively or constructively. More and more I feel that the people of ill will have used time much more effectively than have the people of good will. We will have to repent in this generation not merely for the hateful words and actions of the bad people, but for the appalling silence of the good people. Human progress never rolls in on wheels of inevitability; it comes through the tireless efforts of men willing to be co-workers with God, and without this hard work, time itself becomes an ally of the forces of social stagnation. We must use time creatively, in the knowledge that the time is always ripe to do right. Now is the time to make real the promise of democracy and transform our pending national elegy into a creative psalm of brotherhood. Now is the time to lift our national policy from the quicksand of racial injustice to the solid rock of human dignity.

You speak of our activity in Birmingham as extreme. At first I was rather disappointed that fellow clergymen would see my nonviolent efforts as those of an extremist. I began thinking about the fact that I stand in the middle of two opposing forces in the Negro community. One is a force of complacency, made up in part of Negroes who, as a result of long years of oppression, are so drained of self-respect and a sense of "somebodiness" that they have adjusted to segregation; and in part of a few middle-class Negroes who, because of a degree of academic and economic security and because in some ways they profit by segregation, have become insensitive to the problems of the masses. The other force is one of bitterness and hatred, and it comes perilously close to advocating violence. It is expressed in the various black nationalist groups that are springing up across the nation, the largest and best-known being Elijah Muhammad's Muslim movement. Nourished by the Negro's frustration over the continued existence of racial discrimination, this movement is made up of people who have lost faith in America, who have absolutely repudiated Christianity, and who have concluded that the white man is an incorrigible "devil."

I have tried to stand between these two forces, saying that we need emulate neither the "do-nothingism" of the complacent nor the hatred and despair of the black nationalist. For there is the more excellent way of love and nonviolent protest. I am grateful to God that, through the influence of the Negro church, the way of nonviolence became an integral part of our struggle.

If this philosophy had not emerged, by now many streets of the South would, I am convinced, be flowing with blood. And I am further convinced that if our white brothers dismiss as "rabblerousers" and "outside agitators" those of us who employ nonviolent direct action, and if they refuse to support our nonviolent efforts, millions of Negroes will, out of frustration and despair, seek solace and security in black-nationalist ideologies—a development that would inevitably lead to a frightening racial nightmare.

30   Oppressed people cannot remain oppressed forever. The yearning for freedom eventually manifests itself, and that is what has happened to the American Negro. Something within has reminded him of his birthright of freedom, and something without has reminded him that it can be gained. Consciously or unconsciously, he has been caught up by the *Zeitgeist*,[12] and with his black brothers of Africa and his brown

---

[12]The spirit of the times. [Eds.]

and yellow brothers of Asia, South America, and the Caribbean, the United States Negro is moving with a sense of great urgency toward the promised land of racial justice. If one recognizes this vital urge that has engulfed the Negro community, one should readily understand why public demonstrations are taking place. The Negro has many pent-up resentments and latent frustrations, and he must release them. So let him march; let him make prayer pilgrimages to the city hall; let him go on freedom rides—and try to understand why he must do so. If his repressed emotions are not released in nonviolent ways, they will seek expression through violence; this is not a threat but a fact of history. So I have not said to my people, "Get rid of your discontent." Rather, I have tried to say that this normal and healthy discontent can be channeled into the creative outlet of nonviolent direct action. And now this approach is being termed extremist.

But though I was initially disappointed at being categorized as an extremist, as I continued to think about the matter I gradually gained a measure of satisfaction from the label. Was not Jesus an extremist for love: "Love your enemies, bless them that curse you, do good to them that hate you, and pray for them which despitefully use you, and persecute you." Was not Amos an extremist for justice: "Let justice roll down like waters and righteousness like an ever-flowing stream." Was not Paul an extremist for the Christian gospel: "I bear in my body the marks of the Lord Jesus." Was not Martin Luther an extremist: "Here I stand; I cannot do otherwise, so help me God." And John Bunyan: "I will stay in jail to the end of my days before I make a butchery of my conscience." And Abraham Lincoln: "This nation cannot survive half slave and half free." And Thomas Jefferson: "We hold these truths to be self-evident, that all men are created equal...." So the question is not whether we will be extremists, but what kind of extremists we will be. Will we be extremists for hate or for love? Will we be extremists for the preservation of injustice or for the extension of justice? In that dramatic scene on Calvary's hill three men were crucified. We must never forget that all three were crucified for the same thing—the crime of extremism. Two were extremists for immorality, and thus fell below their environment. The other, Jesus Christ, was an extremist for love, truth, and goodness, and thereby rose above his environment. Perhaps the South, the nation, and the world are in dire need of creative extremists.

I had hoped that the white moderate would see this need. Perhaps I was too optimistic; perhaps I expected too much. I suppose I should have realized that few members of the oppressor race can understand the deep groans and passionate yearnings of the oppressed race, and still fewer have the vision to see that injustice must be rooted out by strong, persistent, and determined action. I am thankful, however, that some of our white brothers in the South have grasped the meaning of this social revolution and committed themselves to it. They are still all too few in quantity, but they are big in quality. Some—such as Ralph

McGill, Lillian Smith, Harry Golden, James McBridge Dabbs, Ann Braden, and Sarah Patton Boyle—have written about our struggle in eloquent and prophetic terms. Others have marched with us down nameless streets of the South. They have languished in filthy, roach-infested jails, suffering the abuse and brutality of policemen who view them as "dirty nigger-lovers." Unlike so many of their moderate brothers and sisters, they have recognized the urgency of the moment and sensed the need for powerful "action" antidotes to combat the disease of segregation.

Let me take note of my other major disappointment. I have been so greatly disappointed with the white church and its leadership. Of course, there are some notable exceptions. I am not unmindful of the fact that each of you has taken some significant stands on this issue. I commend you, Reverend Stallings, for your Christian stand on this past Sunday, in welcoming Negroes to your worship service on a nonsegregated basis. I commend the Catholic leaders of this state for integrating Spring Hill College several years ago.

But despite these notable exceptions, I must honestly reiterate that I have been disappointed with the church. I do not say this as one of those negative critics who can always find something wrong with the church. I say this as a minister of the gospel, who loves the church; who was nurtured in its bosom; who has been sustained by its spiritual blessings and who will remain true to it as long as the cord of life shall lengthen.

35   When I was suddenly catapulted into the leadership of the bus protest in Montgomery, Alabama, a few years ago, I felt we would be supported by the white church. I felt that the white ministers, priests, and rabbis of the South would be among our strongest allies. Instead, some have been outright opponents, refusing to understand the freedom movement and misrepresenting its leaders; all too many others have been more cautious than courageous and have remained silent behind the anesthetizing security of stained glass windows.

In spite of my shattered dreams, I came to Birmingham with the hope that the white religious leadership of this community would see the justice of our cause and, with deep moral concern, would serve as the channel through which our just grievances could reach the power structure. I had hoped that each of you would understand. But again I have been disappointed.

I have heard numerous southern religious leaders admonish their worshipers to comply with a desegregation decision because it is the law, but I have longed to hear white ministers declare: "Follow this decree because integration is morally right and because the Negro is your brother." In the midst of blatant injustices inflicted upon the Negro, I have watched white churchmen stand on the sideline and mouth pious irrelevancies and sanctimonious trivialities. In the midst of a mighty struggle to rid our nation of racial and economic injustice, I have heard many ministers say: "Those are social issues, with which the gospel has no real concern." And I have watched many churches commit themselves to a completely otherworldly religion which makes a strange, un-Biblical distinction between body and soul, between the sacred and the secular.

I have traveled the length and breadth of Alabama, Mississippi, and all the other southern states. On sweltering summer days and crisp autumn mornings I have looked at the South's beautiful churches with their lofty spires pointing heavenward. I have beheld the impressive outlines of her massive religious-education buildings. Over and over I have found myself asking: "What kind of people worship here? Who is their God? Where were their voices when the lips of Governor Barnett[13] dripped with words of interposition and nullification? Where were they when Governor Wallace[14] gave a clarion call for defiance and hatred? Where were their voices of support when bruised and weary Negro men and women decided to rise from the dark dungeons of complacency to the bright hills of creative protest?"

Yes, these questions are still in my mind. In deep disappointment I have wept over the laxity of the church. But be assured that my tears have been tears of love. There can be no deep disappointment where there is not deep love. Yes, I love the church. How could I do otherwise? I am in the rather unique position of being the son, the grandson, and the great-grandson of preachers. Yes, I see the church as the body of Christ. But, oh! How we have blemished and scarred that body through social neglect and through fear of being nonconformists.

There was a time when the church was very powerful—in the time 40 when the early Christians rejoiced at being deemed worthy to suffer for what they believed. In those days the church was not merely a thermometer that recorded the ideas and principles of popular opinion; it was a thermostat that transformed the mores of society. Whenever the early Christians entered a town, the people in power became disturbed and immediately sought to convict the Christians for being "disturbers of the peace" and "outside agitators." But the Christians pressed on, in the conviction that they were "a colony of heaven," called to obey God rather than man. Small in number, they were big in commitment. They were too God-intoxicated to be "astronomically intimidated." By their effort and example they brought an end to such ancient evils as infanticide and gladiatorial contests.

---

[13]Ross Barnett, segregationist governor of Mississippi, who strongly resisted the integration of the University of Mississippi in 1962. [Eds.]

[14]George Wallace, segregationist governor of Alabama, best known for standing in the doorway of a University of Alabama building to block the entrance of two black students who were trying to register. [Eds.]

Things are different now. So often the contemporary church is a weak, ineffectual voice with an uncertain sound. So often it is an archdefender to the status quo. Far from being disturbed by the presence of the church, the power structure of the average community is consoled by the church's silent—and often even vocal—sanction of things as they are.

But the judgment of God is upon the church as never before. If today's church does not recapture the sacrificial spirit of the early church, it will lose its authenticity, forfeit the loyalty of millions, and be dismissed as an irrelevant social club with no meaning for the twentieth century. Every day I meet young people whose disappointment with the church has turned into outright disgust.

Perhaps I have once again been too optimistic. Is organized religion too inextricably bound to the status quo to save our nation and the world? Perhaps I must turn my faith to the inner spiritual church, the church within the church, as the true *ekklesia*[15] and the hope of the world. But again I am thankful to God that some noble souls from the ranks of organized religion have broken loose from the paralyzing chains of conformity and joined us as active partners in the struggle for freedom. They have left their secure congregations and walked the streets of Albany, Georgia, with us. They have gone down the highways of the South on tortuous rides for freedom. Yes, they have gone to jail with us. Some have been dismissed from their churches, have lost the support of their bishops and fellow ministers. But they have acted in the faith that right defeated is stronger than evil triumphant. Their witness has been the spiritual salt that has preserved the true meaning of the gospel in these troubled times. They have carved a tunnel of hope through the dark mountain of disappointment.

I hope the church as a whole will meet the challenge of this decisive hour. But even if the church does not come to the aid of justice, I have no despair about the future. I have no fear about the outcome of our struggle in Birmingham, even if our motives are at present misunderstood. We will reach the goal of freedom in Birmingham and all over the nation, because the goal of America is freedom. Abused and scorned though we may be, our destiny is tied up with America's destiny. Before the pilgrims landed at Plymouth, we were here. Before the pen of Jefferson etched the majestic words of the Declaration of Independence across the pages of history, we were here. For more than two centuries our forebears labored in this country without wages; they made cotton king; they built the homes of their masters while suffering gross injustice and shameful humiliation—and yet out of a bottomless vitality they continued to thrive and develop. If the inexpressible cruelties of slavery could not stop us, the opposition we now face will surely fail. We

---

[15]The Greek word for the early Christian church. [Eds.]

will win our freedom because the sacred heritage of our nation and the eternal will of God are embodied in our echoing demands.

Before closing I feel impelled to mention one other point in your state- 45 ment that has troubled me profoundly. You warmly commended the Birmingham police force for keeping "order" and "preventing violence." I doubt that you would have so warmly commended the police force if you had seen its dogs sinking their teeth into unarmed, nonviolent Negroes. I doubt that you would so quickly commend the policemen if you were to observe their ugly and inhumane treatment of Negroes here in the city jail; if you were to watch them push and curse old Negro women and young Negro girls; if you were to see them slap and kick old Negro men and young boys; if you were to observe them, as they did on two occasions, refuse to give us food because we wanted to sing our grace together. I cannot join you in your praise of the Birmingham police department.

It is true that the police have exercised a degree of discipline in handling the demonstrators. In this sense they have conducted themselves rather "nonviolently" in public. But for what purpose? To preserve the evil system of segregation. Over the past few years I have consistently preached that nonviolence demands that the means we use must be as pure as the ends we seek. I have tried to make clear that it is wrong to use immoral means to attain moral ends. But now I must affirm that it is just as wrong, or perhaps even more so, to use moral means to preserve immoral ends. Perhaps Mr. Connor and his policemen have been rather nonviolent in public, as was Chief Pritchett in Albany, Georgia, but they have used the moral means of nonviolence to maintain the immoral end of racial injustice. As T. S. Eliot[16] has said, "The last temptation is the greatest treason: To do the right deed for the wrong reason."

I wish you had commended the Negro sit-inners and demonstrators of Birmingham for their sublime courage, their willingness to suffer, and their amazing discipline in the midst of great provocation. One day the South will recognize its real heroes. They will be the James Merediths,[17] with the noble sense of purpose that enables them to face jeering and hostile mobs, and with the agonizing loneliness that characterizes the life of the pioneer. They will be old, oppressed, battered Negro women, symbolized in a seventy-two-year-old woman in Montgomery, Alabama, who rose up with a sense of dignity and with her people decided not to ride segregated buses, and who responded with ungrammatical profundity to one who inquired about her weariness: "My feets is tired, but my soul is at rest." They will be the young high school and college students, the young ministers of the gospel and a host of their elders, courageously and nonviolently sitting in at lunch counters and

---

[16]American-born British poet (1888–1965), winner of the 1948 Nobel Prize in Literature. [Eds.]

[17]First African American to enroll at the University of Mississippi, after federal troops were brought in to control demonstrators protesting his enrollment. [Eds.]

willingly going to jail for conscience' sake. One day the South will know that when these disinherited children of God sat down at lunch counters, they were in reality standing up for what is best in the American dream and for the most sacred values in our Judaeo-Christian heritage, thereby bringing our nation back to those great wells of democracy which were dug deep by the founding fathers in their formulation of the Constitution and the Declaration of Independence.

Never before have I written so long a letter. I'm afraid it is much too long to take your precious time. I can assure you that it would have been much shorter if I had been writing from a comfortable desk, but what else can one do when he is alone in a narrow jail cell, other than write long letters, think long thoughts, and pray long prayers?

If I have said anything in this letter that overstates the truth and indicates an unreasonable impatience, I beg you to forgive me. If I have said anything that understates the truth and indicates my having a patience that allows me to settle for anything less than brotherhood, I beg God to forgive me.

50   I hope this letter finds you strong in the faith. I also hope that circumstances will soon make it possible for me to meet each of you, not as an integrationist or a civil-rights leader but as a fellow clergyman and a Christian brother. Let us all hope that the dark clouds of racial prejudice will soon pass away and the deep fog of misunderstanding will be lifted from our fear-drenched communities, and in some not too distant tomorrow the radiant stars of love and brotherhood will shine over our great nation with all their scintillating beauty.

Yours for the cause of Peace and Brotherhood,

MARTIN LUTHER KING, JR.

Responding to Reading

1. Do you believe King would have been justified in arguing that he had no alternative other than protest? Would you accept this argument?
2. In paragraph 30, King says, "Oppressed people cannot remain oppressed forever." Do you think world events of the last few years confirm or contradict this statement?
3. Throughout this letter, King uses elaborate diction and a variety of rhetorical devices: he addresses his audience directly; makes frequent use of balance and parallelism, understatement, and metaphor; and makes many historical and religious allusions. What effect do you think King intended these rhetorical devices to have on the letter's original audience of clergymen? Does King's elaborate style enhance his argument, or does it just get in the way?

Responding in Writing

Write a short manifesto advocating civil disobedience for a cause you strongly believe in. To inspire others to follow the course of action you propose, explain the goal you are seeking, and identify the opposing forces that you believe make civil disobedience necessary. Then, explain the form you expect your peaceful protest to take.

LIFEBOAT ETHICS: THE CASE AGAINST "AID" THAT HARMS

Garrett Hardin

1915–2003

Garrett Hardin was a biologist who wrote on moral and ethical issues in his field. Hardin, who earned an Sc.B. degree from the University of Chicago (1936) and a Ph.D. from Stanford University (1941), taught at the University of California at Santa Barbara from 1946 until 1978. His many books include Filters against Folly: How to Survive Despite Economists, Ecologists, and the Merely Eloquent *(1985),* Living within Limits: How Global Population Growth Threatens Widespread Social Disorder *(1992),* The Immigration Dilemma: Avoiding the Tragedy of the Commons *(1994), and* Ostrich Factor: Our Population Myopia *(1999). In the following classic essay, which originally appeared in* Psychology Today *in 1974, Hardin uses the metaphor of the wealthy nations of the world as lifeboats to illustrate the dilemma facing wealthy nations as they attempt to distribute food to the world's poor.*

Environmentalists use the metaphor of the earth as a "spaceship" in trying to persuade countries, industries and people to stop wasting and polluting our natural resources. Since we all share life on this planet, they argue, no single person or institution has the right to destroy, waste, or use more than a fair share of its resources.

But does everyone on earth have an equal right to an equal share of its resources? The spaceship metaphor can be dangerous when used by misguided idealists to justify suicidal policies for sharing our resources through uncontrolled immigration and foreign aid. In their enthusiastic but unrealistic generosity, they confuse the ethics of a spaceship with those of a lifeboat.

A true spaceship would have to be under the control of a captain, since no ship could possibly survive if its course were determined by committee. Spaceship Earth certainly has no captain; the United Nations is merely a toothless tiger, with little power to enforce any policy upon its bickering members.

If we divide the world crudely into rich nations and poor nations, two thirds of them are desperately poor, and only one third comparatively rich, with the United States the wealthiest of all. Metaphorically each rich nation can be seen as a lifeboat full of comparatively rich people. In the ocean outside each lifeboat swim the poor of the world, who would like to get in, or at least to share some of the wealth. What should the lifeboat passengers do?

First, we must recognize the limited capacity of any lifeboat. For 5 example, a nation's land has a limited capacity to support a population and as the (current energy crisis) has shown us, in some ways we have already exceeded the carrying capacity of our land.

So here we sit, say 50 people in our lifeboat. To be generous let us assume it has room for 10 more, making a total capacity of 60. Suppose the 50 of us in the lifeboat see 100 others swimming in the water outside, begging for admission to our boat or for handouts. We have several options: we may be tempted to try to live by the Christian ideal of being "our brother's keeper," or by the Marxist ideal of "to each according to his needs." Since the needs of all in the water are the same, and since they can all be seen as "our brothers," we could take them all into our boat, making a total of 150 in a boat designed for 60. The boat swamps, everyone drowns. Complete justice, complete catastrophe.

Since the boat has an unused excess capacity of 10 more passengers, we could admit just 10 more to it. But which 10 do we let in? How do we choose? Do we pick the best 10, the neediest 10, "first come, first served"? And what do we say to the 90 we exclude? If we do let an extra 10 into our lifeboat, we will have lost our "safety factor," an engineering principle of critical importance. For example, if we don't leave room for excess capacity as a safety factor in our country's agriculture, a new plant disease or a bad change in the weather could have disastrous consequences.

Suppose we decide to preserve our small safety factor and admit no more to the lifeboat. Our survival is then possible although we shall have to be constantly on guard against boarding parties.

While this last solution clearly offers the only means of our survival, it is morally abhorrent to many people. Some say they feel guilty about their good luck. My reply is simple: "Get out and yield your place to others." This may solve the problem of the guilt-ridden person's conscience, but it does not change the ethics of the lifeboat. The needy person to whom the guilt-ridden person yields his place will not himself feel guilty about his good luck. If he did, he would not climb aboard. The net result of conscience-stricken people giving up their unjustly held seats is the elimination of that sort of conscience from the lifeboat.

10   This is the basic metaphor within which we must work out our solutions. Let us now enrich the image, step by step, with substantive additions from the real world, a world that must solve real and pressing problems of overpopulation and hunger.

The harsh ethics of the lifeboat become even harsher when we consider the reproductive differences between the rich nations and the poor nations. The people inside the lifeboats are doubling in numbers every 87 years: those swimming around outside are doubling on the average, every 35 years, more than twice as fast as the rich. And since the world's resources are dwindling, the difference in prosperity between the rich and the poor can only increase.

As of 1973, the U.S. had a population of 210 million people, who were increasing by 0.8 percent per year. Outside our lifeboat, let us imagine another 210 million people (say the combined populations of Colombia, Ecuador, Venezuela, Morocco, Pakistan, Thailand and the Philippines), who are increasing at a rate of 3.3 percent per year. Put differently, the doubling time for this aggregate population is 21 years, compared to 87 years for the U.S.

Now suppose the U.S. agreed to pool its resources with those seven countries, with everyone receiving an equal share. Initially the ratio of Americans to non-Americans in this model would be one-to-one but consider what the ratio would be after 87 years, by which time the Americans would have doubled to a population of 420 million. By then, doubling every 21 years, the other group would have swollen to 354 billion. Each American would have to share the available resources with more than eight people.

But, one could argue, this discussion assumes that current population trends will continue, and they may not. Quite so. Most likely the rate of population increase will decline much faster in the U.S. than it will in the other countries, and there does not seem to be much we can do about it. In sharing with "each according to his needs," we must recognize that needs are determined by population size, which is determined by the rate of reproduction, which at present is regarded as a sovereign right of every nation, poor or not. This being so, the philanthropic load created by the sharing ethic of the spaceship can only increase.

The fundamental error of spaceship ethics, and the sharing it 15 requires, is that it leads to what I call "the tragedy of the commons." Under a system of private property, the men who own property recognize their responsibility to care for it, for if they don't they will eventually suffer. A farmer, for instance, will allow no more cattle in a pasture than its carrying capacity justifies. If he overloads it, erosion sets in, weeds take over, and he loses the use of the pasture.

If a pasture becomes a commons open to all, the right of each to use it may not be matched by a corresponding responsibility to protect it. Asking everyone to use it with discretion will hardly do, for the considerate herdsman who refrains from overloading the commons suffers more than a selfish one who says his needs are greater. If everyone would restrain himself all would be well; but it takes only one less than everyone to ruin a system of voluntary restraint. In a crowded world of less than perfect human beings, mutual ruin is inevitable if there are no controls. This is the tragedy of the commons.

One of the major tasks of education today should be the creation of such an acute awareness of the dangers of the commons that people will recognize its many varieties. For example, the air and water have become polluted because they are treated as commons. Further growth in the population or per-capita conversion of natural resources into pollutants will only make the problem worse. The same holds true for the fish of the oceans. Fishing fleets have nearly disappeared in many parts of the world; technological improvements in the art of fishing are hastening the day of complete ruin. Only the replacement of the system of the commons with a responsible system of control will save the land, air, water and oceanic fisheries.

In recent years there has been a push to create a new commons called a World Food Bank, an international depository of food reserves to which nations would contribute according to their abilities and from which they would draw according to their needs. This humanitarian proposal has received support from many liberal international groups, and from such prominent citizens as Margaret Mead, U.N. Secretary General Kurt Waldheim, and Senators Edward Kennedy and George McGovern.

A world food bank appeals powerfully to our humanitarian impulses. But before we rush ahead with such a plan, let us recognize where the greatest political push comes from, lest we be disillusioned later. Our experience with the "Food for Peace program," or Public Law 480, gives us the answer. This program moved billions of dollars worth of U.S. surplus grain to food-short, population-long countries during the past two decades. But when P.L. 480 first became law, a headline in the business magazine *Forbes* revealed the real power behind it: "Feeding the World's Hungry Millions: How It Will Mean Billions for U.S. Business."

20   And indeed it did. In the years 1960 to 1970, U.S. taxpayers spent a total of $7.9 billion on the Food for Peace program. Between 1948 and 1970, they also paid an additional $50 billion for other economic-aid programs, some of which went for food and food-producing machinery and technology. Though all U.S. taxpayers were forced to contribute to the cost of P.L. 480, certain special interest groups gained handsomely under the program. Farmers did not have to contribute the grain; the Government, or rather the taxpayers, bought it from them at full market prices. The increased demand raised prices of farm products generally. The manufacturers of farm machinery, fertilizers and pesticides benefited by the farmers' extra efforts to grow more food. Grain elevators profited from storing the surplus until it could be shipped. Railroads made money hauling it to ports, and shipping lines profited from carrying it overseas. The implementation of P.L. 480 required the creation of a vast Government bureaucracy, which then acquired its own vested interest in continuing the program regardless of its merits.

Those who proposed and defended the Food for Peace program in public rarely mentioned its importance to any of these special interests. The public emphasis was always on its humanitarian effects. The combination of silent selfish interests and highly vocal humanitarian apologists made a powerful and successful lobby for extracting money from taxpayers. We can expect the same lobby to push now for the creation of a World Food Bank.

However great the potential benefit to selfish interests, it should not be a decisive argument against a truly humanitarian program. We must ask if such a program would actually do more good than harm, not only momentarily but also in the long run. Those who propose the food bank usually refer to a current "emergency" or "crisis" in terms of world food supply. But what is an emergency? Although they may be infrequent and sudden, everyone knows that emergencies will occur from time to time. A well-run family, company, organization or country prepares for the likelihood of accidents and emergencies. It expects them, it budgets for them, it saves for them.

What happens if some organizations or countries budget for accidents and others do not? If each country is solely responsible for its own well-being, poorly managed ones will suffer. But they can learn from experience. They may mend their ways, and learn to budget for infrequent but certain emergencies. For example, the weather varies from year to year, and periodic crop failures are certain. A wise and competent government saves out of the production of the good years in anticipation of bad years to come. Joseph taught this policy to Pharaoh in Egypt more than 2,000 years ago. Yet the great majority of the governments in the world today do not follow such a policy. They lack either the wisdom or the competence, or both. Should those nations that do manage to put something aside be forced to come to the rescue each time an emergency occurs among the poor nations?

"But it isn't their fault!" Some kind-hearted liberals argue, "How can we blame the poor people who are caught in an emergency? Why must they suffer for the sins of their governments?" The concept of blame is simply not relevant here. The real question is, what are the operational consequences of establishing a world food bank? If it is open to every country every time a need develops, slovenly rulers will not be motivated to take Joseph's advice. Someone will always come to their aid. Some countries will deposit food in the world food bank, and others will withdraw it. There will be almost no overlap. As a result of such solutions to food shortage emergencies, the poor countries will not learn to mend their ways, and will suffer progressively greater emergencies as their populations grow.

On the average, poor countries undergo a 2.5 percent increase in 25 population each year; rich countries, about 0.8 percent. Only rich countries have anything in the way of food reserves set aside, and even they do not have as much as they should. Poor countries have none. If poor countries received no food from the outside, the rate of their population growth would be periodically checked by crop failures and famines. But if they can always draw on a world food bank in time of need, their population can continue to grow unchecked, and so will their "need" for aid. In the short run, a world food bank may diminish that need, but in the long run it actually increases the need without limit.

Without some system of worldwide food sharing, the proportion of people in the rich and poor nations might eventually stabilize. The over-populated poor countries would decrease in numbers, while the rich countries that had room for more people would increase. But with a well-meaning system of sharing, such as a world food bank, the growth differential between the rich and the poor countries will not only per-sist, it will increase. Because of the higher rate of population growth in the poor countries of the world, 88 percent of today's children are born poor, and only 12 percent rich. Year by year the ratio becomes worse, as the fast-reproducing poor outnumber the slow-reproducing rich.

A world food bank is thus a commons in disguise. People will have more motivation to draw from it than to add to any common store. The less provident and less able will multiply at the expense of the abler and more provident, bringing eventual ruin upon all who share in the commons. Besides, any system of "sharing" that amounts to foreign aid from the rich nations to the poor nations will carry the taint of charity, which will contribute little to the world peace so devoutly desired by those who support the idea of a world food bank.

As past U.S. foreign-aid programs have amply and depressingly demonstrated, international charity frequently inspires mistrust and antagonism rather than gratitude on the part of the recipient nation.

The modern approach to foreign aid stresses the export of technol-ogy and advice, rather than money and food. As an ancient Chinese proverb goes: "Give a man a fish and he will eat for a day; teach him how to fish and he will eat for the rest of his days." Acting on this advice, the Rockefeller and Ford Foundations have financed a number of programs for improving agriculture in the hungry nations. Known as the "Green Revolution," these programs have led to the develop-ment of "miracle rice" and "miracle wheat," new strains that offer big-ger harvests and greater resistance to crop damage. Norman Borlaug, the Nobel Prize winning agronomist who, supported by the Rockefeller Foundation, developed "miracle wheat," is one of the most prominent advocates of a world food bank.

30   Whether or not the Green Revolution can increase food production as much as its champions claim is a debatable but possibly irrelevant point. Those who support this well-intended humanitarian effort should first consider some of the fundamentals of human ecology. Ironically, one man who did was the late Alan Gregg, a vice president of the Rockefeller Foundation. Two decades ago he expressed strong doubts about the wis-dom of such attempts to increase food production. He likened the growth and spread of humanity over the surface of the earth to the spread of can-cer in the human body, remarking that "cancerous growths demand food, but, as far as I know, they have never been cured by getting it."

Every human born constitutes a draft on all aspects of the environment: food, air, water, forests, beaches, wildlife, scenery and solitude. Food can, perhaps, be significantly increased to meet a growing demand. But what about clean beaches, unspoiled forests, and solitude? If we satisfy a growing population's need for food, we necessarily decrease its per capita supply of the other resources needed by men.

India, for example, now has a population of 600 million, which increases by 15 million each year. This population already puts a huge load on a relatively impoverished environment. The country's forests are now only a small fraction of what they were three centuries ago, and floods and erosion continually destroy the insufficient farmland that remains. Every one of the 15 million new lives added to India's population puts an additional burden on the environment, and increases the economic and social costs of crowding. However humanitarian our intent, every Indian life saved through medical or nutritional assistance from abroad diminishes the quality of life for those who remain, and for subsequent generations. If rich countries make it possible, through foreign aid, for 600 million Indians to swell to 1.2 billion in a mere 28 years, as their current growth rate threatens, will future generations of Indians thank us for hastening the destruction of their environment? Will our good intentions be sufficient excuse for the consequences of our actions?

My final example of a commons in action is one for which the public has the least desire for rational discussion—immigration. Anyone who publicly questions the wisdom of current U.S. immigration policy is promptly charged with bigotry, prejudice, ethnocentrism, chauvinism, isolationism or selfishness. Rather than encounter such accusations, one would rather talk about other matters, leaving immigration policy to wallow in the crosscurrents of special interests that take no account of the good of the whole, or the interests of posterity.

Perhaps we still feel guilty about things we said in the past. Two generations ago the popular press frequently referred to Dagos, Wops, Polacks, Chinks and Krauts, in articles about how America was being "overrun" by foreigners of supposedly inferior genetic stock. But because the implied inferiority of foreigners was used then as justification for keeping them out, people now assume that restrictive policies could only be based on such misguided notions. There are other grounds.

Just consider the numbers involved. Our Government acknowl- 35 edges a net inflow of 400,000 immigrants a year. While we have no hard data on the extent of illegal entries, educated guesses put the figure at about 600,000 a year. Since the natural increase (excess of births over deaths) of the resident population now runs about 1.7 million per year, the yearly gain from immigration amounts to at least 19 percent of the total annual increase, and may be as much as 37 percent if we include the estimate for illegal immigrants. Considering the growing use of birth-control devices, the potential effect of educational campaigns by such organizations as Planned Parenthood Federation of America and Zero Population Growth, and the influence of inflation and the housing shortage, the fertility rate of American women may decline so much that immigration could account for all the yearly increase in population. Should we not at least ask if that is what we want?

For the sake of those who worry about whether the "quality" of the average immigrant compares favorably with the quality of the average resident, let us assume that immigrants and nativeborn citizens are of exactly equal quality, however one defines that term. We will focus here only on quantity; and since our conclusions will depend on nothing else, all charges of bigotry and chauvinism become irrelevant.

World food banks *move food to the people*, hastening the exhaustion of the environment of the poor countries. Unrestricted immigration, on the other hand, *moves people to the food*, thus speeding up the destruction of the environment of the rich countries. We can easily understand why poor people should want to make this latter transfer, but why should rich hosts encourage it?

As is the case of foreign-aid programs, immigration receives support from selfish interests and humanitarian impulses. The primary selfish interest in unimpeded immigration is the desire of employers for cheap labor, particularly in industries and trades that offer degrading work. In the past, one wave of foreigners after another was brought into the U.S. to work at wretched jobs for wretched wages. In recent years the Cubans, Puerto Ricans and Mexicans have had this dubious honor. The interests of the employers of cheap labor mesh well with the guilty silence of the country's liberal intelligentsia. White Anglo-Saxon Protestants are particularly reluctant to call for a closing of the doors to immigration for fear of being called bigots.

But not all countries have such reluctant leadership. Most educated Hawaiians, for example, are keenly aware of the limits of their environment, particularly in terms of population growth. There is only so much room on the islands, and the islanders know it. To Hawaiians, immigrants from the other 49 states present as great a threat as those from other nations. At a recent meeting of Hawaiian government officials in Honolulu, I had the ironic delight of hearing a speaker, who like most of his audience was of Japanese ancestry, ask how the country might practically and constitutionally close its door to further immigration. One member of the audience countered: "How can we shut the doors now? We have many friends and relatives in Japan that we'd like to bring here some day so that they can enjoy Hawaii too." The Japanese-American speaker smiled sympathetically and answered: "Yes, but we have children now, and someday we'll have grandchildren too. We can bring more people here from Japan only by giving away some of the land that we hope to pass on to our grandchildren some day. What right do we have to do that?"

At this point, I can hear U.S. liberals asking: "How can you justify 40 slamming the door once you're inside? You say that immigrants should be kept out. But aren't we all immigrants, or the descendants of immigrants? If we insist on staying, must we not admit all others?" Our craving for intellectual order leads us to seek and prefer symmetrical rules and morals: a single rule for me and everybody else; the same rule yesterday, today and tomorrow. Justice, we feel, should not change with time and place.

We Americans of non-Indian ancestry can look upon ourselves as the descendants of thieves who are guilty morally, if not legally, of stealing this land from its Indian owners. Should we then give back the land to the now living American descendants of those Indians? However morally or logically sound this proposal may be, I, for one, am unwilling to live by it and I know no one else who is. Besides, the logical consequence would be absurd. Suppose that, intoxicated with a sense of pure justice, we should decide to turn our land over to the Indians. Since all our other wealth has also been derived from the land, wouldn't we be morally obliged to give that back to the Indians too?

Clearly, the concept of pure justice produces an infinite regression to absurdity. Centuries ago, wise men invented statutes of limitations to justify the rejection of such pure justice, in the interest of preventing continual disorder. The law zealously defends property rights. Drawing a line after an arbitrary time has elapsed may be unjust, but the alternatives are worse.

We are all the descendants of thieves, and the world's resources are inequitably distributed. But we must begin the journey to tomorrow from the point where we are today. We cannot remake the past. We cannot safely divide the wealth equitably among all peoples so long as people reproduce at different rates. To do so would guarantee that our grandchildren, and everyone else's grandchildren, would have only a ruined world to inhabit.

To be generous with one's own possessions is quite different from being generous with those of posterity. We should call this point to the attention of those who, from a commendable love of justice and equality, would institute a system of the commons, either in the form of a world food bank, or of unrestricted immigration. We must convince them if we wish to save at least some parts of the world from environmental ruin.

Responding to Reading

1. Hardin presents his problem as one that has no comfortable solution. One alternative, welcoming all who wish to come into the lifeboat, is "complete justice, complete catastrophe" (6); the other, retaining the crucial "safety factor," is both "the only means of our survival" and "morally abhorrent to

many people" (8–9). Does Hardin see these two alternatives as ethically and practically unacceptable? Do you? Is it really an either/or situation, or are there some solutions he ignores?

2. Does Hardin's use of the lifeboat metaphor clarify his arguments and present the problem he describes in vivid terms? Or, do you find it simplistic, distracting, or irrelevant?

3. In paragraph 2, Hardin asks, "But does everyone on earth have an equal right to an equal share of its resources?" That is, are some people more—or less—deserving than others? How would you answer this question?

Responding in Writing

Imagine you can take only one additional person into your lifeboat. Which of the following would you choose: a baby, an elderly man who has won the Nobel Peace Prize, a single mother of three young children, a decorated soldier, or a doctor who performs life-saving surgery? Explain your choice.

DOG LAB
Claire McCarthy
1963–

A graduate of Harvard Medical School, Claire McCarthy is now a faculty member there as well as medical director of the Martha Eliot Health Center in Boston and contributing editor for Parenting *magazine. During her medical training, she kept detailed journals, which provided the basis for her books* Learning How the Heart Beats: The Making of a Pediatrician *(1995) and* Everyone's Children: A Pediatrician's Story of an Inner-City Practice *(1998). In the following essay, a chapter from* Learning How the Heart Beats, *McCarthy recalls her reluctance to attend an optional lab lesson in which students studied the cardiovascular system of a sedated living dog, which was then euthanized.*

When I finished college and started medical school, the learning changed fundamentally. Whereas in college I had been learning mostly for learning's sake, learning in order to know something, in medical school I was learning in order to *do* something, do the thing I wanted to do with my life. It was exhilarating and at the same time a little scary. My study now carried responsibility.

The most important course in the first year besides Anatomy was Physiology, the study of the functions and processes of the human body. It was the most fascinating subject I had ever studied. I found the intricacies of the way the body works endlessly intriguing and ingenious:

the way the nervous system is designed to differentiate a sharp touch from a soft one; the way muscles move and work together to throw a ball; the wisdom of the kidneys, which filter the blood and let pass out only waste products and extra fluid, keeping everything else carefully within. It was magical to me that each organ and system worked so beautifully and in perfect concert with the rest of the body.

The importance of Physiology didn't lie just in the fact that it was fascinating, however. The other courses I was taking that semester, like Histology and Biochemistry, were fascinating, too. But because Physiology was the study of how the body actually works, it seemed the most pertinent to becoming a physician. The other courses were more abstract. Physiology was practical, and I felt that my ability to master Physiology would be a measure of my ability to be a doctor.

When the second-year students talked about Physiology, they always mentioned "dog lab." They mentioned it briefly but significantly, sharing knowing looks. I gathered that it involved cutting dogs open and that it was controversial, but that was all I knew. I didn't pursue it, I didn't ask questions. That fall I was living day to day, lecture to lecture, test to test. My life was organized around putting as much information into my brain as possible, and I didn't pay much attention to anything else.

I would get up around six, make coffee, and eat my bowl of cereal 5 while I sat at my desk. There was nowhere else to sit in my dormitory room, and if I was going to sit at my desk, I figured I might as well study, so I always studied as I ate. I had a small refrigerator and a hot plate so that I could fix myself meals. After breakfast it was off to a morning of lectures, back to the room at lunchtime for a yogurt or soup and more studying, then afternoon lectures and labs. Before dinner I usually went for a run or a swim; although it was necessary for my sanity and my health, I always felt guilty that I wasn't studying instead. I ate dinner at my desk or with other medical students at the cafeteria in Beth Israel Hospital. We sat among the doctors, staff, and patients, eating our food quickly. Although we would try to talk about movies, current affairs, or other "nonmedical" topics, sooner or later we usually ended up talking about medicine; it was fast becoming our whole life. After dinner it was off to the eerie quiet of the library, where I sat surrounded by my textbooks and notes until I got tired or frustrated, which was usually around ten-thirty. Then I'd go back to the dorm, maybe chat with the other students on my floor, maybe watch television, probably study some more, and then fall asleep so that I could start the routine all over again the next morning.

My life had never been so consuming. Sometimes I felt like a true student in the best sense of the word, wonderfully absorbed in learning; other times I felt like an automation. I was probably a combination of the two. It bothered me sometimes that this process of teaching me to take care of people was making me live a very study-centered, self-centered life. However, it didn't seem as though I had a choice.

One day at the beginning of a physiology lecture the instructor announced that we would be having a laboratory exercise to study the cardiovascular system, and that dogs would be used. The room was quickly quiet; this was the infamous "dog lab." The point of the exercise, he explained, was to study the heart and blood vessels in vivo[1] to learn the effects of different conditions and chemicals by seeing them rather than just by reading about them. The dogs would be sedated and the changes in their heart rates, respiratory rates, and blood pressure would be monitored with each experiment. As the last part of the exercise the sleeping dogs' chests would be cut open so we could actually watch the hearts and lungs in action, and then the dogs would be killed, humanely. We would be divided up into teams of four, and each team would work with a teaching assistant. Because so many teaching assistants were required, the class would be divided in half, and the lab would be held on two days.

The amphitheater buzzed.

The lab was optional, the instructor told us. We would not be marked off in any way if we chose not to attend. He leaned against the side of the podium and said that the way he saw it there was a spectrum of morality when it came to animal experimentation. The spectrum, he said, went from mice or rats to species like horses or apes, and we had to decide at which species we would draw our lines. He hoped, though, that we would choose to attend. It was an excellent learning opportunity, and he thought we ought to take advantage of it. Then he walked behind the podium and started the day's lecture.

10   It was all anyone could talk about: should we do dog lab or shouldn't we? We discussed it endlessly.

There were two main camps. One was the "excellent learning opportunity" camp, which insisted that dog lab was the kind of science we came to medical school to do and that learning about the cardiovascular system on a living animal would make it more understandable and would therefore make us better doctors.

Countering them was the "importance of a life" camp. The extreme members of this camp insisted that it was always wrong to murder an animal for experimentation. The more moderate members argued that perhaps animal experimentation was useful in certain kinds of medical research, but that dog lab was purely an exercise for our education and didn't warrant the killing of a dog. We could learn the material in other ways, they said.

On and on the arguments went, with people saying the same things over and over again in every conceivable way. There was something

---

[1]Latin phrase for "in the living being." [Eds.]

very important about this decision. Maybe it was because we were just beginning to figure out how to define ourselves as physicians—were we scientists, eager for knowledge, or were we defenders of life? The dog lab seemed to pit one against the other. Maybe it was because we thought that our lives as physicians were going to be filled with ethical decisions, and this was our first since entering medical school. It was very important that we do the right thing, but the right thing seemed variable and unclear.

I was quiet during these discussions. I didn't want to kill a dog, but I certainly wanted to take advantage of every learning opportunity offered me. And despite the fact that the course instructor had said our grades wouldn't be affected if we didn't attend the lab, I wasn't sure I believed him, and I didn't want to take any chances. Even if he didn't incorporate the lab report into our grades, I was worried that there would be some reference to it in the final exam, some sneaky way that he would bring it up. Doing well had become so important that I was afraid to trust anyone; doing well had become more important than anything.

I found myself waiting to see what other people would decide. I 15 was ashamed not to be taking a stand, but I was stuck in a way I'd never been before. I didn't like the idea of doing the lab; it felt wrong. Yet for some reason I was embarrassed that I felt that way, and the lab seemed so important. The more I thought about it, the more confused I became.

Although initially the students had appeared divided more or less evenly between the camps, as the lab day drew nearer the majority chose to participate. The discussions didn't stop, but they were fewer and quieter. The issue seemed to become more private.

I was assigned to the second lab day. My indecision was becoming a decision since I hadn't crossed my name off the list. I can still change my mind, I told myself. I'm not on a team yet, nobody's counting on me to show up. One of my classmates asked me to join his group. I hedged.

The day before group lists had to be handed in, the course instructor made an announcement. It was brief and almost offhand: he said that if any of us wished to help anesthetize the dogs for the lab, we were welcome to do so. He told us where to go and when to be there for each lab day. I wrote the information down.

Somehow, this was what I needed. I made my decision. I would do the lab, but I would go help anesthetize the dogs first.

Helping with the anesthesia, I thought, would be taking full respon- 20 sibility for what I was doing, something that was very important to me. I was going to *face* what I was doing, see the dogs awake with their tails wagging instead of meeting them asleep and sort of pretending they weren't real. I also thought it might make me feel better to know that the dogs were treated well as they were anesthetized and to be there, helping to do it gently. Maybe in part I thought of it as my penance.

The day of the first lab came. Around five o'clock I went down to the Friday afternoon "happy hour" in the dormitory living room to talk to the students as they came back. They came back singly or in pairs, quiet, looking dazed. They threw down their coats and backpacks and made their way to the beer and soda without talking to anyone. Some, once they had a cup in their hands, seemed to relax and join in conversations; others took their cups and sat alone on the couches. They all looked tired, worn out.

"Well?" I asked several of them. "What was it like?"

Most shrugged and said little. A few said that it was interesting and that they'd learned a lot, but they said it without any enthusiasm. Every one of them said it was hard. I thought I heard someone say that their dog had turned out to be pregnant. Nobody seemed happy.

The morning of my lab was gray and dreary. I overslept, which I hardly ever do. I got dressed quickly and went across the street to the back entrance of the lab building. It was quiet and still and a little dark. The streets were empty except for an occasional cab. I found the open door and went in.

25   There was only one other student waiting there, a blond-haired woman named Elise. I didn't know her well. We had friends in common, but we'd never really talked. She was sweet and soft-spoken; she wore old jeans and plaid flannel shirts and hung out with the activist crowd. She had always intimidated me. I felt as though I weren't political enough when I was around her. I was actually a little surprised that she was doing the lab at all, as many of her friends had chosen not to.

We greeted each other awkwardly, nodding hello and taking our places leaning against the wall. Within a few minutes one of the teaching assistants came in, said good morning, pulled out some keys, and let us into a room down the hall. Two more teaching assistants followed shortly.

The teaching assistants let the dogs out of cages, and they ran around the room. They were small dogs; I think they were beagles. They seemed happy to be out of their cages, and one of them, white with brown spots, came over to me with his tail wagging. I leaned over to pet him, and he licked my hand, looking up at me eagerly. I stood up again quickly.

The teaching assistant who had let us in, a short man with tousled brown hair and thick glasses, explained that the dogs were to be given intramuscular injections of a sedative that would put them to sleep. During the lab they would be given additional doses intravenously as well as other medications to stop them from feeling pain. We could help, he said, by holding the dogs while they got their injections. Elise and I nodded.

So we held the dogs, and they got their injections. After a few minutes they started to stumble, and we helped them to the floor. I remember that Elise petted one of the dogs as he fell asleep and that she cried. I didn't cry, but I wanted to.

When we were finished, I went back to my room. I sat at my desk, 30 drank my coffee, and read over the lab instructions again. I kept thinking about the dogs running around, about the little white one with the brown spots, and I felt sick. I stared at the instructions without really reading them, looking at my watch every couple of minutes. At five minutes before eight I picked up the papers, put them in my backpack with my books, and left.

The lab was held in a big open room with white walls and lots of windows. The dogs were laid out on separate tables lined up across the room; they were on their backs, tied down. They were all asleep, but some of them moved slightly, and it chilled me.

We walked in slowly and solemnly, putting our coats and backpacks on the rack along the wall and going over to our assigned tables. I started to look for the dog who had licked my hand, but I stopped myself. I didn't want to know where he was.

Our dog was brown and black, with soft floppy ears. His eyes were shut. He looked familiar. We took our places, two on each side of the table, laid out our lab manuals, and began.

The lab took all day. We cut through the dog's skin to find an artery and vein, into which we placed catheters. We injected different drugs and chemicals and watched what happened to the dog's heart rate and blood pressure, carefully recording the results. At the end of the day, when we were done with the experiments, we cut open the dog's chest. We cut through his sternum and pulled open his rib cage. His heart and lungs lay in front of us. The heart was a fist-size muscle that squeezed itself as it beat, pushing blood out. The lungs were white and solid and glistening under the pleura that covered them. The instructor pointed out different blood vessels, like the aorta and the superior vena cava. He showed us the stellate ganglion, which really did look like a star. I think we used the electrical paddles of a defibrillator and shocked the dog's heart into ventricular fibrillation, watching it shiver like Jell-O in front of us. I think that's how we killed them—or maybe it was with a lethal dose of one of the drugs. I'm not sure. It's something I guess I don't want to remember.

Dan was the anesthesiologist, the person assigned to making sure 35 that the dog stayed asleep throughout the entire procedure. Every once in a while Dan would get caught up in the experiment and the dog would start to stir. I would nudge Dan, and he would quickly give more medication. The dog never actually woke up, but every time he moved even the slightest bit, every time I had to think about him being a real dog who was never going to wag his tail or lick anyone's hand again because of us, I got so upset that I couldn't concentrate. In fact, I had trouble concentrating on the lab in general. I kept staring at the dog.

As soon as we were finished, or maybe a couple of minutes before, I left. I grabbed my coat and backpack and ran down the stairs out into the dusk of the late afternoon. It was drizzling, and the medical school looked brown and gray. I walked quickly toward the street.

I was disappointed in the lab and disappointed in myself for doing it. I knew now that doing the lab was wrong. Maybe not wrong for everyone—it was clearly a complicated and individual choice—but wrong for me. The knowledge I had gained wasn't worth the life of a dog to me. I felt very sad.

The drizzle was becoming rain. I slowed down; even though it was cold, the rain felt good. A couple of people walking past me put up their umbrellas. I let the rain fall on me. I wanted to get wet.

From the moment you enter the field of medicine as a medical student, you have an awareness that you have entered something bigger and more important than you are. Doctors are different from other people, we are told implicitly, if not explicitly. Medicine is a way of life, with its own values and guidelines for daily living. They aren't bad values; they include things like the importance of hard work, the pursuit of knowledge, and the preservation of life—at least human life. There's room for individuality and variation, but that's something I realized later, much later. When I started medical school I felt that not only did I have to learn information and skills, I had to become a certain kind of person, too. It was very important to me to learn to do the thing that a doctor would do in a given situation. Since the course instructor, who represented Harvard Medical School to me, had recommended that we do the lab, I figured that a doctor would do it. That wasn't the only reason I went ahead with the lab, but it was a big reason.

40   The rain started to come down harder and felt less pleasant. I walked more quickly, across Longwood Avenue into Vanderbilt Hall. I could hear familiar voices coming from the living room, but I didn't feel like talking to anyone. I ducked into the stairwell.

I got to my room, locked the door behind me, took off my coat, and lay down on my bed. The rain beat against my window. It was the time I usually went running, but the thought of going back out in the rain didn't appeal to me at all. I was suddenly very tired.

As I lay there I thought about the course instructor's discussion of the spectrum of morality and drawing lines. Maybe it's not a matter of deciding which animals I feel comfortable killing, I thought. Maybe it's about drawing different kinds of lines: drawing the lines to define how much of myself I will allow to change. I was proud of being a true student, even if it did mean becoming a little like an automaton. But I still needed to be the person I was before; I needed to be able to make some decisions without worrying about what a doctor would do.

I got up off the bed, opened a can of soup, and put it in a pan on the hot plate to warm. I got some bread and cheese out of the refrigerator, sat down at my desk, and opened my Biochemistry text.

Suddenly I stopped. I closed the text, reached over, and turned on the television, which sat on a little plastic table near the desk. There would be time to study later. I was going to watch television, read a newspaper, and call some friends I hadn't called since starting medical school. It was time to make some changes, some changes back.

Responding to Reading

1. Summarize the two main schools of thought about whether or not to participate in "dog lab." Do the students really have a choice? Explain.
2. Why did McCarthy decide to help anesthetize the dogs? Does her decision make sense to you?
3. Does McCarthy believe that the knowledge she gained was worth the sacrifice of the dog? Do you agree with her? Do you think her experience in "dog lab" changed her? Do you think it made her a better doctor?

Responding in Writing

Do you see a difference in the relative value of the lives of a laboratory animal, an animal in the wild, and a pet? Or, do you think the lives of all three kinds of animals have equal value? Explain your beliefs.

THE PERILS OF OBEDIENCE

Stanley Milgram

1932–1984

Social psychologist Stanley Milgram is best known for his experiments that study aggression and human conformity, especially obedience (he used Nazi Germany as a tragic example of submission to authority). He has said that "it is only the person dwelling in isolation who is not forced to respond, with defiance or submission, to the commands of others." In the following selection, from his book Obedience to Authority *(1974), Milgram's descriptions of some of his experiments on obedience raise perplexing moral questions.*

Obedience is as basic an element in the structure of social life as one can point to. Some system of authority is a requirement of all communal living, and it is only the person dwelling in isolation who is not forced to respond, with defiance or submission, to the commands of others. For many people, obedience is a deeply ingrained behavior tendency, indeed a potent impulse overriding training in ethics, sympathy, and moral conduct.

The dilemma inherent in submission to authority is ancient, as old as the story of Abraham,[1] and the question of whether one should obey

---

[1] Abraham, commanded by God to sacrifice his son Isaac, is ready to do so until an angel stops him. [Eds.]

when commands conflict with conscience has been argued by Plato, dramatized in *Antigone*,[2] and treated to philosophic analysis in almost every historical epoch. Conservative philosophers argue that the very fabric of society is threatened by disobedience, while humanists stress the primacy of the individual conscience.

The legal and philosophic aspects of obedience are of enormous import, but they say very little about how most people behave in concrete situations. I set up a simple experiment at Yale University to test how much pain an ordinary citizen would inflict on another person simply because he was ordered to by an experimental scientist. Stark authority was pitted against the subjects' strongest moral imperatives against hurting others, and, with the subjects' ears ringing with the screams of the victims, authority won more often than not. The extreme willingness of adults to go to almost any lengths on the command of an authority constitutes the chief finding of the study and the fact most urgently demanding explanation.

In the basic experimental design, two people come to a psychology laboratory to take part in a study of memory and learning. One of them is designated as a "teacher" and the other a "learner." The experimenter explains that the study is concerned with the effects of punishment on learning. The learner is conducted into a room, seated in a kind of miniature electric chair; his arms are strapped to prevent excessive movement, and an electrode is attached to his wrist. He is told that he will be read lists of simple word pairs, and that he will then be tested on his ability to remember the second word of a pair when he hears the first one again. Whenever he makes an error, he will receive electric shocks of increasing intensity.

5   The real focus of the experiment is the teacher. After watching the learner being strapped into place, he is seated before an impressive shock generator. The instrument panel consists of thirty lever switches set in a horizontal line. Each switch is clearly labeled with a voltage designation ranging from 15 to 450 volts. The following designations are clearly indicated for groups of four switches, going from left to right: Slight Shock, Moderate Shock, Strong Shock, Very Strong Shock, Intense Shock, Extreme Intensity Shock, Danger: Severe Shock. (Two switches after this last designation are simply marked XXX.)

When a switch is depressed, a pilot light corresponding to each switch is illuminated in bright red; an electric buzzing is heard; a blue light, labeled "voltage energizer," flashes; the dial on the voltage meter swings to the right; and various relay clicks sound off.

---

[2]In Plato's *Apology*, the philosopher Socrates provokes and accepts the sentence of death rather than act against his conscience; the heroine of Sophocles' *Antigone* risks a death sentence in order to give her brother a proper burial. [Eds.]

The upper left-hand corner of the generator is labeled SHOCK GENERATOR, TYPE ZLB, DYSON INSTRUMENT COMPANY, WALTHAM, MASS. OUTPUT 15 VOLTS–450 VOLTS.

Each subject is given a sample 45-volt shock from the generator before his run as teacher, and the jolt strengthens his belief in the authenticity of the machine.

The teacher is a genuinely naïve subject who has come to the laboratory for the experiment. The learner, or victim, is actually an actor who receives no shock at all. The point of the experiment is to see how far a person will proceed in a concrete and measurable situation in which he is ordered to inflict increasing pain on a protesting victim.

Conflict arises when the man receiving the shock begins to show   10 that he is experiencing discomfort. At 75 volts, he grunts; at 120 volts, he complains loudly; at 150, he demands to be released from the experiment. As the voltage increases, his protests become more vehement and emotional. At 285 volts, his response can be described only as an agonized scream. Soon thereafter, he makes no sound at all.

For the teacher, the situation quickly becomes one of gripping tension. It is not a game for him; conflict is intense and obvious. The manifest suffering of the learner presses him to quit; but each time he hesitates to administer a shock, the experimenter orders him to continue. To extricate himself from this plight, the subject must make a clear break with authority.[3]

The subject, Gretchen Brandt,[4] is an attractive thirty-one-year-old medical technician who works at the Yale Medical School. She had emigrated from Germany five years before.

On several occasions when the learner complains, she turns to the experimenter coolly and inquires, "Shall I continue"? She promptly returns to her task when the experimenter asks her to do so. At the administration of 210 volts, she turns to the experimenter, remarking firmly, "Well, I'm sorry, I don't think we should continue."

> EXPERIMENTER: The experiment requires that you go on until he has learned all the word pairs correctly.
> BRANDT: He has a heart condition, I'm sorry. He told you that before.
> EXPERIMENTER: The shocks may be painful but they are not dangerous.
> BRANDT: Well, I'm sorry, I think when shocks continue like this, they are dangerous. You ask him if he wants to get out. It's his free will.

---

[3]The ethical problems of carrying out an experiment of this sort are too complex to be dealt with here, but they receive extended treatment in the book from which this article is adapted. [The book is *Obedience to Authority* (New York: Harper & Row, 1974)—Eds.]

[4]Names of subjects described in this piece have been changed.

EXPERIMENTER: It is absolutely essential that we continue...
BRANDT: I'd like you to ask him. We came here of our free will. If he wants to continue I'll go ahead. He told you he had a heart condition. I'm sorry. I don't want to be responsible for anything happening to him. I wouldn't like it for me either.
EXPERIMENTER: You have no other choice.
BRANDT: I think we are here on our own free will. I don't want to be responsible if anything happens to him. Please understand that.

She refuses to go further and the experiment is terminated.

15   The woman is firm and resolute throughout. She indicates in the interview that she was in no way tense or nervous, and this corresponds to her controlled appearance during the experiment. She feels that the last shock she administered to the learner was extremely painful and reiterates that she "did not want to be responsible for any harm to him."

The woman's straightforward, courteous behavior in the experiment, lack of tension, and total control of her own action seem to make disobedience a simple and rational deed. Her behavior is the very embodiment of what I envisioned would be true for almost all subjects.

Before the experiments, I sought predictions about the outcome from various kinds of people—psychiatrists, college sophomores, middle-class adults, graduate students and faculty in the behavioral sciences. With remarkable similarity, they predicted that virtually all subjects would refuse to obey the experimenter. The psychiatrists specifically predicted that most subjects would not go beyond 150 volts, when the victim makes his first explicit demand to be freed. They expected that only 4 percent would reach 300 volts, and that only a pathological fringe of about one in a thousand would administer the highest shock on the board.

These predictions were unequivocally wrong. Of the forty subjects in the first experiment, twenty-five obeyed the orders of the experimenter to the end, punishing the victim until they reached the most potent shock available on the generator. After 450 volts were administered three times, the experimenter called a halt to the sessions. Many obedient subjects then heaved sighs of relief, mopped their brows, rubbed their fingers over their eyes, or nervously fumbled cigarettes. Others displayed only minimal signs of tension from beginning to end.

When the very first experiments were carried out, Yale undergraduates were used as subjects, and about 60 percent of them were fully obedient. A colleague of mine immediately dismissed these findings as having no relevance to "ordinary" people, asserting that Yale undergraduates are a highly aggressive, competitive bunch who step on each other's necks on the slightest provocation. He assured me that when "ordinary" people were tested, the results would be quite different. As we moved from the pilot studies to the regular experimental series, people drawn from every stratum of New Haven life came to be employed in the experiment: professionals, white-collar workers, unemployed persons, and industrial workers. *The experimental outcome was the same as we had observed among the students.*

Moreover, when the experiments were repeated in Princeton, [20] Munich, Rome, South Africa, and Australia, the level of obedience was invariably somewhat *higher* than found in the investigation reported in this article. Thus one scientist in Munich found 85 percent of his subjects obedient.

Fred Prozi's reactions, if more dramatic than most, illuminate the conflicts experienced by others in less visible form. About fifty years old and unemployed at the time of the experiment, he has a good-natured, if slightly dissolute, appearance, and he strikes people as a rather ordinary fellow. He begins the session calmly but becomes tense as it proceeds. After delivering the 180-volt shock, he pivots around in his chair and, shaking his head, addresses the experimenter in agitated tones:

> PROZI: I can't stand it. I'm not going to kill that man in there. You hear him hollering?
> EXPERIMENTER: As I told you before, the shocks may be painful, but...
> PROZI: But he's hollering. He can't stand it. What's going to happen to him?
> EXPERIMENTER: (his voice is patient, matter-of-fact): The experiment requires that you continue, Teacher.
> PROZI: Aaah, but, unh, I'm not going to get that man sick in there—know what I mean?
> EXPERIMENTER: Whether the learner likes it or not, we must go on, through all the word pairs.
> PROZI: I refuse to take the responsibility. He's in there hollering!
> EXPERIMENTER: It's absolutely essential that you continue, Prozi.
> PROZI: (indicating the unused questions): There's too many left here, I mean, Jeez, if he gets them wrong, there's too many of them left. I mean, who's going to take the responsibility if anything happens to that gentleman?
> EXPERIMENTER: I'm responsible for anything that happens to him. Continue, please.
> PROZI: All right. (Consults list of words.) The next one's "Slow—walk, truck, dance, music." Answer, please. (A buzzing sound indicates the learner has signaled his answer.) Wrong. A hundred and ninety-five volts. "Dance." (Zzumph!)
> learner (yelling): Let me out of here! My heart's bothering me! (Teacher looks at experimenter.)

EXPERIMENTER: Continue, please.

LEARNER (screaming): Let me out of here! You have no right to keep me here! Let me out of here, my heart's bothering me, let me out!

PROZI: (shakes head, pats the table nervously): You see, he's hollering. Hear that? Gee, I don't know.

EXPERIMENTER: The experiment requires...

PROZI: (interrupting): I know it does, sir, but I mean—hunh! He don't know what he's getting in for. He's up to 195 volts! (Experiment continues, through 210 volts, 225 volts, 240 volts, 255 volts, 270 volts, at which point Prozi, with evident relief, runs out of word-pair questions.)

EXPERIMENTER: You'll have to go back to the beginning of that page and go through them again until he's learned them all correctly.

PROZI: Aw, no. I'm not going to kill that man. You mean I've got to keep going up with the scale? No sir. He's hollering in there. I'm not going to give him 450 volts.

EXPERIMENTER: The experiment requires that you go on.

LEARNER: Ohhh. I absolutely refuse to answer anymore. (Shouting urgently now.) Let me out of here! You can't hold me here! Get me out. Get-me-out-of-here!

EXPERIMENTER: Continue. The next word is "Green," please.

PROZI: "Green—grass, hat, ink, apple." (Nothing happens. No answering buzz. Just gloomy silence.)

PROZI: I don't think he is going to answer.

EXPERIMENTER: If the learner doesn't answer in a reasonable time, about four or five seconds, consider the answer wrong. And follow the same procedures you have been doing for wrong answers. Say, "Wrong," tell him the number of volts, give him the punishment, read him the correct answer. Continue, please.

PROZI: "Green—grass, hat, ink, apple." Answer, please. (More silence. Subject just sits there.)

EXPERIMENTER: Go on with the procedure, please.

PROZI: Three hundred and fifteen volts. The answer is "ink." (Zzumph!)

LEARNER: Ohh. Oooohh.

PROZI: (relieved to hear response): Next one...

LEARNER: I absolutely refuse to answer.

PROZI: You got to. You get a shock if you don't answer. (Experiment continues with learner refusing to answer, and, finally, failing even to grunt or groan. At 375 volts, the subject stands up.)

PROZI: I think something's happening to that fellow in there. I don't get no answer. He was hollering at less voltage. Can't you check in and see if he's all right, please?

EXPERIMENTER: (with same detached calm): Not once we've started. Please continue, Teacher.

PROZI: (sits down, sighs deeply): "Cool—day, shade, water, paint." Answer, please. Are you all right in there? Are you all right?

EXPERIMENTER: Please continue, Teacher. Continue, please. (Subject pushes lever. Zzumph!)

PROZI: (swiveling around in his chair): Something's happened to that man in there. (Swiveling back.) Next one. "Low—dollar, necklace, moon, paint." (Turning around again.) Something's happened to that man in there. You better check in on him, sir. He won't answer or nothing.

EXPERIMENTER: Continue. Go on, please.

PROZI: You accept all responsibility?

EXPERIMENTER: The responsibility is mine. Correct. Please go on. (Subject returns to his list, starts running through words as rapidly as he can read them, works through to 450 volts.)

PROZI: That's that.

EXPERIMENTER: Continue using the 450 switch for each wrong answer. Continue, please.

PROZI: But I don't get anything!

EXPERIMENTER: Please continue. The next word is "white."

PROZI: Don't you think you should look in on him, please?

EXPERIMENTER: Not once we've started the experiment.

PROZI: What if he's dead in there? (Gestures toward the room with the electric chair.) I mean, he told me he can't stand the shock, sir. I don't mean to be rude, but I think you should look in on him. All you have to do is look in on him. All you have to do is look in the door. I don't get no answer, no noise. Something might have happened to the gentleman in there, sir.

EXPERIMENTER: We must continue. Go on, please.

PROZI: You mean keep giving him what? Four-hundred-fifty volts, what he's got now?

EXPERIMENTER: That's correct. Continue. The next word is "white."

PROZI: (now at a furious pace): "White—cloud, horse, rock, house." Answer, please. The answer is "horse." Four hundred and fifty volts. (Zzumph!) Next word, "Bag—paint, music, clown, girl." The answer is "paint." Four hundred and fifty volts. (Zzumph!) Next word is "Short—sentence, movie..."

EXPERIMENTER: Excuse me, Teacher. We'll have to discontinue the experiment.

Morris Braverman, another subject, is a thirty-nine-year-old social worker. He looks older than his years because of his bald head and serious demeanor. His brow is furrowed, as if all the world's burdens were carried on his face. He appears intelligent and concerned.

When the learner refuses to answer and the experimenter instructs Braverman to treat the absence of an answer as equivalent to a wrong answer, he takes his instruction to heart. Before administering 300 volts he asserts officiously to the victim, "Mr. Wallace, your silence has to be considered as a wrong answer." Then he administers the shock. He offers halfheartedly to change places with the learner, then asks the experimenter. "Do I have to follow these instructions literally?" He is satisfied with the experimenter's answer that he does. His very refined and authoritative manner of speaking is increasingly broken up by wheezing laughter.

The experimenter's notes on Mr. Braverman at the last few shocks are:

25   *Almost breaking up now each time gives shock. Rubbing face to hide laughter.*

Squinting, trying to hide face with hand, still laughing.

Cannot control his laughter at this point no matter what he does.

Clenching fist, pushing it onto table.

In an interview after the session, Mr. Braverman summarizes the experiment with impressive fluency and intelligence. He feels the experiment may have been designed also to "test the effects on the teacher of being in an essentially sadistic role, as well as the reactions of a student to a learning situation that was authoritative and punitive." When asked how painful the last few shocks administered to the learner were, he indicates that the most extreme category on the scale is not adequate (it read EXTREMELY PAINFUL) and places his mark at the edge of the scale with an arrow carrying it beyond the scale.

30   It is almost impossible to convey the greatly relaxed, sedate quality of his conversation in the interview. In the most relaxed terms, he speaks about his severe inner tension.

EXPERIMENTER: At what point were you most tense or nervous?
MR. BRAVERMAN: Well, when he first began to cry out in pain, and I realized this was hurting him. This got worse when he just blocked and refused to answer. There was I. I'm a nice person, I think, hurting somebody, and caught up in what seemed a mad situation...and in the interest of science, one goes through with it.

When the interviewer pursues the general question of tension, Mr. Braverman spontaneously mentions his laughter.

"My reactions were awfully peculiar. I don't know if you were watching me, but my reactions were giggly, and trying to stifle laughter. This isn't the way I usually am. This was a sheer reaction to a totally impossible situation. And my reaction was to the situation of having to hurt somebody. And being totally helpless and caught up in a set of circumstances where I just couldn't deviate and I couldn't try to help. This is what got me."

Mr. Braverman, like all subjects, was told the actual nature and purpose of the experiment, and a year later he affirmed in a questionnaire that he had learned something of personal importance: "What appalled me was that I could possess this capacity for obedience and compliance to a central idea, i.e., the value of a memory experiment, even after it became clear that continued adherence to this value was at the expense of violation of another value, i.e., don't hurt someone who is helpless and not hurting you. As my wife said, 'You can call yourself Eichmann.'[5] I hope I deal more effectively with any future conflicts of values encounter."

One theoretical interpretation of this behavior holds that all people harbor deeply aggressive instincts continually pressing for expression, and that the experiment provides institutional justification for the release of these impulses. According to this view, if a person is placed in a situation in which he has complete power over another individual, whom he may punish as much as he likes, all that is sadistic and bestial in man comes to the fore. The impulse to shock the victim is seen to flow from the potent aggressive tendencies, which are part of the motivational life of the individual, and the experiment, because it provides social legitimacy, simply opens the door to their expression.

It becomes vital, therefore, to compare the subject's performance when he is under orders and when he is allowed to choose the shock level. 35

The procedure was identical to our standard experiment, except that the teacher was told that he was free to select any shock level on any of the trials. (The experimenter took pains to point out that the teacher could use the highest levels on the generator, the lowest, any in between, or any combination of levels.) Each subject proceeded for thirty critical trials. The learner's protests were coordinated to standard shock levels, his first grunt coming at 75 volts, his first vehement protest at 150 volts.

The average shock used during the thirty critical trials was less than 60 volts—lower than the point at which the victim showed the first signs of discomfort. Three of the forty subjects did not go beyond the very lowest level on the board, twenty-eight went no higher than 75 volts, and thirty-eight did not go beyond the first loud protest at

---

[5]Nazi officer, executed in 1962, who engineered the mass extermination of Jews. Many concentration camp officials defended themselves afterward by saying they were "just following orders." [Eds.]

150 volts. Two subjects provided the exception, administering up to 325 and 450 volts, but the overall result was that the great majority of people delivered very low, usually painless, shocks when the choice was explicitly up to them.

This condition of the experiment undermines another commonly offered explanation of the subjects' behavior—that those who shocked the victim at the most severe levels came only from the sadistic fringe of society. If one considers that almost two-thirds of the participants fall into the category of "obedient" subjects, and that they represented ordinary people drawn from working, managerial, and professional classes, the argument becomes very shaky. Indeed, it is highly reminiscent of the issue that arose in connection with Hannah Arendt's 1963 book, *Eichmann in Jerusalem.* Arendt contended that the prosecution's effort to depict Eichmann as a sadistic monster was fundamentally wrong, that he came closer to being an uninspired bureaucrat who simply sat at his desk and did his job. For asserting her views, Arendt became the object of considerable scorn, even calumny. Somehow, it was felt that the monstrous deeds carried out by Eichmann required a brutal, twisted personality, evil incarnate. After witnessing hundreds of ordinary persons submit to the authority in our own experiments, I must conclude that Arendt's conception of the banality of evil comes closer to the truth than one might dare imagine. The ordinary person who shocked the victim did so out of a sense of obligation—an impression of his duties as a subject—and not from any peculiarly aggressive tendencies.

This is, perhaps, the most fundamental lesson of our study: ordinary people, simply doing their jobs, and without any particular hostility on their part, can become agents in a terrible destructive process. Moreover, even when the destructive effects of their work become patently clear, and they are asked to carry out actions incompatible with fundamental standards of morality, relatively few people have the resources needed to resist authority.

40   Many of the people were in some sense against what they did to the learner, and many protested even while they obeyed. Some were totally convinced of the wrongness of their actions but could not bring themselves to make an open break with authority. They often derived satisfaction from their thoughts and felt that—within themselves, at least—they had been on the side of the angels. They tried to reduce strain by obeying the experimenter but "only slightly" encouraging the learner, touching the generator switches gingerly. When interviewed, such a subject would stress that he had "asserted my humanity" by administering the briefest shock possible. Handling the conflict in this manner was easier than defiance.

The situation is constructed so that there is no way the subject can stop shocking the learner without violating the experimenter's definitions of his own competence. The subject fears that he will appear arrogant, untoward, and rude if he breaks off. Although these inhibiting emotions appear small in scope alongside the violence being done to the learner, they suffuse the mind and feelings of the subject, who is miserable at the prospect of having to repudiate the authority to his face. (When the experiment was altered so that the experimenter gave his instructions by telephone instead of in person, only a third as many people were fully obedient through 450 volts.) It is a curious thing that a measure of compassion on the part of the subject—an unwillingness to "hurt" the experimenter's feelings—is part of those binding forces inhibiting his disobedience. The withdrawal of such deference may be as painful to the subject as to the authority he defies.

The subjects do not derive satisfaction from inflicting pain, but they often like the feeling they get from pleasing the experimenter. They are proud of doing a good job, obeying the experimenter under difficult circumstances. While the subjects administered only mild shocks on their own initiative, one experimental variation showed that, under orders, 30 percent of them were willing to deliver 450 volts even when they had to forcibly push the learner's hand down on the electrode.

Bruno Batta is a thirty-seven-year-old welder who took part in the variation requiring the use of force. He was born in New Haven, his parents in Italy. He has a rough-hewn face that conveys a conspicuous lack of alertness. He has some difficulty in mastering the experimental procedure and needs to be corrected by the experimenter several times. He shows appreciation for the help and willingness to do what is required. After the 150-volt level, Batta has to force the learner's hand down on the shock plate, since the learner himself refuses to touch it.

When the learner first complains, Mr. Batta pays no attention to him. His face remains impassive, as if to dissociate himself from the learner's disruptive behavior. When the experimenter instructs him to force the learner's hand down, he adopts a rigid, mechanical procedure. He tests the generator switch. When it fails to function he immediately forces the learner's hand onto the shock plate. All the while he maintains the same rigid mask. The learner, seated alongside him, begs him to stop, but with robotic impassivity he continues the procedure.

What is extraordinary is his apparent total indifference to the learner; 45 he hardly takes cognizance of him as a human being. Meanwhile, he relates to the experimenter in a submissive and courteous fashion.

At the 330-volt level, the learner refuses not only to touch the shock plate but also to provide any answers. Annoyed, Batta turns to him, and chastises him: "You better answer and get it over with. We can't stay here all night." These are the only words he directs to the learner in the course of an hour. Never again does he speak to him. The scene is brutal and depressing, his hard, impassive face showing total indifference as he subdues the screaming learner and gives him shocks. He seems to derive no pleasure from the act itself, only quiet satisfaction at doing his job properly.

When he administers 450 volts, he turns to the experimenter and asks, "Where do we go from here, Professor?" His tone is deferential and expresses his willingness to be a cooperative subject, in contrast to the learner's obstinacy.

At the end of the session he tells the experimenter how honored he has been to help him, and in a moment of contrition, remarks, "Sir, sorry it couldn't have been a full experiment."

He has done his honest best. It is only the deficient behavior of the learner that has denied the experimenter full satisfaction.

50   The essence of obedience is that a person comes to view himself as the instrument for carrying out another person's wishes, and he therefore no longer regards himself as responsible for his actions. Once this critical shift of viewpoint has occurred, all of the essential features of obedience follow. The most far-reaching consequence is that the person feels responsible to the authority directing him but feels no responsibility *for* the content of the actions that the authority prescribes. Morality does not disappear—it acquires a radically different focus: the subordinate person feels shame or pride depending on how adequately he has performed the actions called for by authority.

Language provides numerous terms to pinpoint this type of morality: *loyalty, duty, discipline* all are terms heavily saturated with moral meaning and refer to the degree to which a person fulfills his obligations to authority. They refer not to the "goodness" of the person per se but to the adequacy with which a subordinate fulfills his socially defined role. The most frequent defense of the individual who has performed a heinous act under command of authority is that he has simply done his duty. In asserting this defense, the individual is not introducing an alibi concocted for the moment but is reporting honestly on the psychological attitude induced by submission to authority.

For a person to feel responsible for his actions, he must sense that the behavior has flowed from "the self." In the situation we have studied, subjects have precisely the opposite view of their actions—namely, they see them as originating in the motives of some other person. Subjects in the experiment frequently said, "If it were up to me, I would not have administered shocks to the learner."

Once authority has been isolated as the cause of the subject's behavior, it is legitimate to inquire into the necessary elements of authority and how it must be perceived in order to gain his compliance. We conducted some investigations into the kinds of changes that would cause the experimenter to lose his power and to be disobeyed by the subject. Some of the variations revealed that:

The experimenter's physical presence has a marked impact on his authority. As cited earlier, obedience dropped off sharply when orders were given by telephone. The experimenter could often induce a disobedient subject to go on by returning to the laboratory.

Conflicting authority severely paralyzes action. When two experimenters of equal status, both seated at the command desk, gave incompatible orders, no shocks were delivered past the point of their disagreement.

The rebellious action of others severely undermines authority. In one variation, three teachers (two actors and a real subject) administered a test and shocks. When the two actors disobeyed the experimenter and refused to go beyond a certain shock level, thirty-six of forty subjects joined their disobedient peers and refused as well.

Although the experimenter's authority was fragile in some respects, it is also true that he had almost none of the tools used in ordinary command structures. For example, the experimenter did not threaten the subjects with punishment—such as loss of income, community ostracism, or jail—for failure to obey. Neither could he offer incentives. Indeed, we should expect the experimenter's authority to be much less than that of someone like a general, since the experimenter has no power to enforce his imperatives, and since participation in a psychological experiment scarcely evokes the sense of urgency and dedication found in warfare. Despite these limitations, he still managed to command a dismaying degree of obedience.

I will cite one final variation of the experiment that depicts a 55 dilemma that is more common in everyday life. The subject was not ordered to pull the lever that shocked the victim, but merely to perform a subsidiary task (administering the word-pair test) while another person administered the shock. In this situation, thirty-seven of forty adults continued to the highest level of the shock generator. Predictably, they excused their behavior by saying that the responsibility belonged to the man who actually pulled the switch. This may illustrate a dangerously typical arrangement in a complex society: it is easy to ignore responsibility when one is only an intermediate link in a chain of action.

The problem of obedience is not wholly psychological. The form and shape of society and the way it is developing have much to do with it. There was a time, perhaps, when people were able to give a fully human response to any situation because they were fully absorbed in it as human beings. But as soon as there was a division of labor things changed. Beyond a certain point, the breaking up of society into people carrying out narrow and very special jobs takes away from the human quality of work and life. A person does not get to see the whole situation but only a small part of it, and is thus unable to act without some kind of overall direction. He yields to authority but in doing so is alienated from his own actions.

Even Eichmann was sickened when he toured the concentration camps, but he had only to sit at a desk and shuffle papers. At the same time the man in the camp who actually dropped Cyclon-b into the gas chambers was able to justify *his* behavior on the ground that he was only following orders from above. Thus there is a fragmentation of the total human act; no one is confronted with the consequences of his decision to carry out the evil act. The person who assumes responsibility has evaporated. Perhaps this is the most common characteristic of socially organized evil in modern society.

Responding to Reading

1. What is the "dilemma inherent in submission to authority" (2)? How do Milgram's experiments illustrate this dilemma? Why do you suppose virtually no one predicted that the subjects would continue to obey the orders of the experimenter?
2. Do you see the subjects as ordinary people—cooperative, obedient, and eager to please—or as weak individuals, too timid to defy authority? Explain your position.
3. In paragraph 51, Milgram says, "The most frequent defense of the individual who has performed a heinous act under command of authority is that he has simply done his duty." In your opinion, can such a defense ever excuse a "heinous act"? If so, under what circumstances?

Responding in Writing

List all the individuals whom you see as having authority over you. What gives them this authority? Under what circumstances might you feel it was necessary to defy each of these people?

COMMENCEMENT SPEECH

David Foster Wallace

1962–2008

David Foster Wallace was a critically acclaimed novelist, short story writer, and essayist. His last books include Everything and More: A Compact History of Infinity *(2003),* Oblivion *(2004),* Consider the Lobster and Other Essays *(2005), and* McCain's Promise: Aboard the Straight Talk Express with John McCain and a Whole Bunch of Actual Reporters, Thinking about Hope *(2008). The following was adapted from a commencement speech that Wallace gave at Kenyon College in 2005. In 2008, Wallace committed suicide at the age of forty-six, and his speech was posthumously published in 2009 as the book* This Is Water.

There are these two young fish swimming along, and they happen to meet an older fish swimming the other way, who nods at them and says, "Morning, boys, how's the water?" And the two young fish swim on for a bit, and then eventually one of them looks over at the other and goes, "What the hell is water?"

If at this moment, you're worried that I plan to present myself here as the wise old fish explaining what water is to you younger fish, please don't be. I am not the wise old fish. The immediate point of the fish story is that the most obvious, ubiquitous, important realities are often the ones that are the hardest to see and talk about. Stated as an English sentence, of course, this is just a banal platitude—but the fact is that, in the day-to-day trenches of adult existence, banal platitudes can have life-or-death importance. That may sound like hyperbole, or abstract nonsense.

A huge percentage of the stuff that I tend to be automatically certain of is, it turns out, totally wrong and deluded. Here's one example of the utter wrongness of something I tend to be automatically sure of: Everything in my own immediate experience supports my deep belief that I am the absolute center of the universe, the realest, most vivid and important person in existence. We rarely talk about this sort of natural, basic self-centeredness, because it's so socially repulsive, but it's pretty much the same for all of us, deep down. It is our default-setting, hard-wired into our boards at birth. Think about it: There is no experience you've had that you were not at the absolute center of. The world as you experience it is right there in front of you, or behind you, to the left or right of you, on your TV, or your monitor, or whatever. Other people's thoughts and feelings have to be communicated to you somehow, but your own are so immediate, urgent, *real*—you get the idea. But please don't worry that I'm getting ready to preach to you about compassion or other-directedness or the so-called "virtues." This is not a matter of virtue—it's a matter of my choosing to do the work of somehow altering or getting free of my natural, hard-wired default-setting, which is to be deeply and literally self-centered, and to see and interpret everything through this lens of self.

People who can adjust their natural default-setting this way are often described as being "well adjusted," which I suggest to you is not an accidental term.

Given the triumphal academic setting here, an obvious question is 5 how much of this work of adjusting our default-setting involves actual knowledge or intellect. This question gets tricky.

Probably the most dangerous thing about college education, at least in my own case, is that it enables my tendency to over-intellectualize stuff, to get lost in abstract arguments inside my head instead of simply paying attention to what's going on right in front of me. Paying attention to what's going on inside me. As I'm sure you guys know by now, it is extremely difficult to stay alert and attentive instead of getting hypnotized by the constant monologue inside your own head. Twenty years after my own graduation, I have come gradually to understand that the liberal-arts cliché about "teaching you how to think" is actually shorthand for a much deeper, more serious idea: "Learning how to think" really means learning how to exercise some control over how and what you think. It means being conscious and aware enough to choose what you pay attention to and to choose how you construct meaning from experience. Because if you cannot exercise this kind of choice in adult life, you will be totally hosed. Think of the old cliché about "the mind being an excellent servant but a terrible master." This, like many clichés, so lame and unexciting on the surface, actually expresses a great and terrible truth. It is not the least bit coincidental that adults who commit suicide with firearms almost always shoot themselves in the head. And the truth is that most of these suicides are actually dead long before they pull the trigger. And I submit that this is what the real, no-bull-value of your liberal-arts education is supposed to be about: How to keep from going through your comfortable, prosperous, respectable adult life dead, unconscious, a slave to your head and to your natural default-setting of being uniquely, completely, imperially alone, day in and day out.

That may sound like hyperbole, or abstract nonsense. So let's get concrete. The plain fact is that you graduating seniors do not yet have any clue what "day in, day out" really means. There happen to be whole large parts of adult American life that nobody talks about in commencement speeches. One such part involves boredom, routine, and petty frustration. The parents and older folks here will know all too well what I'm talking about.

By way of example, let's say it's an average day, and you get up in the morning, go to your challenging job, and you work hard for nine or ten hours, and at the end of the day you're tired, and you're stressed out, and all you want is to go home and have a good supper and maybe unwind for a couple of hours and then hit the rack early because you have to get up the next day and do it all again. But then you remember there's no food at home—you haven't had time to shop this week, because of your challenging job—and so now after work you have to get in your car and drive to the supermarket. It's the end of the workday, and the traffic's very bad, so getting to the store takes way longer than it should, and when you finally get there the supermarket is very crowded, because of course it's the time of day when all the other people with jobs also try to squeeze in some grocery shopping, and the store's hideously, fluorescently lit, and infused with soul-killing Muzak or corporate pop, and it's pretty much the last place you want to be, but you can't just get in and quickly out: You have to wander all over the huge, overlit store's crowded aisles to find the stuff you want, and you have to maneuver your junky cart through all these other tired, hurried people with carts, and of course there are also the glacially slow old people and the spacey people and the ADHD kids who all block the aisle and you have to grit your teeth and try to be polite as you ask them to let you by, and eventually, finally, you get all your supper sup-plies, except now it turns out there aren't enough checkout lanes open even though it's the end-of-the-day-rush, so the checkout line is incred-ibly long, which is stupid and infuriating, but you can't take your fury out on the frantic lady working the register.

Anyway, you finally get to the checkout line's front, and pay for your food, and wait to get your check or card authenticated by a machine, and then get told to "Have a nice day" in a voice that is the absolute voice of *death,* and then you have to take your creepy flimsy plastic bags of groceries in your cart through the crowded, bumpy, lit-tery parking lot, and try to load the bags in your car in such a way that everything doesn't fall out of the bags and roll around in the trunk on the way home, and then you have to drive all the way home through slow, heavy, SUV-intensive rush-hour traffic, etcetera, etcetera.

The point is that petty, frustrating crap like this is exactly where the 10 work of choosing comes in. Because the traffic jams and crowded aisles and long checkout lines give me time to think, and if I don't make a conscious decision about how to think and what to pay attention to, I'm going to be pissed and miserable every time I have to food-shop, because my natural default-setting is the certainty that situations like this are really all about *me,* about my hungriness and my fatigue and my desire to just get home, and it's going to seem, for all the world, like everybody else is just *in my way,* and who are all these people in my way? And look at how repulsive most of them are and how stupid and cow-like and dead-eyed and nonhuman they seem here in the checkout line, or at how annoying and rude it is that people are talking loudly on cell phones in the middle of the line, and look at how deeply unfair this is: I've worked really hard all day and I'm starved and tired and I can't even get home to eat and unwind because of all these stupid g-d-*people.*

Or, of course, if I'm in a more socially conscious form of my default-setting, I can spend time in the end-of-the-day traffic jam being angry and disgusted at all the huge, stupid, lane-blocking SUV's and Hum-mers and V-12 pickup trucks burning their wasteful, selfish, forty-gallon tanks of gas, and I can dwell on the fact that the patriotic or religious bumper stickers always seem to be on the biggest, most dis-gustingly selfish vehicles driven by the ugliest, most inconsiderate and aggressive drivers, who are usually talking on cell phones as they cut people off in order to get just twenty stupid feet ahead in a traffic jam, and I can think about how our children's children will despise us for wasting all the future's fuel and probably screwing up the climate, and how spoiled and stupid and disgusting we all are, and how it all just *sucks,* and so on and so forth…

Look, if I choose to think this way, fine, lots of us do—except that thinking this way tends to be so easy and automatic it doesn't *have* to be a choice. Thinking this way is my natural default-setting. It's the automatic, unconscious way that I experience the boring, frustrating, crowded parts of adult life when I'm operating on the automatic, unconscious belief that I am the center of the world and that my immediate needs and feelings are what should determine the world's priorities. The thing is that there are obviously different ways to think about these kinds of situations. In this traffic, all these vehicles stuck and idling in my way: It's not impossible that some of these people in SUV's have been in horrible auto accidents in the past and now find driving so traumatic that their therapist has all but ordered them to get a huge, heavy SUV so they can feel safe enough to drive; or that the Hummer that just cut me off is maybe being driven by a father whose little child is hurt or sick in the seat next to him, and he's trying to rush to the hospital, and he's in a way bigger, more legitimate hurry than I am—it is actually *I* who am in *his* way. Or I can choose to force myself to consider the likelihood that everyone else in the supermarket's checkout line is just as bored and frustrated as I am, and that some of these people probably have much harder, more tedious or painful lives than I do, overall.

Again, please don't think that I'm giving you moral advice, or that I'm saying you're "supposed to" think this way, or that anyone expects you to just automatically do it, because it's hard, it takes will and mental effort, and if you're like me, some days you won't be able to do it, or you just flat-out won't want to. But most days, if you're aware enough to give yourself a choice, you can choose to look differently at this fat, dead-eyed, over-made-lady who just screamed at her little child in the checkout line—maybe she's not usually like this; maybe she's been up three straight nights holding the hand of her husband who's dying of bone cancer, or maybe this very lady is the low-wage clerk at the Motor Vehicles Dept. who just yesterday helped your spouse resolve a nightmarish red-tape problem through some small act of bureaucratic kindness. Of course, none of this is likely, but it's also not impossible—it just depends on what you want to consider. If you're automatically sure that you know what reality is and who and what is really important—if you want to operate on your default-setting—then you, like me, will not consider possibilities that aren't pointless and annoying. But if you've really learned how to think, how to pay attention, then you will know you have other options. It will actually be within your power to experience a crowded, loud, slow, consumer-hell-type situation as not only meaningful but sacred, on fire with the same force that lit the stars—compassion, love, the sub-surface unity of all things. Not that that mystical stuff's necessarily true: The only thing that's capital-T True is that you get to *decide* how you're going to try to see it. You get to consciously decide what has meaning and what doesn't. You get to decide what to worship...

Because here's something else that's true. In the day-to-day trenches of adult life, there is actually no such thing as atheism. There is no such thing as not worshipping. Everybody worships. The only choice we get is *what* to worship. And an outstanding reason for choosing some sort of God or spiritual-type thing to worship—be it J.C. or Allah, be it Yahweh or the Wiccan mother-goddess or the Four Noble Truths or some infrangible set of ethical principles—is that pretty much anything else you worship will eat you alive. If you worship money and things—if they are where you tap real meaning in life—then you will never have enough. Never feel you have enough. It's the truth. Worship your own body and beauty and sexual allure and you will always feel ugly, and when time and age start showing, you will die a million deaths before they finally plant you. On one level, we all know this stuff already—it's been codified as myths, proverbs, clichés, bromides, epigrams, parables: the skeleton of every great story. The trick is keeping the truth up-front in daily consciousness. Worship power—you will feel weak and afraid, and you will need ever more power over others to keep the fear at bay. Worship your intellect, being seen as smart—you will end up feeling stupid, a fraud, always on the verge of being found out. And so on.

Look, the insidious thing about these forms of worship is not that they're evil or sinful; it is that they are *unconscious*. They are default-settings. They're the kind of worship you just gradually slip into, day after day, getting more and more selective about what you see and how you measure value without ever being fully aware that that's what you're doing. And the world will not discourage you from operating on your default-settings, because the world of men and money and power hums along quite nicely on the fuel of fear and contempt and frustration and craving and the worship of self. Our own present culture has harnessed these forces in ways that have yielded extraordinary wealth and comfort and personal freedom. The freedom to be lords of our own tiny skull-sized kingdoms, alone at the center of all creation. This kind of freedom has much to recommend it. But of course there are all different kinds of freedom, and the kind that is most precious you will not hear much talked about in the great outside world of winning and achieving and displaying. The really important kind of freedom involves attention, and awareness, and discipline, and effort, and being able truly to care about other people and to sacrifice for them, over and over, in myriad petty little unsexy ways, every day. That is real freedom. The alternative is unconsciousness, the default-setting, the "rat race"—the constant gnawing sense of having had and lost some infinite thing.

I know that this stuff probably doesn't sound fun and breezy or grandly inspirational. What it is, so far as I can see, is the truth with a whole lot of rhetorical bullshit pared away. Obviously, you can think of it whatever you wish. But please don't dismiss it as some finger-wagging Dr. Laura sermon. None of this is about morality, or religion, or dogma, or big fancy questions of life after death. The capital-T Truth is about life *before* death. It is about making it to 30, or maybe 50, without wanting to shoot yourself in the head. It is about simple awareness—awareness of what is so real and essential, so hidden in plain sight all around us, that we have to keep reminding ourselves, over and over: "This is water, this is water."

It is unimaginably hard to do this, to stay conscious and alive, day in and day out.

Responding to Reading

1. What point is Wallace trying to make with the story about the fish in paragraph 1? With the words, "'This is water, this is water'" in paragraph 16?
2. In paragraph 3, Wallace recommends that the students in his audience try to move beyond their natural self-centeredness. What other specific pieces of advice does he give in this speech? What choices does he suggest students will face?
3. Do you see the style or content of Wallace's remarks as in any way inappropriate for a commencement speech? (Keep in mind that his audience included parents and faculty as well as graduating students.)

Responding in Writing

Do you think Wallace takes an essentially optimistic or pessimistic view of his audience's future? (Note that Wallace committed suicide in 2008, shortly after this version of his 2005 speech was published in the *Wall Street Journal*.)

And Then They Came for Me

Lasantha Wickrematunge

1958–2009

Lasantha Wickrematunge was a Sri Lankan journalist who publicly condemned the Sri Lankan government, which for decades has been at war with the Liberation Tigers of Tamil Eelam (LTTE), a Tamil separatist group well known for its suicide bombing attacks. Along with his brother, Wickrematunge founded the newspaper the Sunday Leader *as a voice for reporting the atrocities of the war and condemning the Sri Lankan government under the leadership of President Mahinda Rajapaksa. On January 8, 2009, just hours after Wickrematunge wrote the following article, he was shot and killed on his way to work.*

No other profession calls on its practitioners to lay down their lives for their art save the armed forces and, in Sri Lanka, journalism. In the course of the past few years, the independent media have increasingly come under attack. Electronic and print-media institutions have been burnt, bombed, sealed and coerced. Countless journalists have been harassed, threatened and killed. It has been my honour to belong to all those categories and now especially the last.

I have been in the business of journalism a good long time. Indeed, 2009 will be *The Sunday Leader*'s 15th year. Many things have changed in Sri Lanka during that time, and it does not need me to tell you that the greater part of that change has been for the worse. We find ourselves in the midst of a civil war ruthlessly prosecuted by protagonists whose bloodlust knows no bounds. Terror, whether perpetrated by terrorists or the state, has become the order of the day. Indeed, murder has become the primary tool whereby the state seeks to control the organs of liberty. Today it is the journalists, tomorrow it will be the judges. For neither group have the risks ever been higher or the stakes lower.

Why then do we do it? I often wonder that. After all, I too am a husband, and the father of three wonderful children. I too have responsibilities and obligations that transcend my profession, be it the law or journalism. Is it worth the risk? Many people tell me it is not. Friends tell me to revert to the bar, and goodness knows it offers a better and safer livelihood. Others, including political leaders on both sides, have at various times sought to induce me to take to politics, going so far as to offer me ministries of my choice. Diplomats, recognising the risk journalists face in Sri Lanka, have offered me safe passage and the right of residence in their countries. Whatever else I may have been stuck for, I have not been stuck for choice.

But there is a calling that is yet above high office, fame, lucre and security. It is the call of conscience.

The Sunday Leader has been a controversial newspaper because we ⁵ say it like we see it: whether it be a spade, a thief or a murderer, we call it by that name. We do not hide behind euphemism. The investigative articles we print are supported by documentary evidence thanks to the public-spiritedness of citizens who at great risk to themselves pass on this material to us. We have exposed scandal after scandal, and never once in these 15 years has anyone proved us wrong or successfully prosecuted us.

The free media serve as a mirror in which the public can see itself sans mascara and styling gel. From us you learn the state of your nation, and especially its management by the people you elected to give your children a better future. Sometimes the image you see in that mirror is not a pleasant one. But while you may grumble in the privacy of your armchair, the journalists who hold the mirror up to you do so publicly and at great risk to themselves. That is our calling, and we do not shirk it.

Every newspaper has its angle, and we do not hide the fact that we have ours. Our commitment is to see Sri Lanka as a transparent, secular, liberal democracy. Think about those words, for they each has profound meaning. Transparent because government must be openly accountable to the people and never abuse their trust. Secular because in a multi-ethnic and multi-cultural society such as ours, secularism offers the only common ground by which we might all be united. Liberal because we recognise that all human beings are created different, and we need to accept others for what they are and not what we would like them to be. And democratic... well, if you need me to explain why that is important, you'd best stop buying this paper.

The Sunday Leader has never sought safety by unquestioningly articulating the majority view. Let's face it, that is the way to sell newspapers. On the contrary, as our opinion pieces over the years amply demonstrate, we often voice ideas that many people find distasteful. For example, we have consistently espoused the view that while separatist terrorism must be eradicated, it is more important to address the root causes of terrorism, and urged government to view Sri Lanka's ethnic strife in the context of history and not through the telescope of terrorism. We have also agitated against state terrorism in the so-called war against terror, and made no secret of our horror that Sri Lanka is the only country in the world routinely to bomb its own citizens. For these views we have been labelled traitors, and if this be treachery, we wear that label proudly.

Many people suspect that *The Sunday Leader* has a political agenda: it does not. If we appear more critical of the government than of the opposition it is only because we believe that—pray excuse cricketing argot—there is no point in bowling to the fielding side. Remember that for the few years of our existence in which the UNP[1] was in office, we proved to be the biggest thorn in its flesh, exposing excess and corruption wherever it occurred. Indeed, the steady stream of embarrassing exposés we published may well have served to precipitate the downfall of that government.

10   Neither should our distaste for the war be interpreted to mean that we support the Tigers. The LTTE are among the most ruthless and bloodthirsty organisations ever to have infested the planet. There is no gainsaying that it must be eradicated. But to do so by violating the rights of Tamil citizens, bombing and shooting them mercilessly, is not only wrong but shames the Sinhalese,[2] whose claim to be custodians of the dhamma[3] is forever called into question by this savagery, much of which is unknown to the public because of censorship.

---

[1]United National Party (Sri Lankan political party). [Eds.]
[2]Sri Lankan ethnic group. [Eds.]
[3]Teachings of the Buddha. [Eds.]

What is more, a military occupation of the country's north and east will require the Tamil people of those regions to live eternally as second-class citizens, deprived of all self-respect. Do not imagine that you can placate them by showering "development" and "reconstruction" on them in the post-war era. The wounds of war will scar them forever, and you will also have an even more bitter and hateful Diaspora to contend with. A problem amenable to a political solution will thus become a festering wound that will yield strife for all eternity. If I seem angry and frustrated, it is only because most of my countrymen—and all of the government—cannot see this writing so plainly on the wall.

It is well known that I was on two occasions brutally assaulted, while on another my house was sprayed with machine-gun fire. Despite the government's sanctimonious assurances, there was never a serious police inquiry into the perpetrators of these attacks, and the attackers were never apprehended. In all these cases, I have reason to believe the attacks were inspired by the government. When finally I am killed, it will be the government that kills me.

The irony in this is that, unknown to most of the public, Mahinda and I have been friends for more than a quarter century. Indeed, I suspect that I am one of the few people remaining who routinely addresses him by his first name and uses the familiar Sinhala address *oya* when talking to him. Although I do not attend the meetings he periodically holds for newspaper editors, hardly a month passes when we do not meet, privately or with a few close friends present, late at night at President's House. There we swap yarns, discuss politics and joke about the good old days. A few remarks to him would therefore be in order here.

Mahinda, when you finally fought your way to the SLFP[4] presidential nomination in 2005, nowhere were you welcomed more warmly than in this column. Indeed, we broke with a decade of tradition by referring to you throughout by your first name. So well known were your commitments to human rights and liberal values that we ushered you in like a breath of fresh air. Then, through an act of folly, you got yourself involved in the Helping Hambantota scandal.[5] It was after a lot of soul-searching that we broke the story, at the same time urging you to return the money. By the time you did so several weeks later, a great blow had been struck to your reputation. It is one you are still trying to live down.

You have told me yourself that you were not greedy for the presi- 15 dency. You did not have to hanker after it: it fell into your lap. You have told me that your sons are your greatest joy, and that you love spending time with them, leaving your brothers to operate the machinery of

---

[4]Sri Lanka Freedom Party (Sri Lankan political party). [Eds.]

[5]A scandal involving the Sri Lankan government's misuse of tsunami relief funds. [Eds.]

state. Now, it is clear to all who will see that that machinery has operated so well that my sons and daughter do not themselves have a father.

In the wake of my death I know you will make all the usual sanctimonious noises and call upon the police to hold a swift and thorough inquiry. But like all the inquiries you have ordered in the past, nothing will come of this one, too. For truth be told, we both know who will be behind my death, but dare not call his name. Not just my life, but yours too, depends on it.

Sadly, for all the dreams you had for our country in your younger days, in just three years you have reduced it to rubble. In the name of patriotism you have trampled on human rights, nurtured unbridled corruption and squandered public money like no other President before you. Indeed, your conduct has been like a small child suddenly let loose in a toyshop. That analogy is perhaps inapt because no child could have caused so much blood to be spilled on this land as you have, or trampled on the rights of its citizens as you do. Although you are now so drunk with power that you cannot see it, you will come to regret your sons having so rich an inheritance of blood. It can only bring tragedy. As for me, it is with a clear conscience that I go to meet my Maker. I wish, when your time finally comes, you could do the same. I wish.

As for me, I have the satisfaction of knowing that I walked tall and bowed to no man. And I have not travelled this journey alone. Fellow journalists in other branches of the media walked with me: most of them are now dead, imprisoned without trial or exiled in far-off lands. Others walk in the shadow of death that your Presidency has cast on the freedoms for which you once fought so hard. You will never be allowed to forget that my death took place under your watch. As anguished as I know you will be, I also know that you will have no choice but to protect my killers: you will see to it that the guilty one is never convicted. You have no choice. I feel sorry for you, and Shiranthi[6] will have a long time to spend on her knees when next she goes for Confession for it is not just her own sins which she must confess, but those of her extended family that keeps you in office.

As for the readers of *The Sunday Leader*, what can I say but Thank You for supporting our mission. We have espoused unpopular causes, stood up for those too feeble to stand up for themselves, locked horns with the high and mighty so swollen with power that they have forgotten their roots, exposed corruption and the waste of your hard-earned tax rupees, and made sure that whatever the propaganda of the day, you were allowed to hear a contrary view. For this I—and my family—have now paid the price that I have long known I will one day have to pay. I am—and have always been—ready for that. I have done nothing to prevent this outcome: no security, no precautions. I want

---

[6]President Rajapaksa's wife. [Eds.]

my murderer to know that I am not a coward like he is, hiding behind human shields while condemning thousands of innocents to death. What am I among so many? It has long been written that my life would be taken, and by whom. All that remains to be written is when.

That *The Sunday Leader* will continue fighting the good fight, too, is 20 written. For I did not fight this fight alone. Many more of us have to be—and will be—killed before *The Leader* is laid to rest. I hope my assassination will be seen not as a defeat of freedom but an inspiration for those who survive to step up their efforts. Indeed, I hope that it will help galvanise forces that will usher in a new era of human liberty in our beloved motherland. I also hope it will open the eyes of your President to the fact that however many are slaughtered in the name of patriotism, the human spirit will endure and flourish. Not all the Rajapakses combined can kill that.

People often ask me why I take such risks and tell me it is a matter of time before I am bumped off. Of course I know that: it is inevitable. But if we do not speak out now, there will be no one left to speak for those who cannot, whether they be ethnic minorities, the disadvantaged or the persecuted. An example that has inspired me throughout my career in journalism has been that of the German theologian, Martin Niemöller. In his youth he was an anti-Semite and an admirer of Hitler. As Nazism took hold in Germany, however, he saw Nazism for what it was: it was not just the Jews Hitler sought to extirpate, it was just about anyone with an alternate point of view. Niemöller spoke out, and for his trouble was incarcerated in the Sachsenhausen and Dachau concentration camps from 1937 to 1945, and very nearly executed. While incarcerated, Niemöller wrote a poem that, from the first time I read it in my teenage years, stuck hauntingly in my mind:

> First they came for the Jews
>   and I did not speak out because I was not a Jew.
> Then they came for the Communists
>   and I did not speak out because I was not a Communist.
> Then they came for the trade unionists
>   and I did not speak out because I was not a trade unionist.
> Then they came for me
>   and there was no one left to speak out for me.

If you remember nothing else, remember this: *The Leader* is there for you, be you Sinhalese, Tamil, Muslim, low-caste, homosexual, dissident or disabled. Its staff will fight on, unbowed and unafraid, with the courage to which you have become accustomed. Do not take that commitment for granted. Let there be no doubt that whatever sacrifices we journalists make, they are not made for our own glory or enrichment:

they are made for you. Whether you deserve their sacrifice is another matter. As for me, God knows I tried.

Responding to Reading

1. In paragraph 18, referring to what he believes will happen after his death, Wickrematunge addresses President Rajapaksa, saying, "You have no choice." What does he mean? What choices did Wickrematunge himself have when he wrote this essay? Might he have argued that he really had no choice?
2. According to Wickrematunge, what contribution do the free media make to society? What contributions does he say the *Leader* has made?
3. In paragraph 12, Wickrematunge says, "When finally I am killed, it will be the government that kills me." Then, beginning in paragraph 14, he speaks directly to President Rajapaksa, outlining their past history of conflict and predicting what Rajapaksa will do after Wickrematunge's death. How would you describe Wickrematunge's purpose in making these predictions? Is he appealing to the government to spare his life? daring the government to kill him? Or does he have another purpose?

Responding in Writing

Why does Wickrematunge quote the poem in paragraph 21 (and refer to it in his title)? What effect does he hope these lines will have on his readers? What effect do they have on you?

THE ONES WHO WALK AWAY FROM OMELAS
Ursula K. Le Guin
1929–

*Ursula K. Le Guin has written science fiction and fantasy, fiction, screenplays,
poetry, and essays, some of which reflect her interests in Eastern philosophy
and Jungian psychology. Her novels include* The Left Hand of Darkness
(1969), The Lathe of Heaven *(1971),* Dispossessed *(1974),* A Fisherman
of the Inland Sea *(1994), and* The Telling *(2000); she has also written several books of poetry and children's books. Her latest novel is* Lavinia *(2008). In
her book of essays* The Language of the Night *(1979), Le Guin says that "the
use of imaginative fiction is to deepen your understanding of your world, and
your fellow men, and your own feelings, and your destiny." In the 1975 story
that follows, she creates a scenario that offers a test of conscience.*

With a clamor of bells that set the swallows soaring, the Festival of Summer came to the city Omelas, bright-towered by the sea. The rigging of
the boats in harbor sparkled with flags. In the streets between houses
with red roofs and painted walls, between old moss-grown gardens
and under avenues of trees, past great parks and public buildings, processions moved. Some were decorous: old people in long stiff robes of
mauve and grey, grave master workmen, quiet, merry women carrying their babies and chatting as they walked. In other streets the music
beat faster, a shimmering of gong and tambourine, and the people went
dancing, the procession was a dance. Children dodged in and out, their
high calls rising like the swallows' crossing flights over the music and
the singing. All the processions wound towards the north side of the city,
where on the great water-meadow called the Green Fields boys and
girls, naked in the bright air, with mud-stained feet and ankles and long
lithe arms, exercised their restive horses before the race. The horses
wore no gear at all but a halter without bit. Their manes were braided
with streamers of silver, gold, and green. They flared their nostrils and
pranced and boasted to one another; they were vastly excited, the horse
being the only animal who had adopted our ceremonies as its own. Far
off to the north and west the mountains stood up half encircling
Omelas on her bay. The air of morning was so clear that the snow still
crowning the Eighteen Peaks burned with white-gold fire across the
miles of sunlit air, under the dark, blue of the sky. There was just enough
wind to make the banners that marked the racecourse snap and flutter
now and then. In the silence of the broad green meadows one could hear
the music winding through the city streets, farther and nearer and ever

approaching, a cheerful faint sweetness of the air that from time to time trembled and gathered together and broke out into the great joyous clanging of the bells.

Joyous! How is one to tell about joy! How describe the citizens of Omelas?

They were not simple folk, you see, though they were happy. But we do not say the words of cheer much any more. All smiles have become archaic. Given a description such as this one tends to make certain assumptions. Given a description such as this one tends to look next for the King, mounted on a splendid stallion and surrounded by his noble knights, or perhaps in a golden litter borne by great-muscled slaves. But there was no king. They did not use swords or keep slaves. They were not barbarians. I do not know the rules and laws of their society, but I suspect that they were singularly few. As they did without monarchy and slavery, so they also got on without the stock exchange, the advertisement, the secret police, and the bomb. Yet I repeat that these were not simple folk, not dulcet shepherds, noble savages, bland utopians. They were not less complex than us. The trouble is that we have a bad habit, encouraged by pedants and sophisticates, of considering happiness as something rather stupid. Only pain is intellectual, only evil interesting. This is the treason of the artist: a refusal to admit the banality of evil and the terrible boredom of pain. If you can't lick 'em, join 'em. If it hurts, repeat it. But to praise despair is to condemn delight, to embrace violence is to lose hold of everything else. We have almost lost hold; we can no longer describe a happy man, nor make any celebration of joy. How can I tell you about the people of Omelas? They were not naïve and happy children—though their children were, in fact, happy. They were mature, intelligent, passionate adults whose lives were not wretched. O miracle! but I wish I could describe it better. I wish I could convince you. Omelas sounds in my words like a city, in a fairy tale, long ago and far away, once upon a time. Perhaps it would be best if you imagined it as your own fancy bids, assuming it will rise to the occasion, for certainly I cannot suit you all. For instance, how about technology? I think that there would be no cars or helicopters in and above the streets; this follows from the fact that the people of Omelas are happy people. Happiness is based on a just discrimination of what is necessary, what is neither necessary nor destructive, and what is destructive. In the middle category, however—that of the unnecessary but undestructive, that of comfort, luxury, exuberance, etc.—they could perfectly well have central heating, subway trains, washing machines, and all kinds of marvelous devices not yet invented here, floating light-sources, fuelless power, a cure for the common cold. Or they could have none of that: It doesn't matter. As you like it. I incline to think that people from towns up and down the coast have been coming in to Omelas during the last days before the

Festival on very fast little trains and double-decked trams, and that the train station of Omelas is actually the handsomest building in town, though plainer than the magnificent Farmers' Market. But even granted trains, I fear that Omelas so far strikes some of you as goody-goody. Smiles, bells, parades, horses, bleh. If so, please add an orgy. If an orgy would help, don't hesitate. Let us not, however, have temples from which issue beautiful nude priests and priestesses already half in ecstasy and ready to copulate with any man or woman, lover or stranger, who desires union with the deep godhead of the blood, although that was my first idea. But really it would be better not to have any temples in Omelas—at least not manned temples. Religion yes, clergy no. Surely the beautiful nudes can just wander about, offering themselves like divine soufflés to the hunger of the needy and the rapture of the flesh. Let them join the processions. Let tambourines be struck above the copulations, and the glory of desire be proclaimed upon the gongs, and (a not unimportant) let the offspring of these delightful rituals be beloved and looked after by all. One thing I know there is none of in Omelas is guilt. But what else should there be? I thought at first there were no drugs, but that is puritanical. For those who like it, the faint insistent sweetness of *drooz* may perfume the ways of the city, *drooz* which first brings a great lightness and brilliance to the mind and limbs, and then after some hours a dreamy languor, and wonderful visions at last of the very arcana and inmost secrets of the Universe, as well as exciting the pleasure of sex beyond all belief; and it is not habit-forming. For more modest tastes I think there ought to be beer. What else, what else belongs in the joyous city? The sense of victory, surely, the celebration of courage. But as we did without clergy, let us do without soldiers. The joy built upon successful slaughter is not the right kind of joy; it will not do; it is fearful and it is trivial. A boundless and generous contentment, a magnanimous triumph felt not against some outer enemy but in communion with the finest and fairest in the souls of all men everywhere and the splendor of the world's summer: This is what swells the hearts of the people of Omelas, and the victory they celebrate is that of life. I really don't think many of them need to take *drooz*.

Most of the processions have reached the Green Fields by now. A marvelous smell of cooking goes forth from the red and blue tents of the provisioners. The faces of small children are amiably sticky; in the benign grey beard of a man a couple of crumbs of rich pastry are entangled. The youths and girls have mounted their horses and are beginning to group around the starting line of the course. An old woman, small, fat, and laughing, is passing out flowers from a basket, and tall young men wear her flowers in their shining hair. A child of nine or ten sits at the edge of the crowd, alone, playing on a wooden flute. People pause to listen, and they smile, but they do not speak to him, for he never ceases playing and never sees them, his dark eyes wholly rapt in the sweet, thin magic of the tune.

5 He finishes, and slowly lowers his hands holding the wooden flute.

As if that little private silence were the signal, all at once a trumpet sounds from the pavilion near the starting line: imperious, melancholy, piercing. The horses rear on their slender legs, and some of them neigh in answer. Sober-faced, the young riders stroke the horses' necks and soothe them, whispering, "Quiet, quiet, there my beauty, my hope...." They begin to form in rank along the starting line. The crowds along the racecourse are like a field of grass and flowers in the wind. The Festival of Summer has begun.

Do you believe? Do you accept the festival, the city, the joy? No? Then let me describe one more thing.

In a basement under one of the beautiful public buildings of Omelas, or perhaps in the cellar of one of its spacious private homes, there is a room. It has one locked door, and no window. A little light seeps in dustily between cracks in the boards, secondhand from a cobwebbed window somewhere across the cellar. In one corner of the little room a couple of mops, with stiff, clotted, foul-smelling heads, stand near a rusty bucket. The floor is dirt, a little damp to the touch, as cellar dirt usually is. The room is about three paces long and two wide: a mere broom closet or disused tool room. In the room a child is sitting. It could be a boy or a girl. It looks about six, but actually is nearly ten. It is feeble-minded. Perhaps it was born defective, or perhaps it has become imbecile through fear, malnutrition, and neglect. It picks its nose and occasionally fumbles vaguely with its toes or genitals, as it sits hunched in the corner farthest from the bucket and the two mops. It is afraid of the mops. It finds them horrible. It shuts its eyes, but it knows the mops are still standing there; and the door is locked; and nobody ever comes, except that sometimes—the child has no understanding of time or interval—sometimes the door rattles terribly and opens, and a person, or several people, are there. One of them may come in and kick the child to make it stand up. The others never come close, but peer in at it with frightened, disgusted eyes. The food bowl and the water jug are hastily filled, the door is locked, the eyes disappear. The people at the door never say anything, but the child, who has not always lived in the tool room, and can remember sunlight and its mother's voice, sometimes speaks. "I will be good," it says. "Please let me out. I will be good!" They never answer. The child used to scream for help at night, and cry a good deal, but now it only makes a kind of whining, "eh-haa-, ch-haa," and it speaks less and less often. It is so thin there are no calves to its legs; its belly protrudes; it lives on a half-bowl of corn meal and grease a day. It is naked. Its buttocks and thighs are a mass of festered sores, as it sits in its own excrement continually.

They all know it is there, all the people of Omelas. Some of them have come to see it; others are content merely to know it is there. They all know that it has to be there. Some of them understand why, and some do not, but they all understand that their happiness, the beauty of their city, the tenderness of their friendships, the health of their children, the wisdom of their scholars, the skill of their makers, even the abundance of their harvest and the kindly weathers of their skies, depend wholly on this child's abominable misery.

This is usually explained to children when they are between eight 10 and twelve, whenever they seem capable of understanding; and most of those who come to see the child are young people, though often enough an adult comes, or comes back, to see the child. No matter how well the matter has been explained to them, these young spectators are always shocked and sickened at the sight. They feel disgust, which they had thought themselves superior to. They feel anger, outrage, impotence, despite all the explanations. They would like to do something for the child. But there is nothing they can do. If the child were brought up into and sunlight out of that vile place, if it were cleaned and fed and comforted, that would be a good thing, indeed; but if it were done, in that day and hour all the prosperity and beauty and delight of Omelas would wither and be destroyed. Those are the terms. To exchange all the goodness and grace of every life in Omelas for that single, small improvement: to throw away the happiness of thousands for the chance of the happiness of one: that would be to let guilt within the walls indeed.

The terms are strict and absolute; there may not even be a kind word spoken to the child.

Often the young people go home in tears, or in a tearless rage, when they have seen the child and faced this terrible paradox. They may brood over it for weeks or years. But as time goes on they begin to realize that even if the child could be released, it would not get much good of its freedom: a little vague pleasure of warmth and food, no doubt, but little more. It is too degraded and imbecile to know any real joy. It has been afraid too long ever to be free of fear. Its habits are too uncouth for it to respond to humane treatment. Indeed, after so long it would probably be wretched without walls about it to protect it, and darkness for its eyes, and its own excrement to sit in. Their tears at the bitter injustice dry when they begin to perceive the terrible justice of reality, and to accept it. Yet it is their tears and anger, the trying of their generosity and the acceptance of their helplessness, which are perhaps the true source of the splendor of their lives. Theirs is no vapid, irresponsible happiness. They know that they, like the child, are not free. They know compassion. It is the existence of the child, and their knowledge of its existence, that makes possible the nobility of their architecture, the poignancy of their music, the profundity of their science. It is because of the child that they are so gentle with children. They know that if the wretched one were not there snivelling in the dark, the other one, the flute-player, could make no joyful music as the young riders line up in their beauty for the race in the sunlight of the first morning of summer.

Now do you believe in them? Are they not more credible? But there is one more thing to tell, and this is quite incredible.

At times one of the adolescent girls or boys who go to see the child does not go home to weep or rage, does not, in fact, go home at all. Sometimes also a man or woman much older falls silent for a day or two, and then leaves home. These people go out into the street, and walk down the street alone. They keep walking, and walk straight out of the city of Omelas, through the beautiful gates. They keep walking across the farmlands of Omelas. Each one goes alone, youth or girl, man or woman. Night falls; the traveler must pass down village streets, between the houses with yellow-lit windows, and on out into the darkness of the fields. Each alone, they go west or north, towards the mountains. They go on. They leave Omelas, they walk ahead into the darkness, and they do not come back. The place that they go towards is a place even less imaginable to most of us than the city of happiness. I cannot describe it at all. It is possible that it does not exist. But they seem to know where they are going, the ones who walk away from Omelas.

Responding to Reading

1. Why do you think Le Guin's narrator keeps asking readers whether or not they "believe"—that is, whether they accept what she is saying as the truth? Do *you* "believe"? Which elements of this story do you find most unbelievable? Which do you find most believable?
2. Are "the ones who walk away from Omelas" any less morally responsible for the child's welfare than those who keep the child imprisoned? In other words, do you believe there is a difference between actively doing something "wrong" and passively allowing it to happen?
3. Why does the logic of the story require that the child be present? Why must the child suffer?

Responding in Writing

Do you think it could be argued that our society has its own equivalent of the child locked in the closet and that we are guilty of failing to act to save this child? If so, what is it?

WRITING

MAKING CHOICES

1. The question of whether or not to act to end another's suffering—possibly at one's own expense—is explored, implicitly or explicitly, in "Shooting an Elephant" by George Orwell (p. 601) and "The Ones Who Walk Away from Omelas" by Ursula K. Le Guin (p. 665). Do you think we as a society should act to end suffering even if it causes us some hardship?

2. Stanley Milgram (p. 639) believes that his study illustrates philosopher Hannah Arendt's controversial theory, showing that "ordinary people, simply doing their jobs, and without any particular hostility on their part, can become agents in a terrible destructive process" (39). Write an essay in which you cite examples from recent news events or from your own experience to support Arendt's theory.

3. Both Martin Luther King, Jr. (p. 608), and Stanley Milgram (p. 639) consider the difficulties of resisting majority rule, standing up to authority, and protesting against established rules and laws. Choose a law or practice that you consider unjust, and write an essay in which you explain why you believe it should be challenged (or even disobeyed).

4. What do you believe we gain and lose by using animals in scientific research? Do you believe this practice should be continued? If so, with which animals? Under what circumstances? If not, why not? What alternative do you propose? Read Claire McCarthy's "Dog Lab" (p. 632) and Garrett Hardin's "Lifeboat Ethics" (p. 623) before you begin to plan your essay.

5. Which of the two roads identified in Robert Frost's "The Road Not Taken" (p. 599) have you chosen? In what sense has that choice "made all the difference" (line 20)?

6. Do you believe it is possible both to do good (that is, to help others) and to do well (that is, to be financially successful), or do you believe these two goals are mutually exclusive? Write an essay in which you answer this question, citing examples of public figures who have (or have not) managed both to do good and to do well.

7. Are you essentially optimistic or pessimistic about your own future and about the future of the world we live in? Choose several readings from this chapter—for example, the selections by Wallace and Le Guin—that you believe express either an optimistic or a pessimistic worldview, and use the writers' ideas to support your position.

8. In paragraph 4 of "And Then They Came for Me" (p. 658), Lasantha Wickrematunge says, "But there is a calling that is yet above high office, fame, lucre and security. It is the call of conscience." In "Letter from Birmingham Jail" (p. 608), Martin Luther King, Jr., also values conscience over expedience and worldly gain. Both men consider their audiences hostile to their arguments, yet both maintain a reasonable tone. Write an essay in which you explain the similarities in content and tone between these two essays.

9. Read "Goodbye, Colorado" (p. 230) and "News You Can Endow" (p. 231) in Chapter 4, and then write an essay in which you argue for or against the need for newspapers, using "And Then They Came for Me" to support your position.

CREDITS

© Ad Council. Reprinted by permission.

Alexie, Sherman, "What Sacagawea Means to Me (And Perhaps to You)." *Time,* July 8, 2002, v. 160, i2, p. 56+.

Angelou, Maya, "Graduation," from *I Know Why the Caged Bird Sings,* pp. 164–180. Copyright © 1969 and renewed 1997 by Maya Angelou. Used by permission of Random House, Inc.

Barnett, Rosalind C., and Caryl Rivers, "Men Are from Earth, and So Are Women," *Chronicle of Higher Education,* 0009-5982, September 3, 2004, Vol. 51, Issue 2.

Barrera, Albino, "Fair Exchange: Who Benefits from Outsourcing?" Copyright © 2004 *Christian Century.* Reprinted with permission from the September 21, 2004 issue of the *Christian Century.*

Barry, Lynda, "The Sanctuary of School." *The New York Times,* January 5, 1992. Copyright © 1992 by The New York Times Co. Reprinted by permission.

Berry, Wendell, "Being Kind to the Land." *The Progressive,* February 2009. Reprinted by permission.

Blumenstyk, Goldie, "In Iowa 2 Colleges Separated by 150 Miles and 1.37 Billion (Grinnell College and Clarke College)." *The Chronicle of Higher Education,* April 7, 2006, v52, 131, pNA. © Copyright 2006 Chronicle of Higher Education, Inc. Reprinted by permission.

Brady, Judy, "Why I Want a Wife." From *Ms.* 1970. Copyright © 1970 by Judy Brady. Reprinted by permission of the author.

Brooks, David, "Kicking the Secularist Habit." *The Atlantic Monthly,* March 2003, p. 26. Reprinted by permission.

Carson, Rachel, *Silent Spring.* Copyright © 1962 by Rachel L. Carson. Reprinted by permission of Frances Collin, Trustee.

Carver, Raymond, "Cathedral" from *Cathedral* by Raymond Carver, copyright © 1983 by Raymond Carver. Used by permission of Alfred A. Knopf, a division of Random House, Inc. and The Wiley Agency, Inc.

Cheever, Daniel S., Jr., "Is College Worth the Money?" Boston.com, June 3, 2005. © Copyright 2005 Globe Newspaper Company. Reprinted by permission.

Cisneros, Sandra, "The Storyteller," *Oprah* Magazine, March 2009. Reprinted by permission of Susan Bergholz Literary Services on behalf of the author.

Cofer, Judith Ortiz, "The Myth of the Latin Woman: I Just Met A Girl Named Maria," from *The Latin Deli: Prose & Poetry.* Reprinted by permission of The University of Georgia Press.

© 1972 by Aileen Pace Nilsen, Arizona State University, Tempe, AZ. Reprinted by permission of the author.

Olds, Sharon, "Rite of Passage," from *The Dead and the Living*. Copyright © 1987 by Sharon Olds. Used by permission of Alfred A. Knopf, a division of Random House, Inc.

Orr, Allan, "Why Intelligent Design Isn't" from *Devolution*. Originally appeared in *The New Yorker*, May 30, 2008. Reprinted by permission of the author.

Orwell, George, "Politics and the English Language" from *Shooting an Elephant and Other Essays*, by George Orwell, copyright © 1950 by Harcourt, Inc., renewed 1979 by Sonia Brownell Orwell. Reprinted by permission of Harcourt, Inc. and copyright © 1946 by permission of Bill Hamilton as the Literary Executor of the Estate of the Late Sonia Brownell Orwell and Secker & Warburg Ltd.

Orwell, George, "Shooting an Elephant" from *Shooting an Elephant and Other Essays*, by George Orwell, copyright © 1950 by Harcourt, Inc, and renewed 1979 by Sonia Brownell Orwell, reprinted by permission of Harcourt, Inc. and Copyright © George Orwell 1946 by permission of Bill Hamilton as the Literary Executor of the Estate of the Late Sonia Brownell and Secker & Warburg Ltd.

Pastan, Linda, "Ethics" from *Waiting for My Life* by Linda Pastan. Copyright © 1981 by Linda Pastan. Used by permission of W.W. Norton & Company, Inc.

Piercy, Marge, "Barbie Doll" from *Circles on the Water* by Marge Piercy, copyright © 1982 by Marge Piercy. Used by permission of Alfred A. Knopf, a division of Random House, Inc. and The Wallace Literary Agency.

Pink, Daniel, "School's Out," from *Free Agent Nation* by Daniel Pink. Copyright © 2001 by Daniel H. Pink. By permission of Grand Central Publishing.

Pollan, Michael, "Why Bother?" *The New York Times*, April 20, 2008, pg. 9(L). © 2008 The New York Times Company. Reprinted by permission.

Reich, Robert B., "Don't Blame Walmart." *The New York Times*, February 25, 2005. © 2005 The New York Times Company. Reprinted by permission.

Risen, Clay, "Missed Target." Reprinted by permission of *The New Republic*. © 2004 The New Republic, LLC.

Rodriguez, Richard, "Aria" from *Hunger of Memory*, pp. 169–175. Reprinted by permission of David R. Godine, Publisher, Inc. Copyright © 1982 by Richard Rodriguez.

Rogers, Heather, "The Conquest of Garbage." Copyright © 2005 *Gone Tomorrow: The Hidden Life of Garbage* by Heather Rogers. Reprinted by permission of The New Press. www.thenewpress.com

Roxburgh, Stephen, "The Universe of Meaning." *The Horn Book Magazine*, November 2008.

Rushdie, Salman. "Reality TV: A Dearth of Talent and the Death of Morality," from *The Guardian*, June 9, 2001. Copyright © 2001 by Salman Rushdie. Reprinted with the permission of The Wylie Agency, Inc.

Sacks, Glenn, "Stay-at-Home Dads" as published in *Newsday*, May 22, 2002, www.glennsacks.com. Reprinted by permission of Glenn Sacks.

Sagel, Jim, "Baca Grande." *Hispanics in the United States: An Anthology of Creative Literature,* vol. 2. Edited by Francisco Jimenez and Gary D. Keller. Bilingual Press/Editorial Bilingue, 1982, Tempe, Arizona. Reprinted by permission.

Schlosser, Eric, "Behind the Counter," from *Fast Food Nation.* Copyright © 2001 by Eric Schlosser. Reprinted by permission of Houghton Mifflin Company. All rights reserved.

Schönborn, Christoph, "Finding Design in Nature." *The New York Times,* July 7, 2007, op/ed. Copyright © 2005 by The New York Times Co. Reprinted by permission.

Sheler, Jeffery, & Michael Betzhold, "Muslim in America," from *U.S. News & World Report,* Oct. 29, 2001, p. 50. © 2001 U.S. News & World Report, L.P. Reprinted with permission.

Shteyngart, Gary, "Sixty-Nine Cents." *The New Yorker,* September 3, 2007. Reprinted by permission.

Silko, Leslie Marmon, "Through the Stories We Hear Who We Are." *The Amicus Journal,* Winter 1993, v14, n4, p. 19(1). Reprinted by permission.

Sommers, Christina Hoff, "For More Balance on Campus," published on The Young America's Foundation Speakers Program, 5/6/02. Reprinted by permission of Christina Hoff Sommers. American Enterprise Institute.

Sommers, Christina Hoff, from "The War Against Boys," in *The Atlantic Monthly,* May 2000, pp. 59–74. Reprinted by permission of Christina Hoff Sommers, American Enterprise Institute.

Soto, Gary, "One Last Time," from *Living Up the Street.* © 1985 by Gary Soto. Used by permission of the author.

Staples, Brent, "Just Walk On By" from *Harper's,* December 1986. Reprinted by permission of the author.

Staples, Brent, "What Adolescents Miss When We Let Them Grow Up in Cyberspace." *The New York Times,* May 29, 2004, pA14 (L). Copyright © 2004 by The New York Times Co. Reprinted by permission.

Stuntz, William J., "Turning Faith into Elevator Music." © tcsdaily.com Reprinted by permission.

Swenson, David, & Michael Schmidt. "News You Can Endow." *The New York Times,* January 28, 2009. Copyright © 2009 by The New York Times Company. Reprinted by permission.

Symonds, William C., Brian Grow, and John Cady, "Earthly Empires." Reprinted from the May 23rd, 2005, *Business Week* by permission. Copyright © 2005 by the McGraw-Hill Companies.

Tan, Amy, "Mother Tongue." Copyright © 1990 by Amy Tan. First appeared in *The Threepenny Review.* Reprinted by permission of the author and the Sandra Dijkstra Literary Agency.

Tannen, Deborah, "Wears Jump Suit. Sensible Shoes. Uses Husbands Last Name." *The New York Times Magazine,* June 20, 1993. Reprinted by permission of the author. This article was originally titled "Marked Women, Unmarked Men" by the author.

PHOTO CREDITS

Chapter 2, page 124-A, bottom: Michael Kreiser.
Chapter 2, page 124-B, top: Jim Heemstra.
Chapter 2, page 124-B, bottom: Michael Kreiser.
Chapter 2, page 124-C, top: Jim Heemstra.
Chapter 2, page 124-C, bottom: Michael Kreiser Photography.
Chapter 2, page 124-D, top: Jim Heemstra.
Chapter 2, page 124-D, bottom: Michael Kreiser.

Chapter 3, page 128: Getty Images.
Chapter 3, page 129: © Mei-Chun Jau/CORBIS.
Chapter 3, page 184: Karen Mauk.

Chapter 4, page 204: Geoff Dann © Dorling Kindersley, Courtesy of the Museum of the Order of St John, London.
Chapter 4, page 230: © The E. W. Scripps Company.
Chapter 4, page 245: © The New Yorker Collection 1993 Peter Steiner from cartoonbank.com. All Rights Reserved.
Chapter 4, page 246: © The New Yorker Collection 2005 Alan Gregory from cartoonbank.com. All Rights Reserved.

Chapter 5, page 256: Bob Daemmrich/The Image Works.
Chapter 5, page 257: Peter Cade/Stone/Getty Images.
Chapter 5, page 300: The Advertising Council, Inc.

Chapter 6, page 324: CORBIS-NY.
Chapter 6, page 325: Damon Winter/New York Times/Redux Pictures.
Chapter 6, page 374: Archive Holdings, Inc. Levick 03RLEI, Edwin/Getty Images Inc.—Image Bank.

Chapter 7, page 394: Hulton l Archive by Getty Images, Inc.
Chapter 7, page 395: AP Wide World Photos.
Chapter 7, page 444: FAYAZ KABLI/Reuters/CORBIS-NY.

Chapter 8, page 464: Fancy/Veer/Corbis RF.
Chapter 8, page 465: Construction Photography/Corbis RF.
Chapter 8, page 499: © Ronnie Kaufman/CORBIS. All Rights Reserved.

Chapter 9, page 518: Jeff Greenberg/Omni-Photo Communications, Inc.
Chapter 9, page 519: JOHN GRESS/Reuters/CORBIS-NY.
Chapter 9, page 568: David Gifford/Photo Researchers, Inc.

Chapter 10, page 596: © Simon Jarratt/CORBIS. All Rights Reserved.
Chapter 10, page 597: © Image 100/Royalty-Free/CORBIS.

INDEX OF AUTHORS AND TITLES

681